# Lecture Notes in Computer Science 6353

Commenced Publication in 1973
Founding and Former Series Editors:
Gerhard Goos, Juris Hartmanis, and Jan van Leeuwen

Konstantinos Diamantaras   Wlodek Duch
Lazaros S. Iliadis (Eds.)

# Artificial Neural Networks – ICANN 2010

20th International Conference
Thessaloniki, Greece, September 15-18, 2010
Proceedings, Part II

 Springer

Volume Editors

Konstantinos Diamantaras
TEI of Thessaloniki, Department of Informatics
57400 Sindos, Greece
E-mail: kdiamant@it.teithe.gr

Wlodek Duch
Nicolaus Copernicus University
School of Physics, Astronomy, and Informatics
Department of Informatics
ul. Grudziadzka 5, 87-100 Torun, Poland
E-mail: duch@phys.uni.torun.pl

Lazaros S. Iliadis
Democritus University of Thrace, Department of Forestry
and Management of the Environment and Natural Resources
Pantazidou 193, 68200 Orestiada Thrace, Greece
E-mail: liliadis@fmenr.duth.gr

Library of Congress Control Number: 2010933964

CR Subject Classification (1998): I.2, F.1, I.4, I.5, J.3, H.3

LNCS Sublibrary: SL 1 – Theoretical Computer Science and General Issues

ISSN         0302-9743
ISBN-10      3-642-15821-8 Springer Berlin Heidelberg New York
ISBN-13      978-3-642-15821-6 Springer Berlin Heidelberg New York

springer.com

© Springer-Verlag Berlin Heidelberg 2010
Printed in Germany

Typesetting: Camera-ready by author, data conversion by Scientific Publishing Services, Chennai, India
Printed on acid-free paper      06/3180

# Preface

This volume is part of the three-volume proceedings of the 20$^{th}$ International Conference on Artificial Neural Networks (ICANN 2010) that was held in Thessaloniki, Greece during September 15–18, 2010.

ICANN is an annual meeting sponsored by the European Neural Network Society (ENNS) in cooperation with the International Neural Network Society (INNS) and the Japanese Neural Network Society (JNNS). This series of conferences has been held annually since 1991 in Europe, covering the field of neurocomputing, learning systems and other related areas.

As in the past 19 events, ICANN 2010 provided a distinguished, lively and interdisciplinary discussion forum for researches and scientists from around the globe. It offered a good chance to discuss the latest advances of research and also all the developments and applications in the area of Artificial Neural Networks (ANNs). ANNs provide an information processing structure inspired by biological nervous systems and they consist of a large number of highly interconnected processing elements (neurons). Each neuron is a simple processor with a limited computing capacity typically restricted to a rule for combining input signals (utilizing an activation function) in order to calculate the output one. Output signals may be sent to other units along connections known as weights that excite or inhibit the signal being communicated. ANNs have the ability "to learn" by example (a large volume of cases) through several iterations without requiring a priori fixed knowledge of the relationships between process parameters.

The rapid evolution of ANNs during the last decades has resulted in their expansion in various diverse scientific fields, like engineering, computer science, mathematics, artificial intelligence, biology, environmental science, operations research and neuroscience. ANNs perform tasks like pattern recognition, image and signal processing, control, classification and many others.

In 2010 ICANN was organized by the following institutions: Aristotle University of Thessaloniki, University of Macedonia at Thessaloniki, Technological Educational Institute of Thessaloniki, Hellenic International University and Democritus University of Thrace.

The conference was held in the Kapsis Hotel and conference center in Thessaloniki, Greece. The participants were able to enjoy the atmosphere and the cultural heritage of Thessaloniki, which is built by the seaside and has a glorious history of 2300 years.

As a matter of fact, a total of 241 research papers were submitted to the conference for consideration. All of the submissions were peer reviewed by at least two academic referees. The international Program Committee of ICANN 2010 carefully selected 102 submissions (42%) to be accepted as full papers. Additionally 68 papers were selected for short presentation and 29 as posters.

The full papers have up to 10 pages, short ones have up to 6 pages and posters have up to 4 pages in the proceedings.

In addition to the regular papers, the technical program featured four keynote plenary lectures by the following worldwide renowned scholars:

- Prof. Alessandro E.P. Villa: NeuroHeuristic Research Group, Information Science Institute, University of Lausanne, Switzerland and Institut des Neurosciences, Université Joseph Fourier, Grenoble, France. Subject: "Spatiotemporal Firing Patterns and Dynamical Systems in Neural Networks";
- Prof. Stephen Grossberg: Department of Cognitive and Neural Systems, Center for Adaptive Systems, and Center of Excellence for Learning in Education, Science, and Technology, Boston University. Subject: "The Predictive Brain: Autonomous Search, Learning, Recognition, and Navigation in a Changing World";
- Prof. Sergios Theodoridis: Department of Informatics and Telecommunications, National and Kapodistrian University of Athens. Subject: "Adaptive Learning in a World of Projections";
- Prof. Nikola Kasabov: Knowledge Engineering and Discovery Research Institute (KEDRI), Auckland University of Technology. Subject: "Evolving Integrative Spiking Neural Networks: A Computational Intelligence Approach".

Also two tutorials were organized on the following topics:

- Prof. J.G. Taylor: Department of Mathematics, King's College London. Subject: "Attention versus Consciousness: Independent or Conjoined?";
- Dr. Kostas Karpouzis: Image, Video and Multimedia Systems Lab, Institute of Communication and Computer Systems (ICCS/NTUA). Subject: "User Modelling and Machine Learning for Affective and Assistive Computing".

Finally three workshops were organized namely:

- The First Consciousness Versus Attention Workshop (CVA);
- The Intelligent Environmental Monitoring, Modelling and Management Systems for Better QoL Workshop (IEM3);
- The First Self-Organizing Incremental Neural Network Workshop (SOINN).

The ENNS offered 12 travel grants to students who participated actively in the conference by presenting a research paper, and a competition was held between students for the best paper award.

The three-volume proceedings contain research papers covering the following topics: adaptive algorithms and systems, ANN applications, Bayesian ANNs, bio inspired-spiking ANNs, biomedical ANNs, data analysis and pattern recognition, clustering, computational intelligence, computational neuroscience, cryptography algorithms, feature selection/parameter identification and dimensionality reduction, filtering, genetic-evolutionary algorithms, image, video and audio processing, kernel algorithms and support vector machines, learning algorithms and systems, natural language processing, optimization, recurrent ANNs, reinforcement learning, robotics, and self organizing ANNs.

As General Co-chairs and PC Co-chair and in the name of all members of the Steering Committee, we would like to thank all the keynote invited speakers and the tutorial-workshops' organizers as well. Also, thanks are due to all the reviewers and the authors of submitted papers. Moreover, we would like to thank the members of the Organizing Committee headed by Prof. Yannis Manolopoulos and Prof. Ioannis Vlahavas. In particular, we wish to thank Dr. Maria Kontaki for her assistance and support towards the organization of this conference.

Additionally, we would like to thank the members of the Board of the European Neural Network Society for entrusting us with the organization of the conference as well as for their assistance. We wish to give our special thanks to Prof. Wlodzislaw Duch, President of the ENNS, for his invaluable guidance and help all the way.

Finally, we would like to thank Springer for their cooperation in publishing the proceedings in the prestigious series of Lecture Notes in Computer Science. We hope that all of the attendees enjoyed ICANN 2010 and also the conference site in Thessaloniki, both scientifically and socially. We expect that the ideas that have emerged here will result in the production of further innovations for the benefit of science and society.

September 2010

Wlodzislaw Duch
Kostandinos Diamandaras
Lazaros Iliadis

# Organization

## Executive Committee

| | |
|---|---|
| General Chairs | Konstantinos Diamantaras (Alexander TEI of Thessaloniki) Wlodek Duch (Nikolaus Copernicus University, Torun) |
| Program Chair | Lazaros Iliadis (Democritus University of Thrace) |
| Workshop Chairs | Nikola Kasabov (Auckland University of Technology) Kostas Goulianas (Alexander TEI of Thessaloniki) |
| Organizing Chairs | Yannis Manolopoulos (Aristotle University) Ioannis Vlahavas (Aristotle University) |
| Members | Maria Kontaki (Aristotle University) Alexis Papadimitriou (Aristotle University) Stavros Stavroulakis (Aristotle University) |

## Referees

Luis Alexandre
Cesare Alippi
Plamen Angelov
Bruno Apolloni
Amir Atiya
Monica Bianchini
Dominic Palmer Brown
Ivo Bukovsky
F.F. Cai
Gustavo Camps-Valls
Ke Chen
Theo Damoulas
Tharam Dillon
Christina Draganova
Gerard Dreyfus
Peter Erdi
Deniz Erdogmus
Pablo Estevez
Mauro Gaggero
Christophe Garcia
Erol Gelenbe
Christos Georgiadis
Mark Girolami

T. Glezakos
Giorgio Gnecco
G. Gravanis
Barbara Hammer
Ioannis Hatzilygeroudis
Tom Heskes
Timo Honkela
Amir Hussain
Sylvain Jaume
Yaochu Jin
D. Kalles
Achilles Kameas
Hassan Kazemian
Stefanos Kollias
D. Kosmopoulos
Costas Kotropoulos
Jan Koutnik
Konstantinos Koutroumbas
Vera Kurkova
Diego Liberati
Aristidis Likas
I. Maglogiannhs
Danilo Mandic

Francesco Marcelloni
Konstantinos Margaritis
Thomas Martinetz
Matteo Matteucci
Ali Minai
Nikolaos Mitianoudis
Roman Neruda
Erkki Oja
Mihaela Oprea
Karim Ouazzane
Theofilos Papadimitriou
Charis Papadopoulos
Constantinos Pattichis
Barak Pearlmutter
Elias Pimenidis
Vincenzo Piuri
Mark Plumbley
Manuel Roveri
Leszek Rutkowski
Marcello Sanguineti
Mike Schuster
Hiroshi Shimodaira
A. Sideridis
Olli Simula

Athanassios Skodras
S. Spartalis
Alessandro Sperduti
Soundararajan Srinivasan
Andreas Stafylopatis
Johan Suykens
Johannes Sveinsson
Anastasios Tefas
Athanasios Tsadiras
Ioannis Tsamardinos
T. Tsiligkiridis
Marc Van Hulle
Marley Vellasco
Michel Verleysen
Vassilios Verykios
Alessandro E.P. Villa
Jun Wang
Aaron Weifeng
Yong Xue
K. Yialouris
Hujun Yin
Xiaodong Zhang
Rodolfo Zunino

## Sponsoring Institutions

European Neural Network Society (ENNS)
Aristotle University of Thessaloniki
Alexander TEI of Thessaloniki
University of Macedonia
Democritus University of Thrace
International Hellenic University

# Table of Contents – Part II

## Kernel Algorithms – Support Vector Machines

# Knowledge Engineering and Decision Making

# Recurrent ANN

# Reinforcement Learning

# Robotics

## Self Organizing ANN

## Adaptive Algorithms – Systems

## Optimization

# Convergence Improvement of Active Set Training for Support Vector Regressors

Shigeo Abe and Ryousuke Yabuwaki

Graduate School of Engineering
Kobe University
Rokkodai, Nada, Kobe, Japan
abe@kobe-u.ac.jp
http://www2.kobe-u.ac.jp/~abe

**Abstract.** In our previous work we have discussed the training method of a support vector regressor (SVR) by active set training based on Newton's method. In this paper, we discuss convergence improvement by modifying the training method. To stabilize convergence for a large epsilon tube, we calculate the bias term according to the signs of the previous variables, not the updated variables. And to speed up calculating the inverse matrix by the Cholesky factorization during iteration steps, at the first iteration step, we keep the factorized matrix. And at the subsequent steps we restart the Cholesky factorization at the point where the variable in the working set is replaced. By computer experiments we show that by the proposed method the convergence is stabilized for a large epsilon tube and the incremental Cholesky factorization speeds up training.

## 1  Introduction

A support vector machine (SVM) with nonlinear kernels is usually trained in the dual form to avoid explicit treatment of variables in the feature space. In the dual form, the number of variables is the number of training data in pattern classification and twice the number of training data for function approximation. Therefore to reduce the number of variables that are treated simultaneously, decomposition techniques are used. They are classified into fixed-size chunking [1] and variable-size chunking [2]. The most well known training method using fixed-size chunking is sequential minimal optimization (SMO) [3]. It optimizes two data at a time. In variable-size chunking, we keep support vector candidates in the working set and when the algorithm terminates, the working set includes support vectors. Training based on variable-size chunking is sometimes called active set training. Cauwenberghs and Poggio's incremental and decremental training [4] is one type of active set training and it keeps track of the status change among unbounded support vectors, bounded support vectors, and non-support vectors. This method is extended to batch training [5,6,7,8,9].

K. Diamantaras, W. Duch, L.S. Iliadis (Eds.): ICANN 2010, Part II, LNCS 6353, pp. 1–10, 2010.
© Springer-Verlag Berlin Heidelberg 2010

Because the coefficient vector of the hyperplane is expressed by the kernel expansion, substituting the kernel expansion into the coefficient vector, the SVM in the primal form can be solvable. Based on this idea Chapelle [10] proposed training the SVM in the primal form. In [11], this method is extended to dual L2 SVMs, where at each step variables are allowed to be infeasible. Because in the dual form kernel expansion is not used and the coefficient matrix is positive definite, training in the dual form is usually faster than in the primal.

The training methods using variable-size chunking developed for pattern classification are extended to function approximation [12,13,14]. In [14], active set training in [11] was extended to function approximation. This method, however, has a convergence problem for a large epsilon tube.

In this paper we solve the above convergence problem and propose accelerating training L2 SVRs. We use Mattera et al.'s formulation of the SVR [15], whose number of variables is the number of training data. Then the dual variables take real values. The training algorithm in [14] is as follows. Starting from the initial working set, we repeatedly solve the dual quadratic programming problem, delete from the working set the variables which are within the epsilon tube and add to the working set the data which are outside of the epsilon tube until the same working sets are obtained. In this method, at each iteration step we need to calculate the bias term of the separating hyperplane. We find that unstable convergence for a large epsilon tube is caused by the incorrect value of the bias term. Thus, we calculate the bias term according to the signs of the previous variables, not the updated variables. Furthermore, to speed up training, we calculate the inverse of the coefficient matrix incrementally using the Cholesky factorization. Namely, at the first iteration step, we keep the factorized matrix by the Cholesky factorization. Then at the subsequent iteration steps, we restart the Cholesky factorization at the point where the variable in the working set is replaced.

In Section 2, we explain L2 SVRs in the dual form, and in Section 3 we explain the training method of SVRs discussed in [14]. Then, in Section 5, we discuss how to improve convergence and accelerate training. In Section 6, by computer experiment we demonstrate the effectiveness of the proposed method for some benchmark data sets.

## 2  L2 Support Vector Regressors in the Dual Form

Using the $M$ training input-output pairs $(\mathbf{x}_i, y_i)$ $(i = 1, \ldots, M)$, where $\mathbf{x}_i$ is the $i$th training input and $y_i$ is the associated output, we consider determining the regression function:

$$y = \mathbf{w}^\top \phi(\mathbf{x}) + b, \tag{1}$$

where $\phi(\mathbf{x})$ is the mapping function to the feature space, $\mathbf{w}$ is the coefficient vector of the hyperplane in the feature space and $b$ is its bias term.

The L2 SVR is given by

$$\text{minimize} \quad Q(\mathbf{w}, b, \boldsymbol{\xi}, \boldsymbol{\xi}^*) = \frac{1}{2}\|\mathbf{w}\|^2 + \frac{C}{2}\sum_{i=1}^{M}(\xi_i^2 + \xi_i^{*2}) \tag{2}$$

$$\text{subject to} \quad y_i - \mathbf{w}^\top \phi(\mathbf{x}_i) - b \le \varepsilon + \xi_i \quad \text{for} \quad i = 1, \dots, M, \tag{3}$$

$$\mathbf{w}^\top \phi(\mathbf{x}_i) + b - y_i \le \varepsilon + \xi_i^* \quad \text{for} \quad i = 1, \dots, M, \tag{4}$$

$$\xi_i \ge 0, \quad \xi_i^* \ge 0 \quad \text{for} \quad i = 1, \dots, M, \tag{5}$$

where $\varepsilon$ is the parameter to define the epsilon tube, $\xi_i$ and $\xi_i^*$ are slack variables, and $C$ is the margin parameter that determines the trade-off between the magnitude of the margin and the estimation error of the training data.

The above optimization problem can be converted into the dual form introducing nonnegative slack variables $\alpha_i$ and $\alpha_i^*$ associated with the inequality constraints (3) and (4), respectively. Then the number of variables of the support vector regressor in the dual form is twice the number of the training data. But because nonnegative dual variables $\alpha_i$ and $\alpha_i^*$ appear only in the forms of $\alpha_i - \alpha_i^*$ and $\alpha_i + \alpha_i^*$ and both $\alpha_i$ and $\alpha_i^*$ are not positive at the same time, we can reduce the number of variables to half by replacing $\alpha_i - \alpha_i^*$ with $\alpha_i$, which take negative values as well as nonnegative values, and $\alpha_i + \alpha_i^*$ with $|\alpha_i|$ [15]. Then, we obtain the following dual problem for the L2 SVR:

$$\text{maximize} \quad Q(\boldsymbol{\alpha}) = -\frac{1}{2}\sum_{i,j=1}^{M} \alpha_i \alpha_j \left( K(\mathbf{x}_i, \mathbf{x}_j) + \frac{\delta_{ij}}{C} \right)$$

$$-\varepsilon \sum_{i=1}^{M} |\alpha_i| + \sum_{i=1}^{M} y_i \alpha_i \tag{6}$$

$$\text{subject to} \quad \sum_{i=1}^{M} \alpha_i = 0, \tag{7}$$

where $\alpha_i$ are dual variables associated with $\mathbf{x}_i$ and take negative values as well as nonnegative values, $K(\mathbf{x}, \mathbf{x}') = \phi^\top(\mathbf{x})\phi(\mathbf{x})$ is the kernel, and $\delta_{ij}$ is Kronecker's delta function.

The KKT complementarity conditions are

$$\alpha_i \left( \varepsilon + \xi_i - y_i + \mathbf{w}^\top \phi(\mathbf{x}_i) + b \right) = 0 \quad \text{for} \quad \alpha_i \ge 0, \quad i = 1, \dots, M, \tag{8}$$

$$\alpha_i \left( \varepsilon + \xi_i + y_i - \mathbf{w}^\top \phi(\mathbf{x}_i) - b \right) = 0 \quad \text{for} \quad \alpha_i < 0 \quad i = 1, \dots, M, \tag{9}$$

$$C\,\xi_i = |\alpha_i| \quad \text{for} \quad i = 1, \dots, M. \tag{10}$$

Therefore, $b$ is obtained by

$$b = \begin{cases} y_i - \mathbf{w}^\top \phi(\mathbf{x}_i) - \varepsilon - \dfrac{\alpha_i}{C} & \text{for} \quad \alpha_i > 0, \\[2mm] y_i - \mathbf{w}^\top \phi(\mathbf{x}_i) + \varepsilon - \dfrac{\alpha_i}{C} & \text{for} \quad \alpha_i < 0, \quad i \in \{1, \dots, M\}. \end{cases} \tag{11}$$

By the formulation, L2 SVRs are very similar to L2 SVMs. If the value of $\varepsilon$ is very small almost all training data become support vectors. In such a case the L2 SVR behaves very similar to the least squares (LS) SVR. And for $\varepsilon = 0$ the L2 SVR is equivalent to the LS SVR.

## 3  Training Methods

In this section we explain the training method discussed in [14].

We solve the equality constraint (7) for one variable and substitute it into (6). Then the optimization problem is reduced to the maximization problem without constraints. We divide the variables into the working set and the fixed set and solve the subproblem for the working set fixing the variables in the fixed set. In the next iteration process, we delete the variables that are within the $\varepsilon$-tube from the working set and add, from the fixed set, the variables that do not satisfy the KKT conditions and iterate optimizing the subproblem until the same solution is obtained. This method allows variables to change signs jumping over the epsilon tube between the consecutive iteration steps. We discuss the method more in detail.

Consider solving (6) and (7) for the index set $S$. Solving the equality constraint in (7) for $\alpha_s$ ($s \in S$), we obtain

$$\alpha_s = -\sum_{\substack{i \neq s, \\ i \in S}} \alpha_i. \tag{12}$$

Substituting (12) into (6), we obtain the following optimization problem

$$\text{maximize} \quad Q(\boldsymbol{\alpha}_S) = \mathbf{c}_S^\top \boldsymbol{\alpha}'_S - \frac{1}{2} {\boldsymbol{\alpha}'_S}^\top K_S \, \boldsymbol{\alpha}'_S, \tag{13}$$

where $\boldsymbol{\alpha}_S = \{\alpha_i | i \in S\}$, $\boldsymbol{\alpha}'_S = \{\alpha_i | i \neq s, i \in S\}$, $\mathbf{c}_S$ is the $(|S| - 1)$-dimensional vector, $K_S$ is the $(|S| - 1) \times (|S| - 1)$ positive definite matrix, and

$$c_{S_i} = \begin{cases} y_i - y_s & \text{for} \quad D(\mathbf{x}_i, y_i) \geq 0, D(\mathbf{x}_s, y_s) \geq 0 \\ y_i - y_s - 2\varepsilon & \text{for} \quad D(\mathbf{x}_i, y_i) \geq 0, D(\mathbf{x}_s, y_s) < 0 \\ y_i - y_s + 2\varepsilon & \text{for} \quad D(\mathbf{x}_i, y_i) < 0, D(\mathbf{x}_s, y_s) \geq 0 \\ y_i - y_s & \text{for} \quad D(\mathbf{x}_i, y_i) < 0, D(\mathbf{x}_s, y_s) < 0 \quad i \neq s, \quad i \in S \end{cases} \tag{14}$$

$$K_{S_{ij}} = K(\mathbf{x}_i, \mathbf{x}_j) - K(\mathbf{x}_i, \mathbf{x}_s) - K(\mathbf{x}_s, \mathbf{x}_j)$$
$$+ K(\mathbf{x}_s, \mathbf{x}_s) + \frac{1 + \delta_{ij}}{C} \quad \text{for} \quad i, j \neq s, \quad i, j \in S, \tag{15}$$

where $c_{S_i}$ is the $i$th element of $\mathbf{c}_{S_i}$ and $D(\mathbf{x}, y) = y - \phi(\mathbf{x}) - b$.

If $\varepsilon = 0$, in (14), $c_{S_i} = y_i - y_s$ irrespective of the signs of $D(\mathbf{x}_i, y_i)$ and $D(\mathbf{x}_s, y_s)$. Thus, similar to LS SVRs, we can solve (13) by a single matrix inversion.

Initially, for positive $\varepsilon$, we set some indices to $S$ and set $\alpha_i = 0$ ($i \in S$) and $b = 0$. Therefore, $D(\mathbf{x}_i, y_i) = 0$. Thus, in (14), $c_{S_i}$ is set according to the signs of $y_i$ and $y_s$. We solve (13):

$$\boldsymbol{\alpha}'_S = K_S^{-1} \mathbf{c}_S. \tag{16}$$

We calculate $b$ using (11). Because of $\varepsilon$, the $b$ values calculated by different $\alpha_i$ in $S$ may be different. Thus we calculate the average of $b$s. If training data associated with the variables in $S$ are within the $\varepsilon$-tube, we delete these variables and add the indices of the variables to $S$ that violate KKT conditions. If the working sets and $\mathbf{c}_{S_i}$ are the same for the consecutive two iterations, the solution is obtained and we stop training. This stopping condition is different from that for the SVM discussed in [11] because of the absolute value of $\alpha_i$ in the objective function.

The procedure for training the L2 SVR is as follows.

1. Set the indices associated with $h$ training data to set $S$ and go to Step 2.
2. Calculate $\boldsymbol{\alpha}'_S$ using (16) and using (12) obtain $\alpha_s$. Calculate $b$s for $i \in S$ using (11) and calculate the average of $b$s.
3. Delete from $S$ the indices of $\mathbf{x}_i$ that satisfy $|D(\mathbf{x}_i, y_i)| \leq \varepsilon$. And add to $S$ the indices associated with at most $h$ most violating data, namely $\mathbf{x}_i$ that satisfy $|D(\mathbf{x}_i, y_i)| > \varepsilon$ from the largest $|D(\mathbf{x}_i, y_i)|$ in order. If the solution is obtained, stop training. Otherwise, go to Step 2.

For a large value of $\varepsilon$, there may be cases where a proper working set is not obtained and thus the solution does not converge. This is because the monotonic decrease of the objective function values is not guaranteed.

## 4   Convergence Improvement

The training method discussed in Section 3 works well for a small epsilon tube, but for a large epsilon tube the numbers of violations of KKT conditions fluctuate considerably and convergence becomes difficult. This occurs because of the incorrect bias term calculation. Thus to avoid this, in calculating the bias term by (11), we use the signs of $\alpha_i$ at the previous step, not the updated $\alpha_i$. As will be shown in the "Performance Comparison" Section, this drastically stabilizes convergence.

In calculating (16), we use the Cholesky factorization. It is known that the Cholesky factorization can be done incrementally [16]. Therefore, we use the incremental Cholesky factorization to speed up training. Suppose that the elements in $S$ are ordered from 1 to $|S|$, the first index in $S$ is set to $s$, and the data associated with $i$th and $j$th indices and index $s$ are used to generate the $(i-1)$th column (row) and $(j-1)$th row (column) of $K_S$. And suppose that at the end of some iteration step, the $i$th index is the highest order among the replaced indices in $S$. Then the first $(i-1) \times (i-1)$ sub-matrix of $K_S$ is the same with that of the previous one. Therefore, the factorized matrices of the sub-matrices are also the same. Thus, keeping the factorized matrix at each step, the Cholesky factorization at the next iteration step can be restarted at the $i$th column and row of $K_S$.

Now discuss the complexity of the proposed training method for $\varepsilon = 0$, where no indices in $S$ are removed from $S$ during training. Then, training proceeds as indices for $h$ data are added to $S$ at the end of each iteration step and training ends after $M/h$ iterations. Because the Cholesky factorization is done incrementally, the computational cost of the Cholesky factorization is $O(N^3)$, where $N$ is the number of support vectors and $N = M$. Because the Cholesky factorization is the most crucial part of computation, computational complexity of the proposed method is $O(N^3)$. For $\varepsilon > 0$ the indices in $S$ are replaced with those in the fixed set. But if in most cases the indices of the less violating variables that are added at the previous step are deleted in the next step, the cost for the Cholesky factorization will still be $O(N^3)$. Thus in this case also, the computational complexity will be assumed to be $O(N^3)$. This will be evaluated in the next section.

## 5   Performance Comparison

Using the benchmark data sets obtained from the home page of LIBSVM [17], we first evaluated the convergence of the proposed method and then compared the training time with that of LIBSVM, which is based on SMO.

We scaled the input range into $[-1, 1]$ and used the polynomial kernels: $K(\mathbf{x}, \mathbf{x}') = (\mathbf{x}^\top \mathbf{x}' + 1)^d / (m + 1)^d$, where $d$ is the polynomial degree and RBF kernels: $\exp(-\gamma \|\mathbf{x} - \mathbf{x}'\|^2 / m)$, where $\gamma$ is the radius of the spread and $m$ is the number of input variables.

To check the convergence of the proposed method, we set two cases of parameter values where number of support vectors is large: $\gamma = 10$, $C = 10$, and $\varepsilon = 0.1$ and small: $\gamma = 0.1$, $C = 10^4$, and $\varepsilon = 1.0$. Changing the value of $h$ we checked the mean absolute error (MAE), the numbers of support vectors (SVs) and iterations, and training time. Table 1 shows the results. Because MAE and SVs were the same for different values of $h$, namely the same solution was obtained, we listed these values only in the first line of the results. Previous time and proposed time denote the training time without and with the incremental Cholesky factorization, respectively. For each problem and each training method, the shortest training time is shown in boldface. The effect of the incremental Cholesky factorization is especially evident for the abalone data set. The values of $h$ that gave the shortest training time were different for different problems. By the incremental Cholesky factorization, the median of the shortest training times is $h = 100$. Therefore, in the following we use $h = 100$.

To check convergence improvement for the large value of $\varepsilon$, we used the abalone problem using the RBF kernel with $\gamma = 0.1$ and polynomial kernels with $d = 3$ and with $C = 10000$ and change the value of $\varepsilon$. Table 2 lists the results. In this table, we also includes the maximum absolute error "Max_E." "Previous" and "Proposed" denote that the bias terms are calculated by the signs of current $\alpha_i$ and one-step-before $\alpha_i$. Using the current $\alpha_i$, the solutions were obtained only for $\varepsilon = 1$ with the maximum iterations of 1000. But for the proposed method, for the RBF kernel, for $\varepsilon = 13$ the number of support vectors is 2 and for $\varepsilon = 14$, the solution process was not monotonic and did not converge. This was because the optimum solution was expressed by a constant with no support vectors and the proposed method did not consider the solution with no support vectors. For the

**Table 1.** Convergence for the change of $h$

| Data | $h$ | $\gamma, C, \varepsilon$ | MAE | SVs | Iters | Previous Time (s) | Proposed Time (s) |
|---|---|---|---|---|---|---|---|
| Housing | 500 | 10, 10, 0.1 | 1.186 | 483 | 4 | **0.406** | 0.375 |
| | 250 | | | | 5 | 0.421 | 0.406 |
| | 100 | | | | 8 | 0.421 | **0.343** |
| | 50 | | | | 13 | 0.484 | 0.359 |
| | 500 | 0.1, $10^4$, 1.0 | 1.927 | 339 | 5 | 0.312 | 0.312 |
| | 250 | | | | 6 | 0.234 | 0.234 |
| | 100 | | | | 11 | **0.218** | **0.171** |
| | 50 | | | | 12 | **0.218** | **0.171** |
| Mg | 1000 | 10, 10, 0.01 | 0.07892 | 1279 | 4 | 8.84 | 7.11 |
| | 500 | | | | 5 | **8.81** | 7.22 |
| | 250 | | | | 8 | 10.9 | **6.25** |
| | 100 | | | | 15 | 13.0 | 6.56 |
| | 50 | | | | 28 | 20.5 | 6.58 |
| | 1000 | 0.1, $10^4$, 0.1 | 0.09981 | 599 | 7 | 3.22 | 3.14 |
| | 500 | | | | 6 | 1.98 | 2.08 |
| | 250 | | | | 7 | 1.50 | 1.27 |
| | 100 | | | | 9 | **1.14** | 0.968 |
| | 50 | | | | 16 | 1.55 | **0.812** |
| Space-ga | 1500 | 10, 10, 0.1 | 0.07872 | 941 | 7 | 24.6 | 24.3 |
| | 1000 | | | | 6 | 14.2 | 14.6 |
| | 500 | | | | 9 | 9.20 | 7.84 |
| | 250 | | | | 10 | 8.75 | 4.92 |
| | 100 | | | | 15 | **8.53** | **4.09** |
| | 50 | | | | 24 | 10.3 | 4.92 |
| | 1500 | 0.1, $10^4$, 1.0 | 0.5093 | 7 | 30 | 20.1 | 20.8 |
| | 1000 | | | | 25 | 9.45 | 9.25 |
| | 500 | | | | 22 | 2.80 | 2.47 |
| | 250 | | | | 29 | 1.41 | 0.968 |
| | 100 | | | | 33 | 0.656 | 0.656 |
| | 50 | | | | 29 | **0.484** | **0.437** |
| Abalone | 1500 | 10, 10, 0.1 | 1.425 | 3961 | 5 | **439** | 310 |
| | 1000 | | | | 7 | 543 | 310 |
| | 500 | | | | 10 | 518 | **228** |
| | 250 | | | | 18 | 742 | 324 |
| | 100 | | | | 11 | 1381 | 281 |
| | 50 | | | | 80 | 2600 | 261 |
| | 1500 | 0.1, $10^4$, 1.0 | 1.533 | 2323 | 5 | 109 | 106 |
| | 1000 | | | | 6 | **101** | 60.1 |
| | 500 | | | | 8 | 105 | 39.7 |
| | 250 | | | | 13 | 129 | **31.5** |
| | 100 | | | | 26 | 177 | 37.3 |
| | 50 | | | | 50 | 328 | 46.7 |

**Table 2.** Convergence for the abalone data set for the change of $\varepsilon$ with $C = 10000$

| Parm. | $\varepsilon$ | MAE | Max_E | SVs | Previous | | Proposed | |
|---|---|---|---|---|---|---|---|---|
| | | | | | Iters | Time (s) | Iters | Time (s) |
| $\gamma 0.1$ | 1 | 1.533 | 14.85 | 2323 | 31 | 35.8 | 25 | 37.3 |
| | 5 | 2.577 | 12.79 | 192 | — | — | 8 | 1.03 |
| | 10 | 4.818 | 10.09 | 5 | — | — | 25 | 0.859 |
| | 13 | 5.689 | 13.00 | 2 | — | — | 47 | 0.984 |
| $d3$ | 1 | 1.482 | 11.40 | 2311 | 31 | 44.4 | 29 | 45.4 |
| | 5 | 2.279 | 9.390 | 229 | — | — | 18 | 2.05 |
| | 7 | 2.970 | 7.683 | 81 | — | — | 311 | 13.2 |

polynomial kernel, for $\varepsilon = 7$ the number of support vectors was 81 and for $\varepsilon = 8$ the solution was not obtained. Therefore, training using RBF kernels is more stable than using polynomial kernels. But because we do not set so large a value to $\varepsilon$ unstable convergence for polynomial kernels may not be a serious problem. In addition by changing the calculation method of the bias terms, convergence was drastically improved.

We compared training time of the proposed method with that of LIBSVM. Because the proposed method is based on the L2 SVR but LIBSVM offers only the L1 SVR, the exact comparison is not possible. Usually the L2 SVR gives larger number of support vectors than the L1 SVR. For each case that tested we carefully checked that the above relation held. Except for the CPUsmall problem, we set $\gamma = 1$ for the RBF kernel, $d = 3$ for the polynomial kernel, and $\varepsilon = 0.1$. For the CPUsmall problem, to obtain solutions with the number of support vectors smaller than 5000, we used the RBF kernel with $\gamma = 0.001$ and linear kernels and $\varepsilon = 20$ for both cases. We changed the values of $C$ and measured the training time using a personal computer (3.16GHz, 3GB memory, Windows XP operating system). For parameter values of LIBSVM other than stated above, we set default values.

Table 3 lists the results. In the "Data" column, in addition to the name of the data set, we included the numbers of inputs and data. The "SVs" column lists the number of support vectors for the proposed method. For each case, the shorter training time is shown in boldface. From the table it is clear that for small values of $C$ LIBSVM is faster but for large value of $C$ LIBSVM slows down.

For the proposed method the training time did not change very much except for the CPUsmall problem with the RBF kernel. For the CPUsmall problem, the number of support vectors reduced significantly as the $C$ value was increased. This led to the shorter training time. Except for the abalone and CPUsmall problems with RBF kernels the proposed method is faster than LIBSVM for large $C$ values.

Assuming that the computational complexity of the proposed method is $O(N^3)$ and the training time of the housing data set with RBF kernels and $C = 100000$,

**Table 3.** Training time comparison in seconds

| Data | C | SVs | RBF Proposed | RBF LIBSVM | SVs | Polynomial Proposed | Polynomial LIBSVM |
|---|---|---|---|---|---|---|---|
| Housing | 10 | 487 | 0.328 | **0.093** | 487 | 0.406 | **0.093** |
| 13 | 100 | 480 | 0.343 | **0.125** | 495 | 0.593 | **0.203** |
| 506 | 1000 | 488 | 0.406 | **0.375** | 489 | **0.656** | 1.02 |
| | 10000 | 486 | **0.421** | 2.67 | 494 | **1.00** | 11.5 |
| | 100000 | 492 | **0.562** | 36.9 | 497 | **1.45** | 284 |
| Mg | 10 | 602 | 0.781 | **0.234** | 573 | 1.00 | **0.296** |
| 6 | 100 | 576 | 0.859 | **0.593** | 562 | **0.921** | 1.31 |
| 1385 | 1000 | 560 | **1.16** | 2.88 | 566 | **1.00** | 8.89 |
| | 10000 | 551 | **1.28** | 29.8 | 564 | **1.28** | 93 |
| | 100000 | 533 | **1.45** | 982 | 564 | **1.71** | 1487 |
| Space-ga | 10 | 1082 | 4.70 | **0.531** | 978 | 3.66 | **0.703** |
| 6 | 100 | 994 | 3.86 | **1.64** | 974 | 4.48 | **3.25** |
| 3107 | 1000 | 976 | **4.98** | 9.09 | 979 | **4.13** | 25.2 |
| | 10000 | 943 | **3.75** | 78.2 | 962 | **4.53** | 259 |
| | 100000 | 887 | **3.84** | 1931 | 959 | **4.92** | 7367 |
| Abalone | 10 | 3968 | 264 | **1.48** | 3977 | 319 | **1.25** |
| 8 | 100 | 3961 | 206 | **1.72** | 3951 | 240 | **1.81** |
| 4177 | 1000 | 3962 | 296 | **3.55** | 3957 | 301 | **7.06** |
| | 10000 | 3962 | 202 | **19.4** | 3956 | 297 | **69.2** |
| | 100000 | 3959 | 238 | **196** | 3962 | **287** | 986 |
| CPUsmall | 10 | 2745 | 241 | **0.609** | 784 | 10.3 | **0.625** |
| 12 | 100 | 1449 | 23.4 | **0.625** | 783 | 9.98 | **0.968** |
| 8192 | 1000 | 953 | 11.4 | **0.609** | 783 | 8.56 | **3.66** |
| | 10000 | 786 | 8.91 | **0.687** | 783 | 9.09 | 22.6 |
| | 100000 | 724 | 8.72 | **0.781** | 783 | 9.19 | 155 |

the training time of the abalone data set with the same condition is estimated to be $(3959/492)^3 \times 0.562 = 293$ (s), which is near to the actual training time of 238 (s).

# 6  Conclusions

In this paper we proposed improving convergence of an active set training method for L2 SVRs. To stabilize convergence for a large epsilon tube, we calculate the bias terms according to the signs of previous variables not the current ones. And to accelerate training, we introduce incremental Cholesky factorization. The computation complexity of the proposed method is the cubic of the number of support vectors. Using the benchmark data sets, we showed that the convergence of the training method was drastically stabilized for a large epsilon tube and by the incremental Cholesky factorization, training was sped up and the proposed method was faster than LIBSVM for large $C$ value for medium size problems.

# References

1. Osuna, E., Freund, R., Girosi, F.: An improved training algorithm for support vector machines. In: Proc. NNSP 1997, pp. 276–285 (1997)
2. Saunders, C., Stitson, M.O., Weston, J., Bottou, L., Schölkopf, B., Smola, A.: Support vector machine: Reference manual, Technical Report CSD-TR-98-03, Royal Holloway, University of London (1998)
3. Platt, J.C.: Fast training of support vector machines using sequential minimal optimization. In: Schölkopf, B., et al. (eds.) Advances in Kernel Methods: Support Vector Learning, pp. 185–208. MIT Press, Cambridge (1999)
4. Cauwenberghs, G., Poggio, T.: Incremental and decremental support vector machine learning. In: Leen, T.K., et al. (eds.) Advances in Neural Information Processing Systems, vol. 13, pp. 409–415. MIT Press, Cambridge (2001)
5. Shilton, A., Palaniswami, M., Ralph, D., Tsoi, A.C.: Incremental training of support vector machines. IEEE Trans. Neural Networks 16(1), 114–131 (2005)
6. Scheinberg, K.: An efficient implementation of an active set method for SVMs. Journal of Machine Learning Research 7, 2237–2257 (2006)
7. Abe, S.: Batch support vector training based on exact incremental training. In: Kůrková, V., Neruda, R., Koutník, J. (eds.) ICANN 2008, Part I. LNCS, vol. 5163, pp. 527–536. Springer, Heidelberg (2008)
8. Gâlmeanu, H., Andonie, R.: Implementation issues of an incremental and decremental SVM. In: Kůrková, V., Neruda, R., Koutník, J. (eds.) ICANN 2008, Part I. LNCS, vol. 5163, pp. 325–335. Springer, Heidelberg (2008)
9. Sentelle, C., Anagnostopoulos, G.C., Georgiopoulos, M.: An efficient active set method for SVM training without singular inner problems. In: Proc. IJCNN 2009, pp. 2875–2882 (2009)
10. Chapelle, O.: Training a support vector machine in the primal. In: Bottou, L., et al. (eds.) Large-Scale Kernel Machines, pp. 29–50. MIT Press, Cambridge (2007)
11. Abe, S.: Is primal better than dual. In: Alippi, C., Polycarpou, M., Panayiotou, C., Ellinas, G. (eds.) ICANN 2009, Part I. LNCS, vol. 5768, pp. 854–863. Springer, Heidelberg (2009)
12. Ma, J., Theiler, J., Perkins, S.: Accurate on-line support vector regression. Neural Computation 15(11), 2683–2703 (2003)
13. Musicant, D.R., Feinberg, A.: Active set support vector regression. IEEE Trans. Neural Networks 15(2), 268–275 (2004)
14. Abe, S.: Active set training of support vector regressors. In: Proc. ESANN 2010, pp. 117–122 (2010)
15. Mattera, D., Palmieri, F., Haykin, S.: An explicit algorithm for training support vector machines. IEEE Signal Processing Letters 6(9), 243–245 (1999)
16. Kaieda, K., Abe, S.: KPCA-based training of a kernel fuzzy classifier with ellipsoidal regions. International Journal of Approximate Reasoning 37(3), 189–217 (2004)
17. Chang, C.-C., Lin, C.-J.: LIBSVM-A library for support vector machines, http://www.csie.ntu.edu.tw/~cjlin/libsvm/

# The Complex Gaussian Kernel LMS Algorithm

Pantelis Bouboulis and Sergios Theodoridis

Department of Informatics and Telecommunications,
University of Athens, Athens, Greece
{bouboulis,stheodor}@di.uoa.gr

**Abstract.** Although the real reproducing kernels are used in an increasing number of machine learning problems, complex kernels have not, yet, been used, in spite of their potential interest in applications such as communications. In this work, we focus our attention on the complex gaussian kernel and its possible application in the complex Kernel LMS algorithm. In order to derive the gradients needed to develop the complex kernel LMS (CKLMS), we employ the powerful tool of Wirtinger's Calculus, which has recently attracted much attention in the signal processing community. Writinger's calculus simplifies computations and offers an elegant tool for treating complex signals. To this end, the notion of Writinger's calculus is extended to include complex RKHSs. Experiments verify that the CKLMS offers significant performance improvements over the traditional complex LMS or Widely Linear complex LMS (WL-LMS) algorithms, when dealing with nonlinearities.

**Keywords:** Kernel Methods, LMS, Reproducing Kernel Hilbert Spaces, Complex Kernels, Wirtinger Calculus, Kernels.

## 1 Introduction

In recent years, kernel based algorithms have become the state of the art for many problems, especially in the machine learning community. The common feature of these problems is that they are casted as optimization problems over a Reproducing Kernel Hilbert Space (RKHS). The main advantage of mobilizing the tool of RKHSs is that the original nonlinear task is "transformed" into a linear one, where one can employ an easier "algebra". Moreover, different types of nonlinearities can be treated in a unifying way, that does not affect the derivation of the algorithms, except at the final implementation stage. The main concepts of this procedure can be summarized in the following two steps: 1) Map the finite dimensionality input data from the input space $F$ (usually $F \subset \mathbb{R}^\nu$) into a higher dimensionality (possibly infinite) RKHS $\mathcal{H}$ and 2) Perform a linear processing (e.g., adaptive filtering) on the mapped data in $\mathcal{H}$. The procedure is equivalent with a non-linear processing (non-linear filtering) in $F$.

An alternative way of describing this process is through the popular *kernel trick* [1], [2]: "Given an algorithm, which is formulated in terms of dot products, one can construct an alternative algorithm by replacing each one of the dot products with a positive definite kernel $\kappa$". The specific choice of kernel,

K. Diamantaras, W. Duch, L.S. Iliadis (Eds.): ICANN 2010, Part II, LNCS 6353, pp. 11–20, 2010.

implicitly, defines a RKHS with an appropriate inner product. Furthermore, the choice of a kernel also defines the type of nonlinearity that underlies the model to be used. Although there are several kernels available in the relative literature, in most cases the powerful real Gaussian kernel is adopted.

The main representatives of this class of algorithms are the celebrated *support vector machines* (SVMs), which have dominated the research in machine learning over the last decade. Moreover, processing in Reproducing Kernel Hilbert Spaces (RKHSs) in the context of online adaptive processing is also gaining in popularity within the signal processing community [3], [4], [5], [6], [7]. Besides SVMs and the more recent applications in adaptive filtering, there is a plethora of other scientific domains that have gained from adopting kernel methods (e.g., image processing and denoising [8], [9], principal component analysis [10], clustering [11], e.t.c.).

Although the real Gaussian RBF kernel is quite popular in the aforementioned context, the existence of the corresponding complex Gaussian kernel is relatively unknown to the machine learning community. This is partly due to the fact, that in classification tasks (which is the dominant application of kernel methods) the use of complex kernels is prohibitive, since no arrangement can be derived in complex domains and the necessary separating hyperplane of SVMs cannot be defined. Consequently, all known kernel based applications, since they emerged from the specific background, use real-valued kernels and they are able to deal with real valued data sequences only. While the complex gaussian RBF kernel is known to the mathematicians (especially those working on Reproducing Kernel Hilbert Spaces or Functional Analysis), it has remained in obscurity in the machine learning society. In this paper, however, we use the complex gaussian kernel to address the problem of adaptive filtering of complex signals in RKHSs, focusing on the recently developed Kernel LMS (KLMS) [3], [12]. The main goals of this paper are: a) to elevate from obscurity the complex Gaussian kernel as an effective tool for kernel based adaptive processing of complex signals, b) the extension of *Wirtinger's Calculus* in complex RKHSs as a means for the elegant and efficient computation of the gradients, that are involved in many adaptive filtering algorithms, and c) the development of the Complex Kernel LMS (CKLMS) algorithm, by exploiting the extension of Wirtinger's calculus and the RKHS of complex gaussian kernels. Wirtinger's calculus [13] is enjoying increasing popularity, recently, mainly in the context of *Widely Linear* complex adaptive filters [14], [15], [16], [17], [18], providing a tool for the derivation of gradients in the complex domain.

The paper is organized as follows. In section 2 we provide a minimal introduction to complex RKHSs focusing on the complex gaussian kernel and its relation with the real one. Next, in section 3 we summarize the main notions of the extended Wirtinger's Calculus. Section 4 presents the gaussian complex kernel LMS algorithm. Finally, experimental results and conclusions are provided in Section 5. We will denote the set of all real and complex numbers by $\mathbb{R}$ and $\mathbb{C}$ respectively. Vector or matrix valued quantities appear in boldfaced symbols.

## 2  Reproducing Kernel Hilbert Spaces

In this section we briefly describe the Reproducing Kernel Hilbert Spaces. Since we are mainly interested on the complex case, we recall the basic facts on RKHS associated with complex kernels. The material presented here may be found with more details in [19] and [20]. Given a function $\kappa : X \times X \to \mathbb{C}$ and $x_1, \ldots, x_N \in X$, the matrix[1] $K = (K_{i,j})^N$ with elements $K_{i,j} = \kappa(x_i, x_j)$, for $i, j = 1, \ldots, N$, is called the *Gram matrix* (or *kernel matrix*) of $\kappa$ with respect to $x_1, \ldots, x_N$. A complex hermitian matrix $K = (K_{i,j})^N$ satisfying

$$c^H \cdot K \cdot c = \sum_{i=1,j=1}^{N,N} c_i^* c_j K_{i,j} \geq 0,$$

for all $c_i \in \mathbb{C}$, $i = 1, \ldots, N$, is called *Positive Definite*[2]. Let $X$ be a nonempty set. Then a function $\kappa : X \times X \to \mathbb{C}$, which for all $N \in \mathbb{N}$ and all $x_1, \ldots, x_N \in X$ gives rise to a positive definite Gram matrix $K$ is called a *Positive Definite Kernel*. In the following we will frequently refer to a positive definite kernel simply as *kernel*.

Next, consider a linear class $\mathcal{H}$ of complex valued functions $f$ defined on a set $X$. Suppose further, that in $\mathcal{H}$ we can define an inner product $\langle \cdot, \cdot \rangle_{\mathcal{H}}$ with corresponding norm $\| \cdot \|_{\mathcal{H}}$ and that $\mathcal{H}$ is complete with respect to that norm, i.e., $\mathcal{H}$ is a Hilbert space. We call $\mathcal{H}$ a *Reproducing Kernel Hilbert Space (RKHS)*, if for all $x \in X$ the evaluation functional $T_x : \mathcal{H} \to \mathbb{C} : T_x(f) = f(x)$ is a continuous (or, equivalently, bounded) operator. If this is true, then by the Riesz's representation theorem, for all $x \in X$ there is a function $g_x \in \mathcal{H}$ such that $T_x(f) = f(x) = \langle f, g_x \rangle_{\mathcal{H}}$. The function $\kappa : X \times X \to \mathbb{C} : \kappa(y, x) = g_x(y)$ is called a *reproducing kernel* of $\mathcal{H}$. It can be easily proved that the function $\kappa$ is a positive definite kernel.

Alternatively, we can define a RKHS as a Hilbert space $\mathcal{H}$ for which there exists a function $\kappa : X \times X \to \mathbb{C}$ with the following two properties:

1. For every $x \in X$, $\kappa(\cdot, x)$ belongs to $\mathcal{H}$.
2. $\kappa$ has the so called *reproducing property*, i.e.

$$f(x) = \langle f, \kappa(\cdot, x) \rangle_{\mathcal{H}}, \text{ for all } f \in \mathcal{H}, \tag{1}$$

in particular $\kappa(x, y) = \langle \kappa(\cdot, y), \kappa(\cdot, x) \rangle_{\mathcal{H}}$.

It has been proved (see [21]) that to every positive definite kernel $\kappa$ there corresponds one and only one class of functions $\mathcal{H}$ with a uniquely determined inner product in it, forming a Hilbert space and admitting $\kappa$ as a reproducing kernel. In fact the kernel $\kappa$ produces the entire space $\mathcal{H}$, i.e., $\mathcal{H} = \overline{\text{span}\{\kappa(x, \cdot) | x \in X\}}$. The map $\Phi : X \to \mathcal{H} : \Phi(x) = \kappa(\cdot, x)$ is called the *feature map* of $\mathcal{H}$. Recall, that in the case of complex Hilbert spaces the inner product is sesqui-linear and

---

[1] The term $(K_{i,j})^N$ denotes a square $N \times N$ matrix.

[2] In matrix analysis literature, this is the definition of the positive semidefinite matrix.

Hermitian. In the real case the condition $\kappa(x, y) = \langle \kappa(\cdot, y), \kappa(\cdot, x)\rangle_{\mathcal{H}}$ may be replaced by the well known equation $\kappa(x, y) = \langle \kappa(\cdot, x), \kappa(\cdot, y)\rangle_{\mathcal{H}}$. However, since in the complex case the inner product is Hermitian, the aforementioned condition is equivalent to $\kappa(x, y) = (\langle \kappa(\cdot, x), \kappa(\cdot, y)\rangle_{\mathcal{H}})^*$.

Consider the complex valued function

$$\kappa_{\sigma, \mathbb{C}^d}(\boldsymbol{z}, \boldsymbol{w}) := \exp\left(-\frac{\sum_{i=1}^{d}(z_i - w_i^*)^2}{\sigma^2}\right), \tag{2}$$

defined on $\mathbb{C}^d \times \mathbb{C}^d$, where $\boldsymbol{z}, \boldsymbol{w} \in \mathbb{C}^d$, $z_i$ denotes the $i$-th component of the complex vector $\boldsymbol{z} \in \mathbb{C}^d$ and exp is the extended exponential function in the complex domain. It can be shown that $\kappa_{\sigma, \mathbb{C}^d}$ is a $\mathbb{C}$-valued kernel on $\mathbb{C}^d$, which we call the *complex Gaussian kernel* with parameter $\sigma$. Its restriction $\kappa_\sigma := \left(\kappa_{\sigma, \mathbb{C}^d}\right)_{|\mathbb{R}^d \times \mathbb{R}^d}$ is the well known *real Gaussian kernel*:

$$\kappa_{\sigma, \mathbb{R}^d}(\boldsymbol{x}, \boldsymbol{y}) := \exp\left(-\frac{\sum_{i=1}^{d}(x_i - y_i)^2}{\sigma^2}\right). \tag{3}$$

An explicit description of the RKHSs of these kernels, together with some important properties can be found in [22].

# 3    Wirtinger's Calculus in Complex RKHS

Wirtinger's calculus [13] has become very popular in the signal processing community mainly in the context of complex adaptive filtering [14], [23], [15], [16], [24], as a means of computing, in an elegant way, gradients of real valued cost functions defined on complex domains ($\mathbb{C}^\nu$). The Cauchy-Riemann conditions dictate that such functions are not holomorphic and therefore the complex derivative cannot be used. Instead, if we consider that the cost function is defined on a Euclidean domain with a double dimensionality ($\mathbb{R}^{2\nu}$), then the real derivatives may be employed. The price of this approach is that the computations become cumbersome and tedious. Wirtinger's calculus provides an alternative equivalent formulation, that is based on simple rules and principles and which bears a great resemblance to the rules of the standard complex derivative. A self-consistent presentation of the main ideas of Wirtinger's calculus may be found in the excellent and highly recommended introductory report of K. Kreutz-Delgado [25].

In the case of a simple non-holomorphic complex function $T$ defined on $U \subseteq \mathbb{C}$, Wirtinger's calculus considers two forms of derivatives, the $\mathbb{R}$-*derivative* and the *conjugate* $\mathbb{R}$-*derivative*, which are defined as follows:

$$\frac{\partial T}{\partial z} = \frac{1}{2}\left(\frac{\partial u}{\partial x} + \frac{\partial v}{\partial y}\right) + \frac{i}{2}\left(\frac{\partial v}{\partial x} - \frac{\partial u}{\partial y}\right),$$

$$\frac{\partial T}{\partial z^*} = \frac{1}{2}\left(\frac{\partial u}{\partial x} - \frac{\partial v}{\partial y}\right) + \frac{i}{2}\left(\frac{\partial v}{\partial x} + \frac{\partial u}{\partial y}\right)$$

where $T(z) = T(x + iy) = T(x, y) = u(x, y) + iv(x, y)$. Note that any such non-holomorphic function can be written in the form $T(z, z^*)$. Having this in mind, $\frac{\partial T}{\partial z}$, can be easily evaluated as the standard complex partial derivative taken with respect to $z$ (thus treating $z^*$ as a constant). Consequently, $\frac{\partial T}{\partial z^*}$ is evaluated as the standard complex partial derivative taken with respect to $z^*$ (thus treating $z$ as a constant). For example, if $T(z, z^*) = z(z^*)^2$, then $\frac{\partial T}{\partial z} = (z^*)^2$, $\frac{\partial T}{\partial z^*} = 2zz^*$. Similar principles and rules hold for a function of many complex variables (i.e., $U \subseteq \mathbb{C}^\nu$) [25].

Wirtinger's calculus has been developed only for operators defined on finite dimensional spaces, $\mathbb{C}^\nu$. Hence, this calculus cannot be used in RKH spaces, where the dimensionality of the function space can be infinite, as, for example, it is the case for the Gaussian RKHSs. To this end, Wirtinger's calculus needs to be generalized to a general Hilbert space. A rigorous presentation of this extension is out of the scope of the paper (due to lack of space). Nevertheless, we will present the main ideas and results. We employ the Fréchet derivative, a notion that generalizes differentiability on abstract Banach or Hilbert spaces. Consider a Hilbert space $H$ over the field $F$ (typically $\mathbb{R}$ or $\mathbb{C}$). The operator $T : H \to F$ is said to be *Fréchet differentiable* at $f_0$, if there exists a $u \in H$, such that

$$\lim_{\|h\|_H \to 0} \frac{T(f_0 + h) - T(f_0) - \langle u, h \rangle_H}{\|h\|_H} = 0, \tag{4}$$

where $\langle \cdot, \cdot \rangle_H$ is the dot product of the Hilbert space $H$ and $\| \cdot \|_H = \sqrt{\langle \cdot, \cdot \rangle_H}$ is the induced norm. The element $u$ is usually called the gradient of $T$ at $f_0$.

Assume that $\boldsymbol{T} = (T_1, T_2)^T$, $\boldsymbol{T}(\boldsymbol{f}) = \boldsymbol{T}(f_1 + if_2) = \boldsymbol{T}(f_1, f_2) = T_1(f_1, f_2) + iT_2(f_1, f_2)$, is differentiable as an operator defined on the RKHS $\mathcal{H}$ and let $\nabla_1 T_1$, $\nabla_2 T_1$, $\nabla_1 T_2$ and $\nabla_2 T_2$ be the partial derivatives, with respect to the first $(f_1)$ and the second $(f_2)$ variable respectively. It turns out, proofs are omitted due to lack of space, that if $\boldsymbol{T}(f_1, f_2)$ has derivatives of any order, then it can be written in the form $\boldsymbol{T}(\boldsymbol{f}, \boldsymbol{f}^*)$, where $\boldsymbol{f}^* = f_1 - if_2$, so that for fixed $\boldsymbol{f}^*$, $\boldsymbol{T}$ is $\boldsymbol{f}$-holomorphic and for fixed $\boldsymbol{f}$, $\boldsymbol{T}$ is $\boldsymbol{f}^*$-holomorphic. We may define the $\mathbb{R}$-derivative and the conjugate $\mathbb{R}$-derivative of $\boldsymbol{T}$ as follows:

$$\nabla_{\boldsymbol{f}} \boldsymbol{T} = \frac{1}{2} (\nabla_1 T_1 + \nabla_2 T_2) + \frac{i}{2} (\nabla_1 T_2 - \nabla_2 T_1) \tag{5}$$

$$\nabla_{\boldsymbol{f}^*} \boldsymbol{T} = \frac{1}{2} (\nabla_1 T_1 - \nabla_2 T_2) + \frac{i}{2} (\nabla_1 T_2 + \nabla_2 T_1). \tag{6}$$

The following properties can be proved (among others):

1. The first order Taylor expansion around $\boldsymbol{f} \in \mathcal{H}$ is given by

$$\boldsymbol{T}(\boldsymbol{f} + \boldsymbol{h}) = \boldsymbol{T}(\boldsymbol{f}) + \langle \boldsymbol{h}, (\nabla_{\boldsymbol{f}} \boldsymbol{T}(\boldsymbol{f}))^* \rangle_{\mathcal{H}} + \langle \boldsymbol{h}^*, (\nabla_{\boldsymbol{f}^*} \boldsymbol{T}(\boldsymbol{f}))^* \rangle_{\mathcal{H}}.$$

2. If $\boldsymbol{T}(\boldsymbol{f}) = \langle \boldsymbol{f}, \boldsymbol{w} \rangle_{\mathcal{H}}$, then $\nabla_{\boldsymbol{f}} \boldsymbol{T} = \boldsymbol{w}^*$, $\nabla_{\boldsymbol{f}^*} \boldsymbol{T} = \boldsymbol{0}$.
3. If $\boldsymbol{T}(\boldsymbol{f}) = \langle \boldsymbol{w}, \boldsymbol{f} \rangle_{\mathcal{H}}$, then $\nabla_{\boldsymbol{f}} \boldsymbol{T} = \boldsymbol{0}$, $\nabla_{\boldsymbol{f}^*} \boldsymbol{T} = \boldsymbol{w}$.
4. If $\boldsymbol{T}(\boldsymbol{f}) = \langle \boldsymbol{f}^*, \boldsymbol{w} \rangle_{\mathcal{H}}$, then $\nabla_{\boldsymbol{f}} \boldsymbol{T} = \boldsymbol{0}$, $\nabla_{\boldsymbol{f}^*} \boldsymbol{T} = \boldsymbol{w}^*$.
5. If $\boldsymbol{T}(\boldsymbol{f}) = \langle \boldsymbol{w}, \boldsymbol{f}^* \rangle_{\mathcal{H}}$, then $\nabla_{\boldsymbol{f}} \boldsymbol{T} = \boldsymbol{w}$, $\nabla_{\boldsymbol{f}^*} \boldsymbol{T} = \boldsymbol{0}$.

An important consequence of the above properties is that if $T$ is a real valued operator defined on $\mathcal{H}$, then its first order Taylor's expansion is given by:

$$\begin{aligned} T(f+h) &= T(f) + \langle h, (\nabla_f T(f))^* \rangle_{\mathcal{H}} + \langle h^*, (\nabla_{f^*} T(f))^* \rangle_{\mathcal{H}} \\ &= T(f) + \langle h, \nabla_{f^*} T(f) \rangle_{\mathcal{H}} + (\langle h, \nabla_{f^*} T(f) \rangle_{\mathcal{H}})^* \\ &= T(f) + 2 \cdot \Re\left[ \langle h, \nabla_{f^*} T(f) \rangle_{\mathcal{H}} \right]. \end{aligned}$$

However, in view of the Cauchy Riemann inequality we have:

$$\Re\left[ \langle h, \nabla_{f^*} T(f) \rangle_{\mathcal{H}} \right] \le |\langle h, \nabla_{f^*} T(f) \rangle_{\mathcal{H}}| \le \|h\|_{\mathcal{H}} \cdot \|\nabla_{f^*} T(f)\|_{\mathcal{H}}.$$

The equality in the above relationship holds if $h \propto \nabla_{f^*} T$. Hence, the direction of increase of $T$ is $\nabla_{f^*} T(f)$. Therefore, any gradient descent based algorithm minimizing $T(f)$ is based on the update scheme:

$$f_n = f_{n-1} - \mu \cdot \nabla_{f^*} T(f_{n-1}). \tag{7}$$

## 4   Complex Kernel LMS

As an application of the complex gaussian kernel in adaptive filtering of complex signals, we focus on the recently developed *Kernel Least Mean Squares Algorithm* (KLMS), which is the LMS algorithm in RKHSs [3], [12]. KLMS, as all the known kernel methods that use real-valued kernels, was developed for real valued data sequences only. Here, the KLMS is extended to include the complex case. To our knowledge, no kernel-based strategy has been developed, so far, that is able to effectively deal with complex valued signals. Wirtinger's calculus is exploited to derive the necessary gradient updates.

Consider the sequence of examples $(z(1), d(1)), (z(2), d(2)), \dots, (z(N), d(N))$, where $d(n) \in \mathbb{C}$, $z(n) \in V \subset \mathbb{C}^\nu$, $z(n) = x(n) + iy(n)$, $x(n), y(n) \in \mathbb{R}^\nu$, for $n = 1, \dots, N$. We map the points $z(n)$ to the gaussian complex RKHS $\mathcal{H}$ using the feature map $\Phi$, for $n = 1, \dots, N$. The objective of the complex Kernel LMS is to minimize $E[\mathcal{L}_n(w)]$, where

$$\begin{aligned} \mathcal{L}_n(w) &= |e(n)|^2 = |d(n) - \langle \Phi(z(n)), w \rangle_{\mathbb{H}}|^2 \\ &= (d(n) - \langle \Phi(z(n)), w \rangle_{\mathbb{H}}) (d(n) - \langle \Phi(z(n)), w \rangle_{\mathbb{H}})^* \\ &= (d(n) - \langle w^*, \Phi(z(n)) \rangle_{\mathbb{H}}) (d(n)^* - \langle w, \Phi(z(n)) \rangle_{\mathbb{H}}), \end{aligned}$$

at each instance $n$. We then apply the complex LMS to the transformed data, using the rules of Wirtinger's calculus to compute the gradient $\nabla_{w^*} \mathcal{L}_n(w) = -e(n)^* \cdot \Phi(z(n))$. Therefore the CKLMS update rule becomes $w(n) = w(n-1) + \mu e(n)^* \cdot \Phi(z(n))$, where $w(n)$ denotes the estimate at iteration $n$.

Assuming that $w(0) = 0$, the repeated application of the weight-update equation gives:

$$w(n) = \sum_{k=1}^{n} e(k)^* \Phi(z(k)). \tag{8}$$

Thus, the filter output at iteration $n$ becomes:

$$\hat{d}(n) = \langle \Phi(z(n)), w(n-1) \rangle_{\mathbb{H}} = \mu \sum_{k=1}^{n-1} e(k) \langle \Phi(z(n)), \Phi(z(k)) \rangle_{\mathbb{H}}$$

$$= \mu \sum_{k=1}^{n-1} e(k) \kappa_{\sigma, \mathbb{C}^\nu}(z(n), z(k)).$$

It can readily be shown that, since the CKLMS is the complex LMS in RKHS, the important properties of the LMS (convergence in the mean, misadjustment, e.t.c.) carry over to CKLMS. Furthermore, note that using the complex gaussian kernel the algorithm is automatically normalized. The CKLMS algorithm is summarized in Algorithm 1. Although it is developed in the context of the complex gaussian kernel, it may be used with any other complex reproducing kernel.

---

**Algorithm 1.** Normalized Complex Kernel LMS

**INPUT:** $(z(1), d(1)), \ldots, (z(N), d(N))$
**OUTPUT:** The expansion
$w = \sum_{k=1}^{N} a(k) \kappa(z(k), \cdot)$.

**Initialization:** Set $a = \{\}$, $Z = \{\}$ (i.e., $w = 0$). Select the step parameter $\mu$ and the parameter $\sigma$ of the complex gaussian kernel.
    **for** n=1:N **do**
        Compute the filter output: $\hat{d}(n) = \sum_{k=1}^{n-1} a(k) \cdot \kappa_{\sigma, \mathbb{C}^\nu}(z(n), z(k))$.
        Compute the error: $e(n) = d(n) - \hat{d}(n)$.
        $a(n) = \mu e(n)$.
        Add the new center $z(n)$ to the list of centers, i.e., add $z(n)$ to the list $Z$, add $a(n)$ to the list $a$.
    **end for**

---

In CKLMS, we start from an empty set (usually called the *dictionary*) and gradually add new samples to that set, to form a summation similar to the one shown in equation (8). This results to an increasing memory and computational requirements, as time evolves. To cope with this problem and to produce sparse solutions, we employ the well known *novelty criterion* [26], [12]. In novelty criterion online sparsification, whenever a new data pair $(\Phi(z_n), d_n)$ is considered, a decision is immediately made of whether to add the new center $\Phi(z_n)$ to the dictionary of centers $\mathcal{C}$. The decision is reached following two simple rules. First, the distance of the new center $\Phi(z_n)$ from the current dictionary is evaluated: $dis = \min_{c_k \in \mathcal{C}} \{\|\Phi(z_n) - c_k\|_{\mathbb{H}}\}$. If this distance is smaller than a given threshold $\delta_1$ (i.e., the new center is close to the existing dictionary), then the center is not added to $\mathcal{C}$. Otherwise, we compute the prediction error $e_n = d_n - \hat{d}_n$. If $|e_n|$ is smaller than a predefined threshold $\delta_2$, then the new center is discarded. Only if $|e_n| \geq \delta_2$ the new center $\Phi(z_n)$ is added to the dictionary.

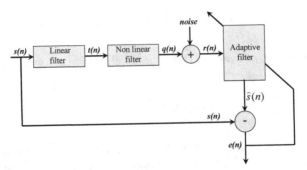

**Fig. 1.** The equalization problem

## 5   Experiments

We tested the CKLMS using a simple nonlinear channel equalization problem (see figure 1). The nonlinear channel consists of a linear filter: $t(n) = (-0.9 + 0.8i) \cdot s(n) + (0.6 - 0.7i) \cdot s(n-1)$ and a memoryless nonlinearity $q(n) = t(n) + (0.1 + 0.15i) \cdot t^2(n) + (0.06 + 0.05i) \cdot t^3(n)$. At the receiver end of the channel, the signal is corrupted by white Gaussian noise and then observed as $r(n)$. The input signal that was fed to the channel had the form

$$s(n) = 0.70(\sqrt{1 - \rho^2}X(n) + i\rho Y(n)), \tag{9}$$

where $X(n)$ and $Y(n)$ are gaussian random variables. This input is circular for $\rho = \sqrt{2}/2$ and highly non-circular if $\rho$ approaches 0 or 1 [15]. The aim of channel equalization is to construct an inverse filter which taking the output $r(n)$, reproduces the original input signal with as low an error rate as possible. To this end we apply the NCKLMS algorithm to the set of samples

$$\left((r(n+D), r(n+D-1), \ldots, r(n+D-L))^T, s(n)\right),$$

where $L > 0$ is the filter length and $D$ the equalization time delay.

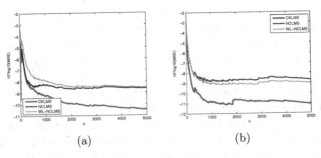

(a)                                      (b)

**Fig. 2.** Learning curves for KCLMS, ($\mu = 1$) CLMS ($\mu = 1/16$) and WL-CLMS ($\mu = 1/16$) (filter length $L = 5$, delay $D = 2$) in the nonlinear channel equalization, for the (a) circular input case and (b) the non-circular input case

Experiments were conducted on a set of 5000 samples of the input signal (9) considering both the circular and the non-circular case. The results are compared with the NCLMS and the WL-NCLMS algorithms. In all algorithms the step update parameter $\mu$ is tuned for best possible results. Time delay $D$ was also set for optimality. Figure 2 shows the learning curves of the NCKLMS with $\sigma = 5$, compared with the NCLMS and the WL-NCLMS algorithms. Novelty criterion was applied to the CKLMS for sparsification with $\delta_1 = 0.1$ and $\delta_2 = 0.2$. In both examples, CKLMS considerably outperforms both the NCLMS and the WL-NCLMS algorithms. However, this enhanced behavior comes at a price in computational complexity, since the CKLMS requires the evaluation of the kernel function on a growing number of training examples.

# References

1. Schölkopf, B., Smola, A.J.: Learning with Kernels. MIT Press, Cambridge (2002)
2. Theodoridis, S., Koutroumbas, K.: Pattern Recognition, 4th edn. Academic Press, London (2009)
3. Liu, W., Pokharel, P., Principe, J.C.: The kernel least-mean-square algorithm. IEEE Trans. Sign. Proc. 56(2), 543–554 (2008)
4. Kivinen, J., Smola, A., Williamson, R.C.: Online learning with kernels. IEEE Trans. Sign. Proc. 52(8), 2165–2176 (2004)
5. Engel, Y., Mannor, S., Meir, R.: The kernel recursive least-squares algorithm. IEEE Trans. Sign. Proc. 52(8) (2004)
6. Slavakis, K., Theodoridis, S., Yamada, I.: On line classification using kernels and projection based adaptive algorithm. IEEE Trans. Signal Process. 56(7), 2781–2797 (2008)
7. Slavakis, K., Theodoridis, S., Yamada, I.: Adaptive constrained learning in reproducing kernel hilbert spaces: The robust beamforming case. IEEE Trans. Signal Process. 57(12), 4744–4764 (2009)
8. Kim, K., Franz, M.O., Scholkopf, B.: Iterative kernel principal component analysis for image modeling. IEEE Trans. Pattern Anal. Mach. Intell. 27(9), 1351–1366 (2005)
9. Bouboulis, P., Slavakis, K., Theodoridis, S.: Adaptive kernel-based image denoising employing semi-parametric regularization: Image Processing. IEEE Transactions. 19(6), 1465–1479 (2010)
10. Smola, A.J., Schölkopf, B., Muller, K.R.: Kernel principal component analysis. In: Gerstner, W., Hasler, M., Germond, A., Nicoud, J.-D. (eds.) ICANN 1997. LNCS, vol. 1327, pp. 583–588. Springer, Heidelberg (1997)
11. Filippone, M., Camastra, F., Masulli, F., Rovetta, S.: A survey of kernel and spectral methods for clustering. Pattern Recognition 41(1), 176–190 (2008)
12. Liu, W., Principe, J.C., Haykin, S.: Kernel Adaptive Filtering. Wiley, Chichester (2010)
13. Wirtinger, W.: Zur formalen theorie der functionen von mehr complexen veränderlichen. Math. Ann. 97, 357–375 (1927)
14. Picinbono, B., Chevalier, P.: Widely linear estimation with complex data. IEEE Trans. Signal Process. 43(8), 2030–2033 (1995)
15. Adali, T., Li, H.: Complex-valued adaptive signal processing. In: Adali, T., Haykin, S. (eds.) Adaptive Signal Processing: Next Generation Solutions, Hoboken, NJ. Wiley, Chichester (2010)

16. Adali, T., Li, H., Novey, M., Cardoso, J.F.: Complex ICA using nonlinear functions. IEEE Trans. Signal Process. 56(9), 4536–4544 (2008)
17. Mattera, D., Paura, L., Sterle, F.: Widely linear decision-feedback equalizer for time-dispersive linear MIMO channels. IEEE Trans. Signal Process. 53(7), 2525–2536 (2005)
18. Navarro-Moreno, J.: ARMA prediction of widely linear systems by using the innovations algorithm. IEEE Trans. Signal Process. 56(7), 3061–3068 (2008)
19. Saitoh, S.: Integral Transforms, Reproducing Kernels and their applications. Longman Scientific & Technical, Harlow (1997)
20. Paulsen, V.I.: An introduction to the theory of reproducing kernel hilbert spaces, http://www.math.uh.edu/~vern/rkhs.pdf
21. Aronszajn, N.: Theory of reproducing kernels. Transactions of the American Mathematical Society 68(3), 337–404 (1950)
22. Steinwart, I., Hush, D., Scovel, C.: An explicit description of the reproducing kernel hilbert spaces of gaussian rbf kernels. IEEE Transactions on Information Theory 52(10), 4635–4643 (2006)
23. Mandic, D., Goh, V.S.L.: Complex Valued Nonlinear Adaptive Filters. Wiley, Chichester (2009)
24. Cacciapuoti, A.S., Gelli, G., Paura, L., Verde, F.: Widely linear versus linear blind multiuser detection with subspace-based channel estimation: Finite sample-size effects. IEEE Trans. Signal Process. 57(4), 1426–1443 (2009)
25. Kreutz-Delgado, K.: The complex gradient operator and the $\mathbb{CR}$-calculus, http://citeseerx.ist.psu.edu/viewdoc/download?doi=10.1.1.86.6515&rep=rep1&type=pdf
26. Platt, J.: A resourse allocating network for function interpolation. Newral Computation 3(2), 213–225 (1991)

# Support Vector Machines-Kernel Algorithms for the Estimation of the Water Supply in Cyprus

Fotis Maris[1], Lazaros Iliadis[1], Stavros Tachos[2], Athanasios Loukas[3],
Iliana Spartali[2], Apostolos Vassileiou[1], and Elias Pimenidis[4]

[1] Democritus University of Thrace Greece
liliadis@fmenr.duth.gr
[2] Aristotle University of Thessaloniki Greece
[3] University of Thessaly Greece
[4] University of East London, UK

**Abstract.** This research effort aimed in the estimation of the water supply for the case of "Germasogeia" mountainous watersheds in Cyprus. The actual target was the development of an ε-Regression Support Vector Machine (SVMR) system with five input parameters. The 5-Fold Cross Validation method was applied in order to produce a more representative training data set. The fuzzy-weighted SVR combined with a fuzzy partition approach was employed in order to enhance the quality of the results and to offer an optimization approach. The final models that were produced have proven to perform with an error of very low magnitude in the testing phase when first time seen data were used.

**Keywords:** support vector machines, water supply, kernel algorithms, 5 fold cross validation.

## 1 Introduction

The "Germasogeia" watershed is located northeast of Lemessos and it has an area of 157 km². The maximum water supply is 0.42 m³/sec whereas its forest cover is 57.7% (33.7% brush lands). A large dam with a capacity of 13 million m³ has been constructed in the watershed of *Germasogeia* in Cyprus. Traditional approaches for the estimation of water supply use too many data features, they are complicated and time consuming. This modeling effort uses the same input data with the UBC watershed model (University of British Columbia) (Quick and Pipes, 1977) and it is cheap and very fast (Loukas, 2009). The UBC method creates a computational representation of the hydrological behavior of the watershed. It divides the watershed in altitude zones and the daily rain height and daily temperature values (min and max) are used as input. The input data features used in this modeling approach were meteorological, such as daily rain height, maximum and minimum daily temperatures. The data were measured by three meteorological stations located in 75, 100 and 995 meters respectively. For the control of the output, actual measurements of the water supply of the main water stream were used. The data concern the period 1986-1997.

K. Diamantaras, W. Duch, L.S. Iliadis (Eds.): ICANN 2010, Part II, LNCS 6353, pp. 21–29, 2010.

## 1.1  Literature Review

SVMR, and other machine learning soft computing and adaptive approaches have been used recently by other research scientists in hydrological applications (Lin et al., 2006), (Lobbrecht and Solomatine, 1999), (Iliadis et al. 2010) and more specifically for hydrological cases in Cyprus island (Iliadis and Maris, 2007). The following figure 1 presents clearly the evolution of the maximum and minimum temperatures (MAX TEMP, MIN TEMP), of the rainfall (in the three meteorological stations RAINFALL1, 2,3) and of the runoff values (RUN OFF) in the area under research for 1997.

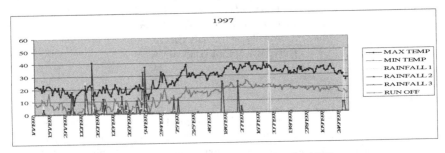

**Fig. 1.** Graphical display of the data for 1997

## 2  Material and Methods

The actual amount of data comprised of 4018 records, whereas the actual values of the parameters were located in the interval $[0,33]$. Due to the very wide range of the features' values, they were normalized by a scaling process before their potential use as input vectors. More specifically, this was done so that the features with a wide range of values should not prevale over the ones with a narrow range. The scaling was done by associating each parameter with a typical normal distribution, which has a standard deviation $\sigma^2 = 1$ and an average value of $\mu = 0$. It is well known that the 99.7% of the values of a parameter that follows a normal distribution can be found in the interval $[-3\sigma, +3\sigma]$ and hence in $[-3,3]$ since $\sigma = \sigma^2 = 1$. The first column in the tabular data is the output parameter. According to the above, the values of each feature were scaled based on the following function 1:

$$Z_j = \frac{X_j - \mu_j}{\sigma_j} \tag{1}$$

where $X_j$ is the $j^{th}$ parameter, $Z_j$ is the scaled variable following a normal distribution and $\sigma_j, \mu_j$ are the standard deviation and the mean value of the $j^{th}$ parameter. After the calculation of the estimated value $\hat{Y}$ of the scaled data, it was restored in the actual range of the output parameter based on the following function 2:

$$\hat{y} = \sigma_1 \cdot \hat{Y} + \mu_1 \tag{2}$$

It should be clarified that the average value in function 2 is always related to the first field data.

## 2.1 The 5-Fold-Cross Validation Approach

Cross-validation is the process where training and validation sets must cross-over in successive rounds such that each data point has a chance of being validated against. The general form of cross-validation is k-fold cross-validation (Refaeilzadeh et al.,2008). The 5-Fold-Cross Validation modeling method was also applied. The data was split in 5 groups (folds) of equal size and the $\varepsilon$-regression algorithm was executed 5 times. Every time a different fold was chosen to serve as the training set. This approach does not allow the existence of extreme values which are not representative for the training set. The division of the data set was done by the use of MATLAB's *crossvalind*, which is included in the Bioinformatics Toolbox.

## 2.2  ε-SV Regression (ε-SVR)

Support Vector Machines (SVM) were initially developed aiming in pattern recognition (Boser, Guyon & Vapnik 1992). The support vectors are a small subset of the training set. Vapnik (Vapnick, 1997), (Kecman, 2001) introduced the following loss function (3) that ignores errors less than a predefined value $\varepsilon > 0$

$$\left| y - f\left(\vec{x}\right) \right|_\varepsilon = \max\left\{ 0 \ , \ \left| y - f\left(\vec{x}\right) \right| - \varepsilon \right\} \tag{3}$$

In this way the ε-SVR algorithm was developed which offers the optimal function of the form: $f\left(\vec{x}\right) = k\left(\vec{w}, \vec{x}\right) + b \qquad \vec{w}, \vec{x} \in R^N, \ b \in R$ (4). This is achieved based on the training set $\left(\vec{x_1}, y_1\right), ..., \left(\vec{x_p}, y_p\right) \in R^N \times R$ (5). The target of this process is the search of a function $f$ with a small testing error which is described by the above function 3. However it is not possible to minimize function 3 because the probability distribution $P$ is unknown. Thus the solution is the minimization of the following normalized risk function 5

$$\frac{1}{2}\left\| \vec{w} \right\|^2 + C_{SVR} \cdot R_{emp}^\varepsilon \left[ f \right] \tag{5}$$

where $R_{emp}^\varepsilon \left[ f \right]$ is the function of empirical risk $R_{emp}\left[ f \right] = \frac{1}{p}\sum_{i=1}^{p} L\left( f, \vec{x_i}, y_i \right)$ (6) and the

loss function is $L(f, \vec{x_i}, y_i) = \left| y_i - f\left(\vec{x_i}\right) \right|_\varepsilon$ (7) that ignores errors less than $\varepsilon$ . $\left\| \vec{w} \right\|^2$ is related to the complexity of the model, whereas $C_{SVR}$ is a constant value determining the point that relates $R_{emp}^\varepsilon \left[ f \right]$ to $\left\| \vec{w} \right\|^2$ (Davy, 2005).

Minimization of function 5 is based on the following optimization problem with constrains: Minimize

$$\tau\left(\vec{w}, \vec{\xi}, \vec{\xi^*}\right) = \frac{1}{2}\left\| \vec{w} \right\|^2 + C_{SVR} \cdot \frac{1}{p}\sum_{i=1}^{p}\left( \xi_i + \xi_i^* \right) \tag{8}$$

subject to $\left(k\left(\vec{w},\vec{x_i}\right)+b\right)-y_i \leq \varepsilon+\xi_i$ (9) to $y_i-\left(k\left(w\cdot x_i\right)+b\right)\leq \varepsilon+\xi_i^*$ (10) and

to $\xi_i,\xi_i^* \geq 0$ (11). Obviously, $\xi_i^*,\xi_i$ are the distances of the training data set points from the zone where the errors les than $\varepsilon$ are ignored. If the $i-$ training point is located above the zone then its distance from the zone is represented by $\xi_i$ , whereas if it is below its distance is denoted as $\xi_i^*$ . Using Lagrange multipliers the problem can be faced as a double optimization one as follows: Maximize

$$W\left(a,a^*\right)=-\varepsilon\sum_{i=1}^{p}\left(a_i^*+a_i\right)+\sum_{i=1}^{p}\left(a_i^*-a_i\right)y_i-\frac{1}{2}\sum_{i,j=1}^{p}\left(a_i^*-a_i\right)\left(a_j^*-a_j\right)k\left(x_i,x_j\right)$$  (12)

subject to $\sum_{i=1}^{p}\left(a_i-a_i^*\right)=0$ (13) and $a_i^{(*)}\in\left[0,\dfrac{C_{SVR}}{p}\right]$ (14). According to Vapnik (Vapnick, 1997), (Kecman, 2001) the solution of the above problem is found in the form of the following linear extension of the kernel functions (15) and (16)

$$w = \sum_{i=1}^{p}\left(a_i^*-a_i\right)\vec{x_i}$$  (15)

$$f\left(\vec{x},a,a^*\right) = \sum_{i=1}^{p}\left(a_i^*-a_i\right)k\left(\vec{x},\vec{x_i}\right)+b$$  (16)

where b is estimated by the following function:

$$b = average_i\left\{\varepsilon\cdot sign\left(a_i-a_i^*\right)+y_k-\sum_j\left(a_j-a_j^*\right)k\left(\vec{x_j},\vec{x_i}\right)\right\}$$  (17)

The vectors $\vec{x_i}$ of the training set that correspond to nonzero values of $\left(a_i-a_i^*\right)$ are called SVM. If in 16 the Radial Basis function (RBF) kernel is employed, then the function estimated by the ε-SVR will be the following:

$$f\left(\vec{x},a,a^*\right) = \sum_{i=1}^{p}\left(a_i^*-a_i\right)\exp\left\{\dfrac{-\left\|\vec{x}-\vec{x_i}\right\|^2}{2\cdot\sigma_{RBF}^2}\right\}+b$$  (18)

The following parameters $\{\sigma_{RBF},\gamma,\varepsilon\}$ play a significant role in the success of the ε-SVR where $\sigma_{RBF}$ is the RBF kernel's standard deviation, $\gamma$ is a constant defining the point where the empiric error is related to complexity and $\varepsilon$ is the width of the ε-zone.

## 3  Fuzzy Weighted SVR with Fuzzy Partition

The Fuzzy Weighted Support Vector Regression with a Fuzzy Partition (FWSVRFP) has been introduced by (Chuang, 2007). This approach manages to take advantage of the local behavior of a model (meaning the response differentiation between two or more inputs which differ to each other slightly), due to the use of fuzzy C-means clustering (Cox, 2005). The initial problem is divided to many smaller ones, which results in the more enhanced study of the training set and also the independent study of

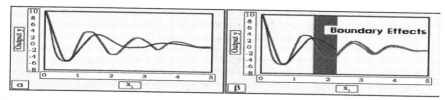

**Fig. 2.** a) System with bad performance of the model's local behavior b) System with boundary effects phenomena

each partition under a separate ε-SVR. On the other hand it might result in the appearance of boundary effects. Boundary effects exist when sudden and significant differentiations in the response between neighboring points occur. In order to extinguish such problems the suggested method integrates the partial responses of the ε-SVR by using the *Takagi-Sugeno-Kang* fuzzy model (Schnitman et al., 1998).

In case a) the model's local behavior output is not good. The blue line corresponds to the training set whereas the black line is the model's output. In case b, the blue line is related to the training set, the black line is the output of group 1, and the red the output of group 2.

The first step in this process is the application of fuzzy c-means clustering. Each cluster has its own center $\overrightarrow{\beta_j}$ and its own width for each input dimension $\delta_j^s$ (Cox, 2005). For example if we have a two dimensional input, then $\delta_3^1$ is the width of the third cluster in the first dimension. In this way local Regression Models (LRMs) are created by using ε-SVR. The local results of the LRMs are used for the integration of the overall output through a fuzzy weighted approach that employs Triangular membership functions to weight the output of each LRM, by using the center and the width of its corresponding cluster.

The integration of the partial output of the $LRM_{SVR}^k$, requires knowledge of the degree of membership of each training vector to each of the clusters. Based on the cluster centers $\overrightarrow{\beta_k}$ and on the corresponding widths of the clusters, the k $k = 1,...,C$ triangular membership functions are created. From the triangular membership functions the weights $w_k^s\left(x_i^s\right)$ are obtained for $i = 1, 2,..., p$, $k = 1, 2,$ $...,C$, $s = 1,...,q$

$$w_k^s\left(x_i^s\right) = \max\left(\min\left(\frac{x_i^s\left(\beta_k^s - \eta \cdot \delta_k^s\right)}{\beta_k^s - \left(\beta_k^s - \eta \cdot \delta_k^s\right)}, \frac{\left(\beta_k^s + \eta \cdot \delta_k^s\right) - x_i^s}{\left(\beta_k^s + \eta \cdot \delta_k^s\right) - \beta_k^s}\right), 0\right) \tag{19}$$

The degree of belonging of $\overrightarrow{x_i}$ to the $k$ − cluster is obtained by function 20.

$$W_k\left(\overrightarrow{x_i}\right) = w_k^1\left(x_i^1\right) \cdot w_k^2\left(x_i^2\right) \cdots w_k^q\left(x_i^q\right) \tag{20}$$

The overall output of the proposed fuzzy weighted SVR with fuzzy partition is obtained by the following De-fuzzifier.

$$\hat{y}\left(\overrightarrow{x}_i\right) = \frac{\sum_{k=1}^{C} W_k\left(\overrightarrow{x}_i\right) LRM_{SVR}^{k}\left(\overrightarrow{x}_i\right)}{\sum_{k=1}^{C} W_k\left(\overrightarrow{x}_i\right)} \tag{21}$$

The Root Mean Square Error (RMSE) $RMSE = \sqrt{\dfrac{\sum_{j=1}^{N}(y_j - \hat{y}_j)^2}{N}}$ (22) is used as an evaluation instrument. Where N is the number of the training vectors, $y_j$ is the actual output of the $j$ − training or testing data and $\hat{y}_j$ is the corresponding estimated output.

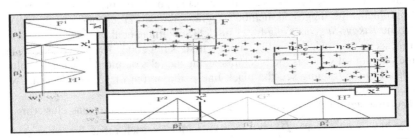

**Fig. 3.** Triangular membership functions for the estimation of the weight $v\, W_k^{s}$ of point $\overrightarrow{x}_i$ . A case with a two dimensional input and C=3 *LRMs*.

## 4   Application

The following chapter presents the application results of the Global SVR and FWSVR approaches in the total data set. According to Global SVR a global regression model was obtained for all of the data set, whereas with the FWSVR several local regression models LRMs were constructed. By the use of the 5-Fold Cross Validation, the regression algorithm was executed five times for 3214 training records and 804 testing ones.The regression was performed by the use of the LIBSVM v2.9 (http://www.csie.ntu.edu.tw/~cjlin/libsvm/) (Chang, 2009) which is encoded in C++ and offers a Matlab Interface. In this specific application the RBF-Kernel was applied. In both cases, the SVR-parameters' values $\{\sigma_{RBF}, \gamma, \varepsilon\} = \{9, 6, 0.02\}$ were used respectively as the optimal ones. They were chosen because after several trial and error experiments they were proven to offer better performance in the model. For the FWSVR the value of $\eta = 2$. As it can be seen the best performance was achieved for $C = 2$ where $RMSE \approx 0.7$. Considering that the range of the output values was $[0, 33]$, one can conclude that the error was more or less equal to the 2.12% of the values' range which can be an acceptable. However a second optimization approach was performed after partitioning the data records in two subsets.

**Table 1.** Performance using the Global SVR and FWSVR approaches with $\{\sigma,\ \gamma,\ \varepsilon\}=\{9,\ 6,\ 0.02\}$ respectively and $\eta=2$

| Method | Group | RMSE | |
|---|---|---|---|
| | | Training | Testing |
| Global SVR | - | 1.163 | 1.167 |
| Fuzzy Weighted SVR | 2 | 0.72 | 0.699 |
| | 3 | 0.722 | 0.699 |
| | 4 | 0.95 | 0.934 |
| | 5 | 0.906 | 0.786 |
| | 6 | 0.834 | 0.835 |
| | 7 | 0.887 | 0.864 |
| | 8 | 0.952 | 0.934 |
| | 9 | 0.98 | 0.861 |
| | 10 | 0.948 | 0.9 |

## 4.1 Optimizing the Performance

A optimization effort has been done by partitioning the data properly. Based on a closer look in the data, it can be seen that from the 4018 data records, the 3660 (the 91.09%) had an output in the range $[0,1]$. Consequently for this data group an error of the 0.7 magnitude was significant. In order to phase this problem the data set was divided in two groups. The first one contained the data vectors with an output in the interval $[0,1]$ and the second in the interval $(1,33]$. The SVM regression algorithms were applied for each group of data separately.

## 4.2 The 5-Fold Cross Validation for the Data Group in the Interval $[0,1]$

The regression algorithm was executed five times, whereas 2928 training data records and 732 testing ones were used in each execution. In both of the cases cases the SVR-parameters applied were $\{\sigma_{RBF},\gamma,\varepsilon\}=\{9,\ 6,\ 0.02\}$ respectively and $\eta=2$. As it can be seen in the above table 2, the optimal performance was achieved for the FWSVR and for $C=2$, where the obtained root Mean Square Error was $RMSE\approx0.2$. This error was actually very small and acceptable.

## 4.3 Results for the Data Group with Output in the Interval $(1,33]$

The second data group that was formed by the partitioning process, contained only 385 data records. By employing the 5-Fold Cross Validation method 308 training data records and 77 testing ones were used in each of the five executions. The values of the SVR-parameters were $\{\sigma_{RBF},\gamma,\varepsilon\}=\{12,\ 5,\ 0.02\}$ respectively and $\eta=2$.

As it can be seen in table 3, the best performance was achieved by using the FWSVR and $C=3$, where $RMSE\approx2.45$. This error was very low compared to the output values.

**Table 2.** Performance using the Global SVR and the FWSVR approaches with $\{\sigma, \gamma, \varepsilon\}=\{9, 6, 0.02\}$ respectively and $\eta=2$. Application for the data records having an output in the interval *[0,1]*

| Method | Group | RMSE | |
|--------|-------|------|------|
| | | Training | Testing |
| Global SVR | - | 0.211 | 0.212 |
| Fuzzy Weighted SVR (FWSVR) | 2 | 0.201 | 0.202 |
| | 3 | 0.202 | 0.203 |
| | 4 | 0.209 | 0.209 |
| | 5 | 0.208 | 0.209 |
| | 6 | 0.208 | 0.209 |
| | 7 | 0.207 | 0.21 |
| | 8 | 0.209 | 0.211 |
| | 9 | 0.211 | 0.213 |
| | 10 | 0.21 | 0.213 |

**Table 3.** Performance by using Global SVR and FWSVR with $\{\sigma, \gamma, \varepsilon\}=\{12, 5, 0.02\}$ respectively and $\eta=2$ Application for the region (1,33]

| Method | Groups | RMSE | |
|--------|--------|------|------|
| | | Training | Testing |
| Global SVR | - | 3.342 | 3.341 |
| Fuzzy Weighted SVR | 2 | 2.516 | 2.442 |
| | 3 | 2.547 | 2.407 |
| | 4 | 2.582 | 2.648 |
| | 5 | 3.022 | 2.617 |
| | 6 | 3.016 | 2.839 |
| | 7 | 2.8 | 2.8 |
| | 8 | 2.962 | 2.466 |
| | 9 | 2.987 | 2.503 |
| | 10 | 2.976 | 2.5 |

## 5   Conclusions

Initially a 5-Fold Cross Validation approach was performed for the integrated data set and the best achieved performance had an error value $RMSE \approx 0.7$.

Afterwards another 5-Fold Cross Validation optimization approach was performed by dividing the actual data records in two partitions according to the range of their expected output. Based on the results of the employed approach, the general conclusions were the following: Every time that the prediction of the performance is required for a new set of input vectors it is well known that the value of the actual output is located in the closed interval [0,1] with a probability of $\frac{4018}{3660}=91.09\%$. Respectively, the value of the actual output might be in the closed interval (1,33] with a probability of

$\frac{4018}{358} = 8.91\%$. So by using a heuristic approach, the user can use his experience in the input data vectors in order to expect the output in the one of the two intervals of values. In the first case when the output values are expected to be low, then the first model should be used with a very low expected error $RMSE \approx 0.2$. In the opposite case the second regression model should be applied with an error more or less $RMSE \approx 2.45$. The models obtained by this research effort are quite promising and they produce RMSE values of a very low magnitude in the testing phase.

# References

1. Boser, B., Guyon, I., Vapnik, V.: A training algorithm for optimal margin classifiers. In: Fifth Annual Workshop on Computational Learning Theory, Pittsburgh, pp. 144–152. ACM, New York (1992)
2. Chang, C.C., Lin, C.J.: LIBSVM A Library for Support Vector Machines (2009), http://www.csie.ntu.edu.tw/~cjlin/libsvm/
3. Chuang, C.: Fuzzy Weighted Support Vector Regression with a Fuzzy Partition. IEEE Transactions on Systems, Man and Cybernetics Part B: Cybernetics 37(3) (2007)
4. Cox, E.: Fuzzy Modeling and Genetic Algorithms for Data Mining and Exploration. Elsevier Science, USA (2005)
5. Davy, M.: An Introduction to Support Vector Machines and other kernel algorithms. In: Proc. of the 9th Engineering Applications of Neural Networks Conference, Lille, France (2005)
6. Iliadis, L., Maris, F.: An Artificial Neural Network model for Mountainous Water-Resources Management: The case of Cyprus Mountainous Watersheds Environmental Modeling and Software 22(7), 1066–1072 (2007)
7. Iliadis, L., Spartalis, S., Tachos, S.: Kernel methods and neural networks for water resources management. Journal Environmental Engineering and Management 9(2) (2010)
8. Kecman, V.: Learning and Soft Computing. MIT Press, London (2001)
9. Kotoulas, D.: Hydrology and Hydraulics of Natural Environment. Aristotle University of Thessaloniki, Greece (2001)
10. Lin, J.Y., Cheng, C.T., Chau, K.W.: Using support vector machines for long-term discharge prediction. Hydrological Sciences Journal 51, 599–612 (2006) (in French)
11. Lobbrecht, A.H., Solomatine, D.P.: Control of water levels in polder areas using neural networks and fuzzy adaptive systems. In: Savic, D., Walters, G.A. (eds.) Water Industry Systems: Modelling and Optimization Applications, vol. 1, pp. 509–518. Research Studies Press, Baldock (1999)
12. Loukas, A.: Class Notes of Laboratory of Hydrology and Water Resources Systems Analysis (2009)
13. Quick, M.C., Pipes, A.: U.B.C. watershed model. Hydrological Sciences-Bulletin-des Sciences Hydrologiques XXII, 1 3/1977 (1977)
14. Refaeilzadeh, P., Tang, L., Liu, H.: Cross-Validation. Arizona State University, USA (2008), http://www.public.asu.edu/~ltang9/papers/ ency-cross-validation.pdf
15. Schnitman, L., Felippe de Souza, J.A.M., Yoneyama, T.: Takagi-Sugeno-Kang Fuzzy Structures in Dynamic System Modeling Issues of Linear Takagi-Sugeno Fuzzy Models. IEEE. Trans. on Fuzzy Systems 6(3), 402–410 (1998)
16. Vapnik, V.N., Golowich, S., Smola, A.: Support Vector method for function approximation regression estimation and signal processing. In: Mozer, M., Jordan, M., Petsche, T. (eds.) Advances in Neural Information Processing Systems, vol. 9, pp. 281–287. MIT Press, Cambridge (1997)

# Faster Directions for Second Order SMO

Álvaro Barbero * and José R. Dorronsoro*

Universidad Autómoma de Madrid and Instituto de Ingeniería del Conocimiento
Francisco Tomás y Valiente 11, 28049, Madrid, Spain
{alvaro.barbero@,jose.dorronsoro@}uam.es

**Abstract.** Second order SMO represents the state–of–the–art in SVM training for moderate size problems. In it, the solution is attained by solving a series of subproblems which are optimized w.r.t just a pair of multipliers. In this paper we will illustrate how SMO works in a two stage fashion, setting first the values of the bounded multipliers to the penalty factor $C$ and proceeding then to adjust the non–bounded multipliers. Furthermore, during this second stage the selected pairs for update often appear repeatedly during the algorithm. Taking advantage of this, we shall propose a procedure to combine previously used descent directions that results in much fewer iterations in this second stage and that may also lead to noticeable savings in kernel operations.

## 1   Introduction

Given a training sample $\mathcal{S} = \{(X_i, y_i) : i = 1, \ldots, N\}$ with $y_i = \pm 1$, SVM training seeks [1] to find a separating hyperplane in the form $W \cdot X + b$ with maximal margin by solving the dual problem

$$\min_{\alpha} f(\alpha) = \frac{1}{2}\alpha^T Q \alpha - e \cdot \alpha \quad s.t. \quad \begin{cases} 0 \leq \alpha \leq C \\ \alpha \cdot y = 0 \end{cases} \tag{1}$$

where $Q = (Q_{ij})$ with $Q_{ij} = y_i y_j X_i \cdot X_j$, $e$ is an all-ones vector, $\alpha^T$ denotes the transpose of $\alpha$, $\cdot$ indicates the standard dot product and $C$ is a penalty parameter. Once the problem is solved, the primal problem solution can be obtained as well using $W = \sum_i \alpha_i y_i X_i$ and computing $b$ though the Karush–Kuhn–Tucker optimality conditions [1]. At first sight, this problem is a relatively simple constrained quadratic minimization problem and, as such, easy to solve. However, $\dim(\alpha) = N$ and so we may not be able to store the full matrix $Q$ into memory, even for moderate size problems. Furthermore, non-linearity is usually introduced in the SVM by using the kernel trick as $Q_{ij} = y_i y_j K(X_i, X_j)$, making the entries of $Q$ costly to evaluate, as non-linear Kernel Operations (KOs) are required. These conditions make impossible to apply standard and fast inner point solvers to the problem. The solution to this are decomposition

* All authors have been partially supported by Spain's TIN 2007–66862 and "Cátedra IIC Modelado y Prediccion". The first author is kindly supported by the FPU–MEC grant reference AP2006–02285.

K. Diamantaras, W. Duch, L.S. Iliadis (Eds.): ICANN 2010, Part II, LNCS 6353, pp. 30–39, 2010.
© Springer-Verlag Berlin Heidelberg 2010

methods, where iteratively a series of subproblems are solved, each of them involving only a small number $q$ of the multipliers. Among the most effective decomposition procedures is Joachims' SVM–Light [2] where the subproblem multipliers are chosen using gradient information. For $q = 2$ SVM–Light reduces to Sequential Minimal Optimization (SMO) [3], that iteratively changes $\alpha$ to $\alpha' = \alpha + \delta(e_U - y_U y_L e_L)$ for appropriate $L, U$ and $\delta$ (see below).

However, decomposition methods are not problem free, because as we will see, the gradient of $f(\alpha)$ needs to be updated at every iteration, which requires at least $N \times q$ KOs. Therefore, if the number of iterations does not decrease substantially, the cost in KOs of a $q$–multiplier procedure may degrade as $q$ grows [4]. The SMO method has a cost of $2N$ KOs per iteration and benefits from the ability of solving its corresponding subproblems in closed form. Therefore, as implemented for instance in the LIBSVM package [5] (also known as second order SMO) is often the most efficient choice, at least for moderate size problems.

In the experimental use of SMO there are two folk observations. The first one is that the initial iterations of second order SMO concentrate predominantly on the bounded multipliers, i.e., those $\alpha_i$ for which at the optimum $\alpha_i^* = C$, as their number increases until it becomes stable. Then SMO focuses on the unbounded multipliers, which are adjusted to arrive at their optimal values $0 < \alpha_i^* < C$. The decrease of $f(\alpha)$ is very fast in the first phase but much slower in the second one. The second observation is that there are often several pairs that are selected repeatedly, particularly as SMO training advances. These observations suggest that, in order to improve the speed of SMO, one should concentrate in this second stage and try to exploit the repeated pairs to derive better descent directions.

In this paper we present an improvement over SMO, which constructs accelerating directions much in the way the Hooke–Jeeves (H–J) method improves cyclic coordinate descent [6], therefore allowing for updating directions unavailable to standard SMO while keeping the burden in KOs under control. Whereas in H–J an accelerating direction is built after a fixed number of iterations, here we will attempt to do so each time an updating pair of multipliers reappears during the optimization process. We shall briefly review first and second order SMO in section 2 and in section 3 we will give the details of our accelerated version. Both second order SMO procedures are compared in section 4 and the paper ends with a short discussion.

## 2 First and Second Order SMO

In principle, the SMO updates would be of the form $\alpha' = \alpha + \delta_U e_U + \delta_L e_L$, where $e_i$ is an all-zeros vector except for the $i - th$ component which is valued 1, i.e. only two coefficients are allowed to change. However the constraint $y \cdot \alpha = 0$ implies that $\delta_L y_L + \delta_U y_U = 0$; that is, $\delta_L = -\delta_U y_L y_U$. Therefore, the SMO updates become $\alpha' = \alpha + \delta(e_U - y_U y_L e_L)$ where we write $\delta$ instead of $\delta_U$. Note that this update can be thought as performing a step of size $\delta$ in the direction $d_{U,L} = (e_U - y_U y_L e_L)$. As a consequence of this and if we ignore the problem's constraints for the moment, by solving $\frac{\partial}{\partial \delta} f(\alpha + \delta d_{U,L}) = 0$ we obtain optimal an step $\delta^*$ as

$$\delta^* = \frac{d_{U,L} \cdot (\alpha - Q\alpha)}{d_{U,L}^T Q d_{U,L}} = \frac{-d_{U,L} \cdot \nabla f(\alpha)}{d_{U,L}^T Q d_{U,L}} = -y_U \frac{\Delta_{U,L}}{Z_{U,L}} = -y_U \lambda^* \qquad (2)$$

where $\nabla f(\alpha)$ stands for the gradient of $f(\alpha)$ and we write $\Delta_{U,L} = y_U \nabla f(\alpha)_U - y_L \nabla f(\alpha)_L$, $Z_{U,L} = d_{U,L}^T Q d_{U,L} = K(X_U, X_U) + K(X_L, X_L) - 2K(X_L, X_U)$ and $\lambda^* = \Delta_{U,L}/Z_{U,L}$. The corresponding multiplier updates can be expressed as $\alpha'_L = \alpha_L + y_L \lambda^*$, $\alpha'_U = \alpha_U - y_U \lambda^*$ and $\alpha'_j = \alpha_j$ for any other $j$.

Several proposals can be found in the literature regarding how to choose the updating pair $(L, U)$. In the so-called first order SMO, also known as Modification 2 [3], $L$ and $U$ are chosen as the pair that most violates at $\alpha$ the Karush–Kuhn–Tucker optimality conditions, i.e.

$$L = \arg \min_j \{y_j \nabla f(\alpha)_j : j \in I_L\}, \quad U = \arg \max_j \{y_j \nabla f(\alpha)_j : j \in I_U\}, \quad (3)$$
$$I_L = \{j | (y_j = -1, \alpha_j > 0) \text{ or } (y_j = 1, \alpha_j < C)\},$$
$$I_U = \{j | (y_j = -1, \alpha_j < C) \text{ or } (y_j = 1, \alpha_j > 0)\}.$$

Notice that this choice implies $\Delta_{U,L} > 0$ and $\lambda^* > 0$, and the restrictions on the $\alpha$ multipliers are needed so that we have $0 \leq \alpha'_L \leq C$, $0 \leq \alpha'_U \leq C$. Moreover, the initial $\lambda^*$ value given by (2) may have to be clipped down so that these bounds hold.

Note also that, since $\Delta_{U,L} = y_U \nabla f(\alpha)_U - y_L \nabla f(\alpha)_L$, we have $\Delta_{U,L} \geq \Delta_{j,i}$ for any other feasible direction $d_{j,i}$, and it follows that the most violating pair $U, L$ choice also gives the feasible direction more aligned with $\nabla f(\alpha)$. In other words, $d_{U,L}$ is the best first order feasible descent direction. However, if no clipping is needed for $\lambda^*$, is is easy to see [7] that the gain can also be written as $f(\alpha) - f(\alpha') = \frac{\Delta_{U,L}^2}{Z_{U,L}}$. This suggests a second order choice of $L, U$ (see [7] for more details) as the pair for which the full gain is maximal. To avoid a nested loop on $L$ and $U$, one chooses first $L$ as in (3) and then $U$ is selected as

$$U = \arg \max_j \left\{ \frac{\Delta_{j,L}^2}{Z_{U,L}} : j \in I_U, \Delta_{j,L} > 0 \right\}. \qquad (4)$$

These second order index choices result in a much faster convergence of SMO and are implemented, for instance, in the latest versions of LIBSVM [5], the SVM training tool that can be considered representative of the current state-of-the-art.

To close this section we remark that we have to keep track of the gradient in order to compute the optimal $L, U$ indices at each. After an $\alpha$ update we can also update the gradient efficiently using

$$\nabla f(\alpha + \delta d) = \nabla f(\alpha) + \delta Q d = \nabla f(\alpha) + \delta(Q_U - y_U y_L Q_L),$$

where $Q_i$ stands for the $i$-th column of $Q$. It follows that SMO requires essentially $2N$ KOs at each iteration.

## 3   Better Directions for Second Order SMO

In this section we will propose a way to improve SMO convergence speed by combining recently used descent directions. Let $d^t = d_{L_t, U_t}$ denote a certain update vector that we assume has appeared again after $K$ steps from a former use as the update vector $d^{t-K}$; in other words, we are assuming that $L_t = L_{t-K}, U_t = U_{t-K}$. Consider then $v = \sum_{j=1}^{K} \delta_{t-j} d^{t-j}$, with $\delta_{t-j}$ the optimal updating coefficient at step $t - j$.

Clearly, $v$ would have been a better descent direction at $\alpha^{t-K}$ than $d^{t-K}$, as we would have arrived to $\alpha^t$ (or another $\alpha'$ such that $f(\alpha') < f(\alpha^t)$) in just one iteration, i.e., it is able to provide greater decrease in $f(\alpha)$. Thus, it makes sense to consider using $v$ as a descent direction at $\alpha^T$ alternative to $d^t$, as it might still be a better direction; to choose the best option we have to compare the $\partial_1 = -\nabla f(\alpha^t) \cdot d^t$ and $\partial_2 = -\nabla f(\alpha^t) \cdot v$ values, i.e., the directional derivatives at $\alpha^t$ with respect $d^t$ and $v$ respectively, and decide on the most negative one. That is, we will be choosing the direction with largest negative steep. The computation of $\partial_1$ is straightforward, as $\partial_1 = \Delta_{U,L}$, and that of $\partial_2$ is only slightly more complex. In fact, we have

$$\nabla f(\alpha^t) \cdot v = \sum_{j=1}^{K} \delta_{t-j} \nabla f(\alpha^t) \cdot d^{T-j}$$

$$= \sum_{j=1}^{K} \delta_{t-j} (\nabla f(\alpha^t)_U - y_{U_{t-j}} y_{L_{t-j}} \nabla f(\alpha^t)_L)$$

which can be computed without needing any KO. Once we have decided to perform an update in the $v$ direction, observe that the value of the objective function will change as $f(\alpha + \lambda v) = f(\alpha) + \frac{1}{2}\lambda^2 v^T Q v + \delta v^T Q \alpha - \delta v \cdot \alpha$, and so the optimal stepsize ignoring constraints can be obtained as

$$\lambda^o = \frac{-v \cdot \nabla f(\alpha)}{v^T Q v} = \frac{-\partial_2}{v^T Q v}. \tag{5}$$

As $v$ is sparse by construction, at most $2K$ entries are non-zero, and so $v^T Q v$ can be computed efficiently by defining $R_i = Q_i v = \sum_{v_j \neq 0} Q_{ij} v_j$ and using $v^T Q v = \sum_{v_j \neq 0} v_j R_j$, which requires at most $2KN$ kernel operations. Furthermore the vector $R$ can be used to update the gradient as $\nabla f(\alpha + \lambda v) = \nabla f(\alpha) + \lambda R$.

Now, taking the constraints back into account note that by using $v$ as updating direction the $\alpha$ will be modified as $\alpha_i^{t+1} = \alpha_i^t + \lambda v_i \; \forall \; v_i \neq 0$. Therefore we must have $0 \leq \alpha_i^{t+1} = \alpha_i^t + \lambda v_i \leq C$. Thus, if $v_i > 0$, the relevant bound is the right one, while the left one has to be met when $v_i < 0$. Define $M_C = \min\{(C - \alpha_i^t)/v_i : v_i > 0\}$ and $M_0 = \min\{-\alpha_i^t/v_i : v_i < 0\}$. By clipping $\lambda^o$ from above as $\lambda^* = \min\{\lambda^o, M_0, M_C\}$ we guarantee feasibility.

Finally, to detect a repetition of the $L_t, U_t$ indices, we keep them in a circular queue $\mathcal{Q}$ which is searched from its beginning each time a new pair $L, U$ is selected. If the search fails we insert the pair in $\mathcal{Q}$, but if a previous copy

$(L_{t-K}, U_{t-K})$ is found we check, as mentioned before, whether the updating vector $V$ actually defines a descent direction with larger steep than the standard updating direction. If it does so, we will perform a $v$ update and reset $\mathcal{Q}$ afterwards. Conversely, if it does not, we will remove the previous appearance $(L_{t-K}, U_{t-K})$ from $\mathcal{Q}$ and, in order to keep the temporal structure of the $(L, U)$ index pairs in $\mathcal{Q}$, we will also remove all pairs from $\mathcal{Q}$'s front up to the $(L_{t-K}, U_{t-K})$ position. All in all, the overall cost of a $v$ update can be regarded as $O(2KN)$ KOs plus other non-KOs operations involving the queue management, which results in roughly $K$ times the cost of standard SMO. Therefore a global speed-up will only happen if the total number iterations the algorithm requires to achieve convergence is sufficiently reduced to make up for the additional costs for these accelerating iterations. An outline of the algorithm is presented in 1.

## 4    Numerical Experiments

In this section we will compare the performance of standard second order SMO (SO) and of our accelerated procedure (AccSO) on the datasets taken from G. Rätsch's benchmark repository [8]. Unless otherwise stated, we shall always use Gaussian kernels with parameter values $C$ and $2\sigma^2$ as reported in [8]. The stopping criterion will be that the maximum KKT violating value $\Delta$ be smaller than a tolerance $\epsilon = 10^{-5}$ and the initial $\alpha$ multipliers values are 0.

First we will briefly illustrate the two–stage nature of SO. Figure 1 shows the evolution of the number of multipliers at the $C$ bound (upper bounded) and of unbounded multipliers ($0 < \alpha < C$) for each of the datasets when SO is applied. A general trend among datasets can be noticed, in which during a first phase of the algorithm most of the updates are displacing multipliers to the upper bound, while a lesser quantity get moved to an unbounded state. Next,

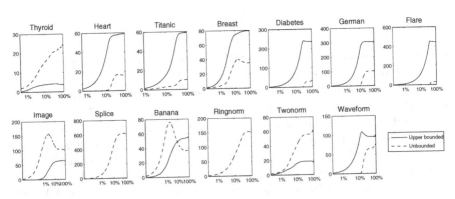

**Fig. 1.** Evolution of the number of bounded and unbounded $\alpha$ coefficients for every dataset. The x-axis represents the percentage of iterations performed by the algorithm (in logarithmic scale), while the y-axis stands for the number of upper bounded or unbounded coefficients.

**Algorithm 1.** Accelerated SMO

```
1: initialize α = 0, ∇f(α) = 0p, Q = ∅ ;
2: while (stopping condition == FALSE) do
3:   find (L,U) second (4) order SMO rules ;
4:   if pair (L,U) is found in Q then
5:     build accelerating direction v ;
6:     if v is feasible and ∂₂ < ∂₁ then
7:       compute R, optimal unbounded stepsize λ° using (5) ;
8:       clip λ° to meet constraints → λ* ;
9:       α = α + λ*v, ∇f(α) = ∇f(α) + λ*R, Q = ∅ ;
10:    else
11:      remove (L,U) and previous updates from Q ;
12:      perform standard SMO update using (L,U), add (L,U) to Q ;
13:    end if
14:  else
15:    perform standard SMO update using (L,U), add (L,U) to Q ;
16:  end if
17: end while
```

the number of upper bounded and unbounded multipliers becomes stable, and only slight changes in their numbers are made until the end of the algorithm. Notice also that some datasets differ from this behaviour. In the case of Heart, Diabetes and Flare datasets unbounded multipliers are only generated after a number of iterations have been completed. On the other hand, in Splice and Ringnorm datasets no upper bounded coefficients appear at all. As we will later see, these datasets present no improvement under our procedure.

While we cannot give a rigorous argument for the generalized two–phase regime, notice that at the early stages of SMO any pair $L, U$ would be eligible and the gain will be large when we have $X_L \simeq X_U$ but $y_L \neq y_U$, as $Z_{L,U} \simeq 0$ and $\Delta_{L,U} = y_U \nabla f(\alpha)_U - y_L \nabla f(\alpha)_L = W \cdot X_U - y_U - (W \cdot X_L - y_L) \simeq -2y_U$. If this is the case, either $X_L$ or $X_U$ will not be correctly classified and the corresponding multiplier will be set to $C$ and it is likely that it will stay there. On the other hand, if we set $\mathcal{O}(\alpha) = \{i : \alpha_i = 0\}$ and $\mathcal{C}(\alpha) = \{i : \alpha_i = C\}$, it can be shown [9] that for a large enough $t_0$ we will have $\mathcal{O}(\alpha^t) \subset \mathcal{O}(\alpha^*)$ and $\mathcal{C}(\alpha^t) \subset \mathcal{C}(\alpha^*)$ for $t \geq t_0$, with $\alpha^*$ the optimal multiplier vector. Thus, the stabilization of the number of 0 and $C$ bounded multipliers is to be expected (this is also the reason why shrinking works).

Turning now our attention to our method, before performing any comparisons we should note that this method introduces a new parameter $\tau$ into the SVM training, which stands for the maximum length of the circular queue $\mathcal{Q}$. Small values of $\tau$ might overlook some $(L, U)$ pair repetitions, while large $\tau$ values might detect lengthy, spurious cycles which provide small improvement at a high computational cost. To analyse the influence of this parameter we run our method for a range of $\tau$ values from 1 to 100 and measure the percentage of reduction in KOs when compared against the standard second order procedure, computed as $p = 100 \frac{KOs(AccSO)}{KOs(SO)}$. Results are plotted in figure 2 for all

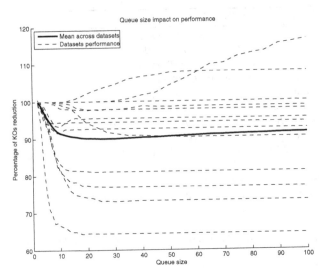

**Fig. 2.** Percentage of reduction achieved as a function of the queue size. Reductions for each dataset are plotted as dashed lines, while the solid line stands for an average reduction across datasets.

the datasets, along a global reduction value averaged across datasets. It can be observed that in most of the datasets AccSO obtains an improvement in the number of KOs, although there is no reduction or even a worsening in performance in some cases. Note also that on average a good choice of $\tau$ seems to be any value in the interval $[20 - 35]$. However, it should be pointed out that the

**Table 1.** Average and std. deviation values of the number of KOs (in thousands) and execution times (in milliseconds) by our second order SMO code (SO) and its accelerated version (AccSO) ; the reduction in % also is given.

| | KOs | | | RUNNING TIME | | |
|---|---|---|---|---|---|---|
| DATASET | SO | AccSO | RED. | SO | AccSO | RED. |
| BANANA | 13576 ± 8377 | 8751 ± 4813 | 64,5 √ | 456,3 ± 246,88 | 306,74 ± 146,09 | 67,22 √ |
| IMAGE | 56304 ± 8776 | 41728 ± 5336 | 74,1 √ | 1666,87 ± 258,06 | 1605,91 ± 205,26 | 96,34 √ |
| BREAST | 703 ± 270 | 543 ± 181 | 77,3 √ | 27,87 ± 10,7 | 20,76 ± 6,89 | 74,49 √ |
| HEART | 131 ± 36 | 106 ± 23 | 81,2 √ | 5,39 ± 1,53 | 4,31 ± 0,94 | 79,96 √ |
| FLARE | 1130 ± 594 | 1047 ± 420 | 92,6 √ | 49,18 ± 26,58 | 46,51 ± 19,22 | 94,57 √ |
| GERMAN | 2595 ± 269 | 2444 ± 229 | 94,2 √ | 107,23 ± 16,8 | 106,03 ± 14,33 | 98,88 √ |
| TITANIC | 50 ± 9 | 48 ± 7 | 94,4 √ | 1,89 ± 0,35 | 1,8 ± 0,28 | 95,24 √ |
| THYROID | 64 ± 20 | 61 ± 18 | 95,4 √ | 2,28 ± 0,74 | 2,15 ± 0,65 | 94,3 √ |
| TWONORM | 365 ± 49 | 356 ± 46 | 97,7 √ | 15,15 ± 3,16 | 14,37 ± 3 | 94,85 √ |
| DIABETES | 451 ± 58 | 441 ± 52 | 97,9 √ | 18,27 ± 2,56 | 17,72 ± 2,2 | 96,99 √ |
| SPLICE | 9613 ± 399 | 9613 ± 399 | 100,0 ≈ | 312,37 ± 37,86 | 308,01 ± 34,34 | 98,6 √ |
| RINGNORM | 487 ± 41 | 487 ± 41 | 100,0 ≈ | 21,46 ± 3,38 | 21,57 ± 3,41 | 100,51 × |
| WAVEFORM | 340 ± 39 | 347 ± 39 | 102,2 × | 13,7 ± 2,6 | 13,9 ± 2,59 | 101,46 × |

queue management also implies a computational burden scaling proportionally to the queue size. This extra cost, although small in comparison to the cost of computing KOs, cannot be neglected. Hence, we shall use a value of $\tau = 20$ for the rest of our experiments.

Table 1 shows the detailed results in KOs for that selection of $\tau$: the table's datasets are sorted with respect to the percentage of reduction achieved. Additionally, a $\sqrt{}$ symbol denotes a significant improvement in a Wilcoxon rank–sum test at a 10% level, whereas $\times$ stands for significant worsening and $\approx$ for no significant difference. AccSO requires more KOs for the Waveform dataset, ties with SO over Splice and Ringnorm and wins in the other ten datasets. We can thus conclude that AccSO may lead to sizeable savings in KOs when compared with SO and, most likely, with the state–of–the–art SMO packages. Moreover, when this is not the case, AccSO does not seem to add such a great complexity burden as to discourage its use. Additionally, also in table 1 we provide the corresponding execution times, where we can check that the amount of reduction is roughly the same as the observed in KOs for most of the datasets.

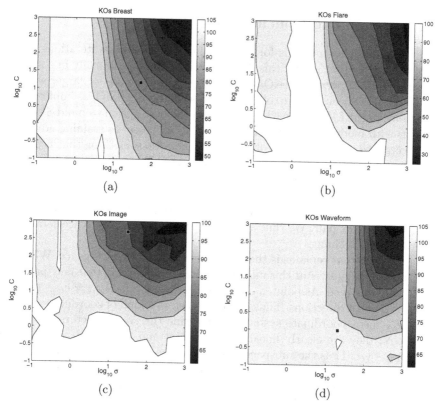

**Fig. 3.** Percentage of KOs reduction in AccSO for different settings of $C$ and $\sigma$ parameters. The squared dots represent the values recommended in [8] for the dataset.

Finally, it is of interest to test whether different values for the SVM parameters $C$ and $\sigma$ would provide a different degree of improvement. To do this we measure the performance of SO and AccSO for a grid of $C$ and $\sigma$ values in the range $[0.1, 1000]$. We depict the percentage of reduction achieved for this range of values as contour maps in figure 3 for the datasets Breast, Flare, Image and Waveform, the rest of the datasets showing similar behaviours. It can be observed that the degree of reduction achieved by the method depends heavily on the SVM parameters, the best results being obtained when both of them have large values. Note that $C$ and $\sigma$ are normally selected through a cross–validation procedure, and so their values will depend on the problem at hand. So, AccSO might be able to provide larger improvements in performance depending on the dataset. On the other hand, note that for most of the parameter space either a notable reduction or no reduction at all is obtained. Worsenings only appear in small areas. Therefore, it is advisable to apply AccSO over SO regardless of the dataset, as generally no increase in computational cost will take place. Also, due to these same reasons, the method could be specially useful to improve running times of a cross-validation procedure that requires training the SVM for a large number of points in the parameter space.

## 5   Discussion and Conclusions

While decomposition methods for SVM training result in less iterations as the size of the working set grows, this does not translate automatically in a smaller number of kernel operations (KOs), that in fact may increase for larger working sets. The practical consequence of this is that second order SMO, as implemented for instance in the LIBSVM packages, is often the best option to build SVMs on problems with moderately large sample sizes. In any case, as training advances, the convergence speed of second order SMO decreases, something that is usually accompanied by the repeated appearance of some descent directions.

In this work we have numerically shown how there is a further speed gain in second order SMO if its standard descent directions are replaced, when appropriate, by the combination of the successive descent steps between two appearances of a repeated index pair. We thus arrive at a simple procedure to accelerate second order SMO training.

The question that remains is the reason for this faster convergence. While we do not have a full answer at this moment, there are some facts that may partially explain why this is so. As pointed out above, SMO uses the $d_{L,U} = e_U - y_U y_L e_L$ vectors as descent directions. Thus, it can be seen as a kind of coordinate descent on the $d_{i,j}$ meta–coordinate system. If we define the $N - 1$ vectors $\chi_i = d_{i,1}$, $2 \leq i \leq N$, they are clearly linearly independent and we have $d_{L,1} = \chi_L$ and $d_{L,U} = \chi_L - \chi_U$. Thus the subspace spanned by the $d_{i,j}$ directions used in SMO is at most $N - 1$ dimensional but if we center our attention on SMO's second training phase, the subspace dimension would be much smaller, as we replace $N$ by the number of unbounded support vectors.

On the coordinates associated to these directions, first order SMO can be seen as a kind of Gauss–Southwell (GS) minimization method, as the $d_{L,U}$

coordinate chosen is precisely the one associated to the largest negative gradient component. Second order SMO becomes then an improved GS variant. The GS method is essentially an improvement on basic cyclic coordinate descent, where one sequentially explores the coordinate descent directions (see [6], chapter 8). A frequent observation on these methods is that their simple descent directions can be sequentially combined to obtain a new direction that leads to a faster convergence. Examples of this are the acceleration step for cyclic coordinate descent or the Hooke–Jeeves (H–J) method [6] that for a $D$–dimensional space combines $D$ standard coordinate descent steps with a single step on a certain combination of previously taken directions. As such, it cannot be applied in an SMO setting, as the dimension $D$ might be too large, but our method detects direction cycles and combines the previously taken directions in a way not too far away from those in the H–J algorithm and, as it is the case with H–J, that leads to a convergence speed up.

In any case, further work is required to obtain insights into the method, that may also suggest other ways to improve second order SMO performance.

# References

1. Schölkopf, B., Smola, A.J.: Learning with Kernels: Support Vector Machines, Regularization, Optimization and Beyond. In: Machine Learning. MIT Press, Cambridge (2002)
2. Joachims, T.: Making Large-Scale Support Vector Machine Learning Practical. In: Advances in Kernel Methods: Support Vector Learning, pp. 169–184. MIT Press, Cambridge (1999)
3. Keerthi, S.S., Shevade, S.K., Bhattacharyya, C., Murthy, K.R.K.: Improvements to Platt's SMO Algorithm for SVM Classifier Design. Neural Computation 13(3), 637–649 (2001)
4. Collobert, R., Bengio, S.: Svmtorch: Support vector machines for large-scale regression problems. Journal of Machine Learning Research 1, 143–160 (2001)
5. Chang, C.C., Lin, C.J.: LIBSVM: a Library for Support Vector Machines (2001)
6. Bazaraa, M., Sherali, D., Shetty, C.: Nonlinear Programming: Theory and Algorithms. Wiley-Interscience Series in Discrete Mathematics and Optimization. Wiley, Chichester (1992)
7. Fan, R.E., Chen, P.H., Lin, C.J.: Working Set Selection using Second Order Information for Training Support Vector Machines. Journal of Machine Learning Research 6, 1889–1918 (2005)
8. Rätsch, G.: Benchmark Repository (2000), Datasets available at http://ida.first.fhg.de/projects/bench/benchmarks.htm
9. Stefano, L., Laura, P., Risi, A., Sciandrone, M.: A convergent hybrid decomposition algorithm model for svm training. IEEE Transactions on Neural Networks 20(6), 1055–1060 (2009)

# Almost Random Projection Machine with Margin Maximization and Kernel Features

Tomasz Maszczyk and Włodzisław Duch

Department of Informatics, Nicolaus Copernicus University
Grudziądzka 5, 87-100 Toruń, Poland
{tmaszczyk,wduch}@is.umk.pl
http://www.is.umk.pl

**Abstract.** Almost Random Projection Machine (aRPM) is based on generation and filtering of useful features by linear projections in the original feature space and in various kernel spaces. Projections may be either random or guided by some heuristics, in both cases followed by estimation of relevance of each generated feature. Final results are in the simplest case obtained using simple voting, but linear discrimination or any other machine approach may be used in the extended space of new features. New feature is added as a hidden node in a constructive network only if it increases the margin of classification, measured by the increase of the aggregated activity of nodes that agree with the final decision. Calculating margin more weight is put on vectors that are close to the decision threshold than on those classified with high confidence. Training is replaced by network construction, kernels that provide different resolution may be used at the same time, and difficult problems that require highly complex decision borders may be solved in a simple way. Relation of this approach to Support Vector Machines and Liquid State Machines is discussed.

**Keywords:** Neural networks, machine learning, random projections, liquid state machines, boosting.

## 1 Introduction

Although backpropagation of errors (BP) algorithm [1] has been very useful and is still widely used it has several well-known drawbacks and is not a good candidate for a model of neurobiological learning. Alternative models, such as Leabra, use a combination of Hebbian learning with error-correction, creating sparse, simple representation in their hidden layers [2], but so far they have not been too useful in practical applications to approximation or classification problems. The simplest model that has good biological foundation treats microcircuits in neural minicolumns as a kind of neural liquid that resonates in a complex way when a signal comes [3]. Liquid State Machines [4], and echo state networks [5] are now investigated in the "reservoir computing" field, assuming that a large number of randomly connected neurons form a reservoir providing memory for different aspects of signals [6]. Readout neurons extract from this reservoir stable information in real-time reacting to transient internal states formed by microcircuits in this high dimensional system. Projections into high dimensional space increase

K. Diamantaras, W. Duch, L.S. Iliadis (Eds.): ICANN 2010, Part II, LNCS 6353, pp. 40–48, 2010.

the probability of data separation, as proved by Cover [7]. This is the main reason for success of the kernel methods in machine learning [8]. It also agrees with the boosting principle [9], treating each projection as a week classifier.

Following these inspirations we have introduced the almost Random Projection Machine (aRPM) algorithm [10], a single hidden layer constructive network based on random projections that are added only if the new node contains useful information. This was determined by checking if the projection contains an interval of relatively pure (single-class) vectors that could be potentially useful. Such localized linear projections are able to solve highly-non-separable problems [11]. They may be further optimized using projection pursuit algorithms based on Quality of Projected Clusters (QPC) indices [12], but this would increase computational costs of the method. So far transformations used to create hidden nodes in aRPM were based on linear projections followed by non-linear separation of intervals, and filtering based on simple correlation coefficient.

Hidden neurons should maximize information transmission, a principle used in deriving learning rules for spiking networks [13]. One can assume that readout neurons with rich connections to different brain areas should be able to discover useful features correlated with a given tasks if they are already present in the neural reservoir, and Hebbian correlation-based learning should be sufficient to form strong weights. In particular, similarity to already learned objects, captured by various kernels, may be quite useful. Therefore instead of using projections based on input features, kernel-based features should also be added to the hidden nodes. Adding new types of features extends the hypothesis space that simple voting or linear discrimination methods are able to explore. Linear kernels define new features $t(x; w) = K_L(x, w) = x \cdot w$ based on a projection on the $w$ direction, or distance along $t(x, w)$ line. Gaussian kernels $g(x, w) = \exp(-||x - w||/2\sigma^2)$ evaluate similarity between two vectors using weighted radial distance function. Support Vector Machines (SVM) find large margin linear discriminators in these spaces without explicitly constructing the feature space. The final discriminant function is constructed as a linear combination of such kernels, creating in fact a weighted nearest neighbor solution. Each support vector used in a kernel may provide a useful feature, but this type of solution is optimal only for data with particular distributions, and will not work well for example on parity data [14] or other problems with complex logical structure [15].

Creating support features directly instead of using kernels based on support vectors $w$ has some advantages, allowing for judicious design of the feature space, optimization of parameters of individual features, selection of features, increased comprehensibility of solutions. Transfer of knowledge between learning of different tasks can be easily implemented by borrowing good non-linear features from other algorithms (learning from others), for example using features corresponding to fragments of path derived from decision trees [16].

In this paper we focus on margin maximization in the aRPM algorithm. New projections should be added only if they increase correct classification probability of those examples that are either on the wrong side, or are close to the decision border. In the next section aRPM algorithm with margin maximization is formally introduced. Section three presents empirical tests and comparisons with standard machine learning methods, and the last section contains discussion and conclusions.

## 2  Almost Random Projections with Margin Maximization

In essence the aRPM algorithm [10] transforms the input features space $\mathcal{X}$ into the support feature space $\mathcal{H}$ discovering various kinds of useful features. The final analysis in the $\mathcal{H}$ space may be done by any machine learning method. In this paper we shall use only the majority voting as it is the simplest model, and linear discrimination, but once a proper information is extracted other classification methods may benefit from it. The emphasis is thus on generation of new features. If linear discrimination with wide margin is used (linear SVM is a very good choice here), and support features are generated using specific kernel $z(x; w) = K(x, w)$, results will be equivalent to the kernel-based SVM. Creating support feature space in an explicit way does not require $O(n^2)$ operations to calculate the full kernel, which for a large number of vectors $n$ may be quite costly. Mixing features from different kernels, using *a priori* knowledge, or adding interesting features extracted from other models, is quite easy. In this paper we shall use only features generated by random projection and Gaussian kernels, filtered by an index that estimates classification margin.

It is convenient to identify each new candidate feature with a class-labeled hidden node $h(x; w)$ in a constructive network. Projections on random directions $t(x; w_i) = x \cdot w_i$ are especially useful if the direction $w = x/\|vx\|$ is taken as a point $x$ close to the decision border. Selecting such points may be done in a rough way by starting from projections on a line connecting centers of the classes, and finding the overlapping regions.

Although some projections may not be very useful as a whole, but the distribution of the training data along $t(x; w_i)$ direction may have a range of values that includes a pure cluster of projected patterns sufficient large to be useful. For example, in case of parity problems [11,15] linear projections never separate all vectors labeled as even and odd, but projections on diagonal $[1, 1..1]$ direction show alternating large even or odd pure clusters. One can model posterior probability $\mathcal{P}(C|t_i)$ along the $t_i = t(x; w_i)$ direction, separating such clusters using $[t_a, t_b]$ intervals. This creates binary features $b_i(x) = t(x; w_i, [t_a, t_b]) \in \{0, 1\}$, based on linear projection in the direction $w_i$, restricted to a slice of the input space perpendicular to the $w_i$ direction.

Good candidate feature should cover some minimal number $\eta$ of training vectors. The optimal number may depend on the data, and the domain expert may consider even a single vector to be a significant exception. Here $\eta$ has been optimized in CV in the 4-15 range, but simply fixing it to $\eta = \max[3, 0.1 NC_{\min}]$ value, where $NC_{\min}$ is the number of vectors in the smallest class, is usually sufficient. This condition avoids creation of overspecific features and is applied to all features. After a new feature has been accepted search for new projection is continued few times (here $N_{rep}$ is simply set to 20), and if no new features is accepted the procedure is stopped and other types of features are generated.

To determine interval $[t_a, t_b]$ that extracts a cluster from projection $t(x; w)$ sort all projected values and call them $t_1 \le t_2 \le ...t_n$. Now count how many vectors, starting from $t_a = t_1$, are from the same class $C$ as vector $x$ projected at $t_a$; find the first vector $t_k$ on the ordered list that is from a different class $C' \ne C$. If $k - 1 \ge \eta$ the interval $[t_a, t_b = (t_k - t_{k-1})/2]$ contains sufficient number of vectors to be included and new candidate feature is created. Start again from $t_a = t_b$ and repeat the procedure to check if more intervals may be created using the same projection.

Even the simplest version of aRPM is thus non-linear, and is capable of solving highly-nonseparable problems [10], posing a real challenge to traditional neural networks and SVMs, for example the parity problem for a large number of bits [14].

The second type of features considered here are based on kernels. While many kernels may be mixed together, here only Gaussian kernels with several values of dispersion $\sigma$ are used for each potential support vector $g(x; x_i, \sigma) = \exp(-||x_i - x||^2/2\sigma^2)$. Local kernel features have values close to zero except around their support vectors $x_i$. Therefore their usefulness is limited to the neighborhood $O(x_i)$ in which $g_i(x) > \epsilon$. In this neighborhood we should have at least $\eta$ vectors, otherwise candidate feature will be rejected. To create a multi-resolution kernel features based on a few support vectors, candidate features with large $\sigma$ are first created, providing smooth decision borders. Then significantly smaller $\sigma$ values are used to create features more strongly localized. In our case 5 values $\sigma = \in \{2^5; 2^2; 2^{-1}; 2^{-4}; 2^{-7}\}$ have been used.

The candidate feature is converted into a permanent node only if it increases classification margin. In SVM classification margin is simply related to the norm of the weight vector $w$ in the kernel space. It is optimized in a fixed feature space using quadratic programming, reducing the number of support vectors and therefore removing some dimensions from the feature space. In our case we have incremental algorithm, expanding feature space until no improvements are made. Expanding the space should move vectors away from decision border. However, only those vectors that are on the wrong side or rather close to the decision border should be moved in the direction of correctly classified vectors, while the remaining vectors may even move slightly towards the decision border. This idea is similar to boosting [9], with each feature treated as a weak classifier, except that these classifiers have high specificity with low recall. We shall use here a simple confidence measure based on the winner-takes-all principle (WTA), summing the activation of hidden nodes. Projections with added intervals give binary activations $b_i(x)$, but the values of kernel features $g(x; x_i, \sigma)$ have to be summed, giving a total activation $A(C|x)$ for each class. Although probability of classification $p(C|x)$ may be estimated by dividing this value through total activation summed over all classes information about confidence will be lost. Plotting $A(C|x)$ versus $A(\neg C|x)$ for each vector leads to scatterograms shown in Fig. 1, giving an idea how far is a given vector from the decision border.

In the WTA procedure the difference $|A(C|x) - A(\neg C|x)|$ estimates distance from the decision border. Specifying confidence of the model for vector $x \in C$ using logistic function: $F(x) = 1/(1 + \exp(-(A(C|x) - A(\neg C|x))))$ gives values around 1 if $x$ is on the correct side and far from the border, and goes to zero if it is on the wrong side. Total confidence in the model may then be estimated by summing over all vectors, and it should reach $n$ for perfect separation. The final effect of adding new feature $h(x)$ to the total confidence measure is therefore:

$$U(\mathcal{H}, h) = \sum_x (F(x; \mathcal{H} + h) - F(x; \mathcal{H}))$$

If $U(\mathcal{H}, h) > \alpha$ than the new feature is accepted, contributing to a larger margin. Parameter $\alpha$ has been fixed at 0.01, lower values will lead to faster expansion of the feature space. Note that the mislabeled cases that fall far from the decision borders will have large number of votes for the wrong class and thus will fall into the saturation region of the confidence functions $F(x; \mathcal{H})$, so they will have little influence on the $U(\mathcal{H}, h)$ change. This is in contrast to the mean square error or other such measures that would encourage features pushing mislabeled cases strongly towards the decision border.

To make final decision aRPM with margin maximization uses winner-takes-most mechanism or linear discrimination. We have tested also several other models (Naive Bayes, decision trees, neural networks and nearest neighbor methods) in the final $\mathcal{H}$ space, and results in all cases are significantly improved comparing them to the original feature space. The aRPM algorithm is summarized in Algorithm 1. The initial space $\mathcal{H}$ is created treating the single features $x_i$ in the same way as projections $t(vx)$, without checking confidence measures. In this way simple original features that may be very useful, are preserved (note that they are never used in SVMs).

---

**Algorithm 1.** aRPM with margin

---

**Require:** Fix the values of internal parameters $\eta$, $\alpha$ parameters and the set of $\sigma$ dispersions (sorted in descending order).

1: Standardize the dataset, $n$ vectors, $d$ features.
2: Set the initial space $\mathcal{H}$ using input features $x_i$, with $i = 1..d$ features and $n$ vectors.
3: **for** $k = 0$ to $N_{rep}$ **do**
4:    Randomly generate new direction $w \in [0, 1]^d$
5:    Project all vectors on direction $t(x) = w \cdot x$
6:    Sort $t(x)$ values in ascending order, with associated class labels.
7:    Analyze $p(t|C)$ distribution to find all intervals with pure clusters defining binary features $b_i(x; C)$.
8:    **if** the number of vectors covered by the feature $b_i(x; C) > \eta$ and $U(\mathcal{H}, b_i) > \alpha$ **then**
9:        accept new binary feature $b_i(x)$ creating class-labeled hidden network node.
10:        **goto 3**
11:    **end if**
12: **end for**
13: **for** $j = 1$ to $n_\sigma$ **do**
14:    Set the Gaussian dispersion to $\sigma = \sigma_j$.
15:    Create kernel features $g_i(x) = \exp(-||x_i - x||^2 / 2\sigma^2)$.
16:    **if** $U(\mathcal{H}, g_i) > \alpha$ **then**
17:        accept new kernel feature $g_i(x)$ creating class-labeled hidden network nodes.
18:    **end if**
19: **end for**
20: Sum the activity of hidden node subsets for each class to calculate network outputs.
21: Classify test data mapped into enhanced space.

---

aRPM with margin maximization may be presented as a constructive network, with new nodes representing transformations and procedures to extract useful features, and additional layers analyzing the image of data in the feature space created in this way. The algorithm has only a few parameters that in the experiments reported below have been fixed at values given above in this section. Although in tests all vectors have been used as potential Gaussian kernel support features, leading to $O(n^2)$ complexity, in practice only a few such features are accepted.

# 3 Illustrative Examples

The usefulness of algorithm described in this paper has been evaluated on six datasets downloaded from the UCI Machine Learning Repository. A summary of these datasets is presented in Tab. 1. These datasets are standard examples of benchmark type and are used here to enable typical comparison of different learning methods. To compare aRPM with and without margin maximization with other popular classification methods 10-fold crossvalidation tests have been repeated 10 times and average results collected in Table 2, with accuracies and standard deviations for each dataset. Results of Naive Bayes, kNN (with optimized $k$ and the Euclidean distance), SSV decision tree [17], SVM with optimized linear and Gaussian kernels are given for comparison.

**Table 1.** Summary of datasets

| Title | #Features | #Samples | #Samples per class | Source |
|---|---|---|---|---|
| Appendicitis | 7 | 106 | 85 / 21 | [18] |
| Diabetes | 8 | 768 | 500 / 268 | [18] |
| Glass | 9 | 214 | 70 / 76 / 17 / 13 / 9 / 29 | [18] |
| Heart | 13 | 297 | 160 absence / 137 presence | [18] |
| Liver | 6 | 345 | 145 / 200 | [18] |
| Wine | 13 | 178 | 59 / 71 / 48 | [18] |
| Parity8 | 8 | 256 | 128 even, 128 odd | artificial |
| Parity10 | 10 | 1024 | 512 even, 512 odd | artificial |

**Table 2.** 10 x 10 crossvalidation accuracy and variance

| Dataset | Method | | | | | | | |
|---|---|---|---|---|---|---|---|---|
| | NB | kNN | SSV | SVM(L) | SVM(G) | aRPM-no | aRPM (WTA) | aRPM(LDA) |
| Append. | 83.1 ± 10.2 | 87.0 ± 10.6 | 87.9 ± 7.4 | 85.1 ± 6.0 | 85.9 ± 6.4 | 82.6 ± 9.3 | 87.7 ± 8.1 | 88.0 ± 6.7 |
| Diabetes | 68.1 ± 2.3 | 75.2 ± 4.1 | 73.7 ± 3.8 | 76.4 ±4.7 | 75.7 ± 5.9 | 67.7 ± 4.2 | 61.2 ± 5.7 | 76.7 ± 4.4 |
| Glass | 68.6 ± 9.0 | 69.7 ± 7.4 | 69.7 ± 9.4 | 40.2 ±9.6 | 63.2 ± 7.7 | 65.0 ± 9.9 | 60.3 ± 8.5 | 68.9 ± 8.3 |
| Heart | 76.5 ± 8.6 | 82.8 ± 6.7 | 74.7 ± 8.7 | 83.2 ±6.2 | 83.5 ± 5.3 | 78.3 ± 4.2 | 80.1 ± 7.5 | 83.1 ± 4.7 |
| Liver | 58.6 ± 3.8 | 62.6 ± 8.5 | 68.9 ± 9.7 | 68.4 ±5.9 | 69.0 ± 8.4 | 61.1 ± 5.1 | 67.5 ± 5.5 | 72.7 ± 7.9 |
| Wine | 98.3 ± 2.6 | 94.9 ± 4.1 | 89.4 ± 8.8 | 96.0 ± 5.9 | 97.8 ± 3.9 | 68.6 ± 7.8 | 94.3 ± 5.8 | 97.7 ± 4.0 |
| Parity8 | 28.9 ± 4.6 | 100 ± 0 | 49.2 ± 1.0 | 34.1 ±11.7 | 15.6 ± 22.7 | 99.2 ± 1.6 | 100 ± 0 | 34.7 ± 3.8 |
| Parity10 | 38.1 ± 3.3 | 100 ± 0 | 49.8 ± 0.3 | 44.1 ±5.0 | 45.6 ± 4.3 | 99.5 ± 0.9 | 100 ± 0 | 40.3 ± 2.7 |

The aRPM-no column gives results of our algorithm without margin optimization [10], and the next two columns with margin, using WTA output and linear discrimination output (calculated here with linear SVM). In all cases adding margin optimization has improved results and linear discrimination in the enhanced space achieves the best results, or at least statistically equivalent. In most cases results are better than linear and Gaussian kernel SVM. The only highly non-separable problem here is the 8 and 10 bit parity that is perfectly handled thanks to the projected binary features even with the WTA output.

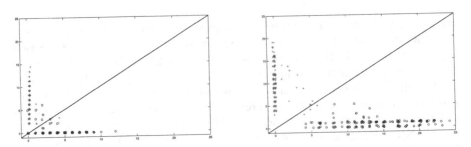

**Fig. 1.** Output of aRPM algorithm for the Heart data, without and with margin optimization

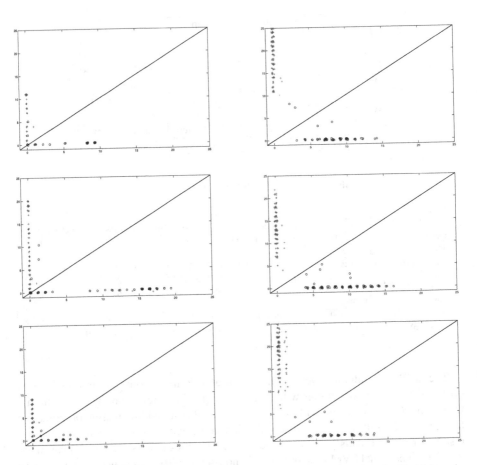

**Fig. 2.** Output of aRPM algorithm for the Wine data, without (left column) and with (right column) margin optimization. Each row present different class (one class vs rest).

Only a few kernel features have been selected in most cases, showing that localized projections are able to provide quite good model of the data. This does not mean that a simpler model would not be created if kernel features will be analyzed before projections. An interesting solution that has not been checked yet is to create first low resolution features, with projections and intervals that cover large number of vectors (large $\eta$), followed by large kernels, and than remove vectors that are correctly handled and progressively reduce $\eta$ to account for the remaining errors. The final model may be then analyzed in terms of general rules and exceptions.

The effect of margin optimization is clearly seen in scatterograms, Fig. 1 and 2. Most vectors that were not classified with high confidence are removed now away from the decision border (which is at the diagonal), activating many units, except for those that cannot be classified correctly. Some vectors that were far from decision border have moved a bit closer to it.

# 4   Conclusions

Almost Random Projection Machine algorithm [10] has been improved in two ways, by adding selection of network nodes to ensure wide margins, and by adding kernel features. Relations to kernel SVM, Liquid State Machines, reservoir computing, and boosting on the machine learning side, and biological plausibility on the other side, make aRPM a very interesting subject of study. In contrast to typical neural networks that learn by parameter adaptation there is no learning involved, just generation and selection of features. Shifting the focus to generation of new features followed by the winner-takes-all algorithm (or linear perceptron), makes it a candidate for a fast-learning neural algorithm that is simpler and learns faster than MLP or RBF networks. Features discovered solving other tasks may be transfered to new tasks facilitating faster learning. Kernel features may be related to neural filters that evaluate similarity to previous complex stimuli. Although kernels have been recommended in cognitive science for analysis of categorization experiments and behavioral data [19] the view expressed in this paper offers a simpler and more comprehensible explanation. Feature selection and construction, finding interesting views on the data is the basis of natural categorization and learning processes.

Results on benchmark problems show improvements of aRPM(LDA) over all other classifiers over the most cases, and results of aRPM(WTA) on the parity problem (and other Boolean functions, not showed here) show that this approach will be particularly useful in solving difficult problems with inherent complex logic. Calculations on much larger datasets from the NIPS 2003 competition [20] are in progress. These datasets have been selected because they are very difficult to analyze correctly by standard MLPs, Support Vector Machines or other machine learning algorithms.

Scatterogram of WTA output shows the effect of margin optimization, and allows for estimation of confidence in classification of a given data. Further improvements to the aRPM algorithm will include admission of impure clusters instead of binary features, with modeling actual $\mathcal{P}(C|t(\boldsymbol{x}))$ distribution along projection directions, use of other kernel features, judicious selection of candidate vectors to define support features and optimization of the algorithm.

# References

1. Rumelhart, D.E., Hinton, G.E., Williams, R.J.: Learning internal representations by error propagation. In: Rumelhart, D.E., McCleland, J.L. (eds.) Parallel Distributed Processing: Explorations in Microstructure of Congnition. Foundations, vol. 1, pp. 318–362. MIT Press, Cambridge (1986)
2. O'Reilly, R., Munakata, Y.: Computational Explorations in Cognitive Neuroscience. MIT-Press, Cambridge (2000)
3. Buonomano, D., Maass, W.: State-dependent computations: Spatiotemporal processing in cortical networks. Nature Reviews in Neuroscience 10(2), 113–125 (2009)
4. Maass, W., Natschläger, T., Markram, H.: Real-time computing without stable states: A new framework for neural computation based on perturbations. Neural Computation 14, 2531–2560 (2002)
5. Jaeger, H., Haas, H.: Harnessing nonlinearity: Predicting chaotic systems and saving energy in wireless communication. Science 304, 78–80 (2004)
6. Jaeger, H., Maass, W., Principe, J.: Introduction to the special issue on echo state networks and liquid state machines. Neural Networks 20(3), 287–289 (2007)
7. Cover, T.M.: Geometrical and statistical properties of systems of linear inequalities with applications in pattern recognition. IEEE Transactions on Electronic Computers 14, 326–334 (1965)
8. Schölkopf, B., Smola, A.: Learning with Kernels. In: Support Vector Machines, Regularization, Optimization, and Beyond. MIT Press, Cambridge (2001)
9. Schapire, R., Singer, Y.: Improved boosting algorithms using confidence-rated predictions. Machine Learning 37, 297–336 (1999)
10. Duch, W., Maszczyk, T.: Almost random projection machine. In: Alippi, C., Polycarpou, M., Panayiotou, C., Ellinas, G. (eds.) ICANN 2009. LNCS, vol. 5768, pp. 789–798. Springer, Heidelberg (2009)
11. Duch, W.: $k$-separability. In: Kollias, S.D., Stafylopatis, A., Duch, W., Oja, E. (eds.) ICANN 2006. LNCS, vol. 4131, pp. 188–197. Springer, Heidelberg (2006)
12. Grochowski, M., Duch, W.: Projection Pursuit Constructive Neural Networks Based on Quality of Projected Clusters. In: Kůrková, V., Neruda, R., Koutník, J. (eds.) ICANN 2008, Part II. LNCS, vol. 5164, pp. 754–762. Springer, Heidelberg (2008)
13. Buesing, L., Maass, W.: A spiking neuron as information bottleneck. Neural Computation 22, 1–32 (2010)
14. Brown, D.: N-bit parity networks. Neural Networks 6, 607–608 (1993)
15. Grochowski, M., Duch, W.: Learning highly non-separable Boolean functions using Constructive Feedforward Neural Network. In: de Sá, J.M., Alexandre, L.A., Duch, W., Mandic, D.P. (eds.) ICANN 2007. LNCS, vol. 4668, pp. 180–189. Springer, Heidelberg (2007)
16. Duch, W., Maszczyk, T.: Universal learning machines. In: Chan, J.H. (ed.) ICONIP 2009, Part II. LNCS, vol. 5864, pp. 206–215. Springer, Heidelberg (2009)
17. Grąbczewski, K., Duch, W.: The separability of split value criterion. In: Proceedings of the 5th Conf. on Neural Networks and Soft Computing, Zakopane, Poland, pp. 201–208. Polish Neural Network Society (2000)
18. Asuncion, A., Newman, D.: UCI machine learning repository (2009), http://www.ics.uci.edu/~mlearn/MLRepository.html
19. Jäkel, F., Schölkopf, B., Wichmann, F.A.: Does cognitive science need kernels? Trends in Cognitive Sciences 13(9), 381–388 (2009)
20. Guyon, I., Gunn, S., Nikravesh, M., Zadeh, L.: Feature extraction, foundations and applications. Physica Verlag, Springer, Heidelberg (2006)

# A New Tree Kernel Based on SOM-SD

Fabio Aiolli, Giovanni Da San Martino, and Alessandro Sperduti

Dept. of Pure and Applied Mathematics, Via Trieste 63, 35131 Padova, Italy

**Abstract.** Many different paradigms have been studied in the past to treat tree structured data, including kernel and neural based approaches. However, both types of methods have their own drawbacks. Kernels typically can only cope with discrete labels and tend to be sparse. On the other side, SOM-SD, an extension of the SOM for structured data, is unsupervised and Markovian, i.e. the representation of a subtree does not consider where the subtree appears in a tree. In this paper, we present a hybrid approach which tries to overcome these problems. In particular, we propose a new kernel based on SOM-SD which adds information about the relative position of subtrees (the route) to the activation of the nodes in such a way to discriminate even those subtrees originally encoded by the same prototypes. Experiments have been performed against two well known benchmark datasets with promising results.

**Keywords:** Tree Kernels, Kernel Methods, SOM, Supervised Learning.

## 1 Introduction

Recently, there has been a great interest in the study of techniques able to learn in structured domains with no need to represent data in vectorial form. For example, kernels for structured domains (see [7] for an overview), allow for a direct exploitation of the structural information obtaining very good results in practice.

However, kernel for structures have the well known disadvantage that, in the case of large structures and many symbols, the feature space implicitly defined by these kernels is very sparse [10]. In fact, these kernels are usually defined in terms of the number of matching subparts and, whenever many different types of these parts can be found in data, these matches tend to be barely observed. As a result, kernel based learning methods like Support Vector Machines (SVM) [5] using these standard kernels cannot be trained effectively. They will tend to generate several support structures thus leading to a final model which is similar to the nearest neighbor rule. It is then clear that any kernel machine cannot work well when used together with these kernels.

A completely different approach for the treatment of structured data has been presented in [8], a neural network based method, called SOM-SD. This is an unsupervised learning algorithm which extends the SOM to structured domains. As SOMs, SOM-SD organizes data (structures in this case) onto a topological discrete lattice. Moreover, the neural approach is well suited to cope with structures having real valued labels, while in the case of standard kernels for trees labels are assumed to be discrete.

The ability of the SOM-SD to represent the data onto a lattice preserving as much as possible their topology in the original space provides a viable technique for defining

K. Diamantaras, W. Duch, L.S. Iliadis (Eds.): ICANN 2010, Part II, LNCS 6353, pp. 49–58, 2010.

similarity functions based on matching of non identical structures in the original space. This idea has been exploited by the Activation Mask Kernels family of kernels (see [1,3]), defined on top of a SOM-SD with the aim of exploiting both its compression and "topology" preserving capabilities. Experimental results with these kernels provided evidence that, when sparsity on the data was present, they were able to improve the overall categorization performance over each method taken individually, i.e. either SVM using tree kernels or SOM-SDs equipped with a 1-NN classification rule. This also demonstrates that, neither tree kernels nor SOM-SDs are always able to retain all the relevant information for classification.

One issue with the SOM-SD type of algorithms, and SOM-SD activation based kernels consequently, is that they are computed by almost neglecting the contextual information of substructures. More specifically, the path linking the root of a tree to the root of the subtree we want to represent is not actually considered when training takes place. This can be a problem when this type of information is relevant for a given task.

In this paper, we propose a new method which tries to fill this gap. The proposed method can be though of as a hybrid method which combines the SOM-SD neural approach, and the Activation Mask kernels, in conjunction with a standard kernel for trees devised in [2]. Specifically, we propose to add additional (contextual) information to the activations of the nodes in such a way to discriminate between subtrees encoded by the same prototypes. Then we propose to add a type of information which is orthogonal to the one processed by the SOM-SD, i.e. information about the antecedents of the root of a given subtree (here referred to as a *route*).

Experiments performed with this new kernel against two well known competition datasets have shown a systematic improvement with respect to baseline approaches.

## 2   Background

In the following sections, the SOM-SD, an extension presented in [1,3] of the Self Organizing Maps for structured data, and the Activation Mask Kernel presented in [2], are sketched. Please, see the referred paper for details on these algorithms.

### 2.1   Self-Organizing Maps for Structured Data

The SOM-SD extends the Self Organizing Map (SOM) approach [9] by allowing to process structured input. In this paper we are interested in structures in the form of (positional) trees, where each node $v$ of a tree $T$ can have a label (e.g., a real valued vector) $\mathbf{v}$ attached to it. Moreover, we assume that each child of a node $v$ is associated to a specific position out of a maximum number $o$ of available positions (the maximum out-degree of the trees we are interested in.) The $i$-th child of $v$ will be denoted by $ch_i[v]$.

The SOM-SD can be understood as the recursive application of a standard SOM to individual nodes in a tree $T$ where the input is properly coded to take into consideration the structural information. As for the standard SOM, the SOM-SD consists of a number of neurons which are organized in a $q$-dimensional grid (usually $q = 2$). A codebook vector $\mathbf{m}$ is associated with each neuron. Given an input vector $\mathbf{x}$, let $\mathbf{y}_\mathbf{x}$ denote the coordinate vector of the winning neuron.

The network input for SOM-SD is a vector $\mathbf{x}_v$ representing the information of a node $v \in T$, and it is built through the concatenation of the data label $\mathbf{v}$ attached to $v$ and the coordinates obtained by the mapping of its child nodes on the same map, so that $\mathbf{x}_v = [\mathbf{v}, \mathbf{y}_{\mathbf{x}_{ch_1[v]}}, \ldots, \mathbf{y}_{\mathbf{x}_{ch_o[v]}}]$. In this representation, the "impossible" coordinate $(-1, -1)$, is used to represent a missing child. As a result, the input dimension is $n = p + 2o$, where $p$ is the dimension of the data label and the constant 2 refers to the number of dimensions of the map which is the most commonly used. The codebook vectors $\mathbf{m} \equiv [\mathbf{m}^{label}, \mathbf{m}^{ch}]$ are of the same dimension.

A number of parameters need to be set before starting the training of a SOM-SD. These parameters (network dimension, learning rate, number of training iterations) are problem dependent and are also required for the standard SOM. The weight value $\mu$ introduced with the SOM-SD is an additional parameter which can be computed while executing the training through a statistical analysis of the size and magnitude of the data labels which typically remain constant during training, and the coordinate vectors which can change during training. In other words, $\mu$ can be used to weight the input vector components so as to balance their influence on the distance measure in Step 1. In practice, however, it is often found that a smaller value for $\mu$ can help to improve the quality of the mappings. This is due to the recursive nature of the training algorithm and to the fact that a stronger focus on structural information helps to ensure that structural information is passed on more accurately to all causally related nodes when processing a tree.

The SOM-SD then is able to map structures in input onto a discrete low dimensional lattice with the aim to preserve the topology of the input data. Structures which are similar tend to be mapped onto closer neurons. This is a key property for the intuition behind this paper. Figure 1 gives an examples of how trees are mapped into a SOM-SD. One can note similar (sub)trees are mapped close each other.

**Fig. 1.** Example of a SOM-SD mapping of a set of trees and their subtrees

## 2.2 The Activation Mask Kernel

The unsupervised SOM-SD model can also be used to define a kernel for trees [1,3]. The idea is to define a feature space having one dimension associated to each neuron of the map. Then a vectorial representation for a tree can be obtained by considering which ones of these neurons are activated for the nodes of the tree. Once the above representation has been computed for any pair of trees, a kernel can be promptly defined as the dot product of these representations.

More formally, given a SOM-SD map, let $\text{ne}_\epsilon[\mathbf{y}(i)]$ denote the set of neurons (coordinates) in the $\epsilon$-neighborhood of neuron $i$, i.e. $\{\mathbf{y}(j)|\Delta_{\mathbf{y}(i)\mathbf{y}(j)} \leq \epsilon\}$, where $\mathbf{y}(i) = (x_i, y_i)$ is the coordinate vector associated to neuron $i$, and $\Delta$ is the topological distance defined on the 2-dimensional map. Given two trees $T_1$ and $T_2$, we define the set of neurons (coordinates) shared by the two $\epsilon$-neighbors related to nodes $v_1 \in T_1$ and $v_2 \in T_2$ as

$$I_\epsilon(v_1, v_2) = \text{ne}_\epsilon[\mathbf{y}_{\mathbf{x}_{v_1}}] \cap \text{ne}_\epsilon[\mathbf{y}_{\mathbf{x}_{v_2}}]. \tag{1}$$

Then, the Activation Mask Kernel is defined by taking:

$$K_\epsilon(T_1, T_2) = \sum_{\substack{v_1 \in T_1, \\ v_2 \in T_2, \\ \mathbf{y} \in I_\epsilon(v_1, v_2)}} Q_\epsilon(\mathbf{y}, \mathbf{y}_{\mathbf{x}_{v_1}}) Q_\epsilon(\mathbf{y}, \mathbf{y}_{\mathbf{x}_{v_2}}), \tag{2}$$

where $Q_\epsilon(\mathbf{y}, \mathbf{y}')$ is inversely proportional to the distance $\Delta_{\mathbf{y}\mathbf{y}'}$ between map neurons with coordinates $\mathbf{y}$ and $\mathbf{y}'$ and $Q_\epsilon(\mathbf{y}, \mathbf{y}') = 0$ when the neurons are not in the $\epsilon$-neighborhood of each other, i.e. when $\Delta_{\mathbf{y}\mathbf{y}'} > \epsilon$. In [1], $Q_\epsilon(\mathbf{y}, \mathbf{y}')$ is defined as

$$Q_\epsilon(\mathbf{y}, \mathbf{y}') = \begin{cases} \epsilon - \eta\Delta_{\mathbf{y}\mathbf{y}'} & \text{if } \Delta_{\mathbf{y}\mathbf{y}'} \leq \epsilon \\ 0 & \text{otherwise} \end{cases} \tag{3}$$

where $0 \leq \eta \leq 1$ is a parameter determining how much the distance influences the neighborhood activation.

Thus, the representation of a tree $T$ into the feature space induced by the map is defined as the vector $\phi(T)$ with $i$-th component $\phi_i(T) = \sum_{v \in T} Q_\epsilon(\mathbf{y}(i), \mathbf{y}_{\mathbf{x}_v})$.

Figure 2 gives an example of construction of the feature space representation of 3 trees according to the AM-kernel ($\epsilon = 2$, $\eta = 1$). On the lower part of the image three simple trees selected from the INEX 2005 dataset (see section 4.1) and on the right part their activation masks referring to a $5 \times 4$ map. The height of each element of the map corresponds to the value of the activation. Note that the tree at the left side is more similar to the tree at the center than to the tree at the right side, and this is reflected in the activation masks.

In [1,3] it has been shown that the similarity function $K_\epsilon(T_1, T_2)$ is a kernel for any choice of $Q_\epsilon(\mathbf{y}, \mathbf{y}')$ and that the complexity of its evaluation is $O(a \cdot b \cdot (|T_1| + |T_2|))$, where $a \cdot b$ is the size of the map. The overall computational complexity is not affected by the required initial training of the SOM-SD as it is performed only once.

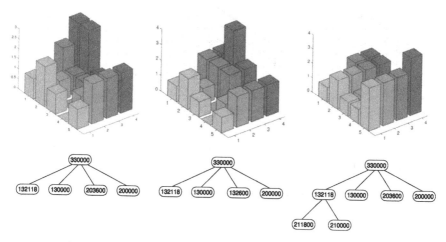

**Fig. 2.** Example of feature space construction for the AM-Kernel ($\epsilon = 2$, $\eta = 1$). The figure presents three trees (bottom) and the corresponding feature mapping onto a $5 \times 4$ map. Note that the feature maps of the first two trees are quite similar while they both differ from the third one, as expected.

# 3    Adding Route Information to the Activation Mask Kernel

In this section, we introduce the main contribution of the paper, i.e. the extension of the feature space of the Activation Mask Kernel with features that are based on route information. Intuitively, a route in a tree explicitly keeps information about the position of the nodes with respect to adjacent nodes.

**Definition 1 (Route).** *Let $T$ be a (positional) tree, $v_1, v_2 \in T$ any two nodes in the tree, with $v_2$ being a descendant of $v_1$. Then the route from $v_1$ to $v_2$ in $T$, denoted by $\pi(v_1, v_2)$, is the sequence of indexes of edges connecting the consecutive nodes in the path connecting nodes $v_1$ and $v_2$.*

Figure 3 gives an example of a tree and a route computed between nodes **a** and **e**. The nodes connected by red edges represent the path connecting nodes **a** and **e**. The route connecting nodes **a** and **e** is represented by the sequence $(2, 3)$, since node **b** is the second child of **a** and node **e** is the third child of **b**. It must be pointed out that a route is not a path, since a path can be understood as a route where we retain the information about the label attached to each node belonging to the path.

The concept of route is useful for those tree domains where it may be important to "recognize" that a specific subtree, or family of subtrees, occurs into a specific "location" within a tree, e.g. at the end of a specific route, with no consideration of the labels attached to nodes crossed by the route. It must be noticed that, because of the causal style of processing, SOM-SD cannot discriminate among different occurrences of the same subtree within the same or different trees. In fact, when computing the winning neuron for a node in a tree, no information about the node's ancestors is used (see Fig. 4). It is true that the Activation Mask Kernel can actually exploit information

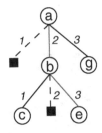

**Fig. 3.** An example of a route connecting nodes labeled with **a** and **e**. The positional nature of the tree is shown in the figure by representing missing edges by dashed lines and missing nodes by black squares. Edges crossed by the route are colored in red. The route is formed by the sequence 2, 3 since node **b** is the second child of **a** and node **e** is the third child of **b**.

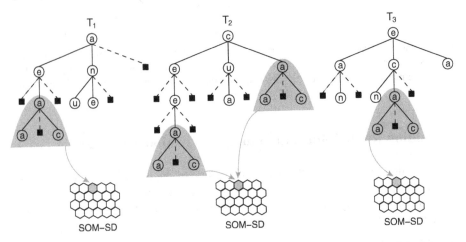

**Fig. 4.** Since SOM-SD is a causal model, the different occurrences of subtree **a(a,_,c)** in the trees $T_1$, $T_2$, $T_3$, get the same winner

about the node's ancestors, since the activation map used by the kernel is obtained by collecting the information about winners for all the nodes in the tree. However, this information is heavily dependent on the label attached to each node. This can be easily understood by recalling that the winner neuron is determined by combining the information about labels and structure. Thus, the feature space exploited by the Activation Mask Kernel does not possess single features based on route information.

Our proposal is to enrich the feature space of the Activation Mask Kernel by introducing explicit information about routes. Let $v$ be a node belonging to a tree $T$, and let $\pi_v^T$ be the route associated to it. Then, we define $\mathrm{ne}_\epsilon^\pi[\mathbf{y}_{\mathbf{x}_v}] = \{\pi_u^T | u \in T, \Delta_{\mathbf{y}_{\mathbf{x}_v}, \mathbf{y}_{\mathbf{x}_u}} \leq \epsilon\}$. Notice that for $\epsilon = 1$, $\mathrm{ne}_\epsilon^\pi[\mathbf{y}_{\mathbf{x}_v}]$ just contains routes of nodes of $T$ that share the same winning neuron with coordinate vector $\mathbf{y}_{\mathbf{x}_v}$, i.e. if $\pi_v^T \in \mathrm{ne}_0^\pi[\mathbf{y}_{\mathbf{x}_v}]$ and $\pi_u^T \in \mathrm{ne}_0^\pi[\mathbf{y}_{\mathbf{x}_v}]$, with $u \neq v$, then $\mathbf{y}_{\mathbf{x}_v} = \mathbf{y}_{\mathbf{x}_u}$. Given two trees $T_1$ and $T_2$, we define the set of routes shared via SOM-SD by the two $\pi$-$\epsilon$-neighbors related to nodes $v_1 \in T_1$ and $v_2 \in T_2$ as

$$I_\epsilon^\pi(v_1, v_2) = \mathrm{ne}_\epsilon^\pi[\mathbf{y}_{\mathbf{x}_{v_1}}] \cap \mathrm{ne}_\epsilon^\pi[\mathbf{y}_{\mathbf{x}_{v_2}}]. \qquad (4)$$

Then, we define the kernel contribution of the routes as:

$$K_\epsilon^\pi(T_1, T_2) = \sum_{\substack{v_1 \in T_1, v_2 \in T_2 \\ \mathbf{y}_{\mathbf{x}_{v_1}} = \mathbf{y}_{\mathbf{x}_{v_2}} \\ \pi' \in I_\epsilon^\pi(v_1, v_2)}} Q_\epsilon(\mathbf{y}_{\mathbf{x}_{v_1}}, \mathbf{y}_{\mathbf{x}_{\pi'|T_1}}) Q_\epsilon(\mathbf{y}_{\mathbf{x}_{v_2}}, \mathbf{y}_{\mathbf{x}_{\pi'|T_2}}), \qquad (5)$$

where $\pi'|T_i$ refers to the node reached by following route $\pi'$ starting from the root of $T_i$. Note that eq. 5 can be computed efficiently by explicitly representing each feature since the number of distinct routes for a tree is at most $|T|$.

The final kernel is defined as $\hat{K}_\epsilon(T_1, T_2) = K_\epsilon(T_1, T_2) + K_\epsilon^\pi(T_1, T_2)$. In Fig. 5 we give an example of how routes are exploited.

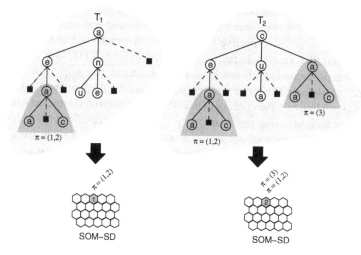

**Fig. 5.** In the proposed representation, the activation mask for each tree is enriched by associating to each neuron the routes to (sub)trees for which the neuron is a winner. In the figure, two examples are shown, where only the contribution of subtree **a(a,_,c)** is reported.

# 4  Experiments and Results

In order to test the effectiveness of the proposed approach, two experiments on multi-class classification problems were performed. The datasets considered are derived from the INEX 2005 and INEX 2006 competitions [6], respectively.

## 4.1  Data Description and Experimental Setting

The INEX 2005 Competition dataset is formed by XML documents describing movies from the IMDB site[1]. The dataset employed in the experiments is obtained from the (m-db-s-0) corpus of INEX 2005 after a preprocessing phase. It consists of 9631 documents

---

[1] http://www.imdb.com

containing XML tags only. The data are divided into 11 classes. The preprocessing is described in detail in [11]. The choice of such preprocessing is motivated by the need to obtain input structures of manageable size and to compare to the techniques which won the competition. The mean size of the input structures has been reduced from 684191 vertices with maximum out-degree 6418 to 124359 vertices with maximum outdegree 32. The data are divided into training, validation and test sets containing 3397, 1423 and 4811 documents, respectively. The dataset is unbalanced and sparse with respect to two of the most popular kernels for trees: the Subtree (ST) and the Subset tree kernels (SST) [4]. Their sparsity index, computed as the proportion of example pairs in the dataset whose kernel value is 0, is 0.54 (see [1] for details).

The INEX 2006 dataset is derived from the IEEE corpus and it's composed of 12107 scientific articles from IEEE journals in XML format. It includes XML formatted documents, each from one of 18 different journals. Each different journal corresponds to one class. The data have been preprocessed with the same methodology used for INEX 2005. The data is again split into training, validation and test sets containing 4251, 1802 and 6054 documents, respectively. The dataset is unbalanced and non sparse with respect to ST and SST kernels. In fact, their sparsity index is 0.002489.

Experiments proceeded as follows. First, for each dataset, five maps were trained with the SOM-SD software[2]. The maps were chosen among the 45 described in [1] by sorting them in ascending order according to the classification error, computed with a 1-NN procedure, and then selecting one map every 11. This choice allows us to investigate the dependency of the error of our kernel from the map. Only 5 maps were selected because of the need to reduce the duration of the experiments. The maps selected for INEX 2005 and INEX 2006 are listed in table 1 and table 2, respectively. The parameters not listed in the two tables are kept fixed: $\alpha = 1$, neighbourhood radius=18, type of $\alpha$ decrease=sigmoidal, map topology=hexagonal. Given a map, the set of features of the activation mask kernel with information about the routes, were computed as described in sections 2.2 and 3. Experiments with the SVM[3] and the proposed kernel, AM$\pi$, were performed by selecting, on the validation set, the $\epsilon$ of the AM kernel and the $c$ of the SVM among these values: $1 \leq \epsilon \leq 6, c \in \{0.001, 0.01, 0.1, 1, 10, 100, 1000\}$. The parameter $\eta$ of the AM kernel is set to 1. Finally, the performance of the best parameter setting, for each map, was checked on the test set. The classification of a tree according to the SOM-SD is the one of the neuron representing the root of the tree. The class of a neuron is the most frequent class of the trees of the training set represented by such neuron.

## 4.2  Results and Discussion

Table 1 summarizes the results on the INEX 2005 dataset. Note that the results of the AM kernel differ from those in [1] because a newer version of the SVMlight software has been employed. The AM$\pi$ kernel show a clear improvement for all maps both on validation and test with respect to the SOM-SD alone and the AM kernel. The mean classification error of the AM kernel is 7.508 with standard deviation 1.610 on the validation set and 7.158 with standard deviation 1.4 on the test set. The mean classification

---

[2] http://www.uow.edu.au/~markus/apods/software.html

[3] http://disi.unitn.it/moschitti/Tree-Kernel.htm

**Table 1.** Characteristics of the SOM-SD maps trained on the INEX 2005 dataset and classification error for the SOM-SD, AM and AM$\pi$ kernels

| Map # | Size | Learning Iterations | $\mu$ | SOM-SD error % test | AM error % valid | AM error % test | AM$\pi$ error % valid | AM$\pi$ error % test |
|---|---|---|---|---|---|---|---|---|
| 1 | 110 x 80 | 128 | 0.85 | 8.65 | 6.33 | 6.41 | 3.45 | 3.48 |
| 2 | 110 x 80 | 32 | 0.05 | 12.62 | 5.77 | 5.60 | 3.59 | 3.16 |
| 3 | 77 x 56 | 32 | 0.65 | 18.62 | 8.22 | 7.18 | 3.52 | 3.14 |
| 4 | 55 x 40 | 128 | 0.85 | 22.51 | 7.38 | 7.24 | 3.45 | 3.23 |
| 5 | 55 x 40 | 32 | 0.25 | 32.49 | 9.84 | 9.36 | 3.45 | 3.39 |

**Table 2.** Characteristics of the SOM-SD maps trained on the INEX 2006 dataset and classification error for the SOM-SD, AM and AM$\pi$ kernels

| Map # | Size | Learning Iterations | $\mu$ | SOM-SD error % test | AM error % valid | AM error % test | AM$\pi$ error % valid | AM$\pi$ error % test |
|---|---|---|---|---|---|---|---|---|
| 1 | 110 x 80 | 128 | 0.05 | 60.77 | 59.22 | 61.07 | 57.72 | 60.16 |
| 2 | 110 x 80 | 32 | 0.85 | 61.98 | 58.77 | 59.93 | 57.22 | 59.67 |
| 3 | 77 x 56 | 128 | 0.85 | 63.45 | 59.22 | 61.37 | 58.50 | 59.49 |
| 4 | 55 x 40 | 64 | 0.05 | 66.25 | 59.94 | 61.75 | 60.44 | 61.73 |
| 5 | 55 x 40 | 32 | 0.45 | 67.66 | 59.55 | 61.77 | 57.50 | 59.26 |

error of the AM$\pi$ kernel on validation is 3.492 with standard deviation 0.062, and 3.28, with standard deviation 0.148, on the test set. The low values of the mean and standard deviations for the AM$\pi$ kernel suggests that the accuracy of the kernel does not seem to depend on the employed map.

The results on the INEX 2006 dataset are summarized in table 2. Except for one case on the validation set, the AM$\pi$ kernel always improves with respect to the AM kernel and always improves with respect to the SOM-SD alone. The mean classification error of the AM kernel is 59.34 with standard deviation 0.435 on the validation set and 61.178 with standard deviation 0.755 on the test set. The mean classification error of the AM$\pi$ kernel on validation is 58.276 with standard deviation 1.299, and 60.062, with standard deviation 0.989, on the test set. Although AM$\pi$ kernel shows more variability on the results, on average an improvement of 1.116 is obtained on the test set.

# 5   Conclusions

The Activation Mask Kernel is a tree kernel based on SOM-SD. Here we have proposed an extension of the Activation Mask Kernel which adds to the feature space information about routes, i.e. how to reach a specific node in a tree by starting from its root. In our proposal, the contribution to the kernel of two trees given by the sharing of a specific subtree is reinforced if the root of the subtree can be reached by the same route in both trees. The SOM-SD is basically enriched with information about routes, and the new kernel computed by adding to the Activation Mask Kernel the contribution due to routes. This extension is supposed to be particularly effective when the tree domain is such that the relative location of a subtree, or family of subtrees, within the tree is important for the task. Experimental results obtained on XML datasets seem to confirm the usefulness of the proposed approach.

# References

1. Aiolli, F., Da San Martino, G., Hagenbuchner, M., Sperduti, A.: Learning nonsparse kernels by self organizing maps for structured data. IEEE Transactions on Neural Networks 20, 1938–1949 (2009)
2. Aiolli, F., Da San Martino, G., Sperduti, A.: Route kernels for trees. In: International Conference on Machine Learning, p. 3 (2009)
3. Aiolli, F., Da San Martino, G., Sperduti, A., Hagenbuchner, M.: Kernelized self organizing maps for structured data. In: ESANN 2007 Conference, April 24-27 (2007)
4. Collins, M., Duffy, N.: New ranking algorithms for parsing and tagging: Kernels over discrete structures, and the voted perceptron. In: ACL 2002 (2002)
5. Cortes, C., Vapnik, V.: Support-vector networks. Mach. Learn. 20(3), 273–297 (1995)
6. Denoyer, L., Gallinari, P.: Report on the xml mining track at inex 2005 and inex 2006: categorization and clustering of xml documents. SIGIR Forum 41(1), 79–90 (2007)
7. Gartner, T.: A survey of kernels for structured data. SIGKDD Explorations 5(1), 49–58 (2003)
8. Hagenbuchner, M., Sperduti, A., Tsoi, A.C.: A self-organizing map for adaptive processing of structured data. IEEE Transactions on Neural Networks 14(3), 491–505 (2003)
9. Kohonen, T.: Self-Organizing Maps. Springer, Heidelberg (1995)
10. Suzuki, J., Isozaki, H.: Sequence and tree kernels with statistical feature mining. In: Weiss, Y., Schölkopf, B., Platt, J. (eds.) Advances in Neural Information Processing Systems, vol. 18, pp. 1321–1328. MIT Press, Cambridge (2006)
11. Trentini, F., Hagenbuchner, M., Sperduti, A., Scarselli, F.: A self-organising map approach for clustering of xml documents. In: Proceedings of the International Joint Conference on Neural Networks, IJCNN 2006, part of the IEEE World Congress on Computational Intelligence, WCCI 2006, Vancouver, BC, Canada, July 16-21, pp. 1805–1812. IEEE Press, Los Alamitos (2006)

# Kernel-Based Learning from Infinite Dimensional 2-Way Tensors

Marco Signoretto[1], Lieven De Lathauwer[2], and Johan A.K. Suykens[1]

[1] Katholieke Universiteit Leuven, ESAT-SCD/SISTA
Kasteelpark Arenberg 10, B-3001 Leuven, Belgium
[2] Group Science, Engineering and Technology
Katholieke Universiteit Leuven, Campus Kortrijk
E. Sabbelaan 53, 8500 Kortrijk, Belgium

**Abstract.** In this paper we elaborate on a kernel extension to tensor-based data analysis. The proposed ideas find applications in supervised learning problems where input data have a natural $2-$way representation, such as images or multivariate time series. Our approach aims at relaxing linearity of standard tensor-based analysis while still exploiting the structural information embodied in the input data.

## 1 Introduction

Tensors [8] are $N-$way arrays that generalize the ordinary notions of *vectors* (first-order tensors or $1-$way arrays) and *matrices* (second-order tensors or $2-$way arrays). They find natural applications in many domains since many types of data have intrinsically many dimensions. Gray-scale images, for example, are commonly represented as second order tensors. Additional dimensions may account for different illuminations conditions, views and so on [14]. An alternative representation prescribes to *flatten* the different dimensions namely to represent observations as high dimensional vectors. This way, however, important structure might be lost. Exploiting a natural $2-$way representation, for example, retains the relationship between the row-space and the column-space and allows to find structure preserving projections more efficiently [7]. Still, a main drawback of tensor-based learning is that it allows the user to construct models which are linear in the data and hence fail in the presence of nonlinearity. On a different track kernel methods [12],[13] lead to flexible models that have been proven successful in many different context. The core idea in this case consists of mapping input points represented as $1-$way arrays $\{x^l\}_{l=1}^n \subset \mathbb{R}^p$ into a high dimensional inner-product space $(\mathcal{F}, \langle \cdot, \cdot \rangle)$ by means of a *feature map* $\phi : \mathbb{R}^p \to \mathcal{F}$. In this space, standard linear methods are then applied [1]. Since the feature map is normally chosen to be nonlinear, a linear model in the feature space corresponds to a nonlinear rule in $\mathbb{R}^p$. On the other hand, the so called *kernel trick* allows to develop computationally feasible approaches regardless of the dimensionality of $\mathcal{F}$ as soon as we know $k : \mathbb{R}^p \times \mathbb{R}^p \to \mathbb{R}$ satisfying $k(x, y) = \langle \phi(x), \phi(y) \rangle$.

When input data are $N-$way arrays $\{X^l\}_{l=1}^n \subset \mathbb{R}^{p_1 \times p_2 \times \cdots \times p_N}$, nonetheless, the use of kernel methods requires to perform flattening first. In light of this, our

K. Diamantaras, W. Duch, L.S. Iliadis (Eds.): ICANN 2010, Part II, LNCS 6353, pp. 59–69, 2010.

main contribution consists of an attempt to provide a kernel extension to tensor-based data analysis. In particular, we focus on 2−way tensors and propose an approach that aims at relaxing linearity of standard tensor-based models while still exploiting the structural information embodied in the data. In a nutshell, whereas vectors are mapped into high dimensional vectors in standard kernel methods, our proposal corresponds to mapping matrices into high dimensional matrices that retain the original 2−way structure. The proposed ideas find applications in supervised learning problems where input data have a natural 2−way representation, such as images or multivariate time series.

In the next Section we introduce the notation and some basic facts about 2−way tensors. In Section 3 we illustrate our approach towards an operatorial representation of data. On Section 4 we turn into a general class of supervised learning problems where such representations are exploited and provide an explicit algorithm for the special case of regression and classification tasks. Before drawing our conclusions, in Section 5 we present some encouraging experimental results.

## 2    Data Representation through 2-Way Tensors

In this Section we first present the notation and some basic facts about 2-way tensors in Euclidean spaces. In order to come up a with kernel-based extension we then discuss their natural extensions towards infinite dimensional spaces.

### 2.1    Tensor Product of Euclidean Spaces and Matrices

For any $p \in \mathbb{N}$ we use the convention of denoting the set $\{1, \ldots, p\}$ by $\mathbb{N}_p$. Given two Euclidean spaces $\mathbb{R}^{p_1}$ and $\mathbb{R}^{p_2}$ their *tensor product* $\mathbb{R}^{p_1} \bigotimes \mathbb{R}^{p_2}$ is simply the space of linear mappings from $\mathbb{R}^{p_2}$ into $\mathbb{R}^{p_1}$. To each pair $(a, b) \in \mathbb{R}^{p_1} \times \mathbb{R}^{p_2}$ we can associate $a \otimes b \in \mathbb{R}^{p_1} \bigotimes \mathbb{R}^{p_2}$ defined for $c \in \mathbb{R}^{p_2}$ by

$$(a \otimes b)c = \langle b, c \rangle a \tag{1}$$

where $\langle b, c \rangle = \sum_{i \in \mathbb{N}_{p_2}} b_i c_i$. It is not difficult to show that any $X \in \mathbb{R}^{p_1} \bigotimes \mathbb{R}^{p_2}$ can be written as a linear combination of *rank-1* operators (1). Furthermore, as is well known, any such element $X$ can be identified by a matrix in $\mathbb{R}^{p_1 \times p_2}$. Correspondingly $\mathbb{R}^{p_1 \times p_2}$ or $\mathbb{R}^{p_1} \otimes \mathbb{R}^{p_2}$ denote essentially the same space and we may equally well write $X$ to mean the operator or the corresponding matrix. Finally, the Kronecker (or tensor) product between $A \in \mathbb{R}^{w_1} \bigotimes \mathbb{R}^{p_1}$ and $B \in \mathbb{R}^{w_2} \bigotimes \mathbb{R}^{p_2}$, denoted by $A \otimes B$ is the linear mapping $A \otimes B : \mathbb{R}^{p_1} \bigotimes \mathbb{R}^{p_2} \to \mathbb{R}^{w_1} \bigotimes \in \mathbb{R}^{w_2}$ defined by

$$(A \otimes B)X = AXB^\top \tag{2}$$

where $B^\top$ denotes the adjoint (transpose) of $B$. This further notion of tensor product also features a number of properties. If $X$ is a rank-1 operator $a \otimes b$, for example, then it can be verified that $(A \otimes B)(a \otimes b) = Aa \otimes Bb$.

## 2.2    Extension to Hilbert Spaces and Operators

Instead of Euclidean spaces, we now consider more general Hilbert spaces (HSs) $(\mathcal{H}_1, \langle \cdot, \cdot \rangle_{\mathcal{H}_1})$, $(\mathcal{H}_2, \langle \cdot, \cdot \rangle_{\mathcal{H}_2})$. The definitions and properties recalled above have a natural extension in this setting. In the general case, however, additional technical conditions are required to cope with infinite dimensionality. We follow [15, Supplement to Chapter 1] and restrict ourselves to Hilbert-Schmidt operators.

Recall that a bounded operator $A : \mathcal{H}_2 \to \mathcal{H}_1$ has adjoint $A^*$ defined by the property $\langle Ax, y \rangle_{\mathcal{H}_1} = \langle x, A^*y \rangle_{\mathcal{H}_2}$ for all $x \in \mathcal{H}_2$, $y \in \mathcal{H}_1$. It is of *Hilbert-Schmidt type* if

$$\sum_{i \in \mathbb{N}} \|Ae_i\|^2_{\mathcal{H}_1} < \infty \tag{3}$$

where $\|x\|^2_{\mathcal{H}_1} = \langle x, x \rangle_{\mathcal{H}_1}$ and $\{e_i\}_{i \in \mathbb{N}}$ is an orthonormal basis[1] of $\mathcal{H}_2$. The tensor product between $\mathcal{H}_1$ and $\mathcal{H}_2$, denoted by $\mathcal{H}_1 \otimes \mathcal{H}_2$, is defined as the space of linear operators of Hilbert-Schmidt type from $\mathcal{H}_2$ into $\mathcal{H}_1$. Condition (3) ensures that $\mathcal{H}_1 \otimes \mathcal{H}_2$ endowed with the inner-product

$$\langle A, B \rangle_{\mathcal{H}_1 \otimes \mathcal{H}_2} = \sum_{i \in \mathbb{N}} \langle Ae_i, Be_i \rangle_{\mathcal{H}_1} = \operatorname{trace}(B^*A) \tag{4}$$

is itself a HS. As for the finite dimensional case to each pair $(h_1, h_2) \in \mathcal{H}_1 \times \mathcal{H}_2$ we can associate $h_1 \otimes h_2$ defined by

$$(h_1 \otimes h_2)f = \langle h_2, f \rangle_{\mathcal{H}_2} h_1 \ . \tag{5}$$

One can check that (5) is of Hilbert-Schmidt type and hence $h_1 \otimes h_2 \in \mathcal{H}_1 \otimes \mathcal{H}_2$. As for the finite dimensional case, elements of $\mathcal{H}_1 \otimes \mathcal{H}_2$ can be represented as sum of rank-1 operator (5). Finally let $A : \mathcal{H}_1 \to \mathcal{G}_1$ and $B : \mathcal{H}_2 \to \mathcal{G}_2$ be bounded Hilbert-Schmidt operators between HSs and suppose $X \in \mathcal{H}_1 \otimes \mathcal{H}_2$. The linear operator $X \to AXB^*$ is a mapping from $\mathcal{H}_1 \otimes \mathcal{H}_2$ into $\mathcal{G}_1 \otimes \mathcal{G}_2$. It is called Kronecker product between the *factors* $A$ and $B$ and denoted as $A \otimes B$. The sum of elements $A_1 \otimes B_1 + A_2 \otimes B_2$ corresponds to the mapping $X \to A_1 X B_1^* + A_2 X B_2^*$ and scalar multiplication reads $\alpha A \otimes B : X \to \alpha A X B^*$. With these operations the collection of tensor product operators we just defined can be naturally endowed with a vector space structure and further normed according to:

$$\|A \otimes B\| = \|A\| \|B\| \tag{6}$$

where $\|A\|$ and $\|B\|$ denote norms for the corresponding spaces of operators. One such norm is the Hilbert-Schmidt norm

$$\|A\| = \sqrt{\langle A, A \rangle_{\mathcal{H}_1 \otimes \mathcal{H}_1}} \tag{7}$$

where $\langle \cdot, \cdot \rangle_{\mathcal{H}_1 \otimes \mathcal{H}_1}$ is defined as in (4). Another norm that recently attracted attention in learning is the trace norm (a.k.a. Schatten $1-$norm, nuclear norm

---

[1] If $A$ is of Hilbert-Schmidt type then (3) actually holds for *any* basis.

or Ky Fan norm). For[2] $|A| = (A^*A)^{\frac{1}{2}}$ the trace norm of $A$ is defined as:

$$\|A\|_\star = \text{trace}\,(|A|) \ . \tag{8}$$

## 3   Reproducing Kernels and Operatorial Representation

Our interest arises from learning problems where one wants to infer a mapping given a number of evaluations at data sites and corresponding output values. Hence we focus on the case where $(\mathcal{H}_1, \langle \cdot, \cdot \rangle_{\mathcal{H}_1})$ and $(\mathcal{H}_2, \langle \cdot, \cdot \rangle_{\mathcal{H}_2})$ are *Reproducing Kernel* HSs (RKHSs) [3] where such function evaluations are well defined. We briefly recall properties of such spaces and then turn into the problem of representing 2-way tensor input observations as high dimensional operators.

### 3.1   Reproducing Kernel Hilbert Spaces

We recall that given an arbitrary set $\mathcal{X}$, a HS $(\mathcal{H}, \langle \cdot, \cdot \rangle)$ of functions $f : \mathcal{X} \to \mathbb{R}$ is a RKHS if for any $x \in \mathcal{X}$ the *evaluation functional* $L_x : f \mapsto f(x)$ is bounded. A function $k : \mathcal{X} \times \mathcal{X} \to \mathbb{R}$ is called a *reproducing kernel* of $\mathcal{H}$ if $k(\cdot, x) \in \mathcal{H}$ for any $x \in \mathcal{X}$ and $f(x) = \langle f, k(\cdot, x) \rangle$ holds for any $x \in \mathcal{X}$, $f \in \mathcal{H}$. From the two requirements it is clear that $k(x, y) = \langle k(\cdot, y), k(\cdot, x) \rangle$ for any $(x, y) \in \mathcal{X} \times \mathcal{X}$. Hence, $\mathcal{H}$ is an instance[3] of the feature space $\mathcal{F}$ discussed in the introduction as soon as we let $\phi(x) = k(x, \cdot)$. The Moore-Aronszajn theorem [3] guarantees that any *positive definite kernel*[4] is uniquely associated to a RKHS for which it acts as reproducing kernel. Consequently, picking up a positive definite kernel such as the popular Gaussian RBF-kernel [12], implicitly amounts at choosing a function space with certain properties. Finally, the space of continuos linear mappings of a finite dimensional space is the space itself. Hence Euclidean spaces $\mathbb{R}^p$ can be seen as specific instances of RKHSs corresponding to the choice of *linear kernel* $k(x, y) = \sum_{i \in \mathbb{N}_p} x_i y_i$.

### 3.2   2-Way Operatorial Representation

So far we have defined tensor products and characterized the spaces of interest. We now turn into the problem of establishing a correspondence between an input matrix (a training or a test observation) $X \in \mathbb{R}^{p_1} \bigotimes \mathbb{R}^{p_2}$ with an element $\Phi_X \in \mathcal{H}_1 \bigotimes \mathcal{H}_2$. Notice that the standard approach in kernel methods corresponds to (implicitly) mapping $\text{vec}(X)$, where $\text{vec}(X) \in \mathbb{R}^{p_1 p_2}$ is a vector obtained for example by concatenating the columns of $X$. On the contrary, our goal here is to construct $\Phi_X$ so that the structural information embodied in the original representation is retained. Recall that for $p = \min\{p_1, p_2\}$ the thin SVD [6] of a point $X$ is defined as the factorization $X = U \Sigma V^\top$ where $U \in \mathbb{R}^{p_1 \times p}$ and $V \in \mathbb{R}^{p_2 \times p}$ satisfies $U^\top U = I_p$ and $V^\top V = I_p$ respectively and $\Sigma \in \mathbb{R}^{p \times p}$

---

[2] Given a positive operator $T$, by $T^{\frac{1}{2}}$ we mean the unique positive self-adjoint operator such that $T^{\frac{1}{2}} T^{\frac{1}{2}} = T$.

[3] Alternative feature space representations can be stated, see e.g. [5, Theorem 4].

[4] See e.g. [12] for a formal definition.

has its only nonzero elements on the first $r = \operatorname{rank}(X)$ entries along the main diagonal. These elements are the ordered singular values $\sigma_1 \geq \sigma_2 \geq \cdots \geq \sigma_r > 0$ whereas columns of $U$ and $V$ are called respectively left and right singular vectors. Equivalently

$$X = \sum_{i \in \mathbb{N}_r} \sigma_i u_i \otimes v_i \tag{9}$$

where $u_i \otimes v_i$ are rank-1 operators of the type (1) and the set $\{u_i\}_{i \in \mathbb{N}_r} \subset \mathbb{R}^{p_1}$ and $\{v_i\}_{i \in \mathbb{N}_r} \subset \mathbb{R}^{p_2}$ span respectively the column space $\mathcal{R}(X)$ and the row space $\mathcal{R}(X^\top)$. Let $\phi_1 : \mathbb{R}^{p_1} \to \mathcal{H}_1$ and $\phi_2 : \mathbb{R}^{p_2} \to \mathcal{H}_2$ be some feature maps. Based upon $\{u_i\}_{i \in \mathbb{N}_r}$ and $\{v_i\}_{i \in \mathbb{N}_r}$ we now introduce the $mode$-0 operator $\Gamma_U : \mathcal{H}_1 \to \mathbb{R}^{p_1}$ and the $mode$-1 operator $\Gamma_V : \mathcal{H}_2 \to \mathbb{R}^{p_2}$ defined, respectively, by

$$\Gamma_U h = \sum_{i \in \mathbb{N}_r} \langle \phi_1(u_i), h \rangle_{\mathcal{H}_1} u_i \quad \text{and} \quad \Gamma_V h = \sum_{i \in \mathbb{N}_r} \langle \phi_2(v_i), h \rangle_{\mathcal{H}_2} v_i . \tag{10}$$

Recall from Section 2.2 that by $\Gamma_U \otimes \Gamma_V$ we mean the Kronecker product between $\Gamma_U$ and $\Gamma_V$, $\Gamma_U \otimes \Gamma_V : \mathcal{H}_1 \otimes \mathcal{H}_2 \to \mathbb{R}^{p_1} \otimes \mathbb{R}^{p_2}$. Under the assumption that $X \in \mathcal{R}(\Gamma_U \otimes \Gamma_V)$ we finally define $\Phi_X \in \mathcal{H}_1 \otimes \mathcal{H}_2$ by

$$\Phi_X := \arg \min \left\{ \|\Psi_X\|^2_{\mathcal{H}_1 \otimes \mathcal{H}_2} : (\Gamma_U \otimes \Gamma_V)\Psi_X = X, \ \Psi_X \in \mathcal{H}_1 \otimes \mathcal{H}_2 \right\} . \tag{11}$$

In this way the feature representation $\Phi_X$ is chosen as that particular solution of $(\Gamma_U \otimes \Gamma_V)\Psi_X = X$ having minimum energy. Notice that the range $\mathcal{R}(\Gamma_U \otimes \Gamma_V)$ is closed in the finite dimensional space $\mathbb{R}^{p_1} \otimes \mathbb{R}^{p_2}$ and hence $\Phi_X$ is guaranteed to exist. The following result that we state without proof due to space limitations, characterizes $\Phi_X$ by providing a concrete representation.

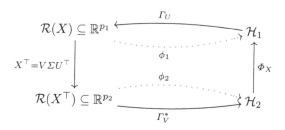

**Fig. 1.** A diagram illustrating the different spaces and mappings that we have introduced. The operator $\Phi_X \in \mathcal{H}_1 \otimes \mathcal{H}_2$ is the feature representation of interest.

**Theorem 1.** *Let $A_U : \mathcal{H}_1 \to \mathbb{R}^r$ and $B_V : \mathcal{H}_2 \to \mathbb{R}^r$ be defined entry-wise as $(A_U h)_i = \langle \phi(u_i), h \rangle$ and $(B_V h)_i = \langle \phi(v_i), h \rangle$ respectively. The unique solution $\Phi_X$ of (11) is then given by*

$$\Phi_X = A_U^* Z B_V \tag{12}$$

*where $Z \in \mathbb{R}^r \otimes \mathbb{R}^r$ is any solution of*

$$K_U Z K_V = \Sigma \tag{13}$$

*where $(K_U)_{ij} = \langle \phi_1(u_i), \phi_1(u_j) \rangle$ and $(K_V)_{ij} = \langle \phi_2(v_i), \phi_2(v_j) \rangle$.*

**Fig. 2.** An image (a) and its feature representation (b) for the case of 2–degree polynomial feature maps. $\Phi_X$ was found based upon (12) and (13).

(a) A $19 \times 18$ image $X$

(b) Its $190 \times 171$ feature representation $\Phi_X$ (not in scale)

The approach can be easily understood for the case of polynomial kernel $k(x, y) = (\langle x, y \rangle)^d$ where $d > 1$ is an arbitrary degree [12]. Suppose this type of kernel is employed and $\phi_1$, $\phi_2$ in (10) denote the corresponding feature maps. Then $K_U$ and $K_V$ are identity matrices, $Z = \Sigma$ and

$$\Phi_X = \sum_{i \in \mathbb{N}_r} \sigma_i \phi_1(u_i) \otimes \phi_2(v_i) . \tag{14}$$

In particular when $d = 1$ (linear kernel), $\phi_1$ and $\phi_2$ denote the identity mapping and the latter formula corresponds to the factorization in (9). Hence, our feature representation (14) has the desirable property to be consistent with the original data representation as soon as we use linear kernels.

## 4　Tensor-Based Penalized Empirical Risk Minimization

We now turn into problem formulations where the generalized tensor-based framework presented might find application. For the 2-way case, existing tensor-based learning algorithms (e.g. [11],[14],[7]) work with input observations $X$ (training or test points) represented as matrices. Instead, our key idea consists in using the corresponding feature representation $\Phi_X$.

### 4.1　A General Class of Supervised Problems

We consider supervised learning and assume we are given a dataset consisting of input-output pairs $\mathcal{D} = \left\{ (X^l, Y^l) \; : \; l \in \mathbb{N}_n \right\} \subset \mathcal{X} \times \mathcal{Y}$ where $\mathcal{X} \subset \mathbb{R}^{p_1} \otimes \mathbb{R}^{p_2}$ and $\mathcal{Y} \subset \mathbb{R}^{w_1} \otimes \mathbb{R}^{w_2}$. The situation where $\mathcal{Y} \subset \mathbb{R}^w$ or simply $\mathcal{Y} \subset \mathbb{R}$ is clearly a special case of this framework. Our goal is then to find a predictive operator

$$F : \Phi_X \mapsto \hat{Y} \tag{15}$$

mapping the operatorial representation $\Phi_X$ into a latent variable $\hat{Y}$. This objective defines a rather broad class of problems that gives rise to different special cases. When the feature maps $\phi_1, \phi_2$ are simply identities, then $\Phi_X$ corresponds to $X$ and we recover linear tensor models. In this case we have $F = A \otimes B :$ $\mathbb{R}^{p_1} \otimes \mathbb{R}^{p_2} \to \mathbb{R}^{w_1} \otimes \mathbb{R}^{w_2}$, $F : X \mapsto AXB^\top$. This is the type of models considered, for example, in [7]. Their problem is unsupervised and amounts to finding a pair of matrices $A \in \mathbb{R}^{w_1 \times p_1}$ and $B \in \mathbb{R}^{w_2 \times p_2}$ such that the mapping $X \mapsto AXB^\top$ constitutes a structure preserving projection onto a lower dimensional space

$\mathbb{R}^{w_1 \times w_2}$. A similar projection-based strategy is followed for a multi-class classification task in [11]. One of the proposed 2-stages algorithms, in fact, is based on firstly finding the dominant subspace for each class. In contrast, here we propose to build the model in a single supervised step as detailed below.

Going back to representations, for general feature maps $\phi_1, \phi_2$, we have $A \otimes B : \mathcal{H}_1 \otimes \mathcal{H}_2 \to \mathbb{R}^{w_1} \otimes \mathbb{R}^{w_2}$ and the predictive model becomes $A\Phi_X B^*$. For nonlinear feature maps, $A\Phi_X B^*$ defines a nonlinear model in $X$ and thus we can account for possible nonlinearities. Here below for both the linear and nonlinear case we write $\Phi^l$ to mean $\Phi_{X^l}$. Extending a classical approach, the problem of finding $A \otimes B$ can be tackled by penalized empirical risk minimization as:

$$\min\left\{\sum_{l \in \mathbb{N}_n} c(Y^l, (A \otimes B)\Phi^l) + \frac{\lambda}{2}\|A \otimes B\|^2 \mid A : \mathcal{H}_1 \to \mathbb{R}^{w_1}, \ B : \mathcal{H}_2 \to \mathbb{R}^{w_2}\right\}$$
(16)

where $c : (\mathbb{R}^{w_1} \otimes \mathbb{R}^{w_2}) \times (\mathbb{R}^{w_1} \otimes \mathbb{R}^{w_2}) \to \mathbb{R}^+$ is a *loss function* and the regularization term is based on the norm defined in (6) as $\|A \otimes B\| = \|A\|\|B\|$. Different norms for the factors are of interest. The use of Hilbert-Schmidt norm (7) corresponds to a natural generalization of the standard $2-$norm regularization used for learning functions [16]. However, recently there has been an increasing interest in vector-valued learning problems [9] and multiple supervised learning tasks [2]. In both these closely related class of problems the output space is $\mathbb{R}^w$. In this setting the nuclear norm (8) has been shown to play a key role. In fact, regularization via nuclear norm has the desirable property of favoring low-rank solutions [10].

Our next goal in this paper is to compare linear versus non-linear approaches in a tensor-based framework. Hence in the next Section we turn into the simpler case where outputs take values in $\mathbb{R}$. Before, we state a general representer theorem for the case where

$$c : \left(Y, \hat{Y}\right) \mapsto \frac{1}{2} \left\|Y - \hat{Y}\right\|_F^2$$
(17)

and $\|\cdot\|_F$ denotes the Frobenius norm. The proof is not reported for space constraints.

**Theorem 2 (Representer theorem).** *Consider problem* (16) *where the loss is defined as in* (17) *,* $\|A \otimes B\| = \|A\|\|B\|$ *is such that* $\|A\|$ *is either the Hilbert-Schmidt norm* (7) *or the nuclear norm* (8) *and B is fixed. Then for any optimal solution $\hat{A}$ there exist a set of functions $\{a_i\}_{i \in \mathbb{N}_{w_1}} \subset \mathcal{H}_1$ such that for any $i \in \mathbb{N}_{w_1}$*

$$(\hat{A}h)_i = \langle a_i, h \rangle_{\mathcal{H}_1}$$
(18)

*and for[5] $p = \min\{p_1, p_2\}$ there is $\alpha^i \in \mathbb{R}^{np}$ so that*

$$a_i = \sum_{\substack{l \in \mathbb{N}_n \\ m \in \mathbb{N}_p}} \alpha_{lm}^i \phi_1(u_m^l) \ .$$
(19)

---

[5] Without loss of generality it is assumed that all the training matrices have rank $p$.

*where $u^l_m$ denotes the $m-$th left singular vector corresponding to the factorization of the $l-$th point $X^l = U_l \Sigma_l V_l^\top$.*

A symmetric result holds if we fix $A$ instead of $B$. This fact naturally gives rise to an alternating algorithm that we fully present for scalar outputs in the next Section.

## 4.2   The Case of Scalar Outputs

In this Section we focus on simple regression ($\mathcal{Y} \subset \mathbb{R}$) or classification ($\mathcal{Y} = \{+1, -1\}$) tasks. With respect to the general formulation (16) in this case the unknown operators are actually linear functionals $A : \mathcal{H}_1 \to \mathbb{R}$, $B : \mathcal{H}_2 \to \mathbb{R}$ and $\| \cdot \|$ boils down to the classical $2-$norm. By Theorem 2, the problem of finding $A$ and $B$ corresponds to finding single functions $a$ and $b$ which are fully identified by respectively $\alpha \in \mathbb{R}^{np}$ and $\beta \in \mathbb{R}^{np}$. On the other hand Theorem 1 ensures that the feature representation of the $l-$th point can be written as $\Phi_l = A^*_{U_l} Z_l B_{V_l}$ where $Z_l$ is any solution of $K^U_{l,l} Z_l K^V_{l,l} = \Sigma_l$ and

$$(K^U_{l,m})_{ij} = \langle \phi_1(u^l_i), \phi_1(u^m_j) \rangle \,, \quad (K^V_{l,m})_{ij} = \langle \phi_2(v^l_i), \phi_2(v^m_j) \rangle \tag{20}$$

where $u^l_i$ (resp. $v^l_i$) denotes the $i-$th left (resp. right) singular vector corresponding to the factorization of the $l-$th point $X^l = U_l \Sigma_l V_l^\top$. Relying on these facts the single task problem can be stated as

$$\min \left\{ \frac{1}{2} \sum_{l \in \mathbb{N}_n} \left( Y^l - \alpha^\top G^U_{:,l} Z_l G^V_{l,:} \beta \right)^2 + \frac{\lambda}{2} (\alpha^\top G^U \alpha)(\beta^\top G^V \beta) \; : \; \alpha \in \mathbb{R}^{np}, \; \beta \in \mathbb{R}^{np} \right\} \tag{21}$$

where $G^U, G^V \in \mathbb{R}^{np} \otimes \mathbb{R}^{np}$ are structured matrices defined block-wise as $[G^U]_{l,m} = K^U_{l,m}$ and $[G^V]_{l,m} = K^V_{l,m}$ and by $G^V_{l,:}$ and $G^U_{:,l}$ we mean respectively the $l-$th block row of $G^V$ and the $l-$th block column of $G^U$. Define now the matrices $S_{\alpha,\beta}, S_{\beta,\alpha} \in \mathbb{R}^n \otimes \mathbb{R}^{np}$ row-wise as

$$(S_{\alpha,\beta})_{l,:} = \left( G^U_{:,l} Z^i G^V_{l,:} \beta \right)^\top \quad \text{and} \quad (S_{\beta,\alpha})_{l,:} = \alpha^\top G^U_{:,l} Z^i G^V_{l,:} \,.$$

A solution of (21) can be found iteratively solving the following systems of linear[6] equations dependent on each over

$$\left( S^\top_{\alpha,\beta} S_{\alpha,\beta} + \lambda_\beta G^U \right) \alpha = S^\top_{\alpha,\beta} y, \quad \lambda_\beta := \lambda (\beta^\top G^V \beta) \tag{22}$$

$$\left( S^\top_{\beta,\alpha} S_{\beta,\alpha} + \lambda_\alpha G^V \right) \beta = S^\top_{\beta,\alpha} y, \quad \lambda_\alpha := \lambda (\alpha^\top G^U \alpha) \,. \tag{23}$$

In practice, starting from a randomly generated $\beta \in \mathbb{R}^{np}$, we alternate between problems (22) and (23) until the value of the objective in (21) stabilizes. Once a solution has been found, the evaluation of the model on a test point $X^\star = U_\star \Sigma_\star V_\star^\top$ is given by $\alpha^\top G^U_{:,\star} Z^\star G^V_{\star,:} \beta$ where $Z^\star$ is any solution of $K^U_{\star,\star} Z^\star K^V_{\star,\star} = \Sigma_\star$, $(K^U_{\star,\star})_{ij} = \langle \phi_1(u^\star_i), \phi_1(u^\star_j) \rangle$ and

$$G^U_{:,\star} = \left[ K^U_{1,\star} \; K^U_{2,\star} \dots K^U_{n,\star} \right]^\top, \quad G^V_{\star,:} = \left[ K^V_{\star,1} \; K^V_{\star,2} \dots K^V_{\star,n} \right] \,.$$

---

[6] The two systems are linear in the active unknown conditioned on the fixed value of the other.

# 5  Experimental Results

In linear tensor-based learning exploiting natural matrix representation has been shown to be particularly helpful when the number of training points is limited [7]. Hence in performing our preliminary experiments we focused on small scale problems. We compared a standard (vectorized) nonlinear kernel-based approach versus our nonlinear tensor method highlighted in Section 4.2. Both the type of kernel matrices in (20) were constructed upon the Gaussian RBF-kernel with the same value of width parameter. As nonlinear kernel-based approach we considered LS-SVM [13] also trained with Gaussian RBF-kernel. This specific choice was considered because the primal problem of LS-SVM share the same quadratic loss used in our problem formulation (21). Also, we did not consider a bias term as this is not present in problem (21) either. In both the cases we took a $20 \times 20$ grid of kernel width and regularization parameter ($\lambda$ in problem (21)) and perform model selection via leave-one-out cross-validation (LOO-CV).

**Robot Execution Failures [4].** Each input data point is here a $15 \times 6$ multivariate time-series where columns represent a force or a torque. The task we considered was to discriminate between two operating states of the robot, namely *normal* and *collision_in_part*. Within the 91 observations available, $n$ were used for training and the remaining $n - 91$ for testing. We repeated the procedure over 20 random split of training and test set. Averages (with standard deviation in parenthesis) of Correct classification rates (CCR) of models selected via LOO-CV are reported on Table 1 for different number $n$ of training points. Best performances are highlighted.

**Table 1.** Test performances for the Robot Execution Failures Data Set

| | Correct Classification rates | | | |
| --- | --- | --- | --- | --- |
| | n=5 | n=10 | n=15 | n=20 |
| RBF-LS-SVM | 0.55(0.06) | 0.64 (0.08) | 0.66 (0.08) | 0.70(0.06) |
| RBF-Tensor | **0.62(0.07)** | **0.66(0.08)** | **0.68(0.10)** | **0.71(0.11)** |

**Optical Recognition of Handwritten Digits [4].** Here we considered recognition of handwritten digits. We took 50 bitmaps of size $32 \times 32$ of handwritten 7s and the same number of 1s and add noise to make the task of discriminating between the two classes more difficult (Figure 3(a) and 3(b)). We followed the same procedure as for the previous example and report results on Table 2.

| Correct Classification rates | | | |
| --- | --- | --- | --- |
| RBF-LS-SVM | | RBF-Tensor | |
| n=5 | n=10 | n=5 | n=10 |
| 0.71(0.20) | 0.85 (0.14) | **0.84 (0.12)** | **0.88(0.09)** |

(a) A noisy 1    (b) A noisy 7

**Fig. 3 & Table 2.** Instances of handwritten digits with high level of noise ((a) and (b)) and CCR on test for different number $n$ of training points

# 6    Conclusions

We focused on problems where input data have a natural 2-way representation. The proposed approach aims at combining the flexibility of kernel methods with the capability of exploiting structural information typical of tensor-based data analysis. We then presented a general class of supervised problems and gave explicitly an algorithm for the special case of regression and classification problems.

## Acknowledgements

Research supported by Research Council KUL: CIF1, STRT1/08/023, GOA Ambiorics, GOA MaNet, CoE EF/05/006 Optimization in Engineering(OPTEC), IOF-SCORES4CHEM. Flemish Government: FWO: PhD/postdoc grants, projects: G0226.06 (cooperative systems and optimization), G0427.10N (Tensors), G.0402.07 (SVM/Kernel), G.0588.09 (Brain-machine) research communities (ICCoS, ANMMM, MLDM); IWT: PhD Grants, Eureka-Flite+, SBO LeCoPro, SBO Climaqs, SBO POM, O&O-Dsquare Belgian Federal Science Policy Office: IUAP P6/04 (DYSCO, Dynamical systems, control and optimization, 2007-2011); EU: ERNSI; FP7-HD-MPC (INFSO-ICT-223854), COST intelliCIS, FP7-EMBOCON (ICT-248940).

## References

1. Aizerman, M., Braverman, E.M., Rozonoer, L.I.: Theoretical foundations of the potential function method in pattern recognition learning. Automation and Remote Control 25, 821–837 (1964)
2. Argyriou, A., Evgeniou, T., Pontil, M.: Multi-task feature learning. In: Advances in Neural Information Processing Systems, vol. 19, p. 41 (2007)
3. Aronszajn, N.: Theory of reproducing kernels. Transactions of the American Mathematical Society 68, 337–404 (1950)
4. Asuncion, A., Newman, D.J.: UCI machine learning repository (2007), http://www.ics.uci.edu/~mlearn/MLRepository.html
5. Berlinet, A., Thomas-Agnan, C.: Reproducing Kernel Hilbert Spaces in Probability and Statistics. Kluwer Academic Publishers, Dordrecht (2004)
6. Golub, G.H., Van Loan, C.F.: Matrix Computations, 3rd edn. Johns Hopkins University Press, Baltimore (1996)
7. He, X., Cai, D., Niyogi, P.: Tensor subspace analysis. In: Advances in Neural Information Processing Systems, vol. 18, p. 499 (2006)
8. Kolda, T.G., Bader, B.W.: Tensor decompositions and applications. SIAM review 51(3), 455–500 (2009)
9. Micchelli, C.A., Pontil, M.: On learning vector-valued functions. Neural Computation 17(1), 177–204 (2005)
10. Recht, B., Fazel, M., Parrilo, P.A.: Guaranteed minimum-rank solutions of linear matrix equations via nuclear norm minimization. To appear in SIAM Review
11. Savas, B., Eldén, L.: Handwritten digit classification using higher order singular value decomposition. Pattern Recognition 40(3), 993–1003 (2007)

12. Schölkopf, B., Smola, A.J.: Learning with kernels: support vector machines, regularization, optimization, and beyond. MIT Press, Cambridge (2002)
13. Suykens, J.A.K., Van Gestel, T., De Brabanter, J., De Moor, B., Vandewalle, J.: Least squares support vector machines. World Scientific, Singapore (2002)
14. Vasilescu, M., Terzopoulos, D.: Multilinear subspace analysis of image ensembles. In: IEEE Computer Society Conference on Computer Vision and Pattern Recognition, vol. 2 (2003)
15. Vilenkin, N.I.A.: Special functions and the theory of group representations. American Mathematical Society, Providence (1968)
16. Wahba, G.: Spline models for observational data. In: CBMS-NSF Regional Conference Series in Applied Mathematics, vol. 59. SIAM, Philadelphia (1990)

# Semi-supervised Facial Expressions Annotation Using Co-Training with Fast Probabilistic Tri-Class SVMs

Mohamed Farouk Abdel Hady*, Martin Schels, Friedhelm Schwenker, and Günther Palm

Institute of Neural Information Processing
University of Ulm
D-89069 Ulm, Germany
{mohamed.abdel-hady,martin.schels,friedhelm.schwenker}@uni-ulm.de,
guenther.palm@uni-ulm.de

**Abstract.** Supervised learning requires a large amount of labeled data but the data labeling process can be expensive and time consuming, as it requires the efforts of human experts. Semi-supervised learning methods that can reduce the amount of required labeled data through exploiting the available unlabeled data to improve the classification accuracy. Here, we propose a learning framework to exploit the unlabeled data by decomposing multi-class problems into a set of binary problems and apply *Co-Training* to each binary problem. A probabilistic version of Tri-Class Support Vector Machine is proposed (*SVM*) that can discriminate between ignorance and uncertainty and an updated version of Sequential Minimal Optimization (SMO) algorithm is used for fast learning of Tri-Class SVMs. The proposed framework is applied to facial expressions recognition task. The results show that *Co-Training* can exploit effectively the independent views and the unlabeled data to improve the recognition accuracy of facial expressions.

## 1 Introduction

Many real-world pattern recognition applications involve a large number of classes. Usually output space decomposition schemes, such as One-Against-One, One-Against-Others and Error-correcting output code (ECOC) are applied. These schemes are supervised learning tasks that require a large amount of labeled data in order to achieve a high classification accuracy. In addition, these applications such as remote sensing image classification, or automated classification of text documents, have often an extremely large pool of unlabeled data available. However, data labeling is often difficult, expensive, or time consuming, as it requires the human efforts.

* This paper is based on work done within the Transregional Collaborative Research Centre SFB/TRR 62 *Companion-Technology for Cognitive Technical Systems* funded by the German Research Foundation (DFG). The first author was supported by a scholarship of the German Academic Exchange Service (DAAD).

K. Diamantaras, W. Duch, L.S. Iliadis (Eds.): ICANN 2010, Part II, LNCS 6353, pp. 70–75, 2010.
© Springer-Verlag Berlin Heidelberg 2010

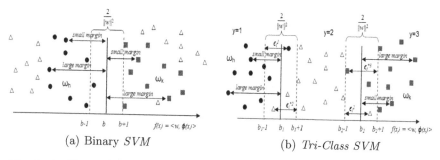

(a) Binary *SVM*          (b) *Tri-Class SVM*

**Fig. 1.** An illustration of the hyperplane(s) that discriminates between $\omega_k$ and $\omega_h$

We propose a learning framework based on *Co-Training* to incorporate un-labeled data into the one-against-one setup. A variant of Sequential Minimal Optimization (*SMO*) algorithm is introduced for fast learning of probabilistic *Tri-Class SVMs*. Gaussian Mixture Model (GMM) supervectors are extracted as features for facial expressions. These are then the inputs to the *Tri-Class SVMs*. Experiments demonstrate that *Co-Training* can automatically improve the recognition of facial expressions in video [1] using a small amount of human-labeled images which minimize the cost of data labeling. The paper is organized as follows: the fast probabilistic *Tri-Class SVM*, is introduced in Section 2. Then the one-against-one *Co-Trainings* framework is discussed in Section 3 and the results are shown in Section 4. Finally, we conclude in Section 5.

## 2   Tri-Class Support Vector Machines

Given a training set $L = \{(x_i, y_i) | x_i \in \mathbb{R}^d, y_i \in \Omega, i = 1, \ldots, n\}$ where $\Omega = \{\omega_1, \ldots, \omega_K\}$ is a predefined set of classes. Let $L_k = \{(x_i, y_i) | y_i = \omega_k\}$ be the set of $n_k = |L_k|$ training examples belonging to class $\omega_k$. If $f_{kh}$ is the optimal hyperplane, then $sign(f_{kh}(x_i))=1$, for $x_i \in L_k$ and $sign(f_{kh}(x_i))= $ -1, for $x_i \in L_h$. Note that the remaining training examples $L - \{L_k \cup L_h\}$ are not considered in the optimization problem. If a hyperplane $f_{kh}$ must classify an example $x$ where $y \neq \omega_k$ and $y \neq \omega_h$, the correct decision is $f_{kh}(x) =0$ which means that the $f_{kh}$ rejects the example $x$. In order to add the reject option to an *SVM*, it must be enforced to produce output $f_{kh}(x) =0$ for all the training examples $x$ that do not belong to the target classes $\omega_k$ and $\omega_h$ (see Figure 1(a)).

Angulo et al. [2] introduced one-against-one *Tri-Class SVMs* that is an extension to the idea used for ordinal regression in [3] to classification. For each pair of classes $\omega_k$ and $\omega_h$, two parallel hyperplanes are trained to separate $L_h$, $L - \{L_k \cup L_h\}$ and $L_k$, respectively where the training set $L$ is divided into three groups, labeled 1, 2, 3 (see Figure 1(b) and Table 1(a)). The primal formulation for the *Tri-Class SVM* is:

$$\min_{w, b_1, b_2, \epsilon, \epsilon^*} \frac{1}{2} \|w\|^2 + C \left( \sum_{i=1}^{n_1} \epsilon_i^1 + \sum_{i=1}^{n_2} \epsilon_i^{*2} + \sum_{i=1}^{n_2} \epsilon_i^2 + \sum_{i=1}^{n_3} \epsilon_i^{*3} \right) \tag{1}$$

subject to the constraints

$$\langle w, x_i^1 \rangle - b_1 \leq -1 + \epsilon_i^1, \quad \epsilon_i^1 \geq 0, \quad i = 1, \ldots, n_1 \quad (for \ x_i^1 \in L_h);$$

$$\langle w, x_i^2 \rangle - b_1 \geq 1 - \epsilon_i^{*2}, \quad \epsilon_i^{*2} \geq 0, \quad i = 1, \ldots, n_2 \quad (for \ x_i^2 \in L - \{L_h \cup L_k\});$$

$$\langle w, x_i^2 \rangle - b_2 \leq -1 + \epsilon_i^2, \quad \epsilon_i^2 \geq 0, \quad i = 1, \ldots, n_2 \quad (for \ x_i^2 \in L - \{L_h \cup L_k\});$$

$$\langle w, x_i^3 \rangle - b_2 \geq 1 - \epsilon_i^{*3}, \quad \epsilon_i^{*3} \geq 0, \quad i = 1, \ldots, n_3 \quad (for \ x_i^1 \in L_k); \quad b_1 \leq b_2$$

where $C$ controls the trade-off between maximizing the margin and minimizing the errors $\epsilon_i^1, \epsilon_i^{*2}, \epsilon_i^2$ and $\epsilon_i^{*3}$. The inequality constraint $b_1 \leq b_2$ is added explicitly to make sure that the hyperplanes are correctly ordered. This primal problem is a convex quadratic optimization problem that can be solved by a modification of the standard *SVM*. Wolfe duality theory is applied to the primal problem to obtain its dual formulation as defined in [2]. Note that the size of the dual optimization problem is $N = 2n - n_1 - n_3$. In [2], this dual problem is solved using the quadratic program-solver provided by Matlab Optimization Toolbox. But quadratic programming algorithms are computationally inefficient because they require an $N \times N$ kernel matrix $H$ be computed and stored in memory. Chu et al. [4] presented a modified version of *SMO* algorithm for ordinal regression which has been adopted in this paper for *Tri-Class SVMs*.

## 2.1  Probabilistic Output for *Tri-Class SVM*

In order for *Tri-Class SVM* to discriminate between uncertainty and ignorance, we derive a probabilistic interpretation for its output $f_{kh}$ through fitting a sigmoid function on the *SVM* output. Therefore, Eq. (2) and Eq. (4) represent the uncertainty and Eq. (3) represents the ignorance degree for an example $x$.

$$P_{kh}(y = 1|x) = P_{kh}(\omega_h|x) = \left( 1 - \frac{1}{1 + exp(-(f_{kh}(x) - b_1))} \right) \tag{2}$$

$$P_{kh}(y = 2|x) = \left( \frac{1}{1 + exp(-(f_{kh}(x) - b_1))} \right) \left( 1 - \frac{1}{1 + exp(-(f_{kh}(x) - b_2))} \right) \tag{3}$$

$$P_{kh}(y = 3|x) = P_{kh}(\omega_k|x) = \left( \frac{1}{1 + exp(-(f_{kh}(x) - b_1))} \right) \left( \frac{1}{1 + exp(-(f_{kh}(x) - b_2))} \right) \tag{4}$$

A decision profile is created for a given example $x$ as in Table(1(b)) based on Eq. (2) to Eq. (4). Then the final probabilistic output of one-against-one ensemble of *Tri-Class SVMs* is defined as follows:

$$P(y = \omega_k|x) = \frac{\sum_{h=1}^{k-1} P_{hk}(y = 1|x) + \sum_{h=k+1}^{K} P_{kh}(y = 3|x)}{\sum_{k'=1}^{K} \sum_{h=1}^{k'-1} P_{hk'}(y = 1|x) + \sum_{h=k'+1}^{K} P_{k'h}(y = 3|x)} \tag{5}$$

# 3  Co-Training for Facial Expressions Annotation

The most confident examples with respect to a single *SVM* are typically not *informative* because these examples have a large margin and therefore have no impact on its decision boundary (see Figure 1(a)). To address this problem, *Co-Training*, introduced by Blum and Mitchell in [5], is applied using an ensemble

**Table 1.** Fusion of One-against-One Probabilistic *Tri-Class SVMs*

(a) Code matrix

| | $f_{12}$ | $f_{13}$ | $f_{14}$ | $f_{23}$ | $f_{24}$ | $f_{34}$ |
|---|---|---|---|---|---|---|
| $\omega_1$ | 3 | 3 | 3 | 2 | 2 | 2 |
| $\omega_2$ | 1 | 2 | 2 | 3 | 3 | 2 |
| $\omega_3$ | 2 | 1 | 2 | 1 | 2 | 3 |
| $\omega_4$ | 2 | 2 | 1 | 2 | 1 | 1 |

(b) One-against-One Decision Profile

| | $\omega_1$ | $\omega_2$ | $\omega_3$ | $\omega_4$ |
|---|---|---|---|---|
| $\omega_1$ | - | $P_{12}(y=3\vert x)$ | $P_{13}(y=3\vert x)$ | $P_{14}(y=3\vert x)$ |
| $\omega_2$ | $P_{12}(y=1\vert x)$ | - | $P_{23}(y=3\vert x)$ | $P_{24}(y=3\vert x)$ |
| $\omega_3$ | $P_{13}(y=1\vert x)$ | $P_{23}(y=1\vert x)$ | - | $P_{34}(y=3\vert x)$ |
| $\omega_4$ | $P_{14}(y=1\vert x)$ | $P_{24}(y=1\vert x)$ | $P_{34}(y=1\vert x)$ | - |

of three *Tri-Class SVMs* (*mvEns*), defined in Eq. (6) as the average of the probabilistic outputs of three *Tri-Class SVMs* (see Eq. (2), Eq. (3) and Eq. (4)). Since the margins assigned by different *SVMs* are not directly related, there may exist a set of examples that have large average margin with respect to the ensemble (*confident*) and have a small or negative margin with respect to an individual machine (*informative*). For each pair of classes $\omega_k$ and $\omega_h$, initially define a labeled data set $L = \{(x_i^{(1)}, x_i^{(2)}, x_i^{(3)}, y_i)\vert x_i^{(j)} \in \mathbb{R}^{d_j}, j = 1, \ldots, 3, y_i \in \{1, 2, 3\}, i = 1, \ldots, n\}$ and an unlabeled data set $U = \{(x_i^{(1)}, x_i^{(2)}, x_i^{(3)})\vert x_i^{(j)} \in \mathbb{R}^{d_j}, j = 1, \ldots, 3, i = n+1, \ldots, m\}$. Then for each view $j$, a *Tri-Class SVM* $f_{kh}^{(j)}$ is trained using the available labeled data $(x_i^{(j)}, y_i)$. Then the following steps are repeated for a given number of iterations $T$ or until the $U$ becomes empty. At each iteration $t$, a pool $U'$ is created by randomly sampling $u$ unlabeled examples from $U$. Then the ensemble *mvEns* is applied to predict the class label of each example $x_u$ in $U'$ and the confidence about its prediction is estimated as follows.

$$P_{kh}(y\vert x_u) = \frac{1}{3} \sum_{j=1}^{3} P_{kh}^{(j)}(y\vert x_u) \text{ and } Confidence(x_u) = \max_{y=1,2,3} P_{kh}(y\vert x_u) \quad (6)$$

The newly labeled examples are ranked in descending order by confidence. Then the three *SVMs* of *mvEns* are retrained using the training set augmented with the most confident examples assigned to each class. In the classification phase, a given sample is classified as defined in Eq. (6) based on *SVMs* created at the last *Co-Training* iteration. Traditional *SVM* $f_{kh}$ can not ignore (reject) the unlabeled examples in $U'$ that belong neither to $\omega_k$ nor to $\omega_h$. These examples may have a margin larger than those belong to $\omega_k$ and $\omega_h$ (see Figure 1(a)). Hence, the most confident examples may have no influence on the decision boundary. To avoid this problem, *Tri-Class SVM* is used instead of the traditional *SVM*.

# 4    Experimental Evaluation

## 4.1    Setup

The Cohn-Kanade dataset [1], is a collection of image sequences with facial expressions that is available for research purposes. As a result of a manual labeling procedure, there are 105, 49, 91, 81, 81 and 25 videos for "happiness" ($\omega_1$), "anger", "surprise" ($\omega_2$), "disgust" ($\omega_3$), "sadness" ($\omega_4$) and "fear", respectively. Due to their sparse appearance, "anger" and "fear" were excluded

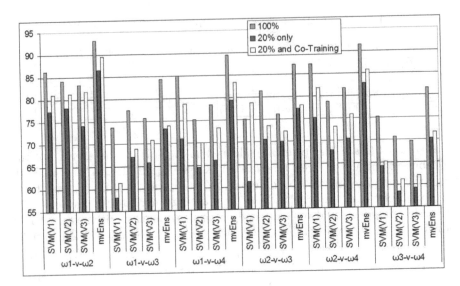

**Fig. 2.** Average test accuracy percentage of *Tri-Class SVMs* and *Co-Training*

from our experiments. Three feature vectors (views) have been extracted to be used for *Co-Training*: orientation histograms from the mouth facial region ($V_1$), in order to represent the facial motion, the optical flow[1] features from pairs of consecutive images have been computed from the full facial region ($V_2$) and from the mouth region ($V_3$). An 8-fold cross validation has been conducted 5 times.

For each fold and each view, the *GMM supervectors* approach, introduced by Campbell et al. in [7], is used to extract the input vectors that are afterward used to train the *Tri-Class SVMs* with the Gaussian kernel function $k(x, x_j) = exp(-\frac{\kappa}{2} \sum_{i=1}^{d}(x_i - x_{ji})^2)$ where $C = 32$, the width of the kernel $\kappa = 0.3$ and tolerance parameter $\tau = 0.001$. For the *GMM*, the number of *GMM* components is set to two and diagonal covariance matrix has been used. Then, the training set of supervectors is split randomly into two sets $L$ and $U$: 20% of the training examples of each class are used in $L$ (18, 16, 14 and 14, respectively), while the remaining are in $U$. For each pair of classes, *Co-Training* has been performed until 3/4 the maximum number of iterations is reached.

### 4.2  Results and Discussion

Figure 2 summarizes the results of all the experiments. We have the following observations from the experimental results.

- For all pair of classes, the ensemble of *Tri-Class SVMs* (*mvEns*) outperforms its members in all cases: using full training set (100%), reduced training

---

[1] A biologically inspired optical flow estimator, which was developed by the Vision and Perception Science Lab of the Institute of Neural Information Processing at the University of Ulm [6].

set (20%) and after *Co-Training*. This indicates that the multi-view *SVMs* are not correlated (diverse) to the extent that their underlying views are independent enough to apply *Co-Training*.

– For all binary problems, the accuracy of individual *SVMs* is improved after *Co-Training* and the improvement ranges between 10.99% and 1.52%.

– Also the performance of the ensembles *mvEns* are improved after *Co-Training* where the improvement ranges between 4.95% and 0.96%.

– In addition, the one-against-one ensemble (*1v1Ens*) consisting of the six ensembles of *Tri-Class SVMs* (*mvEns*) after using the unlabeled image sequences achieves an accuracy 86.95% compared to 91.45% using the full training set. Hence, further investigation is required to minimize this gap.

## 5  Conclusion

The main objective of this paper is to show that there is an improvement from using unlabeled data when training one-against-one ensembles. We proposed a learning framework to combine *Co-Training* and the one-against-one output-space decomposition approach that uses *Tri-Class SVMs* as binary classifiers. In order for *Co-Training* to measure confidence, a probabilistic interpretation for *Tri-Class SVM* outputs is proposed that can differentiate between ignorance and uncertainty. Since the *Tri-Class SVMs* are retrained several times during *Co-Training*, we introduced a variant of SMO algorithm for faster learning. Experiments on facial expressions annotation show that *Co-Training* improves the accuracy when the quantity of labeled videos is small. Also, the *GMM supervectors* approach provides flexible features for the classification of image sequences.

## References

1. Kanade, T., Cohn, J., Tian, Y.L.: Comprehensive database for facial expression analysis. In: Proc. of the 4th IEEE Int. Conf. on Automatic Face and Gesture Recognition, pp. 46–53 (2000)
2. Angulo, C., Ruiz, F.J., González, L., Ortega, J.A.: Multi-classification by using Tri-Class SVM. Neural Processing Letters 23(1), 89–101 (2006)
3. Shashua, A., Levin, A.: Taxonomy of large margin principle algorithms for ordinal regression problems. In: NIPS, vol. 15. MIT Press, Cambridge (2002)
4. Chu, W., Keerthi, S.S.: New approaches to support vector ordinal regression. In: Proc. of the 22nd Int. Conf. on Machine Learning, pp. 145–152 (2005)
5. Blum, A., Mitchell, T.: Combining labeled and unlabeled data with Co-Training. In: Proc. of the 11th Annual Conference on Computational Learning Theory, pp. 92–100. Morgan Kaufmann, San Francisco (1998)
6. Bayerl, P., Neumann, H.: Disambiguating visual motion through contextual feedback modulation. Neural Comput. 16(10), 2041–2066 (2004)
7. Campbell, W.M., Sturim, D.E., Reynolds, D.A.: Support vector machines using GMM supervectors for speaker verification. IEEE Signal Processing Letters 13(5), 308–311 (2006)

# An Online Incremental Learning Support Vector Machine for Large-scale Data*

Jun Zheng[1], Hui Yu[2], Furao Shen[1,2], and Jinxi Zhao[1]

[1] National Key Laboratory for Novel Software Technology, Nanjing University, China
[2] Jiangyin Information Technology Research Institute, Nanjing University, China
junzheng@smail.nju.edu.cn, {frshen,jxzhao}@nju.edu.cn

**Abstract.** Support Vector Machines (SVMs) have gained outstanding generalization in many fields. However, standard SVM and most modified SVMs are in essence batch learning, which makes them unable to handle incremental learning well. Also, such SVMs are not able to handle large-scale data effectively because they are costly in terms of memory and computing consumption. In some situations, plenty of Support Vectors (SVs) are produced, which generally means a long testing time. In this paper, we propose an online incremental learning SVM for large data sets. The proposed method mainly consists of two components, Learning Prototypes (LPs) and Learning SVs (LSVs). Experimental results demonstrate that the proposed algorithm is effective for incremental learning problems and large-scale problems.

**Keywords:** online incremental SVM, incremental learning, large-scale data.

## 1 Introduction

SVM has established itself as the most widely used kernel learning algorithm. The good generalization property of an SVM depends on a subset called Support Vectors (SVs). Unfortunately, the training of traditional SVM is very costly in time and space. Thus it may be intractable for traditional SVM to deal with large-scale problems.

One way apply SVMs for large-scale problems is to adapt SVMs to learn incrementally. Syed, Liu and Sung [1] proposed an incremental SVM (ISVM), and it is one of the earliest attempts to adapt SVM with incremental learning. It re-trains a new SVM by using new examples combined with old SVs. ISVM mainly solves the so-called example-incremental problems. In [2], the old support vectors are more "*costly*" by adding a constant which may vary with different problems. Laskov et al. [3] proposed an online learning algorithm. However, the algorithm suffers from excessive memory consuming.

For large-scale problems, another approach is to scale down the problem size (down-sampling), and the representatives are used for training. Active learning

---

* This work was supported in part by China NSF grant (#60975047, #60723003, #60721002), Jiangsu NSF grant (#BK2009080), and 973 Program (2010CB327903).

K. Diamantaras, W. Duch, L.S. Iliadis (Eds.): ICANN 2010, Part II, LNCS 6353, pp. 76–81, 2010.

[4] chooses the representatives by heuristic; Cluster-based SVM (CB-SVM) [5] recursively selects SV clusters along the cluster tree to get better performance; Cluster-SVM [6] first trains an SVM with cluster algorithm; Core Vector Machine (CVM) [7] chooses a core set by solving the Minimal Enclosing Ball (MEB) problem; Ball Vector Machine (BVM) [8] places the MEB problem with Enclosing Ball (EB) problem, which is seen as a simplified version of MEB. Support Cluster Machine (SCM) [9] exploits a compatible kernel-Probability Product Kernel (PPK) which measures the similarity between data.

In this paper, we try to improve SVM with the following three targets: (1) realize online incremental learning; (2) solve large-scale problem; (3) To save the number of SVs. We designed an online incremental SVM (OI-SVM) to achieve the three targets. OI-SVM can effectively deal with large-scale problems, incremental problems, and online learning problems.

# 2 The Proposed Online Incremental SVM (OI-SVM)

We adapt the traditional SVM into an online incremental version to deal with incremental learning and large-scale problems. For this reason, we name the proposed method online incremental SVM (OI-SVM). One epoch of OI-SVM includes two phases, Learning Prototypes (LPs) and Learning SVs (LSVs). LPs generates prototypes according to the original data. Then LSVs will learn the prototypes of LPs to generate SVs. In the next epoch, the LPs will generate new prototype set. The learned SVs of last epoch will be added to the new prototype set and get a combined prototype set, then the LSVs will learn the combined prototype set to generate new SVs. This procedure will repeat until the whole learning epoches finished.

## 2.1  Learning Prototypes (LPs)

In this section, we will introduce the analysis of LPs. LPs is based on the competitive learning, which tries to learn the prototypes to represent a local subset. Given data $(x_1, d_1)$, $(x_2, d_2)$, $\cdots$, $(x_n, d_n)$, prototypes $(p_1, d_1)$, $(p_2, d_2)$, $\cdots$, $(p_m, d_m)$ are learned ($m$ is much smaller than $n$) to fit the density of the training data. When a new example $(x_i, d_i)$ is input, we insert it to the set directly if the class label $d_i$ is new. If there exists the class $d_i$, we search the trained prototypes to find the nearest neighbor called "$p_{winner}$" and the second nearest neighbor called "$p_{runner-up}$", and a connection between $p_{winner}$ and $p_{runner-up}$ is set. The age of the connection is initialized as '0' when set. If the age of one connection is larger than a predefined parameter ($OldAge$), it will be removed. Now if the distance $\|x_i - w_{p_1}\|$ is larger than $T_{p_1}$, the new example will be inserted to the prototype set as a new prototype. It's also the same as "$p_{runner-up}$". If a new example cannot become a new prototype, we update the weight of the prototypes. This is shown in Algorithm 1. At the same time, some efforts are taken to remove the prototypes caused by noise. Here, we adopt the strategy used in [10]: after every several epochs of learning, those prototypes with only one same class neighbor will be removed. Also these prototypes with no topological neighbors will be removed.

The threshold $T_i$ of a prototype is defined as follows by within-class distance and between-class distance. Within-class distance ($T_{i_{within}}$) means the average distance between $i$ and other prototypes in its neighborhood who have the same label with $i$, and that is $\frac{1}{N_{label_i}} \sum_{(i,j) \in E \wedge label_i = label_j} \|\mathbf{p_i} - \mathbf{p_j}\|$. Between-class distance ($T_{i_{between}}$) is the distance between $i$ and prototypes whose label is different from $i$, and that is $\min_{(k,i) \in E \wedge label_i \neq label_k} \|\mathbf{p_i} - \mathbf{p_k}\|$. So the threshold is defined by $\max \|\mathbf{p_i} - \mathbf{p_k}\|_{label_k \neq label_i} \leq T_{i_{within}} : (k,i) \in E$. The threshold $T_i$ of a prototype is defined as the largest between-class distance that is not larger than $T_{i_{within}}$, where the Euclidean distance is used as the metric and $E$ is the connection set used to store connections between prototypes. The $N_{label_i}$ is the number of the neighbors of target prototype $i$.

## 2.2    Learning SVs (LSVs)

For incremental learning, usually the new examples have "heavier" effects than the old ones. We need to make the old ones "costly", or in terms of SVM, to make the error of the previously learned SVs larger than an error of new examples. SVs are a sufficient representation of the decision hyperplane, but not the all examples. It means that SVs are able to summarize the previous prototypes in a relatively concise way. Therefore, adding previously learned SVs to new SVM training is able to make the previous data more "costly". That is $\phi(w, \xi_i, \xi_i^*) = \frac{1}{2} w^T w + C(\sum_{\xi_i \in P} \xi_i + \sum_{\xi_i \in SV} \xi_i^*)$ where $P$ is the set of prototypes and $SV$ is the set contains SVs. $\xi_i$ is the slack variable of $(x_i, d_i)$. Here we need not the use the additional parameter $L$ in [2], for the reason that the data in the incremental batch have no information about the previous data and the use of $L$ can make much larger error on old SVs. Here, for OI-SVM, the prototypes have already made some error on the old data, thus the combination of SVs with prototypes is enough to make the previous data more "costly". Prototypes produced by LPs may change the original decision bound and generated prototypes are representatives of original data. However, to what extent the obtained prototypes affect the original bound is unknown. Here, we add previously learned SVs into prototypes to train a new SVM, which alleviates the departure of new bound decided by prototypes from original bounds.

The training process only preserve prototypes and SVs. We do not need to store all training data. It means that OI-SVM is available for large-scale problems. With the above discussion, we describe the complete online incremental SVM (OI-SVM) in Algorithm 1. After processing all data, we get the final SVs for testing. In OI-SVM, besides the two parameters in SVM, the regularization parameter $C$ and the parameter of radial-basis-function (RBF) kernel $\gamma$, who are often decided by the grid search, there are another two parameters introduced by the LPs component: $OldAge$ and $\lambda$. According to discussion in [10], the two parameters will be determined by the users, and the generalization ability of the algorithm are not sensitive to the newly introduced parameters.

---

**Algorithm 1.** Online incremental SVM (OI-SVM)

---

1: To simulate incremental learning for off-line data, we partition the whole data into $n$ parts. For online data, the stream data is input to the system directly.

2: Initialize prototype set $G$, support vector set $SV$, and edge set $E$ with $\emptyset$.

3: Load one block of data $TS$ into memory. If $G$ is empty, randomly choose two input data from the training set $TS$, $p_1$ and $p_2$, and insert the two data into $G$. I.e., $G = \{p_1, p_2\}$.

4: Input a new pattern $\xi = (x_i, d_i)$ to the system.

5: Find the winner $p_1$ and runner-up $p_2$ by in set $G$.

6: **if** $N_{label_{x_i}} < 2 or \|x_i - w_{p_1}\| > T_{p_1} or \|x_i - w_{p_2}\| > T_{p_2}$ **then**

7:    Insert $\xi$ into set G. Go to Step(4).

8: **end if**

9: **if** $(p_1, p_2) \notin E$ **then**

10:    $E = E \cup \{(p_1, p_2)\}$

11: **end if**

12: $age_{(p_1, p_2)} = 0$.

13: **for** The neighbor $p_i$ satisfies $(p_1, p_i) \in E$ **do**

14:    Update $age_{(p_1, p_i)} \leftarrow age_{(p_1, p_i)} + 1$

15: **end for**

16: $M_{p_1} \leftarrow M_{p_1} + 1$, $\eta_1 = \frac{1}{M_{winner}}$, and $\eta_2 = \frac{1}{100 M_{winner}}$.

17: **if** $label_\xi = label_{p_1}$ **then**

18:    Update $w_{P_1} \leftarrow w_{P_1} + \eta_1(\xi - w_{P_1})$

19:    **for** The neighbor $p_i$ satisfies $(p_1, p_i) \in E$ and $label_{p_i}! = label_\xi$ **do**

20:       Update $w_{P_i} \leftarrow w_{P_i} - \eta_2(\xi - w_{P_i})$

21:    **end for**

22: **else**

23:    Update $w_{P_1} \leftarrow w_{P_1} - \eta_1(\xi - w_{P_1})$

24:    **for** he neighbor $p_i$ satisfies $(p_1, p_i) \in E$ and $label_{p_i} = label_\xi$ **do**

25:       Update $w_{P_i} \leftarrow w_{P_i} + \eta_2(\xi - w_{P_i})$

26:    **end for**

27: **end if**

28: Delete those edges in set $E$ whose age outstrips the parameter $OldAge$.

29: **if** The number of learned examples is the integer multiple of parameter $\lambda$. **then**

30:    Delete the nodes $p_i$ in set G that have no neighbor node and delete the nodes $p_i$ who has only one neighbor.

31: **end if**

32: **if** All the data in the block $TS$ has been processed. **then**

33:    Combine the prototype set $G$ and the support vector set $SV$ in new set $Temp$: $Temp = G \bigcup SV$.

34:    Train a new SVM with the set $Temp$, get the new support vector set $SV_{p_{new}}$.

35:    Update the old support vector set $SV$. Delete the old support vectors in $SV$ and add the support vectors in $SV_{p_{new}}$ to $SV$, i.e., $SV=\emptyset$, $SV = SV_{p_{new}}$.

36:    Go to Step(3) to continue the learning process.

37: **else**

38:    Go to Step(4) to continue the online learning process.

39: **end if**

40: **if** All the training data has been processed. **then**

41:    **return** set $SV$.

42: **end if**

---

# 3    Experiments

In this section, we do experiments for medium-scale data *optdigits*, *w3a*, *shuttle*, and *ijcnn* and large-scale data *web*, *sensit vehicle (combined)*, and *usps*[11] to test the OI-SVM. The experiments are performed on 3.0 $GHz$ Intel Pentium machine with 512MB RAM. *LibSVM* ($V2.88$) [11], $CVM$ and $BVM$ ($V2.2$) [7] are used to make comparison with OI-SVM. ISVM results are not given here for *LibSVM* has better performance than $ISVM$ [3]. For SVM, it is required to select $C$ and $\gamma$ ( radial-basis-function ). The parameter $C$ is chosen from

$\{2^i : -5 \leq i \leq 5\}$ and the parameter $\gamma$ is in the range of $\{2^j : -5 \leq j \leq 5\}$ except the data set *usps*. For incremental learning, the data are randomly gathered and input into the system continually, then new examples are cooperated to the trained learning system. And all data are divided into 10 parts arbitrarily. Because *LibSVM*, *CVM*, and *BVM* cannot realize incremental learning, here we only give batch learning results. The parameters of OI-SVM for the seven data sets are $(OldAge, \lambda) = (450, 450)$, $(600, 450)$, $(15000, 400)$, $(3000, 500)$, $(500, 100)$, $(500, 500)$, and $(500, 400)$ respectively. For *BVM* and *CVM*, we set the recommended parameter $\varepsilon = 10^{-5}$ [7]. The results are presented in Table 1.

**Table 1.** Experimental results with the accuracy and the number of SVs: comparison with LibSVM, CVM, and BVM

| data | item | LibSVM (batch) | CVM (batch) | BVM (batch) | OI-SVM (batch) | OI-SVM (incremental) |
|------|------|------|------|------|------|------|
| *optdigits* | # of SV | 1594 | 1193 | 2191 | 599 | 987 |
| | Accuracy(%) | 98.37 | 96.38 | 96.38 | 97.33 | 97.33 |
| *w3a* | # of SV | 2270 | 2118 | 952 | 458 | 1359 |
| | Accuracy(%) | 97.85 | 97.81 | 97.88 | 97.40 | 97.56 |
| *shuttle* | # of SV | 733 | 2112 | 2181 | 57 | 115 |
| | Accuracy(%) | 99.83 | 99.74 | 99.70 | 99.68 | 99.77 |
| *ijcnn* | # of SV | 2547 | 9316 | 5271 | 1057 | 4126 |
| | Accuracy(%) | 98.54 | 98.37 | 98.38 | 98.60 | 98.22 |
| *web* | # of SV | 4652 | 9889 | 3540 | 291 | 464 |
| | Accuracy(%) | 99.32 | 99.07 | 99.04 | 98.98 | 98.95 |
| *sv(c)* | # of SV | 30780 | 40595 | 26087 | 6073 | 7490 |
| | Accuracy(%) | 83.88 | 83.94 | 82.49 | 82.20 | 82.06 |
| *usps* | # of SV | 2178 | 4094 | 1426 | 170 | 985 |
| | Accuracy(%) | 99.53 | 99.50 | 99.53 | 98.96 | 99.04 |

According to Table 1, for batch learning, we find that OI-SVM (b) is comparable with others for learning accuracy. For all data sets, OI-SVM generates fewer SVs than others. For incremental learning, even compared with batch learning methods, OI-SVM (i) also gets comparable accuracy. For the number of SVs, OI-SVM (i) gets fewest SVs for *optdigits* and *shuttle*. For *w3a*, many features are zero in the training example. For OI-SVM (i), such duplicated examples will be learned repeatedly and will lead to a little more SVs. For *ijcnn*, the number of SVs generated by OI-SVM (incremental) is less than CVM and BVM, but is greater than LibSVM. For OI-SVM, the number of SVs generated by the incremental learning is often larger than the batch learning. This is because in the incremental learning, OI-SVM works only on a subset of the training examples once a time, and more prototypes are needed to keep more local information and thus get global approximation. In fact, when the number of support vectors is small compared to the size of the training data, the training speed of *CVM* and *BVM* will be fast. However, when the size of SVs is large compared to the size of its training data, the training speed becomes very slow. For *sv(c)*, the training speed of OI-SVM is much faster than BVM, because for BVM, the learned number of SVs is 33% of training data and BVM will be very slow. For *usps*, the training speed of OI-SVM is a little slower than BVM, it is because the number of SVs for BVM is 0.5%. For *web*, the number of SVs for BVM is 7.1%, but BVM works much faster than OI-SVM. It is the same reason with $w3a$. For incremental learning, OI-SVM almost obtains similar results to batch learning. This shows that OI-SVM is able to realize incremental learning very well even for large-scale problem.

## 4   Conclusions

In this paper, we proposed an online incremental SVM (OI-SVM) to deal with large-scale problem. The proposed OI-SVM includes two parts: learning proto-types (LPs) and learning SVs (LSVs). LPs is to learn the proper prototypes to represent the input data, and adjust the prototypes to the concept of new data. LSVs is to learn a new classifier by combining the prototypes representing the data concept with previous learned SVs. OI-SVM can deal with online in-cremental learning as well as batch learning. In the experiments, we compared OI-SVM with typical SVM algorithms such as LibSVM, CVM, and BVM. The experiments on incremental learning for medium-scale data, and large-scale data show the efficiency of the proposed OI-SVM.

## References

1. Syed, N., Liu, H., Sung, K.: Incremental learning with support vector machines. In: Workshop on Support Vector Machines at the International Joint Conference on Articial Intelligence (IJCAI 1999), Stockholm, Sweden (1999b)
2. Stefan, R.: Incremental Learning with Support Vector Machines. In: First IEEE International Conference on Data Mining (ICDM 2001) (2001)
3. Laskov, P., Gehl, C., Krüger, S., Müller, K.: Incremental support vector learning: Analysis implementation and applications. J. of Machine Learning Research 7, 1909–1936 (2006)
4. Schohn, G., Cohn, D.: Less is More: Active learning with support vector machines. In: Proc. of the Intl. Conf. on Machine Learning (2000)
5. Yu, H., Yang, J., Han, J.: Classifying large data sets using SVMs with hierarchical clusters. In: Proc. of the ACM SIGKDD Intl. Conf. on Knowledge Discovery and Data Mining, pp. 306–331 (2003)
6. Boley, D., Cao, D.: Training support vector machine using adaptive clustering. In: 4th SIAM International Conference on Data Mining, pp. 126–137 (2004)
7. Tsang, I.W., Kwok, J.T., Cheung, P.-M.: Core vector machines: Fast SVM training on very large data sets. J. Machine Learning Res. 6, 363–392 (2005)
8. Tsang, I.W., Kocsor, A., Kwok, J.T.: Simpler core vector machines with enclosing balls. In: 24th International Conference on Machine Learning, pp. 911–918 (2007)
9. Li, B., Chi, M., Fan, J., Xue, X.: Support cluster machine. In: 24th International Conference on Machine learning, pp. 505–512 (2007)
10. Shen, F., Hasegawa, O.: An incremental network for on-line unsupervised classica-tion and topology learning. Neural Networks 19, 90–106 (2006)
11. Chang, C.C., Lin, C.J.: LIBSVM: a library for support vector machines (2001), software available at http://www.csie.ntu.edu.tw/~cjlin/libsvm

# A Common Framework for the Convergence of the GSK, MDM and SMO Algorithms

Jorge López and José R. Dorronsoro*

Dpto. de Ingeniería Informática and Instituto de Ingeniería del Conocimiento
Universidad Autónoma de Madrid, 28049 Madrid, Spain

**Abstract.** Building upon Gilbert's convergence proof of his algorithtm to solve the Minimum Norm Problem, we establish a framework where a much simplified version of his proof allows us to prove the convergence of two algorithms for solving the Nearest Point Problem for disjoint convex hulls, namely the GSK and the MDM algorithms, as well as the convergence of the SMO algorithm for SVMs over linearly separable two–class samples.

## 1 Introduction

Given a sample $\mathcal{S} = \{(X_i, y_i) : i = 1, \ldots, N\}$ with $y_i = \pm 1$, let $\mathcal{I}_\pm$ be the set of indices of the patterns $X_i$ belonging to each class. Writing $W = \sum_i \alpha_i y_i X_i = \sum_{i \in \mathcal{I}_+} \alpha_i X_i - \sum_{i \in \mathcal{I}_-} \alpha_i X_i = W_+ - W_-$, we can solve the Nearest Point Problem (NPP) of finding the two closest points in the convex hulls of each class, by:

$$\min \mathcal{D}(\alpha) = \min \tfrac{1}{2} \|W_+ - W_-\|^2 = \min_\alpha \tfrac{1}{2} \sum_i \sum_j \alpha_i \alpha_j y_i y_j X_i \cdot X_j$$

s.t. $\sum_{i \in \mathcal{I}_+} \alpha_i = \sum_{i \in \mathcal{I}_-} \alpha_i = 1$, $\alpha_i \geq 0$ $\forall i$ . To do so, most of the methods proposed in the literature are adaptations of methods for the Minimum Norm Problem (MNP) of finding the point in a convex hull closest to the origin. Classical procedures for MNP are the Gilbert [1] and Mitchell [2] algorithms. These two algorithms were adapted to solve NPP as well as SVM for classification in [3] and [4] respectively. We shall call these NPP adaptations GSK and MDM. We recall that the dual problem solved by an SVM is

$$\min \tilde{\mathcal{D}}(\alpha) = \tfrac{1}{2} \sum_i \sum_j \alpha_i \alpha_j y_i y_i X_i \cdot X_j - \sum_i \alpha_i$$

s.t. $\sum_i \alpha_i y_i = 0$, $\alpha_i \geq 0$ $\forall i$ . Convergence proofs for GSK and MDM were given in [1] and Mitchell [2] (we are not aware of such proofs for their extensions to NPP) and a quite general convergence proof for SMO has been given in [5]; for the linearly separable case a much simpler SMO proof was given in [6]. In this work we propose a unified approach for GSK, MDM and SMO that results in much simpler proofs, again for linearly separable samples. More precisely, we will use a common framework with three basic steps, namely: 1) To bound the distance $\|W^t - W^*\|$ between the iterates

* With partial support of Spain's TIN 2007–66862 project and Cátedra UAM–IIC en Modelado y Predicción. The first author is kindly supported by FPU-MICINN grant AP2007–00142.

K. Diamantaras, W. Duch, L.S. Iliadis (Eds.): ICANN 2010, Part II, LNCS 6353, pp. 82–87, 2010.

$W^t$ and the optimal $W^*$ by a quantity $\Delta^t$ that appears naturally in the algorithms, 2) To show that $\Delta^{t_j} \to 0$ for some subsequence $t_j$ and, therefore, that $W^{t_j} \to W^*$, 3) To conclude that $W^t \to W^*$ for the full sequence $W^t$.

The paper is organized as follows. In section 2 we give an overview of the GSK, MDM and SMO methods. Convergence proofs are given in section 3. Finally, section 4 offers some further discussion and pointers to future research.

## 2  Algorithms for Solving NPP and SVM

GSK uses at each iteration $t$ a single updating pattern to build the new weight vector $W^{t+1}$ by updating one of the components $W^t_\pm$ of the current $W^t = W^t_+ - W^t_-$ through an appropriate convex combination with a pattern $X_{L\pm}$ of the corresponding class. For instance, assuming we use an $X_{L^t_+}$ in the positive class, we have $W^{t+1} = (1-\lambda^t)W^t_+ + \lambda^t X_{L^t_+} - W^t_- = W^t + \lambda^t(X_{L^t_+} - W^t_+)$ and it is shown in [3] that the optimal $\lambda^t$ is

$$\lambda^t = \min\left\{1, \Delta^t_+/\|W^t_+ - X_{L^t_+}\|^2\right\} \;, \tag{1}$$

where we write $\Delta^t_+ = y_{L^t_+} W^t \cdot (W^t_+ - X_{L^t_+})$. Moreover, from the expression above for $W^{t+1}$ we have $\|W^t\|^2 - \|W^{t+1}\|^2 = 2\lambda^t W^t \cdot (W^t_+ - X_{L^t_+}) - (\lambda^t)^2\|W^t_+ - X_{L^t_+}\|^2$. Notice that $\|W^t\|^2 - \|W^{t+1}\|^2 = 2(\mathcal{D}(\alpha^t) - \mathcal{D}(\alpha^{t+1}))$ and if we take an unclipped $\lambda^t$ in (1), we have

$$\mathcal{D}(\alpha^t) - \mathcal{D}(\alpha^{t+1}) = (\Delta^t_+)^2/(2\|W^t_+ - X_{L^t_+}\|^2) \geq (\Delta^t_+)^2/(2D^2) \;, \tag{2}$$

where $D = \max_{i,j} \|X_i - X_j\|$. In this case, the norm decrease is approximately optimal if $\Delta^t_+$ is largest, for which we just choose $L^t_+$ as $L^t_+ = \arg\min_{i \in \mathcal{I}^+}\{y_i W^t \cdot X_i\}$. If, however, clipping takes place we have $\Delta^t_+ \geq \|W^t_+ - X_{L^t_+}\|^2$, which yields

$$\mathcal{D}(\alpha^t) - \mathcal{D}(\alpha^{t+1}) = W^t \cdot (W^t_+ - X_{L^t_+}) - \|W^t_+ - X_{L^t_+}\|^2/2 \geq \Delta^t_+/2 \;. \tag{3}$$

Similar formulae hold when we choose a $X_{L-}$ in the negative class and the class chosen in GSK is the one for which $\Delta^t_+$ or $\Delta^t_-$ is largest. Once the choice is made we just write $\Delta^t$ instead of $\Delta^t_\pm$; see [3] for more details.

Turning our attention to MDM, it updates at each step one of the $W^t_\pm$ components of $W^t$ using now two pattern vectors $X_{L\pm}$ and $X_{U\pm}$. For instance, if we update $W^t_+$ using $X_{L^t_+}$ and $X_{U^t_+}$, we will have $W^t_+ = W^t_+ + \lambda^t(X_{L^t_+} - X_{U^t_+})$ and, therefore, $W^{t+1} = W^t_+ + \lambda^t(X_{L^t_+} - X_{U^t_+}) - W^t_- = W^t + \lambda^t(X_{L^t_+} - X_{U^t_+})$. Now the optimal $\lambda^t$ is chosen as [4]:

$$\lambda^t = \min\left\{\alpha^t_{U^t_+}, \overline{\Delta}^t_+/\|X_{U^t_+} - X_{L^t_+}\|^2\right\} \;, \tag{4}$$

where this time we write $\overline{\Delta}^t_+ = y_{L^t_+} W^t \cdot (X_{U^t_+} - X_{L^t_+})$. If clipping is not needed, taking $\lambda^t = \overline{\Delta}^t_+/\|X_{U^t_+} - X_{L^t_+}\|^2$ in (4) and arguing as done in the GSK case, we obtain

$$\mathcal{D}(\alpha^t) - \mathcal{D}(\alpha^{t+1}) = (\overline{\Delta}^t_+)^2/(2\|X_{U^t_+} - X_{L^t_+}\|^2) \geq (\overline{\Delta}^t)^2/(2D^2) \;, \tag{5}$$

where we used $\|X_{U_+^t} - X_{L_+^t}\|^2 \leq D^2$. The $\mathcal{D}$ decrease is largest when $\overline{\Delta}_+^t$ is largest, which we achieve by choosing $U_+^t = \arg\max_{i \in \mathcal{I}^+ | \alpha_i^t > 0} \{y_i W^t \cdot X_i\}$ and $L_+^t$ as done for GSK. We may have to clip $\lambda^t$ at $\alpha_{U_+^t}^t$ to ensure that the new coefficient of $X_{U_+^t}$ does not become negative. In this case, we obtain

$$\mathcal{D}(\alpha^t) - \mathcal{D}(\alpha^{t+1}) = \alpha_{U_+^t}^t \overline{\Delta}_+^t - (\alpha_{U_+^t}^t)^2 \|X_{U_+^t} - X_{L_+^t}\|^2 / 2 \geq \alpha_{U_+^t}^t \overline{\Delta}^t / 2 \ , \quad (6)$$

since clipping occurs when $\overline{\Delta}_+^t \geq \alpha_{U_+^t}^t \|X_{U_+^t} - X_{L_+^t}\|^2$. Similar formulae hold when we choose $X_{U^t}, X_{L_-^t}$ in the negative class and the class finally selected is the one for which the quantity $\overline{\Delta}_\pm^t$ is largest [4]. Once chosen, we shall just write $\overline{\Delta}^t$.

The SMO updates are of the form $W^{t+1} = W^t + \lambda^t y_{L^t} (X_{L^t} - X_{U^t})$, or, in terms of the $\alpha$ coefficients, $\alpha_{L^t}^{t+1} = \alpha_{L^t}^t + \lambda^t$, $\alpha_{U^t}^{t+1} = \alpha_{U^t}^t - \lambda^t y_{U^t} y_{L^t}$, and the other $\alpha_j$ do not change. An optimal $\lambda^t$ is now chosen so that the decrease in the SVM dual function is largest, which means [6]

$$\lambda^t = y_{L^t} \tilde{\Delta}^t / \|X_{U^t} - X_{L^t}\|^2 = y_{L^t} \mu \ , \quad (7)$$

where we write now $\tilde{\Delta}^t = W^t \cdot (X_{U^t} - X_{L^t}) - (y_{U^t} - y_{L^t})$ and $\mu = \tilde{\Delta}^t / \|X_{U^t} - X_{L^t}\|^2$. Here the $\tilde{\mathcal{D}}$ decrease is largest when $\tilde{\Delta}^t$ is largest, which can be achieved if we select $L^t = \arg\min_{i \in \mathcal{I}_L} \{W^t \cdot X_i - y_i\}$ and $U^t = \arg\max_{i \in \mathcal{I}_U} \{W^t \cdot X_i - y_i\}$, where $\mathcal{I}_L = \{i : y_i = 1 \text{ or } y_i = -1, \alpha_i^t > 0\}$ and $\mathcal{I}_U = \{i : y_i = 1, \alpha_i^t > 0 \text{ or } y_i = -1\}$. As done before, we may have to clip $\mu$ as $\mu^t = \min\{\mu, \alpha_{L^t}^t\}$ if $y_{L^t} = -1$ and as $\mu^t = \min\{\mu, \alpha_{U^t}^t\}$ if $y_{U^t} = 1$. If no clipping is required, making use of (7) yields

$$\tilde{\mathcal{D}}(\alpha^t) - \tilde{\mathcal{D}}(\alpha^{t+1}) = (\tilde{\Delta}^t)^2 / (2\|X_{U^t} - X_{L^t}\|^2) \geq (\tilde{\Delta}^t)^2 / (2D^2) \ . \quad (8)$$

If, however, $\mu$ is clipped at $\alpha_{U^t}^t$, then $\tilde{\Delta}^t \geq \alpha_{U^t}^t \|X_{U^t} - X_{L^t}\|^2$ must hold, yielding

$$\tilde{\mathcal{D}}(\alpha^t) - \tilde{\mathcal{D}}(\alpha^{t+1}) = \alpha_{U^t}^t \tilde{\Delta}^t - (\alpha_{U^t}^t)^2 \|X_{U^t} - X_{L^t}\|^2 / 2 \geq \alpha_{U^t}^t \tilde{\Delta}^t / 2 \ , \quad (9)$$

while we similarly obtain $\tilde{\mathcal{D}}(\alpha^t) - \tilde{\mathcal{D}}(\alpha^{t+1}) \geq \alpha_{L^t}^t \tilde{\Delta}^t / 2$, if $\mu$ is clipped at $\alpha_{L^t}^t$. We refer to [6] for more details.

# 3 Convergence

If the algorithms described previously stop in a finite number $t$ of iterations, the $\Delta^t$, $\overline{\Delta}^t$ and $\tilde{\Delta}^t$ values must be zero, and the KKT conditions imply we are at an optimum. Hence, in the sequel we will consider the case of an infinite number of iterations.

## 3.1 Convergence of GSK and MDM

We give a unified convergence proof for GSK and MDM. As a first step we show the following:

**Proposition 1.** *If $W^*$ is the closest vector between the positive and negative class hulls, then the following hold*

$$\|W^t - W^*\|^2 \le 2\Delta^t \le 2\overline{\Delta}^t \ ,$$ (10)

$$\|W^t - W^*\|^2 \le \|W^t\|^2 - \|W^*\|^2 = 2(\mathcal{D}(\alpha^t) - \mathcal{D}(\alpha^*)) \ .$$ (11)

*Proof.* A simple geometric reasoning in disjoint convex hulls shows that $W^t \cdot W^* \ge \|W^*\|^2$ and, therefore,

$$\begin{aligned}
\|W^t - W^*\|^2 &= \|W^t\|^2 - W^t \cdot W^* - W^t \cdot W^* + \|W^*\|^2 \le \|W^t\|^2 - W^t \cdot W^* \\
&= \|W^t\|^2 - \sum_{i \in \mathcal{I}^+} \alpha_i^* y_i W^t \cdot X_i - \sum_{i \in \mathcal{I}^-} \alpha_i^* y_i W^t \cdot X_i \\
&\le \|W^t\|^2 - \min_{i \in \mathcal{I}^+} \left\{ y_i W^t \cdot X_i \right\} - \min_{i \in \mathcal{I}^-} \left\{ y_i W^t \cdot X_i \right\} \\
&= W^t \cdot W_+^t - \min_{i \in \mathcal{I}^+} \left\{ y_i W^t \cdot X_i \right\} - W^t \cdot W_-^t - \min_{i \in \mathcal{I}^-} \left\{ y_i W^t \cdot X_i \right\} \\
&= \Delta_+^t + \Delta_-^t \le 2\Delta^t \ .
\end{aligned}$$

We show next that $\Delta_+^t \le \overline{\Delta}_+^t$ and that $\Delta_-^t \le \overline{\Delta}_-^t$. In fact

$$\begin{aligned}
\Delta_+^t &= W^t \cdot W_+^t - \min_{i \in \mathcal{I}^+} \left\{ y_i W \cdot X_i \right\} = \sum_{i \in \mathcal{I}^+} \alpha_i y_i W^t \cdot X_i - \min_{i \in \mathcal{I}^+} \left\{ y_i W \cdot X_i \right\} \\
&\le \max_{i \in \mathcal{I}^+ | \alpha_i^t > 0} \left\{ y_i W \cdot X_i \right\} - \min_{i \in \mathcal{I}^+} \left\{ y_i W \cdot X_i \right\} = \overline{\Delta}_+^t \ ,
\end{aligned}$$

and a similar argument works for the other bound. Finally, to prove (11), reasoning as just done at the beginning of the previous argument, we have $\|W^t - W^*\|^2 \le \|W^t\|^2 - W^t \cdot W^* \le \|W^t\|^2 - \|W^*\|^2$. $\qquad \square$

We show next the following.

**Proposition 2.** *For GSK we have $\Delta^t \to 0$ as $t \to \infty$. Moreover, for MDM there is a subsequence $t_j$ such that $\overline{\Delta}^{t_j} \to 0$.*

*Proof.* For GSK (2) and (3) imply $\mathcal{D}(\alpha^t) - \mathcal{D}(\alpha^{t+1}) \ge \min\{(\Delta^t)^2/(2D^2), \Delta^t/2\}$. Thus, since the $\mathcal{D}(\alpha^t)$ sequence decreases and is always positive, it must converge and, therefore, we must have $\mathcal{D}(\alpha^t) - \mathcal{D}(\alpha^{t+1}) \to 0$, so the whole $\Delta^t$ sequence goes to 0.

For MDM, (5) and (6) give $\mathcal{D}(\alpha^t) - \mathcal{D}(\alpha^{t+1}) \ge \min\{(\overline{\Delta}^t)^2/(2D^2), \alpha_{U^t}^t \overline{\Delta}^t/2\}$, and arguing as before, the right hand side must tend to 0. Its first term applies when no clipping is done but, arguing as in [6], it can be proved that clipping cannot occur indefinitely after some $t$. Thus, the bound on $(\overline{\Delta}^t)^2/(2D^2)$ must apply to some subsequence $t_j$ and, therefore, $\overline{\Delta}^{t_j} \to 0$. $\qquad \square$

Now we are ready to show the following.

**Theorem 1.** *The $W^t$ updates of the GSK and MDM algorithms converge to $W^*$ as $t$ goes to $\infty$.*

*Proof.* For GSK, the result is immediate by Proposition 2 and (10).

For MDM, Proposition 2 and (10) imply that $W^{t_j} \to W^*$. By continuity of the dual, $\mathcal{D}(\alpha^{t_j}) \to \mathcal{D}(\alpha^*)$. But the sequence $\mathcal{D}(\alpha^t)$ decreases, so we must then have $\mathcal{D}(\alpha^t) \to \mathcal{D}(\alpha^*)$. Finally, it follows by (11) that $W^t \to W^*$.

### 3.2  Convergence of SMO

The convergence of SMO is also proved along similar lines.

**Proposition 3.** *If $W^* = \sum_i \alpha_i^* y_i X_i$ is the optimal SVM solution, we have*

$$\|W^t - W^*\|^2 \leq (\tilde{\Delta}^t/2) \left( \sum_i \alpha_i^t + \sum_i \alpha_i^* \right) , \tag{12}$$

$$\|W^t - W^*\|^2 \leq 2(\tilde{\mathcal{D}}(\alpha^t) - \tilde{\mathcal{D}}(\alpha^*)) . \tag{13}$$

*Proof.* First, notice that $W^*$ is a primal feasible weight vector (i.e., $y_i(W^* \cdot X_i + b^*) \geq 1$ for all $i$), so we have $W^t \cdot W^* = \sum_i \alpha_i^t y_i W^* \cdot X_i = \sum_i \alpha_i^t y_i(W^* \cdot X_i + b^*) \geq \sum_i \alpha_i^t$. Besides, the KKT conditions imply that $\|W^*\|^2 = \sum_i \alpha_i^*$ and, hence, $\tilde{\mathcal{D}}(\alpha^*) = \|W^*\|^2/2 - \sum_i \alpha_i^* = -\|W^*\|^2/2$. Then

$$\|W^t - W^*\|^2 = \|W^t\|^2 - 2W^t \cdot W^* + \|W^*\|^2 \leq \|W^t\|^2 - 2\sum_i \alpha_i^t + \|W^*\|^2$$

$$= 2(\tilde{\mathcal{D}}(\alpha^t) - \tilde{\mathcal{D}}(\alpha^*)) ,$$

so that (13) holds. Observe that, by the results above, we can also write

$$\|W^t - W^*\|^2 \leq \|W^t\|^2 - \sum_i \alpha_i^t - W^t \cdot W^* + \sum_i \alpha_i^* . \tag{14}$$

For the first two terms, we have

$$\|W^t\|^2 - \sum_i \alpha_i^t = \sum_i \alpha_i^t y_i W \cdot X_i - \sum_i \alpha_i^t y_i^2 = \sum_i \alpha_i^t y_i(W \cdot X_i - y_i)$$

$$= \sum_{\mathcal{I}_+} \alpha_i^t(W \cdot X_i - y_i) - \sum_{\mathcal{I}_-} \alpha_i^t(W \cdot X_i - y_i)$$

$$\leq \left( \max_{\mathcal{I}_U} \{W^t \cdot X_i - y_i\} - \min_{\mathcal{I}_L} \{W^t \cdot X_i - y_i\} \right) \sum_i \alpha_i^t/2$$

$$= (\tilde{\Delta}^t/2) \sum_i \alpha_i^t ,$$

where we use $\sum_{\mathcal{I}_+} \alpha_i^t = \sum_{\mathcal{I}_-} \alpha_i^t = \sum \alpha_i^t/2$. Analogously to what has just been done, we get $W^t \cdot W^* - \sum_i \alpha_i^* \geq (-\tilde{\Delta}^t/2) \sum_i \alpha_i^*$ for the last two terms. Hence, putting it all together in (14), we arrive at (12). $\qquad \square$

We point out that the above argument for inequality (12) can also be applied to complete the partial proof of Lemma 1 in [6] given there.

**Proposition 4.** *There is a subsequence $W^{t_j}$ that tends to $W^*$ as $t \to \infty$.*

*Proof.* As an easy consequence of estimates (8) and (9) we get $\tilde{\mathcal{D}}(\alpha^t) - \tilde{\mathcal{D}}(\alpha^{t+1}) \geq \min\{(\tilde{\Delta}^t)^2/(2D^2), \alpha^t_{U^t}\tilde{\Delta}^t/2, \alpha^t_{L^t}\tilde{\Delta}^t/2\}$. The first term at the right hand side applies when there is no clipping and, as just argued for MDM, clipping cannot go on indefinitely. Thus, there must be a subsequence $t_j$ such that $\tilde{\Delta}^{t_j} \to 0$ and, by Proposition 3, $W^{t_j} \to W^*$, since $\sum_i \alpha^t_i$ can be shown to be bounded [6]. □

Now convergence of the full $W^t$ sequence is proved just as in the MDM case, with Proposition 4 and (13).

**Theorem 2.** *The $W^t$ updates of the SMO algorithm converge to $W^*$ as $t$ goes to $\infty$.*

# 4 Conclusions and Further Work

In this work we present, for linearly separable samples, simple proofs of convergence for the GSK and MDM algorithms for NPP, and the SMO algorithm for SVM training, all three under a common framework. This results in much simpler proofs for GSK and MDM than the ones in [1] and [2], and also generalize them to the NPP case. Our proof for SMO is also simpler than the ones given in [6] and [5], but in its present form it is only applicable to linearly–separable tasks. We are currently working on its extension to the non–linearly separable case.

# References

1. Gilbert, E.G.: Minimizing the Quadratic Form on a Convex Set. SIAM J. Contr. 4, 61–79 (1966)
2. Mitchell, B.F., Dem'yanov, V.F., Malozemov, V.N.: Finding the Point of a Polyhedron Closest to the Origin. SIAM J. Contr. 12, 19–26 (1974)
3. Franc, V., Hlaváč, V.: An Iterative Algorithm Learning the Maximal Margin Classifier. Pattern Recognition 36, 1985–1996 (2003)
4. Keerthi, S.S., Shevade, S.K., Bhattacharyya, C., Murthy, K.R.K.: A Fast Iterative Nearest Point Algorithm for Support Vector Machine Classifier Design. IEEE Transactions on Neural Networks 11(1), 124–136 (2000)
5. Lin, C.-J.: On the Convergence of the Decomposition Method for Support Vector Machines. IEEE Transactions on Neural Networks 12(6), 1288–1298 (2001)
6. López, J., Dorronsoro, J.R.: A Simple Proof of the Convergence of the SMO Algorithm for Linearly Separable Problems. In: Alippi, C., Polycarpou, M., Panayiotou, C., Ellinas, G. (eds.) ICANN 2009, Part I. LNCS, vol. 5768, pp. 904–912. Springer, Heidelberg (2009)

# The Support Feature Machine for Classifying with the Least Number of Features

Sascha Klement and Thomas Martinetz

Institute for Neuro- and Bioinformatics, University of Lübeck

**Abstract.** We propose the so-called Support Feature Machine (SFM) as a novel approach to feature selection for classification, based on minimisation of the zero norm of a separating hyperplane. Thus, a classifier with inherent feature selection capabilities is obtained within a single training run. Results on toy examples demonstrate that this method is able to identify relevant features very effectively.

**Keywords:** Support feature machine, feature selection, zero norm minimisation, classification.

## 1 Introduction

The ever increasing complexity of real-world machine learning tasks requires more and more sophisticated methods to deal with datasets that contain only very few relevant features but many irrelevant noise dimensions. It is well-known that these irrelevant features will distract state-of-the-art methods, such as the support vector machine. Thus, feature selection is often a fundamental preprocessing step to achieve proper classification results, to improve runtime, and to make the training results more interpretable.

For many machine learning tasks, maximum margin methods have been confirmed to be a good choice to maximise the generalisation performance [1]. But, besides generalisation capabilities, other aspects, such as fast convergence, existence of simple error bounds, straightforward implementation, running time requirements, or numerical stability, may be equally important.

In recent years, as complexity and dimensionality of real-world problems have dramatically increased, two other aspects have gained more and more importance. These are sparsity and domain interpretability of the inference model. Both are closely connected to the task of variable or feature selection. Primarily, feature selection aims to improve or at least preserve the discriminative capabilities when using fewer features than the original classifier, regression or density estimator. In the following, we focus on feature selection for classification tasks.

Feature selection as an exhaustive search problem is in general computationally intractable as the number of states in the search space increases exponentially with the number of features. Therefore, all computationally feasible feature selection techniques try to approximate the optimal feature set, e.g. by Bayesian inference, gradient descent, genetic algorithms, or various numerical optimisation methods.

K. Diamantaras, W. Duch, L.S. Iliadis (Eds.): ICANN 2010, Part II, LNCS 6353, pp. 88–93, 2010.

Commonly, these methods are divided into two classes: filter and wrapper methods. Filter methods completely separate the feature selection and the classification task [2]. The optimal feature subset is selected in advance, i.e. filtered out from the overall set of features without assessing the actual classifier. In practise, one could, for example, select those features with the largest Pearson correlation coefficients or Fisher scores before training the classifier.

Wrapper methods make use of the induction algorithm to assess the prediction accuracy of a particular feature subset. Well-known contributions to this class of feature selection algorithms are those of Weston et al. [3], who select those features that minimise bounds on the leave-one-out error, and Guyon et al. [4], who propose the so-called recursive feature elimination. Some types of support vector machines already comprise feature selection to some extend, such as the $l_1$-norm SVM [5] or the VS-SSVM (Variable Selection via Sparse SVMs) [6].

In the following, we propose the so-called Support Feature Machine (SFM) as a novel method for feature selection that is both simple and fast. To assess its performance, we will measure and discuss various aspects of feature selection methods, such as improvements to the test error when using only the selected features, sparsity of the solution, or the ability to identify relevant and irrelevant features.

The following sections are organised as follows. First, we briefly introduce the problem of finding relevant variables by means of zero norm minimisation. This leads to our contribution, the mathematical definition of the SFM. Using artificial linearly separable datasets, we illustrate various aspects of the SFM and compare the results to other feature selection methods.

We conclude with a critical discussion of the achievements and propose further extensions to the SFM.

## 2   Feature Selection by Zero Norm Minimisation

We make use of the common notations used in classification and feature selection frameworks, i.e. the training set

$$\mathcal{D} = \{\boldsymbol{x}_i, y_i\}_{i=1}^{n}$$

consists of feature vectors $\boldsymbol{x}_i \in \mathbb{R}^d$ and corresponding class labels $y_i \in \{-1, +1\}$. First, we assume the dataset $\mathcal{D}$ to be linearly separable, i.e.

$$\exists \boldsymbol{w} \in \mathbb{R}^d, \, b \in \mathbb{R} \quad \text{with} \quad y_i \left(\boldsymbol{w}^{\mathrm{T}} \boldsymbol{x}_i + b\right) \geq 0 \ \forall i \quad \text{and} \quad \boldsymbol{w} \neq \boldsymbol{0}, \qquad (1)$$

where the normal vector $\boldsymbol{w} \in \mathbb{R}^d$ and the bias $b \in \mathbb{R}$ describe the separating hyperplane except for a constant factor. Obviously, if $\boldsymbol{w}$ and $b$ are solutions to the inequalities, also $\lambda \boldsymbol{w}$ and $\lambda b$ solve them with $\lambda \in \mathbb{R}^+$.

In general, there is no unique solution to (1). Our goal is to find a weight vector $\boldsymbol{w}$ and a bias $b$ which solve

$$\text{minimise } \|\boldsymbol{w}\|_0^0 \quad \text{subject to} \quad y_i \left(\boldsymbol{w}^{\mathrm{T}} \boldsymbol{x}_i + b\right) \geq 0 \quad \text{and} \quad \boldsymbol{w} \neq \boldsymbol{0} \qquad (2)$$

with $\|w\|_0^0 = \mathrm{card}\,\{w_i | w_i \neq 0\}$. Hence, solutions to (2) solve the classification problem (1) using the least number of features. Note, that any solution can be multiplied by a positive factor and is still a solution. Weston et al. [7] proposed to solve the above problem with a variant of the Support Vector Machine by

$$\text{minimising } \|w\|_0^0 \quad \text{subject to} \quad y_i\left(w^{\mathrm{T}}x_i + b\right) \geq 1. \tag{3}$$

Indeed, as long as there exists a solution to (2) for which $y_i\left(w^{\mathrm{T}}x_i + b\right) > 0$ is valid for all $i = 1, ..., n$, solving (3) yields a solution to (2). Unfortunately, (2) as well as (3) are NP-hard and cannot be solved in polynomial time. Therefore, Weston et al. [7] proposed to approximate (3) by solving

$$\text{minimise } \sum_{j=1}^{d} \ln\left(\epsilon + |w_j|\right) \quad \text{subject to} \quad y_i\left(w^{\mathrm{T}}x_i + b\right) \geq 1 \tag{4}$$

with $0 < \epsilon \ll 1$. They showed that if $w_0$ and $w^*$ optimise (3) and (4), respectively, then

$$\|w^*\|_0^0 \leq \|w_0\|_0^0 + \mathcal{O}\left(\frac{1}{\ln \epsilon}\right). \tag{5}$$

They also showed that using the following iterative scheme at least a local minimum of (4) is found:

1. Set $z = (1, \ldots, 1)$.
2. Minimise $|w|$ such that $y_i\left(w^{\mathrm{T}}(x_i \cdot z) + b\right) \geq 1$.
3. Set $z = z \cdot w$.
4. Repeat until convergence.

This iterative scheme simply applies linear programming.

## 2.1   Support Feature Machine

Instead of modifying the SVM setting as in (3), we slightly change (2) such that we

$$\text{minimise } \|w\|_0^0 \quad \text{subject to} \quad y_i\left(w^{\mathrm{T}}x_i + b\right) \geq 0 \quad \text{and} \quad w^{\mathrm{T}}u + \bar{y}b = 1 \tag{6}$$

with $u = \frac{1}{n}\sum_{i=1}^{n} y_i x_i$ and $\bar{y} = \frac{1}{n}\sum_{i=1}^{n} y_i$. The second constraint excludes $w = 0$, since otherwise we would obtain $\bar{y}b = 1$ and $y_i b \geq 0$, which cannot be fulfilled for all $i$ (we have labels $+1$ and $-1$). As long as there is a solution to (2) with $y_i\left(w^{\mathrm{T}}x_i + b\right) > 0$ for at least one $i \in \{1, ..., n\}$, also $\sum_{i=1}^{n} y_i\left(w^{\mathrm{T}}x_i + b\right) > 0$ is satisfied. Hence, solving (6) yields a solution to the ultimate problem (2).

Since we have linear constraints, for solving (6) we can employ the same framework Weston et al. [7] used for solving their problem. Also (5) applies. However, our experiments show that by solving

$$\text{minimise } \sum_{j=1}^{d} \ln\left(\epsilon + |w_j|\right) \quad \text{subject to} \quad y_i\left(w^{\mathrm{T}}x_i + b\right) \geq 0 \quad \text{and} \quad w^{\mathrm{T}}u + \bar{y}b = 1$$

with the iterative scheme

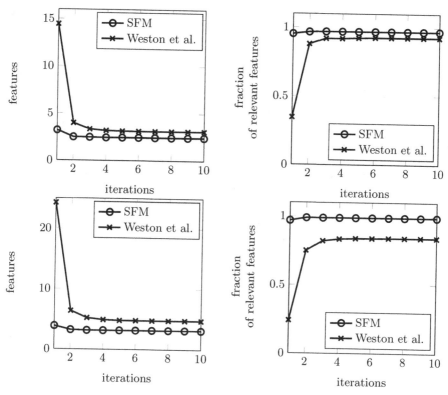

**Fig. 1.** Comparison of the SFM and the method proposed by Weston et al. The top row shows results for $n = 50$ data points, the bottom row for $n = 200$ data points (averaged over 100 runs).

1. Set $z = (1, \ldots, 1)$.
2. Minimise $|w|$ such that $y_i \left( w^{\mathrm{T}}(x_i \cdot z) + b \right) \geq 0$ and $w^{\mathrm{T}}u + \bar{y}b = 1$.
3. Set $z = z \cdot w$.
4. Repeat until convergence

we obtain significantly better solutions to the ultimate problem then by solving (4). It seems that the new cost function is much less prone to local minima.

## 2.2   Experiments

For learning tasks, such as classification or regression, one normally assesses a method's performance via the k-fold cross-validation error, or via the test error on a separate dataset. For feature selection, besides the test error, also the number of selected features and the amount of truly relevant features are important. Since in real-world scenarios these values are almost never known, we used artificial examples to compare the results of the SFM and the method proposed by Weston. The toy examples were constructed according to Weston et al. [7], i.e. the input data consist of 6 relevant but redundant features and 196 noise dimensions. Additionally, we required the datasets to be separable within the 6 relevant dimensions. Figure 1 shows the results for 100 independent runs using $n = 50$ and $n = 200$ data points. Apparently, the SFM returns both a lower total number of features and a higher percentage of truly relevant features. The convergence speed is also slightly better, and already after one iteration the SFM solution is quite close to the final solution.

Next, we evaluated the generalisation performance of the SFM. Table 1 shows mean and standard deviations in comparison to the SVM without feature selection and to the method proposed by Weston et al. For each method and training set size, the experiment was repeated 100 times. Within each repetition 10000 data points were sampled (6 relevant, 196 noise dimensions), $n$ data points were used for training ($n = 20, 50, 100, 200, 500$) and the remaining for evaluating the test error. Again, only linearly separable training datasets were allowed. Obviously, the SFM significantly outperforms a standard SVM approach, but is slightly worse than Weston's method.

**Table 1.** Mean and standard deviation of the test error using different methods and training set sizes for the toy example. The methods are: Standard hard-margin Support Vector Machine (SVM), the method proposed by Weston et al. (Weston) and the Support Feature Machine (SFM).

| n | SVM | Weston | SFM |
|---|---|---|---|
| 20 | 28.8% (± 2.2%) | 8.9% (± 8.0%) | 17.5% (± 7.8%) |
| 50 | 19.0% (± 1.9%) | 2.7% (± 1.5%) | 6.6% (± 3.7%) |
| 100 | 12.2% (± 1.5%) | 1.7% (± 0.7%) | 3.8% (± 1.7%) |
| 200 | 6.7% (± 0.9%) | 1.2% (± 0.5%) | 2.1% (± 0.9%) |
| 500 | 3.1% (± 0.5%) | 0.8% (± 0.2%) | 1.1% (± 0.4%) |

## 2.3  Implementation Issues

As with many machine learning algorithms, normalisation is an essential preprocessing step also for the SFM. For all experiments, we normalised the training datasets to zero mean and unit variance and finally scaled all vectors to have a mean norm of one. This last step is necessary in high-dimensional scenarios to keep the outcome of scalar products in a reasonable range. The test sets were normalised according to the factors obtained from the corresponding training sets.

For solving the optimisation problems, we used the MOSEK optimisation software. To avoid numerical issues, numbers that differed by no more than a specific implementation-dependent number — normally closely connected to the machine epsilon — were considered to be equal.

# 3 Conclusions

We proposed a novel method for combined feature selection and classification — the so-called Support Feature Machine. Experiments on artificial as well as real-world datasets demonstrated that the SFM can identify relevant features very effectively and may improve the generalisation performance significantly with respect to an SVM without feature selection. The implementation only requires linear programming solvers and may therefore be established in various programming environments.

So far, we focused on linear classifiers, mostly for high-dimensional low-sample size scenarios because these scenarios seem to be the most relevant ones in practical applications, such as the analysis of microarray datasets.

In some scenarios, it is necessary to allow for nonlinear classification to achieve proper classification performance. One might think of ways to incorporate kernels into the SFM to allow for arbitrary class boundaries. Nevertheless, the main focus of the SFM was to provide results that may easily be interpreted both in terms of feature selection and classification, so nonlinearities would slacken this demand.

In total, the results we obtained using the SFM approach are quite promising, however, we need to justify our results on real-world datasets. In a follow-up paper, we will show, that even an exponentially increasing number of irrelevant features does not significantly reduce the performance of the SFM. Additionally, we will extend the standard SFM approach to non-separable scenarios. Further work will include experiments on more challenging real-world scenarios with practical relevance. Finally, we seek for an iterative optimisation method to be independent from proprietary optimisation toolboxes.

# References

1. Vapnik, V.: The Nature of Statistical Learning Theory. Springer, New York (1995)
2. Kohavi, R., John, G.H.: Wrappers for feature subset selection. Artificial Intelligence, 273–323 (1997)
3. Weston, J., Mukherjee, S., Chapelle, O., Pontil, M., Poggio, T., Vapnik, V.: Feature Selection for SVMs. In: Advances in Neural Information Processing Systems (2000)
4. Guyon, I., Weston, J., Barnhill, S., Vapnik, V.: Gene selection for cancer classification using support vector machines. Machine Learning 46, 389–422 (2002)
5. Zhu, J., Rosset, S., Hastie, T., Tibshirani, R.: 1-norm support vector machines. In: Thrun, S., Saul, L., Schölkopf, B. (eds.) Advances in Neural Information Processing Systems, vol. 16. MIT Press, Cambridge (2004)
6. Bi, J., Bennett, K.P., Embrechts, M., Breneman, C.M., Song, M.: Dimensionality Reduction via Sparse Support Vector Machines. Journal of Machine Learning Research 3, 1229–1243 (2003)
7. Weston, J., Elisseeff, A., Schölkopf, B., Tipping, M.: Use of the Zero-Norm with Linear Models and Kernel Methods. Journal of Machine Learning Research 3, 1439–1461 (2003)

# Hidden Markov Model for Human Decision Process in a Partially Observable Environment

Masahiro Adomi, Yumi Shikauchi, and Shin Ishii

Graduate School of Informatics, Kyoto University
Gokasho, Uji, Kyoto 611-0011, Japan
{adomi-m,yumi-s}@sys.i.kyoto-u.ac.jp,
ishii@i.kyoto-u.ac.jp

**Abstract.** The environment surrounding us is inevitably uncertain; we cannot perceive all the information necessary for making optimal decision. Even in such a partially observable environment, humans can make appropriate decision by resolving the uncertainty. During decision making in an uncertain environment, resolving behaviors of the uncertainty and optimal behaviors to best suit for the environment are often incompatible, which is termed exploration-exploitation dilemma in the field of machine learning. To examine how we cope with the exploration-exploitation dilemma, in this study, we performed statistical modeling of human behaviors when performing a partially observable maze navigation task; in particular, we devised a hidden Markov model (HMM), which incorporates inference of a hidden variable in the environment and switching between exploration and exploitation. Our HMM-based model well reproduced the human behaviors, suggesting the human subjects actually performed exploration and exploitation to effectively adapt to this uncertain environment.

## 1 Introduction

We, humans can make appropriate decision, even in a complicated environment which may include various kinds of uncertainty. A typical example can be seen when we drive a car through a crossing with bad visibility; in most cases, we can pass through the crossing safely resolving the bad visibility by integrating various signals coming from the environment. Although recent neuroscience studies have revealed neural basis related to such decision making [1,2,3], more concrete mechanisms to perform such decision making are not fully elucidated.

A decision making problem in an uncertain environment, from which all the information necessary for making the optimal decision is not provided, can be formulated as a partially-observable Markov decision process (POMDP) [4]. One possible way to solve a POMDP is to use belief states, which are the sufficient statistics of the state variables, including internal variables, of the environment. In other words, a belief state is the integration of the agent's observation in the past.

During decision making in an uncertain environment, resolving behaviors of the uncertainty and optimal behaviors to best suit for the environment are often

K. Diamantaras, W. Duch, L.S. Iliadis (Eds.): ICANN 2010, Part II, LNCS 6353, pp. 94–103, 2010.

incompatible, which is termed exploration-exploitation dilemma in the field of machine learning [5]. The agent should perform exploration behaviors in some situations, or exploitation in other situations. To examine how one copes with the exploration-exploitation dilemma, in this study, we performed statistical modeling of human behaviors when performing a partially observable maze navigation task formerly devised by ourselves. Our current model is based on Bayesian hidden Markov model (HMM), which was also used in the previous study [6], but directly includes the mechanism of exploration and exploitation. Although another existing study performed an fMRI study in terms of a value-based reinforcement learning model with exploration and exploitation [7], our model does not assume explicitly value function. As a result, our HMM-based model well reproduced the subjects' behaviors, suggesting the subjects actually performed switching between the exploration and exploitation.

# 2 Task

## 2.1 Outline

In this study, human subjects participated in a partially-observable maze navigation task, whose scheme is shown in Fig.1. At the beginning of a single block, the subjects were informed of a goal position on the 2D maze, and then tried to reach the goal after as few trials as possible, based on partial 3D observations which give a cue to identify the current position on the maze. On the day before conducting the maze navigation task, the subject had joined a free exploration task to well identify the maze structure and the mapping from locations on the 2D maze map and 3D views which can be seen at those locations. In the navigation task, we used the same maze as in the preceding free exploration task; then we assume that the subjects were well familiar with the maze structure and the 2D-3D mapping.

## 2.2 The Maze Structure

The maze we used (Fig.2) consists of $9 \times 9$ grid points: 58 vacant squares constituting paths and 23 wall squares. There is no dead-end, cross road, or wide square area. The observation (view) is 3D and partial; at each grid point on the

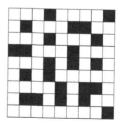

**Fig. 1.** A single block in the maze

**Fig. 2.** Maze 2D structure

maze, the subject may take either of four orientations, north-faced, east-faced, south-faced or west-faced. A single view presents the status, wall or vacant, of six grid points (forward, forward-left, forward-right, left, right and the current position). There are in total seventeen possible views and they actually exist in the used maze. Each location on the maze shares the same view with at least other five different locations on the maze; this maze design did not allow the subject to identify his/her position only from a single 3D view, which made the environment uncertain.

### 2.3   Subjects and Operations

Eight normal human subjects (6 males and 2 females, aged 22-26, right-handed and with normal vision) participated after giving written informed consent. They practiced the free exploration task on the day before they performed the navigation task, and we confirmed that they had sufficiently memorized the maze structure.

In a single trial in a block, after presenting a 3D view, the subject selected one of three possible actions, forward move, left turn and right turn, by a button press. This action selection should be completed within 2 seconds, which defines the maximum reaction time. If the forward move was selected, the location was changed by one grid point to the forward direction, but the other two actions only changed the orientation with letting the subject stay at the same grid point. The subjects reported their actions by their left hand; forward move by a middle finger, right turn by an index finger and left turn by a ring finger.

By using another hand, the subjects were requested to report whether the actual observation was the same as what they had predicted. We assume that the subject could predict the next view before it was presented. The subjects were requested to first press the right-hand button to confirm their prediction and then the left-hand button to select their actions, in each trial. The report by the right hand was optional, but if the subject could not press the action button by their left hand within a allotted time (2 sec.), it caused a miss trial and the subject stayed at the same location with the same orientation.

## 3   Formulation

### 3.1   Optimal Agent and Assumptions on Human Model

To begin with, we modeled an 'optimal' agent; this agent memorizes all the past observations and takes the 'info-max' action which most reduces the possibilities of the agent location in the maze if there is any ambiguity on the position whereas the 'greedy' action to follow the shortest path to the goal if there is no ambiguity.

Our basic assumption is that the subjects would like to behave as the optimal agent, but due to the limited reaction time, their processing should be incomplete. A preliminary analysis has revealed that the subject's behaviors are actually different from those by the optimal agent. Although this partially-observable maze was designed so that subjects can identify their locations after at most four (meaningful) actions starting from any location on the maze, they often took non-optimal actions even after fifth trials. Then, we need to model the incomplete information processing by the subjects, such to include the uncertain (probabilistic) character of the processing, by means of a statistical model.

To get to the goal after as few trials as possible, specifying the present location is the key. Therefore, subjects who are familiar with the maze structure were assumed to employ two policies depending on the situation; one is an exploration policy (to try to specify the present location), and the other is an exploitation policy (to follow the shortest path to the goal). Although the same policies were also implemented in the optimal agent, the exploration and exploitation by human subjects were supposed to be incomplete.

It would be plausible to assume that each subject keeps and maintains a belief state, sufficient statistics of unknowns, which comprises two factors: where the subject thinks he/she is (present location estimated by the subject) on the maze and whether the subject is confident of his/her estimation or not (confidence for estimation). Like the optimal agent, the subject was assumed to take an 'info-max' behavior if he/she is not convinced of his/her position, $c = 0$, or an optimal behavior if he/she is convinced, $c = 1$, even if those behaviors were incomplete; this is the model of decision making by the subject. After getting the new observation, the subject would check if his/her previous guess was correct or not, which would make the confidence to change. Then we formulated these processes in terms of hidden Markov model (HMM).

– Internal state $x_t = (s_t, c_t)$
– Present location estimated by the subject: $s_t$, real location: $s_t^*$
– Confidence for estimation: $c_t$
– Actual action taken by the subject: $a_t$
– Actual observation: $o_t^*$
– Transition probability of the internal state: $p(x_t | x_{t-1}, a_{t-1}, o_t^*)$
– Action selection probability (policy): $p(a_t | x_t)$
– Initial belief $p(x_1 | o_1^*)$

Figure 3 shows the graphical model of the HMM, which expresses the dynamics of the subject's subjective and objective states in the maze environment.

## 3.2    Action Selection Probability

**Exploration policy.** $c_t = 0$ denotes that the subject is not certain about the current position on the maze. The optimal strategy in such a case is to take the 'info-max' behavior; that is, to reduce the number of possible locations on the maze. In typical situations to explore the maze, the subject is able to observe the status of three new grid points by taking a forward movement, or that of two grid points by taking a turn movement. Then the exploration is assumed as follows.

1. If possible, the subject takes the forward movement, to get much new information.

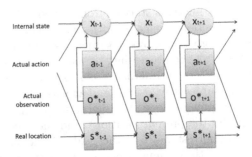

**Fig. 3.** The graphical model of the hidden Markov model

2. If there is a wall to the forward direction but no wall to both of left-hand-side and right-hand-side directions, the subject takes either of turn-to-left or turn-to-right.
3. If the subject is on the L-shape corner, he/she takes the single allowable turn action.

To represent the incompleteness of the exploration by the subjects, $k_{exp}$, which is the preference ratio of exploratory action to non-exploratory one, is introduced so that the policy is given by

$$p(a_t|s_t, c_t = 0) = \begin{cases} k_{exp}/(k_{exp}N_{exp} + (N_a - N_{exp})) & \text{if } a_t \text{ is exploratory} \\ 1/(k_{exp}N_{exp} + (N_a - N_{exp})) & \text{otherwise} \end{cases} \quad (1)$$

Here, $N_a$ and $N_{exp}$ denote the numbers of all allowable actions and exploratory actions defined above, respectively, at $s_t$.

**Exploitation policy.** $c_t = 1$ denotes that the subject is convinced of his/her current location on the maze. Then, the optimal behavior is to follow the shortest path to the goal. Due to the incompleteness of the subject's exploitation process, however, he/she may take some random actions with a probability $\epsilon_{opt}$.

$$p(a_t|s_t, c_t = 1) = \begin{cases} (1 - \epsilon_{opt})/N_{opt} & \text{if } a_t \text{ is exploitative} \\ \epsilon_{opt} & \text{otherwise} \end{cases} \quad (2)$$

Here, $N_{opt}$ denotes the number of optimal actions at the $t$-th trial. Note that it is difficult to discriminate between exploratory actions and exploitative actions only from single actions, because some exploratory actions may also be exploitative and vise versa.

### 3.3  Transition Probability

The subjects were assumed to predict the observation obtained in the next trial. Here, $\hat{s}_t$ and $\hat{o}_t$ denote the predicted position due to mental simulation (deterministic) based on the previous estimation $s_{t-1}$ and the actually taken action

$a_{t-1}$, and the predicted observation at the predicted position, respectively, at the $t$-th trial. Due to the limited reaction time, we assume the subject would perform mental simulation before getting a new observation at the $t$-th trial.

We assume that the subject reexamined his/her position estimate based on the newly available observation; that is, if the new observation was what he/she had expected, he/she became more confident, while if the new observation was found to be different from what he/she had expected, he/she retried the estimation based on the new observation but with low confidence.

More concretely, if the subject was convinced at the $(t-1)$-th trial, $x_{t-1} = (s_{t-1}, c_{t-1} = 1)$, and there was no discrepancy between the predicted observation and the actual observation, $\hat{o}_t = o_t^*$, the estimated location changed to $\hat{s}_t$ with probability 1; that is, the internal state changed to $\hat{x}_t = (\hat{s}_t, c_t = 1)$. But if not convinced at the $(t-1)$-th trial, $x_{t-1} = (s_{t-1}, c_{t-1} = 0)$ and $\hat{o}_t = o_t^*$, he/she remained uncertain with probability $1 - \epsilon_x$ or became convinced with $\epsilon_x$; that is, $x_{t-1}$ changed to $\hat{x}_t = (\hat{s}_t, c_t = 0)$ with probability $1 - \epsilon_x$ or $(\hat{s}_t, c_t = 1)$ with $\epsilon_x$; the latter process represents the change of belief into a confident one.

On the other hand, if there was discrepancy between the prediction and actual, $\hat{o}_t \neq o_t^*$, the new position estimate was uniformly taken from possible positions on the maze whose view was identical to $o_t^*$ with low confidence; that is, $x_{t-1}$ changed to $\hat{x}_t = (s_t', c_t = 0)$. Here, $s_t'$ denotes any possible location whose view is identical to $o_t^*$.

### 3.4    Initial Belief

At the start point, subjects were assumed to be unconvinced of their position, so $p(c_1 = 0) = 1$. And $p(s_1)$ was a uniform distribution over the positions on the maze whose observation was identical to the initial observation $o_1^*$.

## 4    Estimation and Prediction

### 4.1    Estimation for Belief State

The incremental Bayesian estimation provides a way to estimate the belief state [8], i.e., the filtered estimation of the subject's internal state at the $t$-th trial, based on the sequences of actions and observations by the subject before that trial. The policy $p(a_t|x_t)$ was given in Section 3.2, and the state transition $p(x_t|x_{t-1}, a_{t-1}, o_t^*)$ was described in Section 3.3.

$$p(x_t|a_{1:t}, o_{1:t}^*) = \frac{p(a_t|x_t) \sum_{x_{t-1}} p(x_t|x_{t-1}, a_{t-1}, o_t^*) p(x_{t-1}|a_{1:t-1}, o_{1:t-1}^*)}{p(a_t|a_{1:t-1})} \quad (3)$$

On the other hand, by using the whole sequences of actions and observations of the subject until the end of that block, we can obtain the smoothed estimate of the belief state, which would be more reliable than the filtered estimate. Here, $T$ denotes the trial length in the block.

$$p(x_t|a_{1:T}, o_{1:T}^*) = p(x_t|a_{1:t}, o_{1:t}^*) \sum_{x_{t+1}} \frac{p(x_{t+1}|x_t, a_t, o_{t+1}^*) p(x_{t+1}|a_{1:T}, o_{1:T}^*)}{p(x_{t+1}|a_{1:t}, o_{1:t}^*)} \quad (4)$$

## 4.2   Prediction of Action

The incremental Bayesian formulation also provides the way to predict the next action based on the past data as follows. The prediction accuracy is not only the measure of model's predictability (the larger, the better), but also the quantity signifying subjective predictability of human subjects.

$$\hat{a}_t = \arg\max_{a_t} p(a_t|a_{1:t-1}) \tag{5}$$

The concordance rate $\rho$ between the predicted actions $\hat{a}_t$ and the real actions $a_t$ is calculated as $\rho = N_\rho/(T-1)$. $N_\rho$ is the number of trials whose actions were well predicted, $\hat{a}_t = a_t$, in the block $t = 1 : T - 1$. When there were multiple probable actions (given by (5)) as $\hat{a}_t$, we regarded $\hat{a}_t = a_t$ when $a_t$ corresponded to any of those probable actions. In order to evaluate our HMM-based model, its prediction ability was compared with that by the optimal agent. We can evaluate the concordance rate of the optimal agent, $\rho_{opt}$, in a similar fashion to that of the HMM-based model.

## 4.3   Parameter Estimation

According to the incremental Bayesian estimation, we automatically obtain the marginal likelihood, which can be used for the maximum likelihood (ML) estimation of the parameter $\epsilon \equiv (k_{exp}, \epsilon_{opt}, \epsilon_x)$. Here, parameter estimation is crucial because the parameter represents the character of each subject. Given a set ($N$ sequences) of actions and observations of the subject for parameter estimation, $b_k(k = 1, \ldots, N)$, the total marginal likelihood is given by

$$L(\epsilon) = \prod_{k=1}^{N} p(b_k|\epsilon), \tag{6}$$

where the marginal likelihood of a single sequence (block) $p(b|\epsilon)$ is simply given as a normalization constant of the filtered posterior of the internal state at the end of the block:

$$p(b|\epsilon) = p(a_1|\epsilon) \prod_{t=2}^{T} p(a_t|a_{1:t-1}|\epsilon) \tag{7}$$

The ML estimate of the parameter is given by maximizing the total marginal likelihood. Although we can analytically obtain the ML estimate in our HMM's case, we simply applied the grid search heuristics: we discretized each of the parameters, $k_{exp}$, from 1 to 10 by 1, $\epsilon_{opt}$ and $\epsilon_x$, from 0.1 to 1 by 0.1, evaluated the total marginal likelihood on each of the $10 \times 10 \times 10$ grid points, and selected the best point that maximizes the total likelihood.

## 5   Results

### 5.1   Result of Parameter Estimation

Each subject participated in three sessions each of which consisted of 150 trials of the navigation task. When a subject got to a goal, it was the end of a single block, then another block started. The subjects shared the same setting of the task; in the corresponding block, the start and goal positions were the same over the subjects. We performed the parameter estimation for each subject; the ML estimate of the parameter was obtained by using the data in the sessions. The ML estimate was mostly $\epsilon = (k_{exp}, \epsilon_{opt}, \epsilon_x) = (10, 0.1, 0.1)$ or $\epsilon = (10, 0.1, 0.2)$, which was found to be consistent between the subjects.

## 5.2   Result of Action Prediction

We calculated the concordance rate for each subject. The result is shown in Table 1, where the concordance rate $\rho$ by our model was better than that $(\rho_{opt})$ by the optimal agent for almost all the subjects. This result shows that our HMM-based model well reproduces the subject's action which he/she tried to take. When calculating the concordance rate, we performed the parameter estimation for each subject, based on the data during 2 sessions (training data) out of three sessions. We evaluated the prediction performance of our HMM over the blocks in the remaining one session (test data); i.e., the prediction performance is a cross-validated one.

## 5.3   Result of Belief State Estimation

Figure 4 shows an example of the reproduced MAP sequence of the filtered belief during a single block, starting from the filled circle and ending at the star. The real path is shown in Fig. 5, where green open circles show successful trials of the subject's prediction. In the early part of the block in Fig. 4, our

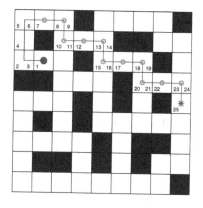

**Fig. 4.** The estimation path reproduced by our HMM. Numbers index the trials in this block. Filled circle, star, red crosses and cyan open circles denote the start position, the goal position, the positions estimated as $c_t = 0$ and the positions estimated as $c_t = 1$.

**Fig. 5.** The actual path taken by the subject. Numbers index the trials in this block. Filled circle and star have the same meaning as in Fig.4. Green open circles show the positions where the subject reported that the observation was what he/she had predicted.

HMM estimated that the subject might have recognized his position but with low confidence ($c_t = 0$, red cross). As the trials proceeded, our HMM estimated that he was confident of his position ($c_t = 1$, cyan open circle), which shows good agreement with the subject's report (green open circle in Fig.5). This example typically shows that our HMM well reproduces the subject's internal processing of resolving uncertainty (his/her position on the maze) in the environment, only from the subject's behaviors.

In order to evaluate further our model, we next calculated the concordance rate of confidence prediction $\rho_{con}$, which is the rate of the trials at which the subjects reported their successful prediction to the trials at which the model evaluated that the subjects were confident; i.e., true positive rate. Here, we defined the criterion of the confidence level; if the probability $\max_{s_t} p(s_t, c_t = 1)$ is bigger than $\max_{s_t} p(s_t, c_t = 0)$, we regard the subject as being confident of his/her estimation, otherwise as uncertain. The result in Table 1 shows that whether he/she was confident or not is well predicted by our HMM-based model.

**Table 1.** Action concordance rate by HMM ($\rho$), that by the optimal agent ($\rho_{opt}$) and the true positive rate of the subjects' confidence ($\rho_{con}$)

| Subject | $\rho(\%)$ | $\rho_{opt}(\%)$ | $\rho_{con}(\%)$ |
|---------|------------|------------------|------------------|
| 1 | 85.8 | 77.2 | 71.3 |
| 2 | 89.5 | 84.0 | 72.2 |
| 3 | 92.5 | 82.2 | 71.6 |
| 4 | 91.4 | 82.4 | 68.1 |
| 5 | 88.5 | 75.5 | 62.9 |
| 6 | 91.6 | 82.9 | 65.9 |
| 7 | 91.9 | 93.3 | 75.2 |
| 8 | 88.2 | 81.7 | 58.7 |

## 6   Conclusion

In this study, we presented a hidden Markov model of human behaviors during performing a partially observable maze navigation task, which directly implemented switching between exploration and exploitation. The high prediction ability of the subject's actions and sufficient reproducibility of the subjects' confidence suggested the plausibility of our model, that is, subjects actually performed exploration and exploitation to appropriately adapt to this uncertain environment.

## References

1. Paulus, M.P., Hozack, N., Zauscher, B., McDowell, J.E., Frank, L., Brown, G.G., Braff, D.L.: Prefrontal, parietal, and temporal cortex networks underlie decision-making in the presence of uncertainty. NeuroImage 13, 91–100 (2001)

2. Dayan, P., Daw, N.D.: Decision theory, reinforcement learning, and the brain. Cognitive, Affective, and Behavioral Neuroscience 8, 429–453 (2008)
3. Daw, N.D., Doya, K.: The computational neurobiology of learning and reward. Current Opinion in Neurobiology 16, 199–204 (2006); Cognitive neuroscience
4. Kaelbling, L.P., Littman, M.L., Cassandra, A.R.: Planning and acting in partially observable stochastic domains. Artificial Intelligence 101, 99–134 (1998)
5. Sutton, R.S., Barto, A.G.: Reinforcement Learning. MIT Press, Cambridge (1998)
6. Yoshida, W., Ishii, S.: Resolution of uncertainty in prefrontal cortex. Neuron 50, 781–789 (2006)
7. Daw, N.D., O'Doherty, J.P., Dayan, P., Seymour, B., Dolan, R.J.: Cortical substrates for exploratory decisions in humans. Nature 441, 876–879 (2006)
8. Kitagawa, G., Sato, S.: Monte carlo smoothing and self-organising state space model. In: Doucet, A., Freitas, N.D., Gordon, N. (eds.) Sequential Monte Carlo Methods in Practice, pp. 177–195. Springer, Heidelberg (2001)

# Representing, Learning and Extracting Temporal Knowledge from Neural Networks: A Case Study

Rafael V. Borges[1], Artur d'Avila Garcez[1], and Luis C. Lamb[2]

[1] Department of Computing
City University London
{Rafael.Borges.1,aag}@soi.city.ac.uk
[2] Institute of Informatics
Federal University of Rio Grande do Sul
LuisLamb@acm.org

**Abstract.** The integration of knowledge representation, reasoning and learning into a robust and computationally effective model is a key challenge in Artificial Intelligence. Temporal models are fundamental to describe the behaviour of computing and information systems. In addition, acquiring the description of the desired behaviour of a system is a complex task in several AI domains. In this paper, we evaluate a neural framework capable of adapting temporal models according to properties, and also learning through observation of examples. In this framework, a symbolically described model is translated into a recurrent neural network, and algorithms are proposed to integrate learning, both from examples and from properties. In the end, the knowledge is again symbolically represented, incorporating both initial model and learned specification, as shown by our case study. The case study illustrates how the integration of methodologies and principles from distinct AI areas can be relevant to build robust intelligent systems.

**Keywords:** Neural Symbolic Integration, Temporal Learning, Temporal Models.

## 1 Introduction

The integration of knowledge representation, reasoning and learning in a robust and computationally effective intelligent platform is one of the key challenges in Computer Science and Artificial Intelligence (AI) [4]. The representation and learning of temporal models in Software Engineering (SE) is an ongoing research endeavour, with several applications widely used in industry [3,5]. Integrating these different dimensions of temporal knowledge aims not only at responding to the challenge put forward in [4], but also at developing a clear abstract representation of dynamic systems, complementing incomplete specifications with observed examples of a system's behaviour. Further, the availability of information about desired properties in a system allows automated evolution of its description, optimizing the processes of specification and verification.

This paper describes a framework that robustly integrates different sources of temporal knowledge: (i) the symbolic knowledge model, (ii) learned observed examples of the system's behaviour, and (iii) an abstract description of properties to be satisfied by the system specification. The paper builds upon principles from two recent applications of machine learning: the first consists in learning an abstract description of a

K. Diamantaras, W. Duch, L.S. Iliadis (Eds.): ICANN 2010, Part II, LNCS 6353, pp. 104–113, 2010.

system through the observation of examples its behaviour [12]; the other consists in the evolution of a specification through the use of examples or abstract descriptions of a system's desired behaviour [1]. Unifying both ideas allows reasoning and adaptation to be integrated into several applications regarding specification of temporal models.

The paper will focus on the evaluation of the framework on a benchmark Software Engineering case study. In the framework, symbolic knowledge is represented by a fragment of a temporal logic, then computed and learned through a connectionist engine. This leads to the construction of an effective, intelligent structure that can be used in the process of development and analysis of a general class of systems. The case study will illustrate the effectiveness of the framework, evaluate its performance in integrating different sources of information, and its applicability to learning from examples and properties, where reasoning and learning are used to evolve temporal models. The paper is organized as follows. Section 2 contains background material. Section 3 describes the temporal reasoning and learning framework. Section 4 discusses the case study in detail. Section 5 concludes and discusses future work.

## 2    Preliminaries: Temporal Learning and Reasoning

Temporal logics have been highly successful in the representation of temporal knowledge about computing systems [5]. For example, LTL (Linear Temporal Logics) and CTL (Computation Tree Logics) are broadly used in computer science, to analyze models and properties of a system [3,5]. However, adding a temporal dimension to knowledge models imposes several challenges to the learning task. Symbolic learning systems such as Inductive Logic Programming (ILP) [11] can in principle be adapted to application in temporal domains, but are considered too brittle for such task [10]. Neural network learning presents itself as an alternative, where a quantitative approach is used in the learning task, which can then be applied to temporal learning through the use recurrent networks or by incorporating memory into the networks [8,9].

One traditional approach to build unified reasoning and learning systems is by translating knowledge from one representation to another. For instance, initial knowledge represented by a symbolic language can be translated into a semantically equivalent neural network. This target network can then be subject to learning through the presentation of examples. In turn, one can then explain the learned knowledge by extracting knowledge from the network into a symbolic representation [2].

Regarding temporal knowledge, the robust integration between learning and reasoning can be used in several ways, as in the modeling and verification of specifications. In Black Box model checking, a symbolic machine learning algorithm is used to acquire an abstract model of a system, and this model is then used to perform automated model checking of the system with no knowledge about its internal structure being provided [7]. Another interesting use of learning in SE consists in applying learning strategies to adapt a model in order to satisfy certain properties or constraints, as done in [1] where a temporal logic description of a model is translated into event calculus; the semantics of the temporal operators is represented through predicates in first-order logics, allowing the application of ILP techniques. In the case study below, we shall discuss the pros and cons of the ILP approach in comparison with our neural network-based approach.

## 3    A Framework for Learning and Reasoning

In order to implement a robust framework to describe, adapt and learn new specifications, we consider three different sources of information: an initial symbolic description, observed examples of the desired behaviour, and properties (or constraints) to be satisfied by the specified system. In the definition of the framework, these different sources of information can be used in the learning task (though none of them is mandatory). This flexibility allows the framework to fulfill the requirements for Black Box checking [7], where a set of examples illustrates how the system works without having an abstract description of its general behaviour. For this purpose, the learning module must be able to build an initial representation of the system from the observed examples. The model is then subject to the presentation of properties that should be satisfied. The framework not only identifies if the model satisfies the properties, but also adapts the model in order to meet a specification. In addition, the presentation of examples and properties to the learning engine can be effected simultaneously. The learning procedure we use can be applied to a model with or without background knowledge of the system.

Consider the diagram of Fig. 1. The core of the system is defined by the *learning engine* (1), which requires different resources to allow the integration of the different sources of information. The initial *model description* (2) is converted into a neural network through the use of a translation algorithm. After that, the network can be subject to learning, considering the information given by the *observed examples* (3) and the *system's properties* (4). In turn, refined knowledge is extracted into a symbolic representation (5), facilitating its analysis. In our system, knowledge is extracted in the form of a *state transition diagram*, which can be converted into a logic program, if needed.

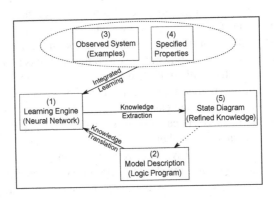

**Fig. 1.** Diagram of our proposed framework

### 3.1    Representing the Model

In order to represent the models, we will use a temporal logic language, similarly to [9]. In this work, we adapt their syntax for the sake of clarity. First, each atom (propositional variable) used in the description of a model will be either an input or a state variable. Input variables are those whose value is set externally to the model, while state variables have their values defined according to the model's behaviour. To represent temporal sequences, we use the $\bigcirc$ (*next time*) operator.

The logical representation can be used to generate the initial architecture of the neural network through an algorithm proposed in [6], which translates a propositional logic program $\mathcal{P}$ into a correspondent neural network $\mathcal{N}$. This translation consists basically in using a hidden neuron to represent the conjunctions of literals in the body of each rule. The input and output neurons represent atoms, where the output neurons compute the disjunction of the rules in which the related atom appears as head. Positive assignments to the variables are represented by positive values close to 1 and negative assignments by values close to -1. The propagation of information through time, to allow the computation of the temporal operators, is represented through recurrent links from the output neuron representing $\bigcirc \alpha$ to the input neuron representing $\alpha$.

Let us illustrate the integration of the different representations of knowledge through a simple example. Consider the monitor of a resource that should allocate such resource between two processes $A$ and $B$. Each process communicates with this monitor through a signal to request the resource (*Req*) and a signal to release it (*Rel*). These signals are considered as input variables to the monitor, that also has two state variables representing if each process has the resource allocated. In Fig. 2, we show a logic program that illustrates how the inputs affect the states, and the network representing this program generated by the translation. Below, a rule of the form $\bigcirc B \leftarrow \sim B, relB$ means that if $relB$ is true and $B$ is false at timepoint $t$ then $B$ should be true at timepoint $t + 1$.

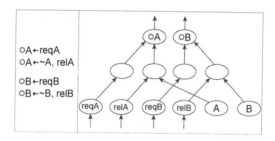

**Fig. 2.** Representation of the monitor example

## 3.2   Learning and Evolving the Model

Our system allows learning from examples and specified properties. Each observed example has values assigned to all the input variables, and to a subset of the state variables. This allows the use of learning from examples when only some of the state variables are observable, such as in the case where these represent the actual outputs of an observed system. We use standard backpropagation [8], as follows. When learning from examples, the input values given by an example are applied to the corresponding input neurons, together with the information about the current state. Information is propagated forward through the network to obtain the output values, and through the network's recurrent connection to obtain the network's next state. If the output information is not present (i.e. not observable), we will consider a null error for this output. Otherwise, the error is calculated using the example and the weights are changed in the usual way.

When learning from properties, instead of standard examples (i.e. input/output patterns), the system is presented with an entire sequence of inputs $I_0, I_1, ...$, states and next states $S_0, S_1$, etc. Hence, the desired output for each timepoint in the backpropagation process must be defined to allow the training of the network. For this purpose, the framework keeps a record of *active properties*, as well as an index $k^X$ for each active property $X$. At every timepoint $t$, if the current state corresponds to the initial condition $S_0^X$ of a property $X$ then $X$ is inserted into the list of active properties, and $k^X$ is set to 0. When an input is applied, the framework verifies if it corresponds to the current position $I_k^X$ of each active property, eliminating from the list all the properties not following this condition. When an active property ends, the state values given by the final state condition $S_n^X$ are used to define the desired output values for the learning process. In Table 1, we can see an example of execution regarding the learning of two properties $X1$ and $X2$ shown on the left. In the table, 1 represents true and $-1$ represents false. Considering that the execution starts with an empty list of active properties, we can notice how the inputs and states affect this list, as well as the definition of the desired output according to property $X2$. The desired output defined by the property will then be integrated with the information from the examples (to avoid conflicts) and then used to define the actual values applied to the network.

**Table 1.** Defining target output values (right) according to specified properties (left)

| Properties | | | Exec | State | | Inputs | | | | Active | Desired |
|---|---|---|---|---|---|---|---|---|---|---|---|
| | $X1$ | $X2$ | Count | A | B | ReqA | RelA | ReqB | RelB | Prop. | Output |
| $S_0$ | $\neg B$ | $\neg A$ | 1 | $-1$ | $-1$ | 1 | $-1$ | $-1$ | $-1$ | $\{X_1(1)\}$ | $\emptyset$ |
| $I_0$ | $ReqA$ | $ReqB$ | 2 | 1 | $-1$ | $-1$ | 1 | $-1$ | $-1$ | $\emptyset$ | $\emptyset$ |
| $I_1$ | $ReqB, \neg RelA$ | $ReqA, \neg RelB$ | 3 | $-1$ | $-1$ | $-1$ | $-1$ | 1 | $-1$ | $\{X_2(1)\}$ | $\emptyset$ |
| $S_2$ | $\neg B$ | $\neg A$ | 4 | $-1$ | 1 | $-1$ | $-1$ | $-1$ | $-1$ | $\{X_2(2)\}$ | $\{\neg A\}$ |

## 3.3 Extracting Knowledge about the Model

We use a pedagogical approach [2] to obtain a symbolic representation of the trained network. Input and output values of the network are sampled and used to infer a general behaviour. The samples used in this procedure can be the same used for learning, but different sets can also be considered to allow a better generalization. In the case of learning through properties, the randomness of the input selection allows different sets of data to be applied to each training epoch; therefore, it is not necessary to create a different procedure to generate the examples for extraction. In this process, for each input applied to the network, a transition $T$ is stored containing information about the current state $S_0^T$, the applied input $I^T$, and the obtained next state $S_f^T$. All the occurrences of transitions $T$ with the same $S_0^T$, $I^T$ and $S_f^T$ are grouped into a unique transition $T'$. Extra variable $count^T$ is also used to give a more quantitative measure when analyzing the extracted knowledge: $count^{T'}$ is the number of transitions grouped into $T'$.

These transitions can be shown in the form of a diagram, but also represented back as a revised temporal logic program. In order to do so, we filter the group of transitions to be used, according to the number of times they appear. Each remaining transition is then rewritten as a set of rules - one rule for each state variable. The body (right-hand side) of all the rules representing $\mathcal{T}$ contains all the input and state variables, in positive or negative form according to the assignments $S_0^{\mathcal{T}'}$ and $I^{\mathcal{T}'}$ of $\mathcal{T}'$. The head (left-hand side) of each rule will be given by one of the variables $\bigcirc\alpha$, if $S^{\mathcal{T}'}$ assigns $\alpha$ to true, or $\bigcirc\neg\beta$ otherwise. To allow a better understanding, this set of rules can also be simplified, through symbolic manipulation of the logic program.

# 4    Validation and Experiments: Case Study

A *pump system* example is used in [1] as a case study to evaluate symbolic strategies to adapt requirements according to properties. Below, we use a version of this problem to verify representation and learning of temporal knowledge from different information sources using neural networks. The pump system monitors and controls the levels of water in a mine to avoid the risk of overflow, through the use of three state variables: $CMet$ indicating a critical level of methane, $HiW$ indicating a high level of water, and $pOn$, indicating that the pump is turned on. In order to turn on and off such indicators, six different signals are considered, as shown below in the rules representing the system:

- $\bigcirc CMet \leftarrow CMet, \sim sCMetOff$
- $\bigcirc CMet \leftarrow \sim sCMetOn$
- $\bigcirc HiW \leftarrow HiW; \sim sLoW$
- $\bigcirc HiW \leftarrow \sim sHiW$
- $\bigcirc POn \leftarrow POn, \sim tPOff$
- $\bigcirc POn \leftarrow \sim tPOn$

Our initial experiments consider three different cases. First, in experiment $a1$, we translated the knowledge described above into a network with 9 neurons in the input layer (representing input and state variables), 6 hidden and 3 output neurons. Next, in experiment $a2$, we considered learning of such relations through the presentation of a sequence of 1000 examples, using a network without background knowledge, but with the same distribution of neurons as in $a1$. Finally, in $a3$, we expressed such relations as properties, and ran the framework again with a similar network. In $a1$ and $a2$, we considered 500 epochs of 1000 presentations, and in $a3$ we used 50 epochs of 10,000 presentations. In the definition of the examples, we considered that only one input is positive at each timepoint, as in [1]. On the other hand, the automatic generation of inputs for learning properties in $a3$ does not have this restriction, requiring a larger sample to get an accurate representation of the possible input configurations.

In Fig. 3, we show a state diagram for the networks before the learning process, the chart depicting the evolution of the root mean square error (RMSE) on output during learning, and a state diagram representing the learned knowledge after training. The state variables $CMet$, $HiW$ and $POn$ are represented by $C$, $H$ and $P$, respectively, in the diagrams. In $a1$, the initial and final diagrams are the same since the knowledge is already built in the network. When learning through examples only ($a2$), the diagrams clearly show that new information was learned about the transitions between states.

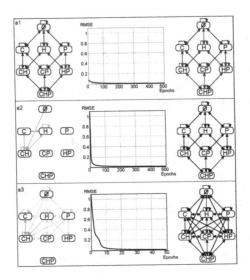

**Fig. 3.** Transition diagram before learning, error evolution and diagram after learning

However, in the learning of properties, in $a3$, the use of many input configurations led to a somewhat confusing diagram. To give a better understanding of the extracted knowledge, we converted such representation into a logic program, also to illustrate the flexibility of our system when presenting extracted information. Below, we show a subset of the program learned for rules regarding the next state of $CMet$.

- $\bigcirc CMet \leftarrow sCMetOn, \sim sCMetOff$
- $\bigcirc CMet \leftarrow \sim CMet, sCMetOn$
- $\bigcirc CMet \leftarrow CMet, \sim sCMetOff$
- $\bigcirc \neg CMet \leftarrow \sim sCMetOn, sCMetOff$
- $\bigcirc \neg CMet \leftarrow \sim CMet, \sim sCMetOn$
- $\bigcirc \neg CMet \leftarrow CMet, sCMetOff$

## 4.1    Integrating Knowledge Sources

Next, we extend the case study to illustrate the framework performance in applications involving incremental learning and interaction between different knowledge sources. We use a state variable $trP$ such that a positive assignment to $trP$ at a timepoint $t$ implies that $POn$ will be true at $t + 1$, independently of the other variables. This is represented through a property $X$. Again, three different cases were considered to evaluate the options on learning: in experiment $b1$, the network was generated by the same translation as in $a1$, extended with a single extra hidden neuron and an extra input and output neurons to represent $trP$. In experiment $b2$, the same extension was applied to the network generated through learning of examples only as in $a2$. In the $b1$ and $b2$ cases, the networks were subject to learning of properties representing the trigger condition. In $b3$ we used a network without background knowledge to learn from the set of examples and property $X$ simultaneously. This network also had ten input, seven hidden and four output neurons. In Fig. 4, we depict the evolution of RMSE in all three cases.

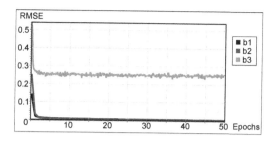

**Fig. 4.** Error evolution when learning the property regarding *trP*

In these experiments, the insertion of an extra variable doubled the number of states in the diagram, making its understanding more complex. Therefore, the extracted logic programs provide a clearer option to analyze the learned knowledge. While the error charts of $b1$ and $b2$ depict a good learning performance, the extracted logic programs do not correspond to the expected behaviour: In $b1$, $POn$ was always true and, in $b2$, a large number of specific rules were generated, without an apparent relation to the knowledge given to the network. Our conjecture as why this has happened is that the original knowledge of the network *fades away* during the learning of the new property, because only the information about $X$ is given to the network during training. Hence, we have decided to improve the framework with the possibility to reinforce the current knowledge of the network during training, by setting the desired output value applied to a neuron to 1 (resp. $-1$) when the obtained output is above a positive threshold $u$ (resp. below $-u$), and no information is given about $\alpha$ by the properties nor the examples. With this modification, we ran $b1$ and $b2$ again, obtaining similar error charts, but.

**Table 2.** Temporal knowledge learned in $b1$, $b2$ and $b3$ - redundant rules omitted in $b3$

| Experiment $b1$ | Experiment $b2$ | Experiment $b3$ |
|---|---|---|
| $\bigcirc POn \leftarrow tPOn$ | $\bigcirc POn \leftarrow tPOn, \sim tPOff$ | $\bigcirc POn \leftarrow tPOn$ |
| $\bigcirc POn \leftarrow trP$ | $\bigcirc POn \leftarrow trP$ | $\bigcirc POn \leftarrow trP$ |
| $\bigcirc POn \leftarrow POn, \sim tPOff$ | $\bigcirc POn \leftarrow POn, \sim tPOff$ | $\bigcirc POn \leftarrow POn, \sim tPOff$ |
| $\bigcirc \neg POn \leftarrow \sim trP, \sim tPOn, tPOff$ | $\bigcirc POn \leftarrow POn, tPOn$ | $...$ |
| $\bigcirc \neg POn \leftarrow \sim POn, \sim trP, \sim tPOn$ | $\bigcirc \neg POn \leftarrow \sim trP, \sim tPOn, tPOff$ | $\bigcirc \neg POn \leftarrow \sim trP, tPOff$ |
|  | $\bigcirc \neg POn \leftarrow \sim POn, \sim trP, tPOff$ | $\bigcirc \neg POn \leftarrow \sim POn, \sim trP, \sim tPOn$ |
|  | $\bigcirc \neg POn \leftarrow \sim POn, \sim trP, \sim tPOn$ |  |

## 4.2 Case Study Discussion

To analyze the importance of the results shown in last section, we will compare our framework to the system proposed in [1] that approach, where the same testbed was used to evaluate the a purely symbolic learning technique to refine a temporal specification. In terms of learning performance, we were able to verify that both approaches were successful in the considered applications. Our case study gave good evidence that our approach is capable of learning, and that the advantages of the use of neural networks, such as noise tolerance, can be verified for the different learning scenarios.

However, a direct comparison between the results of the techniques is difficult due to differences between their structure. The main difference between the approaches regards the actual goal of the learning task: In symbolic techniques such as [1], learning is applied to the task of refinement, i.e., generating a set of hypotheses capable to complement original incomplete knowledge according to the properties to be learned. In our work, the incomplete knowledge is represented into a numeric processor (neural network), that will define an actual (deterministic) transition function even to those cases not specified in the symbolic description. In that way, the learning task will perform a revision of this knowledge, instead of incremental refinement.

This gives to our framework a new and different range of applications. Our system is capable to deal with incorrect symbolic knowledge, instead of just incrementing an existing incomplete specification. The experiments above shown exactly that the networks were capable to change the underlying transition diagram, therefore being using the examples or properties to learn not only how to complement the original incomplete knowledge, but also to correct errors in such description.

It is also important to consider the language used for knowledge representation, when analyzing our framework in comparison with purely symbolic approaches. In our first example, we can see that the learning from properties resulted in a different diagram than the one obtained from learning from examples. This happened because of the limitations of our propositional logic programming language, which do not provide any resource to represent certain relations between variables at the same time point. Other limitation of our representation language is its deterministic nature, which might need to be tackled depending on the focus of the application.

This approach is still clear and powerful enough to the representation of a broad set of cases. Representation systems based on predicate logics might have more representation power, but often falls in issues like decidability and computational complexity. When comparing with the event-calculus based system in [1], one can notice that the different representation structures reflect the very purpose of the application. While event calculus provide powerful constructs to abduction and inductive learning, our logic programming systems present a clear definition of input and state variables, allowing a better integration with the core neural network used for the learning purposes. The simplicity of our language, together with the capacity of the neural networks to perform supervised learning, also caters for the possibility of learning from observed examples, which is an important aspect towards the implementation of Black Box Checking [12].

The numeric representation of the knowledge also allows some interesting possibilities. The association of numeric weights into the extracted transitions allows a probabilistic approach to overcome the deterministic limitation of the representation. Also, the incremental correction of weights in the learning process can be parameterized to give priority to the background knowledge or to the information to be learned, according with the configuration of the problem. In the last experiment, we have shown a simple example of how this can be done, by changing the desired values used on back-propagation according to the obtained output values.

# 5  Conclusions

This paper outlined a framework and presented a case study for representing, adapting and learning temporal knowledge in neural networks. The framework provides integration of different knowledge sources, allowing observed examples and desired properties to be used in the evolution of an initial temporal model, or in learning a completely new model. A case study has shown that the framework can achieve the desired tasks with good performance. The use a neural network caters for noise-tolerance in the learning process, which is useful when treating different sources of information.

We believe the methodology proposed in this work may serve as foundation for the development of richer models for the analysis and evolution of computing systems. Extensions to the formalisms used here to represent models and properties can enhance the applicability of the framework. As further work, we plan to integrate the framework with existing formal verification systems, such as the NuSMV model checker, and apply it to larger-scale testbeds on both reasoning and learning tasks.

**Acknowledgments.** Research supported by the Brazilian Research Council CNPq.

# References

1. Alrajeh, D., Ray, O., Russo, A., Uchitel, S.: Using abduction and induction for operational requirements elaboration. Journal of Applied Logic 7(3), 275–288 (2009)
2. Andrews, R., Diederich, J., Tickle, A.B.: A survey and critique of techniques for extracting rules from neural networks. Knowledge-based Systems 8(6), 373–389 (1995)
3. Clarke, E.M., Emerson, E.A., Sifakis, J.: Model checking: algorithmic verification and debugging. Commun. ACM 52(11), 74–84 (2009)
4. Feigenbaum, E.A.: Some challenges and grand challenges for computational intelligence. Journal of ACM 50(1), 32–40 (2003)
5. Fisher, M., Gabbay, D., Vila, L. (eds.): Handbook of temporal reasoning in artificial intelligence. Elsevier, Amsterdam (2005)
6. d'Avila Garcez, A.S., Zaverucha, G.: The connectionist inductive learning and logic programming system. Applied Intelligence 11(1), 59–77 (1999)
7. Groce, A., Peled, D., Yannakakis, M.: Adaptive model checking. In: Katoen, J.-P., Stevens, P. (eds.) TACAS 2002. LNCS, vol. 2280, pp. 357–370. Springer, Heidelberg (2002)
8. Haykin, S.: Neural Networks: A Compreensive Foundation, 2nd edn. Prentice Hall, Englewood Cliffs (1999)
9. Lamb, L.C., Borges, R.V., d'Avila Garcez, A.S.: A connectionist cognitive model for temporal synchronization and learning. In: AAAI 2007, pp. 827–832 (2007)
10. Mitchell, T.M.: Machine Learning. McGraw-Hill, New York (1997)
11. Muggleton, S., Raedt, L.: Inductive logic programming: Theory and methods. J. Logic Programming 19-20, 629–679 (1994)
12. Peled, D., Vardi, M.Y., Yannakakis, M.: Black box checking. J. Autom. Lang. Comb. 7(2), 225–246 (2001)

# Multi-Dimensional Deep Memory Atari-Go Players for Parameter Exploring Policy Gradients

Mandy Grüttner[1], Frank Sehnke[1], Tom Schaul[2], and Jürgen Schmidhuber[2]

[1] Faculty of Computer Science, Technische Universität München, Germany
[2] IDSIA, University of Lugano, Switzerland

**Abstract.** Developing superior artificial board-game players is a widely-studied area of Artificial Intelligence. Among the most challenging games is the Asian game of Go, which, despite its deceivingly simple rules, has eluded the development of artificial expert players. In this paper we attempt to tackle this challenge through a combination of two recent developments in Machine Learning. We employ Multi-Dimensional Recurrent Neural Networks with Long Short-Term Memory cells to handle the multi-dimensional data of the board game in a very natural way. In order to improve the convergence rate, as well as the ultimate performance, we train those networks using Policy Gradients with Parameter-based Exploration, a recently developed Reinforcement Learning algorithm which has been found to have numerous advantages over Evolution Strategies. Our empirical results confirm the promise of this approach, and we discuss how it can be scaled up to expert-level Go players.

## 1 Introduction

The two-player board game Go is one of the few such games that have resisted a panoply of attempts from Artificial Intelligence at building expert-level players. A broad range of techniques have been used, with some recent successes based on Monte Carlo Tree Search in combination with Reinforcement Learning (see e.g. [1,2]). A large body of research has dealt with the problem using techniques based on Neural Networks (see e.g. [3] for an overview), and that is also the approach taken in this paper.

The recently developed Neural Network architecture called Multi-dimensional Recurrent Neural Networks (MDRNN [4]) has been shown to be highly suited to domains like board games with multi-dimensional inputs. Unlike typical flat networks (e.g. multi-layer perceptrons), they can incorporate spacial structure as well as symmetries in a very natural way. It has also been shown that MDRNNs trained on small game boards can be scaled up to play well on larger game boards, even without further training [5].

Training neural networks to play well with direct policy search (i.e. optimizing the controller network's parameters) can be done in a number of ways. Recent work [5] has used state-of-the-art black-box optimization methods like CMA-ES [6], which unfortunately does not scale well to larger numbers of weights,

K. Diamantaras, W. Duch, L.S. Iliadis (Eds.): ICANN 2010, Part II, LNCS 6353, pp. 114–123, 2010.

as required for more complex playing behavior. Other methods like Evolution Strategies (ES [7]) scale better but suffer from a relatively slow convergence. We therefore train our Go-playing networks using the novel Policy Gradients with Parameter-based Exploration (PGPE, [8]), which have recently been shown to be very successful at optimizing the parameters of large Neural Network controllers [9]. PGPE replaces the usual explicit policy of Reinforcement Learning with an implicit one, defined by a distribution over the parameters of the controller. The fitness for each sequence only depends on one sample and is therefore less noisy.

In section 2.1 we briefly introduce the game of Go and the simplified variant used here. The MDRNN architectures are described in Section 2.2, and sections 2.3. Section 2.4 introduces the three algorithms used (ES, CMA-ES and PGPE, respectively). Then, in section 3, we train MDRNNs using PGPE, CMA-ES and ES to play Go, empirically establishing the advantages of PGPE over ES and CMA-ES. Conclusions and an outlook on future work are presented in Section 6.

## 2  Method

In this section we give the needed background on the game of Go, the Neural Network architectures (MDRNN and MDLSTM) and the training algorithms (ES, CMA-ES and PGPE).

### 2.1  Go and Capture Game

For the comparison of the different methods we are using the Capture Game, a simplified version of the two-player board game Go, a game frequently used to demonstrate the power of algorithms [1,11,12]. In Go, the players alternately make a move by placing a stone on the board. They aim to capture groups of opposing stones by enclosing them, see Figure 1 for an illustration. The goal is to capture more stones and to surround more territory than the opponent (see [3] for more details).

The Capture Game, also called Atari-Go or Ponnuki-Go, uses the same rules as Go, except passing is not allowed and the goal of the game simplified: the first

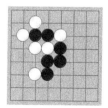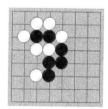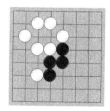

**Fig. 1.** A typical situation in Go: the turn is with white (left), who decides to capture a group of black stones (middle), which is then removed from the board (right)

player who captures at least one opposing stone wins. As this goal is achieved earlier and with less complex strategies, this variant of Go is often used for teaching new players.

Go is very interesting in combination with MDRNNs and MDLSTMs, because scalability is an important issue for board games [10]. The original game board consists of 361 (19x19) fields, but it is possible to use smaller board sizes for teaching, or to shorten the game length. As the main strategies stay the same, it is possible to train on a small board size and then play on bigger ones. In our case we could use small Neural Networks for the training and afterwards use scaled versions to play on bigger boards.

## 2.2    Multi-Dimensional Recurrent Neural Networks

Real world data often consists of multi-dimensional data such as videos, speech sequences or board games (as in our case). To use this data with regular Neural Networks (NN) the data must be transformed into a vector which leads to the loss of topological information about the inputs. Multi-dimensional Recurrent Neural Networks (MDRNN), instead, are capable of using high-dimensional data without this transformation. Furthermore MDRNNs can be trained on small problem instances (e.g. board sizes) and then used on bigger ones, a process we call *scaling*.

Compared to standard Recurrent Neural Networks (RNN), which can only deal with a single (time-)dimension, MDRNNs [4] are able to handle multi-dimensional sequences and were used successfully for vision [13], handwriting recognition [14] and different applications of Go [5,15,10,3].

In the case of Go, the single time dimension is replaced by the two space dimensions of the game board. It would be worthwhile to get information about the whole board. Therefore we introduce *swiping* hidden layers which *swipe* diagonally over the board. The four directions that arise out of the described situation are the following: $D = \{\nearrow, \searrow, \nwarrow, \swarrow\}$.

As exemplary hidden layer we describe the layer $h_\nearrow$, which swipes diagonally over the board from bottom-left to top-right, in detail. At each position $(i, j)$ of the board we define the activation $h_{\nearrow(i,j)}$ as a function of the weighted input $in_{(i,j)}$ and the weighted activations of the previous steps $h_{\nearrow(i-1,j)}$ and $h_{\nearrow(i,j-1)}$ which leads to:

$$h_{\nearrow(i,j)} = f(w_i * in_{(i,j)} + w_h * h_{\nearrow(i-1,j)} + w_h * h_{\nearrow(i,j-1)}) \qquad (1)$$

where $f$ is a function (e.g. $f = tanh$). On the boundaries fixed values are used: $h_{\nearrow(i,0)} = h_{\nearrow(0,i)} = w_b$. An illustration of $h_\nearrow$ for the game Go can be found in Figure 2. The output layer consists of the combination of all swiping directions and could be described as following:

$$out_{i,j} = g\left(\sum_{\diamond \in D} w_o * h_{\diamond(i,j)}\right) \qquad (2)$$

where $g$ is typically the sigmoid function.

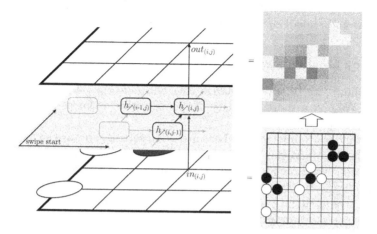

**Fig. 2.** On the left hand side the schematic illustration of a MDRNN shows how the output consists of a swiping hidden layer in one direction. The right hand side illustrates the output (top) to the corresponding input (bottom). The brighter the square, the lower the preference to perform the corresponding move (source [5]).

With the derived equation we have access to the whole game board. Nevertheless the reach of the access is limited by how fast the activations decay through the recurrent connections. This problem could be solved by using Long Short-Term Memory (LSTM) cells [4]. LSTMs are using gates to protect recurrent states over the time and where used successfully in [4,3,13]. The integration of LSTMs in MDRNNs by using swiping layers consisting of LSTM cells is called MDLSTM [5].

## 2.3   Evolution Strategies

Evolution Strategies (ES) are optimization techniques which are based on the principles of natural evolution, producing consecutive generations of individuals. During a generation a selection method is used to select specific individuals which form the new generation by recombination and mutation [16,17]. Individuals can be solution candidates of any problem domain that is fully defined by a parameter set. Neural Networks (NN) and in this case MDRNNs fall into this class of problem domains, assuming the architecture of the NN is kept fixed, as the behavior of the NN is fully defined by its weight matrix.

Adapting continuous paramters by adding normally distributed noise is a typical mutation method. We use for our comparisons the local mutation operator and Covariance Matrix Adaption Evolution Strategy (CMA-ES) [6]. CMA-ES uses a covariance matrix $C \in \mathbb{R}^{n \times n}$, where $n$ is the number of parameters for the mutation and achieves a derandomized correlated mutation. The covariance matrix approach is only feasible in relatively low-dimensional problem domains, because the size of the matrix grows with $n^2$. Here again it is advantageous that

MDRNNs are scalable and that we can train the behavior on smaller instances of the game and scale it up to the full game size after learning.

## 2.4    Policy Gradients with Parameter-Based Exploration

In what follows, we briefly summarize [18], outlining the derivation that leads to PGPE. We give a short summary of the algorithm as far as it is needed for the rest of the paper.

In the standard Reinforcement Learning (RL) setting a reward signal at every time step in the Markovian decision process is given. We can associate a cumulative reward $r$ with each history $h$ by summing over the rewards at each time step: $r(h) = \sum_{t=1}^{T} r_t$. This makes the setting strictly episodic (natural for board games). In this setting, the goal of RL is to find the parameters $\theta$ that maximize the agent's expected reward

$$J(\theta) = \int_H p(h|\theta) r(h) dh \tag{3}$$

An obvious way to maximize $J(\theta)$ is to find $\nabla_\theta J$ and use it to carry out gradient ascent. Noting that the reward for a particular history is independent of $\theta$, and using the standard identity $\nabla_x y(x) = y(x) \nabla_x \log y(x)$, we can write

$$\nabla_\theta J(\theta) = \int_H \nabla_\theta p(h|\theta) r(h) dh = \int_H p(h|\theta) \nabla_\theta \log p(h|\theta) r(h) dh \tag{4}$$

PGPE replaces the probabilistic policy commonly used in PG with a probability distribution over the parameters $\theta$, where $\rho$ are the parameters determining the distribution over $\theta$. The expected reward with a given $\rho$ is

$$J(\rho) = \int_\Theta \int_H p(h, \theta|\rho) r(h) dh d\theta. \tag{5}$$

Noting that $h$ is conditionally independent of $\rho$ given $\theta$, we have $p(h, \theta|\rho) = p(h|\theta)p(\theta|\rho)$ and therefore $\nabla_\rho \log p(h, \theta|\rho) = \nabla_\rho \log p(\theta|\rho)$. Substituting this into Eq. (5) yields Eq. (6) under the notion of several conditionally independencies.

$$\nabla_\rho J(\rho) = \int_\Theta \int_H p(h|\theta)p(\theta|\rho) \nabla_\rho \log p(\theta|\rho) r(h) dh d\theta \tag{6}$$

where $p(h|\theta)$ is the probability distribution over the parameters $\theta$ and $\rho$ are the parameters determining the distribution over $\theta$. Clearly, integrating over the entire space of histories and parameters is unfeasible, and we therefore resort to sampling methods. This is done by first choosing $\theta$ from $p(\theta|\rho)$, then running the agent to generate $h$ from $p(h|\theta)$:

$$\nabla_\rho J(\rho) \approx \frac{1}{N} \sum_{n=1}^{N} \nabla_\rho \log p(\theta|\rho) r(h^n) \tag{7}$$

If we assume that $\rho$ consists of a set of means $\{\mu_i\}$ and standard deviations $\{\sigma_i\}$ that determine an independent normal distribution for each parameter $\theta_i$ in $\theta$. some rearrangement gives the following forms for the derivative of $\log p(\theta|\rho)$ with respect to $\mu_i$ and $\sigma_i$:

$$\nabla_{\mu_i} \log p(\theta|\rho) = \frac{(\theta_i - \mu_i)}{\sigma_i^2} \qquad \nabla_{\sigma_i} \log p(\theta|\rho) = \frac{(\theta_i - \mu_i)^2 - \sigma_i^2}{\sigma_i^3}, \qquad (8)$$

which can then be substituted into (7) to approximate the $\mu$ and $\sigma$ gradients that gives the PGPE update rules. We also used the for PGPE standard Symmetric Sampling (SyS) and the reward normalization commonly used for PGPE. See [18] for details.

## 3    Experiments

In this section we compare PGPE with ES and CMA-ES on different board sizes and with different MDRNNs. For ES we chose a $(\mu, \lambda)$-strategy where the $\mu$ best individuals are chosen from the whole population which has size $\lambda$. In particular, we applied local mutation and used $\mu = 5$ and $\lambda = 30$ which are standard values. The implementations of the Capture Game, the algorithms and the Neural Network architectures are available in the open-source Machine Learning library PyBrain [19].

### 3.1    Fitness Function

The evaluation of the individuals is realized with a Greedy Go Player, implemented in Java using depth-first search. It first checks whether it can capture and thereby defeat the opponent directly. Otherwise it tries to defend its position, by counting the number of liberties for its groups of stones. If one of its groups only has one liberty, and therefore he would be defeated during the next opponents move, the Greedy Player tries to enlarge this group. As a third choice the Greedy player uses a heuristic. Let $p$ and $q$ be the number of liberties of the weakest group of the Greedy Player and the opponent Player. The Greedy Player chooses a valid move which maximizes the sum $p - q$.

By reason of implementation the Greedy Player may pass. As the Capture Game does not allow this move, we replace it with a random move instead. Primarily this happens during games with strong opponents.

To calculate the fitness we averaged 40 games which were played against the Greedy Player. The fitness values are scaled from -1 (individual never wins against Greedy Player) up to +1 (individual always wins against Greedy Player).

### 3.2    Network Topology

With the given architectures of MDRNNs (MDLSTMs) it follows that we have 12 (52) parameters which have to be evaluated. We will give a short calculation for

MDRNNs. As mentioned in 2.2 our network consists of four (identical) hidden layers. The hidden layer is modeled by $k$ neurons. Each neuron is connected with a weight $w_o$ to the output layer and two weights $w_i$ to the input layer. Furthermore the neurons of the hidden layer are fully connected to each other which leads to $k^2$ weights which we call $w_h$. Additionally we have $k$ weights $w_b$ which are fixed and model the boarders of the recurrent connections. All together we get $k + 2k + k^2 + k = 4k + k^2$ weights. Taking into consideration the additional weights of LSTM-cells, a similar reasoning gives us $16k + 5k^2$ weights for MDLSTMs. We decided to use $k = 2$ neurons, the smallest number that allows for qualitatively interesting strategies, which leads to 12 (52) weights. The decisions was taken concerning previous results (see [5]). A larger number of neurons mostly results in a faster conversion, but increases the complexity of the network and therefore the calculation time. However, the use of larger board sizes would make a larger number ($k = 5$) of neurons more feasible.

### 3.3   Results

We trained MDRNNs and MDLSTMs for the board sizes 5 and 7. Furthermore we used 12000 episodes and averaged over 10 independent runs per data point.

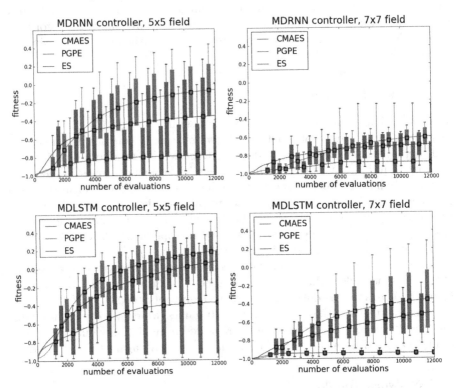

**Fig. 3.** Illustration of the four different types of networks. The plots give the fitness for each of the 12000 episodes as well as the standard deviation and min/max-values (average over 10 independent experiments).

Figure 3 illustrates the results. The fitness value determines the average fitness of a generation. As we can see PGPE mostly converges faster than ES and CMA-ES. Primarily with the increasing of the number of parameters the advantages of PGPE towards ES increase.

Nevertheless neither ES nor PGPE has converged within the 12000 episodes to the maximum fitness value 1. This holds for the best individuals of each generation, too. In our experiments the best result of a single run of PGPE converges to 0.5 which is equivalent to a victory rate of 75% (see Figure 3 MDLSTM controller, 5x5 field). That is why ongoing learning could still improve the results.

Furthermore the use of MDLSTMs leads to better results than MDRNNs. This strength of MDLSTMs is accompanied by a long training time towards MDRNNs. Our observations are similar to [4,5,3].

Another fact we could read from our resulting plots is a big standard deviation. This observation leads to the suggestion (see section 6) that the standard meta parameters for PGPE and ES are not optimal for this problem domain and that meta-parameters that favor a more thorough exploration combined with longer learning cycles should provide better and more stable results.

## 4  Discussion

As is common for PGPE, the results of 3.3 start off with the rather slow phase of searching for the attractor of the global optima. This gives the PGPE curves the typical S-shape [18]. The ES curves form the usual saturation shape, with a faster convergence early on. However, PGPE takes over soon in the convergence process and then converges faster and onto a higher fitness level than ES. The resulting curve of CMA-ES does not reach the results of the other two methods. Especially while using a game board size of 7x7 CMA-ES prematurely converges to a low fitness value. CMA-ES seems to be to greedy for this task and thus converges premature.

One general observation from our experiments was that the longer the episodes and the higher the number of parameters, the more PGPE outperforms ES (in average fitness).

For general Go and other real-world problems more episodes are necessary. Future applications with stacked MDRNNs are possible, as suggested in [10], and for such applications PGPE seems more appropriate than ES or CMA-ES.

In summary, we find that PGPE performs better in finding good game behaviors, already on the smallest scaling level. It also scales better to scenarios with more episodes, and to higher dimensionalities of controllers.

## 5  Future Work

An interesting future application would be the research of the influence of PGPE on scaling MDRNNs as well as determining the best ratio between game board size and PGPE setup (especially using non standard meta-parameters

like smaller step sizes for more thorough exploration and better final behavior).
Besides, PGPE could be used for relearning the scaled controllers.

As suggested for ES in [3], we could use Co-Evolution to further improve
the PGPE results. For PGPE this would mean the fitness is evaluated not only
against the Java Player but also against the best learned controller(s) so far, and
the controller defined by the mean of the current parameter set.

Furthermore, adaptively increasing the number of games per fitness evaluation
could be used to speed up learning. In the early phase of learning, 3-4 games
would be enough for an evaluation step, whereas up to 100 games might be
necessary later on, to calculate a fitness value accurate enough to distinguish
the slight changes in performance at that point.

As mentioned in section 3, the high standard deviation suggests that a higher
rate of exploration would be favorable for the overall performance and stability.
For PGPE this would correspond to decreasing the values of the two step sizes
that are normally set to $\alpha_\mu = 0.2$ and $\alpha_\sigma = 0.1$. Not surprisingly however, this
more thorough exploration comes at the price of longer convergence time.

## 6    Conclusion

In this paper we have introduced different methods of Machine Learning: PGPE,
an algorithm based on a gradient based search through model parameter space,
ES and CMA-ES, based on population based search. We compared these methods
on the task of playing the Capture Game, a variant of Go, on small boards. Our
experiments allow us to conclude that PGPE is advantageous on the given task,
and also appears to scale better to larger and more difficult variants of the Go
game. This is in line with similar results for PGPE on different benchmarks [18].

## References

1. Bouzy, B., Chaslot, G.: Monte-Carlo Go Reinforcement Learning Experiments.
   In: IEEE 2006 Symposium on Computational Intelligence in Games, pp. 187–194.
   IEEE, Los Alamitos (2006)
2. Gelly, S., Silver, D.: Combining online and offline knowledge in UCT. In: ICML,
   vol. 227 (2007)
3. Grüttner, M.: Evolving Multidimensional Recurrent Neural Networks for the Capture Game in Go (2008)
4. Graves, A.: Supervised Sequence Labelling with Recurrent Neural Networks. PhD
   thesis, Technische Universität München (2007)
5. Schaul, T., Schmidhuber, J.: Scalable neural networks for board games. In: Alippi,
   C., et al. (eds.) ICANN 2009. LNCS, vol. 5768, pp. 1005–1014. Springer, Heidelberg
   (2009)
6. Hansen, N., Ostermeier, A.: Completely derandomized self-adaptation in evolution
   strategies. Evolutionary Computation 9, 159–195 (2001)
7. Schwefel, H.: Evolution and optimum seeking. Wiley, New York (1995)
8. Sehnke, F., Osendorfer, C., Rückstieß, T., Graves, A., Peters, J., Schmidhuber, J.:
   Policy gradients with parameter-based exploration for control. In: Kůrková, V.,
   Neruda, R., Koutník, J. (eds.) ICANN 2008, Part I. LNCS, vol. 5163, pp. 387–396.
   Springer, Heidelberg (2008)

9. Rückstieß, T., Sehnke, F., Schaul, T., Wierstra, D., Sun, Y., Schmidhuber, J.: Exploring parameter space in reinforcement learning. Paladyn 1(1), 1–12 (2010)
10. Schaul, T., Schmidhuber, J.: A scalable neural network architecture for board games. In: Proceedings of the IEEE Symposium on Computational Intelligence in Games (CIG 2008) (2008)
11. Konidaris, G., Shell, D., Oren, N.: Evolving Neural Networks for the Capture Game. In: Proceedings of the SAICSIT Postgraduate Symposium (2002)
12. Stanley, K.O., Miikkulainen, R.: Evolving a Roving Eye for Go (2004)
13. Graves, A., Fernández, S., Schmidhuber, J.: Multi-Dimensional Recurrent Neural Networks (2007)
14. Liwicki, M., Graves, A., Fernández, S., Bunke, H., Schmidhuber, J.: A novel approach to on-line handwriting recognition based on bidirectional long short-term memory networks. In: Proc. 9th Int. Conf. on Document Analysis and Recognition, pp. 367–371 (September 2007)
15. Wu, L., Baldi, P.: A scalable machine learning approach to go. In: Advances in Neural Information Processing Systems, vol. 19, pp. 1521–1528. MIT Press, Cambridge (2007)
16. Streichert, F., Ulmer, H.: JavaEvA - A Java Framework for Evolutionary Algorithms. Technical Report WSI-2005-06, Centre for Bioinformatics Tübingen, University of Tübingen (2005)
17. Streichert, F.: Evolutionary Algorithms in Multi-Modal and Multi-Objective Environments. PhD thesis (2007)
18. Sehnke, F., Osendorfer, C., Rückstieß, T., Graves, A., Peters, J., Schmidhuber, J.: Parameter-exploring policy gradients. Neural Networks 23(4), 551–559 (2010)
19. Schaul, T., Bayer, J., Wierstra, D., Sun, Y., Felder, M., Sehnke, F., Rückstieß, T., Schmidhuber, J.: PyBrain. Journal of Machine Learning Research 11, 743–746 (2010)

# Layered Motion Segmentation with a Competitive Recurrent Network

Julian Eggert, Joerg Deigmoeller, and Volker Willert

Honda Research Institute (HRI) Europe GmbH,
Carl-Legien-Str. 30, 63073 Offenbach/Main, Germany
{julian.eggert,joerg.deigmoeller}@honda-ri.de
Technical University of Darmstadt, Control Theory and Robotics Lab,
Landgraf-Georg-Str. 4, 64283 Darmstadt, Germany
volker.willert@rtr.tu-darmstadt.de

**Abstract.** Using local motion information data such as that obtained
from optical flow, we present a network for a multilayered segmentation
into motion regions that are governed by affine motion patterns. Using an
energy-based competitive multilayer architecture based on non-negative
activations and multiplicative update rules, we show how the network
can perform segmentation tasks that require a combination of affine estimation with local integration and competition constraints.

**Keywords:** Motion segmentation, layering, affine, competitive multi-
layer networks, multiplicative gradient descent.

## 1 Introduction

Motion-based segmentation and motion-based layer separation are essential steps
for the decomposition of dynamic visual scenes. The topic has been investigated
in a series of early publications by commonly either combining locally estimated
motion models [1,2] or estimating the spatial support of mixture models [3,4].
The latter frequently appears in the realm of probabilistic approaches, formu-
lating the problem in terms of maximum-likelihood of the observed data.

A common starting point of the approaches is a motion field estimation as
a preprocessing step. Subsequently, they introduce parameterized models for
describing subregions in the motion field, where almost all of these approaches
assume affine motion models. In order to consider spatial constraints, Markov
Random Fields (MRFs) are commonly used to support regions of similar motion
[5,6]. As such approaches optimize conditions in a pixels neighborhood, they do
not explicitly consider model competition at certain pixel positions.

In this paper, we used a dynamic neural network approach to combine the
spatial distribution of labels (*intra-label integration*) with further constraints on
*inter-label competition*. Such a model is motivated by previous work on competitive layer models [7]. The network dynamics within this work are deterministic
and follow a gradient-descent-like update rule, updating motion region *parameter estimation* and motion region *labeling* in alternating steps. The dynamics

K. Diamantaras, W. Duch, L.S. Iliadis (Eds.): ICANN 2010, Part II, LNCS 6353, pp. 124–133, 2010.

can be implemented very efficiently as block operations on a labeling grid. Compared to MRFs which rely on stochastic techniques, this deterministic relaxation method is a computational much faster approach.

Sec. 2 introduces the network for multi-region motion segmentation in detail. As a proof-of-concept, we present results from two motion sequences in Sec. 3. These include the MPEG Flower Garden sequence as well as an example of a moving hand filmed by a moving observer. In Sec. 4, we finally conclude the paper.

## 2   Dynamic Neural Network for Motion Segmentation

In this paper, we start with a sequence of 2D images. For each consecutive pair of images, an approximation of the 2D *motion field* in the images is obtained by calculation of a dense optical flow in the form of velocity vectors $\mathbf{v}(\mathbf{p})$ at positions $\mathbf{p}$. In our particular implementation, we use a spatiotemporally integrating, patch-based method for calculating optical flow [8].

In this section, we introduce the main components of our motion estimation network. In Sec. 2.1, we briefly explain the calculation of parameters for the affine description of motion regions by applying weighted regression on a motion field. In Sec. 2.2, we present a competitive recurrent network for dynamically updating activations that encode the tendency of each image position to belong to the different motion models. In Sec. 2.3, we combine both approaches within a single energy function that drives the entire system.

### 2.1   Motion Fields Described by Affine Models

We assume the motion field to be composed of large spatial regions that can be approximated by *affine homographies*. This is valid if the images recorded by a camera are rectified and the 3D scene contains planar surfaces where changes in depth between objects and camera are small compared to their distance.

In the following, we introduce image coordinates $\mathbf{p} = \{p_x, p_y\}^T$ and motion vectors $\mathbf{v} = \{v_x, v_y\}^T$, as well as homogeneous image coordinates $\hat{\mathbf{p}} = \{p_x, p_y, 1\}^T$ and homogeneous motion vectors $\hat{\mathbf{v}} = \{v_x, v_y, 1\}^T$. The goal is to find $N_A$ affine matrices $A_k$, where each matrix describes the motion field for a certain region. In other words, an assumed affine homography is suitable for describing a region of the image when a large amount of the measured motion vectors $\mathbf{v}(\hat{\mathbf{p}})$ can be approximated by motion vectors $\mathbf{v}_{A_k}(\hat{\mathbf{p}})$:

$$\mathbf{v}(\hat{\mathbf{p}}) \approx \mathbf{v}_{A_k}(\hat{\mathbf{p}}) = A_k \hat{\mathbf{p}} = \begin{pmatrix} a_{k,11} & a_{k,12} & a_{k,13} \\ a_{k,21} & a_{k,22} & a_{k,23} \end{pmatrix} \begin{pmatrix} p_x \\ p_y \\ 1 \end{pmatrix}. \tag{1}$$

Assuming that the motion field has been measured at $N_\mathbf{p}$ positions $\mathbf{p}_i := \{p_{i,x}, p_{i,y}\}^T$, we have $\mathbf{v}_i := \mathbf{v}(\mathbf{p}_i)$. Since we want to describe the entire motion field by all $N_A$ affine models simultaneously, we introduce weight factors $w_{i,k} \geq 0$ which indicate the *affiliation* of a motion vector $\mathbf{v}_i$ to an affine model $A_k$. For fixed weight factors, and assuming the underlying parametric model of residuals $r_{i,k}$ to be Gaussian, we can formulate a cost function $G(\{A_k\})$ that is the weighted Euclidean distance between measured and expected motion:

$$G(\{A_k\}) = \sum_k G_k(A_k) = \sum_k \sum_i w_{i,k}\|\mathbf{v}(\hat{\mathbf{p}}_i) - \mathbf{v}_{A_k}(\hat{\mathbf{p}}_i)\|^2$$
$$= \sum_k \sum_i w_{i,k}\underbrace{\|\mathbf{v}(\hat{\mathbf{p}}_i) - A_k\hat{\mathbf{p}}_i\|^2}_{:=r_{i,k}}. \qquad (2)$$

For this case, a weighted linear regression can be used for the calculation of the affine models. For each affine model $A_k$ describing a region of the motion field characterized by the affiliation weights $w_{i,k}$, the affine parameters are then estimated by minimizing the cost function $G(\{A_k\})$:

$$A_k^* = \arg\min_{A_k} G(\{A_k\}) = \arg\min_{A_k} G_k(A_k). \qquad (3)$$

The cost function gets minimal if:

$$\nabla_{A_k}\left\{\sum_i w_{i,k}[v_{i,x} - (a_{k,11}\ p_{i,x} + a_{k,12}\ p_{i,y} + a_{k,13})]^2\right.$$
$$\left. + \sum_i w_{i,k}[v_{i,y} - (a_{k,21}\ p_{i,x} + a_{k,22}\ p_{i,y} + a_{k,23})]^2\right\} = 0. \qquad (4)$$

This in turn leads to a linear equation system in the coefficients of the $A_k$'s, which can be solved analytically in a straightforward way (see Appendix).

Nevertheless, this only applies for *fixed* affiliation weights $w_{i,k}$. If these are given by some preprocessing step (like segmentation) we would be done. However, we want to simultaneously estimate $A_k$ *and* $w_{i,k}$. The first step towards this is to consider that the affiliation weights act as a kind of affiliation probability, i.e. the different models are loosely coupled via their affiliations by a normalization condition $\sum_k w_{i,k} = 1$ and $w_{i,k} > 0$. Furthermore, beyond the normalization condition, we let the models $A_k$ compete explicitly for their affiliations, i.e., a model $A_k$ which best describes the motion field at location $\mathbf{p}_i$ receives a significant affiliation weight $w_{i,k}$. In the following section, the implementation of this competition by means of a recurrent neural network is presented.

## 2.2   Extraction of Motion Layers with a Recurrent Neural Network

We have seen that the considerations of the previous section assumed the affiliation weights to be fixed or determined by external means. To make affiliation weights compete for their models, we apply a competitive neural network which consists of a grid-like arrangement of neurons at image positions $\mathbf{p}_i$ with activities $a_{i,k}$ for all positions and all models $A_k$.

The network dynamics are determined by energy function $E(\{a_{i,k}\})$ of all neuronal activities $\{a_{i,k}\}$. It can be considered as a layered neural network with a fixed number of $N_A$ layers (indexed here by $k = 1, ..., N_A$), and each layer consisting of $N_\mathbf{p}$ positions (indexed here by $i = 1, ..., N_\mathbf{p}$, but which for practical purposes should be arranged in x and y coordinates so as to map with the input image).

Each neuron receives two sources of input. One, $h_{i,k}$, is a driving input, which originates from outside of the network and conveys a kind of "sensory" support for the neuron $a_{i,k}$. The second is an input originating from recurrent connections from within the network itself, i.e., from the other neurons. This input serves to trigger a competition between the neurons on different layers, and for imposing a spatial coupling between different positions. The energy function therefore comprises three terms, one for the driving input (d), one for the layer competition (l) and one for the spatial coupling term (c):

$$E(\{a_{i,k}\}) = E_d(\{a_{i,k}\}) + E_l(\{a_{i,k}\}) + E_c(\{a_{i,k}\}) = -\lambda_1 \sum_i \sum_k h_{i,k} a_{i,k}$$

$$+\lambda_2 \frac{1}{2} \sum_i \sum_k \sum_{k'} W_k^{k'} a_{i,k'} a_{i,k} - \lambda_3 \frac{1}{2} \sum_i \sum_{i'} \sum_k K_i^{i'} a_{i,k} a_{i',k}. \quad (5)$$

Subsequently, we assume a positivity constraint $a_{i,k} > 0$ and $h_{i,k} > 0$. The energy function should be minimized which is the case e.g., for high activities at those neurons with a large (positive) driving input $h_{i,k}$, and which are consistent with the layer competition and the spatial coupling conditions.

In Eq. (5), we have restricted ourselves to a layer competition term which acts over all layers (corresponding to the motion models $A_k$) but exclusively on neurons at the same position $\mathbf{p}_i$. This is parameterized by the kernel $W_k^{k'}$, which quantifies the competition between the activities $a_{i,k'}$ and $a_{i,k}$. Similarly, we use a kernel $K_i^{i'}$ to express the spatial coupling within one layer. This segregation into inter-layer and spatial coupling is not strictly necessary so that a fully connected network may also be used, but for the purpose presented here it is sufficient. Both kernels $W_k^{k'}$ and $K_i^{i'}$ are chosen to be symmetric and positive. The structure of the neural network, including layerwise and spatial coupling is illustrated in Fig. 1.

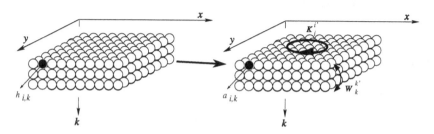

**Fig. 1.** Structure of the recurrent neural network. Each layer of neurons represents the affiliation to a specific motion model through normalized activities $a_{i,k}$ (right). The network is initialized by the driving input $h_{i,k}$ (left).

The dynamics of the activities are motivated by standard gradient descent considerations. We therefore obtain $a_{i,k} \sim -\nabla_{a_{i,k}} E$ with:

$$\nabla_{a_{i,k}} E = -\lambda_1 h_{i,k} + \lambda_2 \frac{1}{2} \sum_{k'} W_k^{k'} a_{i,k'} - \lambda_3 \frac{1}{2} \sum_{i'} K_i^{i'} a_{i',k} . \tag{6}$$

For accurate motion model separation, we would like the activities to be interpretable as affiliation probabilities to different motion models. This implies that the activities should always remain positive and they should always be normalized over the layer index, so that $\sum_k a_{i,k} = 1$. Neither condition is fulfilled by dynamics according to Eq. (6).

We impose the first condition, positivity, by using a multiplicative update rule motivated by exponentiated gradient descent and non-negative matrix factorization (NMF) techniques, similar to [9]. In our case, we separate positive and negative terms of the gradient from Eq. (6) according to:

$$\nabla_{a_{i,k}} E := \nabla_{a_{i,k}} E^+ - \nabla_{a_{i,k}} E^- \tag{7}$$

and express the dynamics by the fixpoint condition:

$$a_{i,k} \leftarrow a_{i,k} \frac{\nabla_{a_{i,k}} E^-}{\nabla_{a_{i,k}} E^+} . \tag{8}$$

Intuitively, as the dynamics approaches the minimum of the energy function, $\nabla_{a_{i,k}} E^+ \to \nabla_{a_{i,k}} E^-$ such that $\frac{\nabla_{a_{i,k}} E^-}{\nabla_{a_{i,k}} E^+} \to 1$ and the activities approach a static state. In addition to the advantage of positivity, the multiplicative update rule does not depend on a step size as gradient descent does.

The second condition, having normalized activities, is not trivial to impose. We cannot modify the activities according to Eq. (8) and then simply normalize the activities at each time step because normalization changes the overall energy $E(\{a_{i,k}\})$ in an unpredictable way, leading for example to a potential energy increase (instead of a decrease). Instead, we can either calculate the gradient and then modify the activities by projecting it onto the "normalized energy submanifold" or we can search for dynamics that have a continuous normalization condition built-in. The latter is the case for energy $E(\{\bar{a}_{i,k}\})$ based on positionwise (resp. columnwise) normalized activities

$$\bar{a}_{i,k} := \frac{a_{i,k}}{\sum_{k'} a_{i,k'}} . \tag{9}$$

Now, we are searching for the dynamics of the activities that minimizes $E(\{\bar{a}_{i,k}\})$ (instead of $E(\{a_{i,k}\})$). This can be done by the multiplicative update rule according to Eq. (8) except that activities are now normalized:

$$a_{i,k} \leftarrow a_{i,k} \frac{\nabla_{a_{i,k}} E^-(\{\bar{a}_{i,k}\})}{\nabla_{a_{i,k}} E^+(\{\bar{a}_{i,k}\})} . \tag{10}$$

Accordingly, the derivative of the energy function changes to $\nabla_{a_{i,k}} E(\{\bar{a}_{i,k}\}) = \sum_{k'} \nabla_{\bar{a}_{i,k'}} E(\{\bar{a}_{i,k}\}) \nabla_{a_{i,k}} \bar{a}_{i,k'}$.

In summary, if we apply the update rule (Eq. (10)) followed by activity normalization (Eq. (9)), we get an activity dynamics that minimizes the energy function under the constraints of positive and normalized activities.

In our implementation, we further used a layer competition kernel $W_k^{k'} := \delta(k, k')$. The detailed activity dynamics from Eq. (10) is then:

$$a_{i,k} \leftarrow a_{i,k} \frac{\lambda_1 h_{i,k} + \lambda_2 \sum_{k'} \bar{a}_{i,k'}^2 + \lambda_3 \sum_{i'} K_i^{i'} \bar{a}_{i',k}}{\lambda_1 \sum_{k'} h_{i,k'} \bar{a}_{i,k'} + \lambda_2 \bar{a}_{i,k} + \lambda_3 \sum_{k'} \sum_{i'} K_i^{i'} \bar{a}_{i',k'} \bar{a}_{i,k'}} \tag{11}$$

which at each update should be followed by normalization Eq. (9). Therefore, Eq. (11) is an iterative descent towards the minimization of the energy $E(\{\bar{a}_{i,k}\})$.

## 2.3  Combined Segregation and Affine Model Estimation

In Sec. 2.1 we explained how to estimate a number of affine models to describe partial motion fields of an image sequence for pre-set model affiliation weights $w_{i,k}$. In Sec. 2.2 we introduced a modified recurrent, layered network to let the affiliation weights compete for their models, triggered by the driving input $h_{i,k}$. The weights are encoded in different layers and incorporate through spatial coupling constraints. In this section, we fuse the energy functions of Sec. 2.1 and Sec. 2.2 by combining the affiliation weights and the driving input. This allows iterative calculations to estimate the motion models and the best affiliation probabilities for the models.

We assume the affiliation weights to be represented directly by the activities of the layered network, i.e., $w_{i,k} \equiv a_{i,k}$. Since by construction the activities $a_{i,k}$ remain positive and normalized if deployed according to the neuronal dynamics from Sec. 2.2, they fulfill the conditions postulated for the weights in Sec. 2.1.

Furthermore, we assume the driving input to originate from the consideration of how well a given model $A_k$ serves to describe a motion flow $\mathbf{v}$ at the positions $\mathbf{p}_i$ indicated by, and weighted with, the model affiliation probabilities $a_{i,k}$. Using the considerations from Sec. 2.1, the driving input should be large when the measured flow and the model-based flow match, in our case by using:

$$h_{i,k} \sim e^{-\frac{1}{2\sigma^2}||\mathbf{v}(\hat{\mathbf{p}}_i) - A_k \hat{\mathbf{p}}_i||^2} . \tag{12}$$

Finally, the complete energy equation becomes:

$$E(\{a_{i,k}\}, \{A_k\}) = -\lambda_1 \sum_i \sum_k e^{-\frac{1}{2\sigma^2}||\mathbf{v}(\hat{\mathbf{p}}_i) - A_k \hat{\mathbf{p}}_i||^2} a_{i,k}$$

$$+\lambda_2 \frac{1}{2} \sum_i \sum_k \sum_{k'} W_k^{k'} a_{i,k'} a_{i,k} - \lambda_3 \sum_i \sum_{i'} \sum_k K_i^{i'} a_{i,k} a_{i',k} . \tag{13}$$

This energy function now has to be solved simultaneously for the models $A_k$ and the activities $a_{i,k}$, with the additional constraints of positive and normalized activities. We then proceed as before with gradient descent, taking

$$\nabla_{a_{i,k}} E(\{\bar{a}_{i,k}\}, \{A_k\}) \tag{14}$$

and

$$\nabla_{A_k} E(\{\bar{a}_{i,k}\}, \{A_k\}) \tag{15}$$

to update the activities and the models in alternating steps for fixed models and activities, respectively. As a shortcut, during the model update according to Eq. (15) we assume that at positions where the layer activity is large, the corresponding model is already matching well (which is the case close to the minimum of the energy function). This means that $\mathbf{v}(\hat{\mathbf{p}}_i) \approx A_k \hat{\mathbf{p}}_i$ and hence we can approximate

$$h_{i,k} \approx 1 - \frac{1}{2\sigma^2}||\mathbf{v}(\hat{\mathbf{p}}_i) - A_k\hat{\mathbf{p}}_i||^2 \tag{16}$$

so that

$$E(\{\bar{a}_{i,k}\}, \{A_k\}) \approx -\lambda_1 N_{\mathbf{p}} \ + \ \lambda_1 \sum_i \sum_k \frac{1}{2\sigma^2}||\mathbf{v}(\hat{\mathbf{p}}_i) - A_k\hat{\mathbf{p}}_i||^2 \ \bar{a}_{i,k}$$

$$+\lambda_2 \frac{1}{2} \sum_i \sum_k \sum_{k'} W_k^{k'} \bar{a}_{i,k'}\bar{a}_{i,k} - \lambda_3 \sum_i \sum_{i'} \sum_k K_i^{i'} \bar{a}_{i,k}\bar{a}_{i',k} \ . \tag{17}$$

Therefore, we get a contribution to the energy function from the driving input which is identical in form to Eq. (2), and hence can be solved using Eq. (4) and Eq. (18).

The full algorithm then reads:

1. Initialize the activities $\{a_{i,k}\}$
2. At each time step:
   (a) Get the motion vector field $\{\mathbf{v}_i\}$
   (b) Calculate the models $\{A_k\}$ according to Eq. (18)
   (c) Calculate the driving input $\{h_{i,k}\}$ according to Eq. (12)
   (d) Update the activities $\{a_{i,k}\}$ according to Eq. (11)
   (e) Normalize the activities $\{a_{i,k}\}$ to 1 according to Eq. (9)
   (f) While a desired energy decrease has not been reached, go to 2 (b)
3. Warp the current activities $\{a_{i,k}\}$ with the calculated affine parameters $A_k$ as prediction for the next time step
4. Go to step 2

The warping step (3) allows to move the activities along with the motion field, which is very useful for temporally persistent, coherent motion. In this case, the affiliation probabilities represented by the activities $a_{i,k}$ are shifted with the stimulus, which requires less repetitions of steps 2(b)-2(f).

## 3   Results

Below, results of the proposed algorithm for two image sequences are presented. The first is the well known MPEG flower garden sequence, available at e.g. [11]. It consists of several planes shifting horizontally due to a moving observer: the tree in front moves fastest, the flower bed moves at intermediate speed and the house moves very slowly. To compute the driving input for the recurrent network, motion vector fields are estimated by the method described in [8]. The second video shows a moving hand in front of a moving background available at [10], including a manually annotated flow field.

For both sequences, the activities of the algorithm have been initialized by zero-mean Gaussian noise. For relaxation, 30 iterations were used for each motion vector field, where iterations 1, 15 and 30 were plotted in Figs. 2 and 3. The first row shows the input images and following rows each represent a motion layer. The $\lambda$s to weight the energy terms have been set to $\lambda_1 = 0.6$, $\lambda_2 = 0.3$ and $\lambda_3 = 0.1$ for all sequences. These heuristically evaluated values represent a good parameterization for a variety of examples.

For the flower garden sequence, the number of models was set to three. It can be seen from the image sequence that after 15 iterations the system starts to converge (2nd column) and already after 30 iterations all models can be clearly separated (3rd column). As described in the previous chapter, activities are warped here to predict the activities for the next input image (see columns three to four). This avoids starting from the scratch for every new incoming image.

For the hand sequence, two models were assumed to be present in the flow field. Again, after 30 iterations the method is able to clearly separate the two layers. For this example, the fitted vector fields are plotted into the layers. This illustrates the close interaction between activities and affine model parameters.

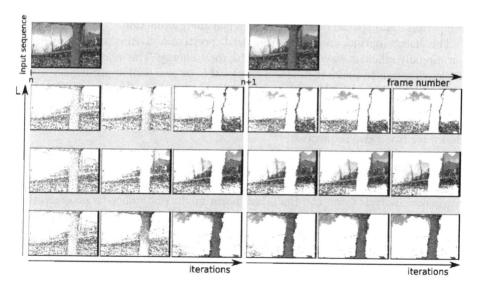

**Fig. 2.** Layer separation for the MPEG flower garden sequence. The first row shows the input images and the next three rows represent the layer activities. Each column of a layer illustrates the activities for the 1st, 15th and 30th iteration step. After the last iteration of the first input image, the activities are warped to predict activities for the next input image as initialization.

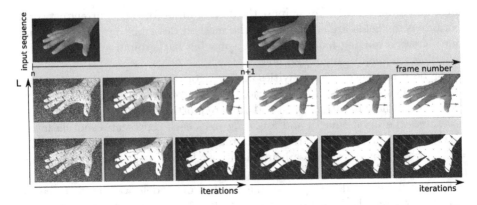

**Fig. 3.** The hand sequence, available at [10]. The first row shows the input images and the next two rows represent the motion layers. Each column of a layer illustrates the activities for the 1st, 15th and 30th iteration step. For each layer, the fitted vector field is plotted as well.

## 4   Conclusion

We have presented a model for motion-based image segmentation into multiple affine motion layers. In contrast to many approaches, we employ a strictly positive dynamic neural network to address the problem of gaining the affiliation parameters for each layer. This allows us to directly combine conditions for layer competition and spatial coherence in a single energy function.

The energy optimization for normalized, positive activities provides a computationally efficient way to minimize the total energy. This allows an effective implementation to make the system employable to practical applications.

The proposed framework makes an important contribution to interpreting and understanding visual scenes containing rigid moving objects. The capability of the algorithms to successfully separate motion in real-world images has been shown for two video sequences.

As the evaluation has shown, the system provides accurate results. This indicates a solid basis for more complex scenarios. Of course, in more challenging scenarios we have to cope with less reliable measured motion. In such cases, the regression analysis using the Euclidean norm might not suffice to satisfactorily fit the motion models. Now, as we have shown the consistency and correct functionality of the implementation, the next step is to prepare the algorithm to be able to deal with outliers and larger uncertainties in the motion data.

## References

1. Wang, J.Y.A., Adelson, E.H.: Representing moving images with layers. IEEE Transactions on Image Processing 3(5) (1994)
2. Ju, S.X., Black, M.J., Jepson, A.D.: Skin and bones: multi-layer, locally affine, optical flow and regularization with transparency. In: IEEE Conference on Computer Vision and Pattern Recognition, San Francisco (1996)

3. Weiss, Y., Adelson, E.H.: Perceptually organized EM: A framework for motion segmentation that combines information about form and motion. M.I.T. Media Lab Perceptual Computing Section Technical Report No. 315, Cambridge (1995)
4. Ayer, S., Sawhney, H.S.: Layered Representation of Motion Video using Robust Maximum-Likelihood Estimation of Mixture Models and MDL Encoding. In: Proceedings of the Fifth International Conference on Computer Vision, Washington (1995)
5. Weiss, Y., Adelson, E.H.: A unified mixture framework for motion segmentation: incorporating spatial coherence and estimating the number of models. In: IEEE Conference on Computer Vision and Pattern Recognition, San Francisco, Ca (1996)
6. Odobez, J.-M., Bouthemy, P.: Direct incremental model-based image motion segmentation for video analysis. Signal Processing 66(2) (1998)
7. Wersing, H., Steil, J.J., Ritter, H.: A Competitive Layer Model for Feature Binding and Sensory Segmentation. Neural Computation (2001)
8. Willert, V., Eggert, J., Adamy, J., Korner, E.: Non-Gaussian velocity distributions integrated over space, time, and scales. IEEE Transactions on Systems, Man, and Cybernetics, Part B: Cybernetics (2006)
9. Eggert, J., Koerner, E.: Sparse coding and NMF. In: IEEE International Joint Conference on Neural Networks, Budapest (2004)
10. Human-Assisted Motion Annotation, http://people.csail.mit.edu/celiu/motionAnnotation/index.html
11. Image Sequences, http://www.cs.brown.edu/~black/images.html

# Appendix: Solution of the Weighted Regression

$$A_k^* = \begin{pmatrix} a_{k,13}^* & a_{k,23}^* \\ a_{k,11}^* & a_{k,21}^* \\ a_{k,12}^* & a_{k,22}^* \end{pmatrix} = \begin{pmatrix} \sum_i w_{i,k} & \sum_i w_{i,k}p_{i,x} & \sum_i w_{i,k}p_{i,y} \\ \sum_i w_{i,k}p_{i,x} & \sum_i w_{i,k}p_{i,x}^2 & \sum_i w_{i,k}p_{i,x}p_{i,y} \\ \sum_i w_{i,k}p_{i,y} & \sum_i w_{i,k}p_{i,x}p_{i,y} & \sum_i w_{i,k}p_{i,y}^2 \end{pmatrix}^{-1}$$

$$\begin{pmatrix} \sum_i w_{i,k}v_{i,x} & \sum_i w_{i,k}v_{i,y} \\ \sum_i w_{i,k}p_{i,x}v_{i,x} & \sum_i w_{i,k}p_{i,x}v_{i,y} \\ \sum_i w_{i,k}p_{i,y}v_{i,x} & \sum_i w_{i,k}p_{i,y}v_{i,y} \end{pmatrix} \tag{18}$$

# Selection of Training Data for Locally Recurrent Neural Network*

Krzysztof Patan and Maciej Patan

Institute of Control and Computation Engineering University of Zielona Góra
{k.patan,m.patan}@issi.uz.zgora.pl

## 1 Problem Formulation

Artificial neural networks of the dynamic type provide an excellent mathematical tool for dealing with non-linear dynamic problems. There are many application domains where the accurate model of a process/plant plays key role. One of the most stimulating practical examples is Fault Detection and Identification (FDI) of industrial systems [1]. Preparation of experimental conditions in order to collect informative measurements can be very expensive and the data acquired form real-world system may be also very noisy, therefore using all the available data may lead to significant systematic modelling errors.

Recently, the problem of optimal selection of input sequences in the context of locally recurrent neural network training has been discussed by the authors in [2,1], where the problem has been formulated in the form of the so-called multiplicative algorithm known from the optimum experimental design theory. The main aim of the research reported here is to propose an alternative approach for the approximated solution of resulting combinatorial optimization problem through adaptation of very efficient algorithm of the exchange-type [3]. It assigns to each sequence the same frequency of its presentation what dramatically simplifies the training process. To illustrate the delineated approach, modelling of a tunnel furnace is presented.

The topology of the neural network considered is analogous to that of the multi-layered feedforward one and the dynamics are reproduced by the so-called dynamic neuron models [4,1]. The dynamic neurons replace the standard static neurons. This network structure does not have any global feedbacks, which complicate the architecture of the network and the training algorithm. Such networks have an architecture that is somewhere inbetween a feedforward and a globally recurrent architecture. In this paper a discrete-time dynamic network with $n$ time varying inputs and $m$ outputs is discussed. The presented structure can be viewed as a network with a single hidden layer containing $v$ dynamic neurons as processing elements and an output layer with linear static elements. For structural details of the network considered, the interested reader is referred to [1].

---

* This work was supported in part by the Ministry of Science and Higher Education in Poland under the grants N N514 1219 33 and N N514 2305 37.

K. Diamantaras, W. Duch, L.S. Iliadis (Eds.): ICANN 2010, Part II, LNCS 6353, pp. 134–137, 2010.

## 2  Optimal Sequence Selection

Let $\boldsymbol{y}^j = \boldsymbol{y}(\boldsymbol{u}^j; \boldsymbol{\theta}) = \{\boldsymbol{y}(k; \boldsymbol{\theta})\}_{k=0}^{L_j}$ denote the sequence of network responses for the sequence of inputs $\boldsymbol{u}^j = \{\boldsymbol{u}(k)\}_{k=0}^{L_j}$ related to the consecutive time moments $k = 0, \ldots, L_j < \infty$ and selected from among an *a priori* given set of input sequences $\mathcal{U} = \{\boldsymbol{u}^1, \ldots, \boldsymbol{u}^P\}$. Here $\boldsymbol{\theta}$ represents a $p$-dimensional unknown network parameter vector which must be estimated via training process using observations of the system. The measurements related to selected input sequences are perturbed with some additive observational noise, which is customary assumed to be zero-mean, Gaussian and white stochastic process [5]. The optimal sequence selection problem consist in choosing the best subset of $S$ sequences from among the set of $P$ given potential ones so as to maximize the determinant of the Fisher Information Matrix (FIM) associated with the parameters to be estimated and constituting the lower bound of the covariance matrix for the parameter estimates [2]. Introducing for each possible sequence $\boldsymbol{u}^i$ ($i = 1, \ldots, P$) a variable $v_i$ which takes the value 1 or 0 depending on whether a sequence is chosen or not, the FIM in the case considered here can be written as [2]

$$M(v_1, \ldots, v_P) = \sum_{i=1}^{P} v_i \frac{1}{SL_i} \sum_{k=0}^{L_i} \left( \frac{\partial \boldsymbol{y}(u, k; \boldsymbol{\theta})}{\partial \boldsymbol{\theta}} \right) \left( \frac{\partial \boldsymbol{y}(u, k; \boldsymbol{\theta})}{\partial \boldsymbol{\theta}} \right)^T \bigg|_{\boldsymbol{\theta} = \boldsymbol{\theta}^0} \tag{1}$$

$\boldsymbol{\theta}^0$ being a prior estimate to the unknown parameter vector $\boldsymbol{\theta}$ which can be obtained from previous experiments or alternatively some known nominal values can be used [6,3]. Then, our design problem consist in finding a sequence $\boldsymbol{v} = (v_1, \ldots, v_N)$ which maximize the criterion $\mathcal{P}(\boldsymbol{v}) = \log \det(\boldsymbol{M}(\boldsymbol{v}))$

$$\text{s.t.} \quad v_i = 0 \text{ or } 1, \quad i = 1, \ldots, N \quad \text{and} \quad \sum_{i=1}^{N} v_i = S. \tag{2}$$

what constitutes a 0–1 integer programming problem. As for its approximate solution a very efficient exchange algorithm can be easily adopted based on a notion of so-called restricted design measures (cf. [5,3] for details) originated from experimental design theory. In the following, a potential of its application to the approach considered here is illustrated by the example of identification of MIMO system.

## 3  Illustrative Example – Tunnel Furnace

*Simulation setting.* As an experimental testbed a laboratory model of tunnel furnace has been used. It contains four electric heaters which are controlled with the continuous input signals and four resistance detectors measuring temperature gradient along the furnace chamber. The control system is based on the industrial programmable logic controllers PACSYSTEMS RX3i produced by GE FANUC Intelligent Platforms and supplemented with touchpad operational panel QUICKPANEL CE. As the input signals the random step functions were selected in order to provide the persistent excitation of the object. The system to be modelled has three inputs (the fourth input is reserved for the diagnostic purposes) and four outputs. In order to model the tunnel furnace the MIMO representation was decomposed into four MISO models. The structure of each neural network model was selected arbitrarily and had the following structure: three inputs, three IIR neurons with second order filters and hyperbolic tangent activation functions, and one linear output neuron. For identifiability purposes the feedforward filter parameter $b_0$ for each hidden neuron is fixed to the value of 1[2]. Firstly, each network was trained in a classical way. Training set contained 500 samples and the training process was carried out off-line for 100 steps using the Levenberg-Marquardt (LM) algorithm. At the second stage of the training process the learning data were split into 60 time sequences, containing 50 consecutive samples each. The design purpose was to choose from this set of all learning patterns the most informative sequences (in the sense of D-optimality).

*Results.* The modelling quality in the form of Sum of Squared Errors (SSE) calculated for each initially trained neural model using the testing set containing 3000 samples are presented in the first column of Table 1. It is obvious that modelling results are not satisfactory with exception of the neural network modelling the 4th output of the system. To achieve more reliable models, the training was continued in three ways: (i) with training sequences selected randomly, (ii) with training sequences selected using the multiplicative algorithm [2], (iii) with training sequences selected using the proposed method.

For each neural model, the multiplicative algorithm selected from 9 to 11 sequences out of 60 as the most informative. In turn, the exchange algorithm selected 10 sequences out of 60 as the most informative. In this algorithm, the number of sequences to be selected is the user defined, but 10 sequences seems to be a good choice taking into account the number of sequences

**Table 1.** Quality of neural models

| Model | Initial model | Random design | Optimal design multiplicative | exchange |
|---|---|---|---|---|
| output 1 | 34.44 | 2.83 | 1.93 | 1.81 |
| output 2 | 11.79 | 3.69 | 2.6 | 1.55 |
| output 3 | 34.78 | 5.96 | 0.8658 | 1.89 |
| output 4 | 0.37 | 0.093 | 0.064 | 0.065 |

selected by the multiplicative method. Analysing the selected sequences one can say that in most cases the both optimum experimental design procedures selected the similar input sequences but the main difference is its presentation frequency. The multiplicative procedure assigns to each sequence the weight showing how frequently this sequence should be presented [2]. The proposed exchange procedure assigns to each sequence the weight of the same value which means that each sequence is presented only once during training.

In the case of the multiplicative algorithm, for a selected design, each distinct sequence is replicated proportionally to its weight in the design with total number of replications assumed to be $P = 20$. It is important to say that sequences are presented to the neural network in a random order. The training procedure was repeated 100 times and the modelling quality, in the form of SSE calculated using 3000 testing samples, for the best achieved models are presented in the fourth column of Table 1.

In the case of the exchange algorithm, for a selected design, each distinct sequence is presented only once, but sequences were presented to the neural network in a random order. The training procedure was repeated 100 times and the modelling quality, in the form of SSE calculated using 3000 testing samples, for the best achieved models are presented in the fifth column of Table 1. The exchange algorithm achieved the comparable results for the first and fourth system output, better results for the second output, and worser for the third. However, it should be pointed out that taking into account the idea behind the methods, the multiplicative procedure should generate slightly better results on the wider number of problems. On the other hand the exchange algorithm is quite easy and fast procedure. Analysing the running time of both planning methods one can conclude that the proposed exchange method works approximately thirty five time faster than the multiplicative one. Tests were performed by repetition of an optimal design algorithm 100 times and the running time was averaged. For the multiplicative algorithm the averaged running time was equal to $0.1855sec.$ and for the exchange one $0.0052sec.$ (PC Core2Duo T7700, 4GB RAM).

In the case of the random design the training sequences were selected randomly from all available with total number of presentations equal to $P = 20$. The training procedure was repeated 100 times and the modelling quality, in the form of SSE calculated using 3000 testing samples, for the best achieved models are presented in the third column of Table 1. Using random designs, the better modelling quality was obtained contrary to the classical training. It is caused by the fact that such a way of training sequences presentation is something inbetween the cross-validation and bootstrap techniques. However, comparing results achieved using random designs with those achieved using optimal designs one can see that the better results are obtained using the latter, especially for the case of the third output of the system.

# References

1. Patan, K.: Artificial Neural Networks for the Modelling and Fault Diagnosis of Technical Processes. LNCIS. Springer, Berlin (2008)
2. Patan, K., Patan, M.: Optimal training sequences for locally recurrent neural network. In: Alippi, C., Polycarpou, M., Panayiotou, C., Ellinas, G. (eds.) ICANN 2009. LNCS, vol. 5768, pp. 80–89. Springer, Heidelberg (2009)
3. Uciński, D.: Optimal Measurement Methods for Distributed Parameter System Identification. CRC Press, Boca Raton (2005)
4. Marcu, T., Mirea, L., Frank, P.M.: Development of dynamical neural networks with application to observer based fault detection and isolation. International Journal of Applied Mathematics and Computer Science 9(3), 547–570 (1999)
5. Fedorov, V.V., Hackl, P.: Model-Oriented Design of Experiments. Lecture Notes in Statistics. Springer, New York (1997)
6. Uciński, D.: Optimal selection of measurement locations for parameter estimation in distributed processes. International Journal of Applied Mathematics and Computer Science 10(2), 357–379 (2000)

# A Statistical Appraoch to Image Reconstruction from Projections Problem Using Recurrent Neural Network

Robert Cierniak

Czestochowa University of Technology, Institute of Computer Engineering,
Armii Krajowej 36, 42-200 Czestochowa, Poland
cierniak@kik.pcz.czest.pl

**Abstract.** This paper is concerned with the image reconstruction from projections problem. The presented paper describes a reconstruction approach based on recurrent neural network. The structure of this network is designed taking into account the probabilistic nature of distortion obesrved in x-ray computed tomography. The reconstruction process is performed using in this way constructed neural network solving the optimization problem. Computer experiments show that the appropriately designed recurrent neural network is able to reconstruct an image with better quality in comparison to the standart analytical reconstruction algorithm.

**Keywords:** image reconstruction from projections, neural networks.

## 1 Introduction

The basic problem arising in X-ray computed tomography (CT) is image reconstruction from projections, which are obtained using a x-ray scanner of a given geometry (in this paper, a solution for tomography with parallel beam geometry is presented). The most popular reconstruction methods are analytical reconstruction algorithms based on convolution and back-projection operations. The algebraic reconstruction technique (ART) was in the past extensivelly explored and are recently applied in practice [5].

In present paper an analytical approach to the reconstruction problem will be presented based on a recurrent neural network [1], [2]. In our reconstruction algorithm a recurrent neural network [3] is proposed to design the reconstruction algorithm.

In the recent investigations on the image reconstruction from projections problem [5], the 3-Dimensional statistical modeling for image quality improvement in cone-beam helical computed tomography is strong considered. We take into considerations this issue in our paper too. The structure of the used in our reconstruction algorithm neural network derives from the error measure imposed on reconstruction process. This measure strongly depends on statistical distribution of the registred signals in CT scanner. We propose an adjusted to statistical

K. Diamantaras, W. Duch, L.S. Iliadis (Eds.): ICANN 2010, Part II, LNCS 6353, pp. 138–141, 2010.

conditions in CT form of error measure and we used it to design recurrent neural network applied to reconstruct image from projections.

# 2    Formulation of Statistical Reconstruction Problem

If we examine a sample of material (such as the human body) using x-rays, we may write

$$p(s, \alpha) = \ln\left(\frac{n_0}{n_{s,\alpha}}\right),$$
(1)

where: $n_0$ is the x-ray intensity emmited by tube (we suppose that $n_0$ is the same for all projections); $n_{s,\alpha}$ is the x-ray intensity after passing through a distance U.

In literature, it is mostly assumed that $N$ is represented by a Poisson-distributed random variable what means that we will register by detector a $n_{s,\alpha}$ number of the x-ray photons with following probability:

$$P(N = n_{s,\alpha}) = \frac{n_{s,\alpha}^{*}{}^{n_{s,\alpha}}}{n_{s,\alpha}!}e^{-n_{s,\alpha}^{*}},$$
(2)

where $n_{s,\alpha}^{*}$ is an expected value of $N$.

In x-ray computed tomography is often used following log form of probability described by (2), and after using of the Stirling's approximation of $\ln n_{s,\alpha}!$ for $n \gg 0$, we obtain

$$LOG_1(n_{s,\alpha}) = n_{s,\alpha}\ln\frac{n_{s,\alpha}^{*}}{n_{s,\alpha}} + n_{s,\alpha} - n_{s,\alpha}^{*}.$$
(3)

The x-ray computed tomography belongs to the transmission tomography group and therefore we have to take into account definition (1) in relation (3). This way we can derive following formula for evaluation of error in transmission tomography:

$$LOG_2(p(s, \alpha)) = -\frac{1}{2}e^{-p(s,\alpha)}(p^{*}(s, \alpha) - p(s, \alpha))^2,$$
(4)

where

$$p^{*}(s, \alpha) = \ln\left(\frac{n_0}{n_{s,\alpha}^{*}}\right)$$
(5)

can be interpreted as expected value of the projection measurment.

In the presented method we take into consideration the discrete form of reconstructed image and we approximate the 2-D convolution using two finite sums of ranges $[1, \ldots, I]$ and $[1, \ldots, J]$. One can formulate relation between the original and the blurred image as follows

$$\hat{\bar{\mu}}(i, j) \approx \sum_{\bar{i}}\sum_{\bar{j}}\hat{\mu}(\bar{i}\bar{j}) \cdot h_{\Delta i, \Delta j},$$
(6)

where

$$h_{\Delta i, \Delta j} = \Delta_\alpha^p \left(\Delta_s\right)^2 \cdot \sum_{\psi_{gf}} \hat{I}\left(|i - \bar{i}|\Delta_s \cos \psi \Delta_\alpha^p + |j - \bar{j}|\Delta_s \sin \psi \Delta_\alpha^p\right). \qquad (7)$$

Equation (6) defines the 2D discrete aproximate reconstruction problem.

We can reformulate equation (4) in following way

$$LOG_3\left(p_\Sigma\left(i,j\right)\right) = -\frac{1}{2}\exp\left(-p_\Sigma\left(i,j\right)\right)\left(p_\Sigma^*\left(i,j\right) - p_\Sigma\left(i,j\right)\right)^2. \qquad (8)$$

The loss function $L3$ from relation (8) takes into account anly one pixel from reconstructed image. For all I·J pixels above measure could be led to the following form:

$$LOG_4 = -\frac{1}{2}\sum_{i=1}^{I}\sum_{j=1}^{J}\exp\left(-\hat{\tilde{\mu}}\left(i,j\right)\right)\left(e_{ij}\right)^2, \qquad (9)$$

where:

$$e_{ij} = \sum_{\bar{i}}\sum_{\bar{j}}\hat{\mu}\left(\bar{i},\bar{j}\right) \cdot h_{\Delta i, \Delta j} - \hat{\tilde{\mu}}\left(i,j\right). \qquad (10)$$

It should be noted that we will assign in further considerations $\hat{\mu}\left(\bar{i},\bar{j}\right)$ to expected value of attenuation coefficients $\hat{\mu}^*\left(\bar{i},\bar{j}\right)$.

Function (9) will be a basic point for the formulation of the new neural reconstruction method.

## 3    Experimental Results

The size of the processed image was fixed at $129 \times 129$ pixels, which determines the number of neurons in each layer of the net. Before the reconstruction process using a recurrent neural network is started, it is necessary to calculate coefficients $h_{\bar{i}\bar{j}}$ using equation (7).

It is very convenient during the computer simulations to construct a mathematical model of the projected object, a so-called phantom, to obtain fan-beam projections. We adopted the well-known Shepp-Logan phantom of the head to our experiments. Such a kind of phantom for parallel beam acquisition was used in many papers, for example [4]. A view of the mathematical model of a phantom is depicted in Table 1a.

The reconstructed image has been evaluated by standard error measures: MSE, where $\mu\left(x,y\right)$ is the original image of the Shepp-Logan mathematical phantom, in the presence of noise with Gaussian probability distribution with the mean $p_0$ and the variance $\sigma^2$ (in our simulations we set $p_0 = 0$ and $\sigma^2 = 0.0025$). Table 1 presents the obtained results of the computer simulations (obtained after 30000 iterations in the case of neural network algorithms).

**Table 1.** View of the images (window: $C=1.02$, $W=0.11$): a) original image b) reconstructed image using standard convolution/back-projection method with rebinning and Shepp-Logan kernel; c) reconstructed image using neural network algorithm described in this paper

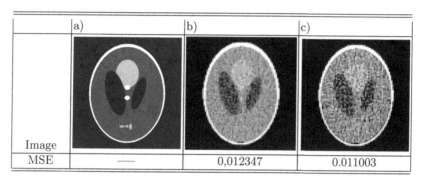

| | a) | b) | c) |
|---|---|---|---|
| Image | | | |
| MSE | — | 0,012347 | 0.011003 |

# 4 Conclusions

The performed simulations showed a convergence of the image reconstruction algorithm based on the statistically tailored recurrent neural networks described in this work. Described in this paper algorithm overperforms standard reconstruction methods in the sense of the mean square error measure.

# Acknowledgement

This work was partly supported by Polish Ministry of Science and Higher Education (Research Project N N516 185235).

# References

1. Cierniak, R.: A new approach to tomographic image reconstruction using a Hopfield-type neural network. International Journal Artificial Intelligence in Medicine 43, 113–125 (2008)
2. Cierniak, R.: New neural network algorithm for image reconstruction from fan-beam projections. Neurocomputing 43, 113–125 (2009)
3. Hopfield, J.J.: Neural networks and physical systems with emergent collective computational abilities. Proc. National Academy of Science USA 79, 2554–2558 (1982)
4. Kak, A.C., Slanley, M.: Principles of Computerized Tomographic Imaging. IEEE Press, New York (1988)
5. Thibault, J.-B., Sauer, K.D., Bouman, C.A., Hsieh, J.: A three-dimensional statistical approach to improved image quality for multislice helical CT. Med. Phys. 34(11), 4526–4544 (2007)

# A Computational System of Metaphor Generation with Evaluation Mechanism*

Asuka Terai and Masanori Nakagawa

Tokyo Institute of Technology, 2-12-1 O-okayama, Meguro-ku, Tokyo, Japan

**Abstract.** This study regards metaphor generation as a process where an expression consisting of a target (A) is modified by certain features to become a metaphorical expression of the form "target (A) like vehicle (B)". A computational system consisting of a metaphor generation process and a metaphor evaluation process is developed. In the metaphor generation process, a metaphor generation model [1] outputs candidate nouns for vehicles from input expressions. In the metaphor evaluation process, the candidate nouns are evaluated based on the similarities between the meanings of metaphors including the candidate nouns and the meaning of the input expression.

## 1 Introduction

The purpose of this study is to construct a computational system that generates metaphors of the form "A (target) like B (vehicle)" from the features of the target based on statistical language analysis and that incorporates an evaluation mechanism. Some computational models of metaphor generation using a corpus have been developed [2][3][1]. For instance, Kitada and Hagiwara[2] constructed a figurative composition support system including a model of metaphor generation based on an electronic dictionary. In contrast, Abe, Sakamoto and Nakagawa's model[3] is based on the results of statistical language analysis, which is more objective than existing dictionaries that must be compiled through the considerable efforts of language professionals. Moreover, Terai and Nakagawa [1] constructed a model that incorporates the dynamic interaction among features using the statistical language analysis.

The earlier models based on a corpus can output candidate nouns from the inputs for the target and its features that are represented by adjectives or verbs. However, the models do not have a mechanism of evaluating the candidate nouns. Abe, et al.'s model and Terai and Nakagawa's model do not evaluate their outputs. Kitada and Hagiwara's model[2] is a support system for metaphorical composition. The system outputs candidate nouns for the vehicle and features that are represented by the metaphor including the candidate noun for the vehicle.

---

* This research is supported by MEXT's program "Promotion of Environmental Improvement for Independence of Young Researchers" under the Special Coordination Funds for Promoting Science and Technology and Grant-in-Aid for Scientific Research (B) (19330156).

K. Diamantaras, W. Duch, L.S. Iliadis (Eds.): ICANN 2010, Part II, LNCS 6353, pp. 142–147, 2010.

Users are responsible for the evaluation and selection of the candidate nouns by referring to the presented features.

Sako, Nakamura and Yoshida[4] constructed a computational model of metaphor generation based on a psychological experiment. The model does not represent the dynamic interaction among features and is not able to technically cover all general metaphors because the model is based on a psychological experiment. However, the model has an advantage over the previous models based on corpus[2][3][1]. The advantage lies in the fact that it has an evaluation mechanism. The model technically consists of a metaphor generation process and a metaphor evaluation process. In the metaphor generation process, the model outputs candidate nouns for the vehicle. In the subsequent metaphor evaluation process, first, each similarity between the target and each candidate noun is computed. Next, the candidate nouns are evaluated based on these similarities. From a cognitive point of view, it is important to evaluate the candidates for the vehicle, in order to generate metaphorical expressions that evoke a common view between speakers and listeners. However, in the metaphor evaluation process, their model does not evaluate the meaning represented by the generated metaphorical expression, but rather it evaluates the figurativeness of the generated metaphorical expression.

The present study implements an evaluation mechanism within the model proposed by Terai and Nakagawa[1], which represents the dynamic interaction among features based on statistical language analysis. Thus, the newly proposed system has two processes: a metaphor generation process and a metaphor evaluation process. In the metaphor generation process, the metaphor generation model[1] outputs candidate nouns for the vehicles from the inputs for the target and its features that are represented by adjectives or verbs. In the metaphor evaluation process, first, the meaning of the metaphor including the candidate noun as the vehicle and the meaning of the expression consisting of the inputs for the target and its features are computed. Next, the similarities between the meaning of the metaphor and the meaning of the input expression are computed and the candidate nouns are evaluated based on these similarities. Thus, the metaphor that is most similar to the input expression is output as the most adequate metaphor.

# 2    A Computational System of Metaphor Generation

## 2.1    Knowledge Structure Based on Statistical Language Analysis

The metaphor generation system is constructed using a knowledge structure based on a statistical language analysis[5], which was also used in previous studies[3][1]. The statistical language analysis[5] estimates latent classes among nouns and adjectives (or verbs) as a knowledge structure using four kinds of frequency data extracted for adjective-noun modifications (Adj) and three kinds of verb-noun modifications: noun(subject)-verb (S-V), verb-noun(modification) (V-M), and verb-noun(object) (V-O). These frequency data are extracted from the Japanese newspaper for the period 1993-2002. The statistical method assumes that $P(n_i^r, a_j^r)$ ($r$ refers to the kind of data set) can be computed using the following formula(1):

$$P(n_i^r, a_j^r) = \sum_k P(n_i^r|c_k^r)P(a_j^r|c_k^r)P(c_k^r),\qquad(1)$$

where $c_k^r$ indicates the $k$th latent class assumed within this method for the $r$ type of modification data. The parameters ($P(n_i^r|c_k^r)$, $P(a_j^r|c_k^r)$, and $P(c_k^r)$) are estimated using the EM algorithm. The statistical language analysis is applied to each set of co-occurrence data fixing the number of latent classes at 200. The conditional probabilities, $P(c_k^r|n_i^r)$ and $P(c_k^r|a_j^r)$, are computed using Bayes' theory. The 18,142 noun types ($n_h^*$) that are common to all four types of modification data and the features are represented as vectors using the following formula,

$$V_p(n_h^*) = P(c_k^r|n_h^*),\qquad(2)$$

$$V_p(a_j^r) = \begin{cases} P(c_k^r|a_j^r) \\ 0 \qquad\qquad \text{else,} \end{cases}\qquad(3)$$

where $V_p(n_h^*)$ indicates the $p$th component of the vector that corresponds to the noun $n_h^*$. $p$ refers to the successive number of latent classes extracted from the four data sets. When $1\le p \le 200$, $r$ indicates the "Adj" modification and $k = p$, when $201\le p \le 400$, $r$ indicates the "S-V" modification and $k = p - 200$, when $401\le p \le 600$, $r$ indicates the "V-M" modification and $k = p - 400$, and when $600\le p \le 800$, $r$ indicates the "V-O" modification and $k = p - 600$.

## 2.2   The Metaphor Generation Process

The metaphor generation process is realized using the metaphor generation model[1]. The model outputs candidate nouns for the vehicles from inputs consisting of the target and its features that are represented by adjectives or verbs. The model consists of three layers: an input layer, a hidden layer, and an output layer. The input layer consists of feature nodes, which each indicating either an adjective or a verb. Each feature node relating to the target has mutual and symmetric connections with the other feature nodes relating to the target. The mutual connections represent the dynamic interaction among features. The hidden layer consists of nodes which indicate the latent classes estimated using the statistical language analysis. The output layer consists of noun nodes. Sets of input expressions, such as "$a_{j_1}^{r_1}$ - $n_h^*$", "$a_{j_2}^{r_2}$ - $n_h^*$", are input into the model. The model outputs each noun's adequacy for the vehicle, which represents a set of input expressions, such as "$n_h^*$ (target) like B (vehicle)".

## 2.3   The Metaphor Evaluation Process

In the metaphor evaluation process, the meanings of the generated metaphorical expressions and the meaning of the expression consist of the inputs for the target and its features are computed, and the candidate nouns are evaluated based on the similarities between the meaning of the metaphor and the meaning of the input expression. These are estimated based on Kintsch's predication algorithm[6]. This algorithm can be used to estimate the meaning vectors of a metaphorical expression and a literal expression using different parameter values. Thus, in this process, the meaning vector of a metaphor including candidate noun and the meaning vector of a set of input literal expressions are computed. Then, the metaphor including the candidate nouns are evaluated based on the similarities between these vectors.

**Estimating the Meaning of the Metaphor Expression.** The meaning of the metaphor consisting of the target and the candidate vehicle is estimated using the meaning vectors. This algorithm represents the class inclusion theory which explains metaphor understanding in terms of class-inclusion statements, where a target is regarded as a member of an ad hoc category of which the vehicle is a prototypical member[7]. For example, in comprehending the metaphor "Hope like glim", the target "hope" can be regarded as belonging to a "transient" category that could be typically represented by a vehicle such as "glim". First, the semantic neighborhood $(N(n_h))$ of a vehicle of size $Sn^m$ is computed on the basis of the similarity to the vehicle, which is represented by the cosine of the angles between the meaning vectors. Next, $S^m$ nouns are selected from the semantic neighborhood $(N(n_h))$ of the vehicle on the basis of their similarity to the target. Finally, a vector $(V(M))$ is computed as the centroid of the meaning vectors for the target, the vehicle and the selected $S^m$ nouns. The computed vector $(V(M))$ indicates the assigned meaning of the target as a member of the ad-hoc category of the vehicle in the metaphor $M$. The category consisting of the vehicle and the selected $S^m$ nouns is regarded as an ad hoc category of which the vehicle is a prototypical member according to class inclusion theory[7].

**Estimating the Meaning of the Input Expression.** The meaning of the expression consisting of the inputs for the target and its features, which is called as the input expression, is also estimated. First, the semantic neighborhood $(N(a_{j_u}^{r_u}))$ of a feature of size $Sn^l$ is computed on the basis of the similarity to the feature, which is represented by the cosine of the angles between feature vectors. Next, $S^l$ features are selected from the semantic neighborhood $(N(a_{j_u}^{r_u}))$ of the feature on the basis of their similarity to the target. Finally, a vector $(V(L))$ is computed as the centroid of the meaning vectors for the target, the vehicle and the selected $S^l$ features. The computed vector $(V(L))$ indicates the meaning of the target, which is modified using the input features as the lateral expression $L$.

### 2.4   Result of the Simulation

In this study[1], the evaluation model simulates using the parameters $Sn^m = 50$, $S^m = 3$, $Sn^l = 10$, $S^l = 3$. It is arranged that the value of $Sn^m$ is higher than

---

[1] The metaphor generation model[1] simulates using the parameters $\alpha = ln(10)$, $\beta = 0.1$, $\gamma = 10$.

**Table 1.** The results of the metaphor evaluation process for the results of the metaphor generation model with interaction and for the model without interaction (similarity:ranking in the generation process)

| | "transient hope", "hope disappear" | |
|---|---|---|
| | the model with an interaction | the model without an interaction |
| 1 | pin money (0.6549:10) | delight (0.5417:8) |
| 2 | light bulb (0.6344:9) | conviction (0.5123:5) |
| 3 | glim (0.5963:4) | interest (0.6552:2) |
| 4 | neon (0.5914:6) | question (0.4889:4) |
| 5 | illuminations (0.5833:5) | motivation (0.4781:6) |
| 6 | lamp (0.5627:3) | requirement (0.4455:9) |
| 7 | celebratory drink (0.5378:2) | disposition (0.5645:10) |
| 8 | candle (0.5144:8) | request (0.6538:3) |
| 9 | afterglow (0.3934:7) | afterglow (0.5928:7) |
| 10 | red light (0.3532:1) | red light (0.5646:1) |

that of $Sn^l$, because it was been reported that the simulation of metaphorical expressions requires a larger semantic neighborhood than literal expressions[6]. The similarity between the metaphorical and input expressions is represented by the cosine of the angles between the vectors of the metaphorical expression ($V(M)$) and of the input expression ($V(L)$). Each similarity between the input target and each candidate noun is computed. The higher the similarity of the candidate noun is, the more adequate the candidate noun is for the vehicle. The results are shown in Table1.

A psychological experiment was conducted in order to verify these results. In the psychological experiment, 14 graduate students were presented with the input set of "transient hope" and "hope disappear". They were asked to answer the vehicle in the metaphor "hope like B" using a noun. The three nouns responded as the vehicle by more than two people were "candle" (by 4 people), "glim" (by 3 people) and "bubble" (by 3 people). The metaphor generation model with interaction estimates "candle" and "glim" among the top 10 candidate nouns but the model without interaction does not. "Glim" is the fourth candidate noun for the metaphor generation process is emphasized as the third candidate noun in the metaphor evaluation process. It can be considered that "red light" is not so transient and so is less adequate for the vehicle than the other candidate nouns. However, it is estimated as the most adequate candidate in the metaphor generation process. In the metaphor evaluation process, it is estimated as the tenth candidate. This result indicates the necessity of the metaphor evaluation process. Furthermore, the similarities of the candidates from the model without interaction are less than those from the model with interaction. The results of the evaluation process indicate that the metaphor generation model with interaction performs better simulations than the model without interaction.

# 3   Discussion

In this study, a computational system of metaphor generation incorporating an evaluation mechanism was constructed based on data obtained through a statistical language analysis[5] using a previous model[1]. Although a noun, which does not represent the image of the input feature, can be estimated as the most adequate candidate within the metaphor generation process, the noun may be estimated as a less than adequate candidate within the evaluation process. In addition, the results of the psychological experiment support the result of the system using the metaphor generation model with interaction[1]. However, the psychological experiment was conducted with only one input expression. In order to examine the more general validity of the system, an experiment should be conducted with a wider range of expression sets. And, it needs to examine an effect of the parameter values on results. In addition, although the participants did not respond with "pin money" for the vehicle, the system output the original metaphor "hope like pin money" as the most adequate metaphor for "transient hope" and "hope disappears". That suggests that the system has the potential to generate more original metaphors than humans.

# References

1. Terai, A., Nakagawa, M.: A Computational Model of Metaphor Generation with Dynamic Interaction. In: Alippi, C., Polycarpou, M.M., Panayiotou, C., Ellinas, G. (eds.) ICANN 2009. LNCS, vol. 5768, pp. 779–788. Springer, Heidelberg (2009)
2. Kitada, J., Hagiwara, M.: Figurative Composition Support System Using Electronic Dictionaries. Transactions of Information Processing Society of Japan 42(5), 1232–1241 (2001)
3. Abe, K., Sakamoto, K., Nakagawa, M.: A Computational Model of Metaphor Generation Process. In: Proc. of the 28th Annual Meeting of the Cognitive Science Society, pp. 937–942 (2006)
4. Sako, T., Nakamura, J., Yoshida, S.: Generation of Metaphorical Expressions using Surface Similarity and Emotional Evaluation between word concepts. IEICE technical report. Natural language understanding and models of communication 37(131), 17–24 (1993)
5. Kameya, Y., Sato, T.: Computation of probabilistic relationship between concepts and their attributes using a statistical analysis of Japanese corpora. In: Proc. of Symposium on Large-scale Knowledge Resources: LKR 2005, pp. 65–68 (2005)
6. Kintsch, W.: Metaphor comprehension: A computational theory. Psychonomic Bulletin & Review 7(2), 257–266 (2000)
7. Glucksberg, S., Keysar, B.: Understanding Metaphorica Comparisons: Beyond Similarity. Psychological Review 97(1), 3–18 (1990)

# Recurrence Enhances the Spatial Encoding of Static Inputs in Reservoir Networks

Christian Emmerich, René Felix Reinhart, and Jochen Jakob Steil

Research Institute for Cognition and Robotics (CoR-Lab),
Bielefeld University, Universitätsstr. 25, 33615 Bielefeld, Germany
{cemmeric,freinhar,jsteil}@cor-lab.uni-bielefeld.de
http://www.cor-lab.de

**Abstract** We shed light on the key ingredients of reservoir computing and analyze the contribution of the network dynamics to the spatial encoding of inputs. Therefore, we introduce attractor-based reservoir networks for processing of static patterns and compare their performance and encoding capabilities with a related feedforward approach. We show that the network dynamics improve the nonlinear encoding of inputs in the reservoir state which can increase the task-specific performance.

**Keywords:** reservoir computing, extreme learning machine, static pattern recognition.

## 1  Introduction

Reservoir computing (RC), a well-established paradigm to train recurrent neural networks, is based on the idea to restrict learning to a perceptron-like read-out layer, while the hidden reservoir network is initialized with random connection strengths and remains fixed. The latter can be understood as a "random, temporal and nonlinear kernel" [1] providing a suitable mixture of both spatial and

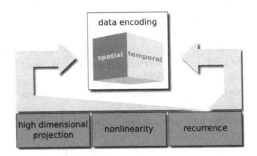

**Fig. 1.** Key ingredients of RC

temporal encoding of the input data in the network's hidden state space. This mixture is based upon three key ingredients illustrated in Fig. 1: (i) the projection into a high dimensional state space, (ii) the nonlinearity of the approach and (iii) the recurrent connections in the reservoir. On the one hand, the advantages of a nonlinear projection into a high dimensional space are beyond controversy: so-called kernel expansions rely on the concept of a nonlinear transformation of the original data into a high dimensional feature space and the subsequent use of a simple, mostly linear, model. On the other hand, the recurrent connections implement a short-term memory by means of transient network states. Due to this

K. Diamantaras, W. Duch, L.S. Iliadis (Eds.): ICANN 2010, Part II, LNCS 6353, pp. 148–153, 2010.

short-term memory, reservoir networks are typically utilized for temporal pattern processing such as time-series prediction, classification and generation [2]. In principle, short term memory can also be implemented in a simpler fashion, e.g. by an explicit delay-line. But we point out that the *combination of spatial and temporal encoding* makes the reservoir approach powerful and can explain the impressive performance on various tasks [3, 4]. It remains nevertheless unclear how the network dynamics influence the spatial encoding of inputs.

Our hypothesis is that the *dynamics* of the reservoir network enhances the spatial encoding of *static* inputs by means of a more nonlinear representation, which consequently improves the task-specific performance. Moreover, we expect an improved performance when applying larger reservoirs, i.e. when using an increased dimensionality of the nonlinear feature expansion. We systematically test the contribution of the network dynamics to the spatial encoding independently from its temporal effects by using attractor-based computation and by considering purely static input patterns, A statistical analysis of the distribution of the network's attractor states allows to access the qualitative difference of the encoding caused by the network's recurrence indepently of the task-specific performance.

# 2   Attractor-Based Computation with Reservoir Networks

We consider the three-layered network architecture depicted in Fig. 2, which comprises a recurrent hidden layer (reservoir) with a large set of nonlinear neurons. The input, reservoir and output neurons are denoted by $\mathbf{x} \in \mathbb{R}^D$, $\mathbf{h} \in \mathbb{R}^N$ and $\mathbf{y} \in \mathbb{R}^C$, respectively. The reservoir state is governed by discrete dynamics

$$\mathbf{h}(t+1) = \mathbf{f}\left(\mathbf{W}^{inp}\,\mathbf{x}(t) + \mathbf{W}^{res}\,\mathbf{h}(t)\right), \qquad (1)$$

where the activation functions $f_i$ are applied componentwise. The reservoir neurons have sigmoidal activation functions such as $f_i(x) = tanh(x)$, whereas the output layer consists of linear neurons, i.e. $\mathbf{y}(t) = \mathbf{W}^{out}\,\mathbf{h}(t)$.

Learning in reservoir networks is restricted to the read-out weights $\mathbf{W}^{out}$. All other weights are randomly initialized and remain fixed. In order to infer a desired input-to-output mapping from a set of training examples $(\mathbf{x}_k^T, \mathbf{y}_k^T)_{k=1,\dots,K}$, the read-out weights $\mathbf{W}^{out}$ are adapted such that the mean square error is minimized. In this paper, we use ridge regression: For all inputs $\mathbf{x}_1, \dots, \mathbf{x}_K$ we collect the corresponding reservoir states $\mathbf{h}_k$ as well as the desired output targets $\mathbf{y}_k$ column-wise in a reservoir state matrix $\mathbf{H} \in \mathbb{R}^{N \times K}$ and a target matrix $\mathbf{Y} \in \mathbb{R}^{C \times K}$, respectively. The optimal read-out weights are determined by the least squares solution with a regularization factor $\alpha \geq 0$: $\mathbf{W}^{out} = \mathbf{Y}\mathbf{H}^T \left(\mathbf{H}\mathbf{H}^T + \alpha\mathbf{1}\right)^{-1}$.

The described network architecture in combination with the offline training by regression is often referred to as echo state network (ESN) [2]. The potential of the ESN approach depends on the quality of the input encoding in the reservoir. To adress that issue, Jaeger proposed to use weights drawn from a uniform distribution in $[-a, a]$, where often a sparsely connected reservoir is preferred.

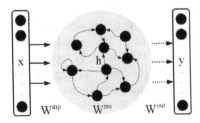

**Fig. 2.** Reservoir network

**Algorithm 1.** Convergence algorithm

**Require:** get external input $\mathbf{x}_k$
1: **while** $\Delta\mathbf{h} > \delta$ and $t < t_{max}$ **do**
2:    apply external input $\mathbf{x}(t) = \mathbf{x}_k$
3:    execute network iteration (1)
4:    compute state change
     $\Delta\mathbf{h} = ||\mathbf{h}(t) - \mathbf{h}(t-1)||^2$
5:    $t = t+1$
6: **end while**

In addtion, the reservoir weight matrix $\mathbf{W}^{res}$ is scaled to have a certain spectral radius $\lambda_{\max}$. There are two basic parameters involved in this procedure: the reservoir's weight connectivity or density $0 \le \rho \le 1$ and the spectral radius $\lambda_{\max}$, which is the largest absolute eigenvalue of $\mathbf{W}^{res}$.

In this paper, an attractor-based variant of the echo state approach is used, i.e. we map the inputs $\mathbf{x}_k$ to the reservoir's related attractor states $\bar{\mathbf{h}}_k$: The input neurons are clamped to the input pattern $\mathbf{x}_k$ until the network state change $\Delta\mathbf{h} = ||\mathbf{h}(t+1) - \mathbf{h}(t)||^2$ approaches zero. This procedure is condensed in Alg. 1. As a prerequisite it must hold that the network always converges to a fix point attractor, which is related to a scaling of the reservoir's weights such that $\lambda_{\max} < 1$. The resulting attractor states $\bar{\mathbf{H}}$ are used for training.

Note that an ESN with a spectral radius $\lambda_{\max} = 0$ or with zero reservoir connectivity ($\rho = 0$) has no recurrent connections at all. Then, the ESN degenerates to a feedforward network with randomly initialized weights. In [5], this special case of RC has been called extreme learning machine (ELM). As our intention is to investigate the role of the recurrent reservoir connections, this feedforward approach obviously is the non-recurrent baseline of our recurrent model and we present all results in comparison to this non-dynamic model.

## 3    Key Ingredients of Reservoir Computing

We investigate the influence of the key ingredients of RC on the network performance for several data sets (Tab. 1) in a static pattern recognition scenario. Except for Wine, all data sets are not linearly seperable and constitute nontrivial classification tasks. The introduced models are used for classification of each data set. We represent class labels $c$ as a 1-of-$C$ coding in the target vector $\mathbf{y}$ such that $y_c = 1$ and $y_i = -1 \ \forall i \ne c$. For classification of a specific input pattern, we apply Alg. 1 and then determine the estimated class label $\hat{c}$ from the network output $\mathbf{y}$ according to $\hat{c} = \arg\max_i y_i$. All results are obtained by either partitioning the data into several cross-validation sets or using an existing partition of the data into training and test set and are averaged over 100 different network initializations. We use normalized data in the range $[-1, 1]$.

## Role of Reservoir Size and Nonlinearity

Fig. 3 shows the impact of the reservoir size to the network's recognition
rate for a fully connected reservoir,
i.e. $\rho = 1.0$, with $\lambda_{max} = 0.9$ and $\alpha$
as in Tab. 1. The number of correctly
classified samples increases strongly
with the number of hidden neurons.
On the one hand, this result shows
that the projection of the input into a
high-dimensional network state space
is crucial for the reservoir approach:
The performance of very small reservoir networks degrates to the performance of a linear model (LM). We
observe also a saturation of the performance for large reservoir sizes. It
seems that the random projection can

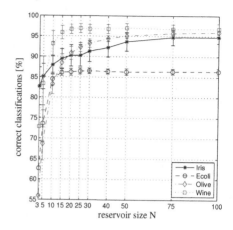

**Fig. 3.** Classification performance depending on the reservoir size $N$

not improve the separability of inputs in the network state space anymore. On
the other hand, note that the nonlinear activation functions of the reservoir neurons are crucial as well: Consider an ELM with linear activation functions, then
the inputs are only transformed linearly in a high dimensional representation.
Hence, the read-out layer can only read from a linear transformation of the input
and the classification performance is thus not affected by the dimensionality of
that representation. Consequently, the combination of a random expansion and
the non-linear activation functions is essential.

## Role of Reservoir Dynamics

In this section, we focus on the role
of reservoir dynamics and restrict our
studies on the Iris data set. We vary
both the spectral radius $\lambda_{max}$ of the
reservoir matrix $\mathbf{W}^{res}$ and the density $\rho$ for a fixed reservoir size of
$N = 50$. Note again that we obtain
an ELM for $\lambda_{max} = 0$ or $\rho = 0$.
Fig. 4 reveals that for recurrent networks the recognition rate increases
significantly with the spectral radius
$\lambda_{max}$ and surpasses the performance
of the non-recurrent networks with
the same parameter configuration. In-

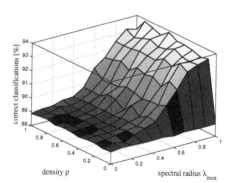

**Fig. 4.** Recognition rate for the Iris data
set depending on $\lambda_{max}$ and $\rho$

terestingly enough, this is not true for the weight density in the reservoir: adding
more than 10% connections inbetween the hidden neurons has only marginal impact on the classification performance, i.e. two many connections neither improve
nor detoriate the performance. Note that there is a trade-off in an increased

number of iterations the network needs for settling in a stable state, which correlates with the spectral radius $\lambda_{\max}$.

## 4    On the Distribution of Attractor States

We give a possible explanation for the improved performance caused by the recurrent connections. Our hypothesis is that these connections spread out the network's attractors to a spatially broader distribution than a non-recurrent approach is capable of, which results in an increasingly nonlinear hidden representation of the network's inputs. Because we perform linear readout, it is reasonable to analyse the encoding $\bar{\mathbf{H}}$ by linear methods, namely PCA. Given the dimension $D$ of the data, we expect the

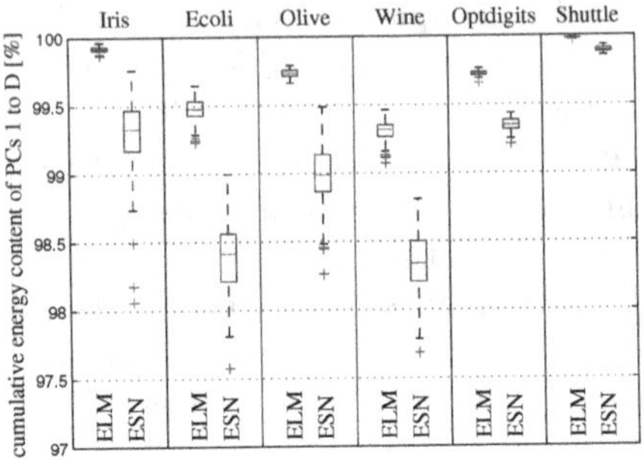

**Fig. 5.** Normalized cumulative energy content $g(D)$ of the first $D$ PCs

hidden representation to encode the input information with a significantly higher number of relevant principle components (PCs). Therefore, we calculate the shift of information or energy content from the first $D$ PCs to the remaining $N - D$ PCs. Let $\lambda_1 \geq \ldots \geq \lambda_N \geq 0$ be the eigenvalues of the covariance matrix $Cov(\bar{\mathbf{H}})$. We calculate the normalized cumulative energy content of the first $D$ PCs by $g(D) = (\sum_{i=1}^{D} \lambda_i)/(\sum_{i=1}^{N} \lambda_i)$, which measures the relevance of the first $D$ PCs. The case of $g(D) < 1$ implicates a shift of the input information to additional PCs, because the encoded data then spans a space with more than $D$ latent dimensions. If $g(D) = 1$, no information content shift occurs, which is true for any linear transformation of data.

Fig. 5 reveals that both approaches are able to encode the input data with more than $D$ latent dimensions. In the case of an ELM, the information content shift is solely caused by its nonlinear activation functions. For recurrent networks, we observe the forecasted effect: The cumulative energy content $g(D)$ of the first $D$ PCs of the attractor distribution is significantly lower for reservoir networks than for ELMs. That is, a reservoir network redistributes more of the existing information in the input data onto the remaining $N - D$ PCs than the feedword approach. This effect, cuased by the recurrent connections, shows the enhanced spatial encoding of inputs in reservoir networks and can explain the improved performance (cf. Fig. 4).

We remark that the introduced measure $g(D)$ does not strictly correlate with the task-specific performance. Although the ESN reassigns a greater amount of information content on the last $N - D$ PCs than the ELM (cf. Fig. 5), this does not improve the generalization performance for every data set (cf. Tab. 1).

**Table 1.** Mean classification rates with standard deviations

| | data set properties | | | classification rate [%] ($L$-fold cross-validation) | | | | network properties | | |
|---|---|---|---|---|---|---|---|---|---|---|
| | $D$ | $C$ | $K$ | $L$ | LM | ELM | ESN | $N$ | $a$ | $\alpha$ |
| Iris [6] | 4 | 3 | 150 | 10 | 83.3 | $88.9 \pm 0.7$ | $92.7 \pm 2.1$ | 50 | 0.5 | 0.001 |
| Ecoli [6] | 7 | 8 | 336 | 8 | 84.2 | $86.6 \pm 0.5$ | $86.4 \pm 0.6$ | 50 | 0.5 | 0.001 |
| Olive [7] | 8 | 9 | 572 | 11 | 82.7 | $95.3 \pm 0.5$ | $95.0 \pm 0.7$ | 50 | 0.5 | 0.001 |
| Wine [6] | 13 | 3 | 178 | 2 | 97.7 | $97.6 \pm 0.7$ | $96.9 \pm 1.0$ | 50 | 0.5 | 0.1 |
| Optdigits [6] | 64 | 10 | 5620 | - | 92.0 | $95.9 \pm 0.4$ | $95.8 \pm 0.4$ | 200 | 0.1 | 0.001 |
| Statlog Shuttle [6] | 9 | 7 | 58000 | - | 89.1 | $98.1 \pm 0.2$ | $99.2 \pm 0.2$ | 100 | 0.5 | 0.001 |

## 5 Conclusion

We present an attractor-based implementation of the reservoir network approach for processing of static patterns. In order to investigate the effect of recurrence on the spatial input encoding, we systematically vary the respective network parameters and compare the recurrent reservoir approach to a related feedforward network. The reservoir dynamics result in an increased nonlinear representation of the input patterns in the network's attractor states which can be advantageous for the separability of patterns in terms of static pattern recognition. In temporal tasks that also require a suitable spatial encoding, the mixed spatio-temporal representation of inputs is crucial for the functioning of the reservoir approach. Incorporating the results reported in [3, 4], we conclude that the spatial representation is not detoriated by the temporal component.

## References

[1] Verstraeten, D., Schrauwen, B.: On the Quantification of Dynamics in Reservoir Computing. In: Alippi, C., Polycarpou, M., Panayiotou, C., Ellinas, G. (eds.) ICANN 2009. LNCS, vol. 5768, pp. 985–994. Springer, Heidelberg (2009)

[2] Jaeger, H.: The echo state approach to analysing and training recurrent neural networks. Technical Report 148, German National Research Center for Information Technology (2001)

[3] Verstraeten, D., Schrauwen, B., Stroobandt, D.: Reservoir-based techniques for speech recognition. In: Proc. IEEE IJCNN, pp. 1050–1053 (2006)

[4] Ozturk, M., Principe, J.: An associative memory readout for ESNs with applications to dynamical pattern recognition. Neural Networks 20(3), 377–390 (2007)

[5] Huang, G., Zhu, Q., Siew, C.: Extreme learning machine: Theory and applications. Neurocomputing 70(1-3), 489–501 (2006)

[6] Frank, A., Asuncion, A.: UCI machine learning repository (2010),
http://archive.ics.uci.edu/ml

[7] Forina, M., Armanino, C.: Eigenvector projection and simplified nonlinear mapping of fatty acid content of italian olive oils. Ann. Chem. (72), 125–127 (1982)

# Action Classification in Soccer Videos with Long Short-Term Memory Recurrent Neural Networks

Moez Baccouche[1,2], Franck Mamalet[1], Christian Wolf[2], Christophe Garcia[1], and Atilla Baskurt[2]

[1] Orange Labs, 4 rue du Clos Courtel, 35510 Cesson-Sévigné, France
firstname.surname@orange-ftgroup.com
[2] LIRIS, UMR 5205 CNRS, INSA-Lyon, F-69621, France
firstname.surname@insa-lyon.fr

**Abstract.** In this paper, we propose a novel approach for action classification in soccer videos using a recurrent neural network scheme. Thereby, we extract from each video action at each timestep a set of features which describe both the visual content (by the mean of a BoW approach) and the dominant motion (with a key point based approach). A *Long Short-Term Memory*-based *Recurrent Neural Network* is then trained to classify each video sequence considering the temporal evolution of the features for each timestep. Experimental results on the *MICC-Soccer-Actions-4* database show that the proposed approach outperforms classification methods of related works (with a classification rate of 77 %), and that the combination of the two features (BoW and dominant motion) leads to a classification rate of 92 %.

## 1 Introduction

Automatic video indexing becomes one of the major challenges in the field of information systems. Thus, more and more works focus on automatic extraction of high-level informations from videos to describe their semantic content. "*Event-based*" and "*Action-based*" classification methods are therefore progressively replacing low-level-based ones, in many applications (closed-circuit television, TV programs structuration...). Especially, sport videos are particularly interesting contents due to their high commercial potential. Several works have dealt with this problem, and can be separated into two main categories. The first one [1] tends to classify sports actions with semantically low-level labels, without using a priori information about the studied sport. On the opposite, the second one [2] extracts high-level semantic information from the sport actions and are domain knowledge-based. Recently, Ballan et al. [3] have proposed a generic approach which is able to semantically classify soccer actions without using a priori information, by relying only on visual content analysis. This approach was experimented on the *MICC-Soccer-Actions-4* database [3], which contains four action classes : *Shot-on-goal*, *Placed-kick*, *Throw-in* and *Goal-kick*. Ballan et al. obtained classification rates of 52, 75 % with a k-NN classifier and 73, 25 % with a SVM-based one.

K. Diamantaras, W. Duch, L.S. Iliadis (Eds.): ICANN 2010, Part II, LNCS 6353, pp. 154–159, 2010.
© Springer-Verlag Berlin Heidelberg 2010

However, most existing methods make little use of the temporal information of the video sequence. In particular, the evolution of shape over time is not treated. In this paper, we advocate the use of learning machines adapted for sequential data. In this context, *Long Short-Term Memory Recurrent Neural Networks* [4] are a particular type of recurrent neural networks that are well-suited for sequence processing due to their ability to consider the context.

In this paper, we propose an LSTM-RNN scheme to classify soccer actions of the *MICC-Soccer-Actions-4* database [3] using both visual and motion contents. The next section describes the outline of the proposed approach. Then, we present in Sect. 3 the visual and dominant motion features that will be used to fed the classifier. LSTM-RNN fundamentals and used architecture will be outlined in Sect. 4, focusing on their abilities to classify sequences. Finally, experimental results, carried out on the *MICC-Soccer-Actions-4* database, will be presented in Sect. 5.

# 2    Proposed Approach

The outline of the proposed approach is shown in Fig. 1. The aim is to classify soccer video sequences that are represented by a sequence of descriptors (one descriptor per image) corresponding to a set of features. The choice of those features is crucial for the successful classification (see Sect. 3). A Recurrent Neural Network (RNN) containing Long Short-Term Memory [4] (LSTM) neurons is trained to categorize each action type based on the temporal evolution of the descriptors. To that aim, descriptors are presented to the neural network (one descriptor per timestep) which makes a final decision based on the accumulation of several individual decisions (see Sect. 4).

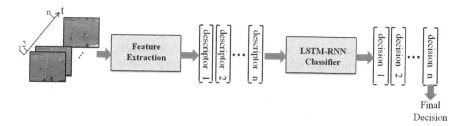

**Fig. 1.** Proposed classification scheme

# 3    Feature Extraction for Action Representation

We have chosen to describe the content of the video sequences by considering both their visual aspect, characterizing the objects appearance, and the motion present in the scene.

### 3.1   Visual Content Representation: A Bag of Words Approach

Bag of words (BoW) are widely used models in image processing, and particularly in object recognition. The main idea is to represent an image by means of an histogram of visual words, corresponding each to a set of local features extracted from the image. In most cases, these features are SIFT descriptors [5].

In the proposed work, the appearance part of our descriptor is inspired by the work of Ballan et al. [3] where a video is represented by means of a sequence of visual BoW (one BoW per frame). To that aim, we generate a codebook of 30 words (empirical choice) resulting of a K-means classification applied to a large number of images extracted from the database. Then, for each video we associate a sequence of descriptors (one per image) having the same size as the codebook and containing values that encode the occurrence frequency of words present in the sequence. Such a representation allows us to take into account the visual content relative to the scene and also to modelize transitions between images by means of the appearance and the disappearance of words.

### 3.2   A SIFT-Based Approach for Dominant Motion Estimation

In addition to the appearance descriptor described above, we propose to introduce another feature, that we called *dominant motion*, to describe the movement represented by the largest number of elements of the scene. Obviously, for a sport video with a global view of the playing field (which is the case of all actions of the database *MICC-Soccer-Actions-4*), the *dominant motion* is assumed to be the one related to the camera. We made the assumption that the camera's movement is affine, which is generally true. The idea is then to estimate the affine transformation $T$ between an image $I_t$ at time $t$ and an image $I_{t+1}$ at time $t+1$.

To that aim, we tend to match SIFT points extracted from each two successive frames of the video. A *Kd-tree* algorithm is used to accelerate the nearest neighbor search process. We reject the interest points corresponding to the TV logos which tend to impose a null motion. Thus, we perform a pre-processing step, inspired by the work in [6], which consists in detecting and blurring these logos. Once SIFT matches are computed, we robustly estimate the affine transformation while ignoring outliers (e.g. moving players) using the RANSAC algorithm [7], aiming at only preserving matches corresponding to the dominant motion.

## 4   Action Classification Using LSTM-RNN

Once the descriptors presented in the previous section are calculated, image by image, for each feature (bag of visual words and dominant motion), the next step consists in using them to classify the actions of the video sequences. We propose to use a particular recurrent neural network classifier, namely Long Short-Term Memory, in order to take benefits of its ability to use the temporal evolution of the descriptors for classification.

## 4.1  Long Short-Term Memory Recurrent Neural Networks

Recurrent Neural Networks (RNN) are a particular category of Artificial Neural Networks which can *remember* previous inputs and use them to influence the network output. This can be done by the use of recurrent connections in the hidden layers. Nevertheless, even if they are able to learn tasks which involve short time lags between inputs and corresponding teacher signals, this *short-term memory* becomes insufficient when dealing with long sequence processing.

The Long Short-Term Memory (LSTM) recurrent architecture was introduced by Schmidhuber et al. [4] in order to provide remedies for the RNN's problem of *exponential error decay*. This is achieved by adding a special node, namely *constant error carousel* (CEC), that allows for constant error signal propagation through time. The second key idea is the use of multiplicative gates to control the access to the CEC.

LSTM have been tested in many applications (CSL learning, music improvisation, phoneme classification...) and generally outperformed existant methods. LSTM have also been used in [8] to structure tennis videos by modelizing transitions between shots, but without analysing their content. In this paper we propose to give as input to the LSTM the extracted features presented in section 3 at each timestep, and train the LSTM network to classify the sport's video sequences.

## 4.2  Network Architecture and Training

In our experiments, we used a recurrent neural network architecture with one hidden layer of LSTM-cells. The input layer has a variable size depending on which features are set as input (see Sect. 5). For the output layer, we used the *softmax* activation function, which is standard for 1 out of $K$ classification tasks [9]. The *softmax* function ensures that the network outputs are all between 0 and 1, and that their sum is equal to 1 at every timestep. These outputs can then be interpreted as the posterior probabilities of the actions at a given timestep, given all the inputs up to the current one. Finally, the hidden layer contains several one-cell unidirectional LSTM neurons fully inter-connected and fully connected to the rest of the network. We have tested several configuration of networks, varying the number of hidden LSTM, and verified that a large number of memory blocks leads to overfitting, and the opposite leads to divergence. Thus, a configuration of 150 LSTM was found to be a good compromise for this classification task. This architecture corresponds to about $10^5$ trainable weights depending on the input size. The network was trained with Online-BPTT with *learning rate* $= 10^{-4}$ and *momentum* $= 0.9$.

## 5  Experimental Results

All the experiments presented in this paper were carried out on the *MICC-Soccer-Actions-4* dataset [3] with a *3-fold cross* validation scheme. In order to

**Table 1.** Summary of obtained results

|  | Classification rate |
|---|---|
| BoW + k-NN [3] | 52,75 % |
| BoW + SVM [3] | 73,25 % |
| BoW + LSTM-RNN | 76 % |
| Dominant motion + LSTM-RNN | 77 % |
| BoW + dominant motion + LSTM-RNN | 92 % |

study the neural classifier's efficiency and to compare to those used in [3], we have learnt such a network taking as input only the BoW descriptors. The codebook described in subsection 3.1 was used to calculate visual word frequency histograms, retaining 30 entries that we use as input of the network. Classification results are reported in table 1, and compared to those presented in [3]. We also present the confusion matrix in Fig. 2-(a).

Table 1 shows that the neural classification scheme largely outperforms the k-NN-based approach and gives better results than the SVM-based one. We have then tested the contribution of the dominant motion descriptors using a network with only 6 inputs (see subsection 3.2). The confusion matrix relative to the classification results is shown in Fig. 2-(b). Results are comparable to those obtained by the BoW-based approach - this is a surprisingly good result given that only camera motion information has been used without any appearance information or local (player) motion.

Furthermore, Fig. 2-(a,b) shows that informations provided by the visual appearance and the dominant motion are complementary. Indeed, the dominant motion-based approach is particularly suited for the classes *throw-in* and *shot-on-goal* because of the representative camera motion existing in these actions (non-moving camera for the first and zoom on the goal-keeper at the end of the action for the last). On the other hand, the classes *goal-kick* and *placed-kick* present highly similar camera movements but distinct characteristic visual words apparition's order.

(a)

|  | Goal-kick | Placed-kick | Shot-on-goal | Throw-in |
|---|---|---|---|---|
| Goal-kick | 0.92 | 0.08 | 0 | 0 |
| Placed-kick | 0.08 | 0.8 | 0 | 0.12 |
| Shot-on-goal | 0 | 0.2 | 0.72 | 0.08 |
| Throw-in | 0.12 | 0.12 | 0.16 | 0.6 |

(b)

|  | Goal-kick | Placed-kick | Shot-on-goal | Throw-in |
|---|---|---|---|---|
| Goal-kick | 0.64 | 0.28 | 0.08 | 0 |
| Placed-kick | 0.08 | 0.68 | 0.08 | 0.16 |
| Shot-on-goal | 0.08 | 0 | 0.88 | 0.04 |
| Throw-in | 0.08 | 0 | 0.04 | 0.88 |

(c)

|  | Goal-kick | Placed-kick | Shot-on-goal | Throw-in |
|---|---|---|---|---|
| Goal-kick | 1 | 0 | 0 | 0 |
| Placed-kick | 0.04 | 0.84 | 0.08 | 0.04 |
| Shot-on-goal | 0 | 0.12 | 0.88 | 0 |
| Throw-in | 0.04 | 0 | 0 | 0.96 |

**Fig. 2.** Confusion matrices : (a) - BoW-based approach (b) - Dominant motion-based approach (c) - Combination of the BoW and the dominant motion

Therefore, we propose to combine both informations and train a network with an input layer's size of 36 (which corresponds to the concatenation of the dominant motion and the BoW). This network enables us to reach a classification rate of 92 % (see table 1 and Fig. 2-(c)), which outperforms the results corresponding to the use of only one type of features, and is, to our knowledge, the best published result on the *MICC-Soccer-Actions-4* dataset.

# 6  Conclusion and Future Work

In this paper, we have presented a recurrent neural scheme for soccer actions classification by considering both visual and dominant motion aspects. Experimental results (see table 1) on the *MICC-Soccer-Actions-4* database show that the LSTM-RNN proposed approach is superior, for this application, to SVM-based and k-NN-based ones. Furthermore, we have demonstrated that camera motion descriptors contain as many discriminant information as visual ones (reaching a classification rate of 77 %). We have also shown that the combination of the two information leads to a classification rate of 92 %, which is the best published result on this dataset. More generally, we have demonstrated that LSTM-RNN are able to learn to classify variable length video sequences taking as input features of different nature automatically extracted from the video.

As future work, we plan to verify the genericity of the approach by testing it on other, more-complex video databases. We also plan to jointly learn feature extractors and classification network using a Convolutional Neural Network-LSTM approach.

# References

1. Ekin, A., Tekalp, A., Mehrotra, R.: Automatic Soccer Video Analysis and Summarization. IEEE Transactions on Image Processing 12(7) (2003)
2. Gong, Y., Lim, T., Chua, H.: Automatic Parsing of TV Soccer Programs. In: IEEE International Conference on Multimedia Computing and Systems, pp. 167–174 (1995)
3. Ballan, L., Bertini, M., Del Bimbo, A., Serra, G.: Action categorization in soccer videos using string kernels. In: Proc. of IEEE CBMI, Chania, Crete (2009)
4. Gers, F., Schraudolph, N., Schmidhuber, J.: Learning precise timing with LSTM recurrent networks. The Journal of Machine Learning Research 3, 115–143 (2003)
5. Lowe, D.: Distinctive image features from scale-invariant keypoints. International journal of computer vision 60(2), 91–110 (2004)
6. Wolf, C., Jolion, J., Chassaing, F.: Text Localization, Enhancement and Binarization in Multimedia Documents. In: Proc. of ICPR (2002)
7. Fischler, M.: RANSAC: A Paradigm for Model Fitting With Applications to Image Analysis and Automated Cartography. Communications of the ACM (1981)
8. Delakis, E.: Multimodal Tennis Video Structure Analysis with Segment Models. PhD thesis, Université de Rennes 1 (2006)
9. Bishop, C.: Neural networks for pattern recognition. Oxford Univ. Press, Inc., Oxford (2005)

# A Hebbian-Based Reinforcement Learning Framework for Spike-Timing-Dependent Synapses

Karim El-Laithy and Martin Bogdan

Faculty of Mathematics and Computer Science
Dept. of Computer Engineering
Universität Leipzig. Germany
kellaithy@informatik.uni-leipzig.de

**Abstract.** In this study a combination of both the Hebbian-based and reinforcement learning rule is presented. The concept permits the Hebbian rules to update the values of the synaptic parameters using both the value and the sign supplied by a reward value at any time instant. The latter is calculated as the distance between the output of the network and a reference signal. The network is a spiking neural network with spike-timing-dependent synapses. It is tested to learn the XOR computations on a temporally-coded basis. Results show that the network is able to capture the required dynamics and that the proposed framework can reveal indeed an integrated version of both Hebbian and reinforcement learning. This supports adopting the introduced approach for intuitive signal processing and computations.

**Keywords:** Hebbian learning, reinforcement learning, spike-time dependent synapses.

## 1 Introduction

Learning in neural networks can be achieved by two main different strategies, namely supervised and unsupervised training [1]. Unsupervised learning is guided by correlations in the inputs to the network. This training strategy has been widely applied to models of, for example, associative memory and self-organizing maps [1]. From a neurobiological point of view, some methods for unsupervised learning have been relatively successful in that they offer an efficient learning strategy and incorporate biologically plausible principles for synaptic modification [2]. Donald Hebb in 1949 [3] postulated that the modifications in the synaptic transmission efficacy are driven by the correlations in the firing activity of the pre- and postsynaptic neurons as described in [2]. One of the attractive models in this regard is the Bienenstock-Cooper-Munro (BCM) model for the development of orientation selective cells in the visual system. The Hebbian learning rule of this model has received considerable support from experiments on long-term potentiation (LTP) and long-term depression (LTD) [4]. Many studies investigated in more details how the hebbian-based learning algorithms can be applied to empower the performance of the artificial neural networks and especially of those realizing the spike-timing dependent activity, see [5,6] for recent reviews. For example, a correlation based hebbian learning rule for spiking neurons was presented in [7] revealing

K. Diamantaras, W. Duch, L.S. Iliadis (Eds.): ICANN 2010, Part II, LNCS 6353, pp. 160–169, 2010.

that correlations between input and output discharges tend to stabilize. In [8] a biologically plausible learning algorithm for multilayer neural networks was studied and it was shown that it enabled the learning of exclusive-Or (XOR) problem without back-propagation with significant robustness against noise. In [9] it was shown that applying both Hebbian and anti-Hebbian rules in a recurrent network that realizes of spike-time dependent plasticity (STDP) leads to approximate convergence of the synaptic weights. These studies were theoretically focused on the computational properties of Hebbian STDP, thus they have illustrated its function in neural homeostasis, supervised and unsupervised learning.

Notably, the theoretical results described in [10] reported that under certain conditions, Hebbian STDP minimizes the postsynaptic neurons variability to a given presynaptic input and anti-Hebbian STDP maximizes this variability. This kind of influence of Hebbian/anti-Hebbian STDP on variability has also been observed at a network level in simulations as in [4] which were done to probe the experimentally observed neural dynamics while learning. By having Hebbian STDP when the network receives positive reward, the variability of the output is reduced, and the network could work the particular configuration that led to positive reward. By having anti-Hebbian STDP when the network receives negative reward, the variability of the networks behavior is increased, and it could thus test various behaviors until it finds one that leads to positive reward. This analysis is conceptually similar to the widely established concepts of reinforcement learning (Rl) which is observed in animal behavior as well, see e.g. [11]. In Rl, a sensory cue is presented to a network, which subsequently gives rise to an output pattern and, as a consequence of this response, a reinforcing feedback from the environment. Rl is, generally, a proven tool for developing an intelligent agent without a teacher (or a supervisor) and without a teaching set [11], in which a reward signal is generated from the interaction with the environment and considered to be the source of supervision, i.e. it represents the teacher in the classical supervised-learning sense.

Although the concept of combining both Hebbian approach and Rl has been not adequately investigated yet, there are some studies that tried to probe the tenability of such integration. For example, in [12] the ability to reduce the required learning steps for certain task in comparison to applying Rl alone was investigated. The task, however, was relatively not well defined to be used for general machine learning regimes. Another study applied the Rl rules to the spike-response-model (SRM) was introduced in [13]. The Hebbian approach was tackled by adding a Hebbian term to the Rl rule. The latter study was directed as well to investigate the influence on the number of learning steps. It is still tempting to ensure whether the Hebbian/anti-Hebbian modulation of STDP with a reward signal can lead to Rl especially for biologically plausible synaptic and neuronal representation that realizes the aspects of temporal dynamics.

Thus, we propose here an *introductory* framework integrating the concepts of both Hebbian/anti-Hebbian and Rl while explicitly using plausible biological neuronal and synaptic representations. To illustrate this, learning the XOR computations is chosen. The biologically plausible neural representations comprises: a) Synaptic representation: one of the well established spike-timing-dependent deterministic synaptic models proposed in [14]; and b) Neuronal representation: leaky Integrate-and-fire neuronal model (IAF) (simulation details are mentioned in section 4). Although other studies have already investigated the issue of either Hebbian or Rl learning in spiking networks using different approaches e.g. [4,15,16,17,13], up to our knowledge this is the first trial to develop the combined Hebbian and Rl framework for the mentioned neural representations. The approach discussed here is inspired from the learning algorithm for stochastic synapses that we have introduced in [18,19]. Here, it is not intended to introduce a novel network-based solution for the XOR problem, however the XOR task is chosen as a classic benchmark problem for learning algorithms. Considering that both Hebbian and Rl are believed to be inherited from the biological neural systems, it makes the biological plausibility of the network components a main aspect here keeping machine learning as a main target. Hence, the core objective in this study is to *propose* an appropriate, but yet simple, learning algorithm which implements both Hebbian- and Rl rules for networks with spike-timing-dependent components, i.e. realizing temporal coding.

## 2   The Model

Neurons are modeled as leaky-IAF neurons usually used in such type of simulations [14]. Each neuron is described by its voltage membrane potential $V$, that follows these dynamics:

$$\tau_V \frac{dV}{dt} = V_{\text{rest}} - V + E_{psp}, \tag{1}$$

where $\tau_V$ is the membrane time constant set at 20 msec, and $E_{psp}$ is the total observed Excitatory postsynaptic potential from all pre-synaptic terminals. When $V(t) \geq V_{\text{th}}$, a spike is generated and $V(t^+) := V_{\text{rest}}$; where $V_{\text{rest}} = 0$ mV and $V_{\text{th}} = 50$mV. Equation 1 is implemented as discrete form introduced by [20] (Please refer to the articles [21,20] for the derivation).

As for the synaptic dynamics, the well-established phenomenological model from Markram et al. [14] for fast synaptic dynamics is used. In particular, synaptic short-term dynamics were determined by the available synaptic efficacy, $R$, and a utilization variable, $u$, which followed the recursive relationship. The mathematical formulations of the model could be expressed as follow (For a better review please refer to [22]):

$$u(n+1) = u(n)e^{\frac{-\Delta t}{\tau_{fac}}} + U_{SE}(1 - u(n)e^{\frac{-\Delta t}{\tau_{fac}}}) \tag{2}$$

$$R(n+1) = R(n)(1 - u(n+1))e^{\frac{-\Delta t}{\tau_{rec}}} + 1 - e^{\frac{-\Delta t}{\tau_{rec}}} \tag{3}$$

$U_{SE}$ is the resting relative amount of synaptic efficacy used per synaptic pulse; and $\tau_{rec}$ and $\tau_{fac}$ are the recovery (from depression) and facilitation time constants for synaptic efficacy. $\Delta t$ is the time difference between the occurrence of the two last action potentials. Let $u(n) \cdot R(n)$ is the response viewed, in an abstract way, as postsynaptic current (PSC); then, $E_{psp}$ is expressed as $E_{psp}(n) = A \cdot u(n) \cdot R(n)$, where $A$ can be viewed as a coupling resistance to the postsynaptic neuron; or it represents the classical synaptic weight. In this synaptic short-term depression, a rise in the presynaptic firing rate causes a transient of synaptic current, which falls off over time according to the equations given above [14].

# 3  Learning Rule

## 3.1  Parameter Update Rule

The Hebbian-based learning concept used in this study was discussed in [20] showing how both the timing parameters and constants of a model can be updated (trained) based on the spiking activity of pre- and postsynaptic neurons. Specifically, the dynamics of synaptic or neuronal activities are governed through the contribution of electrochemical mechanisms. Each of them is represented via a parameter, $m$; e.g. $\tau_{fac}$ or $U_{SE}$ in equation 2. Each mechanism $m$ could contribute to either excitatory or inhibitory regime in the synaptic action; and according to the pre- and postsynaptic activity, the value of $m$ is either increased or decreased following the Hebbian rule [20]. The update of the contribution values of a parameter, $m$, following the Hebbian rule, in general, reads [20]:

$$m_{new} = (1 + \eta)m_{current}, \tag{4}$$

where $|\eta| < 1$ is the learning rate set at 0.01. An arbitrarily chosen sign for the learning rate is set for each parameter. In this study, the training algorithm is restricted, arbitrarily, to the synaptic parameters: $U_{SE}$, $\tau_{fac}$, $\tau_{rec}$ and $A$; their initial values are 0.1, 1.15 sec, 0.05 sec and 0.001 respectively.

The realization of the Hebbian rule in eq. 4 reads [21,20]: the values of parameters contributing to the excitatory mechanisms are increased and the contribution of the inhibitory mechanism are decreased when a spike at the pre-synaptic neuron induce a *desired* spike at the post-synaptic neuron. The term desired here refers to a correct hit. If the pre-synaptic spike does not induce a post-synaptic spike, and no spike is expected the process is flipped. The Anti-Hebbian rules are the inverse process of the Hebbian process [20,18]. Whether the spike is desired or not is judged by comparing to another reference signal. So far, it is supervised learning in full sense.

Concerning RI, it uses a *reward signal*, $K$, applied to the *eligible* synapses to update their parameters. The update process is also meant to change the values of the parameters controlling the process. However, in the proposed approach here, the reward signal is used to both flip the direction and accelerate/decelerate the update process. Thus, on episodic basis (after each simulation run), the sign of the reward value is actually used to alter the direction of the change in the parameter value, either to increase or to decrease the value of the tunned parameter. The value of the reward is used to alter the learning rate. Thus, the learning update rule is rewritten [18]:

$$m_{new} = (1 + \eta \cdot K)m_{current} \tag{5}$$

$K$ can reverse the direction of the updating process of the parameters since it is a signed value, and can in both directions either accelerate or decelerate the learning process.

## 3.2  The Reward Signal

It was described in [18,23], how a reward signal (or a feedback parameter), $K$, can be derived to represent the progress in a desired performance. Accordingly, it can be used to control the direction and the speed of the learning process. Specifically, it is the time derivative of the observed distance, $\mathcal{D}$, between the reference signal, $f(t)$, and the current network output, $g(t)$. Thus, the reward signal via the feedback parameter K reads:

$$K \equiv \frac{\Delta\mathcal{D}(f,\,g)}{\Delta t_{\text{simulation}}} \tag{6}$$

The latter time derivative is observed on an episodic basis, i.e. after each simulation run, and not along each simulation run, as in equation 8. As for this distance measure, in [5] a method was proposed to calculate the difference between an output spike pattern and a correct reference one by subtracting the Gaussian filtered versions of both trains from each other. In [24], van Rossum proposed an algorithm, which we use here, to calculate the distance between two train of spikes. This dimensionless distance calculates the dissimilarity between two spike trains by filtering both spikes trains with exponential filter, and calculating the integrated squared difference of the two trains. By definition, two exact patterns will give the minimum allowed distance of zero. The latter approach is more widely used in the literature that encouraged us to use it here. Hence, $\mathcal{D}$ reads:

$$\mathcal{D}(f,\,g) = \frac{1}{\tau_c} \int_0^\infty [f(t) - g(t)]^2 dt, \tag{7}$$

where $\tau_c$ is time decay constant of the exponential filter. It controls the extent of the effect of each spike on the total spike train, here set at 15 msec. $f(t)$ and $g(t)$ are reference and output signals respectively. Thus, the reward signal is the difference in the observed distance $\mathcal{D}$ from the current run and the previous one; expressed as:

$$K = \mu \left( \mathcal{D}_{\text{current}} - \mathcal{D}_{\text{previous}} \right) \tag{8}$$

$\mu$ is a scaling factor to match the order value of $K$ to the order of the parameter under training.

For Rl, one issue then remains which is eligibility. Eligibility denotes a synapse that has contributed to obtain either the reward or the punishment [11]. Alternatively, the eligibility traces are those values used to tune the value of the reward signal applied to each synapse depending on its activity and location in the network. These traces could be either analytically derived as in [17,10,5] or phenomenologically as in [11,25,26]. The latter approach is the one that is adopted here. In general, this approach depends on the logical understanding of the flow of information within the network. In other words, for a series of neuronal activities, not all synapses of the neural network are contributing to the rewarding. In the study in hands, it is arbitrarily chosen to allow only the forward synaptic connections between the input neurons and the hidden neurons to be learned, Fig. 1. This choice is based on personal observations and other studies [18,19].

Remark, the introduced learning algorithm here performs a kind of gradient descent, that implicitly optimizes a cost function (or an error function) in a heuristic way. This cost/error function is the distance between the reference and output signals.

## 4   Simulation and Results

We use a network setup similar in structure to the one used in [17,10] as shown in the lower part of Fig. 1. There are two input neurons N1 and N2. The input is a set of 600

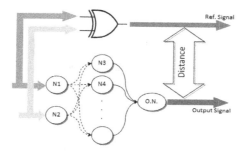

**Fig. 1.** Schematic of network setup and simulation. The input to the network is fed also to an XOR gate to get the reference signal. The details of binning input/output signals are omitted from this illustration for clarity. Dashed arrows represent those synaptic connections allowed for learning. The distance here refers to the calculated distance according to eq. 7.

Poisson distributed trains of spikes with total epoch of 200 msec at 1 msec discretization each. This set is arranged in two subsets, each for one input neuron. These input neurons take two different Poisson distributed input trains from the two subsets per simulation run. The first results are done with a hidden layer of only 4 neurons. The network has one output neuron, i.e. the network size is $N = 7$ neurons[1]. The input and output are temporally coded (or binned) with a time window of certain width, $\mathcal{W}$ taken, first, to be 5 msec. Within each time window, having one or more spikes is interpreted as having digital one (Hi) otherwise it is zero (Low). Thus for a signal of length $L$ msec that is binned with $\mathcal{W}$ msec window, the input and output signals are mapped to shorter digital signals with length $L/\mathcal{W}$. In other words, signal $f(t)$ with 200 msec epoch is mapped to a digital version $F(T)$ that is 40 steps long. An actual XOR output is calculated for the same digital input signals, as in the upper part of Fig. 1 to be the reference signal. The distance $\mathcal{D}$ between the two digital representations of reference signal and network output is calculated per simulation run. As for another indicator for the performance of the network, we use the max. cross correlation coefficient, $\mathcal{X}$, between the Gaussian-filtered versions of F and G, where $F$ and $G$ are the digital versions of the reference and the output signals respectively.

It should be pointed out here that the normal evaluation method of the results, by counting the correct hits of ones and zeros [17,10], seems from our point of view not applicable to our case. The timing of occurrence of input spikes is solely the input feature to the network, since both neuronal and synaptic representation here implement temporal dynamics [22]. Comparing only the counts (hit rates) of the occurrences of ones and zeros in the output and reference signal suppresses all the temporal information and eliminate the involvement of the STDP realized by the synaptic dynamics. Thus, we used the distance between the two digital signals and the coefficient of cross-correlation between them since both measures are directly dependent on the temporal information within the signals.

In Fig. 2 the performance of the learning algorithm in case of 4 neurons in the hidden layer ($N = 7$) and time window of 5 msec is illustrated. Fig. 2(a) shows the progress in

---

[1] The minimum number of perceptrons required to solve the XOR problem is 5 units.

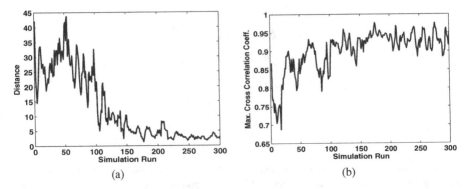

(a)                                                    (b)

**Fig. 2.** a) Simulation results in case of 7 neurons in the hidden layer, at window set to 5 msec: a) Distance between the reference and the output signal, $\mathcal{D}$ as in eq. 7. b) Max. cross correlation coefficient observed between the reference and the output signal.

terms of the distance measure between the digital versions of the reference and output signals, $\mathcal{D}(F,G)$. The value of the distance, started at about 25, experiences an overall decay over time; The mean value over the last 50 simulation runs in the observed distance is $4.98 \pm 4.15$. The second indicator of performance of the network, $\mathcal{X}(F,G)$, between the same two signals is shown in Fig. 2(b). Here, the value is climbing up with learning. The mean value over the last 50 simulation runs is $91.6\% \pm 5.9$. The time evolution of two trained parameters is illustrated in Fig. 3(a). In case of 7 neurons in the hidden layer ($N=10$), $\mathcal{D}(F,G)$ and $\mathcal{X}(F,G)$ are $3.21 \pm 2.33$ and $93.09\% \pm 3.0$ respectively.

Relatively larger networks with 13, 17 and 20 neurons in hidden layer ($N = 16$, 20 and 23 respectively) are also investigated. The enhancement in the performance is observed in terms of $\mathcal{X}(F,G)$ to be with an overall improvement of 1%, 1.3% and 1.7%

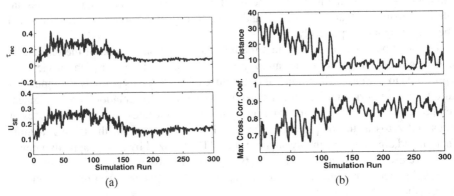

(a)                                                    (b)

**Fig. 3.** a) Evolution of the trained parameters $U_{SE}$ and $\tau_{rec}$ over time. b) Simulation results in case of 7 neurons in the hidden layer, at window set to 4 msec. Upper Panel: the observed distance between the reference and the output signal, while the Lower Panel: Max. cross correlation coefficient observed between the reference and the output signal.

respectively. The effect of changing the time window is also investigated. In Fig. 3(b) both performance measures are illustrated for window value of 4 msec. The mean values at different binning window settings (4, 5 and 7 msec) are summarized in table 1. In case of 4 and 7 msec window, the epoch of the input signals are changed in order to get a final digital version of 40 steps long; i.e. the input signal length is changed to be 160 and 280 msec respectively.

**Table 1.** Summary of performance measures, Distance and coefficient of cross correlation, for the network with 7 neurons in the hidden layers for different window values. Both measure are given as the mean value over the last 50 simulation runs.

| Window $\mathcal{W}$ | Distance $\mathcal{D}(F, G)$ | Max. cross-correl. coeff. $X(F, G)(\%)$ |
|---|---|---|
| 4 msec | 4.63 ± 5.12 | 89.50 ± 6.01 |
| 5 msec | 3.21 ± 2.33 | 93.09 ± 3.04 |
| 7 msec | 6.83 ± 5.41 | 94.42 ± 3.01 |

# 5  Discussion

Developing this framework was basically motivated by the need for both a proper and simple learning algorithm for the spiking networks that utilize spike-timing dependent synapses. In these networks, the synapses are not represented as weighting factors. Hence, altering the synaptic response via the classical back-propagation or the δ-rule is not appropriate [10]. Moreover, the analytical derivation, for example, in [17] and other similar studies are based, for certain extent, on the assumption that the neurotransmitter (Nt) release is independent of the spike generation process at any particular time. Although this is not wrong as an assumption, it limits the application of their techniques to be extended for the stochastic synaptic models, in which the probabilistic nature of the Nt is only responsible for the spike generation.

The results reported here show that the introduced framework enabled the network to perform the XOR computations at the basic network size of 7 neuron at 4 msec binning window. The model still performs well with larger networks and at different binning time-windows. The results with larger networks show slight enhancement on the performance. We believe that a much better enhancement in the performance shall be accomplished by the introduction of feedback connections within the network. Moreover, the network proposed here uses purely excitatory connections. Therefore, realizing both feedback connections and inhibitory ones within the network shall raise the performance of the network in general [9] which is left for a further study. Comparing our results to those reported e.g. in [10] as the count of correct hits may be still investigated in a further study, although, considering the temporal dynamics in the output represents a key issue that distinguish the framework presented in this study from former ones. The output of the network in our case is highly characterized by its temporal features.

We believe that the approach presented here is more useful in such cases where the use of stochastic and biological plausible representations is needed [18]. The results support using our approach for tasks that require intuitively signal processing and computational capabilities. Moreover, since the results confirm that the proposed framework can indeed lead to Rl, the concept of integrating the Hebbian-rules and the Rl for the utilized neural representations agrees, thus, with the remarks discussed in [4]; these remarks indicated that the bidirectional dependence of synaptic plasticity, in general, on the synaptic resources (Neurotransmitter and/or calcium), which observed in biological synapses, represents a kind of combined supervised and unsupervised learning. This sheds more light on the importance of developing Rl frameworks that can specifically "teach" the internal neuronal/synaptic dynamics according to predefined inputs/outputs combinations. Considering the simple mathematical implementation of the update rule and calculation of the reward signal values, this framework can used as an online adaptive scheme for controlling the network performance assuming availability of the reference signal.

This study is an introductory case to be followed in order to extend the presented approach and investigate it with larger networks that may comprises multi layers. Also the use of other neuronal and synaptic representation still represent a coming task to be tackled. Besides, the algorithm has not been proven to be optimal in the sense of learning speed or convergence to minimal error, it may be amenable to improvement.

# 6  Conclusion

In this study a phenomenological online learning rule is presented. It is based on the Hebbian/anti-Hebbian basics of updating the values of the parameters affecting the neural dynamics. It is controlled via an episodic reward signal derived from the comparison between the output of the network and a reference signal. Since both Hebbian and Rl are believed to be inherited from the biological neural systems, the biological plausibility of the approach is a main aspect in this study considering machine learning as a main target. In other words and within the class of error-driven learning models that have some probability of being neurobiologically relevant, our approach then presents an alternative to classical reinforcement learning, which relies on the controversial assumption of a diffusible reinforcement signal. As such, it brings models for reinforcement learning closer to plausible models of unsupervised learning while realizing the Hebbian perspectives.

# References

1. Hopfield, J.J.: Brain, neural networks, and computation. Rev. Mod. Phys. 71(2), S431–S437 (1999)
2. Gerstner, W., Kistler, W.: Mathematical Formulations of Hebbian Learning. Biological Cybernetics 87(5-6), 404–415 (2002)
3. Hebb, D.O.: The Organization of Behavior. Wiley and Son, New York (1949)
4. Pennartz, C.: Reinforcement learning by hebbian synapses with adaptive thresholds. Neuroscience 81(2), 303–319 (1997)
5. Farries, M.A., Fairhall, A.L.: Reinforcement Learning With Modulated Spike Timing Dependent Synaptic Plasticity. J. Neurophysiol. 98(6), 3648–3665 (2007)
6. Urbanczik, R., Senn, W.: Reinforcement learning in populations of spiking neurons. Nature Neuroscience 12(3), 250–252 (2009)

7. Kempter, R., Gerstner, W., van Hemmen, J.: Hebbian learning and spiking neurons. Phys. Rev. E 59(4), 4498–4514 (1999)
8. Klemm, K., Bornholdt, S., Schuster, H.G.: Beyond hebb: Exclusive-or and biological learning. Physical Review Letters 84, 3013 (2000)
9. Carnell, A.: An analysis of the use of hebbian and anti-hebbian spike time dependent plasticity learning functions within the context of recurrent spiking neural networks. Neurocomput. 72(4-6), 685–692 (2009)
10. Florian, R.V.: Reinforcement learning through modulation of spike-timing-dependent synaptic plasticity. Neural Computation 19(6), 1468–1502 (2007)
11. Lee, K., Kwon, D.S.: Synaptic plasticity model of a spiking neural network for reinforcement learning. Neurocomputing 71(13-15), 3037–3043 (2008)
12. Bosman, R.J.C., van Leeuwen, W.A., Wemmenhove, B.: Combining hebbian and reinforcement learning in a minibrain model. Neural Networks 17(1), 29–36 (2004)
13. de Queiroz, M.S., de Berrdo, R.C., de Pdua Braga, A.: Reinforcement learning of a simple control task using the spike response model. Neurocomputing 70(1-3), 14–20 (2006)
14. Markram, H., Wang, Y., Tsodyks, M.: Differential signaling via the same axon of neocortical pyramidal neurons. Proc. of the Nat. Academy of Sciences of the USA 95(9), 5323–5328 (1998)
15. Song, S., Miller, K.D., Abbott, L.F.: Competitive Hebbian learning through spike-timing-dependent synaptic plasticity. Nature Neuroscience 3(9), 2259 (2000)
16. Seung, H.: Learning in spiking neural networks by reinforcement of stochastic synaptic transmission. Neuron 40(6), 1063–1073 (2003)
17. Xie, X., Seung, H.S.: Learning in neural networks by reinforcement of irregular spiking. Phys. Rev. E 69(4), 69–79 (2004)
18. El-Laithy, K., Bogdan, M.: Synchrony state generation in artificial neural networks with stochastic synapses. In: Alippi, C., Polycarpou, M., Panayiotou, C., Ellinas, G. (eds.) ICANN 2009. LNCS, vol. 5768, pp. 181–190. Springer, Heidelberg (2009)
19. El-Laithy, K., Bogdan, M.: Predicting spike-timing of a thalamic neuron using a stochastic synaptic model. In: ESANN Proceedings, pp. 357–362 (2010)
20. Namarvar, H.H., Liaw, J.S., Berger, T.W.: A new dynamic synapse neural network for speech recognition. In: Proc. IEEE Int. Conf. Neural Networks, pp. 2985–2990 (2001)
21. Liaw, J., Berger, T.W.: Dynamic synapse: A new concept of neural representation and computation. Hippocampus 6, 591–600 (1996)
22. Morrison, A., Diesmann, M., Gerstner, W.: Phenomenological models of synaptic plasticity based on spike timing. Science 98, 459–478 (2008)
23. El-Laithy, K., Bogdan, M.: On the Role of Synaptic Dynamics in the Generation of Synchrony States (2010)
24. van Rossum, M.C.W.: A Novel Spike Distance. Neural Comp. 13(4), 751–763 (2001)
25. Kimura, D., Hayakawa, Y.: Reinforcement learning of recurrent neural network for temporal coding. Neurocomputing 71(16-18), 3379–3386 (2008)
26. Fiete, I.R., Seung, H.S.: Gradient learning in spiking neural networks by dynamic perturbation of conductances. Physical Review Letters 97(4), 048104 (2006)

# An Incremental Probabilistic Neural Network for Regression and Reinforcement Learning Tasks

Milton Roberto Heinen and Paulo Martins Engel

UFRGS – Informatics Institute
Porto Alegre, CEP 91501-970, RS, Brazil
mrheinen@inf.ufrgs.br, engel@inf.ufrgs.br

**Abstract.** This paper presents a new probabilistic neural network model, called IPNN (for Incremental Probabilistic Neural Network), which is able to learn continuously probability distributions from data flows. The proposed model is inspired by the Specht's general regression neural network, but have several improvements which makes it more suitable to be used on-line in and robotic tasks. Moreover, IPNN is able to automatically define the network structure in an incremental way, with new units added whenever necessary to represent new training data. The performed experiments shows that IPNN is very useful in regression and reinforcement learning tasks.

**Keywords:** Probabilistic neural networks, General regression neural networks, Incremental learning, Gaussian mixture models, Reinforcement learning.

## 1 Introduction

Probabilistic neural network (PNN) [1, 2] is a feed-forward artificial neural network (ANN) based on the Bayes strategy for decision making and on nonparametric estimators of conditional probability density functions (pdf). Its most important advantage over other ANN models is that the training is easy and instantaneous. In fact, in a PNN learning occurs after a single presentation of each pattern (the procedure is not iterative), and new information can be used whenever it becomes available. Another advantage of PNN is that it is guaranteed to asymptotically approach the Bayes' optimal decision surface provided that the class pdf's are smooth and continuous [3].

The main limitation of the original PNN architecture proposed by Specht [1, 2] is that it requires a separate neuron for each training pattern, which makes the computation very slow for large databases requiring a large amount of space in memory. To avoid this limitation, in [4] a clustering algorithm based on stochastic gradient descent is proposed to find a reduced set of representative exemplars to be used as the nodes for PNN. Unfortunately, the solution proposed in [4] requires labeled training samples, which can only be applied for classifying data. For the general regression neural network (GRNN) [5], which is the probabilistic network model used for estimation of continuous variables, the Traven's algorithm is not directly applicable. Moreover, it uses radially symmetric pdf's, i.e., covariance matrices of the form $\mathbf{C} = \sigma^2 \mathbf{I}$ (where $\sigma$ is a smoothing parameter and $\mathbf{I}$ is the identity matrix), which according to [6] is not robust with respect to affine transformations of the feature space and requires a careful adjustment of the smoothing parameter $\sigma$.

K. Diamantaras, W. Duch, L.S. Iliadis (Eds.): ICANN 2010, Part II, LNCS 6353, pp. 170–179, 2010.

In [7] the Tråvén's work is extended so that no constraints are imposed on the covariance structure of the mixture components (pattern units). However, in this algorithm the number of mixture components is assumed to be fixed, which prevents its use in continuous learning tasks. Although other algorithms have been proposed to automatically set the mixture components of both PNN and GRNN [3, 8–11], most of them are based on off-line methods (e.g. the EM algorithm [12]), which requires that the complete training set is previously known and fixed [13]. For on-line applications, in which learning must occur continuously (e.g. mobile robotics [14]), these algorithms are not very useful.

In this paper a new probabilistic neural network model, called IPNN (for Incremental Probabilistic Neural Network), is proposed. It is based on the Specht's GRNN model [5], but have several improvements which makes it more suitable to be used in on-line applications operating in stochastic environments. The main advantages of IPNN over other probabilistic models are:

- IPNN does not require a separate neuron for each training pattern;
- The number of pattern units is not limited nor fixed (new units are incrementally added when necessary);
- Full covariance matrices are used in the pattern units;
- The pattern units are continuously adjusted to fit the distributions of the input data;
- The learning algorithm operates in an on-line and continuous way without requiring that the complete training set be previously known and/or fixed (each training data can be immediately used and discarded);
- It is not necessary any normalization of the input data.

The rest of this paper is organized as follows. Section 2 describes the proposed model in details. Section 3 presents some experiments involving reinforcement learning and regression tasks. Finally, Section 4 provides some final remarks and perspectives.

# 2  Incremental Probabilistic Neural Network

This section describes the new probabilistic neural network proposed in this paper, called IPNN. It is based on Specht's PNN [2] and GRNN [5] models, but has several improvements which makes it more adequate to be used in on-line and continuous learning tasks. Figure 1 shows a diagram of the IPNN model. Its structure is similar to the RBF network [15], but the learning algorithm (Subsection 2.1) is quite different.

As other neural network models, the first layer of IPNN has just distribution units, but unlike GRNN and PNN in the proposed model it is not necessary to normalize the input variables (in Specht's models this is necessary because the kernels have the same width in each direction). The second layer, composed by probabilistic neurons (called pattern units in the Specht's model), is implemented using multivariate Gaussian distributions, i.e., the component densities $p(\mathbf{x}|j)$ are computed through:

$$p(\mathbf{x}|j) = \frac{1}{(2\pi)^{D/2}\sqrt{|\mathbf{C}_j|}} \exp\left\{ -\frac{1}{2}(\mathbf{x} - \boldsymbol{\mu}_j)^T \mathbf{C}_j^{-1}(\mathbf{x} - \boldsymbol{\mu}_j) \right\} \qquad (1)$$

where $\mathbf{x}$ is an input data vector, $D$ is the dimensionality of $\mathbf{x}$ (number of input variables), $\boldsymbol{\mu}_j$ is the mean and $\mathbf{C}_j$ is the covariance matrix of the $j$th pattern unit. The third layer,

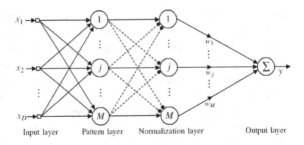

**Fig. 1.** Diagram of the IPNN model

which has always the same size of the pattern layer, computes the posterior probability $p(j|\mathbf{x})$ for each unit $j$ using the Bayes rule:

$$p(j|\mathbf{x}) = \frac{p(\mathbf{x}|j)\,p(j)}{\sum_{q=1}^{M} p(\mathbf{x}|q)\,p(q)} \qquad (2)$$

where is $p(j)$ is the prior probability of $j$. The dotted lines in Figure 1 represent inhibitory connections used for normalization in (2). The fourth layer computes the actual network output $y$ through:

$$y = \sum_{j=1}^{M} w_j\,p(j|\mathbf{x}) \qquad (3)$$

where $M$ is the current number of pattern units. Although Figure 1 shows just one unit in the output layer, IPNN can have an arbitrary number of outputs (i.e., $y$ can be a vector). As described above, in IPNN the number of pattern units is not predefined or fixed. Moreover, it uses non-restricted, full multivariate covariance matrices in the pattern units. These improvements are possible because IPNN uses a new learning algorithm, described in the next subsection, which is able to incrementally learn Gaussian mixture models in an on-line and continuous way.

## 2.1  Learning Algorithm

This subsections presents a detailed description of the learning algorithm used by IPNN, which is based on our previous work in statistical learning [16]. Like other supervised ANN models, IPNN has two operation modes, called *learning* and *regression*. But unlike most part of these models, in IPNN these operations don't need to occur separately, i.e., the learning and regression tasks can be intercalated. In fact, even with just one training pattern the neural network can be used in the regression mode (IPNN can immediately use the acquired knowledge), and the estimates become more precise as more training data arrive. Moreover, the learning process can occur perpetually, i.e., the neural network can always be updated as new input data arrive.

Initially the IPNN network has no units in the pattern layer. When the first training data vector arrives, the first pattern unit is created centered on this input vector, i.e., the distribution parameters are initialized through:

$$\boldsymbol{\mu}_1 = \mathbf{x}^1; \; \mathbf{C}_1 = \sigma_{ini}^2 \mathbf{I}; \; w_1 = d^1; \; p(1) = 1; \; sp_1 = 1,$$

where $\sigma_{ini}$ is a configuration parameter which defines the initial radius of $\mathbf{C}$ (the pdf is initially circular but it changes to reflect the actual data distribution as new input data arrive), $d^1$ is the desired output received at time $t = 1$, $p(1)$ is the prior probability of the first unit and $sp$ is an accumulator which stores the summation of the posterior probabilities $p(j|\mathbf{x})$ (it is required that $\sum_{j=1}^{M} sp_j = 1$):

$$sp_j = \sum_{t=1}^{T} p(j|\mathbf{x}^t) \qquad (4)$$

where $T$ is the current time instant of and $\mathbf{x}^t$ is the input vector received at time $t$. To avoid an eventual saturation of $sp_j$ it is periodically restarted to a fraction $\gamma$ of its value:

$$\text{if}\left(\sum_{q=1}^{M} sp_q\right) \geq sp_{max} \text{ then } sp_j = \gamma sp_j, \; \forall j$$

where $sp_{max}$ can be a huge value (e.g. $sp_{max} = 10^{32}$). It is important to say that a normalization unit is created whenever a new unit is added to the pattern layer, i.e., both layers have always the same size.

When a new training vector arrives, the pattern layer is activated and the component densities $p(\mathbf{x}|j)$ of each unit $j$ are computed using Equation 1. The algorithm then decides if it is necessary to create a new component for the current data point $\mathbf{x}^t$ based on the posterior probabilities $p(\mathbf{x}|j)$ of component membership according to the test:

$$p(\mathbf{x}|j) < \frac{\tau_{nov}}{(2\pi)^{D/2}\sqrt{|\mathbf{C}_j|}}, \; \forall j \qquad (5)$$

where $\tau_{nov}$ is a configuration parameter which specifies a minimum value for the acceptable likelihood. If (5) returns true, the new input vector $\mathbf{x}$ is not considered as a member of any existing component. In this case, a new unit $k$ is created centered on $\mathbf{x}^t$:

$$\boldsymbol{\mu}_k = \mathbf{x}^t; \; \mathbf{C}_k = \sigma_{ini}^2\mathbf{I}; \; w_j = d^t; \; p(k) = \left(\sum_{j=1}^{M} sp_j\right)^{-1}; \; sp_k = 1.$$

After this, the prior probabilities of all $j$ units are adjusted to sum one through

$$p(j) = \frac{p(j)}{\sum_{q=1}^{M} p(q)} \qquad (6)$$

Otherwise (if Equation 5 returns false for at least one unit), the existing mixture model is updated using the following recursive equations:

$$sp_j^{new} = sp_j^{old} + p(j|\mathbf{x}) \qquad (7)$$

$$\boldsymbol{\mu}_j = \boldsymbol{\mu}_j^{old} + \frac{p(j|\mathbf{x})}{sp_j^{new}}\left(\mathbf{x} - \boldsymbol{\mu}_j\right) \qquad (8)$$

$$\mathbf{C}_j = \mathbf{C}_j^{old} - (\boldsymbol{\mu}_j - \boldsymbol{\mu}_j^{old})(\boldsymbol{\mu}_j - \boldsymbol{\mu}_j^{old})^T + \frac{p(j|\mathbf{x})}{sp_j^{new}}\left[(\mathbf{x} - \boldsymbol{\mu}_j)(\mathbf{x} - \boldsymbol{\mu}_j)^T - \mathbf{C}_j^{old}\right] \qquad (9)$$

$$p(j) = \frac{sp_j^{new}}{\sum_{q=1}^{M} sp_q^{new}} \qquad (10)$$

where $p(j|\mathbf{x})$ is the posterior probability computed by (2) and $\mu_j^{old}$ refers to the value of $\mu_j$ at time $t-1$ (i.e., before updating). Finally, the output weight $w_j$ is updated using the desired output $d^t$:

$$w_j = w_j + \frac{p(j|\mathbf{x})}{sp_j^{new}} (d^t - w_j) \tag{11}$$

The learning algorithm used by IPNN has just two configuration parameters, the initial radius $\sigma_{ini}$ and the novelty parameter $\tau_{nov}$. The initial radius is similar to the Traven's smoothing parameter [1], but in IPNN $\sigma_{ini}$ defines just the initial radius of the pdf's (their size and shape rapidly change as new training data arrive) and thus is not critical. The only requirement for $\sigma_{ini}$ is to be large enough to avoid singularities. In our experiments, described in the next section, we made $\sigma_{ini}$ an arbitrary fraction (10%) of the range of the input data, i.e.: $\sigma_{ini} = (\mathbf{x}_{max} - \mathbf{x}_{min})/10$.

The $\tau_{nov}$ parameter, on the other hand, is more critical and must be defined carefully. It indicates how distant $\mathbf{x}$ must be from $\mu_j$ to be consider a non-member of $j$. For instance, $\tau_{nov} = 0.01$ indicates that $p(\mathbf{x}|j)$ must be lower than one percent of the Gaussian height (probability in the center of the Gaussian) for $\mathbf{x}$ be considered a non-member of $j$. If $\tau_{nov} < 0.01$, few pattern units will be created and the regression will be coarse. If $\tau_{nov} > 0.01$, more pattern units will be created and consequently the regression will be more precise. In the limit, if $\tau_{nov} = 1$ one unit per training pattern will be created, which corresponds to the Traven's model [5] but using multivariate Gaussian kernels. Next section describes some experiments performed to evaluate the proposed model in regression tasks.

## 2.2 Reinforcement Learning

Traditional reinforcement learning (RL) techniques (e.g., Q-learning and Sarsa) generally assume that states and actions are discrete, which seldom occurs in real mobile robot applications, by instance [17]. To allow continuous states and actions in RL applications without discretization it is necessary to use function approximators like MLP [18] or RBF [19, 20] neural networks. According to [21], for a function approximator to be used successfully in reinforcement learning tasks (i.e., for it to converge to a good solution) it must be: (i) incremental (it should not have to wait until a large batch of data points arrives to start the learning process); (ii) aggressive (it should be capable of producing reasonable predictions based on only a few training points); (iii) non-destructive (it should not be subject to destructive interference or "forgetting" past values); and (iv) must provide confidence estimates of its own predictions. Thus, according with this principles IPNN is very adequate to reinforcement tasks, i.e., it satisfies all the requirements described above.

Implementing a reinforcement learning algorithm using IPNN may be straightforward – we just need to use the state and action vectors as inputs and the $Q$ value as output in the IPNN network. Unfortunately, using this strategy the action selection process becomes a general optimization problem far from trivial [21]. We considered that states are conditionally independent from the actions, which simplifies the covariance matrices and allows an efficient action selection mechanism, as will be described bellow. This was implemented in the proposed model using two separate covariance matrices for states $\mathbf{C}^s$ and actions $\mathbf{C}^a$ (and the corresponding $\mathbf{x}^s$, $\mathbf{x}^a$, $\boldsymbol{\mu}_j^s$ and $\boldsymbol{\mu}_j^a$ as well), and the posterior probabilities $p(j|\mathbf{x})$ are computed during learning by:

$$p(j|\mathbf{x}) = \frac{p(\mathbf{x}^s|j)\,p(\mathbf{x}^a|j)\,p(j)}{\sum_{q=1}^{M} p(\mathbf{x}^s|q)\,p(\mathbf{x}^a|q)\,p(q)} \tag{12}$$

where $p(\mathbf{x}^s|j)$ and $p(\mathbf{x}^a|j)$ are computed by (1) using $\mathbf{C}_j^s$ and $\mathbf{C}_j^a$, respectively. To find out the best action for the current state $s$ the posterior probability $p(j|\mathbf{x})$ is computed using only $p(\mathbf{x}^s|j)$ (this is possible because state and actions are treated as conditionally independent) and the best action $a^*$ is estimated for the current state using the maximum likelihood hypothesis $j^* = \max_j p(j|\mathbf{x}^s)$, i.e., $a^* = \boldsymbol{\mu}_{j^*}^a$.

To allow exploration in the proposed model the actions are selected randomly using a Gaussian distribution with mean $\boldsymbol{\mu}_{j^*}^a$ and covariance matrix $\mathbf{C}_{j^*}^a$, which enables high exploration rates in the beginning of the learning process (when the Gaussian distributions are larger) and this exploration is reduced when the confidence estimates become stronger. Therefore, this action selection mechanism does not require any optimization technique, which makes the algorithm very fast. Moreover, it allows an exploration strategy based on statistical principles which does not require *ad-hoc* parameters.

In [19, 22] another algorithm is presented, called continuous actor-critic, which also uses Gaussian units in the hidden layer (it uses normalized RBF networks). But unlike IPNN, in [19, 22] the Gaussian units are previously configured and maintained fixed during the learning process. Next section describes some experiments performed to evaluate the proposed model in regression and reinforcement learning tasks.

# 3   Experiments

This section describes the experiments performed to evaluate with the proposed model in regression and reinforcement learning tasks. The configuration parameters used in these experiments are $\tau_{nov} = 0.01$ and $\sigma_{ini} = (\mathbf{x}_{max} - \mathbf{x}_{min})/10$. It is important to say that no exhaustive search was performed to optimize these parameters.

## 3.1   Estimating the Outputs of a Complex Plant

In the first experiment the regression technique needs to identify a complex plant, originally introduced in [23] for the control of nonlinear dynamical systems using backpropagation neural networks, described by:

$$u(k) = \begin{cases} \sin(2\pi k/250) & \text{if } k \le 500 \\ 0.8\sin(2\pi k/250) + 0.2 sin(2\pi k/25) & \text{if } k > 500 \end{cases}$$

where $k$ is an integer value in the interval $[1, 1000]$ (i.e., 1000 training samples were used). This plant was also used in [5] to highlight the GRNN advantages over other ANN models. Figure 2(a) shows the results obtained in this experiment. In this figure, the training samples are shown using red dots, and the output estimated by IPNN is shown using a blue line. The normalizaed root mean square (NRMS) error obtained in

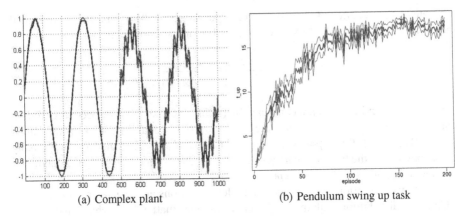

(a) Complex plant                    (b) Pendulum swing up task

**Fig. 2.** Results obtained by IPNN in regression and reinforcement learning tasks

this experiment was 0.0325, and 43 units were added during the learning process. The time needed to perform the learning process was 0.11 seconds in a typical computer[1].

Comparing these results with those presented in [5], it can be noticed that IPNN is able to obtain a similar performance (although in [5] the NRMS error is not informed) using less pattern units than the GRNN model (the Specht's GRNN model would create one pattern unit for each training data, i.e., 1000 pattern units). Moreover, the IPNN learning process was completely on-line and incremental, not requiring the selection of specific patterns for training.

### 3.2   A Reinforcement Learning Task

In the next experiment the proposed model was used to control a pendulum with limited torque using reinforcement learning. The dynamics of the pendulum are given by $\dot{\theta} = \omega$ and $ml^2\dot{\omega} = -\mu\omega + mgl\sin\theta + \mu$ [19], where $\theta$ is the pendulum angle and $\dot{\theta}$ is the angular velocity. The physical parameters are mass $m = 1$, pendulum length $l = 1$, gravity constant $g = 9.81$, time step $\Delta t = 0.02$ and maximum torque $T_{max} = 5.0$. The reward is given by the height of the tip of the pendulum, $R(\mathbf{x}) = cos\theta$, and the discount factor is $\gamma = 0.9$. Each episode starts from an initial state $x(0) = (\theta(0), 0)$, where $\theta(0)$ is selected randomly in $[-\pi, \pi]$. An episode lasted for 20 seconds unless the pendulum is over-rotated ($|\theta| > 5\pi$). These parameters are the same used in [19] for the continuous actor-critic. Due to the stochastic nature of the RL action selection mechanism, this experiment was repeated 50 times using different random seeds, and the mean of the obtained results is shown in Figure 2(b).

In Figure 2(b) the $x$ axis represents the learning episode, and the $y$ axis represents the time in which the pendulum stayed up ($t_{up}$) i.e., when $|\theta| < \pi/4$ (this is the same evaluation criteria used in [19]). The red line in Figure 2(b) represents the mean and the blue lines represent the 95% confidence interval of the obtained results. Comparing these results with those presented in [19] it can be noticed that our model has a performance

[1] All experiments were executed in a Dell Optiplex 755 computer, Intel(R) Core(TM)2 Duo CPU 2.33GHz processor and 1.95GB of RAM.

slightly superior of the Doya's continuous actor-critic, without requiring any previous configuration of the radial basis functions. The average number of probabilistic units added by IPNN was 109.41.

### 3.3 Predicting the Motor Actions in a Robotic Task

As a final example, the proposed model was used to compute the desired speeds for a mobile robot following the walls of the environment shown in Figure 3(a) (this environment was originally used in [24]), where the squares represent the robot trajectory (each color represents the most active pattern unit at each time) and the black arrow shows the robot starting position and direction. This experiment is relevant because in most mobile robot control tasks it is not possible to predict all situations that may occur in the real world, an thus the mobile robot needs to learn from experience while it is interacting with the environment. Moreover, for a mobile robot to adapt to new situations the learning process must occur continuously.

In this experiment, the input data consist of a sequence of 4 continuous values $(s_1, s_2, s_3, s_4)$ corresponding to the readings of a sonar array located at the left/right side $(s_1, s_4)$ and at $-10°/ +10°$ from the front $(s_2, s_3)$ of a robot, generated using the Pioneer 3-DX simulator software ARCOS (Advanced Robot Control & Operations Software). The output data correspond to the speeds to be applied to the right $(v_1)$ and left $(v_2)$ motors of the mobile robot. In these experiments, the robot was manually controlled to perform one loop in the environment shown in Figure 3(a), and the task consists in predicting the next motor actions at each time $t$.

Figure 3(b) shows the results obtained in this experiment, where the $x$ axis corresponds to the simulation time $t$ in seconds and the $y$ axis corresponds to the difference between the right and left speeds, i.e., $y_d(t) = v_1 - v_2$. A positive value in $y_d(t)$ corresponds to a left turn in the robot trajectory and a negative value corresponds to a right turn. The red line in Figure 3(b) represents the desired $y_d(t)$ values and the blue line represents the difference between the IPNN outputs, i.e.: $y_o(t) = y_1 - y_2$. It is important to say that the IPNN used in this experiment has really two outputs, i.e., the difference $y_o(t)$ was used in Figure 3(b) just for visualization purposes.

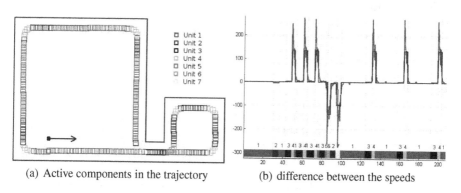

(a) Active components in the trajectory          (b) difference between the speeds

**Fig. 3.** Results obtained in the robotic task (NRMS = 0.050373)

It can be noticed in Figure 3(b) that IPNN was able to approximate the desired output with reasonable accuracy (the NRMS error was 0.050373) using few probabilistic units (just seven) and no memory of past perceptions and actions (e.g., recurrent connections). The main differences between $y_d(t)$ and $y_o(t)$ are in the extremes, i.e., the approximation performed by IPNN is smoother than the target function.

Another interesting feature which can be noticed from this experiment is that IPNN is able to create useful representations in the pattern and normalization layers. This can be observed in Figure 3(a), where the colors in the robot's trajectory represent the units with the highest posterior probability $p(\mathbf{x}|j)$ (i.e., the so called *maximum likelihood hypothesis*). It can be noticed in Figure 3(a) that the pattern units are related to some persistent "concepts" like *wall at right* (1: red), *corridor* (2: blue), *curve at left* (4: cyan), *curve at right* (6: green) and so on. The lower band in Figure 3(b) also shows the maximum likelihood hypothesis at each time step, which stands out the network outputs produced by each probabilistic unit.

## 4   Conclusion

In this paper a new probabilistic neural network model, called IPNN (for Incremental Probabilistic Neural Network), is proposed. This proposed model, which can be considered an improved version of the Specht's general regression neural network (GRNN) [5], is able to perform regression tasks in an incremental and continuous way. Moreover, it uses full multivariate Gaussian probability density functions (pdf) in the probabilistic units, which allows more precise approximations using less artificial neurons in the pattern layer. The experiments performed using the proposed model show that IPNN can be successfully used in function approximation and reinforcement learning tasks. Besides, the learning process occurs in an on-line and incremental way without requiring that the complete training set is previously known and fixed. This is necessary if the neural network has to be used in continuous learning tasks as in robotic control in unexplored environments. Future developments will use the proposed model in control and learning tasks using a real Pioneer 3-DX mobile robot.

## Acknowledgment

This work is supported by CNPq, an entity of the Brazilian government for scientific and technological development.

## References

1. Specht, D.: Probabilistic neural networks for classification, mapping, or associative memory. In: Proc. IEEE Int. Conf. Neural Networks, San Diego, CA, vol. 1, pp. 525–532 (July 1988)
2. Specht, D.F.: Probabilistic neural networks. Neural Networks 3, 109–118 (1990)
3. Rutkowski, L.: Adaptive probabilistic neural networks for pattern classification in time-varying environment. IEEE Trans. Neural Networks 15(4), 811–827 (2004)
4. Tråvén, H.G.H.: A neural network approach to statistical pattern classification by "semi-parametric" estimation of probability density functions. IEEE Trans. Neural Networks 2(3), 366–377 (1991)

5. Specht, D.F.: A general regression neural network. IEEE Trans. Neural Networks 2(6), 568–576 (1991)
6. Montana, D.: A weighted probabilistic neural network. In: Advances in Neural Information Processing Systems, vol. 4, pp. 1110–1117. Morgan Kaufmann, San Francisco (1992)
7. Ćwik, J., Koronacki, J.: Probability density estimation using a gaussian clustering algorithm. Neural Computing and Applications 4, 149–160 (1996)
8. Berthold, M.R., Diamond, J.: Constructive training of probabilistic neural networks. Neurocomputing 19, 167–183 (1998)
9. Delgosha, F., Menhaj, M.B.: Fuzzy probabilistic neural networks: A practical approach to the implementation of bayesian classifier. In: Reusch, B. (ed.) Fuzzy Days 2001. LNCS, vol. 2206, pp. 76–85. Springer, Heidelberg (2001)
10. Chang, R.K.Y., Loo, C.K., Rao, M.V.C.: Enhanced probabilistic neural network with data imputation capabilities for machine-fault classification. Neural Computing and Applications 18, 791–800 (2009)
11. Polat, O., Yildirim, T.: FPGA implementation of a general regression neural network: An embedded pattern classification system. Digital Signal Processing 20, 881–886 (2010)
12. Dempster, A.P., Laird, N.M., Rubin, D.B.: Maximum likelihood from incomplete data via the EM algorithm. Journal of the Royal Statistical Society 39(1), 1–38 (1977)
13. Tan, P.N., Steinbach, M., Kumar, V.: Introduction to Data Mining. Addison-Wesley, Boston (2006)
14. Thrun, S., Burgard, W., Fox, D.: Probabilistic Robotics. In: Intelligent Robotics and Autonomous Agents. MIT Press, Cambridge (2006)
15. Haykin, S.: Neural Networks and Learning Machines, 3rd edn. Prentice-Hall, Upper Saddle River (2008)
16. Engel, P.M., Heinen, M.R.: Incremental learning of multivariate gaussian mixture models. In: Proc. 20th Brazilian Symposium on AI (SBIA), São Bernardo do Campo, SP, Brazil. LNCS. Springer, Heidelberg (October 2010) (to appear)
17. Sutton, R.S., Barto, A.G.: Reinforcement Learning: An Introduction. MIT Press, Cambridge (1998)
18. Utsunomiya, H., Shibata, K.: Learning with a recurrent neural network in a continuous state and action space task. In: Köppen, M., Kasabov, N., Coghill, G. (eds.) ICONIP 2008, Part II. LNCS, vol. 5507, pp. 970–978. Springer, Heidelberg (2009)
19. Doya, K.: Reinforcement learning in continuous time and space. Neural Computation 12(1), 219–245 (2000)
20. Basso, E.W., Engel, P.M.: Reinforcement learning in non-stationary continuous time and space scenarios. In: Anais do VII Brazilian Meeting on Artificial Intelligence ENIA, Bento Gonçalves, RS, Brazil. SBC Press (2009)
21. Smart, W.D.: Making Reinforcement Learning Work on Real Robots. Ph.d. thesis, Brown Univ., Providence, Rhode Island (May 2002)
22. Doya, K.: Temporal difference learning in continuous time and space. In: Advances in Neural Information Processing Systems, vol. 8, pp. 1073–1079 (1996)
23. Narendra, K.S., Parthasarathy, K.: Identification and control of dynamical systems using neural networks. IEEE Trans. Neural Networks 1, 4–27 (1990)
24. Nolfi, S., Tani, J.: Extracting regularities in space and time through a cascade of prediction networks: The case of a mobile robot navigating in a structured environment. Connection Science 11(2), 125–148 (1999)

# Using Reinforcement Learning to Guide the Development of Self-organised Feature Maps for Visual Orienting

Kevin Brohan[1], Kevin Gurney[2], and Piotr Dudek[1]

[1] The University of Manchester,
School of Electrical and Electronic Engineering,
Manchester M13 9PL, United Kingdom
kevin.brohan@postgrad.manchester.ac.uk,
p.dudek@manchester.ac.uk
[2] University of Sheffield,
Department of Psychology,
Sheffield S10 2TP, United Kingdom
k.gurney@sheffield.ac.uk

**Abstract.** We present a biologically inspired neural network model of visual orienting (using saccadic eye movements) in which targets are preferentially selected according to their reward value. Internal representations of visual features that guide saccades are developed in a self-organised map whose plasticity is modulated under reward. In this way, only those features relevant for acquiring rewarding targets are generated. As well as guiding the formation of feature representations, rewarding stimuli are stored in a working memory and bias future saccade generation. In addition, a reward prediction error is used to initiate retraining of the self-organised map to generate more efficient representations of the features when necessary.

**Keywords:** saccade, oculomotor system, visual search, action selection, system model, self-organised map, internal representation, saliency.

## 1 Introduction

Artificial behaving systems must address a number of problems related to action selection and the organisation of knowledge. In particular, we are interested in establishing how an agent can develop useful internal representations of world-related information acquired via sensory inputs and potential rewards associated with various actions; how it can use this information to decide what action to perform next and how can it alter its strategies to adapt to changing circumstances in the outside world? Previous models, which address the learning of internal representations of the behavioural context in which actions take place, include the models of Dominey [1], Cisek [2] and Wilimzig et al. [3].

We address these issues within the context of a visual search task. A virtual eye explores a 2D scene containing a large number of cues by foveating to one cue at a time (Fig. 1). At any point in time, the retinal image contains many cues, and the system must determine which of these cues will become the next target. Some cues are

K. Diamantaras, W. Duch, L.S. Iliadis (Eds.): ICANN 2010, Part II, LNCS 6353, pp. 180–189, 2010.

associated with a reward, though the rewarding cues may change over time, and the task is to learn which categories of cue are rewarding and to foveate to them as often as possible.

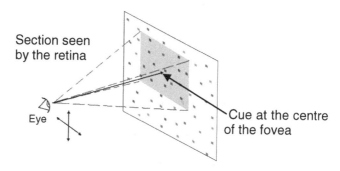

**Fig. 1.** Schematic of the experiment: the retina views a section of the world image at any point in time, making saccades so that a cue always falls on the centre of the fovea (solid black arrow). The target of the saccade may be rewarding, which trains a short term memory and biases the eye to search for similar cues.

The system model is broadly inspired by the visual pathways for saccade generation in the mammalian brain. In the model, low-level feature extraction is followed by a split in processing between two streams: a colour-sensitive 'what' pathway which subserves feature and object detection and a monochromatic 'where' pathway which subserves spatial processing. This scheme is related to that for biological visual processing, in which simple features are first extracted in visual area 1 (V1): these signals are then passed to a dorsal stream devoted largely to spatial (and motion) processing, and a ventral stream which largely subserves feature recognition (which may include a colour dimension) culminating in object identification in inferotemporal cortex (IT) [4]. In the primate brain, neuronal tunings in the dorsal stream show a retinotopic organisation [5][6] and there is evidence for topographic organisation of neuronal responses in IT such that neurons which respond to similar features are located close together in cortex [7]. We deploy similar signal representations in our model. There is also evidence that information from both ventral and dorsal streams is combined into a variety of salience maps (for example, in frontal eye fields) which represent candidate targets for saccades. The competition between these possible targets is resolved in looped circuits through the basal ganglia before the signal is expressed in the superior colliculus which, in turn, drives saccades via the saccadic generator in brainstem [8]. Behaviourally relevant information is maintained in prefrontal working memory [9] and there are several processes devoted to biasing saccades from previous targets under so-called inhibition of return (IOR) [10].

In our model, the action selection problem is addressed through a saliency map that combines bottom-up processing of sensory cues with an IOR mechanism and top-down memory signals that bias saccades towards features that are expected to be rewarding. The model has two novel features: firstly, sensory cues are internally represented in a self-organised map (SOM) of feature space and a working memory of rewarding cues is topographically projected onto this map. Secondly, we bias the development of the

SOM with a reward prediction error signal. The development of the SOM is thus modulated to facilitate the efficient allocation of limited computational resources towards resolving uncertainty in the predicted reward associated with cues.

In the next section, the operation of the model will be overviewed. Implementation details will be given in Section 3. Section 4 contains results of simulations and discussion of these results. Conclusions are presented in Section 5.

## 2   Model Overview

The overview of the model is presented in Fig. 2. The world image $S^W$ is composed of a large number of colour cues on a black background. The retina contains a sub-window of the world image, as determined by the gaze coordinates. The retinal image is split into the luminance channel $R^L$ which is processed in the retinotopic space ('where' pathway) and three colour channels $R^R$, $R^G$, $R^B$ which together form a retinotopic feature vectors $C$ and are further processed in the feature space ('what' pathway). It should be noted that we chose to operate with colour cues for simplicity, but retinotopic maps of other features (e.g. orientations etc.) could be considered.

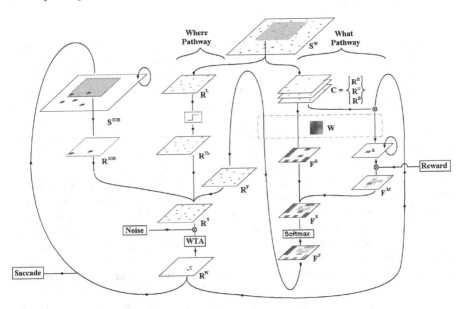

**Fig. 2.** Schematic of the neural network:  the retinal image is divided into feature-based and retinotopic channels. See text for details.

The feature vectors $C$ from each retinal location are classified using a self-organised map $W$, and results are pooled into a feature map $F^R$ which develops an internal representation of the observed stimuli.  A small number of nodes are used in the SOM in order to force the inputs to compete for representation on the map. The SOM can reorganise and its plasticity is modulated by the reward signals, so that behaviourally relevant features are given more precise representations. The balance between the stability and adaptability of the representation is determined by the overall success of the system in predicting the reward associated with various cues.

In the task, a reward is given for making saccades to cues of some determined colours. A working memory ($\mathbf{F}^M$) is topographically mapped onto $\mathbf{F}^R$ and activity in this layer represents reward expectation for a feature at the corresponding location in the $\mathbf{F}^R$. The feature saliency map $\mathbf{F}^S$ is developed combining bottom-up classification of features in the scene by $\mathbf{F}^R$ and top-down memory of rewarding features $\mathbf{F}^M$. The $\mathbf{F}^F$ layer "sharpens" the activity of the $\mathbf{F}^S$ layer such that the activity of the most active units is increased. The "sharpened" feature saliency $\mathbf{F}^F$ is then transformed back to the retinotopic coordinate frame, providing a map $\mathbf{R}^F$, which associates the reward expectation assigned to the features with their locations.

The visual saliency map $\mathbf{R}^S$ is formed by combining the feature-based saliency map $\mathbf{R}^F$, a bottom-up cue-background separation map $\mathbf{R}^{Th}$ (obtained in the 'what' pathway from the luminance map $\mathbf{R}^L$) and inhibition of return map $\mathbf{R}^{IOR}$. The activity in the visual saliency map $\mathbf{R}^S$ represents the reward anticipation at a given cue location. Competition between locations is resolved stochastically and the next saccadic target ($\mathbf{R}^W$) is determined. The saccadic target is classified by the self-organised map ($\mathbf{F}^W$), and if a saccade is made to a rewarding target, the activity in the corresponding location in $\mathbf{F}^M$ is increased. If a target is unrewarding, then the activity in that region of $\mathbf{F}^M$ is reduced.

After a saccade has been made, the target location is activated on a world-centric $\mathbf{S}^{IOR}$ map which prevents the eye from returning to that position for a short period of time.

## 3  Implementation Details

In the first stage of processing, previously visited locations are inhibited by using current gaze coordinate information to map the spatial inhibition field ($\mathbf{S}^{IOR}$) onto retinotopic coordinates ($\mathbf{R}^{IOR}$). The inhibition of return world map $\mathbf{S}^{IOR}$ contains traces of previously visited locations. After a saccade is made, the activity in $\mathbf{S}^{IOR}$ is increased with a Gaussian profile centred at the target location. $\mathbf{S}^{IOR}$ is implemented as a leaky integrator and the activity decays over time.

The feature map $\mathbf{F}^R$ represents the retinotopic RGB vectors of $\mathbf{C}$ on a self-organising 2D map. The function of the $\mathbf{F}^R$ layer is to pool the feature classification results across a retinotopic array of shared-weight SOM classifiers. As in the classical SOM [12], the neurons of the $\mathbf{F}^R$ layer are tuned to preferred input vectors ($\mathbf{W}$). For each retinal location $i$, the best matching unit (BMU) is calculated as the location $j$ in the SOM with the shortest distance between its preferred vector $\mathbf{W}_j$ and the feature vector $\mathbf{C}_i$. The results are pooled across the retina so that the activity of neuron at location $j$ in $\mathbf{F}^R$ is equal to 1 if a feature is present and 0 if a feature is not present in the visual scene, regardless of how many retinotopic locations activate the point $j$ in the SOM:

$$\mathbf{F}^M_j = \begin{cases} 1 & \text{,if } \exists\, i \,:\, j = \arg\min_m \left\{ \left\| \mathbf{C}_i - \mathbf{W}_m \right\| \right\} \\ 0 & \text{otherwise} \end{cases} \tag{1}$$

The activity of the feature saliency map $\mathbf{F}^S$ is calculated as the summation of the activities of the feature memory $\mathbf{F}^M$ and the $\mathbf{F}^R$ layer:

$$\mathbf{F}^S = \mathbf{F}^M + \mathbf{F}^R \tag{2}$$

The $\mathbf{F}^S$ activity is then mapped back to retinotopic space as $\mathbf{R}^F$ such that the strength of a feature in $\mathbf{F}^S$ is reflected in the retinotopic locations at which this feature is present:

$$R_i^F = F_j^S : j = \arg\min_m \left\{ \left\| \mathbf{C}_i - \mathbf{W}_m \right\| \right\} \tag{3}$$

The top-down modulatory activity ($\mathbf{R}^F$) is combined with the bottom-up cue segmentation (thresholded luminance activity $\mathbf{R}^{Th}$) and the previously inhibited locations ($\mathbf{R}^{IOR}$) to form the combined retinotopic saliency map $\mathbf{R}^S$:

$$\mathbf{R}^{Th} = H\left(\mathbf{R}^L - T\right) \tag{4}$$

$$\mathbf{R}^S = \mathbf{R}^{Th}(1 + \frac{1}{2}\mathbf{R}^F) - \mathbf{R}^{IOR} \tag{5}$$

where $T$ is the luminance threshold and H is the Heaviside step function. To implement stochastic competition, the saliency ($\mathbf{R}^S$) is multiplied by an array of white noise ($\mathbf{N}$) and the maximum activity is selected as the target location $x$ for the next saccade:

$$x = \arg\max_i \left\{ R_i^S N_i \right\} \tag{6}$$

In the next stage, the weights $\mathbf{W}$ of the SOM layer are trained. The winning unit $k$ corresponding to the feature vector at saccade target $x$ is located in the map space by calculating the BMU:

$$k = \arg\min_j \left\{ \left\| \mathbf{C}_x - \mathbf{W}_j \right\| \right\} \tag{7}$$

If a cue is rewarding ($r = 1$), some activity is introduced to the location surrounding $k$ in the learning layer $\mathbf{F}^M$ while if a cue is unrewarding, ($r = 0$) the activity at the point $k$ is reduced:

$$\Delta F_j^L = \begin{cases} G(j,k,A,\sigma_L) & ,r = 1 \\ -B & ,r = 0, j = k \\ 0 & ,r = 0, j \neq k \end{cases} \tag{8}$$

where $G$ is a Gaussian function in map space centred on neuron $k$ with amplitude $A = 1$, spread $\sigma_L = 0.25$ and $B = 0.25$.

The SOM weights are modified such that the distance between each weight $\mathbf{W}_j$ and the input vector of the winning unit $\mathbf{C}_x$ is reduced. The degree to which a weight is modified $\Delta\mathbf{W}_j$ decreases as a Gaussian function of the topographic distance from the BMU in the map space. The strength of the change is modulated by the learning rate $\alpha_t$:

$$\Delta\mathbf{W}_j = \alpha_t \left\| \mathbf{C}_x - \mathbf{W}_j \right\| G(j,k,\sigma_t) \tag{9}$$

where G is a Gaussian function of constant area. The SOM weights are initialised with very small values. In the classical SOM global organisation is generated across the map by constantly decreasing values of $\alpha_t$ and $\sigma_t$ over time. This slowly 'freezes' the weights across the map and allows increasingly finer details to be represented on the SOM [12].

Since the stimuli and rewards may change over time, we introduce in our model a feature that allows the SOM weights to become plastic again. If the network is unable to predict rewards with sufficient success, we should assume that the internal representation of that stimulus is not sufficiently resolved on the SOM and that it may be useful to 'unfreeze' the SOM weights and to attempt to generate a new representation of the stimulus. The values of $\alpha_t$ and $\sigma_t$ are thus modulated by the reward history, in the following way:

The reward prediction error $\delta$ is a measure of the surprise when an expected reward is undelivered or a reward is received from an unexpected source. It is defined as the absolute value of the difference between the received reward $r$ and the expected reward, represented by the activity of the winning neuron in the working memory layer $F_k^M$:

$$\delta(r) = \left| r - F_k^M \right| \qquad (10)$$

A non-linear function of the reward prediction error is integrated over time with a leaky neuron of output $\xi$.

$$\xi_t = (1 - \gamma)\xi_{t-1} + \gamma \frac{\delta(r)}{1 - \delta(r) + \theta} \qquad (11)$$

where $\theta$ was equal to 0.1, and g is the leak rate, which was equal to 0.05.

If the value of $\xi$ exceeds a predefined threshold, which occurs at a time $t_{th}$, the variables $\xi$, $\alpha_t$ and $\sigma_t$ are reset to their initial values of 0, $\alpha_0$ and $\sigma_0$. The values of $\alpha_t$ and $\sigma_t$ decrease linearly with decay rate $\lambda$ after reset time $t_{th}$.

$$\alpha_t = \max\{-\lambda(t - t_{th}) + \alpha_0, 0\} \quad , \quad \sigma_t = \max\{-\lambda(t - t_{th}) + \sigma_0, \varepsilon\} \qquad (12)$$

and $\varepsilon$ is a small positive number (1E-5 in this paper) which prevents $\sigma_t$ from decreasing to zero. The time course of the variables associated with the modulation of the SOM during a typical experiment is shown Figure 3.

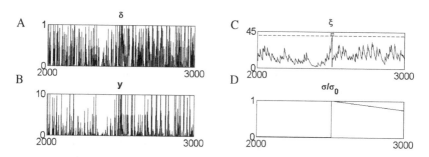

**Fig. 3.** Representation of the modulation of $\alpha_t$ and $\sigma_t$ in the neural network. A) $\delta$ is the reward prediction error; B) y is a non-linear function of the error, which filters out small errors. C) $\xi$ is the leaky integration of y, in which the dashed line marks the threshold. D) $\sigma/\sigma_0$, $\alpha/\alpha_0$ are the modulated learning parameters.

## 4 Results

The model was implemented on a desktop PC in APRON software, a tool for implementing neural simulations on massively parallel processor arrays [13]. In the first experiment, we test the performance of the working memory during a rewarding search task with static SOMs. In the second experiment we examine the effectiveness of the reward-modulated SOM in adapting to a changing reward scenario. In both cases, experiments ran for 10000 time steps, with 10 trials per experiment. The world image is of dimensions 256 x 256 pixels and contains 256 2 x 2 pixel colour cues. The squares were chosen from a set of 64 distinct colours and each colour appears in the world image at four locations. The positions of the cues are random and repeated across trials, and the colours are randomly assigned to the cue positions at the beginning of each trial. The retina views a 128 x 128 pixel region of the world, in which the mean number of cues on the retina at any time is 46.0, with a standard deviation of 14.3.

### 4.1 Experiment I

In the first experiment, SOMs were trained for 200000 steps with constant linear decay throughout, and $\alpha_0$ and $\sigma_0$ values of 0.02 and 0.05 respectively. A new SOM was generated for each trial and no rewards were given in the control experiment. The same SOMs were used during the experiment and the control stages and the SOM did not develop during either the experiment or the control.

There were four different reward epochs in the experiment, each lasting for 2500 time steps. For the first 2500 steps, a reward was presented for foveating to a single orange cue (RGB = {1, .85, 0}). For the second epoch, a reward was presented for foveating to one of two green cues (RGB = {0, 1, 0.07} or RGB = {0, 1, 0.17}). For the third epoch, a reward was present for foveations to one blue cue (RGB = {0, 0.24, 1}). Finally, for the fourth epoch, rewards were given for foveating to one of two magenta cues (RGB = {1, 0, 0.73} or RGB = {1, 0, 0.64}).

Figure 4(A, B) shows the number of saccades made to each colour in this experiment. In the case with working memory (Fig. 4B), saccades were preferentially made to rewarding cues.

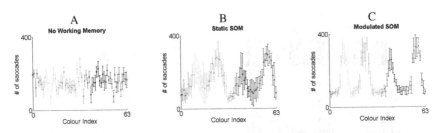

**Fig. 4.** The y axis represents the total number of saccades across 10000 time steps to each possible colour with A) no working memory, B) working memory & static SOM and C) working memory & modulated SOM

Figure 5 (A, B) shows the number of saccades made to each colour in time bins of 100 steps. In the case with working memory (Fig. 5B), saccades were biased towards the rewarding cues, and cues which were similar. In the case without working memory (Fig. 5A), the system had no significant preference for any cue colour.

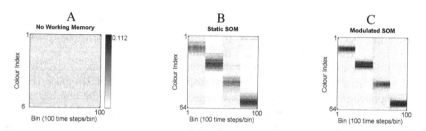

**Fig. 5.** The system learned to distinguish between the rewarding and the unrewarding cues. In the control experiment the rate of detection was approximately the same for all colours. The pixel values represent the average across 10 trials. A) No working memory, B) working memory & static SOM and C) working memory & modulated SOM.

## 4.2 Experiment II

In the second experiment, we investigated the effect of modulating the learning rate $\alpha_t$ and influence $\sigma_t$ online. The results from experiment I are used as the control for this experiment. Figure 4(C) shows the number of saccades made to each cue type in this experiment. The modulated SOM was far more successful at creating a useful representation of the rewarding cues than the static SOM and it shows much better discrimination between rewarding and unrewarding stimuli. Far fewer saccades were being made to unrewarding objects when compared with the control, as is clear from the broadness of the peaks in Fig. 4(B, C). This result is to be expected as the modulated SOM is able to re-train when the rewarding colour changes, allowing the network to re-deploy its limited resources to address the new scenario.

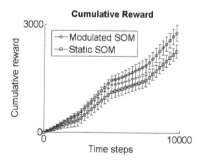

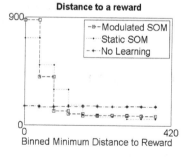

**Fig. 6.** The total number of rewards received over time. The error bars mark one standard deviation across 10 trials. For clarity, every $250^{th}$ point is plotted.

**Fig. 7.** Number of saccades to each colour plotted against the distance between a cue and a reward in RGB space normalised by the number of cues per bin

Figure 5(C) shows the number of saccades made to each colour in time bins of 100 steps. Again, the peaks are more intense and more tightly tuned around the rewarding cues.

When rewarding cues were present on the retinal image, saccades were preferentially made to the rewarding cues during each epoch. Results from the static SOM were similar to those from the modulated SOM, though the static SOM had more difficulty in resolving between rewarding and unrewarding cues. Figure 6 shows the cumulative number of rewards received over time. The modulated model proved far more effective at finding rewarding cues than the static model.

For both experiments, we investigated the mean number of times a saccade was made to a cue as a function of cue distance from the reward in RGB space (Fig. 7). Distances between cue and reward were assigned to 10 bins and the number of cues per bin was counted. The number of saccades per bin was normalised by the number of different cues that were assigned to each distance bin. In the modulated SOM, saccades are more tightly tuned towards rewarding units.

## 5  Conclusions

We have presented a neural network model of working memory on a self-organised feature map as a solution to an action selection problem. The model contains the novel features of a) generating internal representations of stimuli and reward expectation values for different cues and b) using a reward prediction error to remap the SOM when the rewarding stimuli are not sufficiently resolved.

This model is an example of a self-organised map being implemented as part of a larger dynamic neural network system. Rewarding features are learned as activity in the working memory, which is topographically projected onto a self-organised feature map. The working memory biases the system towards saccadic targets which are expected to be rewarding.

By purposely limiting computational resources (restricting the number of nodes in the SOM) we addressed the issue of efficient internal representations of the feature space. The feature maps adapt and self-reorganise to make the model more effective at recognising behaviourally relevant stimuli.

We have demonstrated that the model successfully learns to search for rewarding stimuli, and that the search performance is improved through the action of the modulated SOM.

## Acknowledgment

This work was supported by EPSRC Grant no. EP/C516303.

## References

1. Dominey, P.F.: Complex sensory-motor learning based on recurrent state representation and reinforcement learning. Biol. Cybern. 73, 265–274 (1995)
2. Wilimzig, C., Schneider, S., Schöner, G.: The time course of saccadic decision making: Dynamic field theory. Neural Networks (19), 1059–1074 (2006)

3. Cisek, P.: Integrated Neural Processes for Defining Potential Actions and Deciding between Them: A Computational Model. J. Neurosci. 26(38), 9761–9770 (2006)
4. Mishkin, M., Ungerleider, L.G.: Contribution of Striate Inputs to the Visuospatial Functions of Parieto-Preoccipital Cortex in Monkeys. Behavioural Brain Research 6, 57–77 (1982)
5. Colby, C.L., Goldberg, M.E.: Space and Attention in Parietal Cortex. Annu. Rev. Neurosci., 319–349 (1999)
6. Larsson, J., Heeger, D.J.: Two Retinotopic Visual Areas in Human Lateral Occipital Cortex. J. Neurosci., 13128–13142 (2006)
7. Tanaka, K.: Inferotemporal Cortex and Object Vision. Annu. Rev. Neurosci. 19, 109–139 (1996)
8. Gurney, K., Prescott, T., Redgrave, P.: A computational model of action selection in the basal ganglia. i. a new functional anatomy. Biol. Cybern. 84(6), 401–410 (2001a)
9. Rao, S.C., Rainer, G., Miller, E.K.: Integration of What and Where in the Primate Prefrontal Cortex. Science 276, 821–824 (1997)
10. Posner, M.I., Cohen, Y.: Components of visual orienting. In: Bouma, H., Bouwhuis, D. (eds.) Attention and Performance, vol. X, pp. 552–556. Erlbaum, Mahwah (1984)
11. Sapir, A., Soroker, N., Berger, A., Henik, A.: Inhibition of return in spatial attention: direct evidence for collicular generation. Nature Neuroscience 2, 1053–1054 (1999)
12. Kohonen, T.: Self-Organized Formation of Topologically Correct Feature Maps. Biol. Cybern. 43, 59–69 (1982)
13. Barr, D.R.W., Dudek, P.: APRON: A Cellular Processor Array Simulation and Hardware Design Tool. EURASIP J. Adv. Sig. Pr, Article ID: 751687 (2009)

# Exploring Continuous Action Spaces with Diffusion Trees for Reinforcement Learning

Christian Vollmer, Erik Schaffernicht, and Horst-Michael Gross

Neuroinformatics and Cognitive Robotics Lab
Ilmenau University of Technology
98693 Ilmenau, Germany
christian.vollmer@tu-ilmenau.de
http://www.tu-ilmenau.de/neurob

**Abstract.** We propose a new approach for reinforcement learning in problems with continuous actions. Actions are sampled by means of a diffusion tree, which generates samples in the continuous action space and organizes them in a hierarchical tree structure. In this tree, each subtree holds a subset of the action samples and thus holds knowledge about a subregion of the action space. Additionally, we store the expected long-term return of the samples of a subtree in the subtree's root. Thus, the diffusion tree integrates both, a sampling technique and a means for representing acquired knowledge in a hierarchical fashion. Sampling of new action samples is done by recursively walking down the tree. Thus, information about subregions stored in the roots of all subtrees of a branching point can be used to direct the search and to generate new samples in promising regions. This facilitates control of the sample distribution, which allows for informed sampling based on the acquired knowledge, e.g. the expected return of a region in the action space. In simulation experiments, we show how this can be used conceptually for exploring the state-action space efficiently.

**Keywords:** reinforcement learning, continuous action space, action sampling, diffusion tree, hierarchical representation.

## 1 Introduction

Reinforcement learning in continuous domains is an area of active research. Conventional algorithms are only proven to work well in environments where action space and state space are both discrete [1]. To extend those algorithms to continuous domains a common approach is to discretize the state space and the action space and apply discrete algorithms [2]. This, however, usually reduces the performance of the approaches [3]. One major issue when applying reinforcement learning to continuous domains is the lack of techniques to represent and update knowledge over continuous domains efficiently. Several successful approaches have been proposed that represent knowledge by means of parametric function approximators [3] or sample-based density estimation.

K. Diamantaras, W. Duch, L.S. Iliadis (Eds.): ICANN 2010, Part II, LNCS 6353, pp. 190–199, 2010.

In this work, we present a novel approach to reinforcement learning in continuous action spaces, based on action sampling. In action-sampling-based approaches, the agent stores knowledge by means of a set of discrete samples, which are generated successively by a certain technique, one per learning step, and executed and evaluated thereafter by the agent. To store knowledge efficiently, those samples have to be concentrated on regions with high interest. Therefore, the sampling-technique has to use the knowledge acquired so far, to make the sampling process as informed as possible. In our approach, actions are sampled by means of a diffusion tree, which organizes samples from a continuous space and knowledge about the underlying domain in a hierarchical structure. Higher levels in the hierarchy represent knowledge about bigger regions in the action space. Evaluation of knowledge is done by recursively walking the tree from its root to its leaves. In a balanced tree, evaluation therefore is efficient. While walking down the tree, the stored knowledge is used to control the sample distribution. In this paper, we only outline the theoretical concept and validate it in a proof-of-concept manner. Further research has to be done to proof the full validity of the approach for real-world applications.

This paper is organized as follows. Section 2 briefly introduces the state of the art in sampling-based approaches to reinforcement learning. As a basis of our approach the Dirichlet Diffusion Tree is introduced in section 3. Our proposed algorithm is described in section 4. Section 5 shows results of two simple experiments conducted to conceptually validate our approach. Conclusions and an outlook to future work are stated in section 6.

## 2    State of the Art

Much research has been done in the field of reinforcement learning in continuous domains. In this section, we will outline a few techniques, strongly related to our proposed approach. Our algorithm belongs to the group of sampling-based approaches. Algorithms of that group typically represent knowledge by means of samples drawn from the underlying domain.

In [4] an approach is presented that extends the traditional dynamic programming to continuous action domains. However, the state space remains discrete. Values for states are stored in a table, one value per state. The policy is also represented as a table, where for every state an action is stored. Multilinear interpolation is used to compute values in the continuous state domain. In every iteration of the presented algorithm, a sweep through the whole state space is done where for every state a new action and a new value is computed. Therefore, an action is being sampled uniformly for every state. If the action is better than the previously stored one w.r.t. the expected return, the old action is discarded and the new one is stored instead. Unfortunately, this approach is not suited for real-time exploration and learning, due to the computational cost for the sweeps. Also sampling actions uniformly does not incorporate any knowledge about promising actions for a state seen so far and, thus, is inefficient for fast exploration. In [5,6] the idea of sampling actions is extended to a so-called tree-based sampling approach. For a state, a set of action samples is drawn. For every action the resulting successor state is simulated. In that simulated state again a set of action samples is drawn and again the next state is evaluated. That way a look-ahead tree is built. Based on that tree the expected long-term return of an action in the current state can be estimated. For this approach a generative process model is required, which narrows the applicability in practice. In [7] a sampling-based actor-critic approach is presented which operates on a discrete state space. For every state a set of action samples is maintained. With every action sample an importance weight is associated. Together, all samples for a state approximate a probability density function (PDF) over the continuous action space for that state. New action samples are drawn from that distribution by means of importance sampling. The weight of a sample is set proportional to the expected return of that action. Therefore, the approximated PDF has high values where actions are promising w.r.t. the expected return and thus are sampled and executed more often.

## 3   Mathematical Foundations

In this section, the necessary mathematical foundations will be introduced. We start with a brief definition of our notation for reinforcement learning and then introduce the formalism of the Dirichlet Diffusion Tree, which serves as a basis for our approach.

*Reinforcement Learning:* Our proposed approach is based on the idea of Q-Learning [1], a well known approach to reinforcement learning. The reader is assumed to be fairly familiar with this topic. We refer to [8] for a good and comprehensive introduction. In the following our notation of Q-Learning will be defined. The state of the agent will be denoted by $s \in S$, actions will be assumed to be equal for all states and will be noted by $a \in A$. The reward function is given by by $r = r(s, a) : S \times A \to \mathbb{R}$. Estimated action-values are defined by $\hat{Q}(s, a) = r(s, a) + \gamma \, \hat{V}(s')$. Where $\hat{V}$ is the estimated state value and $\gamma$ is the discounting factor.

*Dirichlet Diffusion Tree:* Our approach is based on the idea of the Dirichlet Diffusion Tree (DDT) introduced in [9], in particular on the construction of such a tree, which will be outlined in the following (see Fig. 3. In a DDT samples are generated sequentially, each one by a stochastic diffusion process of duration $t = D$. The time evolution of a sample $i$ is represented by a random variable $X_i(t)$ with $t \in [0, D]$. The start location of the first sample is set to $X_1(0) = 0$. The location of the sample an infinitesimal time step $dt$ later is determined by $X_1(t + dt) = X_1(t) + N(t)$, where $N(t)$ is multivariate Gaussian with zero mean and covariance $\sigma^2 I dt$. The values $N(t)$ for distinct values of $t$ are i.i.d., thus the time evolution of $X_1(t)$ is a Gaussian process. Lets call the so generated path $X_1$ (see Fig. 1(a)). For the second sample the start point of the new diffusion process, the path $X_2$, is set to the start point of the first one, hence $X_2(0) = X_1(0)$. The second sample then shares the path of the first sample up to a randomly sampled

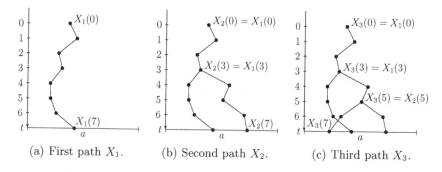

(a) First path $X_1$.     (b) Second path $X_2$.     (c) Third path $X_3$.

**Fig. 1.** Evolution of a Dirichlet Diffusion Tree for three successively sampled paths with a length of $D = 7$. The first path (*left*) is sampled by accumulation of gaussian increments. The second path (*middle*) diverges from the first at time $t = 3$. The third path (*right*) shares the first part with the first path then goes along the second path and diverges at time $t = 5$.

divergence time $T_d$, where it diverges from the first path and goes its own way, which is again determined by a Gaussian process (see Fig. 1(b)). Thus for $t \le T_d$ the paths are the same and for $t > T_d$ they are different. $T_d$ is a random variable and is determined by a divergence function $a(t)$. The probability of diverging in the next infinitesimal interval $dt$ is given by $p(T_d \in [t, t + dt])dt = a(t)dt$, where $a(t)$ is an arbitrary monotonically increasing divergence function (see [9] for details). As a result the probability of divergence increases monotonically in time during the diffusion process. Lets assume $X_2$ diverged from $X_2$ at time $T_d = t_0 = 3$.

Now the third path $X_3$ is being sampled. Lets assume, the point of divergence of the third path is $t_1 > t_0$, i.e. $X_3$ diverges later the $X_2$ did and $X_1(t) = X_2(t) = X_3(t)$ for $t \in [0, t_0]$,. Thus, when the process reaches $t_0 = 3$ a decision has to be made whether it should follow $X_1$ or $X_2$ until it diverges at $t = t_1 = 5$ (see Fig. 1(c)). This decision is done by randomly choosing from one of the branching paths with probability proportional to the number of previous times the respective path was chosen. Thus paths that have often been chosen before, are more likely to be chosen again. The concept of preferring what has been chosen before is called reinforcement of past events by [9] and is one of the main reasons which motivates the use of the DDT in our work. [9] further introduces an additional way to implement this concept by reducing the probability of divergence from a path $X_i$ proportional to the number of times the path has been travelled before. Thus it is less likely to diverge from a path that has been used by many samples before.

After generating $N$ paths $X_1, \ldots, X_N$, the values $X_1(D), \ldots, X_N(D)$ represent the set of samples generated if the DDT is viewed as a black-box sampling technique. We call those values final samples, as they are the final outcome of each diffusion process.

## 4  Our Algorithm

The algorithm proposed here borrows heavily from the idea of the diffusion tree and thus is called DT-Learning, where DT stands for diffusion tree. Like most other sampling-based approaches it operates on a discrete state space $S = \{s_i\}_{i=1,...,N_s}$. To represent values and actions, we maintain a diffusion tree for every state, where the domain of the samples is the action space of the agent. The following paragraph introduces the structural elements that make up a diffusion tree as used in our approach.

*Structural Elements of Our Diffusion Tree:* Unlike the continuous notion of the diffusion tree as presented in [9], the paths of our diffsion tree are discrete in time and consist of a sequence of concrete samples of the diffusion process, which we further call nodes. Further, we extend the notion of the diffusion tree by a structural element called segment, which comprises the set of nodes from one divergence point to another (see Fig. 2).

Let $c$ be a segment and let $c[i]$ be the i-th node of $c$. That way, the segments themselves comprise a tree structure, where a segment has one parent segment and arbitrarily many child segments. One particular segment has no parent segment and is called the root segment. Segments without child segments are called leaf segments. The last node of a leaf segment is also a leaf node of the entire tree. In order to ease notation we will use a functional notation for attributes of an entity (a tree, a segment, or a node) in the following. Let $rt(s)$ be the root segment of the tree of state $s$. Let $pa(c)$ be the parent segment of a segment $c$ and let $ch(c)$ be the set of child segments of segment $c$. In case $c$ is a leaf segment, $ch(c) = \emptyset$. Let further $leaf(c)$ denote the last node of a segment $c$. If $c$ is a leaf segment, $leaf(c)$ is also leaf node of the tree. A leaf node of the tree represents a final sample from the underlying domain. All intermediate nodes of all segments in the tree are just a byproduct of the sampling and have no particular use. Put differently, if we interpret the diffusion tree as a black-box sampling mechanism which just generates samples in the action space, we would only see the final samples represented by the leaf nodes. The remaining tree structure would be hidden in the box.

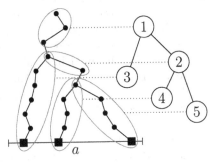

**Fig. 2.** Abstraction of a diffusion tree (*left*) to a tree of segments (*right*). Nodes in the diffusion tree make up a segment (*ellipses*). The segments themselves form a tree (*right*). Segment 1 is the root segment, segments 3,4, and 5 are leaf segments. The rectangular leaf nodes (*left*) are the final action samples, placed continuously in the action space.

*Hierarchical Representation of Knowledge:* Besides the structural relations, several elements carry further information as attributes. The attribute $counter(c)$ counts the number of paths that share the segment $c$, i.e. the number of paths that went $c$ before they diverged and went their own way. The attribute $val(c)$ carries the q-value of a segment. The q-value of a segment is our way of representing the estimated long-term return of a state or state-action pair and is defined recursively as follows. The value of a leaf segment $c$ of the tree in state s is $val(c) = \hat{Q}(s, a)$, where $a = leaf(c)$ is the final action sample of the segment. The quantity $\hat{Q}(s, a)$ is the estimated long term return, when executing action $a$ in state $s$ and is obtained in the real-time run when the agent enters the resulting successor state $s'$ and is given by $\hat{Q}(s, a) = r(s, a) + \gamma \hat{V}(s')$. The value of a non-leaf segment $c$ is defined by the maximum value over all it's children. By applying this rule recursively bottom-up the value of root segment of state $s$ becomes the maximum value of all action samples generated by the diffusion tree in that state and thus $val(rt(s)) = \hat{V}(s)$ is the expected long term return for state $s$ when acting greedy, i.e. always executing the action that maximizes expected long-term return.

*Controlled Exploration by Informed Sampling:* In order to direct our search for good action samples we need to control our action sampling process. We do this by controlling the divergence time and by controlling the choice of path to go at a divergence point. For the first one, we use the approach from the original DDT, which is decreasing the probability of divergence from a segment $c$ with increasing counter $counter(c)$. This way we implement the principle of reinforcement of past events. For the latter one, we will describe our approach in the following.

The information available at a branching point $leaf(c)$ is the set of children $c'$ of the segment $c$ and all information those children are attributed with, in particular each one's $val(c')$, which represents the expected action-value of the region covered by the subtree of $c'$. Based on that information, we can make a decision about which path to choose in numerous ways, each with different effects on the resulting sample distribution. The original heuristics of [9] is to randomly choose a child with probability proportional to the child's counter. This heuristic results in an accumulation of samples in regions where already many samples are, because counters of segments leading to those regions are high. However, to facilitate efficient exploration we wish to accumulate samples in regions with high expected long-term return instead. A straight forward approach to implement this idea is to deterministically choose the child with the maximum value. This will ultimately lead to accumulation of samples in regions with high expected long-term return. However, this statement is only valid, if the tree has 'seen' values in all promising regions of the underlying domain, i.e. it has some samples evenly distributed over the underlying domain. If we choose this heuristic right from the start of the learning process, the tree will concentrate its samples to local optima it encounters in the first few sampling steps. A common way to circumvent this issue in conventional approaches is to choose actions randomly at the beginning of the learning process which accounts for the uncertainty of knowledge about the utility of the actions and to increase the trust on the knowledge obtained by decreasing the random proportion in decision making over time. To implement this idea we use Boltzmann Selection, where the probability of choosing a child is given by $p_c = \exp\left(val(c)/\tau\right) / \sum_{c' \in ch(pa(c))} \exp\left(val(c')/\tau\right)$. Thus, at the beginning of the learning process we set $\tau$ to a high value to account for the uncertainty of knowledge. Choices will be made purely randomly and final samples will be evenly spread over the action space. Over time we decrease $\tau$, and thus the choice will be increasingly deterministic to account for the increasing certainty of the acquired knowledge about high expected return.

*Algorithmic Description:* Algorithm 1 shows the pseudocode of our approach. Knowledge is acquired by incrementally building diffusion trees in the states. Every time the agent visits a state, it generates a new path (line 2) in the diffusion tree and thereby samples an action $a$ to be executed. In the beginning

---

**Algorithm 1.** DT_LEARNING(s).

---

1: **repeat**
2:    $c \leftarrow SAMPLE\_PATH(s)$
3:    $a \leftarrow leaf(c)$
4:    execute $a$, observe result state $s'$ and reward $r$
5:    $PROPAGATE\_UP(c, r, val(rt(s')))$
6:    $s \leftarrow s'$
7: **until** $s$ is goal state
**procedure** $SAMPLE\_PATH(s)$
8: **if** $rt(s) = 0$ **then**
9:    $rt(s) \leftarrow$ sample new segment starting at t=0 and a=0
10:    **return** $rt(s)$
11: **else**
12:    $c \leftarrow rt(s)$
13:    **loop**
14:        $d \leftarrow$ sample divergence time $\in [start(c), D]$ // with $start(\cdot) \equiv$ start time
15:        **if** $d \leq end(c)$ **then** // with $end(\cdot) \equiv$ end time
16:            $c' \leftarrow$ sample new segment starting at t=d and a=c[d]
17:            $pa(c') \leftarrow (c)$ and $ch(c) \leftarrow ch(c) \cup \{c'\}$
18:            **return** $c'$
19:        **else if** $d > end(c)$ **then**
20:            $c \leftarrow$ choose child $c' \in ch(c)$ by Boltzmann Selection
**procedure** $PROPAGATE\_UP(c, r, v)$
21: $val(c) \leftarrow r + \gamma \cdot v$
22: **repeat**
23:    $c \leftarrow pa(c)$;
24:    $e \leftarrow r + \gamma\, v - val(c)$
25:    **if** $e > 0$ **then**
26:        $val(c) \leftarrow val(c) + \alpha\, e$ // with $\alpha \equiv$ learning rate
27: **until** $c$ has no parent

---

of a run the diffusion trees in all states are empty, i.e. they have no path. On the first visit of a state $s$ the agent generates the first path, which will be the first segment $c$ of the tree in $s$ and thus $rt(s) = c$ (line 9). The leaf node of $c$ represents the final action sample $a$ and thus $leaf(rt(s)) = a$ (line 3). The agent will now execute $a$ leading into state $s'$, observe the reward $r(s, a)$ (line 4) and update the value of the three in $s$ (line 5) by first setting the value of $c$ according to value update equation (line 21) and then recursively updating the value of the parents (line 22). When entering a state with a tree that has at least one segment, we walk down the tree by sampling a divergence time (line 14) and choosing between children (line 20) until divergence (line 15). Figure 3 shows a run of an agent in a world with two states and two actions.

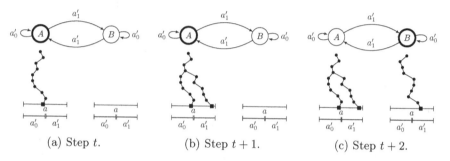

(a) Step $t$.                (b) Step $t + 1$.                (c) Step $t + 2$.

**Fig. 3.** Successive sampling of paths. The upper part of each figure shows the state transition graph of a simple abstract world with two discrete states and two discrete actions, where the current state is painted with a thick line width. Below the states $A$ and $B$ the diffusion trees of those states are shown. The interval lines below the trees illustrate the mapping from continuous action samples to the two discrete actions utilized in the selected exemplary application.

## 5    Experiments

In order to validate our approach we conducted two experiments in simulation. The experiments serve to validate the value of informed sampling against un-informed sampling. Therefore we compare two algorithms, DT-Learning (DTL) and a simple random scheme we call Random Sampling Q-Learning (RSQL). In RSQL, with probability $\nu$ an action-sample is drawn uniformly in every state and kept in case its resulting estimated return is greater than the return of the best action-sample kept so far for that state. With probability $1 - \nu$ the best action obtained so far is executed. The parameter $\nu$ is set to a value near one at the beginning and is decreased over time to account for the uncertainty of knowledge in the beginning. Thus, RSQL is the simplest sampling scheme possi-ble as it is as uninformative as possible while still fulfilling all necessities of the Q-learning framework.

The task in the first experiment is to find the shortest path from a start location to a goal location in a grid world. The states space consists of the two-dimensional locations in the grid. The actions $a'$ in a gridworld consist of the five

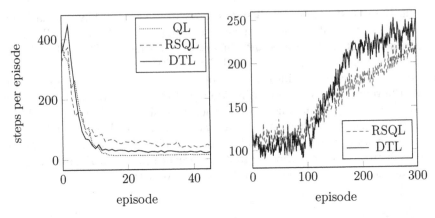

**Fig. 4.** Performance of the algorithms DT-Learning (*DTL*), RSQ-Learning (*RSQL*), and Q-Learning (*QL*) on the two test tasks to reach a goal cell (*left*) and to stabilize a pendulum (*right*)

choices to go up, down, west, east and to stay, i.e. $a' \in \{0, \ldots, 4\}$. To apply the action-continuous approaches, their continuous outputs $a \in [0, 5]$ are mapped to those five actions by $a' = \lfloor a \rfloor$. The agent receives a positive reward when it enters the goal cell and a negative one, when it bumps into a wall. We chose this discrete world, because it is simple and facilitates easy analysis of the key properties of our algorithm. We evaluated the average number of steps until the agent reaches the goal point during a number of successive learning episodes, where the agent keeps its knowledge over the different episodes. Figure 4 (left) shows the results, averaged over 10 trials each. We applied Q-learning (QL) in its original action-discrete fashion, to serve as a base line for comparison. As can be seen the convergence of both sampling-based algorithms is worse than Q-learning. This is because Q-Learning, working with the five discrete actions, is naturally the best fit for this task. The convergence of DTL is better than the one of RSQL, due to DTL sampling more actions in regions with high expected return, whereas RSQL acts ignorant about the knowledge obtained earlier and thus generates samples that lead into walls with relatively high probability.

In a second experiment we tested our algorithm on the task to stabilize a pendulum in an upright position. To ease the task, the starting position for every episode is the upright position. During an episode the number of steps is counted until pendulum crosses the horizontal position. The two-dimensional state space, consisting of angle $\phi \in [0, 2\pi]$ and angular velocity $\omega \in [-10\frac{rad}{s}, 10\frac{rad}{s}]$, was discretized into 41 equally sized intervals per dimension. The action space was the angular acceleration $A = [-10 \ Nm, 10 \ Nm]$. Figure 4 (right) shows the results of the two algorithms RSQL and DTL. As can be seen DT-Learning converges slightly faster. Again, this is due to the more efficient exploration resulting from controlled sampling of actions in regions with higher expected return. We omitted Q-Learning here, because the necessary discretization of the action space would render the results incomparable.

# 6   Conclusion

In this work we presented an approach for reinforcement learning with continuous actions. We were able to show the benefits of informed sampling of actions by efficiently using hierarchically structured knowledge about values of the actions space. The computational cost of sampling an action is of logarithmic order in the number of action samples, as is typical for tree-based approaches. In comparison to a very simple, uninformed sampling scheme our approach showed better convergence rates. However, some open issues remain. Due to the discretization of the state space, there is a discontinuity in the value of a particular action between two states. This could be handled by an interpolation between two trees. Another issue concerns the aging of information in unused parts of the trees. Because memory requirements for our approach are relatively high, a technique must be found to prune subtrees based on the utility of their contained information. These issues will be subject to further research.

# References

1. Watkins, C.J., Dayan, P.: Q-learning. Machine Learning 8, 279–292 (1992)
2. Gross, H.M., Stephan, V., Boehme, H.J.: Sensory-based robot navigation using self-organizing networks and q-learning. In: Proceedings of the 1996 World Congress on Neural Networks, pp. 94–99. Psychology Press, San Diego (1996)
3. Gaskett, C., Wettergreen, D., Zelinsky, A., Zelinsky, E.: Q-learning in continuous state and action spaces. In: Australian Joint Conference on Artificial Intelligence, pp. 417–428. Springer, Heidelberg (1999)
4. Atkeson, C.G.: Randomly sampling actions in dynamic programming. In: 2007 IEEE Symposium on Approximate Dynamic Programming and Reinforcement Learning (ADPRL 2007), pp. 185–192 (2007)
5. Kearns, M., Mansour, Y., Ng, A.Y.: A sparse sampling algorithm for near-optimal planning in large markov decision processes. Machine Learning 49, 193–208 (2002)
6. Ross, S., Chaib-Draa, B., Pineau, J.: Bayesian reinforcement learning in continuous pomdps with application to robot navigation. In: 2008 IEEE International Conference on Robotics and Automation (ICRA 2008), pp. 2845–2851. IEEE, Los Alamitos (May 2008)
7. Lazaric, A., Restelli, M., Bonarini, A.: Reinforcement learning in continuous action spaces through sequential monte carlo methods. In: Platt, J., Koller, D., Singer, Y., Roweis, S. (eds.) Advances in Neural Information Processing Systems, vol. 20, pp. 833–840. MIT Press, Cambridge (2008)
8. Sutton, R.S., Barto, A.G.: Reinforcement Learning: An Introduction. The MIT Press, Cambridge (March 1998)
9. Neal, R.M.: Density modeling and clustering using dirichlet diffusion trees. In: Bayesian Statistics 7: Proceedings of the Seventh Valencia International Meeting, pp. 619–629 (2003)

# An Alternative Approach to the Revision of Ordinal Conditional Functions in the Context of Multi-Valued Logic

Klaus Häming and Gabriele Peters

University of Applied Sciences and Arts,
Computer Science, Visual Computing,
Emil-Figge-Str. 42, D-44221 Dortmund, Germany

**Abstract.** We discuss the use of Ordinal Conditional Functions (OCF) in the context of Reinforcement Learning while introducing a new revision operator for conditional information. The proposed method is compared to the state-of-the-art method in a small Reinforcement Learning application with added futile information, where generalization proves to be advantageous.

## 1 Introduction

An autonomous learning system tries to figure out which actions are beneficial and which have to be avoided. Starting with three system requirements we developed the work described in this paper. These requirements are the following.

First, an autonomous learning system should be able to learn from experience. It should have some kind of memory that, e.g., enables it to decide not to fall over a cliff again in case it proved harmful the last time. A widely adopted approach to incorporate such a property is given by Reinforcement Learning (RL) [10].

Second, the system should generate a representation of its belief that allows further reasoning. In this area Belief Revision (BR) techniques can be found. We will examine the usefulness of Ordinal Conditional Functions (OCF) [4,7] in this work.

Third, and most important, we want both mentioned approaches to benefit from each other. This kind of mixture of low-level learning-by-doing and high level deduction abilities is called a two-level learning approach. Psychological findings [6] indicate that such two-level learning principles can explain some of the human learning abilities. While humans are able to learn both, in a top-down and bottom-up way[9], we will focus on the bottom-up part only.

A combination of RL and BR has been proposed recently [5], influenced by [8] and [11]. In this work, we will shed light onto a rather small but important detail of this approach.

## 2 Reinforcement Learning and OCF

In Reinforcement Learning, we have a set of states $\mathfrak{S}$, a set of actions $\mathfrak{A}$, a transition function $\delta : \mathfrak{S} \times \mathfrak{A} \to \mathfrak{S}$, and a reward function $r : \mathfrak{S} \times \mathfrak{A} \to \mathbb{R}$. Belief

K. Diamantaras, W. Duch, L.S. Iliadis (Eds.): ICANN 2010, Part II, LNCS 6353, pp. 200–203, 2010.

about good and poor actions is learned by applying a learning scheme, in this case we use $Q$-learning. The experience is captured in the $Q$(uality)-function, that assigns an expected reward to each state-action-pair. One can interpret the $Q$-function in such a way, that an action $A$ is *believed* to be best, if it has the highest $Q(S, A)$ value for a given state $S$. This is where we establish a connection to the high-level belief using BR.

BR is a theory of maintaining a belief base in such a way, that the current belief is reflected in a consistent manner (cf. [2] and [1]). We model our belief base $\kappa$ as an OCF. This is a ranking function that maintains a list of all models, which are propositional information in the form of conjunctions. The models the system believes in are set to rank 0, while all ranks greater than 0 reflect an increasing disbelief. We denote the rank an OCF $\kappa$ assigns to a model $M$ as $\kappa(M)$. By convention, contradictions shall have the rank $\infty$.

However, during the exploration the information gathered and the information needed is in the form of conditionals, not conjunctions. To check, whether an OCF believes a conditional, it is sufficient to compute the belief ranks $r_1 = \kappa(SA)$ and $r_2 = \kappa(S\overline{A})$. If $r_1 < r_2$, the conditional is believed.

More difficult then querying the belief base, is its update, called *revision*. The revision operator is "$*$".

Conditionals in BR are usually denoted as $(A|S)$, where $S$ is the antecedent and $A$ the consequent. The meaning of $(A|S)$ is not exactly the same as $S \Rightarrow A$ [4]. The latter means that $S$ implicates $A$ irrespective of the values of other variables. In contrast, $(A|S)$ expresses that $A$ is believed if $\kappa$ is conditioned with $S$ and $S$ alone. In contrast, a revision $(\kappa * (ST))$ may not result in $A$ being believed.

The revision described in [5], conforms to $(\kappa * (A|S))$. The new revision we introduce is $(\kappa * (S \Rightarrow A))$. It needs a new operator $\kappa[A]$, which shall return the highest disbelief among all models of $A$. $(\kappa * (S \Rightarrow A))$ is defined as follows: If $\kappa(SA) < \kappa(S\overline{A})$, do nothing. If $\kappa(SA) \geq \kappa(S\overline{A})$, then the OCF $\kappa'$ derived from $\kappa$ by rearranging the models using

$$\forall M \in \mathfrak{M} : \kappa'(M) := (\kappa * (S \Rightarrow A))(M)$$

$$= \begin{cases} \kappa(M) - \kappa(S \Rightarrow A), & \text{if } M \text{ is a model of } S \Rightarrow A \\ \kappa[SA] + 1 - \kappa(S \Rightarrow A) + \kappa(M) - \kappa(S\overline{A}), & \text{if } M \text{ is a model of } S\overline{A} \end{cases} \quad (1)$$

will result in $\kappa'(SA) < \kappa'(S\overline{A})$. Consequently, $\kappa'$ expresses the belief in $S \Rightarrow A$.

Concerning the insurance of actual belief, this method works just as good as $(\kappa * (A|S))$, but introduces greater changes. The justification for these changes is its behavior toward sequences of belief changes, especially in the context of multi-valued logic, where $(\kappa * (A|S))$ fails to produce consistent results when considering negation and generalization.

# 3    Application

We examine the effect of the proposed algorithm in a cliff-walk gridworld [10] (Figure 2). For this application, three cases are examined, which are plain

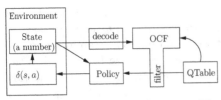

**Fig. 1.** OCF-augmented RL system. The OCF acts as a filter that limits the choices of the policy.

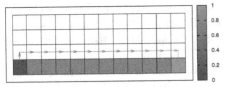

**Fig. 2.** Cliff-walk gridworld. The goal of a moving agent is to reach the green square, starting from the red one. Entering the dark squares (representing a cliff) results in a high negative reward. Superimposed is the learned path after 100 episodes. The path color indicates the expected reward by displaying the value of $\min(1, \frac{\text{expected reward}}{\text{goal reward}})$ using the displayed color key.

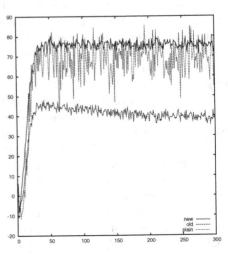

**Fig. 3.** Results. The diagrams show the rewards over a series of 300 episodes. *plain* shows the result of a plain Q-learner, *old* shows the result of revisions with ($\kappa * (A|S)$), and *new* shows the result of revisions with ($\kappa * (S \Rightarrow A)$). The values are averages of 1000 runs.

Q-learning, OCF-augmented Q-learning with application of ($\kappa * (A|S)$), and OCF-augmented Q-learning with application of ($\kappa * (S \Rightarrow A)$). An OCF-augmented Q-learner is a Q-learner that has conditionals extracted from its Q-Table. These conditionals revise the learner's OCF and this OCF acts as a filter for the choice of actions afterwards. Figure 1 shows this architecture.

We add futile information to model the case where the agent perceives properties of its environment that are not helpful with regard to its goal. The OCF-augmented Q-learners are expected to be able to generalize and therefore identify the futile information. The generalization is performed in the same way as in [5] by counting the pattern frequency. The general idea is to keep track of how often sub-patterns of antecedents are used in the context of particular consequents. If they occur frequently enough, we revise the OCF with the sub-pattern instead of the complete state description. The state description is also adopted from [5], where a qualitative description is used which consists of the relative position of the agent towards the goal (north, south, east, west) and a distance (near, middle, far) amended with information on adjacent obstacles. Reaching the goal triggers a reward of 100, getting closer towards it is rewarded with 0.5. Stepping into the chasm is punished by $-10$, every other step gets a $-1$. After 100 steps the episode is forced to end. The results are depicted in Figure 3. It is evident that a revision with ($\kappa * (S \Rightarrow A)$)clearly outperforms a revision with ($\kappa * (A|S)$).

The latter is worse than a plain Q-learner and even seems to deteriorate over time. An explanation for this may lie in the fact that the OCF gets contaminated by harmful conditionals. However, this has not been examined in this work.

# 4  Conclusion

There are some questions left open. Clearly, the use of an OCF speeds up the learning process (measured in the number of episodes). However, the role of futile information has to be examined in more detail. The performance of the proposed method surpasses the plain Q-learner's. Since off-policy learning usually shows a worse performance than on-policy learning, OCF-augmentation could be a way to ease this weakness. Finally, it may be interesting to examine the use of an OCF directly as a Q-function to create a Relational Reinforcement Learning system[3].

**Acknowledgments.** This research was funded by the German Research Association (DFG) under Grant PE 887/3-3.

# References

1. Alchourron, C.E., Gardenfors, P., Makinson, D.: On the logic of theory change: Partial meet contraction and revision functions. J. Symbolic Logic 50(2), 510–530 (1985)
2. Darwiche, A., Pearl, J.: On the logic of iterated belief revision. Artificial intelligence 89, 1–29 (1996)
3. Dzeroski, S., De Raedt, L., Driessens, K.: Relational reinforcement learning. Machine Learning 43, 7–52 (2001)
4. Kern-Isberner, G.: Conditionals in nonmonotonic reasoning and belief revision: considering conditionals as agents. Springer, New York (2001)
5. Leopold, T., Kern Isberner, G., Peters, G.: Combining reinforcement learning and belief revision: A learning system for active vision. In: BMVC 2008, pp. 473–482 (2008)
6. Reber, A.S.: Implicit learning and tacit knowledge. Journal of Experimental Psycology: General 3(118), 219–235 (1989)
7. Spohn, W.: Ordinal conditional functions: A dynamic theory of epistemic states. In: Causation in Decision, Belief Change and Statistics, pp. 105–134 (August 1988)
8. Sun, R., Merrill, E., Peterson, T.: From implicit skills to explicit knowledge: A bottom-up model of skill learning. Cognitive Science 25, 203–244 (2001)
9. Sun, R., Zhang, X., Slusarz, P., Mathews, R.: The interaction of implicit learning, explicit hypothesis testing, and implicit-to-explicit knowledge extraction. Neural Networks 1(20), 34–47 (2006)
10. Sutton, R.S., Barto, A.G.: Reinforcement Learning: An Introduction. MIT Press, Cambridge (1998)
11. Ye, C., Yung, N.H.C., Wang, D.: A fuzzy controller with supervised learning assisted reinforcement learning algorithm for obstacle avoidance. IEEE Transactions on Systems, Man, and Cybernetics, Part B 33(1), 17–27 (2003)

# One-Shot Supervised Reinforcement Learning for Multi-targeted Tasks: RL-SAS

Johane Takeuchi and Hiroshi Tsujino

Honda Research Institute Japan Co., Ltd.
8-1 Honcho, Wako-shi, Saitama 351-0188, Japan
{johane.takeuchi,tsujino}@jp.honda.ri.com

**Abstract.** Our ultimate goal is to realize artificial agents, which can be taught and can behave appropriately in volatile environments. Supervised reinforcement learning (SRL) will play a crucial role in this endeavor as SRL enables agents to function in situations that partly deviate from what has been taught. Currently reinforcement learning (RL) is typically implemented for single tasks, which restricts teaching plural behavioral sequences. Herein we introduce a SRL scheme, which exploits explicit state-action lists to facilitate reuse of learned behavioral sequences. By combining the constructed learning system with a standard RL algorithm, the system could solve a problem in one-shot for the supervised portions and use RL to compensate for the unsupervised portions.

Future robots/agents are expected to support humans in a multitude of environments. On-line learning systems will be necessary to achieve user specific behavior/dialog controls because real situations are diverse and volatile. In order to adapt to user's situations, learning from user's instructions seem to be effective for humans, however, it may often be incorrect and inappropriate for machines. Moreover, just recalling learned behavioral sequences in response to user's demands is inefficient in real diverse environments. In order to achieve those final goals, this paper focuses on one type of learning problem as a first step, called simple partially supervised tasks (SPSTs). A SPST requires a learning agent to reach several specified target states by performing sequential behaviors acquired through explicit supervision by others as well as trial-and-error learning by itself. Each supervised behavioral sequence is simple, and we expect the agent to acquire the supervised sequence in one-shot. Figure 1 depicts the test set for SPST. In this test, supervision is executed in an interactive manner, so when the agent observes a state, a proper action is suggested for each step. Episodes A, B, and C are exhibited to the agent in a stepwise fashion, and the agent is taught that these patterns are good sequences. Additionally, the agent learns episode D is a bad example by interactive supervision. These episodes are taught to a learning agent only once. Next the agent should attain the indicated problems by executing proper behavior. For example, in the case of problem 1, the agent should perform behaviors of episode B after those of episode A. Although systems that test this via an appropriate search method may be implemented, they tend to be insufficient. A satisfactory system should coincide with behavioral learning without supervision. Otherwise, it is difficult to maintain consistencies between behaviors learned with supervision from those without supervision. Moreover, situations during problems can differ from those during supervision. The

K. Diamantaras, W. Duch, L.S. Iliadis (Eds.): ICANN 2010, Part II, LNCS 6353, pp. 204–209, 2010.

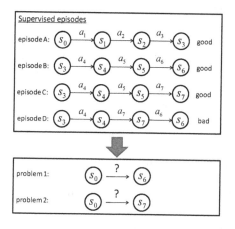

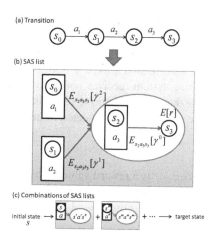

**Fig. 1.** Simple test problem set. $s_n$ is a fixed observed state and $a_m$ is a fixed action.

**Fig. 2.** Schematic diagram of a SAS list

actual transitions of the problems might be changed from deterministic to probabilistic. Additionally, part of the sequence can vary from supervised ones; thus, the system should be complemented by trial-and-error learning.

Reinforcement learning (RL) [1] actualizes unsupervised behavioral learning through trial-and-error. RL consists of two aspects: statistical evaluation of past behaviors based on reward signals and behavior generation with respect to the evaluation results. It is possible to complement behavior generation by combining it with supervised methods, which we call supervised reinforcement learning (SRL). RL and SRL are, however, typically implemented for single tasks, which has difficulties learning plural behavior sequences necessary for multi-targeted tasks. In RL and SRL, a device to distinguish between problem 1 and problem 2 in Figure 1 does not exist. Future agents should behave by corresponding to user's demands. A mechanism, which enables an artificial agent to memorize behavioral sequences in a form that facilitates reuse, is needed to evaluate memorized behaviors and autonomously modify them. Intrinsically motivated reinforcement learning (IMRL) studies [2] represent acquired skills of agents by virtue of options [3]. IMRL studies have suggested a method to acquire options by introducing intrinsic motivations where specified salient events are temporal motivations to acquire and modify new options. Because options are not aimed at supervised learning, applying them to SRL is not straightforward.

Herein we propose to decompose value functions of RL in accordance with search techniques such as the best-first search method [4]. Our algorithm works as an auxiliary device to supplement RL. In addition, RL usually takes a long time to learn because its premise is only trial-and-error learning. Thus, we aim to realize effective combinations of RL and supervision to achieve one-shot learning with supervision. Our aim is not to solve static problems rather to tackle dynamic and volatile environments. Then, we do not stick to theoretical optimal solutions, rather we aim at constructing a practical algorithm which may achieve sub-optimal or *appropriate* solutions.

# 1   Decomposition of Expected Rewards by Targets

We postulate that the Markov decision process (MDP) consists of a fixed observable state space $S$ and a fixed action set $A$. We assume sparse reward functions where the learning system receives non-zero rewards only at the end of sequential episodes because these types of sparse rewards are tractable to design in practical applications. For these conditions, the expected future rewards under a policy $\pi$ become:

$$R^\pi(s_t, a_t) = E^\pi[\gamma^{k-1}r_{t+k}|s_t, a_t] \quad (0 < \gamma < 1), \tag{1}$$

where $r_{t+k}$ is a reward value at the end of an episode and the $t + k$ is the time at the end of an episode. $\gamma$ is the discount rate, $s_t$ is an observed state $s \in S$ at time $t$, and $a_t$ is the selected action $a \in A$ at time $t$. In MDP, equation (1) can be decomposed into:

$$\begin{aligned} R^\pi(s_t, a_t) &= \sum_{\gamma^{k-1}r_{t+k}} \gamma^{k-1}r_{t+k}P^\pi(\gamma^{k-1}r_{t+k}|s_t, a_t) \\ &= \sum_{(S,A,S')} E^\pi_{S,A,S'}[\gamma^{k-1}r_{t+k}|s_t, a_t], \end{aligned} \tag{2}$$

We denote the tuple $(s_{t+k-1}, a_{t+k-1}, s_{t+k})$ as $(S, A, S')$, which consists of a state-action pair that occurs before observing a targeted state and the target state $s_{t+k}$. $E^\pi_{S,A,S'}[\gamma^{k-1}r_{t+k}|s_t, a_t]$ is a *partial* expected reward decomposed by $(S, A, S')$. Equation (2) indicates that each state-action pair $(s_i, a_j)$ can be grouped by each $(S, A, S')$. Hence, we named our algorithm 'RL-SAS'. Each grouping is called an 'SAS list'. Each state-action pair $(s_i, a_j)$ is allowed to be a member of several SAS lists. The expected reward $R^\pi(s_t, a_t)$ is obtained by adding all $E^\pi_{S,A,S'}[\gamma^{k-1}r_{t+k}|s_t, a_t]$.

We simplify equation (2) by assuming that $P^\pi(k|r_{t+k}, s_t, a_t) \sim P^\pi(k|s_t, a_t)$, where $P^\pi(k|\cdot)$ is the probability that an episode terminates at time step $t + k$. Then we can calculate equation (2) by multiplying two expectations:

$$E^\pi_{S,A,S'}[\gamma^{k-1}r_{t+k}|s_t, a_t] \sim E[r_{t+k}|S, A, S'] \cdot E^\pi_{S,A,S'}[\gamma^{k-1}|s_t, a_t], \tag{3}$$

where

$$E[r_{t+k}|S, A, S'] = \sum_{r_{t+k}} r_{t+k}P(r_{t+k}|S, A, S'), \tag{4}$$

and, to simplify implementation, $P^\pi(k|s_t, a_t)$ and $P^\pi(S, A, S'|s_t, a_t)$ are assumed to be independent. Then

$$E^\pi_{S,A,S'}[\gamma^{k-1}|s_t, a_t] = \sum_k \gamma^{k-1}P^\pi(k, S, A, S'|s_t, a_t). \tag{5}$$

Figure 2(b) shows the schematic diagram of an SAS list. Each episodic transition (Figure 2(a)) is transferred into the form of a SAS list with the above estimated averages. Moving averages (MAs) are utilized to estimate the averages described in equations (4) and (5). A simple moving average (SMA) is the partial average of the previous $n$ data points. The number $n$ should be a small value like 10 so that the system can be changed in accordance with a volatile environment. To achieve specified targets, better actions from experienced sequential actions represented by each SAS list and combination of them must be searched (Figure 2(c)). We employ the best-first search method [4], which can search the best combinations of SAS lists in the expected future rewards to achieve specified targets. The expected rewards of the combinations are roughly estimated from $\mathrm{ma}[r|S, A, S']$ and $\mathrm{ma}_{SAS'}[\gamma|s, a]$ as:

$$\mathrm{ma}_{s'a's''}[\gamma|s, a]\mathrm{ma}[r|s', a', s'']+$$
$$\mathrm{ma}_{s'a's''}[\gamma|s, a]\mathrm{ma}_{s'''a'''s''''}[\gamma|s'', a''] \times \mathrm{ma}[r|s''', a''', s''''] + \cdots. \quad (6)$$

Although these estimates of the combined expected reward may not be guaranteed as a normative value function, the aim is to let the system attend to a suggested action with plausible estimations along a search path.

## 2    Simulation Results

This section describes empirical evaluations of our proposed model using partially supervised tasks described in Figure 1. Herein, we combine RL-SAS with the SARSA($\lambda$) algorithm. Because SARSA is on-policy learning, we anticipated that learning would follow the supervised sequences. We demonstrate an efficiency of RL-SAS as an auxiliary system for RL by comparing our constructed model RL-SAS+SARSA($\lambda$) with single SARSA($\lambda$). This algorithm is denoted RL-SAS+SARSA($\lambda$). We set up the RL-SAS algorithm as an auxiliary device to RL. Thus, RL-SAS indirectly affects RL through action selections and does not disturb RL itself. If an effective supervision is given, the system selects a supervised action. Otherwise, RL-SAS affects the consequence. If a valid goal state is provided, then best-first search [4] is executed to find a path from the state to the provided goal state. The algorithm searches a path to the specified goal with the best combinations of expected rewards calculated by equation (6). If the search succeeds, the system modifies the action-value so that the action selector likely selects the action to follow the identified path. This search is repeatedly executed in each step, even if the perfect path to the goal is found. This repetition ensures the system functions in probabilistic transitions and even uncertain consequences. The softmax action selection rule is engaged in to decide the action. We also implemented a mechanism that autonomously acquires SAS lists. When the agent earns a non-zero reward $r_{t+1}$, the system searches the already acquired SAS lists, which contains the target state-action as $(S, A, S') = (s_t, a_t, s_{t+1})$. If none of the SAS lists contain the target state-action tuple $(s_t, a_t, s_{t+1})$, then the system generates an SAS list targeting $(s_t, a_t, s_{t+1})$ and copies some state-action pairs to the list. If the system finds an SAS list where $(S, A, S')$ is $(s_t, a_t, s_{t+1})$, the system tries to extend the corresponding list.

Based on Figure 1, we conducted a test, which consisted of 20 trials. The first four trials were supervised. In the first trial, the agent was taught episode A in Figure 1 in a stepwise manner. The initial state was $s_0$ and all the actions were selected by a supervisor until the learning agent reached state $s_3$. Simultaneously, the agent received a positive reward $r = 1$. Similarly, episodes B and C were presented in the second and third trials, respectively. In the forth trial, episode D was taught to the agent with a negative reward $r = -1$. The next sixteen trials were problem trials. In the fifth trial,

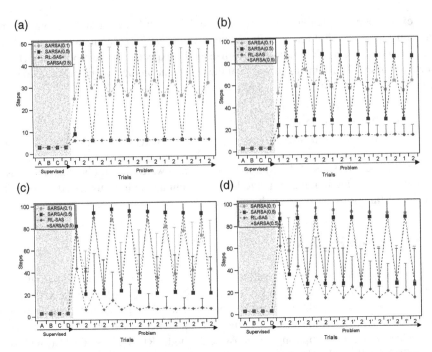

**Fig. 3.** Averaged performances of partially supervised tasks. Ordinate indicates the number of steps to earn a positive reward within a fixed time. Abscissa indicates the number of trials the agent attempted in each set. 'SARSA' is the result of the SARSA algorithm and the figures in parentheses are $\lambda$ values. RL-SAS+SARSA(0.5) is the result of our proposed learning model.

the agent was to solve problem 1 within a fixed number of steps. The next trial (the sixth) was problem 2. Alternately these problem trials were repeated until the 20th trial. In these problem trials, the agent received a positive reward $r = 1$ when it successfully achieved the specified target. Similar to episode D, if the agent chose the transition from $s_4$ to $s_7$ during the trials for problelm 1, the agent earned a negative reward $r = -1$. In the trials of problem 2, the agent could not directly transit from $s_4$ to $s_7$.

Figure 3(a) shows the average performances of the above test. These data were averaged over 1000 trial sets. SARSA(0.1) rarely achieved each target within 50 steps in the problem trials, whereas, the result of SARSA(0.5) tended to learn only problem 1, which seemed to depend on the order of the trials and learning steps. It is difficult to adjust parameters for a single SARSA($\lambda$) to accomplish these tests. For example, if the maximum number of steps for each trial was set to 100, SARSA($\lambda$) repeatedly relearned each problem in each trial and never converged for both problems. On the other hand, our proposed model RL-SAS+SARSA(0.5) repeatedly achieved each specified target with a minimum steps (six) without errors. Additionally, we investigated the performances in a probabilistic environment. Only in the problem trials were the transitions changed into probabilistic ones where the probability of each transition was set to 0.8. If the agent failed to transit to the next step, the state turned into the initial state $s_0$. RL-SAS could appropriately guide the learning agent to each specified target, as shown in Figure 3(b). Only the case of RL-SAS+SARSA(0.5) achieved problem trials with the ideal minimum steps without choosing incorrect actions. RL-SAS explicitly treats specified target states in decisions to select actions, which enables one-shot learning. For SARSA($\lambda$), standard RL lacks a device to exploit the information of expressly provided targets. Hence, RL must repeat trial-and-error learning every time, which can be an obstacle for multi targeted tasks that are more realistic in practical applications. Here, we just try to show that RL-SAS can suppress an aversive effects of RL and can exploit the provided target states.

Nonetheless, RL is an efficient learning algorithm to determine proper actions through trial-and-error. Figure 3(c) depicts the case of a deterministic transition ,which contains partially unknown transitions. In the problem 1 trial, if the agent chose action $a_2$ at state $s_1$, it transited to $s_7$ instead of $s_2$. Afterwards, the agent had to choose action $a_3$ to transit to $s_3$. Because this transition was not taught in advance, the agent must acquire the correct behavioral pattern through trial-and-error. In the figure, this problem is denoted by $1'$. The problem 2 trial did not differ from the original one. Only RL-SAS+SARSA(0.5) exhibited a tendency to converge. Figure 3(d) are the results of mixed conditions with (b) and (c). Hence, the transitions were probabilistic and partially unknown. Thus, RL-SAS enables RL to function in multi-targeted tasks with supervision.

# 3 Conclusion

RL-SAS combined with SARSA($\lambda$) could learn several deviated versions of problems depicted in Figure 1, which we call SPST. For sequence portions supervised in advance, RL-SAS maintained sustained action selections. RL depended on learning conditions, including supervising orders, trial orders, and even the number of maximum steps. RL-SAS suppressed such adverse effects of trial-and-error learning. Additionally RL-SAS+SARSA($\lambda$) was effective in the problems including probabilistic and partially unsupervised ones, where the conditions were different from those which were supervised. Our aim is not to solve static problems rather to tackle dynamic and volatile environments. Rather we require the learning system that is able to function in changing environments. RL-SAS enables the immediate combinations experienced sequential behaviors and one-shot learning. We conclude that the proposed combined system has the potential to be applied to future robots/agents behaving in volatile real environments.

# References

1. Sutton, R.S., Barto, A.G.: Reinforcement Learning: An Introduction. MIT Press, Cambridge (1998)
2. Singh, S., Barto, A.G., Chentanez, N.: Intrinsically motivated reinforcement learning. In: Advances in Neural Information Processing Systems, vol. 17, pp. 1281–1288. MIT Press, Cambridge (2005)
3. Sutton, R.S., Precup, D., Singh, S.P.: Between MDPs and semi-MDPs: A framework for temporal abstraction in reinforcement learning. Artificial Intelligence 112, 181–211 (1999)
4. Pearl, J.: Heuristics: intelligent search strategies for computer problem solving. Addison-Wesley Pub., Boston (1984)

# An Oscillatory Neural Network Model for Birdsong Learning and Generation

Maya Manaithunai[1], Srinivasa Chakravarthy[1], and Ravindran Balaraman[2]

[1] Department of Biotechnology, Indian Institute of Technology Madras,
Chennai 600036, India
[2] Department of Computer Science, Indian Institute of Technology Madras,
Chennai 600036, India

**Abstract.** We present a model of bird song production in which the motor control pathway is modeled by a trainable network of oscillators and the Anterior Forebrain Pathway (AFP) is modeled as a stochastic system. We hypothesize 1) that the songbird learns only *evaluations* of songs during the sensory phase; 2) that the AFP plays a role analogous to the Explorer, a key component in Reinforcement Learning (RL); 3) the motor pathway learns the song by combining the evaluations (Value information) stored from the sensory phase, and the exploratory inputs from the AFP in a temporal stage-wise manner. Model performance from real birdsong samples is presented.

**Keywords:** Birdsong, reinforcement learning, chunking, actor-critic-explorer schema, central pattern generators, Anterior Forebrain Pathway(AFP).

## 1 Introduction

The process of song learning in birds shares many similarities with that of human speech learning [1]. Hence it is a potential model system for investigating the mechanisms of motor skill acquisition and the role of various brain regions in the same. Song learning in birds takes place in three stages: the *sensory stage*, during which the birds listens to and memorizes the song, the *sensori-motor stage*, when the bird learns the memorized song by self-feedback and the *crystallized stage*, when the bird has developed a stable song matching that of the tutor.

### 1.1 Neuroanatomy of Birdsong

Fig. 1 shows the neural pathways in the birdbrain involved in song learning. There are two major pathways involved in the song learning process: the Motor Pathway and the Anterior Forebrain Pathway (AFP), an avian analogue of mammalian basal ganglia. AFP consists of 3 major sets of nuclei - Area X, Dorso-Lateral Thalamus (DLM) and Lateral Magnocellular Nucleus of the Anterior Neostriatum (LMAN). Motor Pathway runs between two nuclei – the HVC and the Robust nucleus of the Archistriatum (RA). It also receives dense dopaminergic projections from the midbrain region called the Ventral Tegmental Area (VTA). HVC receives inputs from the auditory system (Field L) and sends glutamatergic projections to the RA and Area X,

K. Diamantaras, W. Duch, L.S. Iliadis (Eds.): ICANN 2010, Part II, LNCS 6353, pp. 210–215, 2010.
© Springer-Verlag Berlin Heidelberg 2010

a region of the AFP. The RA has two different sets of motor neurons innervating the syringeal muscles and the respiratory muscles. Lesioning studies [2] suggest that song learning can be described within the Reinforcement Learning (RL) framework and the AFP probably plays the role of the *explorer* [3].

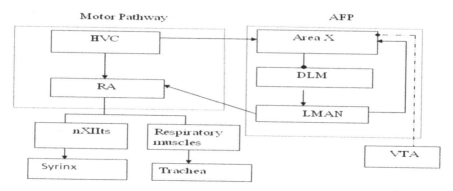

**Fig. 1.** Neuroanatomy of Birdsong.AFP- Anterior Forebrain Pathway,RA- Robust nucleus of the Archistriatum, DLM- Dorso-Lateral Thalamus, LMAN - Lateral Magnocellular Nucleus of the Anterior Neostriatum, VTA – Ventral Tegmental Area, Glu- Glutamate, GABA – Gamma-Amino-Butyric Acid, DA –Dopamine (Lines ending with circles indicate inhibitory connections, lines ending with squares indicate dopaminergic connections,arrows indicate excitatory connections)

### 1.2  Previous Models

Accordingly several RL-based computational models of song learning have been proposed. In [4], the AFP stores in it a 'song template' which it compares with the bird's own song to adaptively train the song bird. The synaptic perturbations were provided by LMAN in the AFP. Doupe et al [5] proposed a model based on the 'AFP comparison hypothesis' in which the AFP evaluates the birdsong by producing a prediction of the feedback of the syllable, the 'efference copy'. Seung et al [6] proposed a spiking neuron model involving the motor pathway and the LMAN nuclei. These models have focused on elucidating the role of various regions within the song system with a specific function during the song learning process. Yet the role of dopamine in the learning process has not been considered by these models. Considering the fact that the AFP functions in a manner analogous to the BG in humans, it would be interesting to understand the exact role of dopamine in the AFP during learning. In our model, this has been modeled as a Temporal Difference error in the RL framework.

## 2  Model Description

We propose a model of song learning based on reinforcement learning where the HVC – RA system is modeled by 2 sets of Hopf oscillators, which act as Central Pattern Generator (CPG) circuits. The AFP is modeled as a random noise source, which perturbs the output of the oscillatory networks. The outputs of the two networks, with the noise added from the AFP, are fed to the model of the bird vocal organ, the syrinx. The output of the syrinx in turn is fed to a vocal filter which plays the role of analogous to the bird's beak.

Figure 2 gives a broad overview of the proposed model.

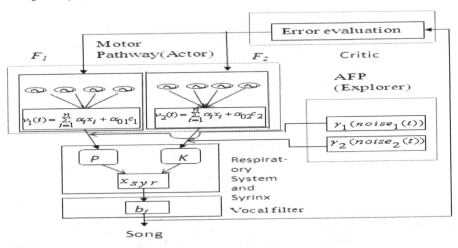

**Fig. 2.** The Actor-Critic-Explorer schema of the proposed model with the various components. AFP- Anterior Forebrain Pathway. For explanation of the notations refer text.

## 2.1 The Motor Pathway Model

We use a network of Hopf oscillators to model the motor pathway [7]. During the training process, the learning signal is fed as a forcing function to each of the oscillators in the network.

The governing equations for the variables of the oscillators are given as:

$$\frac{dx}{dt} = \gamma(\mu - r^2)x - \omega y + \varepsilon F(t).\tag{1}$$

$$\frac{dy}{dt} = \gamma(\mu - r^2)y - \omega x.\tag{2}$$

$$\frac{d\omega}{dt} = -\varepsilon\eta\left(\frac{y}{r}\right)F(t).\tag{3}$$

$$\frac{d\alpha}{dt} = \eta x(t)F(t).\tag{4}$$

$$\frac{d\alpha_0}{dt} = \eta c_1 F(t).\tag{5}$$

where, $\mu$ is a parameter that controls the amplitude of oscillations, $\omega$ is the intrinsic frequency of the oscillators, $\varepsilon$ is a coupling constant and $\gamma$ is the learning rate, $\alpha$ denotes the weights of the oscillators, $\alpha_0$ denotes the baseline values of the weights and $x$ and $y$ denote the state variables of the oscillator. Eqns. (1,2) denote oscillator dynamics, eqns. (3,4,5) denote learning dynamics of the parameters $\omega$, $\alpha$ and $\alpha_0$. Note that the learning described above is a supervised form of learning. In the present model, the above learning mechanism is reformulated as a RL mechanism.

We use the above two- network model to simulate the outputs from the motor pathway to the syringeal and respiratory muscles. The outputs of the two oscillatory networks are:

$$v_1(t) = \sum_{i=1}^{n} \alpha_i x_i + \alpha_{01} c_1. \tag{6}$$

$$v_2(t) = \sum_{i=1}^{n} \alpha_i x_i + \alpha_{02} c_2. \tag{7}$$

## 2.2 The Anterior Forebrain Pathway in the Model

We propose that the AFP plays the role of an 'explorer' in the Reinforcement learning framework. This pathway serves as the source of chaotic perturbations to the motor pathway. This is evident from the remodelling of the LMAN-RA synapses observed during song learning [8] and the reduced variability in the song following LMAN lesions [2]. At the onset of learning, the LMAN-RA projections are diffuse and the bird produces highly variable notes (*subsong*). During the process of learning, refinement of LMAN-RA synapses takes place (*plastic song*) and at the end of *crystallised song* phase, the number of LMAN-RA synapses decreases substantially. The output of AFP to RA is modeled by a two-dimensional random vector, where each component is a random variable with mean 0 and standard deviation 0.25. The outputs of RA (*v(t)*) and LMAN ($\zeta_i$) are combined and given as input to the vocal organ:

$$u(t) = v(t) + (\chi)\zeta. \tag{8}$$

The term $\chi$ controls the exploratory drive to the oscillatory networks. This in turn is controlled by a variable δ, which denotes the Temporal Difference (TD) error term in the RL framework [4], given by

$$\delta = \tanh(s.e_{avg}(t) - err(t)) \tag{9}$$

where, $s$ is a constant, $e_{avg}(t)$ is the average error of the previous training stage and *err(t)* is the current error.

## 2.3 The Respiratory System and Syrinx Model

The respiratory system and syrinx module used in the present model is modeled after [9]. Equations are omitted for reasons of space.

## 2.4 The Vocal Filter Model

The output of syrinx module is fed to a vocal filter model, which is modeled after [9]. Equations of the model are omitted for reasons of space.

## 2.5  Training Algorithm

The model is trained in a temporal stage-wise manner. The signal received by the motor system is processed by dividing the signal into smaller segments. Each segment is processed based on the goodness of fit of the previous segment. This kind of segmentation process, referred to as 'chunking' of sensory information, has been observed to occur in the case of performing a sequential visuomotor task. [10]. In the model, training is done by comparing the instantaneous error in the system's output with the average error over the previous segment using a TD learning algorithm. Training is performed if the TD error at a given instant is lesser than that of the previous trained segment. The error is computed as a weighted average of errors in the peak frequency, peak amplitude and baseline values of the signal over a small time window.

## 3  Results

The model was tested on two different zebra finch song syllables. The results of one of the syllables is shown in Figure 3.

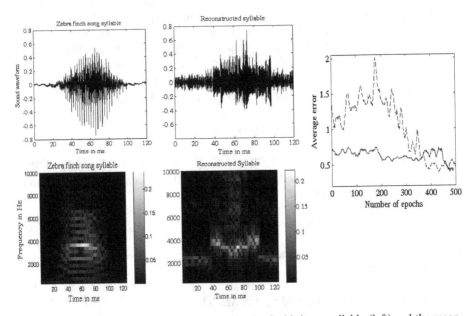

**Fig. 3.** (a) Sound pressure waveforms (normalised) of a birdsong syllable (left) and the reconstructed waveform obtained from the model( right).(b) Power spectrums of an actual birdsong syllable and the reconstructed waveform obtained from the model are shown below.(c) The error plot for the different stages in the training is shown. The solid line indicates the first stage of training where the error is the weighted average of errors in the peak frequency, peak amplitude and baseline values of the signal over a small time window. The dashed line indicates the second stage training where the error is the average value of instantaneous error over a small time window.

# 4  Discussion

Our model of song learning was constructed on the premise of error-driven learning observed in real zebra finches. According to our model, song learning proceeds in a stage-wise manner, similar to the chunking mechanism observed in humans. The precise mechanism for song learning is not known. It was observed that different juvenile birds exposed to the same tutor song learnt the song by using different strategies [11]. Of considerable importance is also the fact that, in humans, this kind of chunking in information processing is thought to be mediated by the basal ganglia [12], which in our avian model corresponds to the AFP. It would be interesting to observe by further experiments, the exact role of the AFP in vocal learning, which would help us get closer to the understanding of basal ganglia function in general.

# References

1. Doupe, J.A., Kuhl, K.P.: Birdsong and Human Speech: Common Themes and Mechanisms. Annual Rev. Neurosc. 22, 22–567 (1999)
2. Doupe, A.J., Perkel, D.J., Reiner, A., Stern, E.A.: Birdbrains could teach Basal Ganglia Research a New Song. Trends Neurosci. 28, 353–363 (2005)
3. Sutton, R.S., Barto, A.G.: Reinforcement Learning: An Introduction. MIT Press, Cambridge (1998)
4. Doya, K., Sejnowski, J.T.: A Novel Reinforcement Model of Birdsong Vocalization Learning. In: Advances in Neural Information Processing Systems, vol. 7, pp. 101–108 (1995)
5. Troyer, T.W., Doupe, A.J.: An Associational Model of Birdsong Sensorimotor Learning: Efference Copy and the Learning of Song Syllables. J. Neurophysiol. 84, 1024–1223 (2000)
6. Fiete, I.R., Fee, M.S., Seung, H.S.: Model of Birdsong Learning Based on Gradient Estimation by Dynamic Perturbation of Neural Conductances. J. Neurophysiol. 98, 2038–2057 (2007)
7. Righetti, L., Buchli, J., Ijspeert, A.J.: Dynamic Hebbian Learning in Adaptive Frequency Oscillators. Physica D 216, 269–281 (2006)
8. Iyengar, S., Bottjer, S.J.: Development of Individual Axon Arbors in a Thalamocortical Circuit Necessary for Song Learning in Zebra Finches. J. Neurosci. 22(3), 901–911 (2002)
9. Gardner, T., Cecchi, G., Magnasco, M., Laje, R., Mindlin, G.B.: Simple motor gestures for birdsongs. Phy. Rev. Lett. 87, 208101 (2001)
10. Sakai, K., Kitaguchi, K., Hikosaka, O.: Chunking during Human Visuomotor Sequence Learning. Exp. Brain Res. 152, 229–242 (2003)
11. Liu, W.-c., Gardner, T.J., Nottebohm, F.: Juvenile zebra finches can use multiple strategies to learn the same song. PNAS 101, 18177–18182 (2004)
12. Boyd, L.A., Edwards, J.D., Siengsukon, C.S., Vidoni, E.D., Wessel, B.D., Linsdell, M.A.: Motor Sequence Chunking is Impaired by Basal Ganglia Stroke. Neurobiol. Learn. Mem. 92(1), 35–44 (2009)

# A Computational Neuromotor Model of the Role of Basal Ganglia and Hippocampus in Spatial Navigation

Deepika Sukumar and Srinivasa Chakravarthy

Department of Biotechnology, Indian Institute of Technology Madras, Chennai, India

**Abstract.** A computational model of the Basal Ganglia and the Hippocampus as key players in solving a navigation task is presented. The roles played by the above-mentioned neural substrates in navigation are demonstrated by an exploration task performed by a model rat in a simulated Morris Water Maze. To highlight the role of hippocampus in navigation, the agent is made to adopt a context-based navigation strategy. To demonstrate the role of BG in navigation, the agent is made to adopt a visual cue-based navigation strategy. The models are developed based on "actor-critic" architecture and trained using reinforcement learning. The above two models are integrated into a complete model which incorporates the above two forms of navigation.

**Keywords:** basal ganglia, hippocampus, navigation, reinforcement learning, dopamine, temporal difference learning, actor, critic.

## 1 Introduction

Animals follow a variety of strategies to find their way around in the environment [1]. For example, when the goal location is signaled by a visible cue, the animal adopts a type of strategy known as the *cue-based* navigation which is thought to be subserved by the Basal Ganglia (BG). In other cases, animals navigate by an internal spatial model of the environment. This type of navigation, known as the *place-based* navigation, is subserved by the hippocampus. Navigation is controlled by both wandering/searching and goal-directed movements. A model of navigation must include a component with stochastic dynamics (corresponding to wandering movements) and another component, which guides the agent towards the goal using a certain "salience" function. An abstract integrated model of spatial navigation involves both BG and hippocampus, but in a lumped form in [2]. We present an integrated model of spatial navigation involving both BG and hippocampus, in which the role of the indirect pathway of BG in exploratory behavior is highlighted.

## 2 A Model to Demonstrate the Role of BG in Navigation

The model developed (Fig.1) is based on "actor-critic" architecture [4] of Reinforcement Learning (RL). The Motor Cortex (MC) serves as the Actor and the striatum as the Critic. The BG is perceived to have two competing elements: a movement facilitating mechanism mediated by the direct (striatum → GPi) pathway and a movement

K. Diamantaras, W. Duch, L.S. Iliadis (Eds.): ICANN 2010, Part II, LNCS 6353, pp. 216–221, 2010.

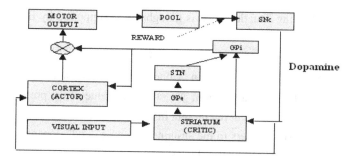

**Fig. 1.** Architecture of the model developed to demonstrate the role of BG in navigation

inhibiting mechanism mediated by the indirect (striatum → GPe→ STN → GPi) pathway. The relative activity of the two pathways is controlled by dopamine signal of the SNc. Experiments in [3] have suggested a link between activities of mesencephalic dopaminergic neurons and a quantity from Reinforcement Learning known as Temporal Difference error (TD error). Thus the general consensus in BG modeling literature regarding correspondence between RL components and BG nuclei is as follows: MC→ Actor, Striatum → Critic, DA signal → TD error. Another major component in RL machinery is the Explorer, which explores the space of possible actions and discovers rewarding actions. In [5] it was hypothesized that the indirect pathway is the Explorer within BG, which is adopted in the present model.

In the present model, a rat is made to search for a visible platform (cue-based) and an invisible platform (place-based with context) in a simulated Morris Water Maze. Spatial context is provided by poles of various heights, placed around the pool. The height of retinal image of each pole, which lies within the visual field of the model rat, is calculated according to Eqn (1).

$$ret\_ht \ = \ ht \ / \ (\lambda_{\times} rad_{\times} d) \tag{1}$$

where $ret\_ht$ is the height of the retinal image of each pole viewed by the model rat, $ht$ is the height of each pole, $\lambda$ is a constant, $rad$ is the radius of the pool and $d$ is the distance between the model rat and the pole.

This visual input is presented to both MC and BG, both of which produce outputs contributing to the rat's next move as described in Eqn (2).

$$g = tanh(\ \alpha g_{actor} + \beta g_{BG}) \tag{2}$$

where $g$ is the final output which controls the movement of the model rat, $\alpha$ and $\beta$ are the weighting factors for MC output and BG output respectively and $g_{actor}$ and $g_{BG}$ are the outputs of the MC and BG respectively.

Mesencephalic dopamine neurons are activated when an animal receives rewarding stimuli from the environment. Dopamine release is further classified in terms of the time-scale at which the release occurs. Phasic dopamine release is a transient phenomenon. The TD error, which represents phasic dopamine in the model, stands for the difference between the total actual reward and the total predicted future reward (Eqn (3)). This signal is used to reinforce actions that yield reward and attenuate those that lead to unrewarding situations. RL is thought to be supported by BG with dopamine playing the role of TD error.

$$\delta = \gamma v(t) - v(t-1) + r(t) \tag{3}$$

where $\delta$ is the temporal difference in Value, $\gamma$ is a constant discounting factor, $v(t)$ is the Value of the current position, $v(t-1)$ is the Value of the previous position and $r(t)$ is the reward received at the present instant of time.

Tonic dopamine, which refers to the sustained, "background" dopamine release, is calculated in the model according to Eqn (4).

$$\bar{r}(t) = \delta(t) + \gamma\delta(t-1) + \gamma^2\delta(t-2) + \dots \tag{4}$$

where $\bar{r}(t)$ is the tonic dopamine level at time $t$, $\delta$'s the TD errors at the different time instants and $\gamma$ the discounting factor.

The BG pathways (DP and IP) are modeled as a function of both, $\delta$ and $\bar{r}$. When $\delta$ is positive and high, exploitation behavior (following the Value gradient) is required and not exploration (search for new directions). In this scenario, DP response should be high. If $\delta$ is negative and high in magnitude, the direction of navigation should be reverted. Hence, DP response is modeled as a tanh (.) function of $\delta$ (Eqn (5)). If $\delta$ is low, it indicates that the rat is away from the goal. In this situation, more of exploratory behavior is required. Hence, IP response is modeled as a Gaussian function of $\delta$, with the mean at 0 (Eqn (6)). When $\bar{r}$ value is high, indicating that the rat has almost reached the goal, neither DP nor IP response should be selected. Instead, the final output should be dominated by the MC output. Hence, IP and DP responses are modeled as exponentially decreasing functions of $\bar{r}$ (Eqns (5) and (6)).

$$y_{dp}(t) = (1 - \frac{1}{1+e^{-\lambda\bar{r}}}) \times tanh(\delta) \times y_{bg}(t-1) \quad (5) \qquad y_{ip}(t) = (1 - \frac{1}{1+e^{-\lambda\bar{r}}}) \times e^{-\frac{\delta^2}{2\sigma}} \times \psi \quad (6)$$

$$y_{bg}(t) = y_{dp}(t) + y_{ip}(t) \tag{7}$$

where $y_{dp}$ is the output of the direct pathway, $y_{ip}$ the output of the indirect pathway, $\psi$ a noise term arising out of IP, $\lambda$ a constant, $\sigma$ the standard deviation of the Gaussian used to compute the response of the indirect pathway.

The Critic is modeled as a multilayer perceptron (MLP) with a single hidden layer consisting of 30 sigmoidal neurons. The input layer of the MLP receives external visual input in the form of a view vector of size 8x1. The training of the MLP for the Critic is done as in Eqns (8-13).

$$\Delta w_{c_{jk}}^f = \eta \delta_{c_j}^f x_k \qquad (8) \qquad \Delta b_{c_j}^f = -\eta \delta_{c_j}^f \tag{9}$$

$$\Delta w_{c_j}^s = \eta \delta_c^s y_{c_j} \qquad (10) \qquad \Delta b_c^s = -\eta \delta_c^s \tag{11}$$

$$\delta_c^s = \delta \qquad (12) \qquad \delta_{c_j}^f = w_{c_j}^s \delta_c^s \tag{13}$$

where $W_c^f$ is the set of weights between the input layer and the hidden layer in the Critic network, $W_c^s$ the set of weights between the hidden layer and the output layer,

$\Delta w c_{jk}^f$ and $\Delta w c_j^s$ weight updates, $\Delta b c_j^f$ and $\Delta b c^s$ bias updates, $\eta$ the learning rate, $\delta c_j^f$ and $\delta c^s$ the back-propagation errors, $\delta$ the TD error, $x_k$ the view vector, $y_{c_j}$ Critic's hidden layer output.

The output layer comprises a single neuron which indicates the Value at each position calculated as the output of the MLP using Eqns (14) and (15).

$$y_{c_j} = tanh(\sum_k w c_{jk}^f x_k - b c_j^f) \qquad (14) \qquad v_t = \sum_j w c_j^s y_{c_j} - b c^s \qquad (15)$$

The Critic network thus maps a view in the input space to a measure of how good the current position of the model rat is with respect to the goal (Value of the current position in the pool). Training of the Critic is performed in a progressive manner starting with a small circular ring around the platform region during the initial training cycles and proceeding gradually to include the entire space. The discount factor ($\gamma$) is gradually increased with training to obtain a gradually expanding Value profile.

The Actor is modeled as a MLP with a single hidden layer consisting of 100 sigmoidal neurons. The visual input and perturbations to motor cortex from BG, in combination with TD error are used to train the Actor as in Eqns (16-21).

$$\Delta w a_{jk}^f = \eta \delta a_j^f x_k \qquad (16) \qquad \Delta b a_j^f = -\eta \delta a_j^f \qquad (17)$$

$$\Delta w a_{jl}^s = \eta \delta a_l^s y a_j \qquad (18) \qquad \Delta b a_l^s = -\eta \delta a_l^s \qquad (19)$$

$$\delta a_l^s = \delta y_{bg_l} \qquad (20) \qquad \delta a_j^f = \sum_l w a_{jl}^s \, \delta a_l^s \qquad (21)$$

The output layer comprises 2 neurons which encode directions ($\Delta$x and $\Delta$y) of movement. The MC's output i.e. its contribution to the rat's transition to the next position, is calculated using the Eqns (22) and (23).

$$y a_j = tanh(\sum_k w a_{jk}^f x_k - b a_j^f) \qquad (22) \qquad y_{act_l} = \sum_j w a_{jl}^s y a_{jl} - b a_l^s \qquad (23)$$

Reward-based learning is implemented to train the MC as follows. If the rat accidentally bumps into the platform, thanks to its wandering movements, it receives a reward. Similarly, if the rat hits the wall of the pool, it receives a punishment. Elsewhere, the rat wanders freely receiving neither reward nor punishment.

# 3   An Integrated Model for Navigation

The integrated model developed (Fig. 2) includes two modules: one for place-based strategy and another for cue-based strategy, competing with each other to assist navigation. Spatially selective "place cells" in CA1/CA3 region of hippocampus contribute to the formation of a cognitive map of space [6]. Hence, involving the hippocampus becomes essential in context-based navigation. A Self-organized Map in cascade with a Continuous Attractor Neural Network is used to model the hippocampus [7]. Stimulus-response is based on associating a sensory cue to a specific response. *In cue-based module, visual input is based on the visible platform. In the place-based module, visual input is based on the spatial context, of the poles surrounding the pool.* The integrated model includes two Actor networks, two Critic networks, two Explorers and two TD

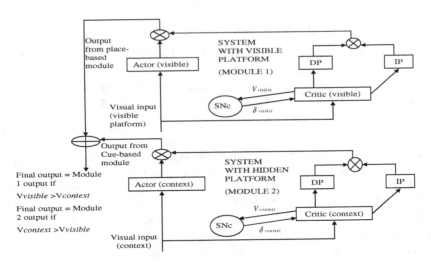

**Fig. 2.** Architecture of the integrated model that adopts both navigation strategies

error signals, one for each of the modules. At any given instant, of the two systems, the system which has higher Value is selected for guiding navigation.

An experimental training and evaluation procedure for simultaneous learning by both modules has been devised [8]. Rats are trained for 9 days, interleaving trials in the visible and hidden versions of the water maze. Along similar lines, the interleaving training procedure (as in Table 1) is followed in the model also where 1 day is equivalent to 200 training cycles.

**Table 1.** Comparison of performance in experiment and simulation during training phase

| Day of the training phase | Training procedure | Result in experiment (escape latency in seconds) | $\gamma$ in the model | Model result (escape latency in seconds) |
|---|---|---|---|---|
| Day1 | Critic of cue-based module trained | 19 | 0.3 | 8.70 |
| Day2 | Critic of cue-based module trained | 9 | 0.7 | 5.00 |
| Day3 | Critic of place-based module trained | 20 | 0.3 | 13.33 |
| Day4 | Actor of cue-based module trained | 5 | - | 4.25 |
| Day5 | Actor of cue-based module trained | 3 | - | 2.77 |
| Day6 | Critic of place-based module trained | 17 | 0.7 | 6.67 |
| Day7 | Actor of cue-based module trained | 3 | - | 2.20 |
| Day8 | Actor of place-based module trained | 21 | - | 7.71 |
| Day9 | Actor of place-based module trained | 3 | - | 2.50 |

Cue-based and place-based modules compete to drive navigation. When the model rat selects context-based response, it is directed towards the location of the platform occupied during training phase, forming a clutter of trajectories (Fig. 3a). When it exhibits cue-based response, it proceeds towards the visible platform which is now in a new location (Fig. 3b).

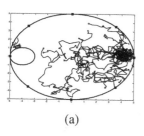

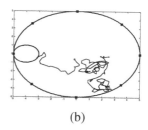

(a)                                                      (b)

**Fig. 3.** (a)Trajectories of the model rat when place-based response is dominant; (b) Trajectories of the model rat when place-based response is dominant

# 4  Conclusions

The models developed bring to light the nuances in the roles played by the BG and Hippocampus in different navigation strategies. They highlight the role of the Basal Ganglia in reward-based learning, action selection and exploratory behavior and that of the Hippocampus in spatial representation. In a real life scenario, an animal uses both stimulus-response strategy and context information to solve navigation tasks. The role of the Indirect Pathway of the Basal Ganglia which is proposed to be the neural substrate for exploratory behavior is demonstrated in the models developed.

# References

1. Redish, A.: Beyond the Cognitive Map, From Place Cells to Episodic Memory. MIT Press, Bradford Books (1999)
2. Lozano, R.C.: Spatial Learning and Navigation in the rat: A Biomimetic Model (2005)
3. Schultz, W.: Predictive Reward Signal of Dopamine Neurons. Journal of Neurophysiology 80, 1–27 (1998)
4. Foster, D.J., Morris, R.G.M., Dayan, P.: A Model of Hippocampally Dependent Navigation, Using the Temporal Difference Learning Rule. Hippocampus 10, 1–16 (2000)
5. Devarajan, S., Prashanth, P.S., Chakravarthy, V.S.: The Role of the Basal Ganglia in Exploratory Behavior in a Model Based on Reinforcement Learning. In: Proc. International Conference on Neural Information Processing, pp. 70–77 (2004)
6. O'Keefe, J., Dostrovsky, J.: The hippocampus as a spatial map, preliminary evidence from unit activity in the freely moving rat. Brain Research 34, 171–175 (1971)
7. Carpenter, G.A., Grossberg, S.: The Art of Adaptive Pattern-Recognition by A Self-Organizing Neural Network. Computer 21, 77–88 (1988)
8. Devan, B.D., White, N.M.: Parallel information processing in the dorsal striatum: relation to hippocampal function. Journal of Neuroscience 19(7), 2789–2798 (1999)

# Reinforcement Learning Based Neural Controllers for Dynamic Processes without Exploration

Frank-Florian Steege[1,2], André Hartmann[2],
Erik Schaffernicht[1], and Horst-Michael Gross[1]

[1] Ilmenau Technical University, Neuroinformatics and Cognitive Robotics Lab,
P.O. Box 100565, D-98684 Ilmenau, Germany
[2] Powitec Intelligent Technologies GmbH, 45219 Essen-Kettwig, Germany
frank-florian.steege@stud.tu-ilmenau.de

**Abstract.** In this paper we present a Reinforcement Learning (RL) approach with the capability to train neural adaptive controllers for complex control problems without expensive online exploration. The basis of the neural controller is a Neural fitted Q-Iteration (NFQ). This network is trained with data from the example set enriched with artificial data. With this training scheme, unlike most other existing approaches, the controller is able to learn offline on observed training data of an already closed-loop controlled process with often sparse and uninformative training samples. The suggested neural controller is evaluated on a modified and advanced cartpole simulator and a combustion control of a real waste-incineration plant and can successfully demonstrate its superiority.

**Keywords:** Neural Control, Adaptive Control, Exploration-Exploitation.

## 1 Introduction

In the area of industrial process control most problems are still solved via conventional solutions from the field of control engineering. The problem with such conventional systems is that they are not able to adapt to changes of the systems to be controlled. In case of a change, the expert who designed the controller has to adapt the parameters of the controller again. For the described problem, it is desirable to use a self-learning controller which is able to adapt to changing dynamics.

Several approaches with learning controllers for unknown processes have been published in recent years. Examples are Reinforcement Learning (RL) Systems such as Q-Learning ([1]), Neural-fitted Q-Iteration (NFQ, [2], [3]) or Bayesian RL ([4], [5]) . Unfortunately, most of the RL-approaches rely on the assumption that it is possible to learn the optimal policy online and/or to explore different strategies for industrial control problems, such as the control of a waste incineration plant, this assumption is not realistic. An online learning phase of an agent

K. Diamantaras, W. Duch, L.S. Iliadis (Eds.): ICANN 2010, Part II, LNCS 6353, pp. 222–227, 2010.

with an inefficient or too explorative strategy at the beginning could commit serious damage to the plant. That means the learning process has to be done completly offline based on observed data. To complicate matters further, the observed data is taken from a closed-loop process where the acting controller is a conventional system which reacts with exactly the same action every time it observes the same state (see Fig. 1). This results in training data less informative than from real exploration periods and causes serious problems for the training of self-learning function approximators. To the best knowledge of the authors, no RL-approach has been published so far which is able to control the key elements of an industrial combustion process due to the charges and restrictions concerning exploration and training data mentioned above.

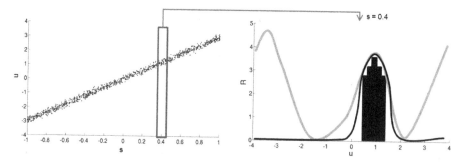

**Fig. 1.** *Left:* Training data set with the state $s$ and control force $u$ from a process controlled by a PI-Controller. *Right:* Action histogram at the state $s = 0.4$ (black boxes) and two possible reward estimations (black and lightgrey lines). Due to the unbalanced distribution of examples in the action space, neural networks can approximate very different reward functions for non-observed actions. Both reward functions would show the same approximation error but cause completly different agent policies.

In this paper, we present an RL-system which meets the demands of the described combustion control systems. The basis of our approach is a NFQ network as presented in [2]. We use the capability of the NFQ to add artificial data-points to the training set to ensure a correct learning of a good policy despite of the less informative nature of the observed data.

# 2  Problem Description and Experimental Setup

## 2.1  Application Domain

In a waste incineration plant the system dynamics are very complex and only partially known. Due to the changing process dynamics most existing control systems are set to cope with all appearing dynamics in general. This solution passes up chances to optimize the combustion for each single process dynamic. Therefore, an adaptive self-learning controller could significantly improve the combustion control.

We applied our controller to a plant with a forward-acting reciprocating grate (see Fig. 2). The stirring of the firebed by the movement of the grates is the main factor for the intensity of the combustion process and is the actuating variable of our controller.

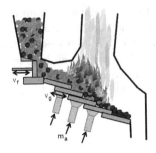

**Fig. 2.** Waste incineration plant. The feeder plunger brings the waste upon the combustion grate with the speed $v_f$. Air with the mass $m_a$ is blown into the combustion zone. The grate elements are locomotive with the speed $v_g$.

## 2.2    Cartpole-Simulator

The cartpole problem is frequently used as a benchmark for RL solutions [3]. In order to take characteristic demands of a combustion process, like aforementioned changes of the system dynamics into consideration the simulator split the simulation into three sequent phases. In every phase, the parameters of the cart and so the dynamics of the system are slightly different. Only the mass of the cart $(5.0kg)$ and the gravity $(9.81\frac{m}{s^2})$ are unchanged. The following table lists the parameters of the cart simulator for every phase:

| Parameter | Phase 1 | Phase 2 | Phase 3 |
|---|---|---|---|
| Mass Pole $(m_p)$ | 2.0kg | 2.0kg | 2.5kg |
| Pole Length $(l_p)$ | 1.0m | 1.0m | 0.75m |
| max. Random Force $(F_r)$ | 1.0N | 1.0N | 1.0N |

Since the focus of this paper lies on training a neural controller which could observe only data from an already controlled process, our simulator also utilizes a conventional PID-controller for controlling the actions of the cart. The maximum Control Force was limited to $5.0N$ for the NFQ and the PID-Controller.

## 3    Algorithm

Our approach aims at training an adaptive controller for an already controlled closed loop process which is

1. not worse than the existing controller,
2. shows a behaviour similar to the old controller
3. but is able to adapt to changes of the process dynamics.

The problem with data observed from a process which is controlled by a conventional deterministic controller is shown in Fig. 1. To each state $s$ the controller only chooses very few different actions from the possible pool of actions $a$. A function approximator, which approximates the reward for the whole action space can calculate very different values for the reward of actions not observed without an increase of the training error (see Fig. 1).The policy choosen by such a net would be very different to the policy of the old controller which is very critical for a serious industrial application.

So, the basic idea of our approach is to label those actions which have not yet been observed with a low reward without worsening the approximation of observed actions and the generalisation-capabilities of the network for not observed states.

NFQ as presented in [2] requires only very few parameters which can influence the training process and have to be optimised, and offers the possibility to insert artificial data into the training set in a very elegant and simple way. An artifical point is a tuple $(s, a, f, Q)$ consisting the state $s$, action $a$ and Q-Value $Q$. A flag $f$ is used to signal the artifical state. We identify non-observed actions by histogramms build over clusters in the state space of the observed dataset (see Fig. 1). The insertion of the artificial data and the training of the NFQ is done as follows:

1. Input $=$ exampleset $X$ where $x_i = (s, a, s', Q)$, $x_i \in X$, $i = 1..n$
2. Cluster $X$ into $m$ cluster $C$ depending on the state $s$, $C_i = (S_{C_i}, A_{C_i}, S'_{C_i}, Q_{C_i})$, $C_i \in C$, where $S_{C_i}$, $A_{C_i}$, $S'_{C_i}$ and $Q_{C_i}$ are sets of all $s$, $a$, $s'$ and $Q$ in the cluster $C_i$
3. For every $C_i$ build a histogram with $k$ bins of actions $A_{C_i}$ appearing
4. If there are action bins with no examples, insert new examples $x_{new}$ into the exampleset $X$ where $x_{new} = (s_{new}, a_{new}, f, Q_{new})$
   $s_{new} = \frac{1}{l} \sum_{i=1}^{l} s_i, s_i \in S_C, l = |S_C|$
   $a_{new} = $ action value of the empty histogram bin
   $f = $ binary flag to label as *artificial data*
   $Q_{new} = min(Q_{C_i}) - Q_{offset}$; $Q_{offset} = $ Reward-Offset to penalize non-observed actions
5. Train NFQ as described in [2] with the new exampleset $X_{new}$

By this algorithm, artificial examples with lower reward are created for all non-observed actions in observed states. This prevents that a function approximator estimates high rewards for such actions, and the policy of the trained agent does not choose them. The number of the artificial data points inserted at a certain state depends on the number of already observed data points in that state. This is important because the lower reward of the artificial points is used to decrease the value of unobserved actions, but should not change the value of a state compared to the value of other states. If a sufficient number of new samples is collected, the agent is retrained with the new data. So the adaptive nature of the controller to changes of the process dynamics is realised.

# 4   Experimental Evaluation of the Approach

The experiments on a real combustion process were executed on a waste incineration plant in Germany with a steam production of 30 t/h. The new NFQ-controller was trained with seven days of data observed from the conventional controllers. After training, the NFQ was tested on the plant. The test phase covered eight days which were split between the NFQ and the PID-controllers. Both controllers acted with a clock of five seconds which results in 17,280 actions per day. The achieved experimental results are as follows:

| Controller | ØCD Steam | Max(CD Steam) | ØCO | ØNOx |
|---|---|---|---|---|
| PID-Controller | 1.61% | 22.2% | 12.77 | 87.06 |
| NFQ with art.data | 1.45% | 16.1% | 11.21 | 86.95 |
| NFQ without art.data | canceled (>10%) | canceled (>25%) | canceled | canceled |

CD is the abbreviation for control deviation and is specified in % of the total amount of steam production. The emissions of carbon monoxide (CO) and nitrogen oxide (NOx) were measured in $mg/Nm^3$. The NFQ which was trained with additional data achieved a better control deviation and reduced noxious gases better than the classical PID-controller. A comparison with a NFQ-Controller without insertion of artificial data had to be canceled after a while because the policy of the NFQ without artificial data was not similar to the policy of the old controller and caused a continuous control deviation of more than 15%. This dangerous policy was the result of a wrong reward approximation as it was shown in Fig. 1.

The cartpole simulator was configured as described in section 2.2. At first the cartpole was controlled by a PID-Controller. 3,000 samples of this experiment were recorded as training samples for the improved NFQ training described in section 3. We inserted 4 virtual points for non-observed actions per real data point. After training, we created two instances of the cartpole simulator. Both instances received the same sequence of random forces affecting the pole. One of the instances was controlled by the PID the other one was controlled by the improved NFQ. Both instances were simulated for 15,000 steps, and each experiment was repeated 10 times with different random sequences:

| Controller | Balancing steps | ØControl error | SD Control error |
|---|---|---|---|
| PID-Controller | 15,000 | 0.0739 | 0.0015 |
| NFQ without art.data | 5 | 1.5707 | 0.0001 |
| NFQ with art.data | 15,000 | 0.0575 | 0.0018 |

The NFQ without artificial samples in the training set was not able to balance the pole for more than 5 steps. Contrary, the NFQ with artificial samples was able to balance the pole and had a lower control error than the conventional PID-controller.

As we explained in section 1, the main advantage of a self-learning conroller is its ability to adapt itself to the process. For the next experiment we collected a data set of 3,000 samples from the runtime of the PID-controller and 3,000 samples of the runtime of the NFQ-controller described above. With this data we trained a new NFQ. The results are as follows:

| Controller | Balancing steps | ØControl error | SD Control error |
|---|---|---|---|
| PID-Controller | 15,000 | 0.0735 | 0.0014 |
| NFQ with art.data | 15,000 | 0.0469 | 0.0010 |

While the results of the PID-controller are the same as in the first experiment, the NFQ-controller was able to improve its result from the first test by 19%. It should be explicitly mentioned, that all results were achieved without explicit exploration phases, all controllers were run in exploitation mode the whole time.

# 5  Conclusion and Outlook

The paper presents a new approach to train neural controllers with data from closed loop processes without exploration. Through the insertion of virtual points with state-depending Q-Values, neural controllers were able to control processes. The same controllers failed if no virtual points were inserted. The new approach offers the possibility to replace conventional controllers through neural adaptive controllers without expensive exploration phases.

Our further research is supposed to concentrate on increasing the applicability of the controller. The possibility to insert artificial data to the training set could allow us to influence the controller in many ways. Expert knowledge about very rare special states and the right control-action could be integrated into the controllers. Such knowledge is extremly valuable because rare special states might not be observed in the example set and the desired policy for these states may differ from the normal policy observed in common states.

# References

1. Watkins, C.: Learning from delayed rewards, PhD Thesis, University of Cambridge, England (1989)
2. Riedmiller, M.: Neural fitted Q-Iteration - First Experiences with a Data Efficient Neural Reinforcement Learning Method. In: Gama, J., Camacho, R., Brazdil, P.B., Jorge, A.M., Torgo, L. (eds.) ECML 2005. LNCS (LNAI), vol. 3720, pp. 317–328. Springer, Heidelberg (2005)
3. Riedmiller, M.: Neural Reinforcement Learning to Swing-Up and Balance a Real Pole. In: Proc. Int. Conf. SMC, vol. 4, pp. 3191–3196 (2005)
4. Price, B., Boutilier, C.: A Bayesian Approach to Imitation in Reinforcement Learning. In: Proc. IJCAI, pp. 712–720 (2003)
5. Schaffernicht, E., Stephan, V., Debes, K., Gross, H.-M.: Machine Learning Techniques for Selforganizing Combustion Control. In: Mertsching, B., Hund, M., Aziz, Z. (eds.) KI 2009. LNCS, vol. 5803, pp. 395–402. Springer, Heidelberg (2009)

# A Neurocomputational Model of Nicotine Addiction Based on Reinforcement Learning

Selin Metin[1] and Neslihan Serap Şengör[1]

Istanbul Technical University, Electrical and Electronics Engineering Faculty,
Maslak 34469, Istanbul, Turkey
selinmetin@gmail.com, sengorn@itu.edu.tr

**Abstract.** Continuous exposure to nicotine causes behavioral choice to be modified by dopamine to become rigid, resulting in addiction. In this work, a computational model for nicotine addiction is proposed and the proposed model captures the effect of continuous nicotine exposure in becoming addict through reinforcement learning. The computational model is composed of three subsystems each corresponding to neural substrates taking part in nicotine addiction and these subsystems are realized by nonlinear dynamical systems. Even though the model is sufficient in acquiring addiction, it needs to be further developed to give a better explanation for the process responsible in turning a random choice into a compulsive behavior.

**Keywords:** computational model, dynamic system, nicotine addiction, reinforcement learning.

## 1 Introduction

The value of an experience or an action is imposed by the reward gained afterwards. An action inducing a greater reward is sensed as a better action, and thus rewarding it is repeated frequently [1]. In the case of addiction, the abusive substance (nicotine, drugs, etc.) has a greater value in the brain than other forms of reward imposing actions. It is believed that some persistent modifications in the synaptic plasticity is the cause of addiction, thus we can define addiction as a disorder in the mesolimbic system which modifies responses of rewarding actions. Mislead by overemphasized reward sensations addicts compulsively seek the object of their addiction. As the reward mechanism has persistently changed, addicts are usually not completely cured and relapse into drug use after treatment [2].

The two main approaches in explaining addiction are the opponent process theory and reward related learning [3,4,5]. Using reinforcement learning theory, addiction is explained as the cumulative result obtained by the administration of a drug as a positive reinforcer [5,6,7]. The opponent-process theory of motivation [3] is used to explain the conditioning principles leading to pleasurable and compulsive activity. According to this model, emotions are paired and when one emotion in a pair is experienced, the other is suppressed. In [8], these two approaches are considered together in deriving a computational model for nicotine addiction.

K. Diamantaras, W. Duch, L.S. Iliadis (Eds.): ICANN 2010, Part II, LNCS 6353, pp. 228–233, 2010.

The hypothesis we considered in this work claims that nicotine addiction is a transition from impulsive behavior to compulsive behavior developed through reinforcement learning. While developing the model considering this view, neural substrates taking part in cognitive processes related to addiction as action selection and value evaluation is considered like in [9]. The proposed model is simulated with an m-file created in MATLAB.

## 2  The Proposed Model for Nicotine Addiction

Nicotine addiction, as with all other kinds of abusive substance addictions, develops with the malfunctioning of the reward mechanism. Nicotine effects the VTA DA signaling, which in turn modify the glutamatergic processes responsible in learning. The behavioral choices depend on the learned situations, in nicotine addiction this choice is in favor of obtaining more nicotine. Continuous exposure to nicotine causes behavioral choice modified by DA to become rigid, resulting in addiction. The proposed model captures this property through reinforcement learning which adapts a parameter that denotes the effect of VTA DA signaling on action selection.

### 2.1  Implementation of the Model

The model has two parts: a DA signaling module which is triggered by nicotine presence and an action-selection module (Figure 1). A-S module is a well-studied cortex-basal ganglia-thalamus dynamical system [10,11,12,9]. The DA signaling module is composed of an action evaluation part, the operation of which is based on the presence of nicotine and a value assignment part which calculates the rewards assigned to the actions and expectation error. The DA signaling module drives the A-S loop with the representation of hedonic value of the previous actions.

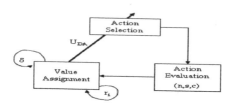

**Fig. 1.** The main blocks of the nicotine addiction model

As in [8] the effect of DA is demonstrated by a DA module which is represented by a difference equation in order to model the dynamic behavior of the process (1):

$$u_{DA}(k+1) = u_{DA}(k) + \mu_{DA}(-u_{DA}(k) + s_{DA}(ri, Ni)) \tag{1}$$

The activation function $s_{DA}$ is a sigmoidal function given as (2):

$$s_{DA}(ri, Ni) = 0.5(1 + \tanh(Ni * ri - \theta_{DA}))$$ (2)

$Ni$ is nicotine uptaking represented by the product of the values of n and s signals when nicotine injection stops (Appendix 1). $\theta_{DA}$ is the threshold setting the minimum tonic DA. We took $\theta_{DA}=0.01$. ri is the reward signal initiated by nicotine taking. $\mu_{DA}$ is the learning rate in the DA subsystem.

The action-selection module used here is acquired from [10,9] which is expressed with the following equations where premotor (pm) and motor (m) loops model the cortex-basal ganglia-thalamus (C-BG-TH) loops (3, 4, 5).

$$\begin{aligned}
p_{pm}(k + 1) &= f(\lambda p_{pm}(k) + m_{pm}(k) + W_{c_{pm}}I(k)) \\
m_{pm}(k + 1) &= f(p_{pm}(k) - d_{pm}(k)) \\
r_{pm}(k + 1) &= W_{r_{pm}}f(p_{pm}(k)) \\
n_{pm}(k + 1) &= f(p_{pm}(k)) \\
d_{pm}(k + 1) &= f(W_{d_{pm}}n_{pm}(k) - r_{pm}(k))
\end{aligned}$$ (3)

$$\begin{aligned}
p_m(k + 1) &= f(\lambda p_m(k) + m_m(k) + \beta p_{pm} + \text{noise}) \\
m_m(k + 1) &= f(p_m(k) - d_m(k)) \\
r_m(k + 1) &= W_{r_m}f(p_m(k)) \\
n_m(k + 1) &= f(p_m(k)) \\
d_m(k + 1) &= f(W_{d_m}n_m(k) - r_m(k))
\end{aligned}$$ (4)

$$f = 0.5(1 + \tanh(a(x - 0.45)))$$ (5)

$W_{d_{pm/m}}$ adds the diffusive effect of subthalamic nucleus and is a symmetrical matrix. The diagonal matrix $W_{r_{pm}}$ represents the effect of ventral striatum (nucleus accumbens) on dorsal striatum (caudate nucleus and putamen). The representation of stimulus is formed by the matrix $W_{c_{pm}}$. The adaptation of weights $W_{c_{pm}}$ and $W_{r_{pm}}$ is done as below (6):

$$W_{c_{pm}}(k + 1) = W_{c_{pm}}(k) + \eta_c\delta(k)p_m(k)I(k)''$$ (6)

$$W_{r_{pm}}(k + 1) = W_{r_{pm}}(k) + \\
\eta_r((\overline{U_{DA}} + Ni)(U_{DA} - \theta_{w_{DA}})''(p_m(k) - \theta))''f(p_m(k))r_m(k)$$

The factors are the phasic DA activitiy $U_{DA}$, running average of 10 steps denoted as in [8] by $\overline{U_{DA}}$. $W_{r_{pm}}$ is calculated only after the reward signal ri becomes greater than 0.5. Thresholds for $U_{DA}$ and $p_m$, respectively, are $\theta_{DA}$ and $\theta$, and are taken as 0.1 times their respective signal. The learning rate $\eta$ is taken as 0.1. The variable $\delta$ represents the error in expectation and is calculated as (7):

$$\delta(k) = ri(k) + \mu V(k + 1) - V(k)$$ (7)

The evaluation of the action selection based on the cortex input and the corresponding reward is given as the value signal (8):

$$V(k) = (W_v + \text{base})I(k) \tag{8}$$

Here, $W_v$ is a row vector and the term base is a row vector with identical entries. $I(k)$ corresponds to input, which in this case is the action performed as a result of (3, 4, 5), and corresponds to "smoke" or "not smoke". An expectation signal based on the value signal is generated which, together with ri, gives rise to the error $\delta$. The error signal represents the modulating role of the neurotransmitters and modulates the behavior of dorsal striatum stream via $W_{r_{pm}}$. The error signal strengthens the representation of the input via $W_{c_{pm}}$ and updates the value of stimuli via $W_v$ are as below (9):

$$W_v(k+1) = W_v(k) + \eta_v \delta(k) I(k)' \tag{9}$$

## 2.2   The Simulation Results

To measure the performance of the proposed model, the response to nicotine uptaking is considered. At the beginning reward value is very small (like 0.01). Each time the selected action is smoking, ri is multiplied by 2 until ri=1.

The action selected by the A-S module is determined by calculating the solution of $p_m$. The value function and the error function are calculated, and using these calculations the weight matrices $W_{c_{pm}}$, $W_{r_{pm}}$, and $W_v$ are updated. The simulation stops if the smoking action is selected successively for 20 times in a given time frame. After numerous trials, it is observed that 20 successive smoking decisions are enough for the system to be considered as a model of an addict. Otherwise, it is decided that addiction is not established.

The parameter values used in the simulation are $\lambda$=0.5, $\beta$=0.03, a=3, $\mu_{DA}$=0.1, $\eta_c$=0.1, $\eta_v$=0.1, $\eta_r$=0.1 and base is 0.2. The initial values of the weight matrices $W_c$ and $W_v$ are generated randomly with small positive real numbers. The initial value of the diagonal matrix $W_{r_{pm}}$ is ones. During the updating phase the matrix values $W_{c_{pm}}$ and $W_{r_{pm}}$ are normalized. The matrices $W_{d_{pm/m}}$ and $W_{rm}$ are composed of 0.5's and they are constant. The noise signal is generated as a very small random number. The action outputs are coded as [1 0]' for smoking, [0 1]' for nonsmoking, and [1 1]' for indecisive behaviors.

In 20 of the 50 successive runs the model completed the task of becoming an addict. The average number of trials to become addict is 346 out of 1000 trials, with a standard deviation of 265.7671. The final matrices for a successful trial are given as follows (10):

$$W_{r_{pm}} = \begin{bmatrix} 1 \\ 0.6179 \end{bmatrix}, \quad W_{c_{pm}} = \begin{bmatrix} 0.8569 & 0.2965 \\ 0.16 & -0.4331 \end{bmatrix} \tag{10}$$

The expectation error signals for two different cases are given in Figure 2. $\delta$ remains constant if the same choice is made successively, and changes otherwise.

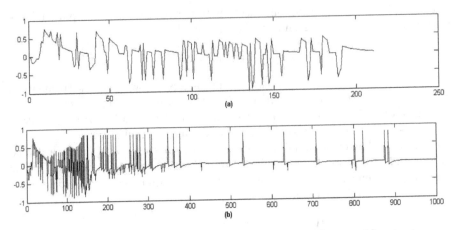

**Fig. 2.** Reinforcement error signal $\delta$ when addiction is a) set up b) not set up

## 3    Discussion and Conclusion

Our work proposes a cortico-striato-thalamic A-S circuit driven by the effects of nicotine uptaking as a model for nicotine addiction. The A-S circuit has two components: an action selection component corresponds to the dorsal stream which simulates behavioral choices, and the other component corresponds to the ventral stream which simulate the evaluation of the action choices and modulates the action selection. The A-S circuit utilizes a competitive learning which is modified with the VTA DA signaling affected by the nicotine. While the structure of the A-S circuit is interconnected nonlinear dynamical systems corresponding to premotor and motor loops, the modification is realized changing a parameter in premotor loop. While in [8], the A-S module is a winner-take-all system, in this work a dynamical system triggered by previous actions, and their evaluation is utilized for A-S. Furthermore, the n-s-c circuit used here is novel. Thus, the system proposed in [10,9] for A-S is enhanced in this work for a more complicated process where reward has more importance on the overall process.

The aim in this work is to support the idea that addiction develops as a form of goal-directed behavior, and therefore the interaction of cortico-striato-thalamic action selection loops have an important role in the development of addiction.

## References

1. Hyman, S.E., Malenka, R.C., Nestler, E.J.: Neural Mechanisms of Addiction: The Role of Reward-Related Learning and Memory. Annual Review of Neuroscience 29, 565–598 (2006)
2. Spanagel, R., Heilig, M.: Addiction and Its Brain Science. Addiction 100(12), 1813–1822 (2005)
3. Solomon, R.L., Corbit, J.D.: An Opponent-Process Theory of Motivation. The American Economic Review 68(6), 12–24 (1978)

4. Koob, G.F., Le Moal, M.: Neurobiological mechanisms for opponent motivational processes in addiction. Phil. Trans. R. Soc. B 363, 3113–3123 (2008)
5. Dayan, P.: Dopamine, Reinforcement Learning, and Addiction Pharmacopsychiatry. Addiction 42, 56–65 (2009); 100(12), 1813–1822 (2005)
6. Peele, S., Alexander, B.K.: The Meaning of Addiction Chapter 3: Theories of Addiction, http://www.peele.net/lib/moa3.html
7. Delgado, M.R.: Reward-Related Resposes in the Human Striatum. Annals of the New York Academy of Sciences 1104, 70–88 (2007)
8. Gutkin, B.S., Dehaene, S., Changeux, J.P.: A Neurocomputational Hypothesis for Nicotine Addiction. PNAS 103(4), 1106–1111 (2006)
9. Metin, S., Sengor, N.S.: Dynamical System Approach in Modeling Addiction. Accepted to be published in Proceedings of BICS (2010)
10. Sengor, N.S., Karabacak, O., Steinmetz, U.: A Computational Model of Cortico-Striato-Thalamic Circuits in Goal-Directed Behavior. In: Kůrková, V., Neruda, R., Koutník, J. (eds.) ICANN 2008, Part I. LNCS, vol. 5163, pp. 328–337. Springer, Heidelberg (2008)
11. Taylor, J.G., Taylor, N.R.: Analysis of Recurrent Cortico-Basal Ganglia-Thalamic Loops for Working Memory. Biological Cybernetics 82, 415–432 (2000)
12. Gurney, K., Prescott, T.J., Redgrave, P.: A Computational Model of Action Selection in the Basal Ganglia I: A New Functional Anatomy. Biological Cybernetics 84, 401–410 (2001)

# Appendix 1

Initial values of n, s, and c are all 0.1. Parameters used in equations are as follows: $\theta_n$=0.6, $\theta_s$=0.7, $\theta_c$=0.7, $\beta_s$=0.4, $\beta_c$=0.4. nicotine level is taken as 0.3 if k is less than 500, 0 otherwise. Rates used in the equations are $\mu$=0.1, $\tau_n$=0.25, $\tau_s$=1, $\tau_c$=2.

Activation functions (11):

$$\alpha_n(k) = 0.5(1 + \tanh(nicotine - \theta_n))$$
$$\alpha_s(k) = 0.5(1 + \tanh(n(k) - \theta_s))$$
$$\alpha_c(k) = 0.5(1 + \tanh(s(k) - \theta_c)) \quad (11)$$
$$\beta_n(k) = 0.5(1 + \tanh(c(k) - \theta_n))$$

Dynamic equations of n, s, and c (12):

$$n(k+1) = n(k) + \mu(1/\tau_n)[-\beta_n(k)c(k) + \alpha_n(k)(1 - n(k)c(k))]$$
$$s(k+1) = s(k) + \mu(1/\tau_s)[-\beta_s s(k) + \alpha_s(k)(1 - s(k))] \quad (12)$$
$$c(k+1) = c(k) + \mu(1/\tau_c)[-\beta_c c(k) + \alpha_c(k)(1 - c(k))]$$

# Teaching Humanoids to Imitate 'Shapes' of Movements

Vishwanathan Mohan, Giorgio Metta, Jacopo Zenzeri, and Pietro Morasso

Robotics, Brain and Cognitive Sciences Department,
Italian Institute of Technology, Via Morego 30, Genova, Italy
{vishwanathan.mohan,pierto.morasso}@iit.it,
{jacopo.zenzeri,giorgio.metta}@iit.it

**Abstract.** Trajectory formation is one of the basic functions of the neuromotor controller. In particular, reaching, avoiding, controlling impacts (hitting), drawing, dancing and imitating are motion paradigms that result in formation of spatiotemporal trajectories of different degrees of complexity. Transferring some of these skills to humanoids allows us to understand how we ourselves learn, store and importantly, generalize motor behavior (to new contexts). Using the playful scenario of teaching baby humanoid iCub to 'draw', the essential set of transformations necessary to enable the student to 'swiftly' enact a teachers demonstration are investigated in this paper. A crucial feature in the proposed architecture is that, what iCub learns to imitate is not the teachers 'end effector trajectories' but rather their 'shapes'. The resulting advantages are numerous. The extracted 'Shape' being a high level representation of the teachers movement, endows the learnt action natural invariance wrt scale, location, orientation and the end effector used in its creation (ex. it becomes possible to draw a circle on a piece of paper or run a circle in a football field based on the internal body model to which the learnt attractor is coupled). The first few scribbles generated by iCub while learning to draw primitive shapes being taught to it are presented. Finally, teaching iCub to draw opens new avenues for iCub to both gradually build its mental concepts of things (a star, house, moon, face etc) and begin to communicate with the human partner in one of the most predominant ways humans communicate i.e. by writing.

**Keywords:** Shape, Imitation, iCub, Passive Motion Paradigm, Catastrophe theory.

## 1 Introduction

Behind all our incessant perception-actions underlies the core cognitive faculty of 'perceiving and synthesizing' shape. Perceiving affordances of objects in the environment for example a cylinder, a ball, etc, or performing movements ourselves, shaping ones fingers while manipulating objects, reading, drawing or imitating are some examples. Surprisingly, it is not easy to define 'shape' quantitatively or even express it in mensurational quantities. Vaguely, shape is the core information in any object/action that survives the effects of changes in location, scale, orientation, end effectors/bodies used in its creation, and even minor structural injury. It is infact this invariance that makes the abstract notion of 'shape' a crucial information in all our sensorimotor interactions. How do humans effortlessly perceive and synthesize

K. Diamantaras, W. Duch, L.S. Iliadis (Eds.): ICANN 2010, Part II, LNCS 6353, pp. 234–244, 2010.

'shape' during their daily activities and what are the essential set of computational transformations that would enable humanoids to do the same? In this paper, we describe our attempts to understand this multidimensional problem using the scenario of teaching baby humanoid iCub to draw shapes on a drawing board after observing a demonstration and aided by a series of self evaluations of its performance.

It is quite evident that scenario of iCub learning to draw a trajectory after observing a teachers demonstration embeds the central loop of imitation i.e transformation from the visual perception of a teacher to motor commands of a student. The social, cultural and cognitive implications of imitation are well documented in literature today [9, 11-12]. In the recent years, a number of interesting computational approaches like direct policy learning, model based learning, learning attractor landscapes using dynamical systems [4] have been proposed to tackle parts of the imitation learning problem [12]. Based on the fact that usually a teacher's demonstration provides a rather limited amount of data, best described as "sample trajectories", various projects investigated how a stable policy can be instantiated from such small amount of information. The major advancement in these schemes was that the demonstration is used just as a starting point to further learn the task by self improvement. In most cases, demonstrations were usually recorded using marker based optical recording and then either spline based techniques or dynamical systems were used to approximate the trajectories. Compared to spline based techniques, the dynamical systems based approach have the advantage of being temporally invariant (because splines are explicitly parameterized in time) and naturally resistant to perturbations. The approach has been has been successfully applied in different imitation scenarios like learning the kendama game, tennis stokes, drumming, generating movement sequences with an anthropomorphic robot [2].

The approach proposed in this paper is also based on nonlinear attractor dynamics and has the flavour of self improvement, temporal invariance (through terminal attractor dynamics [15]) and generalization to novel task specific constraints. However, we also go beyond this in the sense that what iCub learns to imitate is the 'Shape' a rather high level invariant representation extracted from the demonstration. It is independent of scale, location, orientation, time and also the end effector/body chain that creates it (for example, we may draw a circle on a piece of paper or run a circle in a football field). The eyes of iCub are the only source of gathering information about the demonstration. No additional optical marker equipments recording all joint angles of the teacher are employed. In any case, very use of joint information for motion approximation/generation makes it difficult to generalize the learnt action to a different body chain, which is possible from the high level action representations acquired using our approach. Figure 1 shows the high level information flows between different sub modules in the loop starting from the teachers demonstration and culminating in iCub learning to perform the same. The perceptual subsystems are shown in pink background, the motor subsystems in blue and learning modules in green. Section 2 briefly summarizes the perceptual modules that ultimately lead to the creation of a motor goal in iCub's brain. Section 3 and 4 focus on the central issue of this paper about how iCub learns to realize this motor goal (i.e. imitate the teachers' performance), along with experimental results. A brief discussion concludes.

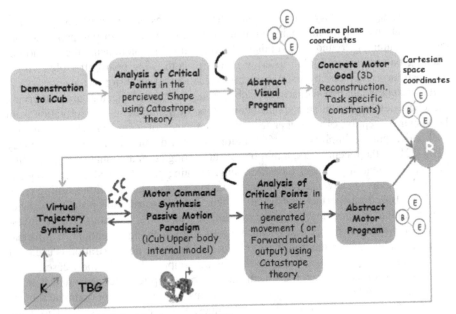

**Fig. 1.** Shows the overall high level information flows in the proposed architecture, beginning with the demonstration to iCub (for example a 'C'). A preprocessing phase extracts the teachers end effector trajectory from the demonstration. This is followed by characterization of the 'shape' of the extracted trajectory using Catastrophe theory [13-14], that leads to the creation of an abstract visual program (AVP). Since the AVP is created out of visual information coming from the two cameras, it is represented in camera plane coordinates. Firstly we need to reconstruct this information to iCub's ego centric frame of reference. Other necessary task specific constraints (like, prescription of scale, end effector/body chain involved in the motor action etc) are also applied at this phase. In this way, the context independent AVP is transformed into a concrete motor goal for iCub to realize. CMG forms the input of the virtual trajectory generation system (VTGS) that synthesizes different virtual trajectories by pseudo randomly exploring the space of virtual stiffness (K) and timing (TBG). These virtual trajectories act as attractors and can be coupled to the relevant internal body model of iCub to synthesize the motor commands for action generation (using Passive Motion Paradigm [5]). In the experiments presented in this paper, the torso-left arm-paint brush chain of iCub is employed. Analysis of the forward model output once again using catastrophe theory extracts the 'shape' of the self generated movement. This is called as the Abstract motor program. Abstract visual and motor information can now be directly compared to self evaluate a score of performance. A learning loop follows.

## 2  Extracting the 'Shape' of a Visually Observed End Effector Movements (of Self and Others)

As seen in figure 1, the stimulus to begin with is the teacher's demonstration. This demonstration is usually composed of a sequence of strokes, each stroke tracing a finite, continuous line segment inside the visual workspace of both cameras. These strokes are created using a green pen i.e. the optical marker iCub track. The captured video of the demonstration undergoes a preprocessing stage, where the location of the marker in each frame (for both camera outputs) is detected using a simple colour segmentation module. If there are N frames in the captured demonstration, the information at the end of the pre-processing phase is organized in the form of a Nx4 matrix, $N^{th}$ row containing the detected location of the marker $(U_{left}, V_{left}, U_{right}, V_{right})$ in the left and right cameras during the $N^{th}$ frame. In this way the complete trajectory traced by the teacher (as observed in the camera plane coordinates) is extracted. The next stage is to create a abstract high level representation of this trajectory, by extracting its shape. A systematic treatment of the problem of shape can be found in a branch of mathematics known as Catastrophe theory (CT) originally proposed in late 1960's by French mathematician Rene Thom, further developed by Zeeman[14], Gilmore[3] among others and applied to a range of problems in engineering and physics. According to CT the overall shape of a smooth function, f(x), is determined by special local features like "peaks", "valleys" etc called as critical points (CP). When all the CP of a function is known, we know its global shape. Further developing CT, [1] have shown that following 12 CP's (pictorially shown in figure 2a) are sufficient to characterize the shape of any line diagram: Interior Point, End Point, Bump (i.e maxima or minima), Cusp, Dot, Cross, Contact, Star, Angle, Wiggle, T and Peck. These 12 critical points, found in many of the worlds scripts, can be computed very easily using simple mathematical operations [1]. In this way the shape of the trajectory demonstrated by the teacher can be described using a set of critical points that describe its 'essence'. For example, the essence of the shape 'C' of figure 1, is the presence of a bump (maxima) in between the start and end points. As shown in figure 2b, for any complex trajectory, the shape description takes the form of a graph with different CP at the graph nodes.

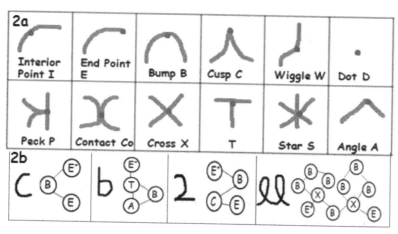

**Fig. 2.** (a) Pictorially illustrates the 12 primitive shape critical points derived in [1] using catastrophe theory. (b) Shows the extracted shape descriptors for four demonstrated trajectories.

By extracting the shape descriptors, we have effectively reduced the complete demonstrated trajectory to a small set of critical points (their type and location in camera plane coordinates). We call this compact representation as the abstract visual program (AVP). AVP may be thought as a high level visual goal created in iCub's brain after perceiving the teachers demonstration. To facilitate any action generation to take place, this visual goal must be transformed into an appropriate motor goal in iCub's egocentric space. To achieve this, we have to transform location of the shape critical points computed in the image planes of the two cameras ($U_{left}$, $V_{left}$, $U_{right}$, $V_{right}$) into corresponding points in the iCub's egocentric space (x,y,z) by a process of 3D reconstruction. Of course the 'type' of the CP is conserved i.e a bump/maxima still remains a bump, a cross is still a cross in any coordinate frame. Reconstruction is achieved using Direct Linear Transform (Shapiro, 1978) based stereo camera calibration and 3D reconstruction system [8] already functional in iCub [5-6]. The set of transformations leading to the formation of the Concrete motor goal is pictorially shown in figure 3. Also note that since critical points analysis using CT can be used to extract shapes of trajectories in general, the same module is reused to extract the shape of iCub's end effector trajectory (as predicted by the forward model) during action generation process. This is called as the abstract motor program (AMP). Since AMP and CMG contain shape description (and also in the same frame of reference), they can directly be compared to evaluate performance and trigger learning in the right direction.

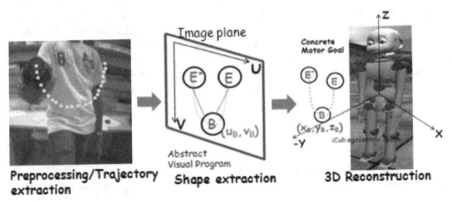

**Fig. 3.** Pictorially shows the set of transformations leading to the formation of concrete motor goal.

## 3   Virtual Trajectory Synthesis and Learning to Shape

The CMG basically consists of a discrete set of critical points (their location in iCub's ego centric space and type), that describe in abstract terms the 'shape' iCub must now create itself. For example, the CMG of the shape 'U' (figure 3) has three CP's (2 end points 'E', and one bump 'B' in between them). Given any two points in space, an infinite number of trajectories can be shaped passing through them. How can iCub learn to synthesize a continuous trajectory similar to the demonstrated shape using a discrete set of critical points in the CMG? In this section we seek to answer this question.

The first step in this direction is the synthesis of virtual trajectory between the shape critical points in the CMG. Synthesized virtual trajectories do not really exist in space and must not be confused with the actual shapes drawn by iCub. Instead, they act as attractors and play a significant role in the generation of the motor action that creates the shape. Let $X_{ini} \in (x,y,z)$ be the initial condition i.e. the point in space from where the creation of shape is expected to commence (usually initial condition will be one of the end points in CMG). If there are N CP's in the CMG, the spatiotemporal evolution of virtual trajectory $(x,y,z,t)$ is equivalent to integrating a non-linear differential equation that takes the following form:

$$
\begin{cases}
\dot{x}_{ini} = \sum_{i=1}^{N} K_i \gamma_i(t) \cdot \left( x_{CP_i} - x_{ini} \right) \\[2mm]
\gamma(t) = \dfrac{\dot{\xi}}{1 - \xi} \\[2mm]
\xi(t) = 6 \left( \dfrac{t}{\tau} \right)^5 - 15 \left( \dfrac{t}{\tau} \right)^4 + 10 \left( \dfrac{t}{\tau} \right)^3
\end{cases}
\tag{1}
$$

Intuitively, as seen in figure 4, we may visualize $X_{ini}$ as connected to all the shape CP's in the CMG by means of virtual springs and hence being attracted by the force fields generated by them $F_{CP}=K_{CP}(x_{CP}-x_{ini})$. The strength of these attractive force fields depends on: 1) the virtual stiffness '$K_i$' of the spring and 2) time varying modulatory signals $\gamma_i(t)$ generated by their respective time base generators (TBG), that basically weigh the influence of different CP's through time. Note that he function $\gamma(t)$ implements the terminal attractor dynamics [15], a mechanism to control the timing of the relaxation of a dynamical system to equilibrium. The function $\xi(t)$ is a minimum jerk time base generator . The virtual trajectory is the set of equilibrium points created during the evolution $X_{ini}$ through time, under the influence of the net attractive field generated by different CP's. Further, by simulating the dynamics of equation 1, with different values of K and $\gamma$, a wide range of virtual trajectories can be obtained passing through the CP's. Inversely, learning to 'shape' translates into the problem of learning the right set of virtual stiffness and timing such that the 'Shape' of the trajectory created by iCub correlates with the shape description in CMG.

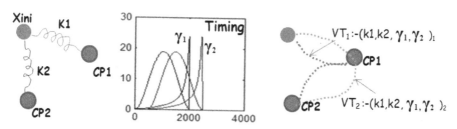

**Fig. 4.** Intuitively, we may visualize $X_{ini}$ as connected to all the shape CP's in the CMG by means of virtual springs. The attractive fields exerted by different CP's at different instances of time is a function of the virtual stiffness (k) and the timing signal $\gamma$ of the time base generator. The virtual trajectory is the set of equilibrium points created during the evolution $X_{ini}$ through time, under the influence of the net attractive field generated by different CP's. For different sets of K and $\gamma$ we get different virtual trajectories.

The site of learning i.e virtual stiffness matrix 'K' of equation 1 are basically open parameters (positive definite). One may intuitively imagine the procedure of estimating the correct values of 'K' analogous to a manual eye testing scenario, where the optician is faced with the problem of estimating the right optical power of the eye glasses necessary for a patient. Just by exploring a fixed range of test lenses, and aided by the feedback of the patient, the optician is able to quickly estimate the dioptric value of the lens required for the patient. Since this procedure is mainly pseudo-random exploration, questions regarding convergence and fast learning are critical. The answer lies in inherent modularity in our architecture. Once iCub learns to draw the 12 shape primitives of figure 2a, it can exploit this motor knowledge to compose more complex shapes (that can be described as combinations of these primitive shape features as in figure 2b). Moreover, using a bump, cusp and straight line all other primitives of 2a can be created (example, peck is a composition of straight line and cusp and so on). Hence once iCub learns to draw a straight line, bump and cusp it can exploit this motor knowledge to draw the other shape primitives, and this can be further exploited during the creation of more complex line diagrams.

Considering that the behaviour of neuromuscular system is predominantly spring like, we consider only symmetric stiffness matrix K, with all non diagonal elements zero (In other words, the resulting vector fields have zero curl). Regarding straight lines, it is well known that human reaching movements follow straight line trajectories with a bell shaped velocity profile. This can be achieved in the VTGS by keeping components of matrix K equal in equation 1 ($K_{xx}=K_{yy}=K_{zz}$). More curved trajectories can be obtained otherwise. Figure 5 shows some of the virtual trajectories generated by titillating the components of the K matrix numerically from 1-9 and simulating the dynamics of equation 1. As seen, a gamut of shapes, most importantly cusps and bumps can be synthesized by exploring this small range itself. Essentially what matters is not the individual values of the components, but the balance between them which goes on to shape the net attractive force field to the CP. Once iCub learns to draw straight lines, bumps and cusps, it can exploit this motor knowledge to learn the other primitives, and through 'composition' any complex shape.

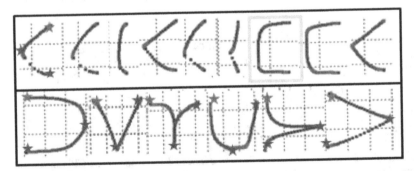

**Fig. 5.** Top Panel shows the range of virtual trajectories synthesized while learning do draw a 'C', with the best solution highlighted. Bottom panel shows other goal shapes learnt. All these shapes can be created by pseudo randomly titillating the components of the matrix K in the fixed range of 1-9.

## 4  Motor Command Synthesis: Coupled Interactions between the Virtual Trajectory and Internal Body Model

In this section, we deal with the final problem of motor command synthesis, that will ultimately transform the learnt virtual trajectory into a real trajectory created by iCub. We use the passive motion paradigm (PMP) based forward/inverse model for upper body coordination of iCub (figure 6) in the action generation phase [5-6]. This interface between the virtual trajectory and the PMP based iCub internal body model is similar to the coordination of the movements of a puppet, virtual trajectory playing the role of the puppeteer. As the strings pull the finger tip of the puppet to the target, the rest of the body elastically reconfigures to achieve a posture that is necessary to position the end effector to the target. If motor commands (trajectory of joint angles) derived by this process of relaxation is actively fed to the actuators, iCub will physically create the shape (hence transforming the virtual trajectory into a real trajectory). This is the central hypothesis behind the VTGS-PMP coupling. The evolving virtual trajectory generates an attractive force field $F=K(x_{VT}-x)$ applied at the end effector, hence leading the end effector to track it (figure 7, top left panel). This field is mapped from the extrinsic to the intrinsic space by means of the mapping $T=J^TF$ that yields an attractive torque field in the intrinsic space ($J$ is the Jacobian matrix of the kinematic transformation). The total torque field induces a coordinated motion of all

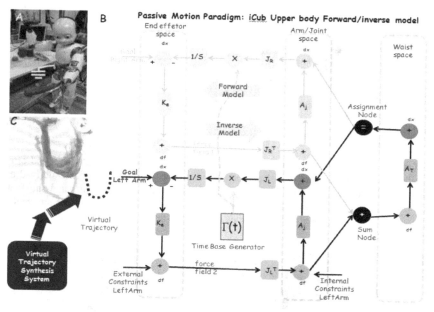

**Fig. 6.** The PMP Forward/Inverse model for iCub upper body coordination. The torso/left arm chain is used in the iCub drawing experiments (Panel A), hence the right arm chain is deactivated. The evolving virtual trajectory acts as an attractor to the PMP system and triggers the synthesis of motor commands (This process is analogous to the coordinating a puppet, the VT serving the role of the puppeteer). Panel C shows the scanned image of drawings of iCub while learning to draw a 'U'.

the joints in the intrinsic space according to an admittance matrix A. The motion of the joints now, determines the motion of the end-effector according to the following relationship: $\dot{x} = J\,\dot{q}$. Ultimately, the motion of the kinematic chain evoked by the evolving VT is equivalent to integrating non-linear differential equations that, in the simplest case in which there are no additional constraints, takes the following form:

$$\dot{x} = \Gamma(t)\, J\, A\, J^T\, K\,(x_{VT} - x) \qquad (2)$$

At the end of the PMP relaxation, we get two trajectories, a trajectory of joint angles (10 DoF (3 torso and 7 left arm) X 3000 iterations in time) and the end effector trajectory (predicted forward model output as a consequence of the motor commands, which is used for monitoring and performance evaluation). As seen in the results of figure 7, when the motor commands are buffered to the actuators, iCub creates the shape, hence transforming the virtual trajectory into a real trajectory (drawn by it).

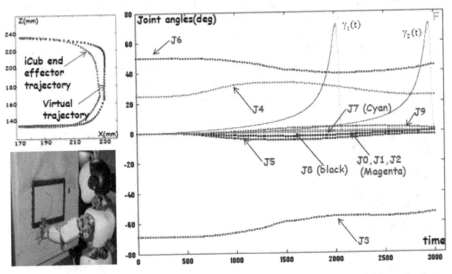

(a) Top left panel shows both the learnt virtual trajectory (attractor) and iCub's end effector trajectory (predicted forward model output) as a result of the motor commands derived using PMP (10 DoF torso/left arm chain X 3000 iterations in time). Bottom left panel shows iCub drawing the shape. The drawing were created on a drawing board, with paper attached to a layer of soft foam. The foam and the bristles of the paint brush provide natural compliance and allow safe interaction.

(b) The first 'scribbles'

**Fig. 7.**

# 5 Discussion

Using the scenario of gradually teaching iCub to draw, a minimal architecture that intricately couples the complementary operations of shape perception/synthesis in the framework of a 'teacher-learner' environment was presented in this article. The proposed action-perception loop also encompasses the central loop of imitation (specifically, end effector trajectories), with the difference that what iCub learns is not to reproduce a mere trajectory in 3D space by means of a specific end-effector but, more generally, to produce an infinite family of 'shapes' in any scale, in any position, using any possible end-effector/body part. We showed that by simulating the dynamics of VTGS using a fixed range of virtual stiffness' a diversity of shapes, mainly the primitives (derived using CT) can be synthesized. Since complex shapes can be efficiently 'decomposed' into combinations of primitive shapes (using CT), inversely the actions needed to synthesize them can 'composed' using combinations of the corresponding 'learnt' primitive actions. Ongoing experiments clearly show that motor knowledge gained while learning a 'C' and 'U' can be systematically exploited while learning to draw a 'S' and so on. Thus, there is a delicate balance between exploration and compositionality, the former dominating during the initial phases to learn the basics, the later dominating during the synthesis of more complex shapes. Finally, teaching iCub to draw opens new avenues for iCub to both gradually build its mental concepts of things (a star, house, moon, face etc) and begin to communicate with the human partner in one of the most predominant ways humans communicate i.e. by writing.

**Acknowledgments.** The research presented in this article is being conducted under the framework of the EU FP7 project ITALK. The authors thank the European Commission for sustained financial support and encouragement.

# References

1. Chakravarthy, V.S., Kompella, B.: The shape of handwritten characters. In: Pattern recognition letters. Elsevier science B.V., Amsterdam (2003)
2. Billard, A.: Learning motor skills by imitation: A biologically inspired robotic model. Cybernetics and Systems 32, 155–193 (2000)
3. Gilmore, R.: Catastrophe Theory for Scientists and Engineers. Wiley-Interscience, New York (1981)
4. Ijspeert, J.A., Nakanishi, J., Schaal, S.: Movement imitation with nonlinear dynamical systems in humanoid robots. In: International Conference on Robotics and Automation (ICRA 2002), Washington, May 11-15 (2002)
5. Mohan, V., Morasso, P., Metta, G., Sandini, G.: A biomimetic, force-field based computational model for motion planning and bimanual coordination in humanoid robots. Autonomous Robots 27(3), 291–301 (2009)
6. Morasso, P., Casadio, M., Mohan, V., Zenzeri, J.: A neural mechanism of synergy formation for whole body reaching. Biological Cybernetics 102(1), 45–55 (2010)
7. Mohan, V., Morasso, P., Metta, G., Kasderidis, S.: Actions and Imagined Actions in Cognitive robots. In: Taylor, J.G., Tishby, N., Hussain, A. (eds.) Perception-Reason-Action cycle: Models, algorithms and systems. Series in Cognitive and Neural Systems, pp. 1–32. Springer, USA (2010) ISBN: 978-1-4419-1451-4

8. Mohan, V., Morasso, P.: Towards reasoning and coordinating action in the mental space. International Journal of Neural Systems 17(4), 1–13 (2007)
9. Rizzolatti, G., Fogassi, L., Gallese, V.: Neurophysiological mechanisms underlying action understanding and imitation. Nat. Rev. Neurosci. 2, 661–670 (2001)
10. Sandini, G., Metta, G., Vernon, D.: RobotCub: An Open Framework for Research in Embodied Cognition. In: Proceedings of IEEE-RAS/RSJ International Conference on Humanoid Robots (Humanoids 2004), pp. 13–32 (2004)
11. Schaal, S.: Is imitation learning the route to humanoid robots? Trends in Cognitive Sciences 3, 233–242 (1999)
12. Schaal, S., Ijspeert, A., Billard, A.: Computational approaches to motor learning by imitation. Philosophical Transaction of the Royal Society of London: Series B, Biological Sciences 358(1431), 537–547 (2003)
13. Thom, R.: Structural Stability and Morphogenesis. Addison-Wesley, Reading (1989)
14. Zeeman, E.C.: Catastrophe Theory-Selected Papers 1972–1977. Addison-Wesley, Reading (1977)
15. Zak, M.: Terminal attractors for addressable memory in neural networks. Phys. Lett. A 133, 218–222 (1988)

# The Dynamics of a Neural Network of Coupled Phase Oscillators with Synaptic Plasticity Controlling a Minimally Cognitive Agent

Renan C. Moioli[1], Patricia A. Vargas[2], and Phil Husbands[1]

[1] Centre for Computational Neuroscience and Robotics, Univ. of Sussex, UK
[2] ISL, Dept. of Computer Science, Heriot-Watt Univ., UK
r.moioli@sussex.ac.uk

**Abstract.** This work explores the neuronal synchronisation and phase information dynamics of an enhanced version of the widely used Kuramoto model of phase interacting oscillators. The framework is applied to a simulated robotic agent engaged in a minimally cognitive benchmark task. The outcomes of this research contribute not only to uncover the role of neuronal synchronisation and phase information in the generation of cognitive behaviours but also to the understanding of oscillatory properties in neural networks.

## 1 Introduction

There is increasingly evidence that cognitive processes have a close non-trivial relationship to neural rhythms and oscillations [1]. The importance of considering temporal relations among groups of neurons, either by external influences or sustained by internal mechanisms, has been stressed by various researchers [2–4]. Varela *et. al.*[5] point out that the phase relationships and synchronisation of brain signals would contain a great deal of information on the temporal structure of neural signals, a key factor when analysing communication and information processing in neuronal assemblies [6, 7]. Other authors have emphasized the relationship between phase information and memory formation and retrieval [8–10].

This work explores the neuronal synchronisation and phase information dynamics of a simulated robotic agent engaged in minimally cognitive tasks [11–15]. Basically, two aspects of an active categorical perception task [11, 14, 15] will be studied: (1) the impact of different neural network temporal dynamics and (2) the effect of different phase sensitivity functions on the synchronisation patterns and phase dynamics observed in the neural network. Although there has been much work on coupled oscillator based control of complex motor behaviours, particularly locomotion [16], to date there has been very little research on the wider issues of temporal dynamics in the generation of embodied cognitive behaviours.

The Kuramoto model of coupled oscillators [17] allows for easy inspection of the phase evolution and frequency of each of its elements and is well known for its suitability to investigate large populations of biological oscillators [18, 19].

K. Diamantaras, W. Duch, L.S. Iliadis (Eds.): ICANN 2010, Part II, LNCS 6353, pp. 245–255, 2010.
© Springer-Verlag Berlin Heidelberg 2010

Moreover, it can resemble the behaviour of groups of neurons instead of focusing on single neuron activations [20]. Based on Moioli *et. al.* [21], who applied evolved instances of the Kuramoto model to the generation of minimally cognitive behaviours, the framework used in this paper is an extended version of the model which differs from the original by incorporating a mechanism inspired by the Hebbian theory of synaptic plasticity [22, 23], where the phase differences of each pair of nodes represent their mutual activity, and by considering external inputs. This mechanism was introduced to allow neuronal oscillators with different natural frequencies to recruit and compete for coherence with other oscillators in the neural network [24].

Section 2 defines the model; section 3 describes the experiments and their implementation procedures; section 4 shows the results and provide some analysis and section 5 presents the conclusions and proposes further work.

## 2    The Extended Kuramoto Model

The Kuramoto model is represented by a lattice of coupled oscillators, each with a possible different natural frequency drawn from some distribution, modulated according to a function that depicts their sensitivity to the phase of other nodes (more specifically, the *sine* function is used). Although apparently simple, it can generate a large variety of synchronisation patterns with dynamics that can easily scale up in complexity [18]. It has the form of Equation 1:

$$\frac{d\theta_i}{dt} = \omega_i + \frac{1}{N} \sum_{j=1}^{N} K_{ij} sin(\theta_j - \theta_i) \tag{1}$$

where $\theta_i$ is the phase of the $i$th oscillator, $\omega_i$ is the natural frequency of the $i$th oscillator, $K_{ij}$ is the coupling factor between nodes $i$ and $j$ and $N$ is the total number of oscillators. If the frequency of any two given nodes $i$ and $j$ $(i, j = 1, 2...n)$ are equal, i.e. $d\theta_i - d\theta_j = 0$ or $\theta_i - \theta_j = constant$, the model is said to be globally synchronised.

We have extended the model by incorporating a phase-based plasticity rule, similar to a Hebbian learning rule, to govern $K_{ij}$ (Equation 2).

$$\frac{dK_{ij}}{dt} = \epsilon \left[\alpha cos(\theta_i - \theta_j) - K_{ij}\right] \tag{2}$$

where: $\epsilon$ is a learning rate, $\alpha$ is a learning enhancement factor.

It is clear from Equation 2 that nodes with similar phases tend to increase their coupling whereas out-of-phase nodes tend to have it decreased. Therefore the activity of the nodes has a strong influence on the unfolding dynamics of the model. The importance of this property in mimicking brain related dynamics relies in the fact that different neuronal blocks could dynamically arise, synchronise and influence other blocks, culminating in different cortical areas flexibly establishing communication channels depending on their temporal activity [1].

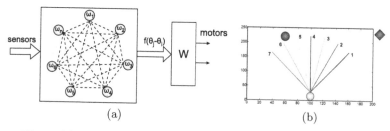

(a)                                                (b)

**Fig. 1.** (a) Network architecture. (b) Experiments 1 and 2 scenario.

The framework implemented to control a simulated robotic agent is composed of a set of fully-connected oscillators, some with connections to the robot's sensors. The frequency of each node is the sum of its natural frequency of oscillation, $w_i$, and the value of the sensory input related to that node (0 if there is no input to it), scaled by a factor $z_i$. The natural frequency $w_i$ can be associated with the natural firing rate of a neuron or a group of neurons, and the sensory inputs mediated by $z_i$ alters its oscillatory behaviour according to environmental interactions, thus improving the flexibility of the model to study neuronal synchronisation [20] within a behavioural context.

At each iteration the phase differences from a given node to all other nodes are calculated following Equation 1 (modified as described in the previous paragraph). A phase-sensitivity function $f(\phi)$ is then applied to each of the phase differences $\phi_{ij}$ from nodes that are connected to sensors. The modified phase differences are then linearly combined by an output weight matrix, $W$, resulting in two signals that will command the left and right motors of the agent (Figure 1). Therefore, there are $n$ inputs to $n$ corresponding nodes in the network of size $N$, with $C_{n,2}$ phase differences, $\phi_{ij}$, being multiplied by a $C_{n,2} \times 2$ matrix, $W$. In this way, the phase dynamics and the environmental input to the robotic agent will determine its behaviour. It is important to stress that nodes that receive no input participate in the overall dynamics of the network, hence their natural activity can modulate the global activity of the network. The next section presents the experimental set-up.

## 3   Methods

In the first experiment an active categorical perception task is performed [11]. It consists of a circular robotic agent constrained to move in 1D (horizontally) along the bottom of a $250 \times 200$ rectangular environment (Figure 1). The agent is required to distinguish between circular and square objects that are dropped from the top of the environment by moving towards the circles and avoiding the squares. The robot has 7 ray sensors, symmetrically displaced in relation to the central ray in intervals of $\pm \pi/12$ radians, and two motors (for left and right movement). An intersection between each sensory ray and an object reflects a reading between 0 and 10, 0 when the ray length is greater than 200 units and 10 when the ray length is 0. In all experiments, there is a saturation of the sensors (they are clamped) when their value is above 9. The square's diagonal, the

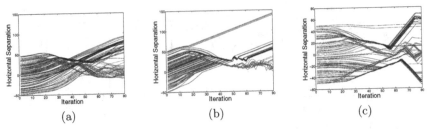

**Fig. 2.** The generalisation performance of the agent over 100 aleatory runs for $t = 1$ (a), $t = 36$ (evolved) (b) and $t = 1$ (evolved) and $f(\phi) = \phi$ (c). The red colour refers to the circle catch behaviour and the blue colour to the square avoidance behaviour.

robotic agent and the circle's radius all measure 15 units. At the beginning of each trial, a circle or a square is dropped from the top at a random horizontal position within a maximum of 50 units from the agent, and moves vertically with a velocity of 3 units/step. This experiment also investigates different temporal dynamics between the network and the agent's actuators, i.e. how the performance and synchronisation patterns are affected when one varies the number of time steps Equation 1 is updated before the phase-differences are used to calculate the motor output. The second experiment studies how the choice of the phase-sensitivity function $f(\phi)$ alters the phase dynamics of the network and in consequence the behaviour displayed by the agent.

A genetic algorithm is used to determine the parameters of the system: the frequency of each node $w_i \in [0, 10]$, the input weights $z_i \in [0, 3]$, the matrix $W_{n,2}$ with elements in the interval $[-2, 2]$, a motor output weight $s \in [0, 10]$, the learning rate $\epsilon \in [0, 10]$, the learning enhancement factor $\alpha \in [0, 10]$ and the network update time $t \in [1, 50]$. For both experiments, a network with 15 nodes (out of which 7 are connected to the agent's sensors) is used, resulting in a genotype of length 68.

The network's genotype consists of an array of integer variables lying in the range $[0, 999]$ which are mapped to the system's parameters. For all the experiments in this paper, a distributed GA was used with a population size of 49, arranged in a $7 \times 7$ grid. A generation is defined as 100 breeding events and the evolutionary algorithm runs for a maximum of 150 generations. There are two mutation operators: the first operator is applied to 20% of the gene and produces a change at each locus by an amount within the $[-10, +10]$ range according to a uniform distribution. The second mutation operator has a probability of 10% and is applied to 40% of the genotype, replacing a randomly chosen gene locus by a new value within the $[0, 999]$ range in a uniform distribution. For further details about the genetic algorithm, the reader should refer to [25].

For both experiments, an evolutionary run corresponds to 28 trials with randomly chosen objects (circles or squares), starting at a uniformly distributed horizontal offset in the interval of $\pm 50$ units from the robotic agent. Fitness is defined as the robotic agent's ability to catch circles and avoid squares, and is calculated according to the following equation: $fitness = \sum_{i=1}^{N} i f_i / \sum_{i=1}^{N} i$, where $f_i$ is the $ith$ value in a descending ordered vector $F_{1,N}$, and is given by $1 - d_i$, in the case of a circle, or by $d_i$ in the case of a square. $d_i$ is the horizontal distance from the robotic agent to the object at the end of the $ith$ trial (when the object reaches the bottom of the scenario), limited to 50 and normalized between 0 and 1. Therefore, a robotic agent with good fitness maximizes its distance from squares and minimizes its distance from circles. Notice that the fitness function pressures for a good performance in all trials in a given evolutionary run, instead of just averaging the performance of each trial.

In the first experiment, two sets of results are obtained: for the parameter $t$ fixed at 1 and for $t$ evolved between 1 and 50, reflecting a single or multiple network update for every motor update. In this first case, $f(\phi) = sin(\phi)$. In the second experiment, $t$ is evolved and the first experiment is replicated using two possible phase-sensitivity functions: $f(\phi) = cos(\phi)$ and $f(\phi) = \phi$. The next section presents the results, considering the highest fitness individual evolved.

# 4   Results

## 4.1   Experiment 1

The evolved individuals for the first case ($t = 1$) will be henceforth called "type 1 agents" and the ones in the second case ($t$ evolved) will be called "type 2 agents". The training fitness of the best individual in the first (second) case was 0.96 (0.91) out of 1.00, and the generalisation fitness over 100 random runs was 0.90 (0.90), which resemble the results that are found in the literature for this task [11, 15]. Figures 2(a) and 2(b) present the resulting behaviour of the agent in the generalisation scenario.

Notice that the circle catch and square avoidance behaviours of type 1 and 2 agents in the first 15 iterations are almost the same, and from this moment on they start to centralize circles and move away from squares. The horizontal separation from objects in type 1 agents vary much more than the trajectories displayed by type 2 agents. In the latter case, the distinction in strategies is clearer: the agent tends to move itself to the right-side of falling objects (hence a positive value for the horizontal separation), gets closer to the objects from iterations 20 to 60 when it finally seems to discriminate between the two different shapes, continuing its movement to the right-side of the object if it is a square or minimizing the horizontal distance if it is a circle. This behaviour has been observed before by Izquierdo [14] and justified by the asymmetric nature of the neural controller, i.e. the neural connection weights and other network parameters are not symmetric in relation to the robotic agent's body.

Consider the centre graphic of the top part of Figure 3(a). In the beginning of the task, as the agent is far from falling objects, the inputs are almost zero and the nodes seem to be converging to a common frequency until iteration 20. At this time, the sensory readings start to increase (the object is closer) and due to the mutual influence of the nodes the network starts to oscillate in a less coherent way. Notice the change in the phase dynamics (rightmost graphic), which becomes less smooth. This variation in the phase dynamics will determine

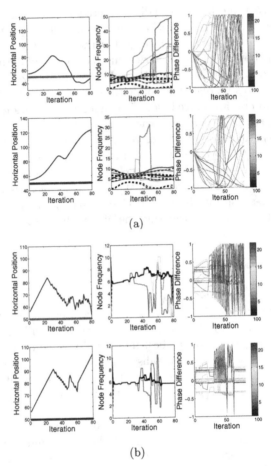

**Fig. 3.** Agent's internal and external dynamics for $t = 1$ (a) and $t = 36$ (evolved) (b). The top three graphics of each figure refer to the circle catch behaviour and the bottom ones to the square avoidance behaviour. The leftmost illustrates the horizontal coordinate of the agent and the object, the middle one shows the frequency of each node of the network as the task progresses (colour lines for nodes with inputs, dashed lines otherwise) and the rightmost ones present the 21 ($C_{7,2}$) possible phase differences.

the approaching the circle behaviour of the agent and also change the nodes' relationship by changing the coupling dynamics. This can be seen in Figure 4(b). The bottom part of Figure 3(a), which reflects the square avoidance behaviour, can be explained by the same reasoning above, but taking into account that the agent moves away from the object and therefore the sensory readings tend to vanish, leading to a much smoother frequency, phase and coupling dynamics.

Figures 3(b) and 4(b) present the results for type 2 agents. In both task scenarios, the network presents a much stronger synchronisation since the first iterations, leading to more stable phase and coupling dynamics until near iteration 30. The robotic agent's motors speed, dictated by the phase differences and

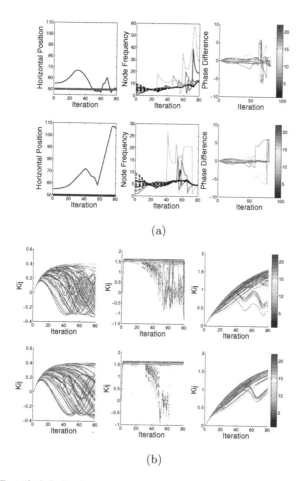

**Fig. 4.** (a) Detailed behaviour of the agent's internal and external dynamics for $t = 1$(evolved) and $f(\phi) = \phi$. (b) coupling dynamics, with each pair in each column representing the scenarios of Figures 3(a), 3(b) and 4(a), respectively.

the output matrix $W$, stabilize in a constant value (leftmost graphics). If a sensory reading increases, the corresponding frequency of the node it is connected to changes, and the different phase dynamics (rightmost part of the graphics) will possibly reduce the coupling strength, reducing at the first moment the influence of that node in the overall behaviour of the network. The conclusion is that the ongoing activity of the network combined with the effects of the modulation caused by external stimulus will determine the agent's behaviour.

Figure 5 shows the detailed sensory input, the motor output, and the frequency of each node. In the top two graphics the sensory input tends to saturate as the robotic agent gets closer to the circle but the frequency of each node has a completely different behaviour. In the beginning of the task, the network rapidly synchronises. As the sensory input starts to increase (due to the circle getting

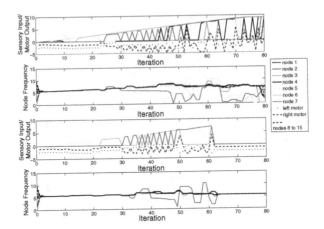

**Fig. 5.** Sensory input and the motor output, and the frequency of each node (upper two graphics refer to circle catch, bottom two for square avoidance, respectively) for the Experiment 1, $t = 36$ (evolved)

closer to the agent), the mean frequency of oscillation changes, but all nodes remain synchronised until near iteration 30, when nodes 5 (yellow) and 7 (magenta) desynchronise and oscillate with different frequencies. One of the reasons this is possible is that the couplings are dynamic, thus adding flexibility to the network. Also, notice that not all nodes can "escape" the entrained oscillatory state of the network, it will depend on the initial values of the node's parameters and the sensory input. The nodes without sensory input (8 in total) reinforce the synchrony, as if they were one oscillator with strong couplings to the others.

Turn to the bottom two graphics now, related to square avoidance. Between iterations 30 and 60 there is a clear variation in the sensory readings of nodes 6 (cyan) and 7 (magenta), but the correspondent oscillatory behaviour of the network changes in a different way, stressing the importance of the ongoing activity of the other nodes. At the end of the trial, with no sensory stimulation, a global synchronisation behaviour is obtained.

### 4.2   Experiment 2

In this experiment, the objective is to investigate the impact of different couplings between the oscillatory network and the agent's motors. In Experiment 1, the phase sensitivity function was $f(\phi) = sin(\phi)$. The functions now investigated are $f(\phi) = cos(\phi)$ and $f(\phi) = \phi$. Everything else is exactly the same.

Evolved agents with good performance could not be obtained using $f(\phi) = cos(\phi)$ - the maximum fitness was 0.78. For the second case ($f(\phi) = \phi$), agents with good performance were obtained. The training fitness for the best evolved individual was 0.97 out of 1.00, and the generalisation fitness over 100 random runs was 0.91. Figure 2(c) illustrates the generalisation test. Notice that the agent's behaviour is completely different from the one displayed in Experiment 1.

It tends to centralize with both circles and squares, and near iteration 55 the discrimination seems to be made, with agents continuing to centre on circles and moving away from squares. It is interesting to see the symmetrical nature of the solutions, specially when comparing with the results of the first experiment. Izquierdo [14] obtained similar results for Experiment 1 using a non-symmetrical artificial neural network and a similar result for Experiment 2 using a symmetrical one. However, in this paper both experiments employ a network with connection strengths that depend on the ongoing activity of the network and the environment, hence no pre-determined structure is forced. A possible conclusion is that the oscillatory activity in the network is influenced by the way the agent's "mind" and "body" are coupled, and not only by the environment.

Analysing Figure 4(a), the synchronisation of the nodes is once more observed, attaining almost complete entrainment near iteration 20. The external stimulus changes the response of some nodes, but most of them remain synchronised during the whole task time. This results in smoother phase dynamics, which also lead to a more stable coupling dynamics (Figure 4(b)).

# 5   Conclusion and Future Work

This work explores the neural synchronisation and phase information dynamics of a simulated robotic agent engaged in minimally cognitive tasks. It extends previous work [21] by adding more nodes to the network and including mechanisms of synaptic plasticity. The objective is to analyse the impact of different neural network temporal dynamics and the effect of different phase sensitivity functions on the synchronisation patterns and phase dynamics observed.

The main contribution of the work is to demonstrate that an enhanced version of a widely used model of phase interacting oscillators, the Kuramoto model, is able to generate interesting embodied behaviours in a benchmark task. The inclusion of synaptic plasticity adds flexibility to the model. The couplings in the network are now not predetermined but established through the interactions of the nodes, which could unveil important emergent processes given that the values of these couplings directly influence the oscillatory behaviour of the model [18]. Specifically, the results showed how the external stimulus modulate the ongoing activity of individual neurons which in turn affect the strength of their synaptic connections, restructuring their mutual interaction and the phase dynamics which control the agent. Internally generated brain activity, regardless of environmental inputs, is stressed by Engel et.al.[4] as one of the key elements in cognitive processes.

Therefore, by exploring a simulated brain/body/environment system, the framework could provide insights on the role of neuronal synchronisation and phase information in the generation of cognitive behaviours. Understanding it could shed light into many different research areas, from the comprehension of the role of oscillatory properties in some diseases (e.g. Parkinson) [5] to the establishment of new parallel computing architectures [26].

Future work would include: investigate the impact and robustness of the model to different initial conditions for the phase and coupling values; gain further insights into how nodes are recruited and cooperate in different neuronal assemblies; based on theoretic predictions [18], calculate and fix the value of the coupling parameter so that the neuronal network is restrained to operate in a metastable zone, studying the resulting dynamics in a more biologically plausible neural network [27].

# References

1. Buzsaki, G.: Rhythms of the Brain. Oxford University Press, Oxford (2006)
2. Singer, W.: Synchronization of cortical activity and its putative role in information processing and learning. Annual Review of Physiology 55, 349–374 (1993)
3. Konig, P., Engel, A., Singer, W.: Integrator or coincidence detector? the role of the cortical neuron revisited. Trends in Neurosciences 19, 130–137 (1996)
4. Engel, A., Fries, P., Singer, W.: Dynamic predictions: oscillations and synchrony in top-down processing. Nat. Rev. Neurosci. 2(10), 704–716 (2001)
5. Varela, F., Lachaux, J., Rodriguez, E., Martinerie, J.: The brainweb: phase synchronization and large-scale integration. Nat. Rev. Neurosci. 2(4) (2001)
6. Von der Malsburg, C.: The correlation theory of the brain. Internal report. Max-Planck-Institute for Biophysical Chemistry, Gottingen, Germany (1981)
7. Friston, K.: The labile brain. i. neuronal transients and nonlinear coupling. Phil.Trans. R. Soc. Lond. B 355, 215–236 (2000)
8. Li, Z., Hopfield, J.: Modeling the olfactory bulb and its neural oscillatory processings. Biological Cybernetics 61(5). Springer, Berlin (1989)
9. Izhikevich, E.: Weakly pulse-coupled oscillators, fm interactions, synchronization, and oscillatory associative memory. IEEE Trans. Neural Networks 10(3), 508–526 (1999)
10. Kunyosi, M., Monteiro, L.: Recognition of noisy images by pll networks. Signal Processing 89 (2009)
11. Beer, R.: The dynamics of active categorical perception in an evolved model agent. Adaptive Behavior 11(4), 209–243 (2003)
12. Seth, A., McKinstry, J., Edelman, G., Krichmar, J.: Visual binding through reentrant connectivity and dynamic synchronization in a brain-based device. Cerebral Cortex 14 (2004)
13. Floreano, D., Husbands, P., Nolfi, S.: Evolutionary Robotics. In: Siciliano, B., Khatib, O. (eds.) Springer Handbook of Robotics, ch. 61. Springer, Heidelberg (2008)
14. Izquierdo, E.: The dynamics of learning behaviour: a situated, embodied, and dynamical systems approach. PhD thesis, CCNR, University of Sussex (2008)
15. Dale, K., Husbands, P.: The evolution of reaction-diffusion controllers for minimally cognitive agents. Artificial Life 16(1), 1–19 (2010)
16. Ijspeert, A., Crespi, A., Ryczko, D., Cabelguen, J.: From swimming to walking with a salamander robot driven by a spinal cord model. Science 315(5817), 1416–1420 (2005)
17. Kuramoto, Y.: Chemical Oscillation, Waves, and Turbulence. Springer, NY (1984)
18. Strogatz, S.: From kuramoto to crawford: exploring the onset of synchronization in populations of coupled oscillators. Physica D 143 (2000)
19. Kitzbichler, M., Smith, M., Christensen, S., Bullmore, E.: Broadband criticality of human brain network synchronization. PLoS Computational Biology 5(3) (2009)

20. Cumin, D., Unsworth, C.: Generalising the kuramoto model for the study of neuronal synchronisation in the brain. Physica D 226(2), 181–196 (2007)
21. Moioli, R., Vargas, P.A., Husbands, P.: Exploring the kuramoto model of coupled oscillators in minimally cognitive evolutionary robotics tasks. IEEE Cong. Evol. Comput. (2010)
22. Hebb, D.: The Organization of Behavior. Wiley, New York (1949)
23. Niyogi, R., English, L., Term, L.: Learning-rate dependent clustering and self-development in a network of coupled phase oscillators. Physical Review E 80(6) (2009)
24. Burwick, T.: Oscillatory networks: pattern recognition without a superposition catastrophe. Neural Computation 18(2) (2006)
25. Husbands, P., Smith, T., Jakobi, N., O Shea, M.: Better living through chemistry: Evolving GasNets for robot control. Connection Science 10, 185–210 (1998)
26. Korniss, G., Novotny, M., Guclu, H., Toroczkai, Z., Rikvold, P.: Suppressing roughness of virtual times in parallel discrete-event simulations. Science 299(677) (2003)
27. Bressler, S., Kelso, J.: Cortical coordination dynamics and cognition. Trends in Cogn. Sci. 5 (2001)

# Integrative Learning between Language and Action: A Neuro-Robotics Experiment

Hiroaki Arie[1], Tetsuro Endo[3], Sungmoon Jeong[2], Minho Lee[2], Shigeki Sugano[3], and Jun Tani[1]

[1] Brain Science Institute, RIKEN
[2] School of Electrical Engineering and Computer Science, Kyungpook National University
[3] Department of Modern Mechanical Engineering, Waseda University

**Abstract.** This paper introduces a model for associative learning combining both linguistic and behavior modalities. The model consists of language and behavior modules both implemented by a hierarchical dynamic network model and interacting densely through hub-like neurons, the so-called parametric biases (PB). By implementing this model for a humanoid robot with the task of manipulating multiple objects, the robot was tutored to associate sentences of two different grammatical types with corresponding sensory-motor schemata. The first type was a verb followed by an objective noun such as "hold red" or "hit blue"; the second was a verb followed by an objective noun and further followed by an adverb phrase such as "Put red on blue". Our analysis of the results of a learning experiment showed that two clusters corresponding to these two types of grammatical sentences appear in the PB activity space, such that a specific micro structure is organized for each cluster.

## 1 Introduction

Compositionality, meaning that a whole can be constituted by reusable parts, is one of the essential human cognitive characteristics [1]. In linguistic processing, diversity of meaning can be generated by combining words by following grammatical rules and semantic constraints. Moreover, diversity in spoken words is originated from compositions through multiple levels from segments to syllables and syllables to lexicons. In the action generation, complex actions can be generated diversely by combining behavior primitives [2]. Both of these compositional systems of language and action have been considered to be organized with specific hierarchy in neuronal anatomy.

In conventional neuroscience, these two types of compositional processing concerned with language and action have been treated as independent processes. Recently, however, some researchers have examined these two functions by utilizing various brain imaging techniques including fMRI, PET and EEG, and their results have begun to suggest that there are certain dependency between

K. Diamantaras, W. Duch, L.S. Iliadis (Eds.): ICANN 2010, Part II, LNCS 6353, pp. 256–265, 2010.

the two. Hauk etal [3] showed in their functional MRI experiment that reading action related words with different end effectors, such as "Lick", "Pick" and "Kick", evoked neural activities in the motor areas those overlap with the local areas responsible for generating motor movements in the face, arm and leg, respectively. This result, as well as [4], suggest that understanding action related words or sentences may require specific motor circuits responsible for generating those actions and, therefore, brain functions for language and actions might be organized as interdependent.

If everyday experience of speech and its corresponding sensory-motor signals tend to overlap during infant development, synaptic connectivity between the two circuits can be reinforced by Hebbian learning, as discussed by Pulvemuller [5]. This suggests the possibility that meaning and concepts of words and sentences can be acquired as associated with the related sensory-motor experiences, as discussed in the usage-based approach [6] in Cognitive Linguistics. Sugita and Tani [7] conducted a synthetic neuro-robotics study to examine the idea of the usage-based approach. They proposed a connectionist architecture which consisted of a linguistic recurrent neural network (RNN) [8] module and an action (RNN) module which interact via associative learning of proto-language and actions of robots. The results of the robot learning experiment showed that the robot can acquire a set of action related concepts by self-organizing certain compositional structure related to verbs and object nouns.

The current paper introduces a trial to extend the aforementioned study [7,9]. The main motivation is to introduce a functional hierarchy for both the linguistic and behavioral modalities by employing a dynamic neural network model, the so-called the multiple timescale RNN (MTRNN) developed by our group [10,11,12]. It was expected that the behavioral modality could have a functional hierarchy where behavior primitives are acquired in a lower level with a fast dynamics network and the action compositions do in a higher level with a slow dynamics network [10]. Also the linguistic modality could be developed with organizing hierarchy consisting of the alphabetical level, the lexical level and the sentence level, by utilizing time scale differences at each level of the network[9]. The processes for these two modalities could be associated by a similar scheme as the PB binding described in [7]. In the current task setting, a humanoid robot learns a set of multiple object manipulation behaviors associated with command sentences. The sentences are comprised of two classes of grammars where one type of sentence is organized as verbs followed by object nouns, such as "Hold Object-A". The other type consists of verbs followed by object nouns, further followed by adverbial phrases, such as "Put Object-A on Object-B". These actions are more complex than those described in [7], because these require adequate visual attention to be paid to the objects, as well as their sequential shifts. The current study examines what sorts of internal representations can be self-organized as a consequence of associative learning of these classes of sentences and the corresponding actions accompanied by visual attention shifts.

# 2  Model

## 2.1  Brain Model

We propose a model inspired by brain function, in which the three cognitive functions of speech comprehension, action generation and visual attention switching are integrated via their mutual interactions. Firstly, the action generation pathway is considered. In [13,11], we hypothesized that the inferior parietal lobe (IPL) may play the role of a sensory forward model for given action programs, as suggested by recent neuro-physiological evidences [14]. This means that the IPL may predicts the coming visuo-proprioceptive sensation flow which is associated with action plans provided from the frontal cortex. For example, when the frontal cortex sends an abstract action plan to the IPL for grasping a mug in front of us, the sensory forward model predicts how our arm and hand postures would change in time, how our hands reaching for the mug would be visually perceived and how the tactile stimulus of touching the mug would arise.

Skilled behaviors of acting toward objects, such as manual object manipulations, require adequate timing of visual attention shifts to the target objects. Here, we consider a functional hierarchy where an abstract plan for a visual attention shift is generated in the frontal eye field (FEF) [15] and the exact eye saccadic movement to achieve the attention shift is generated in the intraparietal sulcus (IPS) [16] in the downstream. The current model assumes that the FEF predicts sequences of shifts of visual attention to particular objects for given action programs and the IPS generates eye movements to the attended objects by following our prior model [17].

Although it has been considered that speech comprehension is performed in Wernicke's area in the temporal cortex, recent evidence [18] has shown that Broca's area in the inferior frontal gyrus, which is considered to be responsible for speech generation, actively participates in the process. Also, Tettamanti etal [4] showed that listening to action related sentences evokes activations spreading from Broca's area to specific premotor and motor cortex regions which are considered to be topographically responsible for generating the corresponding motor activities expressed in the sentences. Here, we could draw a hypothesis from these evidences that listening action related sentences could evoke a corresponding activation in the Broca's area, which can lead to regeneration of neuronal activities in two ways simultaneously. One is an activation in the premotor and motor cortices which generates the corresponding motor imagery and the other is an activation in Wernicke's area to generate the auditory imagery.

The core part of our hypothesis for speech comprehension is that streams of auditory signals might be recognized by inferring the corresponding neural activation patterns in Broca's area, which can regenerate them via a forward model assumed in Broca's area. Furthermore, it is speculated that the forward model is constituted hierarchically by the Broca's area responsible for sentence level, the MTG for lexical level and the STG for phonetic level.

Finally, our basic idea of integrating three neural processing systems of speech comprehension, visual attention and action generation is overviewed. Because all of these neural processing systems seem to constitute a functional hierarchy by connecting different local networks, we propose to model each of them by the MTRNN. Then these three neural processes are integrated with Broca's area as a "hub" to connect these three neural pathways as shown in Fig. 1. For given speech inputs in the STG as targets, the speech comprehension system, consisting of Broca's area, the MTG and the STG, attempt to reconstruct them in their forward computation (depicted by a blue arrow) by inferring adequate activation patterns in Broca's area (depicted by a red dotted arrow). Then, the obtained activation patterns in Broca's area initiate forward computation in the two pathways for the visual attention and action generation. In the visual attention system, the FEF generates predictive sequences of attention shifts from one object to another in the workspace and the IPS generates the corresponding eye saccadic motion while the premotor generates predictive sequences of shifts of behavior primitives and the IPL generates a detailed prediction of the visuo-proprioceptive flow. The prediction of posture changes over time is utilized to compute the necessary motor commands in the motor cortex to achieve the change.

## 2.2   The Computational Model

**Overview.** As described in the previous section, the architecture is based on our prior proposed MTRNN model[10]. In the current study, as shown in Fig. 1, the whole network consists of the behavior module network on the right-hand side, the linguistic module network on the left-hand side and the binding network which may correspond to Broca's area in human brains in the upper part. The binding network contains parametric bias (PB) neurons[7]. The idea is that specific static vector values of the PB map to the generation of a linguistic temporal pattern in the linguistic network and a corresponding behavioral temporal pattern in the behavior network as a generative model.

The behavior network learns to generate two types of sequence patterns, one for proprioception, in terms of the arm posture $p_t$ and the other for so-called visual attention commands $a_t$. The behavior network outputs the attention command, with a specific color category, to the visual attention module. Then, the visual attention module searches for an object of the specified color in the retinal image (see a detailed implementation in [17]). Then, the camera head of the robot moves to target the attended object by means of a hand-coded program. The current angle position of the camera head $v_t$ is fed into the input of the behavior network. In summary, the behavior network predicts the color of the object to be attended to next, and it receives the relative position of the attended object in terms of camera head angle positions. At the same time the network predicts how the arm posture changes in time with the received sensation of the relative position of the currently attended object.

The linguistic network learns to generate alphabetic sequences $l_t$ for command sentences. It can generate sequences autonomously with a closed-loop operation in which the input of the current alphabet $l_t$ is obtained from its prediction in the previous step instead of the one given externally. The behavior network can be operated only with the open-loop with receiving the external input $v_t$ representing the relational position of the attended object.

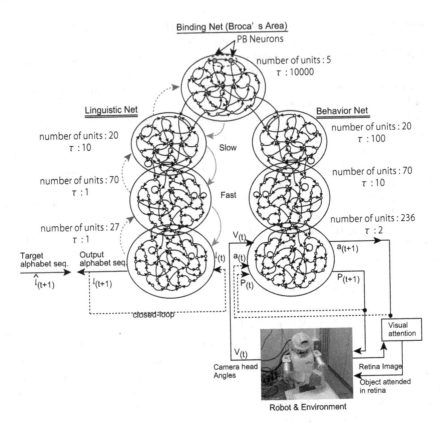

**Fig. 1.** MTRNN Model with Robot Platform

The current model is adopted for a robot task which proceeds with a linguistic phase followed by a behavior phase. In the linguistic phase, the robot receives an alphabetic command sequence without moving, and infers the PB values, as will be detailed later. Then the robot starts to move with the acquired PB values in the following behavioral phase. A associative training is conducted for each pair of alphabetic sequences (a command sentence) and a behavior sequence. The behavior training sequence corresponding to each command sentence is generated by guiding the arm posture associated with the visual attention command at each time step. A set of command sentences and their corresponding behavior sequences can be associated by determining a specific PB value for each pair. The delta errors generated in both module networks during association learning were propagated through both networks to the PB units in the binding network. The PB values responsible for each associative pair in the training sequences are updated by utilizing this delta error, while the optimal synaptic weights for minimizing the learning errors for all training pairs are searched.

After the learning for all pairs converges with respect to minimization of the training error, the robot is tested as follows. A command sentence in terms of alphabetic sequence is shown to the linguistic network as the target to be recognized. This can be done by reconstructing the target sequence by inferring an optimal PB value by back-propagating the error between the target sequence and the regenerated one. Once the PB value is determined, the robot is operated by the behavior network with setting the obtained PB value into the neural units in the binding network.

**Mathematical Detail.** The current model consists of seven groups of neural units as shown in Fig. 1, namely linguistic input-output units ($IO_l$), behavioral input-output units ($IO_b$), linguistic fast context units ($CF_l$), behavioral fast context units ($CF_b$), linguistic slow context units ($CS_l$), behavioral slow context units ($CS_b$) and binding units ($PB$).

The activation value of the $i$-th neural unit at time step $t$ is calculated as follows.

$$y_{t,i} = \begin{cases} \frac{exp(u_{t,i})}{\sum_{j \in IO} exp(u_{t,j})}, & (i \in IO) \\ \frac{1}{1+exp(-u_{t,i})}, & (i \notin IO) \end{cases} \tag{1}$$

$$u_{t,i} = \begin{cases} 0, & (t = 0 \wedge i \notin PB) \\ PB_i, & (t = 0 \wedge i \in PB) \\ (1 - \frac{1}{\tau_i})u_{t-1,i} + \frac{1}{\tau_i}\sum_{j \in I_{all}} w_{ij}x_{t,j}, & (otherwise) \end{cases} \tag{2}$$

$$x_{t,j} = y_{t-1,j} \tag{3}$$

$u_{t,i}$ : internal state of the $i$-th unit at time step $t$

$PB_i$ : neural activation of binding units (PB value)

$\tau_i$ : time constant of $i$-th unit

$w_{ij}$ : connection weight from $j$-th unit to $i$-th unit

$x_{j,t}$ : input from $j$-th unit at time step $t$

The number of neural units and the time constant are shown in Fig. 1. The time constant of the binding network is set to a large value so that the neural activation of binding units can be considered as static vector values like PB.

Connection weights and the PB value are adjusted using the Back Propagation Through Time (BPTT) algorithm, as follows.

$$w_{ij}^{(n+1)} = w_{ij}^n - \eta \frac{\partial E}{\partial w_{ij}} = w_{ij}^n - \frac{\eta}{\tau_i}\sum_t x_{t,j} \frac{\partial E}{\partial u_{t,i}} \tag{4}$$

$$PB_i^{(n+1)} = PB_i^n - \alpha \frac{\partial E}{\partial PB_i} = PB_i^n - \alpha \frac{\partial E}{\partial u_{0,i}} \tag{5}$$

$$E = \sum_t \sum_{i \in IO} y_{t,i}^* log(\frac{y_{t,i}^*}{y_{t,i}}) \tag{6}$$

$$\frac{\partial E}{\partial u_{t,i}} = \begin{cases} y_{t,i} - y_{t,i}^* + (1 - \frac{1}{\tau_i})\frac{\partial E}{\partial u_{t+1,i}} & (i \in IO) \\ y_{t,i}(1 - y_{t,i})\sum_{k \in IO} \frac{w_{ki}}{\tau_k}\frac{\partial E}{\partial u_{t+1,k}} + (1 - \frac{1}{\tau_i})\frac{\partial E}{\partial u_{t+1,i}} & (otherwise) \end{cases} \tag{7}$$

$n$ : iteration number in the updating process

$E$ : prediction error

$y_{t,i}^*$ : value of the current training sequence for the $i$-th neural unit at time step $t$

$\eta, \alpha$ : *learningrate*

The PB values are determined for each training sequence independently whereas the connection weights apply to all sequences. To recognize a linguistic sequence after associative learning, the PB value corresponding to a given alphabetic command sequence is searched for using BPTT with fixed connection weights.

## 3    Experiment

### 3.1    Task Design

A small humanoid robot as shown in Fig. 1 was used as the experimental platform. The robot was fixed to a chair, and a table was set in front of the robot. The robot was supposed to associate a set of alphabetic sequences of two different grammatical types to corresponding behavioral sequence. The first type (Type-1) was a verb followed by an objective noun where the verb could assume the two words "hold" and "up-down" and the objective nouns of "red", "blue" and "green". This generates six sentences. The other type (Type-2) was a verb followed by an objective noun, further followed by an adverbial phrase. In this type the verb was just one word, namely, "put", and both objective nouns and adverbs could assume three words of "red", "blue" and "green". This generates six sentences. For each action, the robot was tutored three times by changing the initial position of the object to be 4cm to the left of the original position, at the original position and 4cm to the right of original one, for the purpose of gaining a generalization of object manipulation behavior. Each action was tutored in every possible combination of object position (left, center and right) and color of the object (red, blue and green). In total, there were 18 behavior sequences for Type-1 and 54 for Type-2.

### 3.2    Results

After training, the robot was tested to see whether it could recognize all 12 linguistic command sentences and generate the corresponding behavior with different object position situations (left, center and right). Recognition was done by searching for optimal PB values. The search calculation was iterated 2000 times with $\alpha = 0.2$ for each linguistic command sentence. The performance was scored in terms of the success rate across all trials. It was considered that a trial was successful if the robot was able to generate a corresponding behavior sequence with the obtained PB values. As the results, it was confirmed that the robot was able to generate the correct behavior with an 82% success rate. It was further confirmed that the robot could recognize all the 12 sentences, because it was able to generate the correct behavior for at least one specific object position case, for each command sentence.

Fig. 2 shows two examples of the time development of sequences. Here it can be seen that the fast context profile contains more complex patterns, as compared to those in the slow context for both the linguistic and behavior networks.

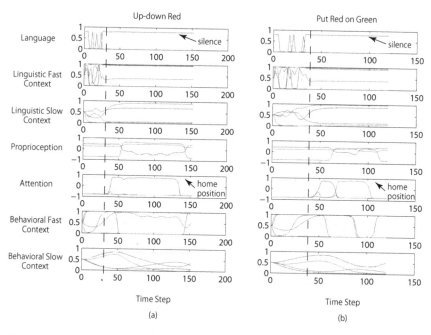

**Fig. 2.** Examples of sequences generated with obtained PB values. (a) shows the "Up Down Red" and (b) shows the "Put Red on Green" case. Vertical dashed lines indicate the onset of the behavioral phase. The first row shows an alphabetic sequence of the representative four characters ("silence", "d", "n" and "o"). The second and third rows show activations of fast and slow context units in the linguistic network. The fourth row shows the joint angles of the right arm of the robot. The fifth row shows the visual attention commands corresponding to "home", "red", "blue" and "green". The sixth and seventh rows show activations of fast and slow context units in the behavior network.

# 4    Analysis

We applied principal component analysis to visualize the structure of the PB space. Fig. 3 shows the 1st and 2nd principal components of the neural activation of binding units (PB). It can be observed that there are two clusters corresponding to Type-1 and Type-2 sentences. The cluster for Type-1 sentences shows that the compositional structure of two verbs multiplied by three objective nouns appears in a two dimensional grid which is similar to the structure observed in our previous study[7]. On the other hand, no systematic structures can be found for Type-2 although the mapping from these sentences to actions was successfully generated, but without the formation of a generalized representation.

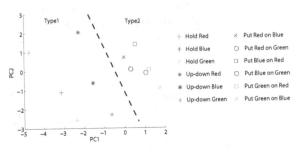

**Fig. 3.** The PB space. The dimensions are reduced from 5 to 2 by PCA. The sentences are clustered, based on their grammatical structure.

## 5   Conclusion

In this paper, we reported on the integrative learning of linguistic and behavioral sequences by the MTRNN. We trained the model with a set of linguistic and behavioral sequences. As a result of our experiment, we found that the model was able to acquire the capability to recognize linguistic sentences and to generate corresponding behavioral sequence patterns. Our analysis showed that the compositional structure could be self-organized for Type-1 sentences, but not for Type-2.

Two possible reasons to account for this result may be as follows. One possibility is that the PB space cannot embed two distinct compositional structures, i.e. Type-1 and Type-2 simultaneously. The other possibility is that the number of examples for learning of Type-2 structures was too low to achieve generalization, as Type-2 was trained only with one verb case of "put", in the current study. A future study will examine these possibilities and also will pursue scaling of the system in terms of the number of words, diversity of grammar types and behavior complexity.

## References

1. Evans, G.: Semantic theory and tacit knowledge. In: Holzman, S., Leich, C. (eds.) Wittgenstein: To Follow a Rule, pp. 118–137. Routledge and Kegan Paul, London (1981)
2. Arbib, M.: Perceptual structures and distributed motor control. In: Handbook of Physiology: The Nervous System, II. Motor Control, pp. 1448–1480. MIT Press, Cambridge (1981)
3. Hauk, O., Johnsrude, I., Pulvermuller, F.: Somatotopic representation of action words in human motor and premotor cortex. Neuron 41(2), 301–307 (2004)
4. Tettamanti, M., Buccino, G., Saccuman, M.C., Gallese, V., Danna, M., Scifo, P., Fazio, F., Rizzolatti, G., Cappa, S.F., Perani, D.: Listening to action-related sentences activates fronto-parietal motor circuits. Journal of Cognitive Neuroscience 17(2), 273–281 (2005)

5. Pulvermuller, F.: Brain mechanisms linking language and action. Nature Reviews Neuroscience 6, 576–582 (2005)
6. Tomasello, M.: Constructing a language: A usage-based theory of language acquisition. Harvard University Press, Cambridge (2003)
7. Sugita, Y., Tani, J.: Learning semantic combinatoriality from the interaction between linguistic and behavioral processes. Adaptive Behavior 13(1), 33–52 (2005)
8. Elman, J.: Finding structure in time. Cognitive Science 14, 179–211 (1990)
9. Hinoshita, W., Arie, H., Tani, J., Ogata, T., Okuno, H.G.: Emergence of hierarchical structure mirroring linguistic compositionality in recurrent neural network. Neural Networks (submitted)
10. Yamashita, Y., Tani, J.: Emergence of functional hierarchy in a multiple timescale neural network model: a humanoid robot experiment. PLoS Computational Biology 4(11) (2008)
11. Nishimoto, R., Namikawa, J., Tani, J.: Learning multiple goal-directed actions through self-organization of a dynamic neural network model: A humanoid robot experiment. Adaptive Behavior 16(2-3), 166–181 (2008)
12. Arie, H., Endo, T., Arakaki, T., Sugano, S., Tani, J.: Creating novel goal-directed actions at criticality: A neuro-robotic experiment. New Mathematics and Natural Computation 5(1), 307–334 (2009)
13. Tani, J., Nishimoto, R., Paine, R.: Achieving "organic compositionality" through self-organization: Reviews on brain-inspired robotics experiments. Neural Networks, 584–603 (2008)
14. Ehrsson, H., Fagergren, A., Johansson, R., Forssberg, H.: Evidence for the involvement of the posterior parietal cortex in coordination of fingertip forces for grasp stability in manipulation. Journal of Neurophysiology 90, 2978–2986 (2003)
15. Bruce, C.J., Goldberg, M.E.: Primate frontal eye fields. i. single neurons discharging before saccades. Journal of Neurophysiology 53(3), 603–635 (1985)
16. Colby, C.L., Goldberg, M.E.: Space and attention in parietal cortex. Annual Review of Neuroscience 22, 319–349 (1999)
17. Jeong, S., Lee, M., Arie, H., Tani, J.: Developmental learning of integrating visual attention shifts and bimanual behavior in object manipulation tasks. In: Proc. of 2010 IEEE 9th International Conference on Development and Learning (2010) (submitted)
18. Wilson, S., Saygin, A., Sereno, M., Iacoboni, M.: Listening to speech activates motor areas involved in speech production. Nature Neuroscience 7(7), 701–702 (2004)

# Sliding Mode Control of Robot Based on Neural Network Model with Positive Definite Inertia Matrix

Jakub Możaryn and Jerzy E. Kurek

Institute of Automatic Control and Robotics, Warsaw University of Technology,
ul. Sw. A. Boboli 8, 02-525 Warsaw, Poland
{j.mozaryn,jkurek}@mchtr.pw.edu.pl

**Abstract.** A synthesis of a sliding mode control law, for a robot arm, based on the robot model with a positive definite inertia matrix, identified with an artificial neural network, is presented. The structure of the neural network resemble a *Lagrange-Euler* mathematical model of the robot, and identifies the positive definite inertia matrix. A design of the neural model is based on the *Cholesky* decomposition of the identified inertia matrix.

**Keywords:** Sliding mode control, Robot control, Neural networks.

## 1 Introduction

A mathematical model of the robot, in a form of *Lagrange-Euler* equations, is useful for the design of the advanced robot control systems. A structure of nonlinear model is known, but it requires the knowledge of exact values of robot kinematical and dynamical parameters, which are hard to obtain [4]. Therefore its calculation is difficult.

There is a growing interest in the identification of the robot model, using the artificial neural networks (ANNs) [8,11,15]. Their advantages are: an approximation of the multivariable nonlinear functions, an easy adaptation of the model parameters and a very rapid calculation of the model equations, which are useful for a real time control. Designing ANN does not require an exact knowledge of the functions, and the physical parameters that describe the model, but only values of the model variables, i.e., generalized coordinates and control signals.

However, there are some drawbacks of this approach. Usually, the structure of ANN does not satisfy the very strict properties of the robot mathematical model. The most important is a positive definiteness of an identified inertia matrix. Lack of this property can result, e.g., in unstable control system. Recently [15], we proposed a new design method of the ANN structure based on the *Cholesky* decomposition [5], which guarantee the identification of the positive definite inertia matrix.

In the article, there is presented the synthesis of the robot sliding mode control (SMC) algorithm, based on the mathematical model, with positive definite

K. Diamantaras, W. Duch, L.S. Iliadis (Eds.): ICANN 2010, Part II, LNCS 6353, pp. 266–275, 2010.

inertia matrix identified by ANN [7,12]. The SMC algorithm was chosen, because according to [1,3,6,7,12] it is robust to the model uncertainties and disturbances.
The article is organized as follows. In section 2, discrete time robot mathematical model in the form of the *Lagrange-Euler* equations, is given. Then, in section 3, the properties of the robot inertia matrix are described. Section 4 introduces the artificial neural network (ANN) for the identification of the robot mathematical model, with positive definite inertia matrix, based on *Cholesky* decomposition. Next, in section 5, there is presented synthesis of ANN robot model and sliding mode control algorithm (SMC-ANN). Section 6 describes results obtained during computer simulations of the control of 2 degree of freedom robot arm using SMC-ANN controller. Finally, in section 7, concluding remarks are given.

## 2   Discrete Time Robot Model

A discrete time model of the robot, with $n$ degrees of freedom, based on *Lagrange-Euler* equations, can be presented as follows [9]

$$M(q,k)\gamma(q,k+1) + P(q,k) = \tau(k) \ , \tag{1}$$

where

$$\gamma(q,k+1) = [\gamma_i(q,k+1)]_n = \frac{q(k+1) - 2q(k) + q(k-1)}{T_p^2} \ , \tag{2}$$

$$P(q,k) = V(q,k) + G(q,k) \tag{3}$$

and $q(k) = [q_i(k)]_n$ is a vector of the generalized joint coordinates, $M(q,k) = [m_{i,j}(q,k)]_{n \times n}$ is a robot inertia matrix, $V(q,k) = [v_i(q,k)]_n$ is a vector of *Coriolis* and centrifugal forces, $G(q,k) = [g_i(q,k)]_n$ is a vector of a gravity forces, $\tau(k) = [\tau_i(k)]_n$ is a vector of control signals, $k$ is a discrete time, $T_p$ is a sampling period $(t = kT_p)$.

## 3   Properties of the Robot Model

There are specific properties [2,8,9,14] of the robot mathematical model

*Property 1.* The inertia matrix is symmetrical

$$M(q,k) = M^T(q,k) \ . \tag{4}$$

*Property 2.* The inertia matrix is positive definite.

$$\forall x \in R^n, x \neq 0 : \ x^T M(q,k) x > 0 \ , \tag{5}$$

$$\det[M(q,k)] \neq 0 \ . \tag{6}$$

*Property 3.* Each element of the inertia matrix $[m_{i,j}(q,k)]_{n\times n}$ depends on $n > \min(i,j)$ joint coordinates

$$m_{i,j}(q,k) = f(q_{\min(i,j)+1}(k), ..., q_n(k)) \ . \tag{7}$$

Properties 1 and 2 can be used for the design of the inertia matrix identification method [15]. Property 3 defines the set of the generalized coordinates, that influence each element of the inertia matrix. Especially, the element $m_{n,n}(q,k)$ does not depend on the joint coordinates, and has a constant value.

## 4    Artificial Neural Network Robot Model

In the robot model (1), the unknown nonlinear elements of $M(q,k)$ and $P(q,k)$ should be identified. For their identification a feed-forward ANN can be used.

Let us describe ANN model for the identification of the model (1). We have assumed, that the inputs to ANN are $q(k-1)$, $q(k)$ and $\gamma(q,k+1)$. The output of ANN is vector $\tau(k)$. ANN preserves the multiple-input-multiple-output structure (MIMO) of the robot model. Each element of $M(q,k)$ and $P(q,k)$ is identified by the distinct subnetwork. Inputs to each subnetwork are determined by Property 3 (7). Identified matrices are denoted as $M_{NN}(q,k) = [m_{NNi,j}(q,k)]_{n\times n}$, $P_{NN}(q,k) = [p_{NNi}(q,k)]_n$. Elements $m_{i,j}(q,k) = m_{j,i}(q,k)$, $i \neq j$ are identified by one subnetwork. Therefore, the identified estimate $M_{NN}(q,k)$ of the inertia matrix is symmetrical.

Fig. 1 shows a structure of a proposed ANN for the identification of the robot with 2 degrees of freedom, and the symmetrical, positive definite inertia matrix. In all nonlinear layers, neurons are described by a nonlinear activation function, e.g., sigmoidal

$$y = f_{NL}(z) = \text{tansig}(z) \ . \tag{8}$$

In linear layers, neurons are described by a linear activation function

$$y = f_L(z) = z \ , \tag{9}$$

where $z = \sum_{i=1}^{L} w_i z_i + b$, $L$ is a number of neuron inputs, $w_i$ is a weight of the $i$-th input to neuron, $z_i$ $i$-th is an input to neuron, $b$ is a threshold offset.

The performance function of ANN was chosen as a mean squared error

$$J = \frac{1}{N} \sum_{k=1}^{N} \sum_{i=1}^{2} [\tau_i(k) - \tau_{NNi}(k)]^2 \ . \tag{10}$$

The element $m_{NN2,2}(q,k)$ is identified using the one layer subnetwork, with the one neuron described by linear activation function (9), as it is presented in Fig. 1, and has a constant value after the identification process.

The elements on the diagonal of the identified matrix $M_{NN}(q,k)$ are calculated as follows [15]

$$m_{NN2,2}(q,k) = \hat{m}_{NN2,2}^2(q,k) + f_2 \ , \tag{11}$$

$$m_{\text{NN1,1}}(q,k) = \hat{m}^2_{\text{NN1,1}}(q,k) + \frac{m^2_{\text{NN1,2}}(q,k)}{m_{\text{NN2,2}}(q,k)} + f_1 , \qquad (12)$$

where $f_i = \text{const}$, $f_i > 0$ are chosen arbitrarily, $\hat{m}_{\text{NN}i,i}(q,k)$ is the output of the subnetwork identifying the element $m_{l,l}(q,k)$, $i = 1, 2$.

The decomposition of positive definite inertia matrix, and calculation of the boundaries of its diagonal elements, are described in detail in [15].

## 5  Application of Artificial Neural Network Model in Sliding Mode Control of Robot

For the robot let us denote

$$\tilde{x}_i(k) = \begin{bmatrix} q_i(k-1) - q_{ri}(k-1) \\ q_i(k) - q_{ri}(k) \end{bmatrix} , \qquad (13)$$

where $q_{ri}(k)$ is the reference generalized coordinate in joint $i$.

The synthesis of SMC control law, and presented ANN model of the robot can be, according to [11], described by the equation

$$\tau(k) = P_{\text{NN}}(q,k) + T_p^{-2}M_{\text{NN}}(q,k)[q_r(k+1) - 2q(k) + q(k-1) + \tau_{\text{sl}}(k)] , \qquad (14)$$

where:

$$\tau_{\text{sl}}(k) = [\tau_{\text{sl}i}(k)]_n , \qquad (15)$$

$$\tau_{\text{sl}i}(k) = -(A_i B_i)^{-1}\Psi_i , \qquad (16)$$

and

$$\Psi_i = T_p\kappa_i\text{sat}[s_i(\tilde{x}_i,k)] + T_p\epsilon_i s_i(\tilde{x}_i,k) - s_i(\tilde{x}_i,k) + A_i A_i \tilde{x}_i(k) \qquad (17)$$

$$A_i = \begin{bmatrix} 0 & 1 \\ 0 & 0 \end{bmatrix} , \qquad B_i = \begin{bmatrix} 0 \\ 1 \end{bmatrix} , \qquad C_i = \begin{bmatrix} 0 & 1 \end{bmatrix} , \qquad (18)$$

$$A_i = \begin{bmatrix} \lambda_i & 1 \end{bmatrix} . \qquad (19)$$

The switching function in (17) is in the form [6]

$$s_i(\tilde{x}_i, k) = A_i \tilde{x}_i(k) , \qquad (20)$$

The saturation function in (16) is calculated as follows

$$\text{sat}(s_i[\tilde{x}_i(k)]) = \begin{cases} +1 & \text{if } s_i[\tilde{x}_i(k)] > \delta_i \\ \frac{s_i[\tilde{x}_i(k)]}{\delta_i} & \text{if } |s_i[\tilde{x}_i(k)]| \le |\delta_i| \\ -1 & \text{if } s_i[\tilde{x}_i(k)] < -\delta_i \end{cases} , \qquad (21)$$

where $\delta_i > 0, i = 1, \ldots, n$ is a switching boundary in joint $i$.

The saturation function eliminates the high frequency oscillations called chattering [3,13], that is typical for the standard SMC control system.

To obtain the stable performance of the sliding mode control system, its parameters should be chosen as follows [11] $\kappa_i > 0$, $\epsilon_i > 0$, $1 - T_p\epsilon_i > 0$, $|\lambda_i| < 1$, $\delta_i > 0$, $i = 1 \ldots n$.

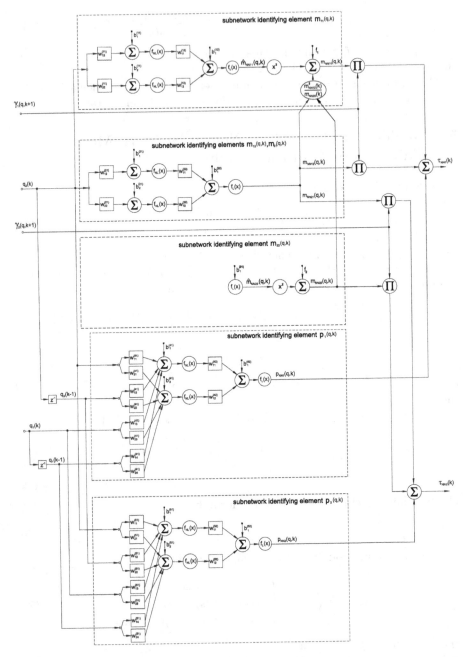

**Fig. 1.** A neural network for the identification of the mathematical model of robot with 2 degrees of freedom

# 6    Experiments and Results

In order to verify the proposed SMC controller with ANN robot model (SMC-ANN), we have calculated an example of the control of the robot with 2 degrees of freedom [2,11]. The physical parameters of the robot are gathered in Table 1 and the robot is shown in Fig. 2.

**Table 1.** Physical parameters of the robot with 2 degrees of freedom assigned according to the *Denavitt-Hartenberg* notation [9,14]

| Link $i$ | $\alpha_i[°]$ | $a_i[m]$ | $\theta_i[°]$ | $d_i[m]$ |
|---|---|---|---|---|
| 1 | 0 | 2.0 | $q_1$ | 0 |
| 2 | 0 | 0.8 | $q_2$ | 0 |
|  | M[kg] | $r_x[m]$ | $r_y[m]$ | $r_z[m]$ |
| 1 | 22 | -1.0 | 0 | 0 |
| 2 | 16 | -0.4 | 0 | 0 |
|  | $I_{xx}[kg \cdot m^2]$ | $I_{yy}[kg \cdot m^2]$ | $I_{zz}[kg \cdot m^2]$ | $J_{xy}, J_{yz}, J_{xz}[kg \cdot m^2]$ |
| 1 | 0 | 22.00 | 22.00 | 0 |
| 2 | 0 | 2.56 | 2.56 | 0 |

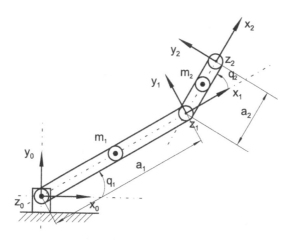

**Fig. 2.** Robot with 2 degrees of freedom, with coordinate systems set according to the *Denavit - Hartenberg* notation spong:robot,siciliano:handbook

For calculation of the training and testing data, a reference trajectory for every joint was set, according to the following formula

$$q_{ri}(k) = \sum_{j=1}^{3} a_{i,j} cos(\varpi_{i,j} k T_p + \varphi_{i,j}), \ i = 1, 2 , \qquad (22)$$

The values of $a_{i,j}$, $\varpi_{i,j}$ and $\varphi_{i,j}$, different for the training and testing trajectories, are given in Table 2.

**Table 2.** The parameters of the training and testing trajectories

| Link $i$ | $a_{i1}[°]$ | $a_{i2}[°]$ | $a_{i3}[°]$ | $\varpi_{i1}[\frac{°}{s}]$ | $\varpi_{i2}[\frac{°}{s}]$ | $\varpi_{i3}[\frac{°}{s}]$ | $\varphi_{i1}[°]$ | $\varphi_{i2}[°]$ | $\varphi_{i3}[°]$ |
|---|---|---|---|---|---|---|---|---|---|
| Link 1, training | 110 | 23 | 47 | 37 | 5 | 8 | 127 | 77 | 54 |
| Link 2, training | 30 | 26 | 124 | 30 | 5 | 15 | 97 | 27 | 125 |
| Link 1, testing | 61 | 92 | 27 | 38 | 6 | 6 | 89 | 161 | 147 |
| Link 2, testing | 104 | 55 | 21 | 29 | 6 | 15 | 52 | 61 | 96 |

Values of SMC-ANN controller parameters, used for the simulations, are gathered in Table 3.

**Table 3.** Parameters of the SMC-ANN controller for the robot with 2 degrees of freedom

| | $\lambda_i$ | $\kappa_i$ | $\delta_i[°]$ | $\epsilon_i[\frac{1}{s}]$ |
|---|---|---|---|---|
| Link 1 | -0.98 | 5 | 5 | 0.2 |
| Link 2 | -0.98 | 5 | 5 | 0.2 |

For identification experiment, a time interval $T = 100[\text{sec}]$ was chosen, with a sampling time $T_p = 0.01[\text{sec}]$. The robot was simulated with given training trajectory, and SMC controller based on the ideal robot model. Therefore, there were $N = 10000$ training data samples - each sample consisted values of $q(k)$, $q(k-1)$, $\gamma(q, k+1)$ and $\tau(k)$.

ANN model of the robot was trained off-line, with the known training data, to identify the model coefficients. Elements $m_{1,1}(q, k)$, $m_{1,2}(q, k) = m_{2,1}(q, k)$ of the robot mathematical model were identified by the subnetworks containing 1 nonlinear hidden layer with 2 neurons, and 1 linear output layer with 1 neuron, as it is given in Fig. 1. ANN was trained using the backpropagation method, and the *Levenberg-Marquardt* method, to update weights in all layers [10]. There were 50 training iterations. Bounding constants in (11) and (12) were chosen arbitrarily, as

$$f_i = 0.001, \; i = 1, 2 . \tag{23}$$

Identified inertia matrix was always positive definite. After identification, the robot with SMC-ANN control system, moving along the reference trajectory, was simulated. At first, as the reference trajectory, the training trajectory was chosen. Next, as the reference trajectory, the testing trajectory was chosen, which parameters are gathered in Table 2. During testing, the time interval was $T = 100[\text{sec}]$, and the sampling time was $T_p = 0.01[\text{sec}]$.

For the evaluation of SMC-ANN control system of the robot, the *average absolute position control error of generalized joint coordinate* was calculated as follows

$$e_{\text{avq}i} = \frac{\sum_{k=1}^{N} |q_{ri}(k) - q_i(k)|}{N}, \; i = 1, 2 , \tag{24}$$

Obtained values of the error (24), for training and testing trajectories, are presented in Table 4. In Fig. 3, there are presented reference testing trajectories,

**Table 4.** The values of the average absolute position control errors of generalized joint coordinates (24), for the robot with SMC-ANN controller

| Training trajectory | | Testing trajectory | |
|---|---|---|---|
| $e_{avq1}$ [rad] | $e_{avq2}$ [rad] | $e_{avq1}$ [rad] | $e_{avq2}$ [rad] |
| 0.09 | 0.12 | 0.20 | 0.33 |

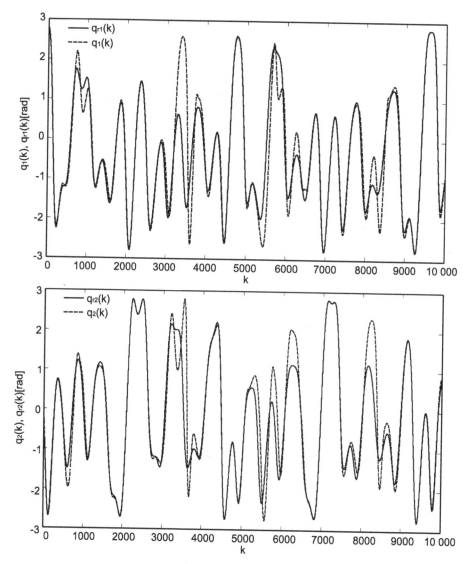

**Fig. 3.** Trajectories in each joint obtained during the simulation of the robot with SMC-ANN controller (dashed line), and reference trajectories (solid line), for testing data

and trajectories obtained for the robot with SMC-ANN controller with identified symmetrical, positive definite inertia matrix.

Obtained results, gathered in Table 4 and presented in Fig. 3, indicate that values of errors (24) can be still too big for some applications. However, presented method has significant properties: the neural network model has the structure that resembles the structure of the *Lagrange-Euler* equations, it is easy to implement, and does not require exact knowledge of the robot physical parameters. Moreover, the identified inertia matrix is positive definite, which is a key feature to design stable control system of the robot.

# 7    Concluding Remarks

This paper presents the synthesis of the sliding mode control system for the robotic manipulator, with structural model of the robot identified by the artificial neural network. Proposed artificial neural network model fulfills strict properties of the mathematical model of the robot, especially, the symmetry and the positive definiteness of the identified inertia matrix. The proposed, new method of the neural network design, is based on the conditions that are calculated using *Cholesky* decomposition of the estimated inertia matrix. Preliminary experimental results show, that the proposed control system is stable and can be used to control the 2 degree of freedom robot arm, with unknown physical parameters.

# References

1. Slotine, J.J., Sastry, S.S.: Tracking control of nonlinear systems using sliding surfaces with aplication to robot manipulators. International Journal of Control 38(2), 465–492 (1983)
2. Tang, K.M.W., Tourassis, V.D.: Systematic simplification of dynamic robot models. In: Proc. Midwest Symp. Circuits Syst., Syracuse, NY, pp. 1031–1034 (1987)
3. Gao, W., Hung, J.C.: Variable structure control of nonlinear systems:a new approach. IEEE Transactions on Industrial Electronics 40, 45–56 (1993)
4. Corke, P.I., Armstrong-Helouvry, B.: A search for consensus among model parameters reported for the PUMA 560 robot. In: Proc. IEEE Int. Conf. Robotics and Automation, San Diego, vol. 1, pp. 1608–1613 (1994)
5. Golub, G.H., Van Loan, C.F.: Matrix Computations, 3rd edn. Johns Hopkins University Press, Baltimore (1996)
6. Edwards, C., Spurgeon, S.K.: Sliding Mode Control: Theory and Applications. Taylor & Francis, Abington (1998)
7. Możaryn, J., Kurek, J.E.: Comparison of sliding mode control and decoupled sliding mode control of robot Puma 560. In: Proc. 9th IEEE Int. Conf. on Methods and Models in Automation and Robotics, MMAR 2003, Międzyzdroje, Poland, vol. 2 (2003)
8. Lewis, F.L., Dawson, D.M., Abdallah, C.T.: Robot Manipulator Control: Theory and Practice. CRC Press, Boca Raton (2004)
9. Spong, M.W., Hutchinson, S., Vidyasagar, M.: Robot Modeling and Control. Wiley, Chichester (2005)

10. Osowski, S.: Neural Networks for Information Processing. OWPW, Warsaw (2006) (in Polish)
11. Możaryn, J., Kurek, J.E.: Synthesis of sliding mode control of robot with neural network model. In: Proc. 12th IEEE Int. Conf. on Methods and Models in Automation and Robotics, MMAR 2006, Międzyzdroje, Poland, vol. 2, pp. 631–636 (2006)
12. Tang, Y., Sun, F., Sun, Z.: Neural network control of flexible-link manipulators using sliding mode. Neurocomputing 70, 288–295 (2006)
13. Leem, H., Utkin, V.I.: Chattering Analysis. In: Edwards, C., Colet, F., Fridman, E. (eds.) Advances in Variable Structure and Sliding Mode Control. Springer, Heidelberg (2006)
14. Siciliano, B., Khatib, O. (eds.): Springer Handbook of Robotics. Springer, Heidelberg (2008)
15. Możaryn, J., Kurek, J.E.: Design of a neural network for an identification of a robot model with a positive definite inertia matrix. In: Rutkowski, L., Scherer, R., Tadeusiewicz, R., Zadeh, L.A., Zurada, J.M. (eds.) ICAISC 2010. LNCS, vol. 6114, pp. 321–328. Springer, Heidelberg (2010)

# Hardware Implementation of a CPG-Based Locomotion Control for Quadruped Robots

Jose Hugo Barron-Zambrano[1], Cesar Torres-Huitzil[1], and Bernard Girau[2]

[1] Information Technology Laboratory, CINVESTAV Tamaulipas, Mexico
{jhbarronz,ctorres}@tamps.cinvestav.mx
[2] Cortex team, LORIA-INRIA Grand Est, Vandoeuvre-les-Nancy Cedex, France
{Bernard.Girau}@loria.fr

**Abstract.** This paper presents a hardware implementation of a controller to generate adaptive gait patterns for quadruped robots inspired by biological Central Pattern Generators (CPGs). The basic CPGs are modeled as non-linear oscillators which are connected one to each other through coupling parameters that can be modified for different gaits. The proposed implementation is based on an specific digital module for CPGs attached to a soft-core processor so as to provide an integrated and flexible embedded system. The system is implemented on a Field Programmable Gate Array (FPGA) device providing a compact and low power consumption solution for generating periodic rhythmic patterns in robot control applications. Experimental results show that the proposed implementation is able to generate suitable gait patterns, such as walking, trotting, and galloping.

## 1 Introduction

The design of locomotion control systems of legged robots is a challenge that has been partially solved. In the literature, broadly, there are two main approaches to the design of locomotion control systems, the mathematical model-based and the biologically inspired approach. In the former, to move a leg in a desired trajectory, the joint angles are calculated in advance, by using a mathematical model that incorporates both robot and environment parameters, to produce a sequence of actions algorithmically scheduled [1]. The second approach uses CPGs which are supposed to play an important role in locomotion. CPGs are comprised of neural oscillators located in the spine of vertebrates and in the segmental ganglia of invertebrates [2]. CPGs are often modeled as oscillators that have mutually coupled excitatory and inhibitory neurons, following a regular structure. The CPGs have the ability to automatically generate complex control signals for the coordination of muscles during rhythmic movements, such as walking, running, swimming and flying [3].

The CPG-based approach for the design of locomotion control systems has several advantages. Due to the limit cycle behavior of neural oscillators, i.e. to produce stable rhythmic patterns, the system rapidly returns to its normal

K. Diamantaras, W. Duch, L.S. Iliadis (Eds.): ICANN 2010, Part II, LNCS 6353, pp. 276–285, 2010.
© Springer-Verlag Berlin Heidelberg 2010

rhythmic behavior after transient perturbations of the state variables. This provides robustness against perturbations. As a result of the natural synchronization and coordination of CPGs, the amount of computations is reduced. The synaptic plasticity of interconnections and feedback signals, used to integrate sensory information, allow CPGs to produce flexible locomotion in unknown environments [4,5]. However, one of the main disadvantages of CPGs is that their parameters have to be tailored for specific applications, and there are few methodologies to generate the rhythmic signals. The parameters are usually tuned either by trial and error method or by some optimization algorithms, genetic algorithms for example. These methodologies are still insufficient to tune the parameters for generating a periodic signal with a specific shape [6].

To address some of the future challenges for robotics, the miniaturization of walking, running and flying robots will be needed, so as to look for real-time adaptability of robots to the environment. These technologies will require small, low-cost, power efficient and adaptive controllers which might greatly benefit from custom bio-inspired hardware. Currently, some researches have used CPG-based locomotion control systems in robots. For example, CPG models have been used for controlling swimming robots, such as a salamander robot [7] and a turtle robot [8]. CPGs also have been used on quadrupeds, hexapods and octopods robots [9,10]. Control systems for quadruped robots using CPGs have been explored by Hiroshi Kimura et al. [11]. Authors have developed a quadruped walking robot capable of adapting to irregular terrain using the Matsuoka oscillator. Other works on CPGs in quadruped robots can be found in Billard et al. [12] and Shan et al. [13]. Many of these applications have been developed using dedicated hardware, both analog and digital [11,12,13]. On one hand, CPGs have been implemented using microprocessors providing high accuracy and flexibility but those systems consume high power and occupy a large area restricting their utility in embedded applications. On the other hand, analog circuits have been already proposed, being computation and power efficient but they usually lack flexibility and dynamics and they involve large design cycles.

In this paper an FPGA-based hardware implementation to generate different gaits for quadruped robots is presented, based on established principles of locomotion that mimics the features of biological CPGs. A custom implementation of the Van Der Pol CPG attached to a Xilinx microblaze processor is presented and discussed. Potentially, this approach might provide modular control circuits that are adaptable and able to generate complex, coordinated movements. The goal of this implementation is to show the feasibility of self-contained locomotion solutions using modular, adaptable and compact modules with a higher degree of programmability to scale up to legged robots with high degrees of freedom.

# 2    CPG-Based Locomotion

## 2.1    Quadruped Gaits

Animal locomotion employs different periodic patterns known as animal gaits. Researchers have established that gaits possess certain symmetries and have

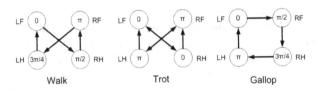

**Fig. 1.** Typical gait patterns in quadruped locomotion and their relative phases between the limbs

modeled the gaits of quadrupeds by a system of coupled cells where each cell is composed of a set of neurons directly responsible to synchronize the movement of their limbs. A simplified mathematical model of CPG-based locomotion consists of using one cell per limb and replacing each cell by a nonlinear oscillator. Thus, quadruped gaits are modeled by coupling four nonlinear oscillators, and by changing the coupling strength, it is possible to reproduce rhythmic locomotion patterns. In rhythmic movements of animals, a transition of the rhythmic movements is often observed. As a typical example, horses choose different locomotive patterns in accordance with their needs, locomotive speeds or the rate of energy consumption. In addition, each gait pattern is characterized by relative phase among the limbs [14]. Figure 1 shows the typical horse gait patterns and its relative phases between the limbs. Here, LF, LH, RF, and RH stand for left forelimb, left hindlimb, right forelimb, and right hindlimb, respectively.

## 2.2   Basic CPG Model

There are several models for neural oscillators to model the basic CPG to control a limb, such as Amari-Hopfield model [15], Matsuoka model [12] and Van De Pol model [16]. In this work, the basic cell is modeled by a Van Der Pol (VDP) oscillator which is a relaxation oscillator governed by a second-order differential equation (equation 1):

$$\ddot{x} - \alpha(p^2 - x^2)\dot{x} + \omega^2 x = 0 \qquad (1)$$

where $x$ is the output signal from the oscillator, $\alpha$, $p$ and $\omega$ are the parameters that tune the properties of oscillators. In general terms, $\alpha$ affects the shape of the waveform, the amplitude of $x$ depends largely on the parameter $p$. When the amplitude parameter $p$ is fixed, the output frequency is highly dependent on the parameter $\omega$. However, a variation of parameter $p$ can slightly change the frequency of the signal, and $\alpha$ also can influence the output frequency. Actually, the VDP equation satisfies the Linard's theorem ensuring that there is a stable limit cycle in the phase space. Using the Linard's transformation, equation 1 can be rewritten as:

$$\begin{aligned}\dot{x} &= y \\ \dot{y} &= \alpha(p^2 - x^2)y + \omega^2 x\end{aligned} \qquad (2)$$

## 2.3    Quadruped CPG Network

In this work, the locomotion control system of a quadruped is modeled as a network of four VDP oscillators as shown in the figure 2a as suggested in most works reported in the literature [4,11]. Each oscillator controls the movement of a single limb. Within the CPG network, oscillators are mutually forced to oscillate in the same period and with a fixed phase difference. The mutual interaction among the VDP oscillators in the network produces a gait. By changing the phase difference between the oscillators, changing the coupling weights, it is posible to generate the three basic gaits. Figures 2b to 2d, present the configurations of the network that generate periodic rhythmic patterns corresponding to each gait (walk, trot, gallop).

The dynamics of the $i$th coupled oscillator in the network is given by:

$$\ddot{x}_c + \alpha(p_c^2 - x_{cj}^2)\dot{x}_c - \omega^2 x_{cj} = 0 \tag{3}$$

For $i = 1, 2, 3, 4$ , where $x_c$ is the output signal from oscillator, $x_{cj}$ denotes the coupling contribution of its neighbors given by the equation 4:

$$x_{cj} = \sum_j \lambda_{cj} x_j \tag{4}$$

Where $\lambda_{cj}$ is the coupling weight that represents the strength of $jth$ oscillator over the current oscillator. The generation of the respective gaits depends on the values of the system parameters.

# 3    Digital Hardware Implementation

In this section, we describe the architecture of the CPG controller for inter-limb coordination in quadruped locomotion. First, the design considerations for the implementation are presented. Next, the basic Van Der Pol Oscillator that constitute a part of the CPG network is given. Finally, the architecture of the complete system is described.

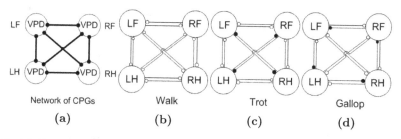

**Fig. 2.** (a) General CPG network. (b)-(c) Functional configurations corresponding to the typical gaits patterns. Black and white dots represent excitatory and inhibitory connections, respectively.

## 3.1   Design Considerations

The Van Der Pol oscillator is suitable for CPG implementation as a digital circuit, however two main factors for an efficient and flexible FPGA-based implementation should be taken into account: a) *arithmetic representation*, CPG computations when implemented in general microprocessor-based systems use floating point arithmetic. An approach for embedded implementations is the use of 2s complement fixed point representation with a dedicated wordlength that better matches the FPGA computational resources and that saves further silicon area at the cost of precision, and b)*efficiency and flexibility*, embedded hard processor cores or configurable soft processors developed by FPGA vendors add the software programmability of optimized processors to the fine grain parallelism of custom logic on a single chip [17]. In the field of neural processing, several applications mix real-time or low-power constraints with a need for flexibility, so that FPGAs appear as a well-fitted implementation solution.

Most of the previous hardware implementation of CPGs are capable of generating sustained oscillations similar to the biological CPGs, however, quite a few have addressed the problem of embedding several gaits and performing transitions between them. One important design consideration in this paper, is that the FPGA-based implementation should be a *platform well suited to explore reconfigurable behavior and dynamics*, i.e., the platform can be switched between multiple output patterns through the application of external inputs.

## 3.2   Module of Van Der Pol Oscillator

From analysis of equation 2, three basic operations were used: addition, subtraction and multiplication. Thus, one block for each operation was implemented with 2's complement fixed-point arithmetic representation. Figure 3a shows a simplified block diagram of the proposed digital architecture for the discretized VDP equation. In the first stage, the value of $X_{ci}$ is calculated: this value depends on the $X_c$-neighbors and the coupling weight values. This stage uses four multipliers and one adder. The square values of $p$, $X_{ci}$ and $\omega$ are calculated in the second stage, it uses three multipliers. In the third stage, the values of $\alpha * y_c$ and $p^2 - X_{ci}$ are calculated, one multiplier and a subtracter are used. The fourth stage computes the values of $\alpha * y_c * (p^2 - X_{ci})$ and $\omega^2 * X_{ci}$. This stage uses two multipliers. For the integration stage, the numerical method of Euler was implemented by using two shift registers and two adders. The integration factor is implemented by a shift register, which shifts six positions the values of $\dot{y}_c$ and $\dot{x}_c$ to provide an integration factor of 1/64. The block labeled as *Reg* stands for accumulators that hold the internal state of the VPD oscillators. Finally, the values $y_c$ and $x_c$ are obtained.

The size word for each block was 18-bit fixed point representation with 11-bit for the integer part and 7-bit for the fractional part. Figure 3b shows the amplitude average error using different precisions for the fractional part. The errors were obtained from the hardware implementation. In figure 3b, it can be appreciated that the average error decreases as the resolution of the input

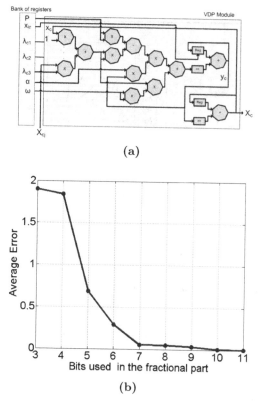

(a)

(b)

**Fig. 3.** (a) Digital hardware architecture for the Van Der Pol oscillator (b) Average error as a function of the bit precision used in the basic blocks

variables is incremented. This reduction is not linear, and the graphic shows a point where such reduction is not significant. Seven bits were chosen as a good compromise for average error and implementation resources.

### 3.3    Quadruped Gait Network Architecture

In the CPG model for quadruped locomotion all basic VDP oscillators are interconnected, as shown on figure 2a, through the connection weights ($\lambda_{ij}$). In order to overcome the partial lack of flexibility of the CPG digital architecture, it has been attached as a specialized coprocessor to a microblaze processor following an embedded system design approach so as to provide a high level interface layer for application development. A bank of registers is used to provide communication channels to an embedded processor. The bank has twenty-three registers and it receives the input parameters from microblaze, $\alpha$, $p^2$, $\omega^2$, $\lambda_{ij}$ and the initial values of each oscillator. The architecture sends output data to specific FPGA pins. Figure 4 shows a simplified block diagram of the VPD network interfacing scheme to the bank registers and the microblaze processor.

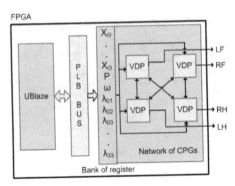

**Fig. 4.** Complete architecture for embedded implementation of a CPG-based quadruped locomotion controller

## 4   Implementation Results

The CPG digital architecture has been modeled using the Very High Speed Integrated Circuits Hardware Description Language (VHDL) and Python was used for the implementation and simulation software. The CPG module has been attached as a slave coprocessor to the microblaze soft-processor using the PLB bus and a set of wrapping libraries according to the Xilinx design flow for embedded systems. The system has been synthesized using ISE Foundation and EDK tools from Xilinx targeted to a Spartan-3E device. To test the hardware implementation, a C-based application was developed on the microblaze to set the values of the parameters in the hardware digital implementation. The implementation was validated in two ways. The first one, the results were sent to the host computer through serial connection to visualize the waveforms generated by the module. Then, the hardware waveforms were compared with the software waveforms. In the second way, results were sent to digital-analog converter (DAC) and the output signal from DAC was visualized on a oscilloscope. Figure 5 shows, the periodic rhythmic patterns corresponding to the gaits (walk, trot, gallop) generated by hardware implementation. The values of weight matrix to configure the CPG network are shown in table 1. The initial values, $x_0 = 1$, $x_1 = 1$, $x_2 = 1$, $x_3 = 1$, $y_0 = y_1 = y_2 = y_3 = 0$, $\alpha = 1$, $p^2 = 2$, $\omega^2 = 20$ were used. The values were calculated experimentally with a software implementation. Figure 5d shows the patterns for two gaits, walk and trot, and the transitions between them. The phase attractors for one VDP oscillator during walking and trotting, are shown in figures 5e and 5f. The phase attractor figures show the adaptability process until the stable cycle in the oscillator is reachieved. The time to reach the stable cycle is around 2 seconds.

The system was synthesized to a Spartan-3E device using Xilinx ISE and EDK tools and tested in the Spartan-3E starter kit development board. Table 2 shows a summary of the FPGA resource utilization of the network architecture.

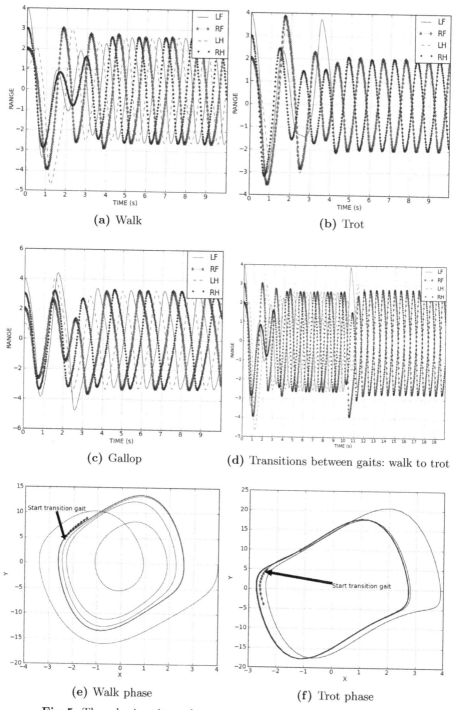

(a) Walk

(b) Trot

(c) Gallop

(d) Transitions between gaits: walk to trot

(e) Walk phase

(f) Trot phase

**Fig. 5.** Three basic gaits and transition between walking and trotting

**Table 1.** Weight matrix to configure the CPG network

| Gait | Walk | Trot | Gallop |
|------|------|------|--------|
| Weight | $\begin{pmatrix} 1.0 & -0.2 & -0.2 & -0.2 \\ -0.2 & 1.0 & -0.2 & -0.2 \\ -0.2 & -0.2 & 1.0 & -0.2 \\ -0.2 & -0.2 & -0.2 & 1.0 \end{pmatrix}$ | $\begin{pmatrix} 1.0 & -0.2 & 0.2 & -0.2 \\ -0.2 & 1.0 & -0.2 & 0.2 \\ 0.2 & -0.2 & 1.0 & -0.2 \\ -0.2 & 0.2 & -0.2 & 1.0 \end{pmatrix}$ | $\begin{pmatrix} 1.0 & 0.2 & -0.2 & -0.2 \\ -0.2 & 1.0 & 0.2 & -0.2 \\ -0.2 & -0.2 & 1.0 & 0.2 \\ 0.2 & -0.2 & -0.2 & 1.0 \end{pmatrix}$ |

**Table 2.** Hardware utilization for implementation of the CPG control for a quadruped targeted to a Xilinx XC3S500e-5fg320 device

| Resource | LTUs | Flip-Flops | Slices | Embedded multipliers | Maximum clock frequency |
|----------|------|------------|--------|----------------------|-------------------------|
| Utilization | 375 | 144 | 221 | 20 | 28 MHz |

## 5   Conclusions and Future Work

This work has presented a hardware digital implementation for Central Pattern Generator suitable for locomotion control of quadruped robots. The implementation takes advantage of the distributed processing of FPGA computational resources. The presented examples show that the measured waveforms from the FPGA-based implementation agree with the numerical simulations. The architecture of the elemental Van Der Pol oscillator was designed and attached as a co-processor to microblaze processor. The implementation provides flexibility to generate different rhythmic patterns, at runtime, suitable for adaptable locomotion and the implementation is scalable to larger networks. The microblaze, allow us to propose an strategy for both generation and control of the gaits, and it is suitable to explore the design with dynamic reconfiguration in the FPGA.

Future work will focus on: (a) explore larger networks for a complete locomotion controller and embedding more diverse transitions (b) incorporate the feedback from the robot body to improve the generation of patterns, (c) integrate visual perception information to adapt the locomotion control in an unknown environment and (d) to scale up the present approach to legged robots with several degrees of freedom to generate complex rhythmic movements and behaviors.

## Acknowledgment

Authors want to thank the partial support received from CONACyT through the research grant number 99912 and the INRIA associate team CorTexMex.

# References

1. Kimura, H., Shimoyama, I., Miura, H.: Dynamics in Dynamic Walk of Quadruped Robot. J. of the Society of Instrument and Control Engineers 29, 220–225 (1990)
2. Delcomyn, F.: Neural Basis of rhythmic behavior in animals. Science 210, 492–498 (1980)
3. Hooper, S.L.: Central Pattern Generator. Current Biology 10(5), 176–177 (2000)
4. Fujii, A., Saito, N., Nakahira, K., Ishiguro, A., Eggenberger, P.: Generation of an adaptive controller CPG for a quadruped robot with neuromodulation mechanism. In: IEEE Int. Conf. Intell. Robots Syst. (2002)
5. Ijspeerta, A.J.: Central pattern generators for locomotion control in animals and robots: A review. Neural Networks 21(4), 642–653 (2002)
6. Zielinska, T.: Coupled oscillators utilized as gait rhythm generators of a two-legged walking machine. Biol. Cybern. 74, 263–273 (1996)
7. Ijspeert, A.J., Crespi, A., Ryczko, D., Cabelguen, J.: From swimming to walking with a salamander robot driven by a spinal cord model. Science 9, 1416–1420 (2007)
8. Zhao, W., Hu, Y., Wang, L.: Construction and Central Pattern Generator-Based Control of a Flipper-Actuated Turtle-Like Underwater Robot. Advanced Robotics 23, 19–43 (2009)
9. Arena, P., Fortuna, L., Frasca, M., Sicurella, G.: n adaptive, self-organizing dynamical system for hierarchical control of bio-inspired locomotion. IEEE Transactions on Systems, Man and Cybernetics, Part B 34(4), 1823–1837 (2004)
10. Inagaki, S., Yuasa, H., Suzuki, T., Arai, T.: Wave CPG model for autonomous decentralized multi-legged robot: Gait generation and walking speed control. Robotics and Autonomous Systems 54(2), 118–126 (2006)
11. Fukuoka, Y., Kimura, H., Cohen, A.H.: Adaptive dynamic walking of a quadruped robot on irregular terrain based on biological concepts. The International Journal of Robotics Research 34, 187–202 (2003)
12. Billard, A., Ijspeert, A.J.: Biologically inspired neural controllers for motor control in a quadruped robot. In: Proceedings of the IEEE-INNS-ENNS international joint conference on neural networks, IJCNN 2000, vol. VI, pp. 637–641. IEEE Computer Society, Los Alamitos (2000)
13. Still, S., Tilden, M.W.: Controller for a four legged walking machine. In: Smith, S., Hamilton, A. (eds.) Neuromorphic Systems: Engineering Silicon from Neurobiology, pp. 138–148. World Scientific, Singapore (1998)
14. Dagg, A.I.: Gait in mammals. Mammal Rev. 3, 135–154 (1973)
15. Amari, S.: Characteristic of the random nets of analog neuron-like elements. IEEE Trans. Syst., Man, Cybern. SMC-2, 643–657 (1972)
16. Van Der Pol, B., Van der Mark, J.: The heartbeat considered as a relaxation oscillation, and an electrical model of the heart. The London, Edinburgh, and Dublin Philosophical Magazine and Journal of Science Ser. 7(6), 763–775 (1928)
17. Torres-Huitzil, C., Girau, B., Gauffriau, A.: Hardware/software co-design for embedded implementation of neural networks. In: Diniz, P.C., Marques, E., Bertels, K., Fernandes, M.M., Cardoso, J.M.P. (eds.) ARCS 2007. LNCS, vol. 4419, pp. 167–178. Springer, Heidelberg (2007)

# Evolutionary Strategies Used for the Mobile Robot Trajectory Tracking Control*

Adriana Serbencu, Adrian Emanoil Serbencu, and Daniela Cristina Cernega

Control Systems and Industrial Informatics Department, Computer Science Faculty,
"Dunarea de Jos" University from Galati, 80021 Str. Domneasca 111, Galati, Romania
{adriana.serbencu,adrian.serbencu,daniela.cernega}@ugal.ro

**Abstract.** This paper addresses the Trajectory Tracking Problem for the Wheeled Mobile Robot, which is a nonlinear system. The trajectory tracking control problem is solved using the sliding mode control. In this paper the Evolution Strategy is investigated in order to obtain the best values for the sliding mode control law parameters. The performances of the control law with the optimum parameters are analyzed. The conclusions are based on the simulation results.

**Keywords:** Sliding Mode Control, Trajectory Tracking, Evolution Strategy.

## 1 Introduction

To solve the trajectory tracking problem for a Wheeled Mobile Robot (WMR) it is used a nonlinear model [1]:

$$x^{(n)} = f(x,t) + b(x,t) \cdot u \tag{1}$$

where $x$ is the state variable; $x^{(n)} = [x, \dot{x}, \ddot{x}, \ldots, x^{(n-1)}]$; $x^{(n)}$ is the $n^{th}$-order derivative of $x$; $f$ is a nonlinear function; $b$ is the gain and $u$ is the control input.

The design of a variable structure control (VSC) [2] for a nonlinear system implies two steps: (1). "reaching mode" or nonsliding mode; (2). sliding mode.

For the reaching mode, the desired response usually is to reach the switching manifold $s$, described by:

$$s(x) = c^T \cdot x = 0 \tag{2}$$

in finite time with small overshoot with respect to the switching manifold.

The distance between the state trajectory and the switching manifold, $s$ is stated as:

$$s(x,t) = \left(\frac{d}{dt} + \lambda\right)^{n-1} \cdot \tilde{x} = 0 \tag{3}$$

---

* This work was supported by the Romanian High Education Scientific Research National Council (CNCSIS), under project PC ID-506.

K. Diamantaras, W. Duch, L.S. Iliadis (Eds.): ICANN 2010, Part II, LNCS 6353, pp. 286–295, 2010.

where $\tilde{x}$ is the tracking error and $\lambda$ is a strictly positive constant which determines the closed-loop bandwidth. For example, if $n = 2$,

$$s = \dot{\tilde{x}} + \lambda \cdot \tilde{x} \tag{4}$$

Hence the corresponding switching manifold is:

$$s(t) = 0 \tag{5}$$

For a system having $m$ inputs, $m$ switching functions are needed.

It is proved that the most important virtue of the VSC systems is robustness. Proper design of the switching functions for a VSC system ensures the asymptotic stability. A number of design criteria exist for this purpose [3],[4].

Sliding Mode is also known to possess merits such as the invariance to parametric uncertainties. Dynamic characteristics of the reaching mode are very important, and this type of control suffers from the chattering phenomenon which is due to high frequency switching over discontinuity of the control signal.

The parameters of the control laws have to be positive, and their values influence the reaching rate and the chattering. The values of these parameters are not specified in the literature. In this paper the optimal values for these parameters will be searched.

The process of optimization gained great importance in many real life engineering problems. Many optimization methods were proposed in literature. Evolution Strategy (ES) [5], [6] is an evolutionary algorithm that is known to be simple and has an excellent global search feature. The ES is presented in Section 2. Section 3 is dedicated to the Trajectory Tracking Problem for the Wheeled Mobile Robot. This problem is solved within the Sliding Mode approach and the result is the sliding-mode trajectory-tracking controller. The parameters $p_i$ and $q_i$ of the control law are not specified in the literature. In Section 4 Evolution strategy is used to determine the optimal values of the control law parameters in order to ensure maximum possible reaching rate of the switching manifold and minimum chattering and the results obtained are presented. Section 5 is dedicated to experimental results. Section 6 is dedicated to the conclusion and future work directions.

## 2 Evolutionary Strategies

In the case of evolutionary computation, there are four historical paradigms that have served as the basis for much of the activity of the field: genetic algorithms [7], genetic programming [8], evolutionary strategies [5], and evolutionary programming [9]. The basic differences between the paradigms lie in the nature of the representation schemes, the reproduction operators and selection methods. Evolution strategy (ES) was created in the early 1960s and developed further along the 70s [5], [6].

The basic version of evolution strategies uses just mutation and selection as search operators. The operators are applied in a loop. An iteration of the loop is called a generation. The sequence of generations is continued a set number of times, or until a stop criterion is met.

As far as real-valued search spaces are concerned, in the ES mutation is usually performed by adding a normally distributed random value to each solution component. The step size or mutation strength is often governed by adaptation.

The selection in evolution strategies is deterministic and based on the fitness rankings. The simplest ES operates on a population of size two: the current point (parent) and the result of its mutation. Only if the mutant's fitness is at least as good as the parent one, it becomes the parent of the next generation. Otherwise the mutant is disregarded. This is a (1 + 1)-ES. More generally, $\lambda$ mutants can be generated and compete with the parent, called (1 + $\lambda$)-ES. In a (1, $\lambda$)-ES the best mutant becomes the parent of the next generation while the current parent is always disregarded. Contemporary versions of evolution strategy often use a population of $\mu$ parents and also recombination as an additional operator (called ($\mu/\rho+$, $\lambda$)-ES) [10]. Using a population of solutions, make ESs less prone to convergence in local optima.

The evolution strategies implementation, that is used, operate on populations $P$ of individuals $a$. An individual $a_k$ with index $k$ comprises not only the specific object parameter set (or vector) $y_k$ and its objective function value $F_k := F(y_k)$, but also a set of endogenous and evolvable strategy parameters $s_k$, $a_k = (y_k, s_k, F(y_k))$.

The endogenous strategy parameters are used to control certain statistical properties of the mutation operator. Endogenous strategy parameters can evolve during the evolution process and are needed in self-adaptive ES [11].

Within one ES generation step, $\lambda$ offspring individuals $\tilde{a}_l$ (note, the tilde is used to mark complete offspring) are generated from the set of $\mu$ parent individuals $a_m$. That is, the size $\lambda$ of the offspring population $P_o$ is usually not equal to the size $\mu$ of the parent population $P_p$. The strategy-specific parameters $\mu$ and $\lambda$ as well as $\rho$ (the mixing number, see below) are called "exogenous strategy parameters" which are kept constant during the evolution run.

The way the offspring population is generated is expressed by the ($\mu/\rho +$, $\lambda$) notation. The $\rho$ refers to the number of parents involved in the procreation of *one* offspring (mixing number).

Selection is the opposite of the variation operators (mutation and recombination). It gives the evolution a direction. In the selection step, a new parental population at $(g + 1)$ is obtained by a deterministic process guaranteeing that only the $\mu$ best individuals from the selection pool of generation $(g)$ are transferred into $P_p(g+1)$.

There are two versions of selection technique, depending on whether or not the parental population at $(g)$ is included in this process, i.e., *plus* selection, denoted by ($\mu + \lambda$), and *comma* selection, denoted by ($\mu$, $\lambda$), respectively. In the case of ($\mu$, $\lambda$) selection, only the $\lambda$ newly generated offspring individuals, i.e. the $P_o(g)$ population, define the selection pool. The plus selection takes the old parents into account. Plus selection is elitist because it guarantees the survival of the best individual found so far an infinitely long time-span.

The mutation operator is the primary source of genetic variation. It is usually a basic variation operator in ES, which assures the search space exploration.

Considering the $\Re^N$ search space and given the standard deviation $\sigma$ (mutation strength) as the only endogenous strategy parameter $s$, the mutation yields

$$\tilde{y} = y + z \tag{6}$$

with
$$z := \sigma(N_1(0, 1), \ldots, N_N(0, 1)) \tag{7}$$

where the $N_i(0,1)$ are random samples from the standard normal distribution.

There are two standard classes of recombination used in ES: "discrete recombination" and the "intermediate recombination".

Given a parental vector $a = (a_1, \ldots, a_D)$ (object or strategy parameter vector), the dominant $\rho$ recombination produces a recombinant $r = (r_1, \ldots, r_D)$ by coordinate wise random selection from the $\rho$ corresponding coordinate values of the parent family

$$(r)_k = (a_{mk})_k, \text{ with } m_k = \text{Random}\{1, \ldots, \rho\} \tag{8}$$

The intermediate recombination simply calculates the center of mass (centroid) of the $\rho$ parent vectors

$$(r)_k = \frac{1}{\rho} \sum_{m=1}^{\rho} (a_m)_k \tag{9}$$

The adaptation of strategy parameters control the statistical properties of the of the mutation operators. It is used the $1/5th$ rule for controlling the mutation strength [12].

# 3 Trajectory Tracking Problem

In this paper the model used for the controlled robot is a 2-order MIMO (Multiply Input Multiply Output) nonlinear system that is "linear in control". The model used is:

$$\ddot{x} = f(x, \dot{x}, t) + B(x, \dot{x}, t) \cdot u \tag{10}$$

where $x = [x_1, x_2, \cdots, x_n]$, $x \in \mathfrak{R}^n$, $f$ is a vector of nonlinear functions, $f \in \mathcal{L}_2^n$, $B$ is a matrix of gains, $B \in \mathfrak{R}^{n \times n}$; $\det(B) \neq 0$; $u \in \mathfrak{R}^n$ is the control vector. The control law is:

$$u = p(x, \dot{x}, t) \tag{11}$$

For the 2nd-order MIMO nonlinear system having the model shown in (11) efficient sliding mode control can be achieved via the following stages (see Fig. 1):

$1^{st}$ reaching phase motion; during this stage the trajectory is attracted towards the switching manifold (if the reaching condition is satisfied); characterized by

$$s_i \neq 0, \tilde{x}_i \neq 0, \dot{\tilde{x}}_i \neq 0 \tag{12}$$

$2^{nd}$ sliding mode motion; during this stage the trajectory stays on the switching manifold, i.e.

$$s_i = 0, \tilde{x}_i \neq 0, \dot{\tilde{x}}_i \neq 0 \tag{13}$$

$3^{rd}$ steady state; during this stage both the state variable and the state velocity will converge to the steady state value, therefore:

$$s_i = 0, \text{ and } \begin{cases} \tilde{x}_i \to 0, \dot{\tilde{x}}_i \to 0 & or \\ x_i = 0, \dot{\tilde{x}}_i = 0 \end{cases} \tag{14}$$

The reaching law is a differential equation which specifies the dynamics of a switching function $s(x)$. The differential equation of an asymptotically stable $s(x)$, is itself a reaching condition. In addition, by the choice of the parameters in the differential equation, the dynamic quality of the VSC system in the reaching mode can be controlled.

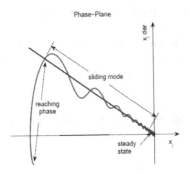

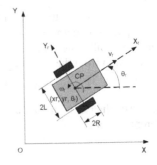

**Fig. 1.** Phase-Plane Diagram for the concept of 3-Stages approach

**Fig. 2.** WMR model and symbols

Gao and Hung [2] proposed a reaching law which directly specifies the dynamics of the switching surface by the differential equation

$$\dot{s} = -Q \cdot sgn(s) - P \cdot h(s) \tag{15}$$

where $Q = diag[q_1, q_2, \cdots, q_n], q_i > 0,$   $P = diag[p_1, p_2, \cdots, p_n], p_i > 0, i = 1,...,n$

and                    $sgn(s) = [sgn(s_1), sgn(s_2), \cdots, sgn(s_n)]^T]$

$$h(s) = [h_1(s_1), h_2(s_2), \cdots, h_n(s_n)]^T; \ s_i \cdot h_i(s) > 0; \ h_i(0) = 0.$$

In this paper, a constant plus proportional rate reaching law proposed in [2] is investigated to control the mobile robot:

$$\dot{s} = -Q \cdot sgn(s) - P \cdot s \tag{16}$$

Clearly, by using the proportional rate term $-P \cdot s$, the state is forced to approach the switching manifolds faster when $s$ is large. The purpose of the trajectory tracking is to control the non-holonomic WMR to follow a desired trajectory, with a given orientation relatively to the path tangent, even when different disturbances exist. In the case of trajectory-tracking the path is to be followed under time constraints. The path has an associated velocity profile, with each point of the trajectory embedding spatiotemporal information that is to be satisfied by the WMR along the path. Trajectory tracking is formulated as having the WMR following a virtual target WMR which is assumed to move exactly along the path with specified velocity profile.

### 3.1 Kinematic Model of a WMR

Fig. 2 shown a WMR with two diametrically opposed drive wheels (radius $R$) and free-wheeling castors (not considered in the kinematic models). $Pr$ is the origin of the robot coordinates system. $2L$ is the length of the axis between the drive wheels. $\omega_R$ and $\omega_L$ are the angular velocities of the right and left wheels. Let the pose of the mobile robot be defined by the vector, $q_r = [x_r \ y_r \ \theta_r]^T$ where $[x_r \ y_r]^T$ denotes the robot position on the plane and $\theta_r$ the heading angle with respect to the $x$-axis. In addition, $v_r$ denotes the linear velocity of the robot, and $\omega_r$ the angular velocity around the vertical axis. For a unicycle WMR rolling on a horizontal plane without slipping, the kinematic model can be expressed by:

$$\begin{bmatrix} \dot{x}_r \\ \dot{y}_r \\ \dot{\theta}_r \end{bmatrix} = \begin{bmatrix} cos\theta_r & 0 \\ sin\theta_r & 0 \\ 0 & 1 \end{bmatrix} \cdot \begin{bmatrix} v_r \\ \omega_r \end{bmatrix} \quad (17)$$

which represents a nonlinear system.

Controllability of the system (17) is easily checked using the Lie algebra rank condition for nonlinear systems. However, the Taylor linearization of the system about the origin is not controllable, thus excluding the application of classical linear design approaches.

## 3.2 Trajectory-Tracking

Without loss of generality, it can be assumed that the desired trajectory $q_d(t) = [x_d(t) \ y_d(t) \ \theta_d(t)]^T$ is generated by a virtual unicycle mobile robot (Fig. 3). The kinematic relationship between the virtual configuration $q_d(t)$ and the corresponding desired velocity inputs $[v_d(t) \ \omega_d(t)]^T$ is analogue with (17):

$$\begin{bmatrix} \dot{x}_d \\ \dot{y}_d \\ \dot{\theta}_d \end{bmatrix} = \begin{bmatrix} cos\theta_d & 0 \\ sin\theta_d & 0 \\ 0 & 1 \end{bmatrix} \cdot \begin{bmatrix} v_d \\ \omega_d \end{bmatrix} \quad (18)$$

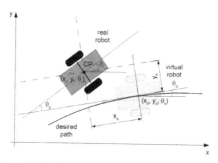

**Fig. 3.** Lateral, longitudinal and orientation errors (trajectory-tracking)

When a real robot is controlled to move on a desired path it exhibits some tracking error. This tracking error, expressed in terms of the robot coordinate system, as shown in Fig. 3, is given by

$$\begin{bmatrix} x_e \\ y_e \\ \theta_e \end{bmatrix} = \begin{bmatrix} cos\theta_d & sin\theta_d & 0 \\ -sin\theta_d & cos\theta_d & 0 \\ 0 & 0 & 1 \end{bmatrix} \cdot \begin{bmatrix} x_r - x_d \\ y_r - y_d \\ \theta_r - \theta_d \end{bmatrix} \quad (19)$$

Consequently one gets the error dynamics for trajectory tracking as

$$\begin{cases} \dot{x}_e = -v_d + v_r \cdot cos\theta_e + \omega_d \cdot y_e \\ \dot{y}_e = v_r \cdot sin\theta_e - \omega_d \cdot x_e \\ \dot{\theta}_e = \omega_r - \omega_d \end{cases} \quad (20)$$

### 3.3  Sliding-Mode Trajectory-Tracking Control

Uncertainties which exist in real mobile robot applications degrade the control performance significantly, and accordingly, need to be compensated. In this section, it is proposed a sliding-mode trajectory-tracking (SM-TT) controller, in Cartesian space, where trajectory-tracking is achieved even in the presence of large initial pose errors and disturbances.

Let us define the sliding surface $s = [s_1 \ \ s_2]^T$ as

$$s_1 = \dot{x}_e + k_1 \cdot x_e \, ; \ s_2 = \dot{y}_e + k_2 \cdot y_e + k_0 \cdot sgn(y_e) \cdot \theta_e \tag{21}$$

where $k_0$, $k_1$, $k_2$ are positive constant parameters, $x_e$, $y_e$ and $\theta_e$ are the trajectory tracking errors defined in (19).

If $s_1$ converges to zero, trivially $x_e$ converges to zero. If $s_2$ converges to zero, in steady-state it becomes $\dot{y}_e = -k_e \cdot y_e - k_0 \cdot sign(y_e) \cdot \theta_e$.

For $y_e < 0 \Rightarrow \dot{y}_e > 0$ if only if $k_0 < k_2 \cdot |y_e| / |\theta_e|$.

For $y_e > 0 \Rightarrow \dot{y}_e < 0$  if only if $k_0 < k_2 \cdot |y_e| / |\theta_e|$. Finally, it can be known from $s_2$ that convergence of $y_e$ and $\dot{y}_e$ leads to convergence of $\theta_e$ to zero. From the time derivative of (21) and using the reaching laws defined in (16), yields:

$$\dot{s}_1 = \ddot{x}_e + k_1 \cdot \dot{x}_e = -q_1 \cdot sgn(s_1) - p_1 \cdot s_1 \tag{22}$$

$$\dot{s}_2 = \ddot{y}_e + k_2 \cdot \dot{y}_e + k_0 \cdot sgn(y_e) \cdot \theta_e = -q_2 \cdot sgn(s_2) - p_2 \cdot s_2$$

From (19), (20) and (22), and after some mathematical manipulation, the output commands of the sliding-mode trajectory-tracking controller result:

$$\dot{v}_c = \frac{-p_1 \cdot s_1 - q_1 \cdot sgn(s_1) - k_1 \cdot \dot{x}_e - y_e \cdot \dot{\omega}_d - \dot{y}_e \cdot \omega_d + v_r \cdot \dot{\theta}_e \cdot sin(\theta_e) + \dot{v}_d}{cos(\theta_e)} \tag{23}$$

$$\omega_c = \frac{-p_2 \cdot s_2 - q_2 \cdot sgn(s_2) - k_2 \cdot \dot{y}_e + x_e \cdot \dot{\omega}_d + \dot{x}_e \cdot \omega_d - \dot{v}_r \cdot sin(\theta_e)}{v_r \cdot cos(\theta_e) + k_0 \cdot sgn(y_e)} + \omega_d$$

Let us define $V = s^T \cdot s / 2$ as a Lyapunov function candidate, therefore its time derivative is

$$\dot{V} = s_1 \cdot \dot{s}_1 + s_2 \cdot \dot{s}_2 = s_1 \cdot (-q_1 \cdot s_1 - p_1 \cdot sgn(s_1)) + \tag{24}$$

$$+ s_2 \cdot (-q_2 \cdot s_2 - p_2 \cdot sgn(s_2)) = = s^T \cdot Q \cdot s - p_1 \cdot |s_1| - p_2 \cdot |s2|$$

For $\dot{V}$ to be negative semi-definite, it is sufficient to choose $q_i$ and $p_i$ such that $q_i$, $p_i \geq 0$. But the optima values for $q_i$, $p_i \geq 0$ will be determined in the next section.

The *signum* functions in the control laws were replaced by *saturation* functions, to reduce the chattering phenomenon [1],

$$sat\left(\frac{s}{\phi}\right) = \begin{cases} \dfrac{s}{\phi} & \text{IF} \left|\dfrac{s}{\phi}\right| \leq 1 \\[2ex] sgn\left(\dfrac{s}{\phi}\right) & \text{IF} \left|\dfrac{s}{\phi}\right| > 1 \end{cases} \tag{25}$$

where constant factor $\phi$ defines the thickness of the boundary layer.

# 4   Sliding Mode Controller Parameters Evaluated with ES

Solving the Trajectory Tracking Problem with a SMC, leads to the reaching laws (23). In literature, the parameters $q1$, $q2$, $p1$ and $p2$ are usual determined through experiments [13] and have great impact on the performance of the controller. $q1$, $q2$ influence the rate at which the switching variable $s(x)$ reach the switching manifold $S$. Parameters $p1$, $p2$ force the state $x$ to approach the switching manifolds faster when $s$ is large. Choosing parameters through experiments only depends on experience or repeated debugging.

In this paper the parameters of the Sliding Mode Controller are selected using the Evolutionary Strategies (ES). The advantages of ES are: simplicity and an excellent global search feature, proven in other parameters training problems [14], [15], [16]. The optimization algorithm is working off-line. The results of the algorithm are the $P$ and $Q$ parameters of the reaching law implemented in the Sliding Mode Controller. The parameters found by ES can be used in real-time implementation of SM-TT controller on PatrolBot Robot.

The objective function used in ES takes into account both the speed of reaching manifolds and the amplitude of the chattering. This is accomplished using the sum of root mean square of the two errors $x_e$ and $y_e$ (19). The evaluation of every set of parameters is achieved after running a numerical simulation of the SM-TT control structure implemented in a Matlab Simulink schema that contains the model of the robot.

The horizon of simulation and initial conditions are chosen to allow a correct comparison between sets of parameters. The step of simulation is selected according to the one used to control the PatrolBot.

# 5   Experimental Results

Based on the above analysis, mathematical simulation software MATLAB was used to accomplish the experiment simulation study.

The mobile robot PatrolBot used in simulation is assumed to have the same structure as in Fig. 2. Parameter values of the PatrolBot are: mass of the robot body 46 [Kg], radius of the drive wheel 0.095 [m], and distance between wheels 0.48 [m]. The parameters of sliding modes were held constant during the experiments: $k_1 = 0.75$, $k_2 = 3.75$, and $k_0 = 2.5$; and the desired trajectory is given by $v_d = 0.5$ [m/s], $\omega_d = 0$ [rad/s].

The experiments were done on the robot with the initial error ($x_e = -0.5$ [m], $y_e = -0.5$ [m], $\theta_e = 0$ [deg]) and used the reaching law (16).

Settings, used in Matlab implementation of ES algorithm are: the size of the parent population is $\mu = 20$; the size $\lambda$ of the offspring population $\lambda=1$; the number of parents involved in the procreation of one offspring $\rho=4$; maximal number of generation 30. The criterion function used for solution evaluation are the sum of root mean square (RMS) of the two errors longitudinal - $x_e$ and lateral - $y_e$. RMS error is an old, proven measure of control and quality. RMS can be expressed as $RMS = \sqrt{\left(\sum x^2(i)\right)/N}$ .

Taking into account that parameters must be positive and large value can causes chattering, the search interval for each SM parameters was selected to be [0.01 5].

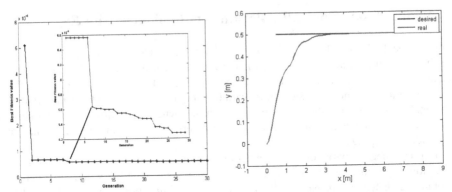

**Fig. 4.** The evolution of best value found by ES of the criterion function

**Fig. 5.** Simulated trajectory with the parameters value found by ES. Experimental SM-TT control starting from an initial error state $(x_e(0) = -0.5, y_e(0) = -0.5, \theta_e(0) = 0)$.

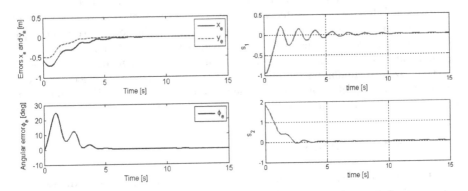

**Fig. 6.** Longitudinal, lateral and orientation errors for experimental SM-TT control

**Fig. 7.** Sliding surface for SM-TT controller

In Fig. 4 the evolution of criterion function best value found by ES is presented. Note that a number of 30 generation are sufficient to find a good set of values of parameters.

The parameter values for the considered PatrolBot, found by ES are $q1$=0.3312, $q2$=0.0340, $p1$=1.0599 and $p2$=4.9295.

In Fig. 5 and 6, the simulation results for the case of optimised parameters are presented.

In Fig. 7 the two sliding manifolds are represented. In Fig. 7 one can also see the value of the reaching time.

## 6   Conclusion

The paper proposed an efficient method to determine the optimum set of parameters for the sliding mode controller. The Evolution Strategy proved to be adequate for this problem because it eliminates the need for repeated simulations in order to find a satisfactory set of parameters.

The tests have proven that this optimization technique is efficient for the problem to be solved. A very good solution without chattering was found in a quite acceptable time interval and number of iterations.

The search of the optimum values for the sliding mode trajectory tracking control laws parameters was done in order to use, in the future, such optimum parameters into a supervised control structure having the ability to switch between different controllers.

# References

1. Slotine, J., Li, W.: Applied Nonliner Control. Prentice Hall, New Jersey (1991)
2. Gao, W., Hung, J.: Variable structure control of nonlinear systems: A new approach. IEEE Transactions on Industrial Electronics 40, 45–55 (1993)
3. Utkin, V., Young, K.: Methods for constructing discontinuity planes in multidimensional variable structure systems. Automation and Remote Control 39, 1466–1470 (1978)
4. Dorling, C., Zinober, A.: Two approaches to hyperplane design in multivariable variable structure control systems. Int. Journal Control 44, 65–82 (1986)
5. Rechenberg, I.: Evolutionsstrategie: Optimierung Technischer Systeme nach Prinzipien der Biologischen Evolution. Frommann-Holzboog, Stuttgart (1973)
6. Schwefel, H.-P.: Numerische Optimierung von Computer-Modellen (PhD thesis) (1974); Reprinted by Birkhäuser (1977)
7. Holland, J.H.: Adaptation in natural and artificial systems. The University of Michigan Press, Ann Arbor (1975)
8. Koza, J.R.: Genetic Programming: On the Programming of Computers by Means of Natural Selection. MIT Press, Cambridge (1992)
9. Fogel, L.J., Owens, A.J., Walsh, M.J.: Artificial Intelligence through Simulated Evolution. John Wiley, NY (1966)
10. Beyer, H.-G., Schwefel, H.-P.: Evolution strategies - A comprehensive introduction. Natural Computing 1(1), 3–52 (2002)
11. Beyer, H.-G., Deb, K.: On self-adaptive features in real-parameter evolutionary algorithms. IEEE Transactions on Evolutionary Computation 5(3), 250–270 (2001)
12. Schwefel, H.-P.: Evolution and Optimum Seeking. Wiley, New York (1995)
13. Solea, R., Cernega, D.C.: Sliding Mode Control for Trajectory Tracking Problem - Performance Evaluation. In: Alippi, C., Polycarpou, M., Panayiotou, C., Ellinas, G. (eds.) ICANN 2009. LNCS, vol. 5769, pp. 865–874. Springer, Heidelberg (2009)
14. Lin, C.-L., Jan, H.-Y.: Application of evolution strategy in mixed H∞/H2 control for a linear brushless DC motor. Advanced Intelligent Mechatronics 1, 1–6 (2003) ISBN: 0-7803-7759-1
15. Iruthayarajan, M.W., Baskar, S.: Evolutionary algorithms based design of multivariable PID controller. Expert Syst. Appl. 36, 9159–9167 (2009)
16. Richter, R., Hofmann, W.: Evolution Strategies Applied to Controls on a Two Axis Robot Source. In: Reusch, B. (ed.) Fuzzy Days 1997. LNCS, vol. 1226, pp. 434–443. Springer, Heidelberg (1997) ISBN:3-540-62868-1

# A Novel Topological Map of Place Cells for Autonomous Robots

Vilson L. DalleMole[1] and Aluizio F.R. Araújo[2]

[1] Federal Technology University of Paraná, Toledo, Br
[2] Federal University of Pernambuco, Recife, Br
vldmole@utfpr.edu.br, aluizioa@cin.ufpe.br

**Abstract.** This paper presents a novel Topological Map of Place Cells model for autonomous robots. In such a model the robot acquires and stores perceptions using a basic memory provided by our proposed growing self-organizing map. Context sensitive cells aim to obtain Place Cells whose activation is dependent on a remembrance process that fires the recollection of stored memories from current robot perceptions. The map is a graph of interconnected and topologically organized Place Cells. The robots notion of localization is primary guided by the recollection process, while vestibular stimuli estimates and a historic of lastly visited places disambiguate conflicting simultaneously activated Place Cells. The results are promising.

**Keywords:** Autonomous Robots, Place Cells, Self-Organizing Maps.

## 1 Introduction

After sensing the environment, an animal can determine its position and the appropriated actions in its memory [1]. Physiological studies identified three different neural substrates as the basis behind the animal navigation skills: (i) Place Cells [2] whose activity is related with the animal position in the environment; (ii) Head Direction Cells (HDC) [3], to integrate visual perceptions and vestibular information about direction changes to yield a notion of direction; and (iii) Grid Cells [4], to produce a local environment representation coupled with the azimuthal plane. The stored content of the substrates is commonly referred as a cognitive map describing the known environment [5]. Naturally, the stored knowledge is related with the individual perceptive capacities and experiences [6].

In this paper we consider an autonomous robot within an unknown environment. The robot navigates exploring its environment while produces an artificial cognitive map starting from its perceptions. An artificial cognitive map should handle place recognition, orientation, anticipation and planning. Such a map could store coordinates in a Cartesian system; positional relations between objects and places; or high level concepts as landmarks. Commonly, a Topological Map is constructed employing the concept of place, a distinctive and remarkable location in the environment whose recognition supplies the robot with a localization notion [7]. Then, we propose a new cognitive model for artificial cognitive processes, such model is composed by four layers having different purposes or functions: (1) perception and vestibular

K. Diamantaras, W. Duch, and L.S. Iliadis (Eds.): ICANN 2010, Part II, LNCS 6353, pp. 296–306, 2010.

systems; (2) basic memory; (3) context mapping; and (4) high cognitive process. Thereafter, we used it together with the concept of Place Cells to develop a new Topological Map Model, which is a graph mapping the basic memory content into contexts describing places in the world. Estimates in a Cartesian coordinate system are used to get topological organization. However, self-localization occurs by place recognition as a result of a remembrance process of environment characteristics.

Section 2 presents and discusses the proposed model while considering its components and their respective backgrounds and the cognitive process that they realize. The results are presented and discussed in the Section 3. Our conclusions and remarks are presented on Section 4.

## 2 The Proposed Model

We have considered a robot immersed into a 3D environment composed by structures as rooms, corridors, stairways and passages. The body of a robot is a box of edges $(l_1, l_2, l_3)$ corresponding to width, height and length. The robot is equipped with six laser sensors, one in each face. Each sensor is capable of sweeping $180°$ in intervals of $1°$ and it can rotate $180°$ around an axis that is orthogonal to the face. We simulate the robot and its environment using OGRE 3D graphics engine [8].

### 2.1 The Cognitive Model

Jean Piaget theory of cognitive development has four stages of a hierarchical process for acquisition of knowledge and skills [6]. Other cognitive processes were considered modular with respect to the processed information [9] or the neural substrates in which they operate [2], [3], [4]. Other evidences [10], [11] suggest the existence of transversal cognitive processes using the output from other processes to produce more elaborated results.

To reproduce animal behaviors, a computational model needs to cope with the features above. Pioneers models, [12], [13], [14] tried it, however, they succeed partially. Our cognitive model aims to support proposition and development of biologically inspired computational models.

The first layer of our model (Fig. 1) works with basic perceptive processes related with acquisition and representation of information from the sensorial flows. The second layer produces the concept of memory, storing and indexing the information

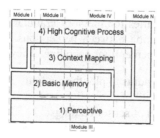

**Fig. 1.** The proposed cognitive model composed by hierarchical layers. Computational modules realizing specific tasks are defined across the layered structure.

produced by the first layer. The third layer is composed of maps binding the stored memories and sensorial information to form contexts, therefore, acting as an elaborated memory. The last layer uses the sensorial information with the stored knowledge and memories producing inferences, actions and behaviors.

## 2.2 The Basic Memory and Encoding Perceptions

We have defined the basic memory as neural substrates able to cluster and organize memories to represent perceptions without associating them with any special meaning. To obtain this artificial basic memory, the Growing Self-Organizing Surface Map (GSOSM) [15], [16] was employed. The GSOSM map is composed of interconnected nodes, each one storing a model vector that represents perceptions within a receptive field. GSOSM learns the input space topology producing a map covering all regions where the density probability function is positive. Some GSOSM characteristics make it a suitable choice to form the neural substrate: (i) no cycle counters; (ii) no error accumulators; (iii) incremental, fast and robust mapping; (iv) ability for indexed recovering of activated memories; and (v) granularity controlled by a single parameter.

GSOSM was originally proposed as a tool for surface reconstruction [15], [16] and then to act as a basic memory. We defined an activation function to determine the similarity between the current perception and the stored memories. This extended model, called Growing Topology Learning Self-Organizing Map (GTLSOM) is not grounded to a specific context. The memory activations are calculated as:

$$a = exp\left(-\frac{\|\omega - \xi\|^2}{2e_{max}^2}\right) \tag{1}$$

where $\omega$ is the stored model vector; $\xi$ is the vector of current perception; $\|\cdot\|$ is the Euclidean distance; and $e_{max}$ is the radius of receptive field of nodes.

The robot acquires information about the local environment layout using its lateral sensor devices. Then, we merged the readings in a circular bitmap image. To obtain translation invariance, the resultant image is repositioned considering its center of mass as image center. Then the perception vector was constructed with the first ten Zernike moments [17] of order greater than zero. Therefore, the perception vector is substantially lighter than the vectors of sensor readings. Moreover, the moments of Zernike present rotation invariance characteristic, allowing direct comparison between two geometric forms, without alignment to the beginning point.

Our topological map model needs three sets of parameters. The first one, for the basic memory, is composed by the GSOSM parameter set [16], being $e_{max}$ the main of them. This parameter specifies the memory granularity controlling its capacity of generalization and differentiation between perceptions. The second parameter set is employed into the process of perceptions encoding. They are:

- $r$ — circular image radius to plot the contour;
- $\hbar$ — the dimensionality of perception vector;
- $\psi$ — maximum depth of sensor readings;
- $\tau$ — a logic value concerning translation invariance.

The last parameter set controls the topological map formation:

- $\rho_{\mathcal{F}s_i}$ – the weight of each flow of perceptions, its value is one by default, however, it needs to be set if more of one perceptive flow is defined;
- $e^{tm}_{max}$ – the expected radius of the receptive field of Place Cells into the topological map;
- $\varepsilon_{min}$ – threshold of activation that fires the insertion of a new Place Cell;
- $\alpha$ – learning rate of the synapses linking memories to the Places Cells.
- $\gamma$ – the minimal activation required for the Place Cell that gives the notion of localization;

## 2.3 Place Cells

Each Place Cell refers to a place in the environment and to a set $\mathcal{L} = \{l_0, ..., l_j, ...\}$ of memories that are simultaneously activated forming a context.

*Determining the Place Cells Activity:* The incoming perceptions trigger the stored memories recall which is activated by (1). New cells have only some associated memories, and then their activations are maintained by vestibular information of displacement and direction changes. Moreover, in a local context the accumulation of integration errors could be considered as despicable. Therefore, using an integration system, the expected vestibular activation can be determined:

$$a^v_{\varsigma_{new}} = exp\left(\frac{-d^2}{2e_{max}{}^2}\right) \quad (2)$$

where $a_{\varsigma_v}$ is the estimated vestibular activation of a new cell $\varsigma_{new}$; $d$ is the estimated distance between the robot's actual position and that defining the center of the cell receptive field.

When the robot moves in the environment, it transfers itself from the receptive field of the current reference cell to the receptive field of another Place Cell. The incoming perceptions induce the activation and recovering of stored memories, and then Place Cells work as an associative memory linking places and perceptions. The recall of stored memories fires the Place Cell activation, a function of memories, $\mathcal{L}^{\mathcal{F}_i} = \{l_0, ..., l_j, ...\}$, activated by the perceptions coming from the $i$-$th$ perceptive flow $\mathcal{F}_i$.

$$a^l_{\varsigma_k} = \sum_i \frac{\sum_j \rho_{\mathcal{F}_i} \cdot i_c \cdot \varrho}{\sum \varrho} \, , \quad \varrho = \frac{1}{\sum(l_j, c)} \quad (3)$$

where $a^l_{\varsigma_k}$ is the activation of the Place Cell $\varsigma_k$; $\rho_{\mathcal{F}_i}$ is the weight of the perceptive flow $\mathcal{F}_i$; $i_c$ is the intensity of the signal emitted by the link between the recollected memory $l_j$ and the Place Cell; $\varrho$ is a measure of the perception singularity and $\sum(l_j, c)$ is the counted places associated to the recollected memory $l_j$.

The Place Cell activation needs a strategy to incorporate the vestibular information. When a cell $\varsigma_k$ wins a competition to be the reference cell for the notion of localization, the robot position is registered. Thereafter, the vestibular estimates of movement and direction changes forms a residual activation factor ($far$) which is calculated using (2) and setting $d$ as the estimated displacement.

If the robot moves towards the direction of Place Cell growth, the vestibular estimates are reinitialized, otherwise the residual activation factor is employed to calibrate it. To the cell $\varsigma_a$, the current notion of localization, the residual activation is:

$$a^r_{\varsigma_a} = arg\,max\left\{ a^{t_i}_{\varsigma_a}, ..., a^{t_j}_{\varsigma_a} \right\} \cdot far \qquad (4)$$

where $a^r_{\varsigma_a}$ is the residual activation of cell $\varsigma_a$; $t_i$ is the time in which $\varsigma_a$ won the competition and $t_j$ is the last time and before the present one.

The activation of the cell $\varsigma_a$ for the current time t $(t = t_j + 1)$ is determined by (5) and by (6) for the other cells.

$$a^t_{\varsigma_a} = \begin{cases} a^l_{\varsigma_a} & if\ a^l_{\varsigma_a} > arg\,max\left\{ a^{t_i}_{\varsigma_a}, ..., a^{t_j}_{\varsigma_a} \right\} \\ a^r_{\varsigma_a} & otherwise \end{cases} \qquad (5)$$

$$a^t_{\varsigma_k} = \begin{cases} a^l_{\varsigma_k} & if\ a^l_{\varsigma_k} > far \cdot a^{t-1}_{\varsigma_k} \\ far \cdot a^{t-1}_{\varsigma_k} & otherwise \end{cases} \qquad (6)$$

Equations (5) and (6) define an iterative process with memory, in which the cell activation propagates over the time. Moreover, action of body rotation could produce different perspectives to sensor devices without affect the activity of cell $\varsigma_a$.

*Inserting Place Cells:* The insertion of a new Place Cell obeys the criterion of a minimum distance, $d_{min} = 2\,e_{max}$, between centers of receptive fields.

The distance $d$ between the robot current position and the center of $\varsigma_a$ can be estimated from its current activation. Then, a new cell should be inserted when $a^t_{\varsigma_a} < \varepsilon_{min} \cong 0,135$ for $d = 2\,e_{max}$. After creating a new Place Cell, a connection is inserted between it and the cell $\varsigma_a$ and the new cell, $\varsigma_{new}$, becomes the reference cell for the notion of localization.

While moving in its environment the robot maintains a list $l_L$ of recollected memory sets. Such recollections should be linked to Place Cells forming contexts to place recognitions if the robot visits them again.

*Swapping the Notion of Localization:* The swapping of the reference point between Place Cells is a local competition defined by a function of the Place Cells activation and needs to satisfy three conditions: (i) the activation of candidate cell is larger than a threshold $\gamma$ ($a^t_{\varsigma_c} > \gamma$); (ii) the activation of candidate cell is larger than that of the actual reference cell ($a^t_{\varsigma_c} > a^t_{\varsigma_a}$); and (iii) the candidate cell $\varsigma_c$ is directly accessible starting from the current reference cell $\varsigma_a$.

Considering the Equation 2, if the robot moves beyond a circle of radius $e_{max}$ the activation of cell $\varsigma_a$ should becomes smaller than 0.6, which is the recommended value for parameter $\gamma$. The second condition is directly verifiable considering the list of candidate cells. The third condition involves remembering the list of visited places and reasoning considering the cognitive map. Therefore, the cognitive map should have shown some spatial organization. When creating the place cells, we used Cartesian estimates to bring topological organization to the map.

*Merging Place Cells:* The insertion of Place cells is made considering the estimated distance of robot to the current reference cell. Hence, it is possible that the center of the inserted cell is within the receptive field of another cell. The Equation 2 suggests that the merging process should be fired even when two cells presents activation levels larger than $\gamma$. However, places at different locations could be perceived as similar considering the robot's perception constraints. Then, the same three conditions applied to allow the swapping of reference cell are used here.

## 2.4 Building a Cognitive Topological Map of Environment

To produce a cognitive topological map of the environment, the robot acquires and organizes knowledge associating it to places. This process is composed of at least four steps: (i) acquisition and storage of perceptions about the environment; (ii) recovery of stored knowledge starting from the current perceptions; (iii) Association of stored knowledge with Place Cells; and (iv) organization of the Place Cells to produce an Extended Topological Map (Fig. 2 (i)).

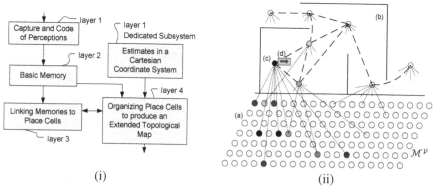

(i)                                    (ii)

**Fig. 2.** Structure of Topological Map Model: i) Diagram of blocks of the cognitive process; ii) Structure of the map: a) Basic memory of perceptions and its activation in gray levels; b) the basic layout of the environment; c) The Place Cells Map and its activation in gray levels as a function of activated memories; and d) the robot.

The first step is a process located at the first layer of our cognitive model, as described early. The subsystem of estimates is also a process located at that first layer and was assumed as ready. The second step uses a basic memory (Subsection 2.2) where the flow of perceptions induces the recollection of memories whose activations are propagated to Place Cells through synapses or links (Fig. 2 (ii)).

The third step produces a mapping selecting and linking recollected memories with places. This is a cognitive process located at the third layer of our cognitive model. Finally, the fourth step produces an Extended Topological Map $M^{te}$ creating and connecting Place Cells while using the estimates to organize it in an oriented graph. The algorithm of this process is the following:

```
1. For each sensor flow F^i
   • Construct a set of perceptions P;
   • Present P to the basic memory M^p, determining the set
     L_a of activated memories
   End_For;
```

2. If $M^{te} = \{\emptyset\}$
   - Create a new Place cell linking the memories in $\mathcal{L}_a$ to it;
   - Go to Step 1;
3. Insert $\mathcal{L}_a$ at the end of the list of recollected memories;

$$l_{\mathcal{L}} = l_{\mathcal{L}} \cup \{(\mathcal{L}_a, a_{\varsigma_a}, \mathbf{E})\} \tag{7}$$

where $l_{\mathcal{L}}$ is the list; $\mathcal{L}_a$ is the set of recollected memories at current position; $a_{\varsigma_a}$ is the activation level of the actual Place Cell; and $\mathbf{E} = [x, y, z]^T$ is the estimated position of $\varsigma_a$.

4. Determine the set $\zeta$ of the Place Cells activated by the memories;
   4.1. If the current reference cell $\varsigma_a$ is not in $\zeta$, add it;
5. Determine the activation level of $\varsigma_a$ and of the other Place Cells $\varsigma_k \in \zeta$, as Equations (5) and (6);
6. Run the merging operator considering the cell $\varsigma_a$ and each other cell $\varsigma_k \in \zeta$;
   6.1. If success, go to Step 1;
7. Run the operator of Localization Notion swap, considering the cell $\varsigma_a$ and each other cell $\varsigma_k \in \zeta$;
   7.1. If success, go to Step 1;
8. If $a_{\varsigma_a} < \varepsilon_{mim}$
   8.1. Run the operator of insertion of a new Place Cell;
9. Go to Step 1;
10.    End.

## 3  Simulations and Results

In this Section we present and discuss the results considering the robot navigating in a plane in a 3D environment.

*Setup:* These results were obtained in a simulated 3D environment employing virtual reality techniques. The dimensions of robot body were $l_1 = 32u, l_2 = 21u, l_3 = 21u$ ($u$=units of length) and its linear velocity was $v_l = 2\,u/s$ and $v_r = 2\,degree/s$ for body rotations. The parameters values for the laser sensor system were $gap = 180°$; step of sweep, $sw = 10°$; max depth $md = 800u$ and rotation sweep $rw = 0°$. The basic memory parameters were $k = 10$; $e_{max} = 10, 20, 40, 60\ and\ 80$; $\alpha = 0.005$; $\beta_{min} = 0,25$; $\theta_{min} = -0,342$; and the edges of KD-Tree hypercube were set to $\epsilon = 3e_{max}$. The perceptive flow $\mathcal{F}^{\wp}$ was for $\varpi = 400, r = 200, \tau = true$. The Topological Map algorithm parameters were $\rho_{\mathcal{F}^{\wp}} = 1,0$; $e_{max} = 10, 20\ and\ 30$; $\gamma = 0,6$; $\varepsilon_{min} = 0,1$; and $\alpha = 0,5$. Therefore, combining the values of parameters $e_{max}$ of the basic memory and of Topological Map, we had fifteen test cases.

*Results:* The results are presented in Table 1, where "$e_{max}^{\mathcal{M}^p}$" stands for the parameter $e_{max}$ of basic memory of perceptions and "$e_{max}^{M^{te}}$" stands for the value of $e_{max}$ for our Topological Map. The columns inform the maximum, minimum and average distance between the robot and the reference cell, the standard deviations are given in the respective columns SD.

The mean values are calculated considering each time instant, whereas the values before the swap consider only the instants immediately before the trade of reference cell. The column "Max" of first group reveals some reference cells remaining active even if the robot runs beyond its expected receptive field, indicating a larger area perceived as similar. However, the column "Avg" and "SD" shows a mean value within the cell receptive field. Moreover, the second group shows that the swap between reference cells occurs next to the areas where their receptive fields collide. However, SD values indicate that the process does not converge to a unique distance because the swap is controlled by the place recognition instead of the distance estimation.

**Table 1.** Distance between the robot and the reference cell

| $e_{max}^{Mp}$ | $e_{max}^{Mte}$ | The mean values | | | | Before swap of reference cell | | | |
|---|---|---|---|---|---|---|---|---|---|
| | | Min. | Max. | Avg. | SD. | Min. | Max. | Avg. | SD. |
| 10 | 10 | 0.0 | 66.8 | 11.3 | 7.0 | 0.3 | 19.9 | 13.0 | 4.8 |
| | 20 | 0.0 | 109.6 | 25.0 | 13.6 | 0.2 | 39.9 | 25.0 | 10.0 |
| | 30 | 0.0 | 148.7 | 31.4 | 19.8 | 1.2 | 59.9 | 37.6 | 15.1 |
| 20 | 10 | 0.0 | 65.1 | 12.5 | 6.8 | 0.2 | 19.9 | 14.3 | 4.6 |
| | 20 | 0.0 | 92.8 | 22.8 | 13.2 | 0.7 | 39.9 | 27.1 | 9.8 |
| | 30 | 0.0 | 126.5 | 32.3 | 18.4 | 2.2 | 59.9 | 41.0 | 14.3 |
| 40 | 10 | 0.0 | 99.8 | 13.5 | 8.3 | 0.1 | 19.9 | 14.4 | 4.6 |
| | 20 | 0.0 | 100.9 | 26.5 | 14.9 | 0.7 | 39.9 | 28.2 | 9.5 |
| | 30 | 0.0 | 155.7 | 36.0 | 20.3 | 1.1 | 59.9 | 41.9 | 14.5 |
| 60 | 10 | 0.0 | 157.3 | 15.6 | 11.1 | 0.4 | 19.9 | 14.9 | 4.6 |
| | 20 | 0.0 | 150.4 | 25.9 | 15.6 | 1.4 | 39.9 | 28.7 | 9.6 |
| | 30 | 0.0 | 159.8 | 38.7 | 23.9 | 0.2 | 59.9 | 42.1 | 15.0 |
| 80 | 10 | 0.0 | 239.6 | 19.7 | 20.2 | 0.7 | 19.9 | 15.1 | 4.6 |
| | 20 | 0.0 | 242.3 | 28.7 | 18.9 | 0.7 | 39.9 | 29.3 | 9.7 |
| | 30 | 0.0 | 201.5 | 41.6 | 25.9 | 0.5 | 59.9 | 42.2 | 14.8 |

The Visual inspection (Fig. 3) shows that the cognitive topological map covers the environment area visited by the robot. Note that the reference Place Cell is partially hidden by the body of robot. Also note the three circled groups of Place Cells, these cells shown activity for the current perceptions. Nonetheless, our algorithm was successful in choosing the correct one.

Table 2 shows the Place Cell distribution considering the distance between each cell and the respective closest neighbor. Note that for $e_{max}^{Mp} = 10$ we have a lot of intersecting cells because the basic memory is fine grained hindering the place recognition and therefore facilitating the insertion of new cells. The best results were obtained using $e_{max}^{Mp} = 20$ and $e_{max}^{Mp} = 40$ as shown the fourth and fifth columns. Whereas, using $e_{max}^{Mp} = 60$ and $e_{max}^{Mp} = 80$ increases the receptive field of Place Cells because a lot of perceptions are grouped into each memory cell. Then the robot recognizes a place considering only coarse features.

The singularity of a memory is a measure defined as the inverse of the number of associated Place Cells.

$$\varrho = \frac{1}{\Sigma(l_j, \varsigma)} \tag{8}$$

where $\varrho$ is the singularity measure and the term $(l_j, \varsigma)$ is used to denote a synapse between a memory $l_j$ and a Place Cell $\varsigma$.

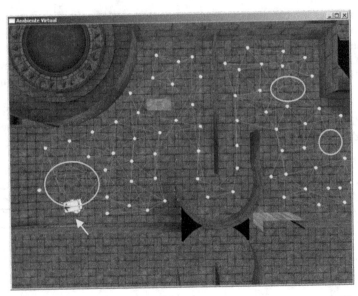

**Fig. 3.** Cognitive Topological map of Place Cells constructed by the robot while wandering into its environment using $e_{max}^{\mathcal{M}^p} = 40$ and $e_{max}^{Mte} = 20$.

**Table 2.** Distance between Place cells

| $e_{max}^{\mathcal{M}^p}$ | $e_{max}^{Mte}$ | Intervals in terms of $e_{max}^{Mte}$ | | | | | |
|---|---|---|---|---|---|---|---|
| | | $[0; 0.5]$ | $]...; 1]$ | $]...; 1.5]$ | $]...; 2]$ | $]...; 2.5]$ | $]2,5; ...[$ |
| 10 | 10 | 37.0 % | 41.1 % | 15.3 % | 5.3 % | 1.1 % | 0.3 % |
| | 20 | 26.1 % | 25.5 % | 18.3 % | 22.2 % | 7.8 % | 0.0 % |
| | 30 | 17.2 % | 27.6 % | 6.9 % | 24.1 % | 22.4 % | 1.7 % |
| 20 | 10 | 6.0 % | 16.1 % | 13.3 % | 44.0 % | 19.8 % | 0.8 % |
| | 20 | 4.1 % | 0.0 % | 5.1 % | 53.1 % | 36.7 % | 1.0 % |
| | 30 | 0.0 % | 0.0 % | 0.0 % | 66.0 % | 31.9 % | 2.1 % |
| 40 | 10 | 2.5 % | 6.0 % | 4.4 % | 49.7 % | 34.0 % | 3.5 % |
| | 20 | 0.0 % | 0.0 % | 2.2 % | 62.9 % | 33.7 % | 1.1 % |
| | 30 | 0.0 % | 0.0 % | 0.0 % | 54.3 % | 43.5 % | 2.2 % |
| 60 | 10 | 6.1 % | 11.3 % | 12.8 % | 39.3 % | 26.5 % | 4.0 % |
| | 20 | 2.2 % | 6.7 % | 5.6 % | 44.9 % | 37.1 % | 3.4 % |
| | 30 | 0.0 % | 0.0 % | 0.0 % | 32.6 % | 67.4 % | 0.0 % |
| 80 | 10 | 1.4 % | 13.1 % | 6.4 % | 40.3 % | 32.2 % | 6.7 % |
| | 20 | 0.0 % | 14.9 % | 5.7 % | 35.6 % | 39.1 % | 4.6 % |
| | 30 | 8.7 % | 6.5 % | 0.0 % | 39.1 % | 43.5 % | 2.2 % |

Table 3 report statistics of memories singularity considering $e_{max}^{\mathcal{M}^p}$ and $e_{max}^{Mte}$.

The columns show the number of nodes into the basic memory; the minimum, maximum and mean singularity values; the percentage of memories whose singularity measure is larger than the average; the median value, the percentage of memories whose singularity measure is larger than it; and the standard deviation of calculated singularities. The values in Table III are coherent with our previous observation.

There is inverse relation between the basic memory granularity and the recognition capacity for a place starting from the current perceptions.

**Table 3.** Sigularity Measures of Place cells

| $e_{max}^{Mp}$ | $e_{max}^{Mte}$ | Singularity = Memories X Associated Place Cells | | | | | | | |
|---|---|---|---|---|---|---|---|---|---|
| | | total | min | max | mean | %>mean | median | %>median | SD |
| 10 | 10 | 24.935 | 0.100 | 1.00 | 0.847 | 72.46 | 1.00 | - | 0.253 |
| | 20 | 24.829 | 0.167 | 1.00 | 0.873 | 76.13 | 1.00 | - | 0.230 |
| | 30 | 25.855 | 0.200 | 1.00 | 0.894 | 79.45 | 1.00 | - | 0.169 |
| 20 | 10 | 5.873 | 0.030 | 1.00 | 0.594 | 38.02 | 0.50 | 38.02 | 0.337 |
| | 20 | 6.179 | 0.059 | 1.00 | 0.630 | 40.08 | 0.50 | 40.08 | 0.317 |
| | 30 | 5.923 | 0.059 | 1.00 | 0.652 | 41.83 | 0.50 | 32.04 | 0.308 |
| 40 | 10 | 734 | 0.006 | 1.00 | 0.446 | 43.18 | 0.33 | 57.49 | 0.336 |
| | 20 | 736 | 0.016 | 1.00 | 0.481 | 48.37 | 0.33 | 65.35 | 0.320 |
| | 30 | 731 | 0.029 | 1.00 | 0.511 | 26.26 | 0.50 | 26.26 | 0.315 |
| 60 | 10 | 200 | 0.004 | 1.00 | 0.388 | 38.50 | 0.25 | 48.50 | 0.323 |
| | 20 | 198 | 0.015 | 1.00 | 0.421 | 39.39 | 0.33 | 55.05 | 0.313 |
| | 30 | 190 | 0.026 | 1.00 | 0.434 | 43.68 | 0.33 | 66.84 | 0.283 |
| 80 | 10 | 79 | 0.004 | 1.00 | 0.321 | 35.443 | 0.20 | 48.10 | 0.311 |
| | 20 | 78 | 0.012 | 1.00 | 0.350 | 35.897 | 0.33 | 55.13 | 0.242 |
| | 30 | 76 | 0.022 | 1.00 | 0.390 | 39.47 | 0.33 | 51.31 | 0.289 |

# 4   Conclusions

We have presented a new model of Cognitive Topological Map of Environment. We also detailed our approach considering its basic elements and operators. Finally, we have presented and discussed the obtained results. Now we argue that the main interesting characteristic of our model is its biological inspiration and functional plausibility. In our model, the robot acquires knowledge about objects in their environment. The stored knowledge reflects the mode as the robot perceives the environment starting from its sensor systems. Moreover, the process of place recognition is a function of recollections fired by its current perceptions. Our proposed model is very simple and does not have special or complex processes to construct its operators.

# References

[1] Ranvaud, R., Nehmzow, U.: The map concept in animal navigation. In: Proc. of Royal Institute of Navigation conference (2005)
[2] O'Keefe, J., Dostrovsky, J.: The Hippocampus as a spatial map. Preliminary evidence from unit activity in the freely moving rat. Brain Research 34(1), 171–175 (1971)
[3] Taube, J.S., Muller, R.U., Ranck, J.B.: Head-direction cells recorded from the postsubiculum in freely moving rats - II. Effects of Environmental Manipulations. J. of Neuroscience 10(2), 436–447 (1990)
[4] Hafting, T., Fyhn, M., Molden, S., Moser, M.-B., Moser, E.I.: Microstructure of a spatial map in the entorhinal cortex. Nature 436(7052), 801–806 (2005)
[5] McNaughton, B.L., Battaglia, F.P., Jensen, O., Moser, E.I., Moser, M.-B.: Path integration and the neural basis of the "cognitive map". Nature Reviews Neuroscience 7, 663–678 (2006)

[6] Gruber, H.E., Voneche, J.J.: The essential Piaget. Basic Books, New York (1977)

[7] Kuipers, B., Beeson, P., Modayil, J., Provost, J.: Bootstrap learning of foundational representations. Connection Science 18(2), 145–158 (2006)

[8] OGRE 3D graphics engine, http://www.ogre3d.org

[9] Scholl, B., Leslie, A.: Modularity, development and theory of mind. Mind and Language 14(1), 131–153 (1999)

[10] McClamrock, R.: Holism without tears: local and global effects in cognitive processes. Philosophy of Science 56, 258–274 (1989)

[11] Fodor, J.A.: The Mind Doesn't Work That Way: The Scope and Limits of Computational Psycology. Theory & Psichology 13, 142–144 (2003)

[12] Kuipers, B.: The spatial semantic hierarchy. J. Artificial Intelligence 119, 191–233 (2000)

[13] Vasudevan, S., Nguyen, V., Siegwart, R.: Towards a cognitive probabilistic representation of space for mobile robots. In: Proc. of IEEE Int. Conf. on Inf. Acquisition, ICIA 2006, pp. 353–359 (2006)

[14] Weng, J.J., Hwang, W.-S.: From Neural Networks to the Brain: Autonomous Mental Development. IEEE Computational Intelligence Magazine, 15–31 (2006)

[15] DalleMole, V.L., Araújo, A.F.R.: The growing Self-organizing surface Map. In: Proc. IEEE Int. Joint Conf. on Neural Networks, pp. 2061–2068 (2008)

[16] DalleMole, V.L., Araújo, A.F.R.: Growing Self-Organizing Surface Map: learning a surface topology from a point cloud. Neural Computation 22(3), 689–729 (2010)

[17] Bailey, R.R., Srinath, M.D.: Orthogonal moment features for use with parametric and nonparametric classifiers. IEEE Trans. on Pattern Analysis and Machine Intelligence 18(4), 389–399 (1996)

# Hybrid Control Structure for Multi-robot Formation

Daniela Cernega and Razvan Solea

Department of Control Systems and Industrial Informatics,
Computer Science Faculty, "Dunarea de Jos" University of Galati,
Domneasca 47, 800008, Galati, Romania
{Daniela.Cernega, Razvan.Solea}@ugal.ro

**Abstract.** In this paper a hybrid control structure to control a multi-robot formation is proposed. The hybrid control structure consists of two control levels: the discrete control level and the continuous control level. The discrete control level ensures the supervisory control and the continuous control level ensures the trajectory tracking control. The trajectory tracking problem is solved using the sliding mode control. The syntheses of the supervisor and of the sliding mode controllers for each discrete state are presented. Simulation example is used to evaluate the sliding-mode algorithm and to show the application of the algorithm in practice. The controller is simply structured and easy to implement.

**Keywords:** Hybrid control, Sliding-mode control, Multi-robot formation control.

## 1 Introduction

The multi robots systems is an important robotics research field. Such systems are of interest for many reasons; tasks could be too complex for a simple robot to accomplish; using several simple robots can be easier, cheaper and more flexible than a single powerful robot [1], [2], [3], [4].

Formation control has been one of the important research topics in multiple robot systems as it is applicable to many areas such as geographical exploration, rescue operations, surveillance, mine sweeping, and transportation. Different approaches have been developed recently, for example, behavior-based control, LQ control, visual servoing control, Lyapunov-based control, input and output feedback linearization control, graph theory, and nonlinear control.

In leader-follower formation control, the most widely used control technique is feedback linearization based on the kinematics model of the system.

In this study the hybrid leader-follower robot formation control is considered. The referenced robot is called *leader*, and the robot following it, is called *follower*. Thus, there are many pairs of leaders and followers and complex formations can be achieved by controlling relative positions of these pairs of robots respectively. This approach is characterized by simplicity, reliability and no need for global knowledge and computation.

The hybrid control structure consists of two levels: the discrete control level implementing the supervisory control, and the numerical control level using a sliding-mode controller to solve the trajectory tracking problem.

K. Diamantaras, W. Duch, L.S. Iliadis (Eds.): ICANN 2010, Part II, LNCS 6353, pp. 307–316, 2010.
© Springer-Verlag Berlin Heidelberg 2010

To control a multi-robot formation as a discrete event system means to follow a desired behavior described through the imposed constraints. The desired behavior is modeled as discrete event system for the entire formation and a supervisor is designed to achieve this behavior. The approach used to design the supervisor is proposed in [5], and in [6].

The discrete control level is coupled with the numerical control level and it detects the functioning situations. Each functioning situation is a discrete state. Each discrete state is characterized with a continuous model as shown in [7]. For each of the situations detected at the discrete event level the appropriate continuous model is selected together with the corresponding continuous controller. For each discrete state the references of the corresponding continuous controllers are also established.

The model for a hybrid automaton (HA), is defined with:

$$HA = \left( X, Q, \mu_1, \mu_2, \Sigma, \mu_3, Q_0, Q_f \right) \tag{1}$$

where: $X$ is the vector space of the system state $x$, the continuous state vector of the system, denoted by $x = [x_1...x_n]^T \in X$, supposed to be continuous observable vector; $Q$ the set of discrete states corresponding to all the possible phases, $Q = \{q_i, i=1...m\}$; the hybrid state of the system is defined within the pair $(x, l) \in X \times Q$; $\mu_1$ is the set of the $m$ vector fields associated to each discrete phase; $\mu_2$ is the set of the constraints associated to each discrete phase; $\Sigma$ is the set of the events; $\mu_3$ is the set of functions associated with the events; $Q_0$ is the set of the initial states and $Q_f$ is the set of final sates.

In the next section the hybrid control system is presented. The discrete dynamic event system model for the multi-robot formation is obtained. The supervisor to ensure the desired behavior of the system is designed. The continuous models for each discrete state are also presented.

The wheeled mobile robot is a nonlinear system. The continuous control level is dedicated to the trajectory tracking control [8] - [12]. The trajectory tracking control problem is solved using the sliding mode control. In the Section 4 this problem is solved and the control laws together with the references for the discrete states are obtained. Section 5 is dedicated to the results obtained after implementing this hybrid structure.

## 2 The Hybrid Control Structure

The hybrid control structure proposed in this paper is shown in Fig.1.

To control the multi-robot formation as a discrete event system leads to a supervisor design. The discrete event model used is the automaton called $G$, defined as follows:

$$G = (Q, \Sigma, \delta, q_0, Q_m) \tag{2}$$

where Q is the set of the discrete states physically possible of the system, $\Sigma$ is the set of all the events, $\delta$ is the transition function of the automaton, $q_0$ is the initial state and $Q_m$ is the set of the marked states of the system. The events in the follow the leader-formation are from two distinctive categories: $\Sigma_u$ is the set of the uncontrollable events and $\Sigma_c$ is the controllable events set. The controllable events are subject of the

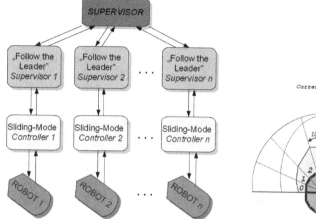

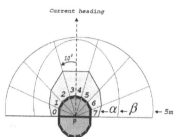

**Fig. 1.** Hybrid Control Structure

**Fig. 2.** The sensitivity sphere of robot

control action and these events can be enabled and disabled at any time i.e. from any state. The uncontrollable events cannot be enabled or disabled by the control action.

Supervisory control for this discrete event system has the objective to ensure the desired behavior of the follower robot according to some constraints imposed.

The supervisor design for this problem is based on sonar data. The *sensitivity sphere* is a concept defined in order to establish the smallest distance equal to the length of the *follower* robot in order to avoid collision with the *leader* or with other obstacles. The sensitivity sphere is represented in Fig. 2.

The analysis of the robot motion according to the defined sensitivity sphere, for this problem generates seven cases:

-*Case 1*: the sonar 3 and 4 detect an object inside the sensitivity sphere and the robot will receive references to move ahead;

-*Case2*: sonar 2 and 3 detect an object inside the sensitivity sphere and the supervisor generates references for the robot motion the constant distance $d$ and the angle $\alpha$;

- *case3*: sonar 4 and 5 detect an object inside the sensitivity sphere and the supervisor generates references for the robot motion the constant distance $d$ and the angle $-\alpha$;

-*Case4*: sonar 1 and 2 detect an object inside the sensitivity sphere and the supervisor generates references for the robot motion the constant distance $d$ and the angle $2\alpha$;

-*Cas5*: sonar 5 and 6 detect an object inside the sensitivity sphere and the supervisor generates references for the robot motion the constant distance $d$ and the angle $-2\alpha$;

-*Case6*: any sonar detects an object inside the sensitivity sphere closer then the minimum allowed distance and the supervisor generates references for the robot to stop;

-*Case7*: no sonar pair detects an object and the supervisor generates references for the robot circular motion in order to search the leader.

These cases are generating the discrete states set, Q, of the automaton $G$, model of the process defined in (2).

The objective of the supervisory control for the *follower* is to track the *leader* when in the environment there are some unknown obstacles identified within the sensitivity sphere, or another leader appears inside the sensitivity zone. The discrete events generating discrete state transitions in this system are:

- $\Sigma_c = \{\ e_{c0},\ e_{c1},\ e_{c2},\ e_{c3},\ e_{c4}\}$, where $e_{c0}$ - the *start* command, $e_{c1}$ - the distance established between the two robots is respected, $e_{c2}$ – start the distance evaluation, $e_{c3}$ – command the robot movement with speed references inside the established limits, $e_{c4}$ - the sonar data are valid;

- $\Sigma_u = \{e_1,\ e_{u1},\ e_{u2},\ e_{u3},\ e_{u4}\}$, where $e_1$ - end initialization, $e_{u1}$ - an obstacle appeared in the interior of the sensitivity sphere, $e_{u2}$ the leader is lost, $e_{u3}$ reading errors from sonar detected, $e_{u4}$ another leader appeared inside the sensitivity sphere.

The discrete state set, Q contains the states defined as follows: $q_1$ robot initialization; $q_2$ sonar reading; $q_3$ nearest limit verification for all the sonar; $q_4$ data analysis from sonar 3 and 4; $q_5$ trajectory tracking algorithm for *case 1*, $q_6$ movement according to *case1* references, $q_7$ data analysis from sonar 2 and 3, $q_8$ trajectory tracking algorithm for *case 2*, $q_9$ movement according to *case2* references; $q_{10}$ data analysis from sonar 4 and 5; $q_{11}$ trajectory tracking algorithm for *case 3*; $q_{12}$ movement according to *case3* references; $q_{13}$ data analysis from sonar 1 and 2, $q_{14}$ trajectory tracking algorithm for *case 4*, $q_{15}$ movement according to *case4* references, $q_{16}$ data analysis from sonar 5 and 6, $q_{17}$ trajectory tracking algorithm for *case 5*, $q_{18}$ movement according to *case5* references, $q_{19}$ 180 degrees rotation, $q_{20}$ STOP, $q_{21}$ corresponds to the situation when an obstacle appears inside the sensitivity sphere during the movement corresponding to one the states $q_6$, $q_9$, $q_{12}$, $q_{15}$, $q_{18}$; this state provides the supervisor the ability to avoid collisions, $q_{22}$ is the state to be avoided with the supervisor control: the collision state.

The transition function, δ, of the automaton is represented in figure 3.

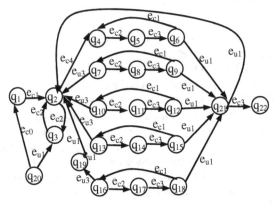

**Fig. 3.** The automaton *G*, model of the discrete event system

## 3  Leader-Following Formation Models

Figure 4 is a leader-following control model where the formation pattern is specified by the separate distance $d$ and the relative bearing $\psi$ for two robots $r_1$ and $r_2$. The desired formation pattern can be defined as the desired separate distance $d^d$ and the relative bearing $\psi^d$. The follower $r_2$ regulates the formation state errors of the separate distance and the relative bearing through its speed control signals $u_{r2} = [v_{xr2} \; \omega_{r2}]^T$.

$$
\begin{bmatrix} \tilde{d} \\ \tilde{\psi} \end{bmatrix} = \begin{bmatrix} d^d \\ \psi^d \end{bmatrix} - \begin{bmatrix} d \\ \psi \end{bmatrix}
\tag{3}
$$

The relative distance between the leader and the follower robot is denoted as $d$, the separation bearing angle is $\psi$, and they are given by:

$$
d = \sqrt{(x_{r1} - x_{c2})^2 + (y_{r1} - y_{c2})^2} \; ; \quad \psi = \pi - [\theta_{r1} - \arctan 2(y_{r1} - y_{c2}, x_{r1} - x_{c2})]
\tag{4}
$$

where: 
$$
x_{c2} = x_{r2} + l \cdot \cos(\theta_{r2}), \quad y_{c2} = y_{r2} + l \cdot \sin(\theta_{r2})
\tag{5}
$$

The formation control can be investigated by modeling the formation state error as follows [13]:

$$
\begin{bmatrix} \dot{\tilde{d}} \\ \dot{\tilde{\psi}} \end{bmatrix} = G \cdot u_{r2} + F \cdot u_{r1}, \quad \dot{\phi} = \omega_{r1} - \omega_{r2}
\tag{6}
$$

and $G = \begin{bmatrix} -\cos(\phi+\psi) & -l \cdot \sin(\phi+\psi) \\ \dfrac{\sin(\phi+\psi)}{d} & -\dfrac{l \cdot \cos(\phi+\psi)}{d} \end{bmatrix}$, $F = \begin{bmatrix} \cos(\psi) & 0 \\ -\dfrac{\sin(\psi)}{d} & 1 \end{bmatrix}$

where: $u_{ri} = [v_{ri} \; \omega_{ri}]^T$, $\phi = \theta_{r1} - \theta_{r2}$ and $l$ is the distance between the robot position $(x_{r2}, y_{r2})$ and the robot hand position $(x_{c2}, y_{c2})$ as shown in Fig. 4.

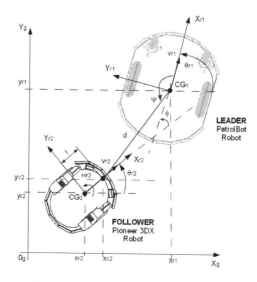

**Fig. 4.** Leader-following formation models

## 4  Sliding-Mode Controller Design

In a leader-follower configuration, with the leader's position given and once the follower's relative distance and angle with respect to the leader are known, the follower's position can be determined. To use the leader-following approach, it is assumed that the angular and linear velocities of the leader are known. In order to achieve and maintain the desired formation between the leader and follower, it is only need to control the follower's angular and linear velocities to achieve the relative distance and angle between them as specified. Therefore, the leader-following based mobile robot formation control can be considered as an extension of the tracking control problem of the nonholonomic mobile robot.

A practical form of reaching the control law (proposed by Gao and Hung [14]) is defined as:

$$\dot{s}_i = -p_i \cdot s_i - q_i \cdot \text{sgn}(s_i), \quad p_i, q_i > 0, \quad i = 1, 2. \tag{7}$$

By adding the proportional rate term $-p_i \cdot s_i$, the state is forced to approach the switching manifolds faster when $s_i$ is large. It can be shown that the reaching time for $x$ to move from an initial state $x_0$ to the switching manifold $s_i$ is finite, and is given by

$t_i = \dfrac{1}{p_i} \cdot \ln \dfrac{p_i |s_i| + q_i}{q_i}$. A new design of sliding surface is proposed, such that distance between the leader and the follower robot, $d$, and the separation bearing angle, $\psi$, are internally coupled with each other in a sliding surface leading to convergence of both variables. For that purpose the following sliding surfaces is proposed:

$$s_1 = \dot{\tilde{d}} + k_d \cdot \tilde{d} \; ; \qquad s_2 = \dot{\tilde{\psi}} + k_\psi \cdot \tilde{\psi} + k_0 \cdot \text{sgn}(\tilde{\psi}) \cdot |\phi| \tag{8}$$

where $k_0$, $k_d$ and $k_\psi$ are positive constant parameters and $\tilde{d}, \tilde{\psi}, \phi$ are defined by (3).

If $s_1$ converge to zero, trivially $\tilde{d}$ converge to zero. If $s_2$ converge to zero, in steady-state it becomes $\dot{\tilde{\psi}} = -k_\psi \cdot \tilde{\psi} - k_0 \cdot \text{sgn}(\tilde{\psi}) \cdot |\phi|$. Since $|\phi|$ is always bounded, the following relationship between $\tilde{\psi}$ and $\dot{\tilde{\psi}}$ holds: IF $\tilde{\psi} < 0 \Rightarrow \dot{\tilde{\psi}} > 0$ and IF $\tilde{\psi} > 0 \Rightarrow \dot{\tilde{\psi}} < 0$.

From the time derivative of (8) and using the reaching law defined in (7) yields:

$$\dot{s}_1 = \ddot{\tilde{d}} + k_d \cdot \dot{\tilde{d}} = -p_1 \cdot s_1 - q_1 \cdot \text{sgn}(s_1) \tag{9}$$

$$\dot{s}_2 = \ddot{\tilde{\psi}} + k_\psi \cdot \dot{\tilde{\psi}} + k_0 \cdot \text{sgn}(\tilde{\psi}) \cdot \text{sgn}(\phi) \cdot \dot{\phi} = -p_2 \cdot s_2 - q_2 \cdot \text{sgn}(s_2) \tag{10}$$

After some mathematical manipulation, one can achieve:

$$\dot{v}_{c2} = \frac{p_1 \cdot s_1 + q_1 \cdot \text{sgn}(s_1) + k_d \cdot \dot{\tilde{d}} - C_1}{\cos(\phi + \psi)} \; ; \quad \dot{\omega}_{c2} = \frac{\left(p_2 \cdot s_2 + q_2 \cdot \text{sgn}(s_2) + k_\psi \cdot \dot{\tilde{\psi}}\right) \cdot d - C_2}{l \cdot \cos(\phi + \psi)} \tag{11}$$

where

$$C_1 = l \cdot \dot{\omega}_{r2} \cdot \sin(\phi + \psi) - d \cdot (\dot{\phi} + \psi) \cdot (\psi + \omega_{r1}) - \dot{v}_{r1} \cdot \cos(\psi) - v_{r1} \cdot \dot{\phi} \cdot \sin(\psi)$$

$$C_2 = k_0 \cdot \text{sgn}(\tilde{\psi} \cdot \phi) \cdot \dot{\phi} \cdot d - \dot{v}_{r2} \cdot \sin(\phi + \psi) + d \cdot (\dot{\phi} + \psi) \cdot (\psi + \omega_{r1}) -$$
$$- \dot{v}_{r1} \cdot \cos(\psi) - v_{r1} \cdot \dot{\phi} \cdot \sin(\psi)$$

The *sgn* functions in the sliding surface were replaced by *saturation* functions, to reduce the chattering phenomenon [15].

# 5 Simulation Results

In this section, some simulation results are presented to validate the proposed control law. To show the effectiveness of the proposed sliding mode control law numerically, experiments were carried out on the multi-robot formation control problem.

High-level control algorithms (including desired motion generation) are written in C++ and run with a sampling time of Ts = 100 ms on a embedded PC, which also provides a user interface with real-time visualization and a simulation environment.

All the simulations were made using the MobileSim. MobileSim is a software for simulating MobileRobots' platforms and their environments, for debugging and experimentation with ARIA. The ARIA software can be used to control the mobile robots like Pionner, PatrolBot, PeopleBot, Seekur etc. ARIA (Advanced Robot Interface for Applications) it is an object-oriented Applications Programming Interface (API), written in C++ and intended for the creation of intelligent high-level client-side software.

Figure 5 shows a block diagram of the proposed sliding-mode controller.

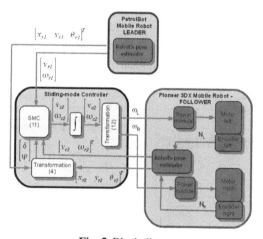

**Fig. 5.** Block diagram

Wheel velocity commands,  $\omega_R = \dfrac{v_{c2} + L \cdot \omega_{c2}}{R}$;  $\omega_L = \dfrac{v_{c2} - L \cdot \omega_{c2}}{R}$  (12)

are sent to the power modules of the follower mobile robot, and encoder measures $N_R$ and $N_L$ are received in the robots pose estimator for odometric computations.

Two simulation experiments were carried out to evaluate the performance of the sliding mode controller presented in Section 4. The first simulation refers to the case of circular trajectory ($v_{r1} = 0.4$ [m/s] and $w_{r1} = 0.1$ [rad/s]). The initial conditions of the leader and the follower are, $x_{r1}(0) = 0$ , $y_{r1}(0) = 0$, $\theta_{r1}(0) = 0$, $x_{r2}(0) = -1$, $y_{r2}(0) = -1$, $\theta_{r1}(0) = 0$, $d^d = 1$ [m], $\psi^d = 135$[deg] (see Fig. 6).

In the second simulation the leader robot execute a linear trajectory but with a non-zero initial orientation ($\theta_{r1} = 45$ [deg]). The initial conditions of the leader and the follower in this second case are, $x_{r1}(0) = 0$, $y_{r1}(0) = 0$, $\theta_{r1}(0) = pi/4$, $x_{r2}(0) = -1$, $y_{r2}(0) = -1$, $\theta_{r2}(0) = 0$, $d^d = 1$ [m], $\psi^d = 120$ [deg] (see Fig. 6).

The good performance for controlling the formation with the developed control law can be observed from Figs. 6 - 9. The outputs of the formation system ($\tilde{d}$ and $\tilde{\psi}$ ) asymptotically converge to zero, as shown in Figs. 8 and 9.

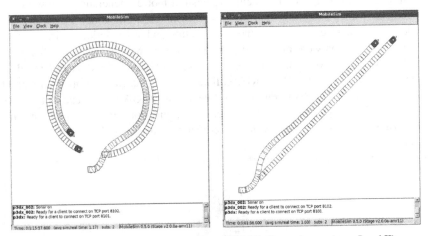

**Fig. 6.** Simulation results using Aria and MobileSim software (case I and II)

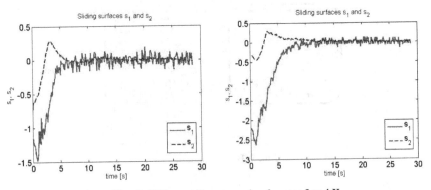

**Fig. 7.** Sliding surfaces $s_1$ and $s_2$ for case I and II

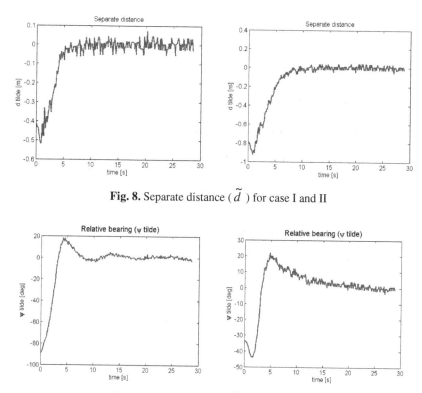

**Fig. 8.** Separate distance ($\tilde{d}$ ) for case I and II

**Fig. 9.** Relative bearing ($\tilde{\psi}$ ) for case I and II

# 6 Conclusions

In this study a hybrid control structure to control a multi-robot formation is proposed. The hybrid control structure consists of two control levels: the discrete control level and the continuous control level. The discrete control level ensures the supervisory control and the continuous control level ensures the trajectory tracking control.

The desired formation, defined by two parameters (a distance and an orientation function) is allowed to vary in time. The effectiveness of the proposed designs have validated via simulation experiments.

Simulation example is used to evaluate the sliding-mode algorithm and to show the application of the algorithm in practice. The controller is simply structured and easy to implement. From the simulation results, it is concluded that the proposed strategy achieves the effectiveness of desired performance.

Future research lines include the experimental validation of our control scheme and the extension of our results to skid-steering mobile robots. For the sake of simplicity in the present paper a single-leader, single follower formation has been considered. Future investigations will cover the more general case of multi leader, multi-follower formations.

**Acknowledgments.** This work was supported by CNCSIS-UEFISCSU, project PNII-IDEI 506/2008.

# References

1. Murray, R.M.: Recent research in cooperative control of multi-vehicle systems. Journal of Dynamic Systems, Measurement and Control 129(5), 571–583 (2007)
2. Klancar, G., Matko, D., Blazic, S.: Wheeled mobile robots control in a linear platoon. Journal of Intelligent and Robotic Systems 54(5), 709–731 (2009)
3. Mazo, M., Speranzon, A., Johansson, K., Hu, X.: Multi-robot tracking of a moving object using directional sensors. In: IEEE International Conference on Robotics and Automation, ICRA 2004, vol. 2, pp. 1103–1108 (2004)
4. Zavlanos, M.M., Pappas, G.J.: Dynamic assignment in distributed motion planning with local coordination. IEEE Transaction on Robotics 24(1), 232–242 (2008)
5. Ramadge, P.J., Wonham, W.M.: Supervisory control of a class of discrete event processes. SIAM J. of Control Optim. 25(1), 206–230 (1987)
6. Queiroz, M.H., Cury, J.E., Wonham, W.M.: Multitasking Supervisory Control of Discrete-Event Systems. Discrete Event Dynamic Systems 15(4) (2005)
7. Antsaklis, P.J., Nerode, A.: Hybrid Control Systems: An Introductory Discussion to the Special Issue. IEEE Trans. on AC 43(4), 457–460 (1998)
8. Chwa, D.: Sliding-mode tracking control of nonholonomic wheeled mobile robots in polar coordinates. IEEE Transactions on Control 12(4), 637–644 (2004)
9. Yang, J.-M., Kim, J.-H.: Sliding mode control for trajectory tracking of nonholonomic wheeled mobile robots. IEEE Transactions on Robotics and Automation 15(3), 578–587 (1999)
10. Floquet, T., Barbot, J.P., Perruquetti, W.: Higher-order sliding mode stabilization for a class of nonholonomic perturbed systems. Automatica 39(6), 1077–1083 (2003)
11. Solea, R., Cernega, D.: Sliding mode control for trajectory tracking problem - performance evaluation. In: Alippi, C., Polycarpou, M., Panayiotou, C., Ellinas, G. (eds.) ICANN 2009. LNCS, vol. 5769, pp. 865–874. Springer, Heidelberg (2009)
12. Solea, R., Nunes, U.: Trajectory planning and sliding-mode control based trajectory-tracking for cybercars. Aided Engineering 14(1), 33–47 (2007)
13. Das, A., Fierro, R., Kumar, V., Ostrowski, J., Spletzer, J., Taylor, C.: A vision-based formation control framework. IEEE Transactions on Robotics and Automation 18(5), 813–825 (2002)
14. Gao, W., Hung, J.C.: Variable structure control of nonlinear systems: A new approach. IEEE Transactions on Industrial Electronics 40(1), 45–55 (1993)
15. Slotine, J.J.E., Li, W.: Applied nonlinear control. Prentice-Hall, Englewood Cliffs (1991)

# From Conditioning of a Non Specific Sensor to Emotional Regulation of Behavior

Cyril Hasson and Philippe Gaussier

Cergy-Pontoise University, CNRS, ENSEA
ETIS laboratory UMR 8051, F-95000

**Abstract.** Inspired by the emotional conditionings performed by the amygdala, we describe a simulated neural network able to learn the meaning of a previously neutral stimulation. A robot using this neural network can learn the conditioning of a non specific sensor activated by the experimentator and its internal state of pain or pleasure. This biologically inspired adaptive and natural way to interact with the robot is tested with a mobile robot learning navigation tasks in a real environment.

## 1 Introduction

This study focuses on the interest of an adaptative and biologically plausible neural network used to interact with a robot in a non predifined but meaningfull way. The ability to give a meaning to a non specific stimulation is used by the robot as a source of information to improve its behavior. This learning by interaction mechanism is congruent with neurobiological studies of emotional conditioning. A large number of studies have shown the implication of the amygdala in emotional conditioning [13] and specifically for both aversive [6,9] and appetitive [5,4] emotionally conditioned behaviors. Anatomical studies [18] have also shown that the amygdala afferent neural pathways are carrying information for both aversive and appetitive events. The main role of amygdala is to give a positive or negative emotional valence to incoming stimulations [17]. Among the many functions of these emotional conditionings, one is to use them to regulate neuromodulation of learning. Computational models of these mechanisms can be found in [2,14]. If the robot is able to express its positive or negative emotional internal state, interactions with the experimentator can teach it the meaning of the stimulation of a sensor through classical conditioning [21,20,19]. Later activation of this sensor can then be used as an external source of positive or negative rewards [3,8]. Our aim is to illustrate the potential of this interactive learning neural network in situations of interaction between the robot and the human. In homing tasks, the robot can easily get lost when moving outside the attraction basin build around the goal. Though, conditioning a non specific sensor to the expression of an internal state of pain or pleasure allows the experimentator to reinforce (positively or negatively) the robot's behavior interactively and teach it to reach the goal. Figure 1 shows the robot and its environment. Section 2 describes the robot sensorimotor navigation and motivation system. Results from

K. Diamantaras, W. Duch, L.S. Iliadis (Eds.): ICANN 2010, Part II, LNCS 6353, pp. 317–326, 2010.

**Fig. 1.** The experimental set-up. The environment is a 6m x 8m area. The robot is a Robulab 10 from Robosoft with a 360 degree pan camera and a magnetic compass.

robotic experiments with traditional supervised learning are shown in section 3. Section 4 describes how to give a meaning to a non specific sensor. Results from robotic experiments with interactive learning using the conditioning of the non specific sensor are shown in section 5. Section 6 contains the discussion.

## 2   Motivated Sensorimotor Navigation

Following the animat appraoch [7], the robot is viewed as an animal motivated to survive by fullfilling its needs [16]. The robot must maintain a set of artificial physiological variables inside safe levels. It has to find in its environment the simulated resource corresponding to its active motivation. When one of these variables gets too low, a pain signal is produced and expressed on a display screen as a corresponding iconic face. Similarly, when the robot finds and consumes a resource it was looking for, a pleasure signal is produced and expressed. The navigation architecture is based on sensorimotor visuo-motor learning [11, 12] inspired by neurobiological models of rodent visual navigation [10,15]. The robot has to manage raw sensory inputs to construct real environment place cells.

**Synthetic physiology and motivational system:** A synthetic physiology simulates the physiological variables dynamical evolution (e.g. food level). These variables levels decrease with time (as the robot consumes its internal resources) and increase by recolting the corresponding simulated resource. Figure 2 describes this system. A low-level drive system reacts to the physiological state perception e.g. as food level gets low, hunger drive gets high. A distinction is made between the inner drives, drives as they are computed directly from the physiological variables levels, and integrated drives, temporal integration of the inner drives. The integrated drives offer the possibility to modulate drives according to higher order sources of information without manipulating the physiological state of the system. The most active drive dictates the robot's behaviour. When a needed resource is detected, the corresponding physiological variable level increases and the temporal integration of the corresponding drive is reset to 0. A pain signal (equation 1) is produced if the level of one physiological variable is critically low (below a definite threshold). A pleasure signal (equation 2)

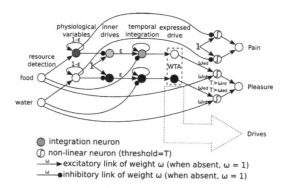

**Fig. 2.** Physiological variables levels decrease with time. Inner drives are the complementary values of physiological variables levels. Integrated drives can be manipulated whitout affecting the inner states of the system and the expressed drive is the most active integrated drive. Pain results from the criticaly low level of a physiological variable and pleasure from the satisfaction of an active drive.

is produced when consumption of a resource satisfies a physiological need. A display interface, allows the robot to express visually, via prototypical expressions of anger and joy, its internal state of pain and pleasure.

$$Pain = \begin{cases} 1 & if \ PV_n(t) \ < \ pain \ threshold \\ 0 & otherwise \end{cases} \tag{1}$$

$$Pleasure = \begin{cases} 1 & if \ R_{detect} * \omega_{rd} + D_r * \omega_{wd} > pleasure \ threshold \\ 0 & otherwise \end{cases} \tag{2}$$

$PV_n(t)$ is the level of the physiological variable $n$ at time t .The pain threshold is a fixed low value. $R_{detect}$ equals 1 when the resource $R$ is detected and $D_r$ equals 1 when the drive corresponding to resource $R$ is active. Pleasure threshold is higher than both $\omega_{rd}$ (connection weight from resource detection) and $\omega_{wd}$ (connection weight from the winner drive) acting as an "AND" operator.

**Visual navigation:** The visual system is a simulated neural network able to characterize different places of the environment learning place cells [15] i.e. neurons that code information about a constellation of local views (visual cues) and their azimuths from of a specific place in that environment [12]. Place cells activity depend on the recognition levels of these visual cues and of their locations. A place cell will then be more and more active as the robot gets closer to its learning location. Associative learning allows sensorimotor learning (place-action groups on figure 3). Place cells are associated with the goal direction to build a visual attraction bassin around the goal. Due to the generalization property of place cells, only a few place cells are necessary to construct an attraction basin.

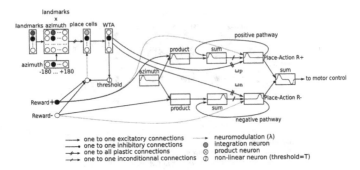

**Fig. 3.** Sensorimotor visual navigation : a visual place cell is constructed from recognition of a specific landmarks-azimuths pattern and an action (a direction) is associated to it. When one neuron of the Place-Action group receives a neuromodulation from the reward (positive reward in this example), it learns the association between the current robot location and its direction. The positive conditioning group activates the learned direction while the negative conditioning inhibits the learned direction.

## 3    Robotic Experiments: Results and Limitations of the Supervised Learning

The environment contains one simulated resource (specific color on the ground). A supervised procedure allows the robot to learn sensorimotor associations (place-actions) around the resource. If the action associated with each place cell is a movement in direction of the resource, an attraction basin is constructed. As long as the robot is in the attraction basin, it can discriminate correctly the different learned places and its actions will lead it to the resource. However, if the robot is too far away from the resource it needs and thus from the associated learned places, it is not able to discriminate them correctly. Figure 4 shows the robot trajectories. When it is placed inside the attraction basin, the robot reachs the resource. When it is placed too far away from the places it has learned, the robot is lost. Being lost, the robot navigation is similar to a random navigation. The robot thus needs a mecanism to extend the frontiers of the attraction basin it has learned.

## 4    Learning a Reinforcement Signal via Stimulation of a Non-specific Sensor

Looking at the robot performing its task, the experimentator is able to evaluate if the robot is doing well or badly i.e. going toward or away from the needed resource. While the robot is lost, reinforcing its actions positively when it is heading toward its goal or negatively otherwise, is a natural, interactive and less constraintfull way to teach the robot to perform a given task than totally supervised learning. But in order to do so, the robot has to learn what is a positive or a negative reinforcement. Our objective is to show that the robot can

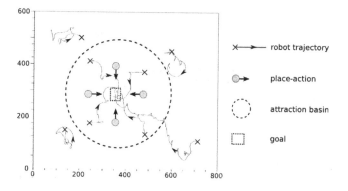

**Fig. 4.** Trajectories of the robot. Place-action associations are learned 0.8 meter from the goal and the attraction basin is approximately 4 meters wide. When the robot is inside its attraction basins, it successfully navigates toward its goal. Outside the attraction basin the robot is lost. Even with this raw strategy, the robot sometimes reachs the attraction basin (by mere chance) and then converges toward its goal. These trajectories are obtained via infra red video tracking.

learn the meaning of an initially non specific sensor (NSS) stimulation through stimulus-stimulus conditionings similar to those performed by the baso-lateral amygdala. Because the robot has the ability to express its internal states of pain and pleasure, the experimentator disposes of the information needed to teach the robot to associate consistently a non-specific sensor stimulation to its internal state of pain or pleasure. The robot learns the association between this stimulation and its internal state making the sensor a specific one through interactive associative learning. The sensor is said to be non specific because the experimentator is entirely free to choose to which internal state he wants to associate the sensor. After this learning has been made, the robot can use this stimulation to reinforce accordingly its behaviors. This learned reinforcement signal can be used to perform an interactive semi-supervised learning in case the robot is lost and cannot use its supervised learned attraction basin to reach the resource. Figure 5 shows the neural network used to enable this learning. A conditioning neuron functionning with the Widrow and Hoff learning rule, the least mean square learning rule [21], uses the difference between its output and the desired output to compute the amount by which the connexions weights have to be changed (weight adaptation due to learning). In our case, conditioning neurons using the least mean square rule learn (equation 3) to predict the pain and pleasure signals from the NSS activity :

$$\Delta w = \epsilon * S(Sd - S) \tag{3}$$

$\Delta w$ is the difference between the old and the new weight, $\epsilon$ is the learning rate (neuromodulation of the neurons), $S$ is the output (of the conditioning neurons) and $Sd$ the desired output (the pain or pleasure signal). As shown in figure 6, the reward signal associated with the sensor activation is the difference between

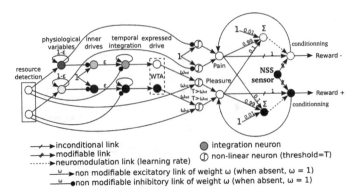

**Fig. 5.** NSS conditioning : neural network used to learn the association of the sensor stimulation and the robot internal state. In this example, a needed resource is detected and a pleasure signal is thus produced (the active drive will then change) The NSS sensor is activated. The robot learns the conditioning of the sensor to its internal pleasure state. The generated reward is used as an AcH neuromodulation signal to control learning of the sensorimotor navigation.

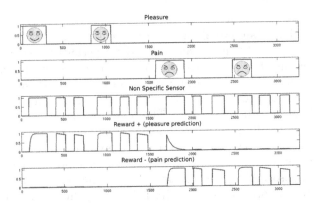

**Fig. 6.** Adaptative learning of how to give a meaning to the NSS (in terms of positive or negative reward). We first conditioned the NSS to predict the robot's pleasure state. Then, the NSS is activated during the robot's pain expressed state. The pleasure conditioning is quickly forgotten while the conditioning between the NSS and the robot's pain expressed state is learned. The NSS now produces a negative reward.

positive and negative (associated with pleasure and pain) predicted rewards. This network learns only when the conditionnal stimulus is present (stimulation of the sensor). The learning control of this network is designed such as when the inconditionnal stimulus is present (the internal state of pain or pleasure), the associated conditioning network learns fast ($\epsilon = 1$) and in absence of the inconditionnal stimulus, the associated conditioning neuron learns slowly ($\epsilon = 0.01$). Furthermore, when one inconditional stimulus is present (e.g. pain), the conditioning neuron associated to the other inconditional stimulus (pleasure) also learns ($\epsilon = 0.1$). This enables this network to learn fast, to forget slowly without any new conditioning and to forget fast in case of a new conditioning. This gives flexibility to this network, allowing the online reconditioning of the NSS from one internal signal to the other. Someone interacting with the robot can teach it the association of two different kinds of reinforcement with the NSS. If the NSS is associated with the pleasure signal expressed by the robot, activation of the sensor gives the robot a positive reinforcement signal. When the robot is lost but is heading toward its goal, activation of the sensor allows the robot to learn visually where it is (visual place cell learning) and associate this perception with its current direction (place-action R+). If however the sensor is associated with the pain signal, activation of the sensor gives the robot a negative reinforcement signal and the robot learns a place cell and associates it with the inhibition of its current direction (place-action R-).

## 5  Robotic Experiments: Learning Interactively to Reach a Goal When the Robot Is Lost

In the following experiments, the robot uses the attraction basin learned in the first experiment. The robot was first trained to associate the NSS with the pleasure signal and thus using it as a source of positive rewards. If the robot seems lost, the experimentator stimulates the sensor whenever he judges the robot's behavior as being the right one. Figure 7 shows the robot trajectories. All trajectories are obtained by infra red video tracking.This interactive learning allows to enlarge to attraction basin around the goal. The robot is now able to reach the goal from farther distances. The robot was then trained to associate the NSS with the pain signal and thus using it as a source of negative rewards. If the robot seems lost, the experimentator stimulates the sensor whenever he judges the robot's behavior as being wrong. Figure 8 shows the robot trajectories.

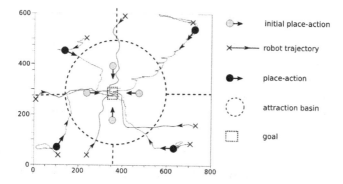

**Fig. 7.** Trajectories of the robot when it is lost but learns interactively to reach its goal. The robot is placed outside the attraction basin and the sensor is associated with the robot's positive emotional state. When the robot behavior is considered as being "good" (e.g. heading toward the attraction basin around the goal), stimulation of the sensor allows the robot to reinforce the current direction.

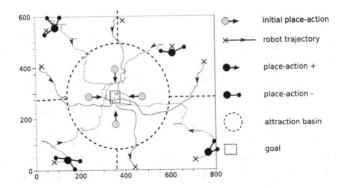

**Fig. 8.** Trajectories of the robot when it is lost but learns interactively to reach its goal. The robot is placed outside the attraction basin and the sensor is associated with the robot's negative emotional state. When the robot behavior is considered as being "bad", stimulation of the sensor allows the robot to learn to inhibit the current direction. Eventually, and by elimination, the robot will head for the attraction basin.

## 6    Conclusions and Perspectives

Robotic experiments are a way to test psychological or neurobiological models. In particular, models of emotional conditionings. The NSS conditioning is inspired by the way baso-lateral amygdala performs stimulus-stimulus conditionings. Figure 9 shows how the robotic control architecture presented in this paper can be understood in terms of a network of cerebral structures. Pain and pleasure signal are constructed from the robot physiological state (hypothalamus). The baso-lateral amygdala learns stimulus-stimulus associations i.e. it learns the conditioning of the NSS perception by the pain or pleasure signals. The ventral tegmental area receives connections from the amygdala and send neuromodulation connections to the amygdala (conditioning learning), the parahippocampus (landmarks-azimuths learning), the enthorinal cortex (place cells learning) and the nucleus accumbens (sensorimotor learning). Furthermore, these experiments showed how someone interacting with a robot could use information displayed by this one about its internal state to teach it the meaning of an otherwise neutral stimulation. The experimentator is able to make the conditioning of any kind of non specific sensor to any kind of the robot's expressed internal state. Different stimulations could then be associated with different robot internal states. One stimulation could also be associated with a combination of expressed internal states. Furthermore, these conditionings allow a very easy and natural way to interact with the robot and to assist its learning.

In this experiment, we used simplified versions of joy and anger expressions to express the pleasure and pain signals. But as the signals to express become more abundant or if the realism and complexity constraints increase, the simplification we used (pleasure equals joy and pain equals anger) becomes an issue of its own. A very promising future development of this architecture would be to give

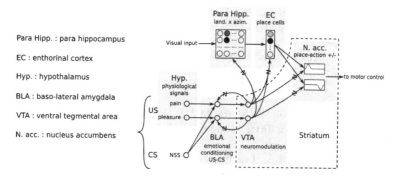

**Fig. 9.** The robot control architecture can be understood as a network involving the following cerebral structures : inner perception of physiological variables are done by the hypothalamus. The baso lateral amygdala learns the conditioning of the NSS with pain or pleasure signals. The ventral tegmental area neuromodulates this conditioning as well as the visual place cell learning. From the parahippocampus (landmark-azimuths) to the enthorinal cortex (place cells). This conditioned signal is used as a reward to control the learning of sensorimotor associations in the nucleus accumbens which are finally used for motor control.

the robot the ability to monitor its progress toward its goals via predictions of its goals through its different perceptions (mainly visual and proprioceptive). Being able to evaluate its behaviors according to its goal should be one of the major source of information to bootstrap the development of emotional behaviors and thus of a greater autonomy. But even if a self monitoring system coupled with a reinforcement learning mechanism is sufficient to discover and learn a solution [1], the interaction with the human in a non predefined way allows the use of the same sensor in different ways a thus speed up learning. In future studies, we plan to test the interactions between the interactive emotional signals (via a non specific sensor and/or via emotional facial expressions recognition) and the robot's own emotional state issued from its automonitoring abilities.

# Acknowledgments

This work has been supported by the european project Feelix Growing.

# References

1. Arleo, A., Gerstner, W.: Spatial cognition and neuro-mimetic navigation: a model of hippocampal place cell activity. Biol. Cybern. (2000)
2. Balkenius, C., Moren, J., Winberg, S.: Interactions between motivation, emotion and attention: From biology to robotics. In: Proceedings of the Ninth International Conference on Epigenetic Robotics (2009)

3. Balkenius, C., Winberg, S.: Fast learning in an actor-critic architecture with reward and punishment. In: Tenth Scandinavian Conference on Artificial Intelligence, SCAI 2008 (2008)
4. Balleine, B.W., Killcross, S.A.: Parallel incentive processing: an integrated view of amygdala function. Trends in Neuroscience (2006)
5. Baxter, M.G., Murray, E.A.: The amygdala and reward. Nature Review of Neuroscience (2002)
6. Blair, H.T., Sotres-Bayon, F., Moita, M.A.P., Leadoux, J.E.: The lateral amygdala processes the value of conditioned and unconditioned aversive stimuli. Neuroscience (2005)
7. Donnart, J.Y., Meyer, J.A.: Learning reactive and planning rules in a motivationally autonomous animat. IEEE Transactions on Systems Man and Cybernetics, Part B (1996)
8. Doya, K.: Reinforcement learning in continuous time and space. Neural Computation (2008)
9. Dunsmoor, J., Schmajuk, N.: Interpreting patterns of brain activation in human fear conditioning with an attentionalassociative learning model. Behavioral Neuroscience (2009)
10. Gallistel, C.R., Cramer, A.E.: Computations on metric maps in mammals: getting oriented and choosing a multi-destination route. Journal of experimental biology (1996)
11. Gaussier, P., Joulain, C., Banquet, J.P., Leprêtre, S., Revel, A.: The visual homing problem: an example of robotics/biology cross fertilization. In: Robotics and autonomous system (2000)
12. Giovannangeli, C., Gaussier, P.: Interactive teaching for vision-based mobile robot: a sensory-motor approach. IEEE Transactions on Man, Systems and Cybernetics, Part A: Systems and humans (2010)
13. Grossberg, S., Bullock, D., Dranias, M.: Neural dynamics underlying impaired autonomic and conditioned responses following amygdala and orbitofrontal lesions. Behavioral Neuroscience (2008)
14. Mannella, F., Zappacosta, S., Mirolli, M., Baldassarre, G.: A computational model of the amygdala nuclei's role in second order conditioning. In: From animals to animats, vol. 10 (2008)
15. O'Keefe, J., Nadel, L.: The Hippocampus as a Cognitive Map. Oxford University Press, Oxford (1978)
16. Oudeyer, P.-Y., Kaplan, F., Hafner, V.: Intrinsic motivation systems for autonomous mental development. IEEE Transactions on Evolutionary Computation (2007)
17. Paton, J.J., Belova, M.A., Morrison, S.E., Salzman, C.D.: The primate amygdala represents the positive and the negative value of visual stimuli during learning. Nature (2006)
18. Pitkanen, A., Jolkkonen, E., Kemppainen, S.: Anatomic heterogeneity of the rat amygdaloid complex. Folia Morphologica (2000)
19. Rescorla, R.A., Wagner, A.R.: A theory of pavlovian conditioning: Variations in the effectiveness of reinforcement and nonreinforcement. Classical conditioning II: Current research and theory (1972)
20. Schmajuk, N.: Computational models of classical conditioning. Scholarpedia (2008)
21. Widrow, B., Hoff, M.E.: Adaptive switching circuits. In: IRE WESCON (1960)

# A Robot Vision Algorithm for Navigating in and Creating a Topological Map of a Reconfigurable Maze

Eleftherios Karapetsas[1] and Demosthenes Stamatis[2]

[1] Department of Electrical Engineering and Information Systems, University of Tokyo
7-3-1 Hongo, Bunkyo-ku, Tokyo 113-8656, Japan
lefteris@realintelligence.net
[2] Department of Information Technology, Alexander TEI of Thessaloniki
P.O. Box 141, 57400, Thessaloniki, Greece
demos@it.teithe.gr

**Abstract.** In this paper we present a neural network approach to solving the problem of a robot agent (Mazebot) navigating in and creating a topological map of a reconfigurable maze. The robotics system used is based on an SRV-1 Robot extended both in hardware and software to accomplish the task. The main algorithm of the system is vision based, requiring only a single camera and a dead reckoning sensor. For the purposes of our algorithm a database of images from various maze configurations has been created. Neural Networks are utilized to train the agent at first and later to analyze features extracted from the images and enable agent navigation inside the maze. The advantage of our approach lies in the minimal number of sensors required by the robot agent to achieve success in its task.

**Keywords:** Robotics, neural networks, machine vision, machine learning.

## 1 Introduction

The problem of a robot correctly navigating inside different kinds of environments has been thoroughly investigated and many different approaches have been shown to work. Each approach depends on a number of factors such as the complexity of the environment itself and the robot's sensing and processing capabilities. Robots with a wide array of sensors have been used to provide a complete view of the environment by fusing input from their various sensors [1], [2]. Furthermore many algorithms have been developed for navigation using vision, either by itself or by combining image data with input from additional sensors to achieve correct movement.

In this paper we tackle this problem by restricting our robot (Mazebot) to a particular environment, a reconfigurable maze, and by utilizing mainly visual processing algorithms, based on neural networks, to achieve movement inside the maze. Our main goal was to create a robotics system that would achieve navigation by using a single camera as its main visual sensor and some kind of odometry sensor for dead-reckoning giving additional feedback to the robot. In comparison to other approaches existing in the literature, we set out to show that this problem can be accurately tackled by a small and lightweight vision-based platform, both in size and processing capabilities. The objectives that we set out to accomplish were:

K. Diamantaras, W. Duch, L.S. Iliadis (Eds.): ICANN 2010, Part II, LNCS 6353, pp. 327–332, 2010.
© Springer-Verlag Berlin Heidelberg 2010

- **Use of a lightweight platform:** Accomplish all of the above without using any other sensor except the camera, thus focusing only on visual processing. Furthermore a requirement we set in our problem definition was that the robot's platform should be lightweight as far as processing and sensing capabilities are concerned.
- **Accuracy of the robot's movement:** The width of each maze corridor has been determined so as to just fit the robot, restricting in effect the movement choices the robot has in its disposal to correctly move inside the maze. This provides it with a challenge to coordinate its movements with great accuracy so it can traverse the maze correctly.
- **Intelligent visual processing:** To add additional hindrances to the robot's task the maze has been constructed so that there is not a clear difference in color between the corridors' floor and the walls. Because of that it is harder to differentiate between different objects of its environment and provide an additional challenge to the task at hand. As a result the machine vision algorithm becomes more reliable.

Creating a lightweight platform was one of our objectives because the robot is used as a teaching tool in the context of an Artificial Intelligence lab course [3]. The robotic platform which we developed to tackle the maze problem is based on the SRV-1 Robot by Surveyor Corporation [9]. That particular robot fit very well with our demand for a lightweight platform based around a single camera sensor. It has a 500MHZ blackfin processor which allows for the implementation of visual processing algorithms in real time. That processing power combined with the camera, long battery life and the option for Wi-Fi access to the robot, rendered the SRV-1 as the perfect foundation for our robotic platform.

In order to overcome a number of shortcomings of SRV-1, we made the following extensions to it:

- a software **FPU emulation** library for floating point arithmetic needed for the calculations of the neural networks,
- a **dead reckoning** sensor interface unit, which helps in the estimation of the distance travelled by the robot.
- a **remote user interface** to be able to control the robot and train the neural networks through a remote PC and
- **customized firmware** to coordinate all functions needed.

We have created a reconfigurable maze (see Fig. 1) to serve as the environment our robot will function in. The goal of the robot is to find the exit of the maze while at the same time treating the maze as a graph that it is trying to map. The graph of the maze serves as the topological map of our environment with corridors representing the edges and crossroads and dead ends acting as the graph's nodes. Each time a new maze is configured the robot can be dynamically ordered to traverse the maze in many different ways by being provided a new search algorithm each time. This provides the students of the Artificial Intelligence lab course with a way to visualize their algorithms in a tangible real-world environment.

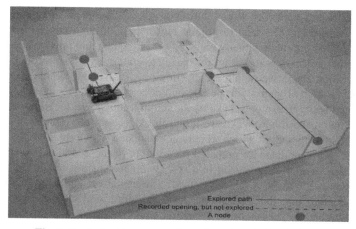

**Fig. 1.** Exploring the maze and creating a topological map

## 2 The Algorithm for Maze Navigation and Topological Map Creation

The problem of navigating inside an environment is not a new one in the field of robotics and computer vision. A lot of work has been done in the field with most of it falling under the category of Simultaneous Localization And Mapping algorithms (SLAM).

Various SLAM-based implementations for robots exist such as in the work of Michael Montemerlo et.al. [4] who utilize the SIFT algorithm combined with stereo vision. In our approach instead of geographical mapping which tends to be error-prone, memory and processing power demanding and as such would contradict our objective for a lightweight robotic platform, we use topological mapping of the environment. An example of using a topological map to create a view of the environment inside a robot can be seen in [5].

Moreover since one of the objectives we set for our robotic platform was that it would be used as an educational tool we needed a testing environment that would be limited and reconfigurable so that it could be easily used by our students. To that end we chose a reconfigurable maze. Many good examples of maze-like environments exist in robotics literature [8].

In our case, the maze is treated as a graph and the robot will map it as such and treat the finding of an exit as a graph search problem. More specifically each cross-road or dead end represents a node in the graph, while the corridors of the maze represent the edges which link the nodes (Fig. 1). In that way, the maze can act as a visualization of various graphs, limited only by its dimensions and the way the walls connect to one another. The robot can then proceed to search for a solution to the maze knowing its starting node and its goal node, using various graph search algorithms, such as Breadth first, Depth First, A* and others.

As far as the navigation algorithm is concerned a database of images from various maze configurations has been created. Feature extraction is performed on these images in the form of edge detection and subsequently these features are used to train the robot's neural networks. When the robot is left alone to traverse the maze, input from the camera and the dead reckoning sensor pass through the trained neural nets and decide what the robot actually sees in its environment and how it should act.

The visual processing algorithm for maze navigation has to go through two stages. During the first stage, we obtain a collection of images from the maze environment, and associate each of them with specific output corresponding to certain goals that the robot should learn. These will make up the initial training sets for the neural networks that will run on the robot. When we tested the algorithm the robot was left alone in the maze gathering images which were later associated with a set of goals.

Having an image database prepared the training of the neural networks can begin. The neural networks were trained in a host computer since it would be possible but very impractical to do it in the robot itself. The neural networks are multi-layer perceptrons trained with the back propagation algorithm and all the usual parameters including momentum. Four different neural networks were created in order for the robot to function properly inside the maze:

1. *Left and right opening:* The job of these neural networks is to detect openings in the walls on the right and left of the robot, thus allowing the robot to map the maze correctly and follow new routes inside it.

2. *Movement/Halt*: This neural network combines input from both the camera and the optical sensor to give an estimation regarding the distance travelled and to inform the robot when it should check for possible openings in the maze.

3. *Wall:* This neural network reads the current camera frame along with measurements from the laser pointers and reaches a decision as to whether there is a wall ahead of the robot or not.

4. *Orientation:* The orientation neural network's job was by far the most challenging. It reads frames from the camera and decides if the robot is properly oriented in the maze's corridor. If it is not looking straight, it can decide the movement needed to correct its orientation and get back on track.

Training the neural networks with a set of images the robot learns about a few different configurations of the maze and is later able to generalize in any possible maze that it is put in. The neural networks do not process raw images but instead canny's edge detection algorithm is applied to the images so that we can perform some form of feature extraction. It is these feature extracted images that are later used in the neural networks. As far as the edge detection algorithm is concerned we made a few minor modifications to the original canny algorithm, such as using a reduced sobel mask, to achieve real time edge detection of the camera's frames.

The training of the neural networks required a considerable number of experiments as far as training parameters were concerned. Furthermore the camera frames contain noise, in the form of unwanted information that can only disrupt the decision process. To solve this problem image masks were used in the training of each network so that only a part of the image would be read for both training and recalling the neural network at hand. Experiments were conducted to figure out which parts of the image are more useful for each network making sure at the same time that no useful information is kept out of the image mask.

During the second stage, the algorithm realizes the actual movement inside the maze combining all of the above. As can be seen through the algorithm's activity

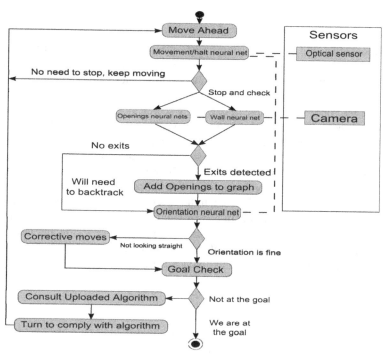

**Fig. 2.** Activity diagram of the algorithm for navigation inside the maze

diagram (Fig. 2), the robot moves continuously while reading input from the optical sensor to get an estimate about its current position. The optical sensor values along with images from the maze are filtered by the "Movement/Halt" network. This network's output determines whether the robot should stop to check for openings.

When it is time to check for exits in either side of the maze's corridors the robot stops momentarily to check for exits. After checking for exits, the "orientation network" is recalled to determine whether the robot's orientation is correct and if it is looking straight inside the corridor or if corrective movements need to be done.

Subsequently the "openings networks" are recalled and inform the robot if there is any opening that it should add in the topological map of the maze. Then the "wall network" along with distance values estimated by the laser pointer's position in the image frame determines if there is a wall in front of the robot and provides us with a distance measurement. This serves the purpose of deciding if going straight ahead is an option or not.

Finally by consulting the algorithm that has been dynamically uploaded to the robot a goal check is performed to assert if we have reached the goal or not and then movement continues towards the direction that the algorithm determines.

By navigating inside the maze in this way the robot creates a topological map of the maze. New openings add new edges to the map while new crossroads and any dead ends that the robot comes across become new nodes in the topological map of the maze. An illustration of this can be seen in Fig. 2 where the robot creates a topological map of the maze while trying to find the exit using the A* graph search algorithm.

## 3  Conclusions

We presented in this paper a vision-based system via which a reconfigurable maze can be accurately navigated by a lightweight robot agent. The robot's movement inside its environment was accurate despite the presented environment related handicaps, thanks to the neural networks based machine vision system that the robot used. Moreover the robot was capable of executing search algorithms dynamically uploaded to it and as such accomplished the role of a teaching assistant to students, by visually displaying the graph search algorithms taught in the class.

Our robotic platform proved to be a success because once properly calibrated and trained from a number of different maze configurations, was able to function correctly in many other new maze configurations. The robot was thoroughly tested and was able to generalize in many different lighting conditions and maze layouts. It succeeded, having never before functioned in many of those conditions and without the need to retrain any of the neural networks, used for machine vision and navigation. A number of test cases together with their video recordings can be seen in MazeBot project web page (http://www.realintelligence.net).

## References

1. Xinqyong, S., Leed, H.-K., Cho, H.: A Sensor Fusion Method for Mobile Robot Navigation. In: SICE-ICASE International Join Conference (2006)
2. Jin, T.-S., Myung, J., Lee, Tso, S.K.: A new approach using sensor data fusion for mobile robot navigation. Robotica 22(1), 51–59 (2004)
3. Karapetsas, E., Stamatis, D.: Teaching AI concepts using a robot as an assistant. In: Fasli, M. (ed.) Proceedings of the 4th Artificial Intelligence in Education Workshop, HEA-ICS 2009, Cambridge, UK (2009)
4. Se, S., Lowe, D., Little, J.: Vision-based mobile robot localization and mapping using scale-invariant features. In: Proceedings of the IEEE International Conference on Robotics and Automation, ICRA (2001)
5. Filliat, D., Meyer, J.A.: Global localization and topological map-learning for robot navigation. In: Proceedings of the seventh international conference on simulation of adaptive behavior on From animals to animats (2002)
6. Fraundorfer, F., Engels, C., Nister, D.: Topological mapping, localization and navigation using image collections. In: IEEE/RSJ International Conference on Intelligent Robots and Systems, IROS 2007 (2007)
7. Goedeme, T., Tuytelaars, T., Gool, L.V.: Visual topological map building in self-similar environment. Informatics in Control Automation and Robotics 15, 195–205 (2006)
8. Wyard-Scott, L., Meng, Q.-H.M.: A potential maze solving algorithm for a micromouse robot. In: Proceedings of the IEEE Conference on Communications, Computers, and Signal Processing (1995)
9. Surveyor corporation SRV-1 robot, http://www.surveyor.com/SRV_info.html

# Generation of Comprehensible Representations by Supposed Maximum Information

Ryotaro Kamimura

IT Education Center,
1117 Kitakaname Hiratsuka Kanagawa 259-1292, Japan
ryo@keyaki.cc.u-tokai.ac.jp

**Abstract.** In this paper, we propose a new information-theoretic method to simplify and unify learning methods in one framework. The new method is called "supposed maximum information," which is used to produce humanly comprehensible internal representations supposing that information is already maximized before learning. The new learning method is composed of three stages. First, without information on input variables, a competitive network is trained. Second, with supposed maximum information on input variables, the importance of the variables is estimated by measuring mutual information between competitive units and input patterns. Finally, with the estimated importance of input variables, the competitive network is retrained to take into account the importance of input variables. The method is applied not to pure competitive learning but to self-organizing maps, because it is easy to demonstrate how well the new method can produce more explicit internal representation intuitively. We applied the method to the well-known SPECT heart data of the machine learning database. We succeeded in producing more comprehensible class boundaries on the U-matrices than did the conventional SOM. In addition, quantization and topographic errors produced by our method were not larger than those by the conventional SOM.

**Keywords:** Competitive learning, self-organizing maps, interpretation, information maximization.

## 1 Introduction

In this paper, we propose a new type of information-theoretic method to produce humanly interpretable representations by maximizing information in input units as well as competitive units. The main characteristics of the new method lie in simplification and unification. First, the method is proposed to simplify the computation of information maximization. In this method, we suppose that information is already maximized before learning. Then, we try to examine what kinds of configuration change can be observed by this supposed maximum information. This is the reason why we call this method "supposed maximum information." Now, information-theoretic methods have been applied to neural networks as well as machine learning, because the information-theoretic methods have made it possible to deal with higher-order statistics and non-linear

K. Diamantaras, W. Duch, L.S. Iliadis (Eds.): ICANN 2010, Part II, LNCS 6353, pp. 333–342, 2010.

problems [1]. Thus, there have been many attempts to formulate learning processes from the information-theoretic points of view [2], [3], [4]. However, one of the major problems of the information-theoretic methods lies in the computational complexity of computing entropy, information and mutual information for learning. Though many computationally feasible methods have been proposed [5], [6], the problem of computational complexity still remain unsolved from our point of view. The supposed maximum information is introduced to overcome the problem, because information to be maximized is supposed to be maximized before learning.

Second, we can see several computational methods in a more unified way, because some methods seem to use this supposed maximum information, though implicitly. Let us take two examples, namely, competitive learning and feature selection. In competitive learning [7], one of the main jobs is to determine a winner by computing distances between input patterns and connection weights. Then, connection weights to the winner with the minimum distance are updated in competitive learning, or the winner with its neighbors in the self-organizing maps [8] must be updated. This winner-take-all algorithm is considered to be one realization of supposed maximum information in our context. This is because in our definition, in a maximum information state, only one competitive unit fires, while all the other competitive units cease to do. Second, the feature selection can be considered to be a method to suppose maximum information, though not so explicitly as in competitive learning. Feature selection have played important roles to improve the performance [9]. Basically, in the feature selection, the number of important variables should be reduced as much as possible with the same precision in errors. In our term, the feature selection correspond to information maximization of input variables. As the information is larger, the number of input variables should be smaller. Thus, it is possible to suppose maximum information in feature selection, meaning that the minimum number of features is already detected. Thus, in our framework, feature selection and competitive learning can be considered and implemented in a framework of the supposed maximum information.

## 2    Theory and Computational Methods

Figure 1 shows a schematic diagram of our method. In the competitive layer in Figure 1(a), the supposed maximum information is realized by the conventional winner-take-all algorithm. In the input layer in Figure 1(b), the new method is composed of three stages. In the first stage, minimum information is supposed in Figure 1(1). On the other hand, maximum information is supposed in the second and third stage in Figure 1(2) and (3).

### 2.1    First Stage: Minimum Information Learning

In Figure 1(0), we have an network architecture at the initial stage, where $x_k^s$, $w_{jk}$ and $v_j^s$ denote the $k$th element of $L$ input units for the $s$th input pattern of

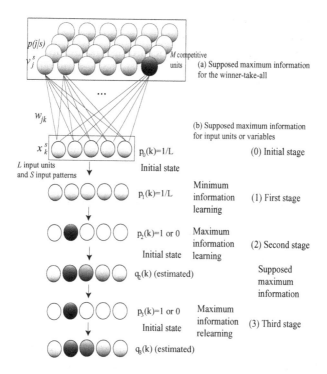

**Fig. 1.** A schematic diagram of three types of information-theoretic learning, namely, minimum information learning (1), maximum information learning (2) and maximum information relearning (3)

$S$ input patterns, connection weights from the $k$th input unit to the $j$th unit of $M$ competitive units and the $j$th competitive unit output, respectively. At the initial stage, shown in Figure 1(0), no information on input units or variables is supposed to be given, and the firing probabilities $p_0(k)$ of the $k$th input unit are supposed to be equi-probable, namely, $p_0(k) = 1/L$. Note that the number zero denotes the specific stage of learning, and without this number, the probability is considered to be a general one.

Figure 1(1) shows the first stage of learning with supposed minimum information. As already mentioned, let us suppose that $p_0(k)$ and $p_1(k)$ represent the supposed firing probabilities of the $k$th input unit at the initial stage and at the first stage, respectively. The supposed information $SI_1$, presuming that no information on input variables exists, is defined by the difference between these two probabilities

$$SI_1 = \sum_{k=1}^{L} p_1(k) \log \frac{p_1(k)}{p_0(k)}. \tag{1}$$

This supposed information is zero, namely, minimum information learning. In the minimum information learning, no information exists with respect to input variables, meaning that $p_1(k)$ is equal to the initial probability $p_0(k)$. For learning, we use the conventional SOM with the batch type learning[1]. In the batch learning, all input patterns must be given before weight update procedures. In each training step, the data set is partitioned according to the Voronoi regions of map vectors. To obtain update rules, we must select the best matching unit (BMU), denoted by $c$:

$$c = \operatorname{argmin}_j \sum_{k=1}^{L} p_1(k)(x_k^s - w_{jk})^2. \tag{2}$$

As shown in Figure 1(a), the winner-take-all algorithm is considered to be a realization of supposed maximum information.

## 2.2    Second Stage: Maximum Information Learning

At the second stage of maximum information learning in Figure 1(2), information on input variables is supposed to be maximized. In a maximum information state, one input unit, for example, the $t$th unit, is turned on, while all the other units should be off. Thus, we have firing probabilities when the $t$th input unit is turned on,

$$p_2(k;t) = \begin{cases} 1, & \text{if } k = t; \\ 0, & \text{otherwise.} \end{cases}$$

When the information on input variables is supposed to be maximized, the supposed information at the second stage of learning is defined by

$$SI_2(t) = \sum_{k=1}^{L} p_2(k;t) \log \frac{p_2(k;t)}{p_0(k)}$$
$$= \log L. \tag{3}$$

We should now examine how this supposed maximum information affects a process of competition. Now, the distance between input patterns and connection weights, when focusing upon the $t$th input unit, is computed by

$$d_j^s(t) = \sum_{k=1}^{L} p_2(k;t)(x_k^s - w_{jk})^2. \tag{4}$$

By using this equation, we have competitive unit outputs for the $t$th input unit

$$v_j^s(t,\sigma) = \exp\left(-\frac{\sum_{k=1}^{L} p_2(k;t)(x_k^s - w_{jk})^2}{2\sigma^2}\right). \tag{5}$$

Normalizing these outputs, we have

$$p(j \mid s; t, \sigma) = \frac{v_j^s(t,\sigma)}{\sum_{m=1}^{M} v_m^s(t,\sigma)}. \tag{6}$$

---

[1] This is a default learning method in the SOM toolbox [10] used in this paper.

The firing probability of the $j$th competitive unit is defined by

$$p(j;t,\sigma) = \sum_{s=1}^{S} p(s)p(j \mid s;t,\sigma).$$ (7)

By using these probabilities, we have mutual information $MI_2$ when the $t$th input unit is turned on:

$$MI_2(t;\sigma) = \sum_{s=1}^{S} \sum_{j=1}^{M} p(s)p(j \mid s;t,\sigma) \log \frac{p(j \mid s;t,\sigma)}{p(j;t,\sigma)}.$$ (8)

This mutual information shows how well an input unit contributes to a process of competition among competitive units [11]. As this mutual information gets larger, the $t$th input variable plays a more essential role in realizing competitive processes, and the variable should be considered to be important in competition.

We approximate the actual firing probabilities of input units by this mutual information, and we have

$$q_2(t;\sigma) \approx \frac{MI_2(t;\sigma)}{\sum_{l=1}^{L} MI_2(l;\sigma)}.$$ (9)

Then, using these estimated firing probabilities, $q_2(t;\sigma)$, the estimated information can defined by

$$EI_2(\sigma) = \sum_{k=1}^{L} q_2(k;\sigma) \log \frac{q_2(k;\sigma)}{p_0(k)}.$$ (10)

This estimated information, $EI_2$, is dependent on the spread parameter $\sigma$. Suppose that the spread parameter $\sigma^*$ can give maximum estimated information, then we have the final estimated firing probability at the second stage

$$q_2(k) = q_2(k;\sigma^*),$$ (11)

and the estimated information

$$EI_2 = EI_2(\sigma^*).$$ (12)

## 2.3   Third Stage: Maximum Information Relearning

In the maximum information relearning in Figure 1(3), by obtained estimated firing probabilities $q_2(k)$ with maximum estimated information, competitive learning is again applied to get the final firing probability of input units. Now, using the estimated firing probabilities obtained by the previous maximum information learning, the final winner can be determined by

$$c = \operatorname{argmin}_j \sum_{k=1}^{L} q_2(k)(x_k^s - w_{jk})^2.$$ (13)

Then, we compute new connection weights and estimated information $MI_3$ by the same equation (8). Then, the final firing probabilities are defined by

$$q_3(k) = \frac{MI_3(k)}{\sum_{l=1}^{L} MI_3(l)}. \tag{14}$$

We use the optimal spread parameter $\sigma^*$ to shorten the computational time, because little change can be observed even if we search for an optimal spread parameter value again. Then, the final estimated information is

$$EI_3 = \sum_{k=1}^{L} q_3(k) \log \frac{q_3(k)}{p_0(k)}. \tag{15}$$

## 3    Results and Discussion

For easy comparison, we use the conventional SOM[2] with the well-known data of the SPECT heart data[3]. The data shows the diagnosing of cardiac Single Proton Emission Computed Tomography (SPECT) images. Each of the patients is classified into two categories: *normal*(0) and *abnormal*(1). The number of input patterns is 80, with 22 input variables. The data were normalized for their values to range between zero and one. To evaluate the performance of competitive networks, we used the quantization and topographic errors. The quantization error is simply the average distance from each data vector to its BMU [12]. The topographic error is the percentage of data vectors for which the BMU and the second-BMU are not neighboring units [13]. The reason why we used these classic measures for evaluation for networks is that the importance is on the easy reproduction of our results presented in this paper. In all experimental results, information on input variables was increased as much as possible by changing the spread parameter $\sigma$. Learning was considered to be finished when the absolute difference between the information at two successive learning stages was less than 0.001.

Figure 2(a) shows the estimated information $EI_2$ at the second stage and $EI_3$ at the third stage. Both types of information increase gradually as the spread parameter is increased from 0.1 to 2.3(final). The estimated information $EI_2$ at the second stage reaches its maximum value of 0.090, while the estimated information $EI_3$ is further increased and reaches its maximum value of 0.145. Figure 2(b) shows quantization errors by the SOM in green, at the second stage in blue and at the third stage in red. The quantization error by the conventional SOM is 0.242. At the second stage, the quantization error is decreased to 0.231, while at the third stage, the quantization error is further decreased to 0.225 ($\sigma = 0.9$). Figure 2(c) shows topographic errors by the SOM in green, at the

---

[2] We used SOM Toolbox 2.0, February 11th, 2000 by Juha Vesanto http://www.cis.hut.fi/projects/somtoolbox/. No special options were used for easy reproduction.

[3] http://www1.ics.uci.edu/ mlearn/MLRepository.html

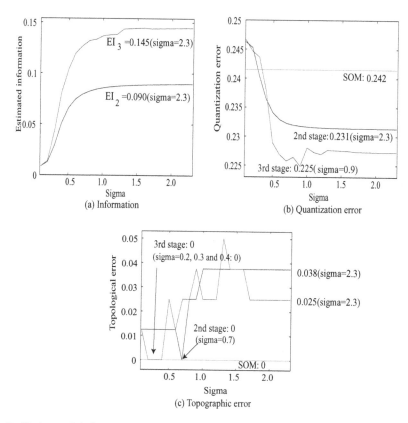

**Fig. 2.** Estimated information for input units (a), quantization errors (b) and topographic errors (c) for the SPECT heart problem

second stage in blue and at the third stage in red. As can be seen in the figure, the topographic error by the SOM is zero. On the other hand, at the second stage, the error is increased to 0.038, and the error at the third stage is slightly decreased to 0.025 at the end of learning. However, when the parameter $\sigma$ is 0.7, the topographic error at the second stage becomes zero. In addition, when the parameter $\sigma$ is 0.2 to 0.4, the topographic error also becomes zero at the third stage of learning. Though we need to take appropriate values of the parameter, the topographic errors can be reduced to zero.

Figure 3 shows the estimated firing probabilities $q_3(k)$ when the spread parameter is increased from 0.1 (a) to 2.3 (b). As can be seen in Figure 3(a), when the spread parameter is 0.1, the firing probabilities are almost flat, and no characteristics can be seen. When the spread parameter is increased to 2.4 (b), several input variables, for example, variables No. 1, No. 5, No.10 and No.13 show larger values. Figure 4 shows U-matrices (1) and labels (2) obtained by the SOM (a) and when the spread parameter is increased from 0.1(b) to 2.4 (f). Figure 4(a) shows a U-matrix and labels obtained by the conventional SOM. The higher values are seen on the lower part of the U-matrix. When the spread

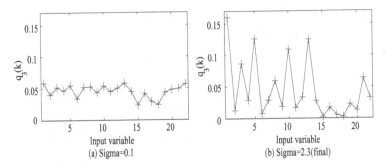

**Fig. 3.** Estimated firing probabilities $q_3(k)$ for the SPECT heart problem

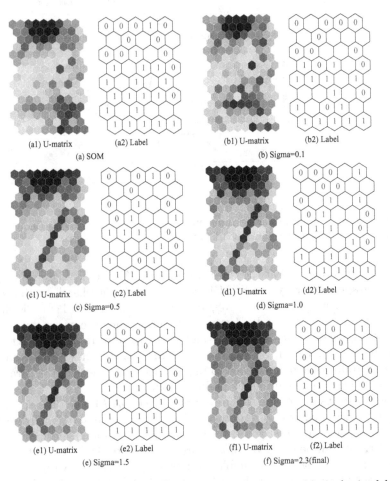

**Fig. 4.** U-matrix (1) and labels (2) for the SPECT heart problem obtained by the conventional SOM (a) when the spread parameter is increased from 0.1(b) to 2.3 (f)

parameter is 0.1, the same kinds of higher values can be seen on the lower side of the map in Figure 4(b). When the spread parameter is increased to 0.5 (c), a warmer-colored and clear boundary on the diagonal position can be seen. This boundary continues to exist as the spread parameter is increased from 1.0 (d) to 2.3 (f). This diagonal property is more accentuated when the spread parameter is increased from 0.5 to 2.3.

We can summarize those experimental results by the following three points. First, as the information on input variables is increased, quantization errors are gradually decreased, while topographic errors are inversely increased. Thus, we need to take the appropriate values of the parameter for better topographic errors. Second, estimated firing probabilities at the third stage are gradually expanded, and stable probabilities can be obtained. Third, on the U-matrices, gradually, clear boundaries on the diagonal position, which reflect the characteristics of the most important input variable, appear.

# 4  Conclusion

In this paper, we have proposed a new type of information-theoretic method that aims to simplify the computation of information and at the same time to unify several methods independently developed in neural networks. The simplification is possible by supposing that information on input variables is already maximized. With this supposed maximum information, we try to examine what kind of change a network has in the course of learning. The unification is also realized by supposing that information is already maximized before learning. The examples in this paper are the winner-take-all algorithm and feature selection to be seen in the same framework. Thus, we have the possibility to unify the winner-take-all and the variable selection in one framework. We applied the method to the well-known data set, namely, the SPECT heart data of the machine learning database. We have shown that information on input variables is increased and finally saturated as the spread parameter $\sigma$ is increased. The quantization errors decrease as the information is increased. However, the topographic errors are not necessarily decreased as the information is increased. Final U-matrices show much clearer class boundaries that reflect the properties of the connection weights into the important input variables.

Though our method is restricted to competitive learning and the determination of the spread parameter should be made clearer, our method certainly shows the possibility of being a new information-theoretic method that includes information content on various components in a network.

# References

1. Torkkola, K.: Feature extraction by non-parametric mutual information maximization. Journal of Machine Learning Research 3, 1415–1438 (2003)
2. Linsker, R.: Self-organization in a perceptual network. Computer 21, 105–117 (1988)

3. Barlow, H.B.: Unsupervised learning. Neural Computation 1, 295–311 (1989)
4. Becker, S.: Mutual information maximization: models of cortical self-organization. Network: Computation in Neural Systems 7, 7–31 (1996)
5. Principe, J.C., Xu, D., Zhao, Q., Fisher III, J.W.: Learning from examples with information theoretic criteria. The Journal of VLSI Signal Processing 26(1-2), 61–77 (2000)
6. Torkkola, K.: Feature extraction by non-parametric mutual information maximization. Journal of Machine Learning Research 3, 1415–1438 (2003)
7. Rumelhart, D.E., Zipser, D.: Feature discovery by competitive learning. Cognitive Science 9, 75–112 (1985)
8. Kohonen, T.: Self-Organizing Maps. Springer, Heidelberg (1995)
9. Guyon, I., Elisseeff, A.: An introduction to variable and feature selection. Journal of Machine Learning Research 3, 1157–1182 (2003)
10. Vesanto, J.: SOM-based data visualization methods. Intelligent Data Analysis 3, 111–126 (1999)
11. Kamimura, R.: Information-theoretic competitive learning with inverse Euclidean distance output units. Neural Processing Letters 18, 163–184 (2003)
12. Xu, R., Wunsch II, D.: Survey of clustering algorithms. IEEE Transactions on neural networks 16, 645–678 (2005)
13. Kiviluoto, K.: Topology preservation in self-organizing maps. In: Proceedings of the IEEE International Conference on Neural Networks, pp. 294–299 (1996)

# Visualization of Changes in Process Dynamics Using Self-Organizing Maps

Ignacio Díaz[1], Abel A. Cuadrado[1], Alberto B. Diez[1],
Manuel Domínguez[2], Juan J. Fuertes[2], and Miguel A. Prada[2]

[1] University of Oviedo, Area de Ingeniería de Sistemas y Automática,
Campus de Viesques s/n, 33204, Gijón, Asturias, Spain
[2] Instituto de Automática y Fabricación, Universidad de León,
Escuela de Ingenierías. Campus Universitario de Vegazana, León, 24071, Spain

**Abstract.** In this paper a new method based on the self-organizing map (SOM) is proposed to track and identify changes in the dynamic behaviour of a physical process. In a first stage, a SOM is trained on a parameter space composed of the coefficients of local dynamic models estimated around different operating points of the process. On execution, new models estimated from process data are compared against the stored models in the SOM to yield *residual models* that contain relevant information about the changes in the process dynamics. This information can be efficiently represented using *time-frequency* visualizations, that reveal unseen patterns in the frequency response and hide those that can be explained by the model.

**Keywords:** Self-organizing maps, data visualization, process monitoring.

## 1 Introduction

Knowledge about the process behaviour is a key factor in today's industry. Precise and timely knowledge about its condition is crucial in order to take actions to improve productivity and quality. Fault detection and identification in large and complex industrial processes is often an unsupervised problem. In most cases, the overwhelming number of factors that intervene in a fault make it virtually impossible to build models or even gather data of all possible faults, and the only available models or data about the process describe it under normal working conditions. The problem of fault detection and identification on the basis of the knowledge of the process under normal conditions is closely related to *novelty detection*, that is the identification of new or unknown data or signal that a machine learning system is not aware of during training [8,9]. The novelty detection problem conceptually involves finding states that lie significantly outside the kernel of the joint probability density function defined by known states. This joint pdf embodies geometric relationships among the process variables $x_1, \cdots, x_n$ and, in fact, can be considered a model of the process under normal conditions.

K. Diamantaras, W. Duch, L.S. Iliadis (Eds.): ICANN 2010, Part II, LNCS 6353, pp. 343–352, 2010.
© Springer-Verlag Berlin Heidelberg 2010

Despite this approach is rather general, when the variables $x_i$ describe process measurements instead of process behaviours, only inherently *static* relationships are considered, which do not have into account possible *dynamical* relationships. When two (or more) variables $x_i$ and $x_j$ are dynamically related –e.g. input force and output position in a spring-damp-mass system–, the relationships, usually described by a differential equation, also depend on time, and the "static model" is no longer valid to detect novel states.

A classical method to consider dynamic processes is the *model based approach* [3]. It consists in the detection of faults in the processes, actuators and sensors by using the dependencies between different measurable signals. These dependencies are expressed by mathematical process models [4,5]. The model based approach, largely used in fault detection and identification literature, is rooted on the idea of *analytical redundancy*, that is based on comparing the process to a "copy" of it (in this case, an analytical model) that is supposed to behave in the same manner as the original process. Any differences between the actual process and its copy reveal, in consequence, potential faulty behaviours. However, one key factor of this class of methods is the availability of a model that explains the process dynamics. Sometimes models are not available or difficult to obtain; also, the process may be multimodal and show many different dynamic behaviours. In those cases automated learning processes may become competitive and less time-consuming to obtain models of the process.

In this work we propose a method to detect novel dynamic behaviours of the process based on the so called *maps of dynamics* [2] consisting of a combination of least squares (LS) system identification and self organizing maps to store models describing all the different dynamic behaviours shown by the process on a training set. After the learning process, the current process dynamics is compared to the best matching model to produce a *residual model*. This residual model allows to detect changes in the dynamic behaviour but also provides qualitative information regarding the nature of the change that has taken place; this information can be efficiently visualized by means of a time-frequency representation that highlights only the frequencies that suffer changes as well as the time when they happen. This paper is organized as follows. In section 2 a brief state of the art of methods to consider dynamics in the SOM is presented followed by a description of the proposed method. In section 3 experimental results with real data are presented for two industrial scale systems, namely, a liquid level control system with modified conditions in the base area of the tank and the visualization of faulty vibration patterns due to chatter effect on a cold rolling mill. Finally section 4 includes a general discussion and concludes the paper.

## 2    Modeling of Dynamics Using SOM on a Parameter Space

In its basic form, the original SOM algorithm is a nonlinear ordered smooth mapping of high dimensional data on a regular low dimensional array [7]. The SOM adapts a low dimensional lattice of codebook vectors to the input dataset preserving at the same time a previously defined topology for the lattice. What the SOM actually learns is a *static* model capturing the geometrical relationships of data in the input space, that does not consider temporal sequences or dynamic relationships. However, it can also be used to model the process dynamics. Several authors have proposed variants of the SOM to learn dynamic behaviour of signals and processes. In [6] Kohonen already describes the *operator maps* as an extension of the SOM that considers local dynamic models on each unit. In [10], a procedure for learning dynamics is described based on training the SOM in a embedded signal space and learning local linear models for each unit from process data close to it. Some architectures, such as the VQTAM, include short term memory to the SOM by considering vectors of time delayed versions of inputs and outputs [1]. Another approach to store dynamics in the SOM is to make it operate in a space of parameters –typically coefficients of dynamic models– so that the SOM builds an ordered map of all dynamic behaviours that can be used for visualization or further retrieval [2]. The proposed method in this paper, rooted in this latter method, is accomplished in four stages: selection of the parametric model structure, system identification of all dynamic states, mapping the dynamics using a SOM and finally retrieval of the best dynamic model and comparison to the current estimated model for further visualization. A description of these stages is done in next subsections.

## 2.1   Selection of a Parametric Model

Let $\{u(k)\}$ and $\{y(k)\}$ be input and ouput sequences of a given process that are supposed to be dynamically related by the parametric model $y(k) = f(\varphi(k), \mathbf{p})$, where $\mathbf{p} = [p_1, \cdots, p_p]^T$ is a *parameter vector* and $\varphi(k) = [y(k-1), \cdots, y(k-n), u(k), \cdots, u(k-m)]^T$ is a *data vector*. Depending on the choice of function $f(.,.)$, the data vector $\varphi(k)$ and the parameter vector $\mathbf{p}$, different model types (ARX, NARX, etc.) and orders can be considered. In this paper we shall choose ARX($n,m$) models

$$y(k) = a_1 y(k-1) + \cdots a_n y(k-n) + b_0 u(k) + \cdots + b_m u(k-m) \qquad (1)$$

which corresponds to the following linear model $y(k) = f_L(\varphi(k), \mathbf{p}) = \mathbf{p}^T \varphi(k)$. This particular case corresponds to an LTI (linear time invariant) model that is equivalent to the following *transfer function* representation

$$G(z, \mathbf{p}) \stackrel{\text{def}}{=} \frac{b_0 + b_1 z^{-1} + \cdots b_m z^{-m}}{1 - a_1 z^{-1} - \cdots - a_n z^{-n}} \qquad (2)$$

being $\varphi(k) = [y(k-1), \cdots, y(k-n), u(k), \cdots, u(k-m)]^T$ the data vector and $\mathbf{p} = [a_1, \cdots, a_n, b_0, b_1, \cdots b_m]^T$ the parameter vector, which defines the transfer function. While this model is simple, it may describe a rather general class of nonlinear global behaviours of the process as an aggregation of local linear models, and at the same time it brings insight to engineers and domain experts, since it allows to exploit the wealth of analysis tools and descriptors available for linear systems commonly used in engineering.

## 2.2  Identification Stage

The available process data can be subdivided into $N$ subsets containing the output and the data vector at different values of $k$ contained in an index set $I_j$

$$\{y(k), \varphi(k)\}_{k \in I_j}, \quad j = 1, \cdots N \tag{3}$$

Each subset should ideally include process data with similar dynamics. For instance a kmeans or another SOM with $N$ units can be trained to cluster the space of variables that define the dynamic state –typically, the operating point– and choose

$$I_j = \{\text{all } k \text{ such that } \|\mathbf{x}_k - \mathbf{m}_j\| < \varepsilon\}$$

where $\mathbf{x}$ is the the process operating point at sample $k$ and $\mathbf{m}_j$ is the $j$-th codebook vector of the SOM or kmeans algorithm.

When the process dynamics change slowly, however, a simpler and practical way to build subsets is to use overlapped windows of length $n$ of the data $I_j = \{k_j - n + 1, k_j - n + 2, \cdots, k_j\}$.

Once the subsets are defined, a system identification can be carried out on each subset using any optimization technique –e.g. a least squares– to produce a parameter set $P = \{\mathbf{p}(1), \cdots, \mathbf{p}(N)\}$ with $N$ points in a parameter space $\mathbb{R}^p$, such that the cost function

$$J = \sum_{k \in I_j} \|y(k) - f(\varphi(k), \mathbf{p}(k))\|^2 \tag{4}$$

is minimized.

## 2.3  SOM Projection Stage

In this stage, a SOM is trained in the parameter space, using the data set $P$ obtained in the previous stage. After training, the codebook vector $\mathbf{m}_i$ of the SOM unit $i$ contains the parameters of a dynamic model whose behaviour can be reproduced using

$$y(k) = f(\varphi(k), \mathbf{m}_i) \tag{5}$$

In consequence, the SOM stores all the dynamic behaviours of the process identified in the previous stage, allowing for visualization of dynamic features, as shown in [2] or, as it will be shown here, to compare the current dynamic behaviour with the stored dynamic behaviours and yield a residual dynamic model that can be visualized.

## 2.4  Visualization of Changes in Dynamic Behaviour

Let's consider a set of process data $\{y(k), \varphi(k)\}_{k \in W_k}$ obtained in a window $W_k = \{k - n + 1, \cdots, k\}$. Using the same identification technique as in the identification stage on this data set, a vector of model parameters $\mathbf{p}(k)$ can be estimated. From this vector, the best matching unit $\mathbf{m}_{c(k)}$ of the SOM can be obtained, such that $c(k) = \arg\min_i\{\|\mathbf{p}(k) - \mathbf{m}_i\|\}$.

Since the current and estimated models of the process dynamics are available, a *residual model* can be defined by comparing both models in a proper way, looking forward to maximize insightfulness. A powerful way to visualize differences between both models is to use the frequency domain

$$\mathbf{R}(e^{j\theta}, k) = \frac{G(e^{j\theta}, \mathbf{p}(k))}{G(e^{j\theta}, \mathbf{m}_{c(k)})} \tag{6}$$

where $\mathbf{R}(e^{j\theta}, k)$ is the *residual frequency response* for window $W_k$. Since residual models can be typically obtained in a sequential way for overlapping windows $W_k$, a *residual spectrogram* can be defined in a straightforward way, providing a time-frequency description of process changes by making a color image representation of a matrix whose columns contain the frequency response of the residual model. Using a logarithmic representation in decibels (dB) –usually more convenient in typical engineering applications– at sample $k$ during the execution with test data, $k$-th column would be,

$$20\log_{10}\left|\frac{G(e^{j\theta}, \mathbf{p}(k))}{G(e^{j\theta}, \mathbf{m}_{c(k)})}\right| = 20\log_{10}\left|\mathbf{R}(e^{j\theta}, k)\right|$$

# 3  Results

## 3.1  Tank Level Control Dynamics

The proposed method was applied to real data from an industrial scale plant composed of 4 tanks, two pumps and three-way valves that allow to derive fluid to any of the tanks. A liquid level control system in one of the tanks was subject to different dynamic conditions by changing the base area of the tank. The liquid level dynamics can be described by the following ordinary differential equation (ODE),

$$A_b\frac{dh(t)}{dt} = q_{in}(t) - A_c\sqrt{2gh(t)} \tag{7}$$

where $A_b$ is the base area of the prismatic tank, and $A_c$ is the section of the sink conduct. It can be easily shown that changes in $A_b$ (due, for instance to the presence of objects inside the tank) lead to changes in the tank dynamics. In our experiment the liquid level in the tank was controlled using a proportional-integral (PI) control law, where the error signal $e(t) = r(t) - h(t)$ is the difference between the setpoint value $r(t)$ and the actual liquid level $h(t)$ –see Fig. 1. The closed loop control system was made to work under 6 different conditions varying $A_b$ as shown in table, by introducing different objects inside the tank.

In order to describe the dynamics of the feedback system –relating the level reference $r$ and the liquid level $h$–, that includes the PI control law and the changing tank dynamics, a second order model was considered

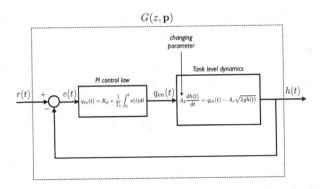

**Fig. 1.** Block diagram of the tank level control system

**Table 1.** The 6 conditions produced by changing the base area of the tank

| Condition | base area | description |
|---|---|---|
| 1 | $A_b = 389.16$ cm$^2$ | (no objects) |
| 2 | $A_b = 332.61$ cm$^2$ | (two small cilindric objects) |
| 3 | $A_b = 332.61$ cm$^2$ | (two small cilindric objects) |
| 4 | $A_b = 282.35$ cm$^2$ | (a large cilindric object + 2 small cilindric objects) |
| 5 | $A_b = 343.80$ cm$^2$ | (a large cilindric object) |
| 6 | $A_b = 389.16$ cm$^2$ | (no objects) |

$$G(z, \mathbf{p}) = \frac{b_0 + b_1 z^{-1} + b_2 z^{-2}}{1 - a_1 z^{-1} - a_2 z^{-2}} \qquad (8)$$

Data acquisition of the reference $r(k)$ and the liquid level $h(k)$ was done at a rate of 8 samples per second. To build the parameter space, windows $W_k$ with a length $n = 500$ samples were regularly taken at intervals of 20 samples, a standard LS identification was used to obtain the parameters.

To learn the process dynamics, parameter data were divided into two sets: a training set including data of conditions 1 and 2 (ranging from $t = 0$ to $t = 45$ min.), that will be considered "normal" and a test set including conditions 3, 4, 5 and 6 (from $t = 45$ min. to the end of the experiment), that includes "normal" dynamic states (conditions 3 and 6) as well as "novel" dynamic states (4 and 5).

A $35 \times 35$ SOM was trained on the parameters estimated from training set, using $\pm 1$ normalization and the batch algorithm with 10 epochs and a gaussian neighborhood with a width $\sigma$ monotonically decreasing from 11.66 ($\frac{1}{3}$ of the grid size) to 1.2. Finally, the residual spectrogram was built on a logarithmic scale as shown in previous section. The residual spectrogram is displayed with the original spectrogram for comparison in Fig. 3.

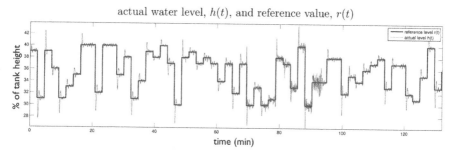

**Fig. 2.** Reference level, $r(t)$, and actual level, $h(t)$, expressed in % of the total tank height (note a different dynamic behaviour approximately between 70 and 110 min.)

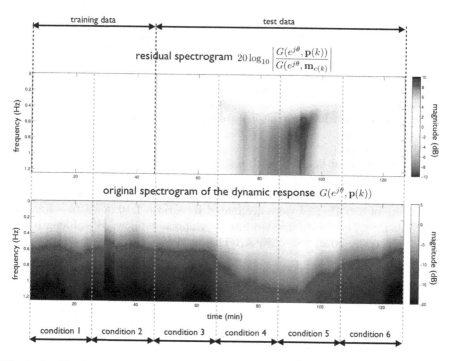

**Fig. 3.** Residuals of the dynamic conditions in tank level control system. Training set contains process in conditions 1 and 2. It can be seen how similar conditions (3 and 6) yield small residuals while conditions 4 and 5 show up the differences in the frequency response.

## 3.2    Isolation of Chatter Effect in Vibration Data of a Rolling Mill

The proposed method was also applied to isolate the chatter effect (unusual vibration mode) in a cold rolling mill. It was applied to data from a 969mm width coil rolled in a 5−stand cold rolling mill to isolate unseen vibration patterns in

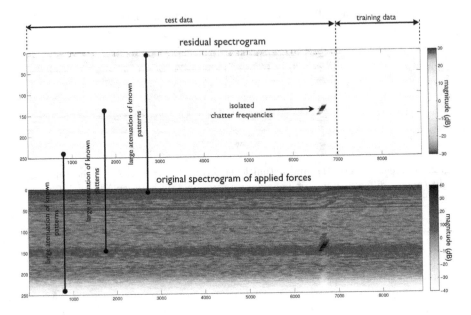

**Fig. 4.** Force vibration residuals in a cold rolling mill during a chattered coil

the roll force $F_5(t)$ at stand 5, with respect to a training set on which the mill run under normal conditions.

Data of the experiment were acquired using a data acquisition board at a sample rate of 5000Hz and were decimated by a ratio 1:10 down to a final 500 Hz sample rate. Data were divided into overlapped windows $W_j$ of length 1000 each, displaced by 10 samples. An AR(110) model,

$$F_5(k) = a_1 F_5(k-1) + \cdots + a_{110} F_5(k-110) + \epsilon \tag{9}$$

was chosen to describe the spectral content of the roll forces on the basis of the level of detail (number of main harmonics) required to define the spectral envelope of the forces. The AR(110) model was estimated for each window $W_j$, on the training set as well as on a test set, using a standard LS parameter fit of eq. (9) within each window, to obtain each parameter vector $\mathbf{p}(j)$. A 30 × 30 SOM was trained on the parameter space spanned by a training set containing samples 7000 to 8889, using the batch algorithm with a gaussian neighborhood for a width factor $\sigma$ decreasing from 10 to 0.7.

The residual spectrogram of Fig. 4 was obtained as described in the previous sections, based on the model trained with data from samples 7000 to 8889. As seen, it highlights only the novelties (time and frequency), and hides "known" spectral patterns making them appear on white color.

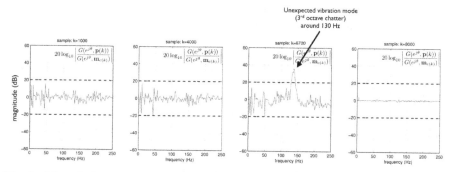

**Fig. 5.** Plot of the residual spectra at four different time instants (columns of the residuals spectrogram). The third one corresponds to sample 6700, when chatter occurs.

# 4   Conclusion

In this paper a novel method to visualize changes in the dynamic response of process has been proposed. The method is rooted on the idea of maps of dynamics, where the self-organizing map is used to learn and map all local dynamic behaviours of the process present in a training data set, and allows to display qualitative information on changes in the dynamic response by means of comparison between the closest stored dynamic model and the current model, following therefore a model based approach. The proposed method not only provides a way to detect the presence of changes, but also gives qualitative information about the nature of the change, showing the affected frequencies. All this information may be efficiently displayed in a time-frequency plot (residual spectrogram) that hides known frequency patterns and shows up novel spectral patterns and the time instant where the changes appeared. The idea is shown on two real data examples: tank level control dynamics and visualization of chatter in a cold rolling mill.

The method can be potentially used in many other ways, admitting a number of possible variations such as using local nonlinear models or developing alternative visualizations such as time-time plots (using e.g. impulse responses of the residual models instead of frequency responses) or plotting meaningful features from the residual models selected on the basis of the problem domain.

**Acknowledgements.** This paper was supported by FEDER funds and MICINN (Spanish Ministry of Science and Innovation) under grants DPI2009-13398-C02-01 and DPI2009-13398-C02-02.

# References

1. Barreto, G.A., Araujo, A.F.R.: Identification and control of dynamical systems using the self-organizing map. IEEE Transactions on Neural Networks 15(5), 1244–1259 (2004)
2. Blanco, I.D., González, M.D., Cuadrado, A.A., Martínez, J.J.F.: A new approach to exploratory analysis of system dynamics using SOM. Applications to industrial processes. Expert Systems with Applications 34(4), 2953–2965 (2008)

3. Gertler, J.J.: Survey of model-based failure detection and isolation in complex plants. IEEE Control Systems Magazine 8(6), 3–11 (1988)
4. Isermann, R.: Supervision, fault-detection and fault-diagnosis methods – an introduction. Control Engineering Practice 5(5), 639–652 (1997)
5. Isermann, R.: Model-based fault-detection and diagnosis-status and applications. Annual Reviews in control 29(1), 71–85 (2005)
6. Kohonen, T.: Self-Organizing Maps. Springer, Heidelberg (1995)
7. Kohonen, T., Oja, E., Simula, O., Visa, A., Kangas, J.: Engineering applications of the self-organizing map. Proceedings of the IEEE 84(10), 1358–1384 (1996)
8. Markou, M., Singh, S.: Novelty detection: a review–part 1: statistical approaches. Signal Processing 83(12), 2481–2497 (2003)
9. Markou, M., Singh, S.: Novelty detection: a review–part 2: neural network based approaches. Signal Processing 83(12), 2499–2521 (2003)
10. Principe, J.C., Wang, L., Motter, M.A.: Local dynamic modeling with self-organizing maps and applications to nonlinear system identification and control. Proceedings of the IEEE 86(11), 2240–2258 (1998)

# Functional Architectures and Hierarchies of Time Scales

Dionysios Perdikis[1], Marmaduke Woodman[1,2], and Viktor Jirsa[1]

[1] Theoretical Neuroscience Group, Institute of Movement Sciences, UMR CNRS 6233 &
University of Mediterranean, 163, Av. de Luminy, F-13288, Marseille cedex 09, France
[2] Center for Complex Systems and Brain Sciences, Florida Atlantic University,
777 Glades Rd, Florida 33431, USA
dionysos.perdikis@etumel.univmed.fr

**Abstract.** Dynamical system theory offers approaches towards cognitive modeling and computation inspired by self-organization and pattern formation in open systems operating far from thermodynamical equilibrium. In this spirit we propose a functional architecture for the emergence of complex functions such as sequential motor behaviors. We model elementary functions as Structured Flows on Manifolds (SFM) that provide an unambiguous deterministic description of the functional dynamics, while still remaining compatible with the intrinsically low dimensionality of elementary behaviors. Pattern competition processes (operating on a hierarchy of time scales) provide the means to compose complex functions out of simpler constituent ones. Our underlying hypothesis is that complex functions can be decomposed in functional modes (simpler building blocks). Simulations of generating cursive handwriting provide proof of concept and suggest exciting avenues towards extending the current framework to other human functions including learning and language.

**Keywords:** cognitive architectures, function, phase flow, self-organization, pattern formation, non-linear dynamics.

## 1 Introduction

It is a common assumption in cognitive modeling and Artificial Intelligence that human function is constituted in a structured manner (even if that structure is as complex as irregular behavior [1,2] or of a purely statistical nature [3,4]. Complex functions are often characterized by the repetition of invariant patterns such as in dancing, musical performance and language related functions including speech, writing and typing. In all these cases, dancing figures, musical notes, elementary conceptual schemas, phonemes, graphemes or keyboard pressings combine to form complex sequences in time. To understand the organization of a complex sequence, the two traditional approaches, symbolic dynamics and connectionism, define functional units as well as a set of operations on them, commonly referred to as "computation". In symbolic dynamics information is represented explicitly as organized symbols and computation takes the form of syntactic rules combining them [5]. In connectionist models on the other hand, patterns of activation, distributed across the nodes of large networks, allow for parallel computations [6]. Moreover, hybrid cognitive architectures involving symbolic knowledge representation with connectionist learning algorithms

K. Diamantaras, W. Duch, L.S. Iliadis (Eds.): ICANN 2010, Part II, LNCS 6353, pp. 353–361, 2010.
© Springer-Verlag Berlin Heidelberg 2010

have also been proposed [7]. It is a common theme, however, that in all but a few cases [2,8,9], functional units are considered as static patterns or "states". Even when a dynamical process is modeled and dealt with in real time (see the broad literature of recurrent neural networks [10,11,12]), it is eventually broken into a succession of discrete states (encoding past context) and treated as such.

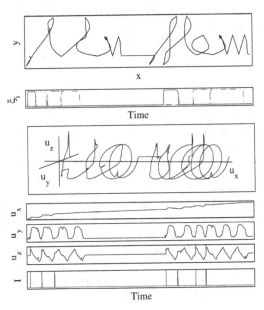

**Fig. 1.** The word *"flow"* is generated by the functional architecture. From top to bottom: (a) workspace output: the trajectory on the plane *x-y*, (b) time series of the slow sequential dynamics $\xi_{1-4}$ (different line styles are used to distinguish among the four functional modes used), (c) functional dynamics: the trajectory in the 3-dimensional phase (state) space spanned by $u_x$, $u_y$ and $u_z$, and the respective time series, and (d) the control signal $I$.

In contrast our here proposed approach is based upon the time structure of complex human function. We propose that complex functional sequences can be decomposed in a dynamical repertoire of functional modes, namely elementary processes (as opposed to static states) that play the role of functional units. Additional processes operating in different characteristic time scales use the latter ones as building blocks of more complex functions. Thus, computation emerges in a self-organized manner. The ensemble of subsystems, acting upon two different time scales, defines a functional architecture allowing for novel forms of biologically inspired computation.

Potential applications of the here proposed functional architecture may be found in motor control where complex movements are composed of elementary building blocks called motor programs [13] or movement primitives [14,15]. Production and comprehension of speech perception in terms of syllables [16,17] or language in terms of basic conceptual schemas [18,19] may serve as another promising field for application. Here we illustrate the basic functional principles in the context of sequential motor behavior because movements constitute dynamical phenomena easily open to observation.

In the following we present the mathematical framework of Structured Flows on Manifolds and then introduce the functional architecture in section 2. In section 3 we demonstrate an application in cursive handwriting as a proof of concept providing the respective computer simulations. Finally, in section 4 we discuss several potential extensions with respect to neural coding, learning, embodied intelligence and analog biological inspired computation.

## 1.1 Structured Flows on Manifolds (SFMs)

We model functional modes as Structured Flows on Manifolds (SFM) that have only recently been proposed [20,21] as a general framework for understanding functional dynamics. Such is accomplished through a fast adiabatic contraction from an inherently high dimensional space to a functionally relevant subset of the phase (state) space, the so-called manifold. On the manifold a phase flow is prescribed and a dynamics evolves for the duration of a specific functional mode. This behavior is mathematically expressed as:

$$\dot{u}_i = -g\left(\{u_i\}, \{s_j\}\right) u_i + \mu f\left(\{u_i\}, \{s_j\}\right)$$

$$\dot{s}_j = -s_j + h\left(\{u_i\}, \{s_j\}\right) \qquad , \qquad (1)$$

$$u \in \mathbb{R}^N, \ s \in \mathbb{R}^M, \ N \ll M$$

where the value of the so called "smallness" parameter $\mu$ is constrained as in $0<\mu\ll 1$, the function $g(.)$ defines the manifold, the function $f(.)$ describes the subsequent flow on it and $h(.)$ the fast variable dynamics that approaches the manifold. The choice for a small value of $\mu$ will ensure that the phase flow dynamics is slow in comparison to the dynamics collapsing on the manifold. The flow can be constrained on the manifold by choosing an appropriate attractive function $g(.)$.

Such a theoretical framework makes reference to the literature of Synergetics [22] and the related research program in behavioral and cognitive neuroscience, namely Coordination Dynamics [1,23]. The former considers the brain as an open multicomponent system that interacts with its environment and is free to exchange matter and energy. In the proximity of instabilities (determined by critical values of control parameters) the dynamics is separated into fast stable and slow variables. The fast variables can be adiabatically eliminated by expressing their dynamics as a function of the slow variables. Thus, reduced descriptions can be derived for the collective dynamics, described by only a few so-called order parameters. Accordingly, the field of Coordination Dynamics searches for low-dimensional patterns emerging in brain function (and human behavior as well) as a result of the tendencies of the brain regions to segregate and integrate based on functional requirements.

However, adiabatic elimination is based on center manifold theory [24], which is a local theory as well as valid only around instabilities. Instead, we require that systems of the form of equations (1) contain an inertial manifold [25], a global structure used in cases of reduction of infinite dimensional dynamical systems to finite dimensional spaces. Systems exhibiting inertial manifolds are dealt with on a case by case basis.

## 1.2 Phase Flows

The SFM framework allows us to model a dynamical repertoire of functional modes that we assume to be available to an agent. At each time moment the dynamics of an agent's function is dominated by a specific functional mode, that is, it evolves on a manifold that is of a much lower dimension than the original functional space and it is described by a structured phase flow (function $f(.)$ of equations (1)) to which we focus in the following.

In a quantitative manner, phase flows determine unambiguously the evolution of a dynamical process in the phase (state) space of an autonomous, deterministic and time continuous system. Thus, from a computational perspective, they can be considered as general forms of computational elements; the vector field describing a phase flow establishes causal relationships among the states of the system by assigning at each state a vector determining the next state.

On the other hand, the phase flow topology uniquely determines a system's qualitative behaviour. In other words, phase flow topologies encode the invariant features of a dynamical process relative to quantitative variation, thus identifying all functional possibilities within a class in a model-independent manner. This means that stability properties or the effect of a small enough perturbation are also encoded. This is an advantage rarely found in other types of functional or computational units, which would correspond to single states or (in the best of cases) to single solutions (trajectories in the phase space) of a phase flow. Consequently, the information contained in phase flows is much greater.

In planar systems (systems of two dimensions), common phase flow topologies are the ones that include point attractors and limit cycles that can be used to model discrete and rhythmic functions respectively, as well as separatrices. The latter ones are structures that locally divide the phase flow into opposing directions, and thus, endow phase flows with threshold properties and multistability [26].

Phase flows have been used in the past to model patterns of behavioural and sensorimotor coordination [26,27] that led to counter-intuitive predictions such us the ones on false starts [28]. Huys *et al.* [29] used the class formation properties of phase flows topologies to establish a taxonomy between discrete and rhythmic movements.

In short, SFMs provide functional modes with properties such as low-dimensionality, class-defining invariance together with within class variation and executive stability (i.e. the maintenance of performance in the presence of perturbations). Another such property, essential for the emergence of complex function, is assemblability, i.e. the notion that functional modes can be assembled and embedded into a larger functional organization.

## 2 Functional Architectures

Once functional modes are identified as SFMs, there is still need for mechanisms to operate on them in order that complex function or computation emerges. We assume that at each time moment a single SFM dominates the dynamics of an agent's function. This SFM is given as a linear combination of all SFMs available in the dynamical repertoire of the agent:

$$\dot{\mathbf{u}} = F(\mathbf{u},t) = \sum_i w_i \left(\xi_i(t)\right) f_i(\mathbf{u}) + I \ , \tag{2}$$

where $\mathbf{u}$ is the state vector and $f_i(.)$ is the vector field of the $i$-th SFM, $F(.)$ denotes the vector field of the expressed SFM as a function of time $t$. The $w_i$s ($w_i \in [0,1]$) act as weighting coefficients for the $i$-th SFM and generally operate on a slower time scale than that of the SFMs (except for fast transitions between SFMs that lead to a fast contraction on the respective manifold). That is, they 'select' a particular component flow $f_j$ (when $w_j=1$ and all other $w_i=0$, for $i \neq j$) during its activation phase.

Apart from the slow dynamics that changes the (expressed) flow topology, the architecture also provides for the optional involvement of a control signal that leaves the flow unaffected, namely an instantaneous one, $I$, that resembles a meaningful perturbation. This signal can temporarily set the system in a desired state or, when combined with phase flows comprising separatrices, may change the dynamics of a functional mode (by, for instance, initiating a process [29]). The functional architecture, thus, combines invariant features (the SFM) with those that are variable across repeated instances of a functional mode's appearance in an agent's behavior. Perdikis & Jirsa [30] provide computational evidence on the efficiency of a control scheme like the one described here.

In summary, the ensemble of subsystems ($f_i(\mathbf{u})$, $w_i$, $I$) operating on distinct time scales ($T_f \ll T_u \ll T_w$), constitutes the proposed functional architecture (see [31,32] for other time hierarchies in brain and cognitive function). In the following subsections we show how the $\xi_i$ dynamics controlling the $w_i$ can be designed to organize functional modes so that more complex functions emerge, such as sequential motor behavior.

## 2.1 Functional Mode Competition

Since, we require that SFMs activations do not overlap, we implement a "winner-take-all competition" (WTA) for the $\xi_i$ dynamics:

$$\dot{\xi}_i = \frac{1}{T_\xi} \left( \lambda_i - C_i \sum_k^N \xi_k^2 \right) \xi_i \ ,$$
$$\lambda_i \in [-1,1], \ C_i \in [1,+\infty) \tag{3}$$

where $T_\xi$ is a time constant ensuring that the competition will evolve fast, $\lambda_i$ controls the availability of a functional mode to take part in the competition and $C_i$ its outcome.

Thus, functional modes are organized by mutual relationships of competition. Such a functional mode decomposition based on a competition scheme follows previous work on the Synergetic Computer [33], which, in turn, is inspired by the physics of pattern formation in non-equilibrium systems. At the same time, it is well established in the literature of biological inspired computation [34]. An alternative could be the winner-less competition principle based on transient heteroclinic sequences [9].

## 2.2 Sequential Dynamics

In order to model sequential behavior, additional "circuitry" is required to activate the functional modes taking part in the sequence, one after the other and with the correct timing. This is achieved by designing suitable dynamics for the $\lambda_j$ parameters that determine which functional modes are going to be available for the competition at each stage of the sequence as well as the duration of activation of every one of them. In addition, the $C_j$ parameters decide about which functional mode will win the competition at each such stage, and thus, the specific order of the sequence. The index $j$ denotes the subset $\mathbf{I}$ of $M$ functional modes that participate in the sequence out of a repertoire of total $N$ modes, indicating also the order of activation.

Thus, parallel representations of the sequence (encoded in the arrays of $\lambda_j$ and $C_j$ parameters) are combined with serial processes of WTA competition at each stage of it. Such an organization makes reference to the well established Competitive Queuing models of sequential behavior [35].

## 3   Implementation of Cursive Handwriting

We demonstrate as proof of concept the application of the functional architecture on a characteristic example of sequential motor behavior, namely handwriting. Here functional modes correspond to characters modeled as 3-dimensional SFMs. The manifold, a cylindrical spiral along the $u_x$ axis, is chosen to be common for all characters for implementation reasons, without loss of generality. Thus, the general form of the functional dynamics (exemplifying equation (2)) is:

$$
\begin{aligned}
\dot{u}_x &= \frac{\mu}{T_u}\sum_i^N\left(|\xi_i|f_{x_i}\left(u_y,\dot{u}_y\right)\right) \\
\dot{u}_y &= \frac{1}{T_u}\left[\left(R^2-u_y^2-u_z^2\right)u_y+\mu\left(\sum_i^N|\xi_i|\right)\left(u_z-u_y\left(u_y-R\right)\left(u_y+R\right)\right)\right], \\
\dot{u}_z &= \frac{1}{T_u}\left[\left(R^2-u_y^2-u_z^2\right)u_z+\mu\sum_i^N\left(|\xi_i|f_{z_i}\left(u_y,u_z\right)\right)\right]+I\left(u_y,\dot{u}_y\right)
\end{aligned}
\tag{4}
$$

where $R$ is the radius of the manifold and $I$ is chosen as a function of position and velocity on the $u_y$ axis, thus, constituting the functional architecture a completely autonomous system. $u_y$ and $u_z$ obey excitator-like dynamics, first proposed as a unifying framework for rhythmic and discrete movements [26]: depending on whether $f_z^{limcycl}(u_y,u_z)=\mu_e(-u_y), f_z^{mono}(u_y,u_z)=\mu_e(-u_y\pm R)$, or $f_z^{bi}(u_y,u_z)=\mu_e(-u_z)$, the system exhibits a limit cycle (rhythmic behavior), a point attractor with a separatrix (monostable system with threshold properties) or two point attractors with a separatrix between them (bistable system) respectively. In any case, a second "smallness" parameter $\mu_e$ guarantees the time scale separation that is necessary for the threshold properties of Excitator systems. In its turn, the form of $f_{xi}(.)$ yields the desired letter shapes. The modeling strategy constitutes modulating the velocity on the $u_x$ axis by the position and velocity on the $u_y$ axis. Of course such modeling of the handwriting functional dynamics is completely arbitrary and far from biological realism. However, our present purpose is to demonstrate the functional architecture, which is compatible with any phase flow choice. The actual phase flows constituting a character should be determined based on real experimental data. Finally, the functional dynamics (properly scaled and after a baseline is chosen for each character) drive the dynamics on the handwriting workspace, that is, the plane $x$-$y$.

Figure 1 demonstrates a simulation of the 'handwritten' word *"flow"* generated by the functional architecture. The system settles on a high dimensional attractor after a short transient. Monostable flows are used to generate letters *"f"*, *"l"* and *"o"* and a limit cycle one for *"w"*. *"f"* is initiated with the appropriate initial conditions, while the control signal $I$ triggers one cycle per stimulus for letters *"l"* and *"o"*.

## 4 Discussion

We proposed a functional architecture based on two main subsystems operating in distinct time scales: a dynamical repertoire of functional modes modeled as SFMs and slower additional mechanisms organizing them, based on the principle of winner-take-all competition.

We demonstrated how the appropriate choice of the functional "circuitry" within the available dynamical repertoire can lead to the emergence of more complex functions such as sequential motor behavior. At this point, we would like to stress the fact that different kinds of such "circuitries" among the functional modes could be designed to prescribe numerous other types of causal relationships between them (apart from the above described sequential one). Thus, a variety of functional architectures can emerge, even conditional ones, mimicking the IF-THEN rules found in traditional Artificial Intelligence. Moreover, a hierarchy of multiple levels of such functional architectures could be designed in order to account for a repertoire of even more complex functions necessary to model higher cognitive functions like language.

The here proposed theoretical framework also suggests that different processes of adaptation or learning are required for complex function to emerge. The acquisition of an initial repertoire of elementary functions would be followed by processes constructing various functional architectures to account for complex behaviors. At the same time, the initial repertoire could be extended with new functional modes by composition of existing ones (for instance through fusion or concatenation). The latter mechanism could provide us with the means to model phenomena found in cognitive linguistics literature such as conceptual metaphors and blends [18,19].

By modeling functional units as dynamical processes instead of states, an attempt to naturalize human function without undesired reductions with respect to its complexity may be possible. Moreover, the hierarchy of time scales as a principle of organization conciliates continuous dynamics with the "discrete" nature of a repertoire of distinct functional modes.

Thanks to these choices the here proposed framework is also compatible with embodied intelligence approaches, since functional modes may correspond to patterns of closed sensorimotor loops or human-environment interactions. In this case they would result out of a process of pattern formation in the structurally coupled [36] agent-environment systems in an autonomous self-organized manner.

Finally, in [21] the foundations are laid for coding SFMs in distributed networks like ones of firing rate neural populations, thus, addressing the problem of the structure-function dipole (see Figure 2 for some preliminary results). From a computational perspective, this could lead to a novel paradigm of analog biologically inspired computation with possible materializations in integrated circuits such as VLSI.

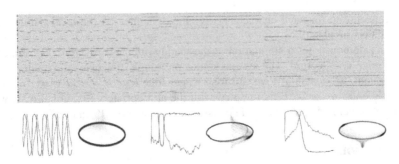

**Fig. 2.** Neural coding of SFMs: A network of 200 firing rate neural populations is simulated with Gaussian noise for 600 *ms*. The network engages in different two dimensional phase flows (from left to right limit cycle, monostable and bistable) in subsequent 200 *ms* segments. At the top, a spatio-temporal plot of each neural population firing rate activity (vertical axis in color coding) in time (horizontal axis) is displayed. There are distinct spatio-temporal patterns corresponding to the SFMs produced by the network. The three pairs of plots at the bottom demonstrate the result of principal components analysis of the network activity for the different SFMs. Each one is comprised of a single trajectory time series plot (first two components) on the left, and a plot of 200 phase space trajectories starting from different initial conditions (first three components) on the right. In the latter plots, it can be viewed that the network dynamics collapses to two dimensional manifolds and exhibits structured phase flows on them.

# References

1. Kelso, S.: Dynamic Patterns: The Self-Organization of Brain and Behavior. A Bradford Book, The MIT Press, Cambridge (1995)
2. Kozma, R., Freeman, W.: The KIV model of intentional dynamics. Neural Networks 22(3), 277–285 (2009)
3. Friston, K., Kilner, J., Harrison, L.: A free energy principle for the brain, pp. 70–87 (2006)
4. Harris, C., Wolpert, D.: Signal-dependent noise determines motor planning. Nature 394, 780–784 (1998)
5. Newel, A.: Unified theories of cognition. Harvard University Press, Cambridge (1990)
6. Kremer, S.: Spatiotemporal connectionist networks: A taxonomy and review. Neural Computation 13, 249–306 (2001)
7. Sun, R., Alexandre, F.: Connectionist-symbolic integration: From unified to hybrid approaches. Lawrence Erlbaum Associates, Mahwah (1997)
8. Rabinovich, M., Muezzinoglu, M.: Mutual emotion-cognition dynamics (September 2009), arXiv:0909.1144
9. Rabinovich, M., Huerta, R., Verona, P., Afraimovich, V.: Transient cognitive dynamics, metastability, and decision making. PLoS Comp. Biol. 4(5) (2008)
10. Kolen, J., Kremer, S.: A field guide to dynamical recurrent networks. Wiley-IEEE Press, New York (2001)
11. Carpenter, G., Grossberg, S.: Adaptive resonance theory. In: Arbib, M. (ed.) The handbook of brain theory and neural networks, 2nd edn., pp. 87–90. The MIT Press, Cambridge (2003)
12. Maass, W., Natschlager, T., Markram, H.: Real-time computing without stable states: A new framework for neural computation based on perturbations. Neural Computation 14, 2531–2560 (2002)

13. Schmidt, R., Lee, T.: Motor control and learning: a behavioral emphasis, 4th edn. Human Kinetics, Leeds (2005)
14. Mussa-Ivaldi, F., Bizzi, E.: Motor learning through the combination of primitives. Phil. Trans. R. Soc. Lond. B 355, 1755–1769 (2000)
15. Morasso, P., Mussa-Ivaldi, F.: Trajectory formation and handwriting: A computational model. Biological Cybernetics 45, 131–142 (1982)
16. Tuller, B., Kelso, S.: The production and perception of syllable structure. Journal of Speech and Hearing Research 34, 501–508 (1991)
17. Poeppel, D., Idsardi, W., van Wassenhove, V.: Speech perception at the interface of neurobiology and linguistics. Phil. Trans. R. Soc. B 363(1493), 1071–1086 (2007)
18. Lakoff, G.: Women, fire, and dangerous things: What categories reveal about the mind. University of Chicago Press, Chicago (1987)
19. Feldman, J.: From molecule to metaphor: A neural theory of language. A Bradford Book, The MIT Press, Cambridge (2006)
20. Jirsa, V., Mersmann, J.: Neuronal network structure and method to operate a neuronal network structure. International Patent Application WO 2009/037526 A1 (2009)
21. Pillai, A.: Structured Flows on Manifolds: Distributed functional architectures. PhD thesis, Florida Atlantic University (2008)
22. Haken, H.: Synergetics: introduction and advanced topics. Springer, Heidelberg (2004)
23. Kelso, S., Jirsa, V.: Coordination dynamics: issues and trends. Springer, Heidelberg (2004)
24. Guckenheimer, J., Holmes, P.: Nonlinear oscillations, dynamical systems, and bifurcations of vector fields. Springer, New York (2002)
25. Constantin, P., Foias, C., Nicolaenko, B., Teman, R.: Intergral manifolds and inertial manifolds for dissipative partial differential equations, 1st edn. Springer, New York (1989)
26. Jirsa, V., Kelso, S.: The excitator as a minimal model for the coordination dynamics of discrete and rhythmic movement generation. J. Mot. Behav. 37(1), 35–51 (2005)
27. Huys, R., Fernandez, L., Bootsma, R., Jirsa, V.: Fitts' law is not continuous in reciprocal aiming, pp. 1179–1184 (2009)
28. Fink, P., Kelso, S., Jirsa, V.: Perturbation-induced false starts as a test of the Jirsa-Kelso excitator model, pp. 147–157 (2009)
29. Huys, R., Jirsa, V., Studenka, B., Rheaume, N., Zelaznik, H.: Human trajectory formation: Taxonomy of movement based on phase flow topology. In: Fuchs, A., Jirsa, V. (eds.) Coordination: neural, behavioral and social dynamics. Springer, Heidelberg (2007)
30. Perdikis, D., Jirsa, V.: How to control complex movements. Poster in Progress in Motor Control, Marseille (2009)
31. Friston, K.: Hierarchical models in the brain. PLoS Comput. Biol. 4(11) (2008)
32. Kiebel, S., von Kriegstein, K., Daunizeau, J., Friston, K.: Recognizing sequences of sequences. PLoS Comput. Biol. 5(8) (2009)
33. Haken, H.: Synergetic computers and cognition: a top-down approach to neural nets, 2nd edn. Springer, Heidelberg (2004)
34. Grossberg, S.: Biological competition: Decision rules, pattern formation and oscillations. Proc. Natl. Acad. Sci. USA 77(4), 2338–2342 (1980)
35. Bullock, D., Rhodes, B.: Competitive queuing for planning and serial performance. In: Arbib, M. (ed.) Handbook of brain theory and neural networks, 2nd edn., pp. 241–244. The MIT Press, Cambridge (2003)
36. Maturana, H., Varela, F.: The tree of knowledge: The biological roots of human understanding Revised edn. Shambhala, Boston (1998)

# A Novel Single-Trial Analysis Scheme for Characterizing the Presaccadic Brain Activity Based on a SON Representation

Konstantinos Bozas[1,*], Stavros I. Dimitriadis[1],
Nikolaos A. Laskaris[1,*], and Areti Tzelepi[2]

[1] Laboratory of Artificial Intelligence & Information Analysis, Department of Informatics,
Aristotle University of Thessaloniki, 54 124, Greece
konmpoz@gmail.com, stdimitr@csd.auth.gr,
laskaris@aiia.csd.auth.gr
[2] ICCS, National Technical University of Athens, Greece
areti@iccs.gr

**Abstract.** We introduce a tactic for single-trial (ST) analysis that incorporates, in the study of saccades, the experimental control of a behavioural variable within the standard paradigm of a repeated execution of a single task. The ubiquitous ST-variability in brain imaging recordings is turned, here, to an additional informative dimension that can be exploited to gain further understanding of brain's function mechanisms.

Our approach builds over a self-organizing neural network (SON) that can efficiently learn and parameterise the variability in the patterning of electro-oculographic (EOG) signals. In a second stage, the STs of encephalographic activity are organized accordingly and the observed variations in the EOG signals are associated with specific brain activations. Finally, complex network analysis is employed as a means to characterize the ST-variability based on modes of functional connectivity.

Using EEG data from a Go/No-Go paradigm, we demonstrate that the spontaneous variations in the execution of a saccade can open a window on the role of different brain regions for ocular movements.

**Keywords:** EEG, EOG, Neural-Gas, phase-locking, network-metrics.

## 1 Introduction

There is nowadays a vast variety of experimental techniques applicable for studying the nervous system, based on diverse instrumentations, with which various brain theories can be brought under test. Usually, neuroscience research proceeds in either of the two following ways: i) the controlled experimental approach and ii) the empirical approach [1]. In the first case, an experiment is conducted for the purpose of determining the effect of a single variable of interest (like stimulus color) on a particular system. The influence of all other variables (attention, habituation etc.) is attempted to

---

* Corresponding author.

K. Diamantaras, W. Duch, L.S. Iliadis (Eds.): ICANN 2010, Part II, LNCS 6353, pp. 362–371, 2010.
© Springer-Verlag Berlin Heidelberg 2010

kept at minimum via appropriate manipulations. On the other hand, the empirical method is based on the collection of a large amount of related data which need, later, to be processed efficiently and sorted accordingly. Data analysis needs to be adjusted not only with respect to the particular recording technique, but also with respect to either of the two experimental approaches. The spirit of regression dominates the analysis of data from controlled experiments, while the notion of classification (mostly in its unsupervised flavor) dominates the empirical studies.

Within the previous experimental manipulations, the extremely popular paradigm of event-related responses is included as well. A particular task (e.g. finger movement, target detection) is repeatedly performed by the subject with the aim of collecting sufficient number of relevant traces of brain activity. The recorded signals, after time-alignment, are processed by averaging so as to diminish the ongoing activity (including spontaneous brain activity) and reveal the task-related component of the signals. In principle, event-related paradigms belong to the category of controlled experiments. However, a thorough study of (a large collection of) actual data can demonstrate the phenomenon of 'ST-variability', which is usually attributed to the non-stationary character of brain and calls for adopting methodologies designed for analyzing data from empirical studies. In a series of previous publications [2]-[5], we experimented with the idea that ST-variability can be treated as a useful signal. The justification was based on the simplest experimental set-up, this of collecting multiple ST-responses during identical sensory stimulation in humans. We have therefore introduced suitable signal-analytic algorithms to manipulate the involved variations in order to gain insights into the brain mechanisms and probe functional associations between different brain areas. In the present study we extend the above consideration in the case of event-related responses, by introducing the concept that the (originally) unduly variations in the performance of a task can be exploited in order to test the role of different brain activations.

Saccade-related activity has been explored in many previous neuroscientific studies [6]-[9], with the involved experiments adopting both the empirical and controlled experimental approaches. It is the scope of this work to introduce a hybrid methodology that works with saccade-related data from a standard EEG experiment where the subject had to execute the movement as fast as possible. First, the EOG signals are grouped, by means of Neural-Gas network, according to the velocity patterning of the executed movement. This partition (into slow, fast and very-fast movements) is then transferred to brain signals in order to detect the temporal modulations of a complex scheme with which the brain controls the response to the external stimulus (the visual cue for the movement). Finally, functionally connectivity analysis is performed - independently for each group of STs- based on a *phase-locking* estimator that associates a functional dependence value to every edge in a graph built over all the placed electrodes.

The rest of the paper is structured as follows. Section 2 has an introductory purpose and reviews shortly well-established knowledge about presaccadic brain activity. Section 3 includes a short description of the available data. Section 4 provides a detailed description of our methodology and Section 5 reports on the new experimental findings.

## 2 Background

Preparing a movement is a complex process. It involves different sensory-motor transformations in the human brain before the movement is finally executed. There has been extensive research of how the central nervous system controls voluntary action. Although today we have a reasonable understanding of the different stages involved in this complex process, some aspects are still not clear. In order to perform a movement, position and the velocity vector (including direction and speed) need to be calculated. Previous research [10] on the encoding of kinematic parameters in the motor cortex while primates performed arm movements showed a direct relationship between kinematics and neural activity over the motor cortex. Many studies later on have confirmed these findings and revealed new aspects of this relationship. However, little is known about the relationship of brain activity to the kinematics of eye movements. We know from previous EEG studies that brain activity preceding an eye movement is similar to the one preceding finger movements [11],[12]. Here, we examine the dependence of saccade velocity on preceding brain activity as recorded with EEG.

## 3 Experimental Data

### 3.1 Experiment Description

In order to explore the relationship between EEG activity and saccadic eye movement, a Go/No-Go experimental design was adopted (See Fig.1). According to the color of the fixation cross, the subject had either to make a saccade (green cross), or ignore (red cross) the lateral target and keep fixating at the center. In the beginning of a trial, a white cross comes on. Then the color of the cross changes (red/green) and at the same time a lateral target (left/right) appears. The subject has to keep fixation on the colored cross. When the color of the cross becomes white again (Go signal), the subject has to make a saccade to the target if the color of the cross was green, or keep fixation ignoring the target otherwise (i.e. in case of a red cross). The last frame (empty frame) provides a relaxation period during which the subject can blink, rest, etc.

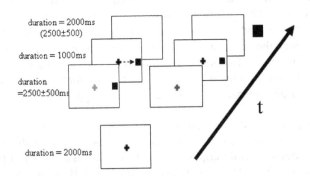

**Fig. 1.** The different periods in the time course of a single trial

Every subject attended 7 to 9 runs and each run consisted of 40 trials. (20 for Go, 20 for No-Go condition). The duration of each trial was 8 seconds. The EEG signals were recorded via 64 electrodes, which were placed according to the international 10-20 electrode position classification system. The EOG signals were simultaneously recorded through two pairs of electrodes attached to the top-bottom side and right-left side of the right eye (vertical and horizontal EOG). All data were sampled at 1024Hz.

### 3.2  EEG Processing and Artifact Rejection

The raw EEG data were filtered by a high-pass filter (cut-off 0.16Hz) and by a low-pass filter (cut-off 100 Hz). The data were further processed so as to, first, remove 'outlying' trials and, then to enhance the SNR in the remaining ones. Since oculo-graphic noise was prevalent in our EEG data (due to the nature of the experiment), we applied the recently introduced (a simple, robust and fully automatic technique) *regression-based EOG reduction method* [13], which suppresses the fast and slow EOG-related artifacts of the multichannel EEG data.

## 4  Methodology

A flowchart of the (main steps of the) introduced methodology is provided in Fig.2. In a nutshell, *Neural-Gas* algorithm splits the EEG STs into different groups based on the corresponding velocity profiles of the EOG-signals. For each group, we measure (across trials) the *phase locking value* for every possible pair of EEG channels. In this way a graph representation of brain-connectivity is formed, in which nodes corresponds to electrodes. The obtained graph is characterized via a *local network metric*, which expresses the segregation and evaluates communication efficiency among the nodes. This characterization is repeated for different time segments of EEG data, and presented in a time-dependent topographic format that facilitates the recognition of brain regions with activation that relates causally with the forthcoming saccade.

### 4.1  Saccadic Onset Detection and  ST-Data Collection

In order to extract segments of brain activity related with the saccade initiation, the saccadic movement onset had to be, first, detected based on the horizontal EOG signal. *Position-variance* and *velocity-based methods* [14] are among the most popular techniques, utilizing the sharp increase/decrease of the EOG signal during eye movement. Marple-Horvat et al. [15] suggested a technique with a linked double window applied to an approximation of the first derivative of the EOG position, which yielded fine identification rates to our data and therefore adopted in this study.

Since the above onset detection technique, occasionally, produced false positives, we incorporated an outlier-detection step just after the onset detection. Based on the onset latencies, a set of EOG signal-segments were first extracted and then fed to an artifact rejection technique [16]. This technique uses signal morphology to compare every segment against each other and then realizes reduced-ordering of the involved EOG-patterns in order to enable the removal of outliers (i.e. segment wrongly recognized as containing saccadic onset). The remaining EOG-segments formed the ensemble of EOG-STs. The corresponding EEG-segments, extracted from the concurrently recorded multichannel signal, formed the ensemble of EEG-STs.

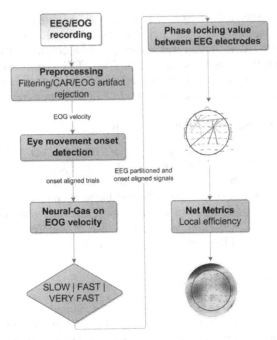

**Fig. 2.** Flowchart of the main steps

## 4.2 Grouping STs with Neural-Gas acting on EOG-Velocity Patterns

In an attempt to link the behavioral response (saccade) with the initiating brain activity, we treat the EOG-segments (from the saccade onset and before) as a set of multivariate patterns. The inherent variations in this set are leaned by means of Neural-Gas network and parameterized in a parsimonious and intelligible way. This included the formation of different groups of EOG-segments, which are sorted according to relevant semantics (that are of interest for the particular study of presaccadic brain activity). Having in mind that oculographic signals are indicative about the velocity of a saccade, we choose to associate with the EOG-segments the corresponding velocity patterns. This can be thought as a feature-extraction step, with which the subsequent learning algorithm is guided to focus on the important aspects of EOG variations. Hence, the N segments of EOG-signals are associated with $\{X_i\}$, i=1,2,...N , i.e. with vectors having as coordinates the estimates of saccade velocity at successive latencies (before the detected onset).

Neural-Gas network is then employed to accomplish the learning task, i.e. to organize the saccades based on their velocity profiles. This algorithm is an artificial neural network model, which converges efficiently to a small, user-defined number $k<N$ of codebook vectors, using a stochastic gradient descent procedure with a "softmax" adaptation rule that minimizes the average distortion error [17]. Following the procedure described in [3], the computed code vectors are then assigned ranks based on their MST graph. Finally, the ordered code vectors $O_j \in \Re^p \; j = 1,2,...,k$ were used in a simple encoding scheme: the nearest code vector was assigned to each $X_i$. This procedure divides the data manifold $V \in R^p$ into k Voronoi-regions.

$$\mathbf{V}_j = \{ X \in \mathbf{V} : \| X - O_j \| \le \| X - O_i \| \forall i, i = 1,2,...,k \cdot \tag{1}$$

From a more practical point of view, the bulk of information contained in the data is represented, in a parsimonious way, by a (Nxk) partition matrix U, with elements $u_{ij}$ such that

$$u_{ij} = \begin{cases} 1 & \text{if } X_i \in V_j \\ 0 & \text{if } X_i \notin V_j \end{cases}, \sum_k^j \sum_{i=1}^N u_{ij} = N \cdot \tag{2}$$

The derived grouping (estimated for EOG-signals) is applied to the corresponding EEG-STs. In this way, groups of multichannel data are emerging which can be compared in order to understand what was the leading cause of the observed variability (i.e. in the patterning of saccade velocity).

The previous steps are exemplified, via Fig.3, in the case of a subject with 58 trials of left saccades. Neural-Gas algorithm was executed using the approximation of the first derivative of the EOG signal (previously used for detecting the onset [15]). The input vectors consisted of 100 samples before the movement onset and 100 after it. Using k=3, we ended up with three groups (containing 18,14,26 trials respectively), which can easily identified as *SLOW, FAST and VERY FAST* saccades (see Fig.3a). By grouping the EEG-STs accordingly and deriving within-group averages, we can provide prototypes of brain activation (see Fig.3b).

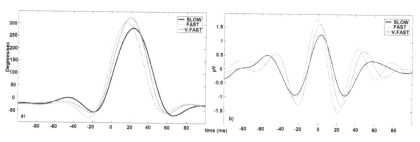

**Fig. 3.** a) Codebook vectors for left saccade velocity profiles. b) Prototypical EEG activity (in beta band), recorded at C2 electrode, for each saccade group.

### 4.3 Between-Groups Comparison of Brain Dynamics

With the scope of identifying the leading causes of the observed variation in behavior, the k-groups of EEG-STs can be contrasted for time-intervals well before the saccade onset. There is a multitude of methods with which the spatiotemporal brain dynamics can be compared based on the corresponding ST-segments of multichannel EEG-data. Spectral characterization, topography of signal activations, event-related synchronization/desynchronization (ERS/ERD) are the most popular approaches to proceed with. However, after experimenting with them, we realized that the most striking between-groups explanations could be provided via a *complex-network approach*, which emphasized neural synchrony and is summarized as follows

(i) First, an estimator of phase synchrony (known as *Phase Locking Value* (PLV) [18]) is applied (using signals filtered within a particular frequency band) to every possible pair of electrodes and for different time windows. The computed estimates were tabulated, for each group of STs independently, in time-series of [64x64] matrices (in which an entry conveys the strength of functional connection between a particular electrode pair). Such a matrix has a natural graph representation, called hereafter as functional connectivity graph (FCG), with nodes being the recording sites and edges the in-between links weighted by the tabulated values. The *PLV* was employed successively between 150ms before the eye movement onset and 25ms after it with a time window of 50ms and 5ms time step, producing 25 *FCG* snapshots in total.
(ii) Each of the formed FCGs is then characterized based on a network metric called *local efficiency.*
(iii) Finally, The k groups of EEG-STs are compared -in a time dependent manner- regarding network-properties.

The employed *PLV* is known to quantify the frequency-specific synchronization between two neuroelectric signals. Hence, with the adopted procedure the role of neural synchrony (as a putative mechanism for long-range neural integration) is explored during saccade planning till movement initiation. For each trial n, n=1 ,..., $N_k$, (in the k-th group) the phase $\varphi(t,n)$ is extracted for all latencies $t$. The *phase locking value (PLV)* is defined at time instant $t$ as the average value:

$$PLV_t = \frac{1}{N_k}\left|\sum_{n=1}^{N_k} exp(\, j\theta(\,t,n\,))\right| \cdot \tag{3}$$

where $\theta(t,\ n)$ is the phase difference $\varphi_1(t,\ n)$ - $\varphi_2(t,\ n)$ between the signals (filtered within a particular frequency range) corresponding to a pair of electrodes. PLV measures the inter-trial variability of this phase difference at t. If the phase difference varies little across the trials, PLV is close to 1; otherwise is close to 0. Usually, the above quantity is integrated over successive latencies so as to achieve a more robust measurement. In our implementation, the EEG signals are filtered within known frequency bands (e.g. $\alpha$-waves, $\gamma$-oscillations ) and the latency-dependent PLV values are averaged over particular time periods before using them as weights for the FCGs.

To characterize each FCG, we measure its *local efficiency* [19]. This metric is known to express how efficiently information is exchanged over the network. By using efficiency, brain neural network is seen as system that is both globally and locally efficient. The local efficiency $E_{loc}$ reveals how much the system is fault tolerant, thus it shows how efficient the communication is between the first neighbors of $i$ when $i$ is removed:

We can characterize the local properties of *FCG* by evaluating for each vertex $i$ the efficiency of its $G_i$ , the subgraph of the neighbors of $i$. We define the *local efficiency* as the average of all individual efficiencies:

$$E_{loc} = \frac{1}{M}\sum_{i\in M}\frac{\sum_{j,h\in G_i, j,h\neq i}(d_{jh})^{-1}}{k_i(k_i-1)} \cdot \tag{4}$$

where $k_i$ corresponds to the total number of neighbors of the current node, M is the set of all nodes in the network and $d$ keeps the shortest absolute path length between every possible pair in the neighborhood of the current node.

# 5  Results

Our experimentations with the previously described characterization of frequency-dependent, time-varying functional connectivity graphs, revealed that *Beta band (13-30Hz)* was the frequency channel that provided the best explanation about the formation of different saccades-groups (slow, fast, very fast). This finding fits well with the widely-known involvement of high-frequency EEG activations during saccade generation [7],[8],[20].

The visualization of the results, as a time-series of topographic maps, from the network analysis (restricted within beta-band) enabled us to track differences during the generation of different groups of saccades and draw conclusions about the local exchange of information in a time-dependent manner (See Fig. 4). These snapshots of brain connectivity clearly indicate that brain's self-organization tendencies should be pursuit within the domain of inter-areal interactions as well (i.e. apart of the signal domain). The thorough examination of the topographies included in Fig.4 facilitates the following observations.

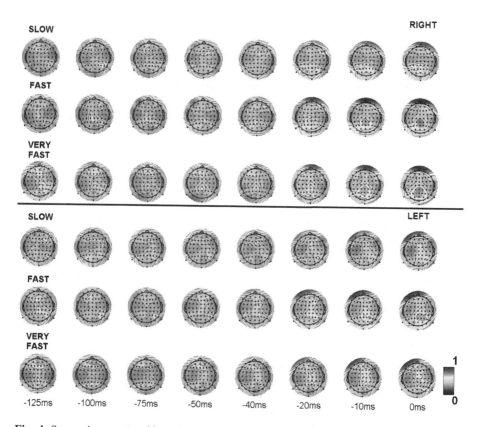

**Fig. 4.** Successive topographies of channelwise local network efficiency ($G_i$) during preparation for right/left saccade (up/down). Time 0 ms corresponds to saccade onset.

In both left and right saccade, there is contralateral activity emerging before the eye movement onset (0ms) in centro-parietal, parietal and occipital brain areas. The results suggest that brain activity just before a saccade is modulated by saccade velocity. The differences were located mainly over parietal cortex. It is well known that posterior parietal cortex is a crucial interface between the motor and perceptual system in mediating sensory-motor transformations [8]. An eye-movement related region within the intraparietal sulcus (IPS) of the posterior parietal cortex sometimes referred to as the "parietal eye filed".

Of great importance is the inter-group comparison that reveals temporal differences following the grouping of saccades according to velocity. In *SLOW* saccades, information exchange begins -10ms before onset, while in *FAST* and *VERY FAST* saccades, starts earlier (-50ms). Interestingly, in the case of *VERY FAST* saccades, this exchange is apparently greater.

# 6  Conclusions

We have introduced a ST-analysis framework for characterizing brain's self-organization in terms of functional connectivity and network properties during the execution of saccades. It can offer novel knowledge about the coding of kinematic parameters related to eye movements. Neural-gas recognizes the different variations of the performed task and network analysis provides their explanations. The methodology is applicable to other cognitive tasks as well, while can be further advanced via affirmative randomization tests. Furthermore, it can be used to study the neural activity related to the kinematics of arm movements in order to drive neural prostheses.

# References

1. Mitra, P.P., Bokil, H.: Observed brain dynamics, 1st edn. Oxford University Press, USA (2007)
2. Laskaris, N.A., Ioannides, A.A.: Exploratory data analysis of evoked response single trials based on minimal spanning tree. Clinical Neurophysiology 112(4), 698–712 (2001)
3. Laskaris, N.A., Fotopoulos, S., Ioannides, A.A.: Mining information from event-related recordings. IEEE Signal Processing Magazine 21(3), 66–77 (2004)
4. Laskaris, N.A., Liu, L.C., Ioannides, A.A.: Single-trial Variability in Early Visual Neuromagnetic Responses: An Explorative Study based on the Regional Activation Contributing to the N70m peak. NeuroImage 20(2), 765–783 (2003)
5. Laskaris, N.A., Fotopoulos, S., Ioannides, A.A.: Mining information from event-related recordings. IEEE Signal Processing Magazine 21(3), 66–77 (2004)
6. Dyckman, K.A., Camchong, J., Clementz, B.A., McDowell, J.E.: An effect of context on saccade-related behavior and brain activity. NeuroImage 36(3), 774–784 (2007)
7. Van Der Werf, J., Jensen, O., Fries, P., Medendorp, W.P.: Gamma-band activity in human posterior parietal cortex encodes the motor goal during delayed prosaccades and antisaccades. J. Neurosci. 28, 8397–8405 (2008)
8. Jerbi, K., Hamame, C.M., Ossandon, T., Dalal, S.S.: Role of posterior parietal gamma activity in planning prosaccades and antisaccades. J. Neurosci. 28, 13713–13715 (2008)

9. Clementz, B.A., Brahmbhatt, S.B., McDowell, J.E., Brown, R., Sweeney, J.A.: When does the brain inform the eyes whether and where to move? An EEG study in humans. Cerebral Cortex 17(11), 2634–2643 (2007)
10. Georgopoulos, A.P., Kalaska, J.F., Caminiti, R., Massey, J.T.: On the relations between the direction of two-dimensional arm movements and cell discharge in primate motor cortex. J. Neurosci. 2, 1527–1537 (1982)
11. Wauschkuhn, B., Wascher, E., Verleger, R.: Lateralised cortical activity due to preparation of saccades and finger movements: a comparative study. Electroencephalogr. Clin. Neurophysiol. 102, 114–124 (1997)
12. Van der Lubbe, R.H., Wauschkuhn, B., Wascher, E., Niehoff, T., Kompf, D., Verleger, R.: Lateralized EEG components with direction information for the preparation of saccades versus finger movements. Exp. Brain Res. 13 (2000)
13. Schlögl, A., Keinrath, C., Zimmermann, D., Scherer, R., Leeb, R., Pfurtscheller, G.: A fully automated correction method of EOG artifacts in EEG recordings. Clinical Neurophysiology 118, 98–104 (2007)
14. Duchowski, A.: Eye Tracking Methodology, Theory and Practice, pp. 137–153. Springer, Heidelberg (2007)
15. Marple-Horvat, D.E., Gilbey, S.L., Hollands, M.A.: A method for automatic identification of saccades from eye movement recordings. Journal of Neuroscience Methods 67, 191–195 (1996)
16. Laskaris, N.A., Bezerianos, A., Fotopoulos, S.: Unsupervised artifact rejection in EP recordings by means of a novel nonlinear technique. Appl. Signal Process. 3, 150–154 (1996)
17. Martinez, T., Berkovich, S., Schulten, K.: Neural-gas network for vector quantization and its application to time series prediction. IEEE Trans. Neural Networks 4(4), 558–569 (1993)
18. Lachaux, J., Rodriguez, E., Martinerie, J., Varela, F.J.: Measuring Phase Synchrony in Brain Signals. Human Brain Mapping 8, 194–208 (1999)
19. Latora, V., Marchiori, M.: Economic small-world behavior in weighted networks. Eur. Phys. J. B 32, 249–263 (2003)
20. Lachaux, J.P., Hoffmann, D., Minotti, L., Berthoz, A., Kahane, P.: Intracerebral dynamics of saccade generation in the human frontaleye field and supplementary eye field. Neuroimage 30, 1302–1312 (2006)

# Web Spam Detection by Probability Mapping GraphSOMs and Graph Neural Networks

Lucia Di Noi[1], Markus Hagenbuchner[2],
Franco Scarselli[1], and Ah Chung Tsoi[3]

[1] University of Siena, Siena, Italy
[2] University of Wollongong, Wollongong, Australia
[3] Hong Kong Baptist University, Hong Kong

**Abstract.** In this paper, we will apply, to the task of detecting web spam, a combination of the best of its breed algorithms for processing graph domain input data, namely, probability mapping graph self organizing maps and graph neural networks. The two connectionist models are organized into a layered architecture, consisting of a mixture of unsupervised and supervised learning methods. It is found that the results of this layered architecture approach are comparable to the best results obtained so far by others using very different approaches.

**Keywords:** Graph Neural Network, Probability Mapping GraphSOM, Web spam detection.

## 1 Introduction

The term *Web spam* refers to the results of the activities directed towards misleading search engines [1] in believing that a particular Web page has a high authority value on a particular query while in actual fact the Web page may contain little relevant information. In the past decade, these types of activities have increased dramatically as a consequence of the growing popularity of Internet search and the importance of being among the top ranked pages by popular search engines[1]. Search engines sort the URLs returned in response to a user query on the basis of a score that is usually composed of two parts: a measure of the relevance of the page content with respect to the query (e.g., see [2]) and a measure of the importance of the page that is obtained using its connectivity (e.g., Google's PageRank [3,4]). In general, spam techniques can be classified into content based or link based spam, according to whether their focus is on the former or on the latter measure, respectively [5].

In this paper, we present a spam detection approach based on a layered architecture, consisting of unsupervised and supervised learning methods. The reason why such a methodology would work is based on the following intuition: given a

---

[1] It is known that most people would only look at the top ranked pages returned on the first page of an Internet search. Being top ranked pages hence would increase the exposure or visibility to readers.

K. Diamantaras, W. Duch, L.S. Iliadis (Eds.): ICANN 2010, Part II, LNCS 6353, pp. 372–381, 2010.
© Springer-Verlag Berlin Heidelberg 2010

set of training examples, if we first run, say, an unsupervised learning algorithm through part or all of the training samples; this will group the training samples together to form clusters. These clusters would be formed based on the "natural" inclination according to the similarity of the features. On the other hand, the distribution of the patterns in cluster may be very complex and, if a supervision is available, the training samples within the same cluster could belong to a number of classes in an interlocking manner, like a Swiss roll. However, if we use a supervised training algorithm on the results of the unsupervised training, we can learn the classification of the clusters more effectively. If this process is repeated a number of times through layers, the approach could produce very respectable results. This compares with the "hard work" which a supervised learning approach would need to do, if there is no pre-screening using the unsupervised approach first, as the supervised approach will need to attempt to "unravel" the intricate interlocking classes from "raw" data. To the best of our knowledge, nobody has ever proved that such an approach would work. However, from practical experience, it is found that this approach often works well, especially in cases where the mapping from clusters to classes is complex (like having many interlocking clusters of different classes).

In this paper, we propose to follow this methodology in processing graph input domains. Here we use two best of its breed algorithms: for supervised learning, we use the Graph Neural Networks (GNNs) [6] and for unsupervised learning, we use Probability Mapping Graph Self Organizing Maps (PM–GraphSOMs) [7]. These models are particularly suited for this task, since the Web is naturally represented by a graph, where the nodes stand for the pages, the edges denote the hyperlinks, and the labels contain features of the pages and the hyperlinks. This approach can deal, at the same time, with both the content based and the link based spams.

We will apply this methodology to a common benchmark problem for web spam detection, namely, WEBSPAM-UK2006 dataset. It is found that the combined approach produced results which are comparable to the best results obtained so far on this dataset by others.

The paper is organized as it follows. In Section 2, we will review briefly the GNN and the PM–GraphSOM models. In Section 3, the proposed approach is discussed, while Section 4 describes the experimental results. Finally, some conclusions are drawn in Section 5.

## 2    GNNs and PM–GraphSOMs

In this section, we will give a very brief description of the concepts underling the Probability Mapping Graph Self Organizing Maps (PM–GraphSOMs), and the Graph Neural Networks (GNNs). We will refer the readers to the original papers [6,7,8] for more details.

In the following, a *graph* $G$ is a pair $(N,E)$, where $N$ is a set of *nodes* (or vertices), and $E \subseteq \{(u,v)|u,v \in N\}$ is a set of *edges* (or arcs) between nodes. For the sake of simplicity, we will assume that the considered graphs are undirected, i.e., $(u, v) = (v, u)$ holds for every edge $(u, v)$. Nodes and edges may have labels, that describe the features of the object represented by a node and the features related to the relationships between objects/nodes, respectively.

## 2.1   The General Framework

GNNs and PM–GraphSOMs belong to a class of connectionist models that have been designed to directly process graphs. Those approaches, which include, for instance, Recursive Neural Networks [9] and SOM for Structured Data [10], are based on the same underling idea. A graph represents a set of objects/concepts (the nodes) and their relationships (the edges). For each node $n$, a *state* $\boldsymbol{x}_n \in \mathbb{R}^s$ is specified, which stores a representation of the corresponding object. Moreover, since every concept is naturally defined by its features and the related concepts, we can assume that $\boldsymbol{x}_n$ depends on the information contained in the neighborhood of $n$ (see Fig. 1). Formally, such a dependence is defined by a parametric function $f_{\boldsymbol{w}}$, called a *local transition function*:

$$\boldsymbol{x}_n = f_{\boldsymbol{w}}(\boldsymbol{l}_n, \boldsymbol{l}_{\text{co}[n]}, \boldsymbol{x}_{\text{ne}[n]}, \boldsymbol{l}_{\text{ne}[n]}),  \tag{1}$$

where $\boldsymbol{l}_n$, $\boldsymbol{l}_{\text{co}[n]}$, $\boldsymbol{x}_{\text{ne}[n]}$, $\boldsymbol{l}_{\text{ne}[n]}$ are respectively the label of $n$, the labels of its edges, and the states and the labels of the nodes in the neighborhood of $n$. An output $\boldsymbol{o}_n$ may also be defined, which depends on the node state and the node label, according to a parametric *local output function* $g_{\boldsymbol{w}}$:

$$\boldsymbol{o}_n = g_{\boldsymbol{w}}(\boldsymbol{x}_n, \boldsymbol{l}_n).  \tag{2}$$

Thus, Eqs. (1) and (2) specify a parametric model that computes an output $\boldsymbol{o}_n = \varphi_{\boldsymbol{w}}(\boldsymbol{G}, n)$ for any node $n$ of the graph $\boldsymbol{G}$, considering all the data in $\boldsymbol{G}$. Interestingly, it was proved that, under some mild assumptions, a very large class of continuous functions on graphs can be approximated in probability, up to any degree of precision, by this model [8].

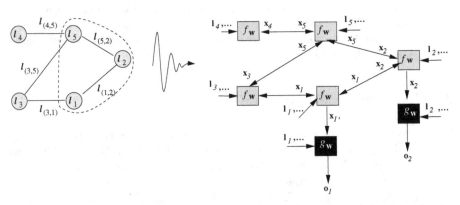

**Fig. 1.** On the left, a graph and the neighborhood of the node with label $l_2$. On the right, the encoding network corresponding to the graph.

Such a framework can be used either for supervised or unsupervised learning. In the supervised case, the training set $\mathcal{L}$ is defined as $\mathcal{L} = \{(\boldsymbol{G}_i, n_{i,j}, \boldsymbol{t}_{n_{i,j}}) \mid 1 \leq i \leq p, 1 \leq j \leq q_i\}$, where each triple $(\boldsymbol{G}_i, n_{i,j}, \boldsymbol{t}_{n_{i,j}})$ denotes a graph $\boldsymbol{G}_i$, one of its nodes $n_{i,j}$ and the desired output at that node, $\boldsymbol{t}_{n_{i,j}}$, while $p$ is the number of graphs in $\mathcal{L}$, and $q_i$ is the number of *supervised nodes*[2] in graph $\boldsymbol{G}_i$. The goal of learning is to estimate the parameters $\boldsymbol{w}$ so that $\varphi_{\boldsymbol{w}}$ approximates the targets on the supervised nodes, which can be obtained by minimizing a quadratic error criterion $e_{\boldsymbol{w}} = \sum_{i=1}^{p} \sum_{j=1}^{q_i} (\boldsymbol{t}_{n_{i,j}} - \varphi_{\boldsymbol{w}}(\boldsymbol{G}_i, n_{i,j}))^2$.

On the other hand, in the unsupervised case, the training set $\mathcal{L}$ does not have targets and the purpose of the learning is to cluster the objects represented in $\mathcal{L}$. Thus, the parameters $\boldsymbol{w}$ are adapted so that $\varphi_{\boldsymbol{w}}(\boldsymbol{G}_i, n_{i,j})$ is close to $\varphi_{\boldsymbol{w}}(\boldsymbol{G}_k, n_{k,s})$, if the objects represented by $n_{i,j}$ and $n_{k,s}$ are similar, and, $\varphi_{\boldsymbol{w}}(\boldsymbol{G}_i, n_{i,j})$ is far from $\varphi_{\boldsymbol{w}}(\boldsymbol{G}_k, n_{k,s})$, if the two objects are different.

## 2.2  GNN and PM–GraphSOM Peculiarities

GNNs and PM–GraphSOMs implement Eqs. (1) and (2) with several differences and peculiarities, the most important of which is the learning framework: the GNN is a supervised model, while the PM–GraphSOM is unsupervised. The other differences are reviewed in the following.

**The transition and the output function implementation.** In GNNs, both $f_{\boldsymbol{w}}$ and $g_{\boldsymbol{w}}$ are implemented by multilayered static neural networks. In this way, Eqs. (1) and (2) define a neural network, called *encoding network* (Fig. 1). The encoding network is obtained by substituting all the nodes of $\boldsymbol{G}$ with $f$–*units*, which compute the function $f_{\boldsymbol{w}_n}$. The $f$–units are connected according to the graph topology and calculate the states locally at each node. For the nodes where the output has to be computed, the $f$–unit is also connected to a $g$–*unit*, that implements the output function $g_{\boldsymbol{w}_n}$.

In PM–GraphSOMs, the transition function $f_{\boldsymbol{w}}$ is based on a Self–Organizing Map (SOM) [11]. Intuitively, the state $\boldsymbol{x}_n$ of each node $n$ stores the activation levels achieved by the neurons of the SOM and the transition function produces such a state using the node label $\boldsymbol{l}_n$ and a vector $\boldsymbol{y}_n$, which contains a summarization of the statistical distribution of the winning codebooks in the neighborhood of $n$. The vector $\boldsymbol{y}_n = [y_{n,1}, \ldots, y_{n,s}]$, whose dimension equals the number of neurons in the SOM, is defined by $y_{n,i} = \sum_{u \in \text{ne}[n]} \sum_{j=1}^{s} \frac{e^{\frac{-\|c(i)-c(k_u)\|^2}{2\sigma(t)^2}}}{\sqrt{2\pi}\sigma(t)}$ , where $c(i)$ denotes the coordinates of the neuron $i$ and $c(k_u)$ the coordinates of the winning neuron of the SOM at node $u$, while $\sigma$ is a function that decreases towards 0 as the training time $t$ increases. Moreover, the output function $g_{\boldsymbol{w}}$ is a simple map that extracts from the state $\boldsymbol{x}_n$ the coordinates of the winning neuron.

**The computation of the states.** Note that the states $\boldsymbol{x}_n$ in Eq. (1) are defined recursively and cannot be computed directly. The states can be calculated

---

[2] The supervised nodes are those for which a desired target exists. In general, the supervision can be on all the nodes or on a subset.

iteratively by the dynamical system $x_n(t) = f_w(l_n, x_{ch[n]}(t-1), l_{ch[n]})$, which describes the behavior of the encoding networks when its units are repeatedly activated. However, such a procedure computes a solution of Eq. (1) only if the dynamical system converges to a stable point. With respect to such a problem, GNNs and PM–GraphSOMs adopts different approaches. PM–GraphSOMs disregard the problem and iterate the dynamical system for a predefined number of times. On the other hand, in GNNs, a penalty term, which forces the dynamical system to be contractive [12], is added to the error function. In this way, it is ensured that Eq. (1) has a unique solution and, at the same time, that the above dynamical system converges exponentially to the desired solution.

**The learning algorithm.** In both models, each epoch of the training procedure consists of two steps: (1) first the states are computed; (2) then the parameters are adapted. The epochs are repeated until a desired stop criterion is satisfied.

GNNs carry out step (2) according to a gradient descent strategy. The gradient is computed by a combination of the BackPropagation Through Structure algorithm, adopted by Recursive Neural Networks [9], and the Almeida–Pineda algorithm [13,14], while the parameters are updated using resilient backpropagation [15]. Similarly, PM–GraphSOMs adopt for step (2) a modified version of the original SOM learning algorithm, where the SOM is trained on a learning set consisting of all the input patterns constructed at different nodes.

## 3   A Layered Architecture for Web Spam Detection

Web Spam Detection can be considered a classification problem in a graph domain. In fact, the Web can be naturally represented as a graph in which the nodes stand for the pages, the labels attached to the nodes represent information about the page contents and the links between the pages denote the hyperlinks. Thus, we can predict which pages contain spam by using a machine learning technique that can process graphs and can learn by examples to classify their nodes.

The model we have adopted is a layered architecture in which unsupervised and supervised learning approaches are deployed. Given a set of training samples (in this case, graphs representing a portion of the Web), the classification of these training samples are known, i.e. if it is a spam site, or a non-spam site. We will first use unsupervised learning approach to cluster the training samples into clusters. Now as the input domain is a graph, hence it makes sense to use a best of breed algorithm which can handle graph domain inputs. In this case, we propose to use the PM–GraphSOM approach. This would produce a low dimensional display space which shows how the training samples are clustered together. Then, as the input in this case is still in a graph format (the display space shows clusters of various sizes on a low dimensional space) with known classifications for each cluster, we can apply a supervised learning technique to classify these clusters. Graph Neural Network (GNN) is a best of its breed algorithm which is capable of handling graph inputs with known output classifications.

Why would such a approach work? Intuitively for a spam web page to work, it must be in some sense close to the normal web pages. In other words, they

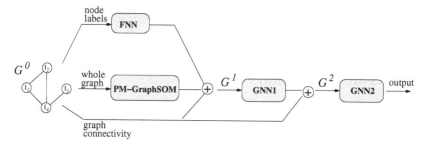

**Fig. 2.** The layered architecture proposed in this paper

"masquerade" as a normal web page[3] Thus, it is expected that such a complex classification problem would be best handled using the layered architecture proposed in this paper in which the input features are first clustered together using an unsupervised approach. In our case, we further use the outputs of a feedforward neural network together with the outputs of the unsupervised approach. These then serve as inputs to a GNN. The GNN can be run once or a number of times (a number of layers of GNNs).

Following this idea, the graph is processed by layers of different kinds of networks, including common feedforward neural networks, PM–GraphSOMs and GNNs. The architecture that achieved the best performance in the experiments is depicted in Fig 2.

1. The node labels $l_n$ of the original graph $G^0$ are processed by a three layered feedforward neural network (FNN), whose goal is to classify the information contained in the pages without considering the Web connectivity.
2. The PM–GraphSOM, whose goal is to extract more condensed information from the inputs, is feded on the original graph $G^0$.
3. For each graph $G^0$, a new graph $G^1$ is constructed by replacing the original labels with a concatenation of the outputs produced by the FNN and the PM–GraphSOM. Formally, the label $l_n^1$ of node $n$ in $G^1$ is $l_n^1 = [o_n^{FNN}, o_n^{PM}]$, where $o_n^{FNN}$, $o_n^{PM}$ are the outputs of the FNN and the PM–GraphSOM, respectively. The graphs $G^1$ are processed by a GNN (GNN1 in Fig 2) the goal of which is to obtain a preliminary classification of the nodes.
4. For each $G^1$, a new graph $G^2$ is constructed having the some connectivity of $G^1$, but whose labels are replaced by the outputs of GNN1: $l_n^2 = o_n^{GNN1}$ holds, where $o_n^{GNN1}$ is the output of the GNN1. The final predictions are computed by a GNN (GNN2 in Fig 2) that takes in input the graph $G_2$.

The learning is carried out layer by layer. Thus, the PM–GraphSOM is trained on the original learning set, disregarding the targets. The FNN is trained on a learning set consisting of pairs $(l_n, t_n)$, where $t_n$ is the original target of node $n$. Finally, the learning set of the GNNs contains triples $(G_i^k, n_{i,j}, t_{n_{i,j}})$ that differ

---

[3] Interestingly, in [16], the authors plotted the dataset WEBSPAM-UK2006, which contains a Yahoo crawling and is used in this paper for the experiments. The plot confirms the intuition that the spam pages are well surrounded by normal pages.

from the original ones only for the graph which is replaced by $G_i^1$, in step 3, and $G_i^2$, in step 4.

## 4    Experimental Results

The proposed approach was assessed on the WEBSPAM–UK2006 dataset [16], a publicly available benchmark introduced, in 2007, by the Web Spam Challenge and the Adversarial Information Retrieval on the Web (AIRWeb) workshop. Such a collection of pages was particularly suitable for our purposes, since it is large and it has been used by other research teams. Moreover, the dataset comes with a predefined splitting into a train set and a test set and it includes a set of precomputed features, which simplifies the preprocessing procedure[4].

The benchmark is based on a crawl of the .uk domain, carried out in May 2006 and it includes 77.9 million pages and over 3 billion links in about 11,400 hosts. The collection was tagged at the host level by a group of volunteers. The assessors labeled 2725 hosts as "normal", "borderline" or "spam".

The dataset contains precomputed features about the hyperlinks and the host contents. The link–based features consist of 41 items and include, for example, the in–degree, the out–degree, the PageRank [3] and the TrustRank [17] of the host home page. The 23 content–based features include several statistical values measuring the distribution of words in the host pages as, for instance, the precision and the recall of the words in a page with respect to the $q$ most frequent terms from a query log, where $q = 100, 200, 500, 1000$, respectively.

In this experimentation, the GNN transition and output functions were implemented by three layered (one hidden layer) static networks with 5 hidden neurons using sigmoidal activation functions. The state dimension was set to 2. Similarly, the FNN network was a three layered static network with 20 hidden neurons. The PM–GraphSOM adopted a SOM whose units were arranged in $50 \times 80$ lattice. The GNNs and the FNNs were trained for $1,000$ epochs, updating the gradient with resilient backpropagation mechanisms.

Those parameters, were selected as a result of a set of preliminary experiments and heuristics that for space reasons cannot be completely discussed here. A first set of experiments was used to find the best architecture using only the training dataset. For instance, Table 1 displays the performance, measured using precision and f-measure, achieved by a simple GNN (not a layered architecture) that is fed with graphs, the labels of which have different combinations of the following features: the link–based features (link), the content–based features (content) and the coordinates of the winning neurons in a PM–GraphSOM (PM–G). The results suggest that without a layered architecture, the features in rows 2, 3, 4 respectively show comparable performances, whereas using only the link–based features the performance is slightly lower, but not by far though.

---

[4] It is worth mentioning that, due to the large number of pages involved, the computation of several features requires a huge amount of computation time and human effort.

**Table 1.** The performance of a simple GNN with graphs having different labels

| Node labels | Accuracy | F-measure |
|---|---|---|
| Link | 80.65% | 0.428 |
| Link + PM–G | 87.63% | 0.576 |
| Link + Content | 88.52% | 0.579 |
| Link + Content +PM–G | 88.18% | 0.575 |

**Table 2.** The Results obtained using different architectures

| Layer 0 | Layer 1 | Layer 2 | Accuracy | F-measure | ROC AUC |
|---|---|---|---|---|---|
| FNN | | | 78.39% | 0.4773 | 0.8602 |
| GNN | | | 90.87% | 0.4081 | 0.7913 |
| FNN, PM–G | GNN | | 91.24% | 0.5890 | 0.9236 |
| GNN | GNN | | 90.70% | 0.4400 | 0.8103 |
| FNN, PM–G, Autoass | GNN | | 90.60% | 0.5308 | 0.8701 |
| Autoass | GNN | | 91.04% | 0.4173 | 0.8070 |
| FNN, PM–G | GNN | GNN | 92.94% | 0.6324 | 0.9362 |

Another set of experiments was conducted to evaluate different layered architectures and some of the results are shown in Table 2. Each row displays an architecture. The first three columns describes the models[5] used in the layers: for instance, the results using the architecture shown in Fig. 2 are displayed in the last row. The last three columns show the accuracy, the f–measure and the area under the receiving operating characteristic curve (ROC AUC). The networks of layer 0 take in input graphs with both link–based and content–based features, whereas the models in other layers take in input graphs where the original labels have been replaced by the outputs provided by the previous layer. A comparison of the architectures[6] suggests that the deeper ones are those with a better performance, even if it is not possible to define a general rule, probably because the architectures mix models with completely different characteristics.

Moreover, the architecture achieving the best result in Table 2, i.e., the one in the last row and depicted in Fig. 2, was evaluated also on the original splitting of the benchmark and compared with the other teams that participated in the challenge. Table 3 shows that our approach equals the best f–measure and it obtains the second best ROC AUC. Interestingly, the other participants have used *ad hoc* features and have exploited algorithms which may depend on the

---

[5] The considered models include also an autoassociator network, the output of which is the difference between the input and the output.

[6] Interestingly, the differences between the architectures are clearer by observing the ROC AUC and the f–measure, than the accuracy measure. Actually, the possible accuracy results are restricted to a small range, because the dataset is unbalanced (it contains few spam pages compared with the number of non–spam pages) and even a very simple predictor can achieve a very high accuracy by classifying every page as non–spam.

Table 3. Web Spam Challenge 2007 results

| Team | F–Measure | ROC AUC |
|------|-----------|---------|
| Benczúr et al. | 0.91 | 0.93 |
| Filoche et al. | 0.88 | 0.93 |
| Geng et al. | 0.87 | 0.93 |
| Abou et al. | 0.81 | 0.80 |
| Fetterly et al. | 0.79 | – |
| Cormack | 0.67 | 0.96 |
| Proposed approach | 0.9169 | 0.9301 |

selected features. On the other hand, the proposed method uses the original features of dataset and no attempt has been made to optimize them. Moreover, the involved machine learning algorithms are general purpose ones and can be used elsewhere without conceptual changes. Those facts suggest that the presented approach is more flexible and it can be more easily extended to process different features or to face similar tasks based on the Web graph.

Finally, it is also worth to mention that, while the training is computational expensive, the test phase of the proposed architecture require a linear time w.r.t. the number of nodes in the graph [6], which allows to apply such an approach also on relatively large datasets.

## 5   Conclusions

In this paper, we have introduced a layered architecture combining an unsupervised and a supervised approach in the processing of graph domain inputs. This approach has been applied on a common web spam detection benchmark. It is shown, through various experiments, that the layered method obtained results which are comparable to the best results achieved using other approaches. It is matter of further research a wider experimentation and a theoretical analysis of the properties of the proposed architecture.

## Acknowledgement

The authors wish to acknowledge the partial financial support received from the Australian Research Council, Discovery Project grant DP0774168 and Linkage International Award grant LX0882106, which made an extended stay of the first author in University of Wollongong possible.

## References

1. Gyöngyi, Z., Garcia-Molina, H., Pedersen, J.: Combating web spam with trustrank. In: Proceedings of the thirtieth international conference on very large data bases, vol. 30, p. 587. VLDB Endowment (2004)

2. Manning, C., Raghavan, P., Schütze, H.: An introduction to information retrieval. Cambridge University Press, Cambridge (2008)
3. Brin, S., Page, L., Motwani, R., Winograd, T.: The PageRank citation ranking: Bringing order to the Web. Technical Report 1999-66, Stanford University (1999), http://dbpubs.stanford.edu:8090/pub/1999-66
4. Bianchini, M., Gori, M., Scarselli, F.: Inside pagerank. ACM Transactions on Internet Technology (TOIT) 5(1), 92–128 (2005)
5. Gyöngyi, Z., Garcia-Molina, H.: Web spam taxonomy. In: 1st International Workshop on Adversarial Information Retrieval on the Web, pp. 39–47 (2005)
6. Scarselli, F., Gori, M., Tsoi, A., Hagenbuchner, M., Monfardini, G.: The graph neural network model. IEEE Transactions on Neural Networks 20(1), 61–80 (2009)
7. Hagenbuchner, M., Zhang, S., Tsoi, A., Sperduti, A.: Projection of undirected and nonpositional graphs using self organizing maps. In: European Symposium on Artificial Neural Networks-Advances in Computational Intelligence and Learning, pp. 22–24 (April 2009)
8. Scarselli, F., Gori, M., Tsoi, A., Hagenbuchner, M., Monfardini, G.: Computational capabilities of graph neural networks. IEEE Transactions on Neural Networks 20(1), 81–102 (2009)
9. Frasconi, P., Gori, M., Sperduti, A.: A general framework for adaptive processing of data structures. IEEE Transactions on Neural Networks 9(5), 768–786 (1998)
10. Hagenbuchner, M., Sperduti, A., Tsoi, A.: A self-organizing map for adaptive processing of structured data. IEEE Transactions on Neural Networks 14(3), 491–505 (2003)
11. Kohonen, T.: Self-organization and associative memory. Springer Information Sciences Series (1989)
12. Khamsi, M.A.: An Introduction to Metric Spaces and Fixed Point Theory. John Wiley & Sons Inc., New York (2001)
13. Almeida, L.: A learning rule for asynchronous perceptrons with feedback in a combinatorial environment. In: Caudill, M., Butler, C. (eds.) IEEE International Conference on Neural Networks, San Diego, vol. 2, pp. 609–618. IEEE, New York (1987)
14. Pineda, F.: Generalization of back–propagation to recurrent neural networks. Physical Review Letters 59, 2229–2232 (1987)
15. Riedmiller, M., Braun, H.: RPROP-A fast adaptive learning algorithm. In: Proc. of ISCIS VII, Universitat (1992)
16. Castillo, C., Donato, D., Gionis, A., Murdock, V., Silvestri, F.: Know your neighbors: web spam detection using the web topology. In: SIGIR 2007: Proceedings of the 30th annual international ACM SIGIR conference on Research and development in information retrieval, pp. 423–430. ACM, New York (2007)
17. Gyöngyi, Z., Garcia-Molina, H., Pedersen, J.: Combating web spam with trustrank. In: International Conference on VLDB, pp. 576–587 (2004)

# Self-Organizing Maps for Improving the Channel Estimation and Predictive Modelling Phase of Cognitive Radio Systems

Aimilia Bantouna, Kostas Tsagkaris, and Panagiotis Demestichas

University of Piraeus, 80 Karaoli Dimitriou str., 18534, Piraeus, Greece

**Abstract.** Rapid evolution of wireless communications, especially in terms of managing and allocating the scarce, radio spectrum in the highly varying and disparate modern environments asks for a technology for its intelligent handling. Cognitive radio systems (CRSs) have been proposed as one. A typical CRS implements a so called "cognition cycle", during which it senses its environment, evaluates a set of candidate radio configurations to operate with and finally decides and adjusts its operating parameters expecting to move the radio toward an optimized operational state. As the process is often proved to be rather arduous and time consuming, learning mechanisms that are capable of exploiting measurements sensed from the environment, gathered experience and stored knowledge can be judged as rather beneficial in terms of speeding it up. Framed within this statement, this paper introduces and evaluates a mechanism which is based on a well-known unsupervised learning technique, called Self-Organizing maps (SOM), and is used for assisting a CRS to predict the bit-rate that can be obtained, when it senses specific input data from its environment, such as Received Signal Strength Identification (RSSI), number of input/output packets etc. Results show that the proposed method is successful up to a percent of 75.4%.

**Keywords:** Cognitive Radio Systems (CRS), Cognition Cycle, Learning, Self-Organizing Maps (SOMs).

## 1 Introduction

Each wireless communication needs its different piece of a specific limited natural source, the electromagnetic radio spectrum, whose current static assignment often leads to its underutilization. Accordingly, the deployment of a technology which will have the ability to exploit the underutilized frequency bands is needed.

Cognitive radio systems have been proposed as a promising technology for this cause [1] [2] due to their ability to adjust their function according to the external, environmental stimuli, the demands of the users/applications and their past experience. Based on this ability, future cognitive systems will be able to change their parameters (carrier frequency, radio access technology, transmit power, modulation type etc), observe the results and decide which is the best combination of those parameters in order to get into a better operational state. So, in terms of flexible spectrum

K. Diamantaras, W. Duch, L.S. Iliadis (Eds.): ICANN 2010, Part II, LNCS 6353, pp. 382–391, 2010.

management concept, use of cognitive systems will allow the use of a spectrum band in different radio access technologies (RATs) [3], [4].

A typical cognitive operation consists of three cooperative phases (**Fig. 2**) [2] [3]. During, the first phase, known as radio scene analysis, the system takes measurements from the environment (e.g. conditions related to interference) and explores of different configurations. In the $2^{nd}$ phase, channel estimation and predictive modeling, the output of the $1^{st}$ phase is used for discovering the capabilities of each candidate configuration, wherein past experience of the system may also be used. Finally, in the last phase, known as "configuration selection", the system adjusts its operation parameters according to its selected best configuration. In particular during the 2nd phase of the cognition cycle, numerous candidate configurations for the CRS need to be evaluated. This is proved to be a very arduous and time-consuming task, which can be relaxed by using learning mechanisms.

Supervised learning through neural networks-based schemes have been used recently in [4] [5]. Bayesian networks have been also used in [3]. Our proposal is an unsupervised neural network technique called Self-Organizing Maps (SOMs). SOM is a technique for representation and classification of multidimensional data into 2D maps. These maps consist of rectangular or hexagonal cells on a regular grid and according to the technique; each data sample correlates with one cell/neuron of the map in order to be closest to those who are most like it. In this term, the created map represents the similarity of the data and their classification. Due to their ability, SOMs are very popular in data mining problems such as identification of illicit drugs [6], chemical analysis [7], document collections [8], speech recognition [9], identification of a cancer cell gene [10], hematopoietic differentiation [11] and more. In our case we examined the possibility of connecting parameters observed during a configuration, such as noise, received signal strength Indication (RSSI), errors (input and output), packets (received and sent) and Bytes (received and sent) with an anticipated QoS metric namely the bitrate that can be achieved under the configuration in question.

Finally, in order to validate the technique, we have setup and executed a program by using MATLAB SOM toolbox. The developed SOMs are trained with measurements that have taken place in a real working environment within our University premises. The method exhibits a satisfactory capability of predicting the achieved bitrate when facing both known and unknown exemplars (combinations of monitored parameters given a configuration).

The rest of the paper is structured as follows: a review of SOM technique and a short analysis of our proposal are presented in section 2. Section 3 presents the results of our test cases, including a comparison of different versions of our program (section 3.1), the choice of the variables of the input data samples (section 3.2), different cases which include different number of data samples (section 3.3) and different evaluating scenarios with different parameters of SOM technique (section 3.4). Finally, the paper is concluded in section 4.

# 2  Self-Organizing Maps (SOMs) and Contribution

SOM, introduced by [12], is a type of neural network that belongs to the set of unsupervised learning techniques. An overview of its theoretical foundation may be found in [13]. It is a technique for representation and classification of multidimensional data into 2D maps. These maps consist of cells, whose shape is rectangular or hexagonal, on a regular grid. According to the technique, each data sample correlates with one cell/neuron of the map, called Best Matching Unit (BMU). The process during which the BMU and a neighborhood around it stretch towards the inserted data sample (**Fig. 1**) is called SOM training and results in an ordered SOM map where similar data samples are close. In this term, the created map represents the similarity of the data and their classification.

Two different training algorithms are used for SOM training: the sequential and the batch training algorithm. In the first algorithm each data sample is inserted in the training process individually, thus affecting its own best matching unit (BMU) and a neighborhood around it. In the 2nd algorithm, all data samples are inserted together in the process and eventually affect their BMUs and neighbors in parallel.

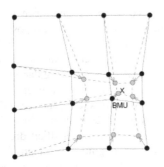

**Fig. 1.** The inserted data sample x affects its BMU and its neighborhood. The solid and dash-doted lines correspond to the situation before and after the input of the data sample [14]

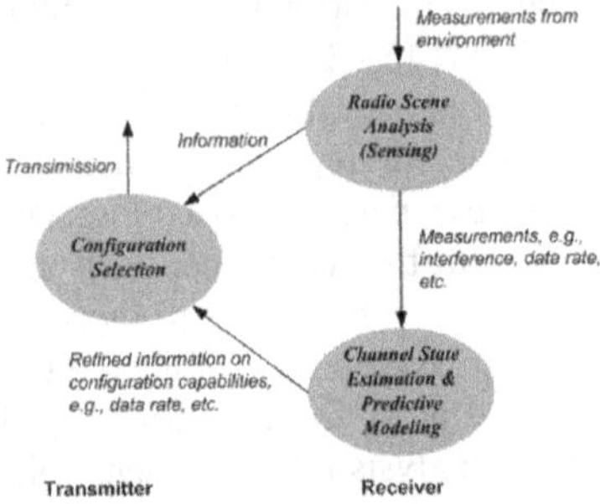

**Fig. 2.** Simplified representation of cognitive radio cycle [2]

As mentioned in section 1, we will examine the possibility of connecting parameters observed during a configuration, such as noise, received signal strength Indication (RSSI), errors (input and output), packets (received and sent) and Bytes (received and sent) with one QoS metric, the bitrate in order to predict it. This is done by using the unsupervised training technique of SOM. However, as also mentioned in section 1, SOM is a technique for representation and classification of multidimensional data into 2D maps. So how could it be useful in our case?

To begin with, measurements that have taken place in a real working environment within the premises of our University were used to create different data files. Each file comprised a different test case including different combinations of our parameters. Each column, apart from the last one, referred to a different parameter of the data sample while each row corresponded to one different data sample (see **Fig. 3**). Finally, the last column of the data file was the measured value of the bitrate which was related to the data sample and was taking part only for distinguishing them. It is essential to mention that no normalization of the data samples has taken place.

In the sequence the created data file and SOM toolbox v.2 of MATLAB [14] were used to train the SOM. For facilitating the analysis, SOM toolbox offers the ability to use labels in order to distinguish the data samples. In our case, each label corresponds to the measured value of the bitrate of the data sample. However, the fact that more than one data samples may have the same BMU ($m_c$) leads to the fact that each cell of the map may have more than one labels appearing more than once. As SOM toolbox offers enough different ways for labeling the map, we used three of them ending up with three different versions of our program. The first way (VOTE) is to put on each cell only the most frequently appearing label, the second one (ADD1) is to put all labels while the third one (FREQ) is to put all labels, like in case of ADD1, but in descending order with respect to their appearance frequency and followed by the number of appearances.

```
 1   5
 2   #n RSSI IPKTS  OPKTS    IBYTES   OBYTES
 3       -35 926    1750     32630    880650   54
 4       -32 908    1680     31932    845424   54
 5       -32 888    1680     31272    845424   54
 6       -35 888    1679     31338    845468   54
 7       -36 890    1683     31338    845598   54
 8       -36 960    1818     33812    915702   54
 9       -36 890    1682     31338    845598   54
10       -36 928    1766     32756    887366   54
11       -34 920    1731     32328    873760   48
12       -33 926    1751     32586    880650   54
13       -33 924    1750     32564    880650   54
14       -32 894    1684     31494    845688   54
```

**Fig. 3.** Matlab Data File: the number of the first line refers to the number of the parameters of the configuration, here equal to 5 (RSSI, Input PacKeTS, Output PacKeTS, Input BYTES, Output BYTES), and the last column refers to the bitrate which was used as label. Each line is a data sample and each column is a different parameter of the configuration.

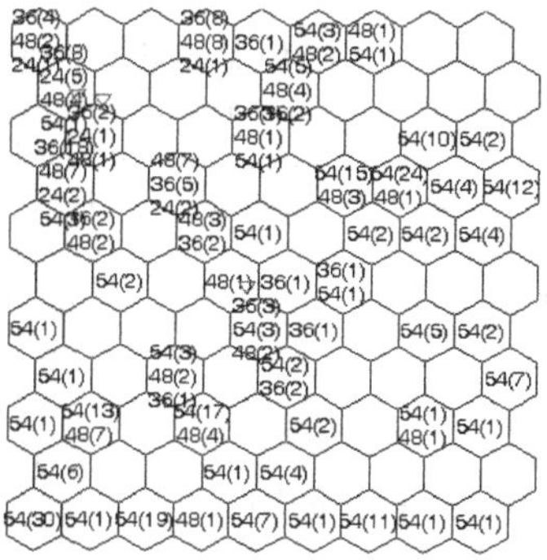

**Fig. 4.** Labeled SOM when using the FREQ version

At this point, the output of our program is a labeled SOM map (**Fig. 4**) and our program may represent a new data sample on the map but cannot predict its bitrate. In order to train our program how to predict the bitrate of a data sample we transformed our visualization into mathematical functions. According to the ability of SOM technique cells which have the same bitrate are expected to comprise a cluster whose center may be calculated by the equations

$$x = \sum_{i}^{n} w_i x_i / n \quad (1) \qquad \text{and} \quad y = \sum_{i}^{n} w_i y_i / n \quad (2),$$

where n is the number of cells which belong to the cluster, $x_i$ and $y_i$ are the coordinates of the cell i and $w_i$ is the weight according to which the cell i participates to the calculation. In the first two versions (VOTE, ADD1) $w_i$ is always set equal to 1 while in the last version $w_i$ is set to be calculated by the following function:

$$w_i = k / r \quad (3),$$

where k is the number of instances of the specific bitrate in the cell i and r is the sum of the instances of all bitrates of the cell.

In order to define the bitrate of a data sample we need to find to which cluster the BMU of the data sample belongs. The BMU is set to belong to the cluster that its center is closest according to the Euclidean Distance. The bitrate of the data sample will be the one that represents the cluster. Finally, for evaluating our process and reaching conclusions our program is able to compare the predicted values of the bitrate of each data sample with its real measured value.

# 3 Test Cases and Results

A number of test cases that correspond to variations of input parameters of the proposed method have been set up in order to reach useful conclusions. In particular, the focus is placed on exploring the following: a) which the best choice between the three versions of the method (VOTE, ADD1 and FREQ) is, b) what variables of our data samples are going to be used, c) how many data samples are needed for the training phase and d) what the training algorithm and the values of its parameters should be. For evaluation and comparison reasons, the higher the percent of the correct prediction is, the better the choice. As a result, the metric used was the number of data samples whose bitrate was correctly predicted (expressed in percent). The different test cases are presented and compared to each other below.

### 3.1 Comparison of the Labelling Versions

Having analyzed the three versions, we need to compare them in order to use the best one according to their results. As mentioned above, the VOTE version uses only the most frequently appeared label when calculating the centres of the clusters. In this case, it is possible that a label doesn't appear in the created SOM even if it has been used as label in a data sample. As a result, labels with fewer instances may not appear in the created SOM. This causes the elimination of one or more clusters as there is no centre of them. In addition to the above, the program terminates a little after the calculation of the centres as according to its programming it needs all four centres. Finally, even if the program wouldn't stop, the data, which are used for evaluation and belong to the eliminated cluster, would be correlated with a wrong label and cluster.

Trying to find a solution to the existing problem of VOTE version, ADD1 version was created. In ADD1 version, all possible labels of each cell participate equally independently of their instances. We executed both versions using same data files in both training and evaluating phases. The result of the tests led to the conclusion that ADD1 version solved the problem of VOTE version but, in cases where VOTE version worked properly, ADD1 version had lower percent of correct predictions.

The above conclusion led us in a new version, the FREQ version. Contrarily to ADD1 version, labels participate in the calculation of the centres of the clusters unequally as a weighted average of their frequency. Having created this version all that was left to be done was its comparison with the VOTE and ADD1 versions. In order to do so, we executed all versions using the same data files in both training and evaluating phase. It is worth mentioning that in all three versions the training parameters were the same. The results of FREQ version were all better (with higher percent of correct predictions of the bitrate) and thus FREQ version is the one that was used in the rest of the experiments.

## 3.2 Selection of the Variables of a Data Sample

The next step of our research concerned the variables of the data samples that suit better for predicting the bitrate. In order to do so we created many different cases and used the FREQ version of our program and the same training variables. These cases used different data files for both training and evaluation phases. The difference between them lied in the number and the type of the variables of the data samples.

At the created cases there were 9 variables of a data sample that were used in different combinations, namely: noise, RSSI (Received Signal Strength Identifier), number of input and output packets, number of input and output error, number of input and output bytes and bitrate.

Comparing these cases we concluded the following:

- ➢ The result does not depend on the fact that data samples are or are not ordered according to the bitrate. The results in both cases are the same.
- ➢ The existence or not of bitrate as variable of the data sample does not influence the results always in the same way. In some cases the result was reduced while in other cases it was increased. Moreover, the highest percent of correct predictions was not one of these whose data file contained the bitrate as a variable.
- ➢ Finally, the case with the highest percent of correct predictions, equal to 71.4%, was the one whose variables were the number of input and output packets and RSSI. Those variables are the ones that are used in the rest of our paper.

## 3.3 Selection of the Number of Data Samples

Having selected the variables of a data sample, we needed to decide the number of data samples to participate in the training process of SOM. In order to do so we created cases which included the variables in which we resulted from the analysis in section 3.2 (number of input and output packets and RSSI) but different number of data samples. For taking results we used once more the same training parameters and the FREQ version.

According to the results, the number of data samples affected the results of our predictions but not always in the same direction. These results are depicted in the following **Fig. 5**:

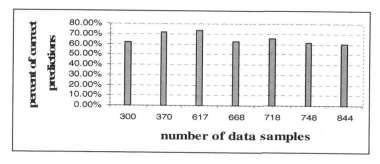

**Fig. 5.** Diagram of the percent of correct predictions of the bitrate according to the number of the used data samples

Finally, the maximum result was 73.6% and appeared when the number of data samples was 617. This number was also the number of the data samples which comprised our cases for the rest of our tests.

## 3.4 Selection of the Training Algorithm and its Parameters

Our next concern was to decide between the two training algorithms and finding the most suitable values for their parameters. In order to make such a decision we firstly defined the most suitable values for each training algorithm separately and then we compared them to each other.

In order to decide which were the most suitable values for the parameters of the batch training algorithm we tried different test cases changing only one parameter at a time. The parameters were tested randomly. Comparing the results it was obvious that the best choice in the case of batch training algorithm is shown in **Table 1**:

**Table 1.** Values of the parameters for the batch training algorithm

| Neighborhood function: Gaussian | | | |
|---|---|---|---|
| Rough Phase | | Fine-tuning Phase | |
| Initial radius | 5 | Initial radius | 1 |
| Final radius | 1 | Final radius | 1 |
| Training length | 6 | Training length | 48 |

**Fig. 6** depicts the diagram of the predicted values of the bitrate, the diagram of the real measured values of the bitrate and a comparison among the two above in case of batch training algorithm.

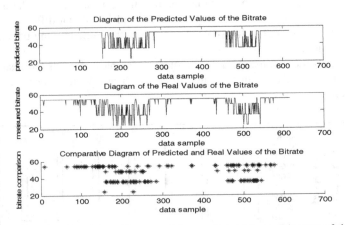

**Fig. 6.** Batch Training Algorithm: Diagram of the predicted bitrate, Diagram of the measured bitrate and a Comparison of the above. The symbol * depicts only the data samples which have different predicted and real values.

In case of sequential training algorithm, we created different test cases as well. Although the technique was the same it's worth mentioning an important difference: in sequential training algorithm the samples do not enter the training phase at the same time. As a result, the order that they enter the system leads to different results. In order to avoid such a situation we selected the entrance of the samples to be ordered according to the data file.

Finally, the best set of values for the sequential training algorithm is shown on **Table 2**:

**Table 2.** Values of the parameters for the sequential training algorithm

| Neighborhood function: Gaussian | | | |
|---|---|---|---|
| Length type: epochs | | | |
| Learning function: inv | | | |
| rough phase | | Fine-tuning phase | |
| Initial radius | 3 | Initial radius | 1 |
| Final radius | 1 | Final radius | 1 |
| Training length | 4 | Training length | 21 |
| Initial alpha | 0.5 | Initial alpha | 0.05 |

As previously, a diagram of the predicted bitrate, a diagram of the measured bitrate and a comparison of the above diagrams is depicted in **Fig. 7**.

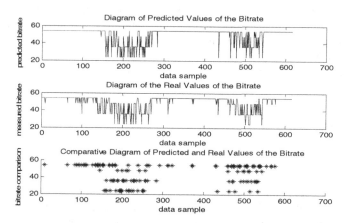

**Fig. 7.** Sequential Training Algorithm: Diagram of the predicted bitrate, Diagram of the measured bitrate and a Comparison of the above. The symbol * depicts only the data samples which have different predicted and real values.

The comparison of the set of the values of the batch training algorithm with the one of the sequential training algorithm reveals that the first result, equal to 74.4%, is a little lower than the second one, equal to 75.4%, giving the impression that the best choice is the sequential training algorithm. However, the time that is needed to complete the training phase of the SOM is sometimes crucial so we measured it as well. According to the program, batch training algorithm is quicker, requiring about 3 to 4 seconds to complete the training phase while sequential one requires about the double time (7-8 seconds). As a result, and because of the fact that the difference between the two results is rather small, the choice between the two algorithms is subjective and depends on the existence of the requirement of a quick training or not.

## 4 Conclusions

Rapid evolution of wireless communications demands the use of systems capable of intelligently adapting to the highly varying and disparate modern environments. In these terms, Cognitive Radio Systems have been a very promising technology but the cognition process, which they utilize in order to monitor, evaluate and select a radio configuration to operate with, is often time-consuming, thus leading to the necessity of a learning technique for speeding it up. In this paper we used an unsupervised leaning technique, Self-Organizing Map, in order to train a CRS to predict the bitrate that can be achieved under a combination of parameters obtained as a result of a specific radio configuration and based on its past experience. Going through numerous test cases we achieved to predict correctly the bitrate at 75.4% of the tested data samples. Such a method is expected to assist CRS to choose among the different candidate configurations by taking into account the predictions of the bitrate that can be achieved.

**Acknowledgments.** This work is performed in the framework of the European-Union funded project OneFIT (Opportunistic NEtworks and cognitive management systems for efficient application provision in the Future InterneT). The project is supported by the European Community's Seventh (7th) Framework Program (FP7). The views expressed in this document do not necessarily represent the views of the complete consortium. The Community is not liable for any use that may be made of the information contained therein.

## References

1. Mitola III, J., Maguire Jr., G.: Cognitive radio: making software radios more personal. IEEE Personal Commun. 6(4), 13–18 (1999)
2. Haykin, S.: Cognitive radio: brain-empowered wireless communications. IEEE Journal on Selected Areas in Communications 23(2), 201–220 (2005)
3. Demestichas, P., Katidiotis, A., Tsagkaris, K., Adamopoulou, E., Demestichas, K.: Enhancing Channel Estimation in Cognitive Radio Systems by means of Bayesian Networks. Wireless Personal Communications 49(1), 87–105 (2009)
4. Katidiotis, A., Tsagkaris, K., Demestichas, K.: Performance Evaluation of Artificial Neural Network-Based Learning Schemes for Cognitive Radio Systems. In: Computers & Electrical Engineering. Elsevier, Amsterdam (in press)
5. Tsagkaris, K., Katidiotis, A., Demestichas, P.: Neural Network-based Learning schemes for Cognitive Radio systems. Computer Communications 31(14), 3394–3404 (2008)
6. Liang, M., Shen, J., Wang, G.: Identification of illicit drugs by using SOM neural networks. Journal of Physics D: Applied Physics 41 (2008)
7. Tokutaka, H., Yoshihara, K., Fujimura, K., Obu-Cann, K., Iwamoto, K.: Application of self-organizing maps to chemical analysis. Applied Surface Science, 144–145, 59–63 (1999)

8. Kaski, S., Hankela, T., Lagus, K., Kohonen, T.: WEBSOM – Self-organizing maps of document collections. Neurocomputing 21, 101–117 (1998)
9. Kohonen, T., Somervuo, P.: Self-Organizing Maps of Symbol Strings with Application to Speech Recognition (1997)
10. Matsuura, Y., Tuoya, S.M., Tokutaka, H., Ohkita, M.: The Identification of a Cancer Cell Gene by using SOM. In: 16th International Conference on Genome Informatics, Yokohama Pacifico, Japan, December 19-21 (2005)
11. Tamayo, P., Slonim, D., Mesirov, J., Zhu, Q., Kitareewan, S., Dmitrovsky, E., Lander, E.S., Golub, T.R.: Interpreting patterns of gene expression with self-organizing maps: Methods and application to hematopoietic differentiation. Proc. Natl. Acad. Sci. USA 96, 2907–2912 (1999)
12. Kohonen, T.: Self-Organizing Maps, 2nd edn. Series in Information Sciences, vol. 30. Springer, Heidelberg (1997)
13. Kohonen, T.: The Self-Organizing map. Neurocomputing 21, 1–6 (1998)
14. Vesanto, J., Himberg, J., Alhoniemi, E., Parhankangas, J.: SOM Toolbox for Matlab 5 (2000)

# Application of SOM-Based Visualization Maps for Time-Response Analysis of Industrial Processes

Miguel A. Prada[1,*], Manuel Domínguez[2], Ignacio Díaz[3], Juan J. Fuertes[2], Perfecto Reguera[2], Antonio Morán[2], and Serafín Alonso[2]

[1] Dept. of Information and Computer Science, Aalto University School of Science and Technology, P.O. Box 15400, FI-00076 Aalto, Espoo, Finland
miguel.prada@tkk.fi
[2] Dept. de Ing. Elétrica y de Sistemas y Automática, Universidad de León, Esc. de Ing. Industrial e Informática, Campus de Vegazana s/n, 24071, León, Spain
{manuel.dominguez,jj.fuertes,prega,a.moran,saloc}@unileon.es
[3] Dept. de Ing. Elétrica, Electrónica, de Computadores y Sistemas, Universidad de Oviedo, Campus de Viesques s/n, Ed. Departamental 2, 33204, Gijón, Spain
idiaz@isa.uniovi.es

**Abstract.** Self-organizing maps have been extensively used for visualization of industrial processes. Nevertheless, most of these approaches lack insight about the dynamic behavior. Recently, an approach to define visualizable maps of dynamics from data has been proposed. We propose the application of this approach to single-input single-output processes by defining several maps related to relevant features in the time-response analysis. This features are commonly used in control engineering. We show that these maps are intuitive and consistent tools for knowledge discovery and validation. They also provide a general overview of the process behavior and can be used along with other previously defined maps for process analysis and monitoring.

**Keywords:** Self-organizing map, visualization, dynamics, industrial processes.

## 1 Introduction

In industry applications, data acquisition allows to gather huge volumes of data from a large number of variables. This has favored the application of methods [1] that, by means of the analysis of process data, lead to models of industrial processes. These techniques can be considered within the scope of data mining and knowledge discovery. A powerful approach in this context is visual data mining [2], i.e., the transformation of data into visual representations that enable a better understanding of the process. This paradigm has been successfully applied to fault and novelty detection, discovery of dependencies or recognition of process conditions from incomplete knowledge [3]. One relevant approach for data visualization is dimensionality reduction, which aims at finding low-dimensional structures that preserve the most important information in data. These unsupervised methods perform a selection or transformation of the set of variables that produces a better representation of relevant features on the low-dimensional display. Many

---

* This work was conducted at the University of León and supported by a research scholarship funded by the Government of Castilla y León and the European Social Fund.

K. Diamantaras, W. Duch, L.S. Iliadis (Eds.): ICANN 2010, Part II, LNCS 6353, pp. 392–401, 2010.

dimensionality reduction techniques have been proposed in the literature, e.g., Principal Component Analysis (PCA) and its nonlinear extensions, multi-dimensional scaling (MDS) methods, or nonlinear algorithms such as Isomap, Laplacian Eigenmaps or Stochastic Neighbor Embedding [4].

A powerful technique for this purpose is the Self-Organizing Map (SOM) [5]. SOM algorithm defines, in an unsupervised way, a projection from a high-dimensional input space onto a regular lattice defined on a low-dimensional space (usually 2D). The resulting projection captures the underlying low-dimensional structure in the input data and, at the same time, preserves the topology defined by the lattice. This feature makes SOM a powerful tool for data visualization, with many applications in industrial process analysis and supervision [6]. For instance, applications were described in pulp and paper and in steel industry, [7] or chemical plants, [8]. These applications are mostly focused on the static analysis of process variables, with the exception of a few works addressing the dynamical analysis of the projected state trajectory [9,10].

Knowledge about the dynamic behavior of the systems is a key issue and there is a need for evidence-based techniques to visualize the dynamics of the processes. The potential of SOM to analyze dynamic behaviors has been explored in some works, addressing topics such as modeling [11] and visualization [12]. This latter work proposed the exploratory analysis of dynamic features in an exhaustive way, including relationships between the process operating point, defined by a set of process variables, and its dynamic state, defined by a set of parameters. For that purpose, the authors defined the maps of dynamics, which allow to visualize different features associated to local parametric models described in terms of transfer functions or even nonlinear dynamical models. These maps are consistent with the component planes, so it is possible to directly search for links between the process operating point and its local dynamical behavior. Some visualizations proposed in the aforementioned work [12] were the parameter component planes, the frequency response maps or the gain maps.

However, the study and application of this technique has still been very limited and new visualizations should be designed to help in the analysis and monitoring of industrial processes. It would be particularly useful to apply this procedure to support common tasks of a control engineer, such as obtaining the time response of a system. The aim, in this case, would be to define visualization maps concerning the most common dynamic features used in the analysis and monitoring of SISO systems. We rely in the hypothesis that these maps are useful for a better understanding of industrial processes and helpful for their further analysis or monitoring.

This rest paper is organized as follows. Section 2.1 describes the method to create the proposed visualization maps. In section 2.3, visualization maps for support of the time-response analysis of second-order systems are proposed. Section 3 describes the experiments designed to test the suitability of these maps and the results obtained. Finally, in section 4, we present the conclusions drawn from the experimental results.

## 2  Maps of Dynamics

### 2.1  Description of the Technique

The basic idea behind the maps of dynamics is to apply a dimensionality reduction mapping on a space of parameters that describe different dynamic models, generally obtained from a previous system identification stage. Let us consider a parametric model

$$y(k) = f(\varphi(k), \mathbf{p}) \tag{1}$$

where the *data vector* $\varphi(k) = [y(k-1), \cdots, y(k-n), u(k), \cdots, u(k-m)]^T$ contains input-output data known at sample $k$ and $\mathbf{p} = [p_1, \cdots, p_p]^T$ is a vector with the model parameters. To build the set of parameter vectors, the whole set of input-output data pairs $\{y(k), \varphi(k)\}$ including the output at sample $k$, $y(k)$, may be subdivided into $N$ subsets for different values of $k$ contained in an index set $I_j$

$$\{y(k), \varphi(k)\}_{k \in I_j} \qquad j = 1 \cdots N \tag{2}$$

The subsets can be defined in different ways, according to the identification procedure or using a clustering algorithm such as the SOM on the signal space [13] or in a space of user-selected variables. Then, a parameter vector can be obtained from each subset using an optimization algorithm, such as least squares if the model is linear, that produces a parameter set $\{\mathbf{p}(1), \cdots, \mathbf{p}(N)\}$ with $N$ points in a parameter space $\mathbb{R}^p$, each of which defines a single dynamical model.

Alternatively, a vector $\mathbf{x} = (x_1, \cdots, x_n)^T$ of descriptive variables defining the operating point of the process can be obtained from each subset, to compose an extended parameter vector $\mathbf{q} = [\mathbf{p}^T, \mathbf{x}^T]^T$. This vector could also include time if a nonstationary behavior is to be analyzed. That results in a *joint space* that combines both dynamic parameters and process variables that are known (or assumed) to define different local dynamic behaviors. These variables are often selected on the basis of prior knowledge or hypotheses. They allow to link dynamic visualizations and the process working point.

Since the main objective is to obtain ordered visual representations of parametric models, a projection of these data is done by means of the SOM. Once trained, each prototype vector $\mathbf{m}_i$ of the SOM contains a set of model parameters $\mathbf{p}_i$ that describe the local dynamics of the process and a set of variables $\mathbf{x}_i$ that define its working point.

Let us define $\mathbf{d} = [d_1, \cdots, d_m]^T$ as the vector of dynamic features that are interesting for possible representation. Since these features express properties of the dynamic behavior, they will depend on the parameters $\mathbf{p}$ of the model, $\mathbf{d} = g(\mathbf{p})$, which is available on each prototype vector $\mathbf{m}_i$. Therefore, it is possible to compute the value of each feature $d_i$ for every SOM unit. A typical approach to represent the feature associates a color level to each 2D position $\mathbf{g}_i$ in the grid, depending on the magnitude of the property. This way, local dynamic behavior can be represented consistently with classical SOM-based maps.

In short, similar behaviors are grouped into regions in an ordered and comprehensive visualization of system dynamics. Since dynamic features have a physical insight, the maps of dynamics provide qualitative information about many aspects of the process behavior. It is possible to establish a synergy between advanced data visualization tools and control engineering concepts that opens a broad horizon for monitoring and exploratory analysis of process dynamics. It enables the analysis of local dynamic modes in nonlinear and/or non-stationary processes and the exploration of the factors with influence on changes of dynamics. Also, intuitive and standardized maps are advantageous, since only expertise in control engineering is required for its interpretation.

## 2.2 Distance in the Extended Parameter Space

In the previous work, Euclidean distance was used as the measure in the input space. Although it is the simpler choice, it could be argued that its application is not justified. There are more suitable measures for certain types of parametric models. For instance, cepstral distance have been proposed as a distance between ARMA models [14] and, therefore, it is applicable for discrete-time transfer functions. Nevertheless, research on time series data mining suggest that the results provided with such a technique might, in some cases, be even worse than with Euclidean distance [15].

In this study, the extended parameter space is composed of real variables and parameters of continuous transfer functions. Some preliminary tests with simple distances, such as Euclidean distance on normalized and unnormalized data, correlation and cosine distance, showed almost identical results regardless of the orientation of the maps. In the rest of this paper, Euclidean distance on normalized data will be used.

## 2.3 Definition of Maps of Dynamics for Time-Response Analysis

During the analysis and design, control engineers manage, on a regular basis, several well-known features associated to the system response [16]. Among them, the ones linked to the behavior of second-order systems are especially relevant, because they approximate the response of many important systems.

Second-order systems are described by the following transfer function

$$G(s) = \frac{K\omega_n^2}{s^2 + 2 \cdot \zeta \cdot \omega_n \cdot s + \omega_n^2}, \tag{3}$$

where $K$ represents the gain, $\zeta$ is the damping ratio and $\omega_n$ the undamped natural frequency. These parameters define the position of the poles and, therefore, the transient response and stability of the system. Other meaningful features can be computed from the response to a unit-step input, such as the rise time, the peak time, the maximum overshoot and the rise time. Maps of dynamics for those features can then be very useful for analysis and monitoring.

Let us describe a trivial example of the way that using maps of dynamics for finding correlations between dynamical parameters can serve that purpose. Given a certain

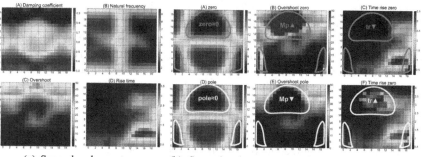

(a) Second-order system.    (b) Second-order systems with additional pole and zero.

**Fig. 1.** Trivial example of the application of maps of dynamics for time-response analysis

second-order system, a correlation between the increase of the damping coefficient and the decrease of the overshoot can be seen in the maps in Fig. 1(a). There it is clearly visible that the transition from blue zones to red zones in the damping coefficient map corresponds with the transition from red to blue in the overshoot map. Likewise, there is a correlation between the natural frequency and the rise time. In the maps of Fig. 1(b) we can see maps of overshoot and rise time of a second-order system with one additional pole and a second-order system with one real and negative additional zero.

If we compare these maps with the position of the corresponding pole in the complex map, it can be easily inferred that values of the pole near the origin (blue zones) correspond with zones where overshoot tends to disappear. In these areas, the pole becomes dominant and determines the system dynamics. However, as the pole moves away from the origin, its influence is smaller. The effect of the additional zero is the opposite, since values close to zero make the overshoot increase and shorten the rise time.

In the next section, experiments to test the usefulness of the approach in a real environment are described and discussed.

## 3   Experiments and Results

The purpose of the experiments is to check whether the proposed maps let the analyst extract relevant information about the dynamic behavior of a real process, detect correlations or recognize different regions. Prior knowledge is useful for evaluation of the conclusions drawn from the visual inspection of the maps, i.e., assessment will be based in the significance and coherence of the maps. Thus, two experiments are proposed. The first one test maps created from a physical model, whereas the second one addresses the generation of maps from sampled data of a real system. Both of them are closely related, since the model for the first experiment is a simplification of the system used for the second one.

We perform an agglomerative clustering of the SOM [17] to generate an additional map that shows the grouping of dynamic behaviors with similar characteristics. The step response of the centroids is also plotted. Single, complete, group average, centroid and Ward's linkages are considered [18]. Davies-Bouldin (DB) is the cluster validity index used to select, among those linkages, the one that maximizes the distance between clusters and minimizes the distance from the centroid to other points within the cluster [18]. For both test cases, centroid linkage was the one that obtained better results.

The **first test case** uses the simulated measurements of a closed-loop level control system on a tank. The schema is depicted in Fig. 2. The controller measures the tank level and operates the pump in order to maintain the setpoint. The maps of time-response features (gain, settling time, peak time, overshoot, rise time, damping coefficient and natural frequency), defined in section 2.3, are visualized.

The variables involved in this model are input and output flows $q_i(t)$ and $q_o(t)$, tank level $h(t)$, tank and output areas $A$ and $a$, pump speed $b(t)$, pump constant $k$, controller constants $k'$ and $k_i$ and acceleration due to gravity $g$. The system is modeled by the mass balance and Bernoulli equations and linearized around $h_0$:

$$A\Delta \frac{dh}{dt} = k\gamma\Delta b - \frac{ag}{\sqrt{2gh_0}}\Delta h, \tag{4}$$

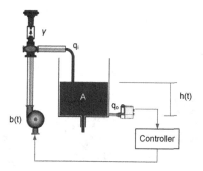

**Fig. 2.** Level control model

After computing its Laplace transform and applying a closed-loop control with a proportional-integral ISA controller, the equation becomes

$$G(s) = \frac{k'k\gamma(s + k_i)}{As^2 + (a\sqrt{\frac{g}{2h_0}} + k'k\gamma)s + k'kk_i\gamma}. \tag{5}$$

The tank area is fixed as $0.04m^2$, whereas the output area as $0.001m^2$ and the pump constant as $4.55 \cdot 10^{-6}m^3/sV$.

The input data for SOM is composed of 480 equilibrium points, obtained by combining 24 levels and 20 valve openings, and their respective dynamic behaviors, computed directly from the equations. Its dimensionality is 7 and includes the valve opening and level as the relevant variables and the coefficients of a second-order transfer function with one zero as dynamical parameters. The normalized input set is used for batch training of a standard SOM with 20 × 24 units and decreasing Gaussian neighborhood along 100 epochs. Normalization is even more advisable than usual, because it is necessary to avoid, as much as possible, changes in the dynamical parameters that may lead to a completely different interpretation of dynamics. For the same reason, map dimensions are selected to minimize distortion of input data. After training, the maps of dynamics are created from the denormalized codebook vectors in such a way that every position $g_i$ is linked to the corresponding value of feature $k_i$, which is a function of $p_{m_i}$. Component maps of the relevant variables, $x_{m_i}$, are computed.

The component planes of level (Fig. 3(a)) and valve opening (Fig. 3(b)) variables make it possible to link local dynamic behaviors with operating points. Indeed, the settling time map (Fig. 3(c)) shows an evident correlation with the level. This can be explained intuitively by the fact that the tank drains faster when the level is higher. On the other hand, the peak time map (Fig. 3(e)) and the rise time map (Fig. 3(f)) show certain relationship with both level and valve opening. Their values rise moderately for small values of the opening variable and more drastically when level is also low. The system is slower because a decrease of level and valve opening implies also a increase in the damping coefficient (Fig. 3(i)) and, therefore, a decrease of maximum overshoot (Fig. 3(d)), Natural frequency (Fig. 3(h)) is correlated with valve opening and gain (Fig. 3(g)), as expected, equals one along the whole operating range.

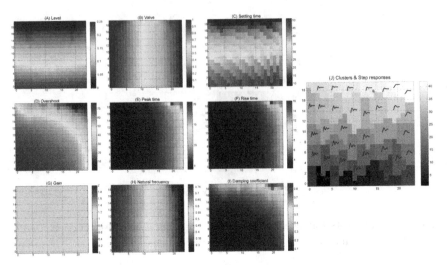

**Fig. 3.** Component planes and maps of dynamics for the mathematical model

The **second experiment** uses also a closed-loop level control system, but this time a real industrial process is sampled. The system used for this test is a 4-variable industrial scale model (see Fig. 4(a)), which consists of a main and two auxiliary circuits and has 4 controllable variables. The main circuit is the one that will be used for the experiment and comprises two cascading tanks with 10 and 15.5 liters each, a centrifugal pump with variable frequency drive that provides a supply flow of up to 22 l/m, a pneumatic valve, a drain electrovalve and sensors for the control loops associated to the variables. The implemented strategy controls filling of the upper tank in the process circuit. The mathematic model used in the previous experiment could be seen as a very simplified model of this system. The network infrastructure of the Remote Laboratory of Automatic Control at Univ. of León was used to easily perform control, data acquisition, storage and recovery. A distributed control system (Opto SNAP B3000-ENET) was used to implement the control strategy, whereas Matlab was used for data analysis.

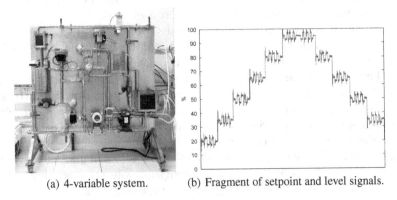

(a) 4-variable system.     (b) Fragment of setpoint and level signals.

**Fig. 4.** 4-variable industrial scale model

Again, the controlled variable is level, measured by means of an ultrasonic sensor, whereas the input is the speed (%) of the variable speed drive. The tank has a volume of 10 liters and a small capacitance, because the drain electrovalve is opened all the time. For that reason, it is difficult to maintain the level. A pneumatic supply valve modifies the input flow. Diameter of supply and drainage pipes is 25mm. Therefore, tank empties very fast and turbulence appear. The loop is closed to stabilize the system with an ISA proportional-integral controller, as in the previous experiment.

In order to obtain valid models around several operating points, the system is excited with different initial values of level and valve opening and, therefore, a step-wise staircase-shaped identification is performed (see Fig. 4(b)) . The equilibrium point of level is increased in 15% steps and later decreased and this process is repeated for different valve openings. A pseudo-random binary sequence (PRBS signal) with levels +2.5 y −2.5 [19] is used to maintain persistent excitation in each step, once the level has been stabilized in the equilibrium point.

Data are acquired by means of the aforementioned network infrastructure with a sampling period of 125ms and stored in a database from which they are recovered later for their analysis. Preprocessing includes removal of erroneous data and centering. In each step, data are divided in training and validation sets, so that a fitting metric of the model can be computed. The model of the process between setpoint and output is obtained for each step by means of a direct identification of the continuous transfer function. This direct identification uses a parameter estimation method, based on prediction error minimization, that exploits the prior knowledge about the system and is available in Matlab [19]. Therefore, the result of the system identification procedure is a set of 60 models, specifically underdamped transfer functions with two poles and one zero. The fitting to validation data is computed as $fit(\%) = 1 - 100 \cdot \|y - \hat{y}\| / \|y - \overline{y}\|$, where $\hat{y}$ is the identified output, $\overline{y}$ is the mean and its value is acceptable: $86.51\%$.

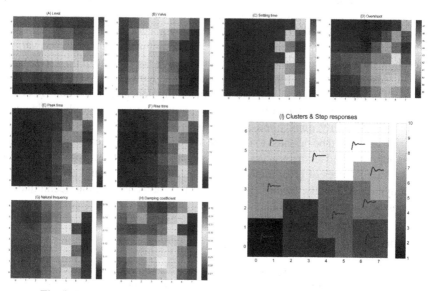

**Fig. 5.** Component planes and maps of dynamics for the real industrial plant

The data set has 60 7-dimensional vectors (level, valve opening and coefficients of the transfer function around the equilibrium point). Again, time-response features are the target of the visualization. The data set is normalized and a $7 \times 8$ SOM is trained with a standard batch algorithm of 100 epochs. Neighborhood is Gaussian and decreasing over time. In this case, the dimension of the map also aims at minimizing distortion. After training, the maps of dynamics, obtained from the denormalized codebook vectors, are visualized. So are the component planes of tank level (Fig. 5(a)) and valve opening (Fig. 5(b)), with the aim of looking for correlations with the dynamic behavior. As in the previous experiment, gain stays approximately constant in all the operating points, as expected, so it is not shown. In this experiment, visual inspection clearly shows that valve opening is the variable that decides the behavior of the system to a larger extent. For small values, i.e., when valve is partially closed, settling (Fig. 5(c)), peak (Fig. 5(e)) and rise (Fig. 3(f)) times are higher. So, in general, the system is slower when the valve opening is small. The interpretation is quite intuitive, since it takes longer to reach the setpoint with a reduced supply of liquid. Apart from making the system slower, small valve opening makes the system more oscillatory, causing a decrease of the damping coefficient (Fig. 5(h)) and an increase of overshoot (Fig. 5(d)). Natural frequency (Fig. 5(g)) decreases in this case. The influence of level is clearly smaller.

## 4 Conclusions

The results obtained in the experiments show again that the maps of dynamics are useful for knowledge discovery or model validation of the process behavior. They provide a comprehensive visualization that spans the whole range of operating points. The user can also establish a visual comparison among the dynamic features or between these and the variables that define the operating point. This allows the analyst to gain deep insight on the correlations that exist in the process. They are also consistent with other existing SOM efforts in the area of industrial process visualizations.

The proposed maps of the time response provide a general and intuitive overview of the process behavior. This allows the engineer to distinguish what areas and variable ranges show up a proper dynamic behavior for the purposes of control or, alternatively, which of these areas require further in-depth analysis. However, as in any data-based technique, the quality of the visualization or modeling depends on the quality of data and its use as support or alternative to analytic models must be carefully evaluated in terms of the availability, quality and cost of process data.

Future work should be oriented to integrate the multiple local linear models approach with this approach and let the process variables be the only input data for training. Also, other dynamic features of great importance in system analysis should give rise to new maps of dynamics. Finally, further efforts in the development of similar techniques for on-line monitoring must be made.

## References

1. Venkatasubramanian, V., Rengaswamy, R., Kavuri, S., Yin, K.: A review of process fault detection and diagnosis part III: Process history based methods. Computers and Chemical Engineering 27(3), 327–346 (2003)

2. Keim, D.A.: Information visualization and visual data mining. IEEE Trans. Vis. Comput. Graph. 8(1), 1–8 (2002)
3. Alhoniemi, E., Hollmén, J., Simula, O., Vesanto, J.: Process monitoring and modeling using the self-organizing map. Integrated Computer-Aided Engineering 6(1), 3–14 (1999)
4. Lee, J.A., Verleysen, M.: Nonlinear Dimensionality Reduction. In: Information Science and Statistics. Springer, Heidelberg (2007)
5. Kohonen, T.: Self-Organizing Maps, 3rd edn. Springer, New York (2001)
6. Kohonen, T., Oja, E., Simula, O., Visa, A., Kangas, J.: Engineering applications of the self-organizing map. Proceedings of the IEEE 84(10), 1358–1384 (1996)
7. Jämsä-Jounela, S.L., Vermasvuori, M., Endén, P., Haavisto, S.: A process monitoring system based on the Kohonen self-organizing maps. Control Eng. Practice 11(1), 83–92 (2003)
8. Abonyi, J., Nemeth, S., Csaba, V., Vesanto, P.A.J.: Process analysis and product quality estimation by self-organizing maps with an application to polyethylene production. Computers in Industry 52(3), 221–234 (2003)
9. Simula, O., Kangas, J.: Process monitoring and visualisation using Self-Organizing Maps. In: Neural Networks for Chemical Engineers, pp. 377–390. Elsevier Science B.V, Amsterdam (1995)
10. Fuertes, J.J., Prada, M.A., Domínguez, M., Reguera, P., Díaz, I., Cuadrado, A.A.: Modeling of Dynamics using Process State Projection on the Self Organizing Map. In: de Sá, J.M., Duch, W., Alexandre, L.A., Mandic, D.P. (eds.) ICANN 2007, Part I. LNCS, vol. 4668, pp. 589–598. Springer, Heidelberg (2007)
11. Principe, J., Wang, L., Motter, M.: Local dynamic modeling with self-organizing maps and applications to nonlinear system identification and control. Proc. IEEE 86(11), 2240–2258 (1998)
12. Díaz, I., Domínguez, M., Cuadrado, A.A., Fuertes, J.J.: A new approach to exploratory analysis of system dynamics using SOM. Applications to industrial processes. Expert Systems with Applications 34(4), 2953–2965 (2008)
13. Cho, J., Principe, J.C., Erdogmus, D., Motter, M.A.: Modeling and inverse controller design for an unmaned aerial vehicle based on the self-organizing map. IEEE Trans. Neural Networks 17(2), 445–460 (2006)
14. Basseville, M.: Distance measures for signal processing and pattern recognition. Signal Processing 18, 349–369 (1989)
15. Keogh, E., Kasetty, S.: On the need for time series data mining benchmarks: A survey and empirical demonstration. In: Proc. of the 8th ACM SIGKDD International Conference on Knowledge Discovery and Data Mining, pp. 102–111 (2002)
16. Ogata, K.: Modern Control Engineering, 4th edn. Prentice Hall, Englewood Cliffs (2001)
17. Vesanto, J., Alhoniemi, E.: Clustering of the self-organizing map. IEEE Transactions on Neural Networks 11(3), 586–600 (2000)
18. Xu, R., Wunsch II, D.C.: Clustering. IEEE Press Series on Computational Intelligence. Wiley-IEEE Press (October 2008)
19. Ljung, L.: System Identification: Theory for the User, 2nd edn. Prentice-Hall, Englewood Cliffs (1999)

# Snap-Drift Self Organising Map

Dominic Palmer-Brown and Chrisina Draganova

London Metropolitan University, Faculty of Computing,
166-220 Holloway Road, London N7 8DB, UK
d.palmer-brown@londonmet.ac.uk, c.draganova@londonmet.ac.uk

**Abstract.** A novel self-organising map (SOM) algorithm based on the snap-drift neural network (SDSOM) is proposed. The modal learning algorithm deploys a combination of the snap-drift modes; fuzzy AND (or Min) learning (snap), and Learning Vector Quantisation (drift). The performance of the algorithm is tested on several well known data sets and compared with the traditional Kohonen SOM algorithm. It is found that the snap mode makes the learning in SDSOM faster than the Kohonen SOM, and that it leads to the formation of more compact maps. When using the maps for classification, SDSOM gives better performance, based on labelled winning nodes, than Kohonen SOM on a variety of data sets.

**Keywords:** Neural networks, Self-organising Map, Snap-drift, modal learning, unsupervised Learning.

## 1 Introduction

The standard snap drift neural network (SDNN) algorithm [1-5] has proved invaluable for continuous learning in many diverse applications. It is essentially a simple modal learning method, which swaps periodically between the two learning modes (snap and drift). The unsupervised snap drift algorithm has previously been successfully applied in several domains including the analysis and interpretation of data representing interactions between trainee computer network managers and a simulated network management system [2], where it helped to identify patterns of the user behaviour. It has also been used in feature discovery and clustering of speech waveforms recorded from non-stammering and stammering speakers [3]. Phonetically meaningful properties of non-stammering and stammering speech were discovered, and rapid automatic classification into stammering and non stammering speech was found to be possible. Most recently, snap-drift has been successfully applied to categorising student responses to multiple choice questions in a virtual learning context [5]. In this work, SDNN is deployed in a self-organising map, to ascertain whether the advantages of snap-drift over LVQ alone (drift, without snap) transfer into the formation of topological maps. We are interested in processing speed, classification performance and data visualisation (the shape of the resultant maps).

The self-organising feature map algorithm developed by Kohonen[6] has been used widely in clustering analysis and visualization of high-dimensional data [7]. The SOMs can be also used for pattern classification by applying fine tuning of the map

K. Diamantaras, W. Duch, L.S. Iliadis (Eds.): ICANN 2010, Part II, LNCS 6353, pp. 402–409, 2010.
© Springer-Verlag Berlin Heidelberg 2010

with LVQ learning algorithms [8, 9, 10]. The Kohonen feature map was inspired by the idea that self-organising maps resemble the topologically organised maps found in the cortices of the brain [11]. The Kohonen SOM algorithm is based on unsupervised learning realised by finding the best matching node (the winner) on the map to the input vector and adapting the weights of the winner and the topological neighbourhood nodes. After the training finishes each node on the map identifies a particular input vector and the organisation of the map reflects the original organisation of the input data.

# 2 Snap-Drift Self-Organising Map

## 2.1 Snap-Drift Algorithm

Snap-drift learning uses a combination of fuzzy AND (or MIN) learning (*snap*), and Learning Vector Quantisation *(drift)* [10]. Abstractly speaking, the Snap-Drift algorithm can be expressed as:

$$Snap\text{-}Drift = \alpha(Snap) + (1\text{-}\alpha)(drift) \tag{1}$$

The weights are updated using the following:

$$w_{ji}^{(new)} = \alpha(I \cap w_{ji}^{(old)}) + (1\text{-}\alpha)(w_{ji}^{(old)} + \beta(I - w_{ji}^{(old)})) \tag{2}$$

where $w_{ji}$ = weights vectors; $I$ = binary input vectors, and $\beta$ = the drift speed constant. When $\alpha = 1$, fast, minimalist (snap) learning is invoked:

$$w_{ji}^{(new)} = I \cap w_{ji}^{(old)} \tag{3}$$

This works for binary data, otherwise equation (3) becomes the fuzzy AND of weight with data, Min($I$, $w_{ji}^{(old)}$). Consequently, Snap encodes, within the weights, the common elements of all patterns that activate the node (neuron) for learning.

In contrast, when $\alpha = 0$, (2) simplifies to:

$$w_{ji}^{(new)} = w_{ji}^{(old)} + \beta(I - w_{ji}^{(old)}) \tag{4}$$

which implements a simple form of clustering (drift) or LVQ, at a speed determined by β. Finally, in the case of either snap or drift, weights are normalized:

$$w_{ji}^{(new)} = w_{ji}^{(new)} / |w_{ji}^{(new)}| \tag{5}$$

The snap and drift modes provide complementary features. Snap capturing the common elements of the group of patterns as represented by the minimum values on each input dimension, whereas drift captures the average values of the group of patterns. Snap also has the effect of contribution to rapid convergence.

## 2.2 SDSOM

We present a new version of Self-organising Map, which combines SOM with the snap-drift algorithm. The SDSOM has the same architecture (Fig.1) as a standard SOM, with a layer of input nodes connecting to the self organising map layer. A shrinking neighbourhood is used during training, as in SOM, with the weight vector of each neighbour of the winning node being adapted according to the input pattern. The key difference in SDSOM is the weight update, which consists of either snap (min of input and weight) or drift (LVQ, as in SOM). The following steps illustrate the SDSOM algorithm:

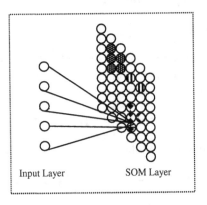

**Fig. 1.** SOM architecture

**Step 1:** Initialize parameters: $\alpha = 1$ (equation (1))
Set size of the SOM layer map.
Initialize neighborhood size.
Initialize weights between input and SOM layer with the values of randomly selected input patterns.
Normalize weights.
Initialize learning rate $\beta$ for drift mode
Initialize maximum number of epochs
**Step 2:** For each epoch (t)
Swap the value of $\alpha$ to 1 or 0
**Step 2.1:** For each input pattern
**Step 2.1.1:** Find the winning node in SOM with the largest net input
**Step 2.1.2:** Update weights of the wining node and its neighbour nodes according to the current learning mode (equation (2))
**Step 2.1.3** Normalize weights (equation (5))
**Step 2.2:** Decrease the neighborhood size with 1
**Step 3:** Terminate when maximum number of epochs is reached
**Step 4:** Evaluate the results by labelling SOM layer nodes

The shaded nodes in Fig. 1 represent different classes or labels. Nodes receive the class label of the majority of the patterns for which they win. There is generally a tendency for neighbouring nodes to have the same class, given the nature of SOMs, but this is not forced by the labelling algorithm.

# 3  Experiments and Results

## 3.1  Data Sets

A range of data sets are chosen, presenting a variety of learning challenges. They vary in terms of the number of input variables, the number of classes, and the level of separability of the classes. Since they are all known and freely available they provide useful benchmark comparators, not only with SOM, but with a number of other neural computing and other machine learning techniques.

The **Animal** data set is artificial and consists of 16 animals described by 13 attributes such as size, number of legs etc. [7]. The 16 animals are grouped into three classes (the first one represents bird, the second represents carnivore and the third represents herbivore).

The **Iris** data set has three classes setosa, virsicolor and virginica [12, 13]. The iris data has 150 patterns, each with 4 attributes. The class distribution is 33.3% for each of 3 classes. One of the classes is linearly separable from the other two, and the two are linearly inseparable from each other.

The **Wine** data set is the result of a chemical analysis of wines grown in the same region in Italy but derived from three different cultivars [14]. The analysis determines the quantities of 13 constituents (input variables) found in each of the three types of wines. There are 178 patterns with the following distribution: class 1 - 59, class 2 – 71, class 3 – 48.

The **Ecoli** data set contains 336 patterns with 7 attributes and 8 classes, which are the 'localization sites', distributed as follows [15]:

| | |
|---|---|
| cp  (cytoplasm) | 143 |
| im  (inner membrane without signal sequence) | 77 |
| pp  (perisplasm) | 52 |
| imU (inner membrane, uncleavable signal sequence) | 35 |
| om  (outer membrane) | 20 |
| omL (outer membrane lipoprotein) | 5 |
| imL (inner membrane lipoprotein) | 2 |
| imS (inner membrane, cleavable signal sequence) | 2 |

## 3.2  Results

In the experiments, 20% selections of the patterns of each data set are allocated for testing and the remaining 80% form the training set. For each run the training and testing patterns are selected at random from the entire data set . SOM is trained for 500 epochs and SDSOM for 200 epochs. This is long enough for the maps to be stable in all cases.

In order to perform a labelling of nodes for the purposes of classification the number of patterns for which the node wins is accumulated for each class and for each node. The majority class, with the highest number of patterns, becomes the class label of that node. The training classification score is the percentage of patterns categorised by nodes of the correct class. The training class labels are retained for use in testing.

**Table 1.** Mean % correct classification for train and test sets based on 5 runs. Standard deviation given in the brackets

| Method/Data set | | Animals | Iris | Wine | Ecoli |
|---|---|---|---|---|---|
| SDSOM | train | 100 (0) | 100 (0) | 100 (0) | 96.2 (0.8) |
| | **test** | **100 (0)** | **99.4 (1.3)** | **92.6 (1.3)** | **84.6 (2.5)** |
| Kohonen SOM | train | 100 (0) | 100 (0) | 100 (0) | 100 (0) |
| | test | 100 (0) | 95 (3.1) | 86 (6.3) | 81 (2.1) |

The percentage of correct classifications is the percentage of patterns for which the winning node has the same class label as the class of the pattern. Nodes in the map that by the end of training have not associated patterns for which they win are not labelled. During testing, if a winning node is unlabelled (which is rare) then the most active labelled node provides the class (correct or incorrect). Each test consists of 5 repeat trainings of the data, with the training set being randomly selected from the whole data set in each case. The maps formed are very similar for each of the repeat trainings, and the classification results presented are the averages for the 5 results. The standard deviations across the 5 tests are also presented in table 1 and for SDSOM it is only about 1%.

The **Animal** data (the maps in Fig. 2) presents a relatively easy classification task because each pattern differs quite significantly, therefore it is a simple challenge for any method to separate or classify them individually without the need for generalised rules. Both SOM and SDSOM perform well. There is however an important qualitative difference between the two results, as Fig. 2a and Fig. 2b clearly shows. SDSOM has projected the classes onto the map in a linearly separable fashion; two straight lines can separate the three animal classes on the map. This is not possible in the SOM, which mixes the herbivores and carnivores to a greater extent. The snap mode finds some common elements that are specific to herbivores that are not based on the overall similarity of herbivores across all dimensions, which is the limitation of LVQ, or any method that calculates overall similarity.

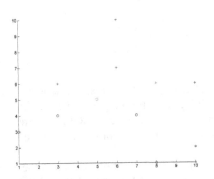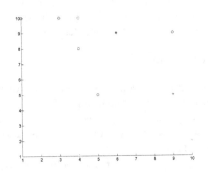

**Fig. 2a.** SDSOM 10x10 applied to Animal Data set + (bird)  o (carnivore)  * (herbivore )        **Fig. 2b.** SOM 10x10 applied to Animal Data set + (bird)  o (carnivore)  * (herbivore )

The **Iris** maps differ substantially between SOM and SDSOM. The SOM map presents a widely dispersed set of points. They are nonetheless in clear regions associated with the three classes. However, the lines between classes in the map are curved with several changes of direction and there is no margin between the classes, even in the case of the linearly separable classes. In the SDSOM map, the margin between setosa and the other two classes is significant, and the linearly inseparable verginica is more tightly grouped than in SOM. These factors give a classification advantage to SDSOM of 99% as opposed to 95%, and the t test (t=2.92, p=0.05) indicates a 95% probability of this 4% difference being statistically significant.

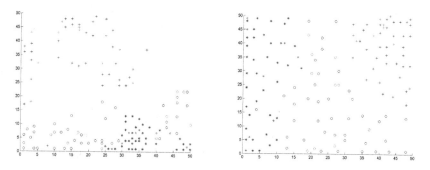

**Fig. 3a.** SDSOM 50x50 applied to Iris Data set o (verisicolor) + (setosa) * (virginica )

**Fig. 3b.** SOM 50x50 applied to Iris Data set + (setosa) o (verisicolor) * (virginica )

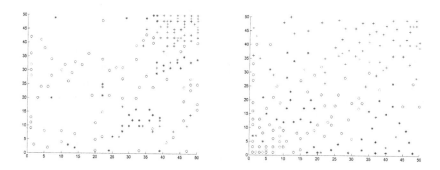

**Fig. 4a.** SDSOM 50x50 applied to Wine Data set + (class 1) o (class 2) * (class 3 ).

**Fig. 4b.** SOM 50x50 applied to Wine Data set + (class 1) o (class 2) * (class 3 ).

The average separation on the **Wine** data map of the classes is larger in SDSOM, and the classification is 92.6% as opposed to 86% with SOM, a result that is 90% likely to be statistically significant (t=2.27, p=0.1).

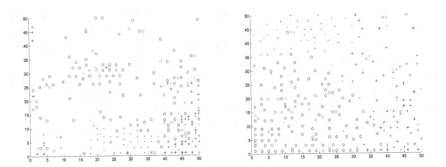

**Fig. 5a.** SDSOM 50x50 applied to Ecoli Data set + (class 1)  o (class 2) * (class 3 ).

**Fig. 5b.** SOM 50x50 applied to Ecoli Data set + (class 1)  o (class 2) * (class 3 ).

The **Ecoli** data set has 8 classes but only 3 are given on the pictures above. The E.coli data is clearly a challenging problem, with a range of methods achieving 81% correct classification, for example using an ad hoc structured probability model, a binary decision tree, or a Bayesian classifier [15]. Similarly, SOM based classification yields 81%. SDSOM achieves 84.6%, with a t test indicating 95% confidence (t=2.45, p=0.05) of the improvement over SOM being statistically significant.

# 4   Conclusion

In this work a method for using the snap-drift principle in the training of a Self Organinzing Map is considered. The resulting algorithm is called snap-drift SOM (SDSOM). SOM is useful for data visualisation and to some extent for classification.  SDSOM explores whether some advantages of the modal combination of LVQ and min learning that has been effective elsewhere with snap-drift can be successfully transferred into SOMs. SDSOM requires fewer epochs than the original SOM because snap is a rapidly convergent form of adaptation, but we also see that there are differences both in terms of the maps that are formed and the classification results obtained from the maps.   Snap-drift creates tighter groupings within the map and typically wider margins between groupings, and where those groupings correspond to classes this supports more effective classification. Because snap modifies drift by minimising or removing dimensions in weight space, fewer input variables are represented in the weight vectors than in LVQ and the feature gradient across the SD Self-organising Map is steeper than in SOM. Consequently, the map class-regions are more compact in SDSOM. When compactness is measured as the average proportion of the map space covered by the outline of the class groupings, the SDSOMs are about 30% more compact than the SOMs. The groupings are also more widely separated. The average distance between the centroids of groupings in the SDSOMs is 35% of the maximum possible separation, compared to 20% in SOMs.

# References

1. Lee, S.W., Palmer-Brown, D., Tepper, J., Roadknight, C.M.: Snap Drift: Realtime Performance guided Learning. In: International Joint Conference on Neural Networks IJCNN, Portland, Oregon, vol. 2, pp. 1412–1416 (2003)
2. Lee, S.W., Palmer-Brown, D., Roadknight, C.M.: Performance guided Neural Network for Rapidly Self Organising Active Network Management. Neurocomputing 61C, 5–20 (2004)
3. Lee, S.W., Palmer-Brown, D.: Phonetic Feature Discovery in Speech using Snap-Drift. In: Kollias, S.D., Stafylopatis, A., Duch, W., Oja, E. (eds.) ICANN 2006, Part II. LNCS, vol. 4132, pp. 952–962. Springer, Heidelberg (2006)
4. Ekpenyong, F., Palmer-Brown, D., Brimicombe, A.: Extracting road information from recorded GPS data using snap-drift neural network. Neurocomputing 73, 24–36 (2009)
5. Palmer-Brown, D., Draganova, C., Lee, S.W.: Snap-Drift Neural Network for Selecting Student Feedback. In: International Joint Conference on Neural Networks IJCNN, Atlanta, pp. 391–398 (2009)
6. Kohonen, T.: Self-Organisation and Asssociative Memory, 3rd edn. Springer, Heilderberg (1989)
7. Ritter, H., Kohonen, T.: Self-Organizing Semantic Maps. Biological Cybernetics 61, 241–254 (1989)
8. Kohonen, T.: Learning Vector Quantisation. Helsinki University of Technology, Laboratory of Computer and Information Science, Report TKK-F-A-601 (1986)
9. Kohonen, T.: Learning Vector Quantisation. Neural Networks 1, 303 (1988)
10. Kohonen, T.: Improved Versions of Learning Vector Quantization. In: IJCNN, vol. 1, pp. 545–550 (1990)
11. Kohonen, T.: Self-organised formation of topologically correct feature maps. In: Biological Cybernetics, vol. 43. Springer, Heilderberg (1982)
12. Fisher, R.A.: The use of multiple measurements in taxonomic problems. Annual Eugenics 7(Part II), 179–188 (1936); also in Contributions to Mathematical Statistics. John Wiley, NY (1950)
13. Duda, R.O., Hart, P.E.: Pattern Classification and Scene Analysis, p. 218. John Wiley & Sons, Chichester (1973)
14. Forina, M.: An Extendible Package for Data Exploration. In: Classification and Correlation. Institute of Pharmaceutical and Food Analysis and Technologies, Genoa, Italy
15. Horton, P., Nakai, K.: A Probablistic Classification System for Predicting the Cellular Localization Sites of Proteins. In: Intelligent Systems in Molecular Biology, pp. 109–115 (1996)

# Fault Severity Estimation in Rotating Mechanical Systems Using Feature Based Fusion and Self-Organizing Maps

Dimitrios Moshou[1], Dimitrios Kateris[1], Nader Sawalhi[2],
Spyridon Loutridis[3], and Ioannis Gravalos[3]

[1] Aristotle University, Agricultural Engineering Laboratory, P.O. 275,
54124 Thessaloniki, Greece
{dmoshou,dkateris}@agro.auth.gr
[2] School of Mechanical and Manufacturing Engineering,
The University of New South Wales,
Sydney 2052, Australia
n.sawalhi@unsw.edu.au
[3] Technological Educational Institute of Larissa,
Departments of Electrical Engineering and Biosystems Engineering,
41110 Larissa, Greece,
{loutridi,gravalos}@teilar.gr

**Abstract.** The capability of Self-Organizing Maps (SOM) to visualize high-dimensional data is well known. The presented work concerns a SOM based diagnostic system architecture for the monitoring of fault evolution in bearings. Bearings form an essential part of rotating machinery and their failure is one of the most common causes of machine breakdowns. A SOM based approach has been used to map time series of feature data produced by acceleration sensors in order to capture the process dynamics. The fusion of specific features and the introduction of new features related to fault severity can enable the monitoring of fault evolution. The evolution of system states showing the bearing health trend has been shown to warn of impeding failure.

**Keywords:** self-organizing maps, bearing faults, feature fusion, condition monitoring, fault evolution.

## 1 Introduction

The bearing is at the heart of rotating machinery which plays a very important role in industrial applications and is mainly used to support the axle in rotating machinery. Their failure during practical operation can lead to machine breakdown. Accordingly, in order to increase reliability and reduce loss of production, condition monitoring of bearings has become important in recent years. The use of vibration signals is quite common in the field of condition monitoring and fault diagnosis of bearings [1]. A comprehensive review on techniques that are used for condition-based rotating machinery prognostics is given in [10].

There is a large body of literature on different usage of signal processing techniques to detect faults in rolling element bearings. To make mention of a few, Fast

K. Diamantaras, W. Duch, L.S. Iliadis (Eds.): ICANN 2010, Part II, LNCS 6353, pp. 410–413, 2010.
© Springer-Verlag Berlin Heidelberg 2010

Fourier Transform, Wigner–Ville distribution [2], wavelets [3] are classic signal processing methods. Newly introduced signal processing techniques include spectral kurtosis [4] and cyclostationary analysis [5]. Intelligent techniques like SOM and multilayer perceptrons have been used for residual life prediction [9].

# 2  Diagnosis of Faults in Rotating Machinery

The use of vibration signals is quite common in the field of condition monitoring of rotating machinery. These signals can also be used to detect the incipient failures of the machine components, through an on-line monitoring system, reducing the possibility of catastrophic damage and the down time.

The Self-Organizing Map also called SOM [6] is a neural network that maps signals from a high-dimensional space into a one- or two-dimensional discrete lattice of neuron units. This study shows how the measurements obtained for a faulty bearing can be mapped into a two dimensional state SOM and the temporal evolution of states can form a trajectory that can be plotted on SOM, in order to visualize the system trend and give an indication about the health status of the bearing.

The data were obtained from the web database of the Bearing Data Center [7]. Three types of fault conditions were accounted for simulating fault development for faults appearing on the same bearing; normal bearing; bearings with a fault width of 0.007 inches and fault width of 0.021 inches at the inner raceway. In the current paper the main objective was the assessment of the severity of the fault. Previous work with the other datasets from the same database has focused on the discrimination of different types of faults depending on their position on the bearing [11].

# 3  SOM Approach for Monitoring Fault Evolution

Feature extraction was performed using two features, Kurtosis and a newly proposed feature consisting of the line integral of the acceleration signal. The introduction of the line integral feature as presented in Eq (2) is justified from the ability of such a feature to represent frequency changes in the signal. The Kurtosis is the fourth moment about the mean normalized with variance and it is given by Eq (1):

$$K = \frac{\sum_{i=1}^{N}(x_i - \mu_X)^4}{N\sigma_X^4} \tag{1}$$

The proposed line integral feature for a sliding window of N sampling points is given by Eq (2):

$$LI = \int_a^b ds \approx \sum_{i=1}^{N}\sqrt{(x(i+1)-x(i))^2 + T_s^2} \approx \sum_{i=1}^{N}|x(i+1)-x(i)| \tag{2}$$

Where N is the number of sample points (equal to 500 for the training set) in the window used to calculate Kurtosis and $T_s$ is the sampling period.

The feature vectors are then fed to the SOM for training. To test the effectiveness of SOM, several snapshots of data corresponding to a fault evolution in a similar bearing but at different horsepower of 1 Hp were used to test the generalization of the SOM. The methodology was implemented by using the SOM Toolbox for Matlab [8].

## 4  Results and Discussion

For the experiments in this paper a map size of 4x67 was used. This specific SOM shape has been selected because it enables the mapping of feature combinations corresponding to fault evolution in a way that different fault classes form distinct zones on the SOM. Following a voting procedure for label allocation, Fig. 1(a) shows clear clusters on the SOM with associated classes corresponding to fault evolution.

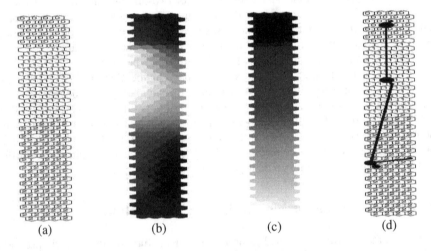

(a)                (b)                (c)                (d)

**Fig. 1.** Different manifestations of the features are shown:

(a) Assigned labels corresponding to different fault widths (0: no fault, 1: width 0.007 inches, 2: width 0.021 inches).
(b) Component map corresponding to Kurtosis with darker areas corresponding to lower relative values.
(c) Component map corresponding to Line integral with darker areas corresponding to lower relative values.
(d) Formation of trajectories for 30 data vectors for testing the correct classification of faults. All faults have been assigned to clusters having the same class as the real fault

The component maps in Figs. 1(b) and 1(c) show the distribution of Kurtosis and line integral values respectively for the units of the SOM. The distribution of Kurtosis as shown in Fig. 1(b) indicates a sensitivity of Kurtosis to minor faults compared to normal bearings and larger faults (of 0.021 inches width). On the other hand the proposed feature of the line integral is more sensitive to extended faults as shown in Fig. 1(c). The fusion (by concatenation) of the features resulted in a more accurate separation of classes related to fault extent. This is evident from the mapping of fault classes in the SOM representation which shows the labels of each SOM unit in Fig. 1(a). The testing of the SOM with fault data from a similar bearing running at a power of 1 Hp shows that the 30 testing samples form a trajectory in Fig. 1(d) that falls by 100% in the correct corresponding classes indicating normal and faulty conditions.

## 5 Conclusions

It has been shown that the SOM can be used to detect faults in roller bearings and assess the severity of the faults, and can therefore prove to be a powerful tool for bearing health monitoring especially regarding monitoring of fault evolution. Different stages of fault evolution may be indicated by a collective response of several features, which may not be obvious by just looking at the data using other diagnostic techniques. It is planned that this work be extended to include more real data, different features and spall sizes for bearings in gearboxes or other machines.

## References

1. Xu, Z., Xuan, J., Shi, T., Wu, B., Hu, Y.: Application of a modified fuzzy ARTMAP with feature-weight learning for the fault diagnosis of bearing. Expert Systems with Applications 36, 9961–9968 (2009)
2. Baydar, N., Ball, A.: A comparative study of acoustic and vibration signals in detection of gear failures using Wigner–Ville distribution. Mechanical Systems and Signal Processing 15(6), 1091–1107 (2001)
3. Wang, C., Gao, R.X.: Wavelet transform with spectral post-processing for enhanced feature extraction. IEEE Transactions on Instrumentation and Measurement 52(4), 1296–1301 (2003)
4. Randall, R.B.: Applications of Spectral Kurtosis in Machine Diagnostics and Prognostics. In: Ostachowicz, W.M., Dulieu-Barton, J.M., Holford, K.M., Krawczuk, M., Zak, A. (eds.) Journal Key Engineering Materials. Damage Assessment of Structures VI, vols. 293-294, pp. 21–32 (2005)
5. Estupiñan, E., White, P., San Martin, C.: A Cyclostationary Analysis Applied to Detection and Diagnosis of Faults in Helicopter Gearboxes. In: Rueda, L., Mery, D., Kittler, J. (eds.) CIARP 2007. LNCS, vol. 4756, pp. 61–70. Springer, Heidelberg (2007)
6. Kohonen, T.: Self-organizing Maps. Springer, Berlin (2001)
7. Bearing Data Center,
   http://www.eecs.case.edu/laboratory/bearing/CWRUFlash.htm
8. URL: SOM Toolbox, http://www.cis.hut.fi/projects/somtoolbox/
9. Huanga, R., Xia, L., Lib, X., Liuc, C.R., Qiud, H., Leed, J.: Residual life predictions for ball bearings based on self-organizing map and backpropagation neural network methods. Mechanical Systems and Signal Processing 21(1), 193–207 (2007)
10. Heng, A., Zhang, S., Tan, A.C.C., Mathew, J.: Rotating machinery prognostics: State of the art, challenges and opportunities. Mechanical Systems and Signal Processing 23(3), 724–739 (2009)
11. Yang, J., Zhang, Y., Zhu, Y.: Intelligent fault diagnosis of rolling element bearing based on SVMs and fractal dimension. Mechanical Systems and Signal Processing 21(5), 2012–2024 (2007)

# Self-Organization of Steerable Topographic Mappings as Basis for Translation Invariance

Junmei Zhu, Urs Bergmann, and Christoph von der Malsburg

Frankfurt Institute for Advanced Studies
Johann Wolfgang Goethe University, 60438 Frankfurt Germany
{jzhu,ubergmann,malsburg}@fias.uni-frankfurt.de

**Abstract.** One way to handle the perception of images that change in position (or size, orientation or deformation) is to invoke rapidly changing fiber projections to project images into a fixed format in a higher cortical area. We propose here a model for the ontogenesis of the necessary control structures. For simplicity we limit ourselves to fiber projections between two one-dimensional chains of units. Our system is a direct extension of a mathematical model [1] for the ontogenesis of retinotopy. Our computer experiments are guided by stability analysis and show the establishment of multiple topographic mappings implementing different translations, each projection associated with a single control unit. The model relies on neural signals with appropriate correlation structure, signals that can be generated by the network as spontaneous noise, so that the proposed mechanism could act prenatally.

## 1 Introduction

When we visually inspect an object, its images on our retina change quickly with motions of the eye and of the object itself, and a challenge to understanding visual perception is to cope with these image transformations. There are mainly two approaches to achieve invariance. One solution is to extract and compare features that are invariant to transformations [2,3,4]. Because it neglects explicit representation of relations, this approach is difficult to handle, for instance, cluttered scenes with multiple objects. In addition, learning high-order features has been achieved only for restricted object classes. General learning is still an unsolved problem.

The other solution that has repeatedly been proposed is based on rapidly switching fiber projections [5,6,7,8,9]. These have to be controlled by specialized units able to gate connections [7,8,9,10], an idea similar to bilinear formulations [11]. There has not been much work on how these transformation representations are developed or learned. A few systems have demonstrated the possibility of learning from images that undergo transformations [12,13]. We are interested in the question whether they can be developed before eye opening. Studies on prenatal development have mainly focused on the formation of topographic mappings between brain areas. One of the most studied problems is retinotopy, the development of a single ordered projection between retina and tectum [14,1,15].

K. Diamantaras, W. Duch, L.S. Iliadis (Eds.): ICANN 2010, Part II, LNCS 6353, pp. 414–419, 2010.

In this paper, we study the development of multiple mappings, each of which representing a different transformation parameter. Our model is guided by a system for the ontogenesis of fixed retinotopic mappings [1], which we call the *Häussler system* and describe briefly in section 2. Section 3 presents our extended system for the development of multiple mappings with linear analysis. Simulation results are given in section 4, and section 5 concludes.

# 2   The Häussler System for Retinotopy

The Häussler system for the ontogenesis of retinotopy [1] describes the establishment of an ordered projection between retina and tectum, each modelled as a closed one-dimensional chain of $N$ elements. The projection between the two domains is represented by a set of links $(\tau, \rho)$, where $\tau$ and $\rho$ are points in the tectum and retina, respectively. The weight $w_{\tau\rho}$ of link $(\tau, \rho)$ indicates the strength with which $\tau$ and $\rho$ are connected, with a value zero representing the absence of a connection. The set of all links forms a mapping $W = (w_{\tau\rho})$.

The Häussler system is described by the set of $N \times N$ differential equations:

$$\dot{w}_{\tau\rho} = f_{\tau\rho}(W) - w_{\tau\rho}B_{\tau\rho}(f(W)) \tag{1}$$

where the growth term $f_{\tau\rho}(W)$ of link $w_{\tau\rho}$ expresses the cooperation from all its neighbors, and $\alpha$ is a non-negative synaptic formation rate: $f_{\tau\rho}(W) = \alpha + w_{\tau\rho}\sum_{\tau',\rho'} C(\tau, \tau', \rho, \rho')w_{\tau'\rho'}$.

The coupling function $C(\tau, \tau', \rho, \rho')$, a monotonically falling function of both $|\tau - \tau'|$ and $|\rho - \rho'|$, describes the mutual cooperative support that link $(\tau, \rho)$ receives from its neighbors $(\tau', \rho')$. The derivation of the $C$ function from signal correlations in retina and tectum can be found in [16]. The second term in (1) describes convergent and divergent competition between synapses and has the form $B_{\tau\rho}(X) = \frac{1}{2N}\left(\sum_{\tau'} X_{\tau'\rho} + \sum_{\rho'} X_{\tau\rho'}\right)$.

An analytical treatment of the system was also provided in [1]. There it was shown that starting from around $W = 1$ (the matrix in which all entries are equal to 1), the system (1) reaches as final state in the form of a diagonal matrix, that is, a precise topographic mapping. Due to periodic boundary conditions (retina and tectum both being circularly closed chains), any of $N$ mappings, related by cyclic permutation (translation) in either retina or tectum, can be reached as final state, the symmetry between them being broken spontaneously by the system.

# 3   The Formation of Multiple Topographic Mappings

## 3.1   System Description

Here we describe the ontogenesis of a system composed again of two cyclic chains of $N$ units. This time, we aim, however, at the development of $M$ different topographic mappings that are related by relative translation. These mappings are to be installed under the control of $M$ units that form a third cyclic chain.

The basis for this functionality are 3-way connections $w_{\tau\rho\sigma}$, by which an active control unit $\sigma$ activates a topographic mapping between the chains with index $\tau$ and $\rho$. The purpose of our system is to organize these 3-way connections. For a preliminary report on a related system see [17].

Our system is a straightforward generalization of the original Häussler system, which is the special case for $M = 1$:

$$\dot{w}_{\tau\rho\sigma} = f_{\tau\rho\sigma}(W) - w_{\tau\rho\sigma}B_{\tau\rho\sigma}(f(W)), \tag{2}$$

$$f_{\tau\rho\sigma}(W) = \alpha + w_{\tau\rho\sigma} \sum_{\tau',\rho',\sigma'} C(\tau,\tau',\rho,\rho',\sigma,\sigma')w_{\tau'\rho'\sigma'}, \tag{3}$$

$$B(X) = \frac{1}{3}\left(\frac{1}{N}\sum_{\tau'}X_{\tau'\rho\sigma} + \frac{1}{N}\sum_{\rho'}X_{\tau\rho'\sigma} + \frac{1}{M}\sum_{\sigma'}X_{\tau\rho\sigma'}\right). \tag{4}$$

$C$ again is a cooperative coupling function, which we assume (as before) to be normalized to sum 1. Fig. 1 shows an example of the $C$ function modelled by a 3D separable Gaussian $C(\tau,\tau',\rho,\rho',\sigma,\sigma') = C_\tau(\tau-\tau')C_\rho(\rho-\rho')C_\sigma(\sigma-\sigma')$.

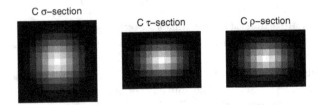

C σ–section     C τ–section     C ρ–section

**Fig. 1.** An example of coupling function $C$, a 3D separable Gaussian. The size and standard deviation in dimensions $\tau,\rho,\sigma$ are $(13,2),(13,2),(9,1.3)$, respectively. Shown are 3 sections of the 3D function (a section $\xi$ ($\xi = \sigma,\tau,\rho$) keeps the $\xi$-dimension constant at $\xi' = \xi$ while plotting the other two dimensions).

## 3.2   Linear Analysis

As in the Häussler system under periodic boundary conditions, the homogeneous state $W_0 = 1$ (i.e., the 3D matrix with all entries equal 1) is a fixed point of the system. Analysis is performed around $W_0$, by introducing the deviation $V = W - W_0$ as a new variable. The system is then

$$\dot{V} = L(V) + Q(V) + K(V),$$

where $L(V), Q(V), K(V)$ are linear, quadratic, and cubic terms, respectively. In particular, the linear term has the form

$$L(V) = -\alpha V + C(V) - B(V) - B(C(V)). \tag{5}$$

We analyze the system based on the expansion of the system state $V$ in terms of eigenfunctions ("modes") of the linear term (5). The eigenfunctions are the complex exponentials

$$e^{klm}(\tau, \rho, \sigma) = \exp(i\frac{2\pi}{N}(k\tau + l\rho) + i\frac{2\pi}{M}(m\sigma)), \tag{6}$$

for $k, l \in \mathbb{Z}_N$ and $m \in \mathbb{Z}_M$.
The corresponding eigenvalues are

$$\lambda^{klm} = \begin{cases} -\alpha - 1, & k = l = m = 0 \\ -\alpha + (\gamma^{klm} - 1)/3 - 2/3, & \text{one of } k, l, m \text{ nonzero, the others zero} \\ -\alpha + 2(\gamma^{klm} - 1)/3 - 1/3, & \text{two of } k, l, m \text{ nonzero, the third zero} \\ -\alpha + \gamma^{klm}, & \text{all } k, l, m \text{ nonzero} \end{cases} \tag{7}$$

where $\gamma^{klm}$ is the eigenvalue of the $C$ function for mode $e^{klm}$.

If we assume the $C$ function to be symmetric, $C_\xi(\xi - \xi') = C_\xi(\xi' - \xi)$ for $\xi = \sigma, \tau, \rho$, the eight modes with the largest eigenvalues are $e^{\pm 1 \pm 1 \pm 1}$ ("principal modes"), all having the same eigenvalue $\lambda = -\alpha + \gamma^{\pm 1 \pm 1 \pm 1}$. The control parameter $\alpha$ can be set such that $\lambda$ is the only positive eigenvalue, leading to the growth of the principal modes only. With that parameter, the eigenvalues of all other modes ("ancillary modes") will be negative, so that the amplitudes of these modes will, in the absence of non-linear interactions, decay to 0.

The principal mode that is favored in the initial condition is the pattern that dominates the linear regime of the dynamics. In each layer spanned by two of the variables $\tau, \rho, \sigma$ the principal modes have the form of a broad diagonal whose position shifts continuously under variation of the third index.

Outside of the linear regime, that is, for final amplitudes in $V$, nonlinearities take effect, and the principal modes excite higher frequency modes of the same orientation and phase. In the end, all excited modes contribute to a narrow diagonal. Rather than giving the detailed analysis, we numerically integrate the system and show the results in the next section.

## 4   Experiments

We here present the simulations of a system with $N = 16$ and $M = 5$ or $M = 16$. The dynamics of the system described in equation (2) is simulated using the fourth-order Runge-Kutta method and starting from an initial state that is close to the stationary state $W_0 = 1$ (each link being perturbed by additive independent random deviations uniformly distributed in the interval $(0, 0.1)$). For the control parameter $\alpha$ we assume the values 0.5 (for $M = 16$) and 0.3 (for $M = 5$). The cooperative function $C$ is a 3D separable Gaussian with standard deviation equals 1 in dimensions $\tau$ and $\rho$, whereas in dimension $\sigma$ the value is either (a) 0.67 for $M = 5$, or (b) 1 for $M = 16$.

Final states are shown in Fig. 2. In the case (a) of $M = 5$ the final state has the form of a diagonal that is a few units wide and the position of which changes progressively with the index $\sigma$, in the case (b) with $M = 16$ the diagonal is one unit wide, again progressing regularly with $\sigma$.

(a)

(b)

**Fig. 2.** Topographic mappings formed. $N = 16$. (a) $M = 5$, and (b) $M = 16$.

## 5    Conclusion and Discussion

We have presented a model for the ontogenesis of multiple topographic fiber projections between two one-dimensional chains of units, each projection implementing one translation parameter. The model only needs correlated noise as input, so the proposed mechanism could act prenatally. Our system is a mathematical idealization which would have to be expanded and modified in various directions to be directly applicable to the biological case or to computer vision. In comparison to realistic models, the autonomously self-organizing system presented in this paper has the advantage of permitting rigorous mathematical analysis.

One direction of expansion is to invariance in other transformation parameters such as orientation and scale. This generalization has one complication. Mutually overlapping transformations, which necessarily share point-to-point links, cannot be straight-forwardly organized with the current approach, in which the domains of different control units compete with each other. For a possible solution see [18]. A more systematic treatment is to expand point-to-point links to include orientation and scale of feature detectors. Correspondingly, also the control space will have to be expanded (where it may be hoped that that space can be covered by a combination of control units in low-dimensional subspaces, combining their control multiplicatively). This inclusion of feature specificity in the projections may solve the above problem of link-wise collision of projections for different scale and orientation, in that links avoid overlap in terms of feature specificity when they overlap in terms of position. When successful, the expansion to two-dimensional case without periodic boundary conditions is straightforward. These and other extensions will have to be the subject of future work.

**Acknowledgement.** Supported by EU project "SECO", BMBF Project "Bernstein Focus Neurotechnology" FKZ 01GQ0840, and by the Hertie Foundation.

# References

1. Häussler, A.F., von der Malsburg, C.: Development of retinotopic projections — an analytical treatment. Journal of Theoretical Neurobiology 2, 47–73 (1983)
2. Selfridge, O.: Pandemonium: a paradigm for learning. In: The mechanisation of thought processes. H.M.S.O., London (1959)
3. Fukushima, K., Miyake, S., Ito, T.: Neocognitron: A neural network model for a mechanism of visual pattern recognition. IEEE Transactions on Systems, Man and Cybernetics 13(5), 826–834 (1983)
4. Riesenhuber, M., Poggio, T.: Models of object recognition. Nature Neuroscience 3, 1199–1204 (2000)
5. Hinton, G.: A parallel computation that assigns canonical object-based frames of reference. In: Proc. of the Seventh IJCAI, Vancouver BC, pp. 683–685 (1981)
6. Lades, M., Vorbrüggen, J., Buhmann, J., Lange, J., von der Malsburg, C., Würtz, R., Konen, W.: Distortion invariant object recognition in the dynamic link architecture. IEEE Transactions on Computers 42(3), 300–311 (1993)
7. Olshausen, B., Anderson, C., Van Essen, D.: A neurobiological model of visual attention and invariant pattern recognition based on dynamic routing of information. The Journal of Neuroscience 13(11), 4700–4719 (1993)
8. Zhu, J., von der Malsburg, C.: Maplets for correspondence-based object recognition. Neural Networks 17(8-9), 1311–1326 (2004)
9. Lücke, J.: Information Processing and Learning in Networks of Cortical Columns. Shaker Verlag, Aachen (2005) (Dissertation)
10. Wolfrum, P., Wolff, C., Lücke, J., von der Malsburg, C.: A recurrent dynamic model for correspondence-based face recognition. Journal of Vision 8(7), 1–18 (2008)
11. Tenenbaum, J., Freeman, W.: Separating style and content with bilinear models. Neural Computation 12, 1247–1283 (2000)
12. Rao, R.P.N., Ruderman, D.L.: Learning lie groups for invariant visual perception. In: Kearns, M.S., Solla, S.A., Cohn, D. (eds.) Advances in Neural Information Processing Systems, vol. 11, pp. 810–816. MIT Press, Cambridge (1999)
13. Memisevic, R., Hinton, G.: Unsupervised learning of image transformations. In: CVPR, pp. 1–8 (2007)
14. Willshaw, D.J., von der Malsburg, C.: A marker induction mechanism for the establishment of ordered neural mappings: its application to the retinotectal problem. Phil. Trans. Roy. Soc. London B B287, 203–243 (1979)
15. Goodhill, G.: Contributions of theoretical modeling to the understanding of neural map development. Neuron 56, 301–311 (2007)
16. von der Malsburg, C.: Network self-organization in the ontogenesis of the mammalian visual system. In: Zornetzer, S.F., Davis, J., Lau, C., McKenna, T. (eds.) An Introduction to Neural and Electronic Networks, 2nd edn., pp. 447–462. Academic Press, London (1995)
17. Bergmann, U., von der Malsburg, C.: Ontogenesis of invariance transformations. In: Computational and Systems Neuroscience, Cosyne (2008)
18. Bergmann, U., von der Malsburg, C.: Self-organization of topographic bilinear networks for invariant recognition (2010) (in review)

# A Self-Organizing Map for
# Controlling Artificial Locomotion

Orivaldo V. Santana Jr and Aluizio F.R. Araújo

Center of Informatics, Federal University of Pernambuco,
Pernambuco, Brazil
{aluizioa,ovsj}@cin.ufpe.br

**Abstract.** This paper investigates the ability of STRAGEN to construct state trajectories so as to control the locomotion of legged robots. STRAGEN is a model of a self-organized artificial neural network which has a variable topology. Two scenarios are developed: one for checking the behavior of STRAGEN vis-à-vis noisy data and other to test the ability of STRAGEN to construct states belonging to different trajectories.

**Keywords:** Central Pattern Generator, Self-Organizing Map.

## 1 Introduction

The control of locomotion and the reproduction of a certain gait, in a robot in which the lower limbs have multiple degrees of freedom, is a complex problem [1]. Some of the most common approaches [2,3,4,5,6] used to solve this problem are related to the CPG (Central Pattern Generator). From the biological point of view, a CPG is a neural circuit, found in vertebrates, capable of producing rhythmic neural signals without receiving rhythmic stimuli. During locomotion neural oscillators produce periodic discharges of nerve impulses that activate the motor neurons, thus producing sequences that alternate between flexion and extension in various muscles of a limb.

To control the gait of legged robots, Ijspeert et al [3,7] drew up a biologically inspired model in which the behavior of CPG is described by a set of systems of coupled non-linear oscillators. Arena et al [5] employed Cellular Nonlinear Networks to play the role of the CPG. These CPG models, based on systems of differential equations, demand adjusting a set of parameters or even modifying these equations so as to produce a desired gait. Such a setting up is based on evolutionary algorithms [7], reinforcement learning [2], or on a specific methodology for adjusting these parameters [5]. This cited models generate a particular gait in accordance with their pre-determined equations and parameters.

STRAGEN (State Trajectories Generator) is able to control the robot based on postures that describe a gait regardless of the approach used to generate these state trajectories. STRAGEN is a self-organizing map with a variable topology able to generate state trajectories [8]. This article investigates the ability of STRAGEN to construct state trajectories for to control the gait of legged robots.

K. Diamantaras, W. Duch, L.S. Iliadis (Eds.): ICANN 2010, Part II, LNCS 6353, pp. 420–425, 2010.

STRAGEN constructs trajectories from a set of posture points by differentiating trajectories with different velocities, autonomously. Therefore, two scenarios were developed: the first tackles the ability of STRAGEN to deal with noisy data and the second checks if STRAGEN constructs states belonging to different trajectories, i.e. constructs different gaits. In addition, this article makes a parametric study of STRAGEN vis-à-vis these scenarios. STRAGEN can construct state trajectories from a databases of individual postures in which it establishes the temporal sequence of states through the determination of states neighborhood, controlling the robot gait. The previous models are limited to generating a particular gait in accordance with their pre-determined equations and parameters.

Section 2 describes STRAGEN. Experiments are shown in Section 3. Finally some conclusions are drawn in Section 4.

## 2   STRAGEN

STRAGEN [8] has a Training Phase to represent the topology of the solution space and to adapt itself while it receives examples from a given set of data. The objective of the Trajectory Generation Phase is to find the best trajectory of a set of states, according to a given criterion. The trajectory is generated by a diffusion algorithm that propagates energy from a final point through the network until it reaches an initial point.

### 2.1   STRAGEN Algorithm

In order to train STRAGEN, consider $C$ the set of connections between these nodes, $\xi$ a sample input, $w$ the vector of weights. Initialize set $A$ with two nodes $n_1$ and $n_2$ placed in $\mathbf{w}_{n_1}$ and $\mathbf{w}_{n_2}$, in $\mathbb{R}^D$, representing two random patterns of the data set, where $D$ is the dimension of the input data, thus $A = \{n_1, n_2\}$.

The vector of weights $w$ may contain heterogeneous information, divided into $m$ groups with elements belonging to one and the same domain. Two groups of these $m$ groups have greater importance in the algorithm: the group $\mathbf{v}_\zeta$ used to calculate the activity of the neuron and the group $\mathbf{v}_\eta$ used to create the network neighborhood. The vector of weights is $\mathbf{w} = [\mathbf{v}_1...\mathbf{v}_\zeta...\mathbf{v}_\eta...\mathbf{v}_m]^T$.

The training algorithm of STRAGEN is presented below:

1. Present a sample $\xi = [\mathbf{v}_1...\mathbf{v}_\zeta...\mathbf{v}_\eta...\mathbf{v}_m]^T$ to the network;
2. For each weight vector in the network, calculate the Euclidean distance to the input stimulus $\|\xi(t)_\eta - \mathbf{w}_{s_1,\eta}\|$, determine the nearest $s_1$ and the second nearest unit to the input sample $s_2$ according to the criterion of the chosen neighborhood, in which $\xi(t)_\eta$ is the group $\mathbf{v}_\eta$;
3. Update the number of wins of the winner;
4. Enter a new connection between $s_1$ and $s_2$, if they do not yet exist;
5. Calculate the activity of the input stimulus $\xi$ in relation to the winner node ($s_1$) for each subgroup of the activity group $\mathbf{v}_\zeta$;

6. If the activity of any subgroup of $\mathbf{v}_\zeta$ is less than a threshold established for this subgroup, then add a new node in the exact location of the example input;
7. If no new node is inserted in the previous step (6), update all elements $\mathbf{v}_i$ of the vector of weights of the winner node $s_1$;
8. Calculate the average size $\mu$ and the standard deviation $\sigma_s$ of all the connections $k = |N_{s_1}|$ emanating from the winner node $s_1$; where $|N_{s_1}|$ is the number of neighbors of $s_1$, e $i \in N_{s_1}$.
9. If $|N_{s_1}| > 2$, remove all the connections from the set $C$ for which: $\mathrm{Dst}(s_1, n_i) > \mu + 0.8 * \sigma_s$, $i \in N_{s_1}$.
10. Remove all nodes without neighbors: $|N_{s_1}| = 0$.
11. Repeat all the steps from step 1 until a maximum number of iterations, or some other stopping criterion has been reached.

A trajectory between two states is yield according to a function of energy propagation in the network. The target node has an assigned energy value of 1.0. The energy flows through the network iteratively, from neighbor to neighbor until it reaches node representing the initial state. A cyclical trajectory comprises a set $P$ of control states that are processed in pairs to form the sub-trajectories that make up the cyclical trajectory. The control states $P = \{p_1, p_2, ..., p_n\}$, are processed as follows:

1. Repeat for $i$ from 1 to $n - 1$:
   (a) Run the algorithm for generating the trajectory passing $p_i$ as the target and $p_{i+1}$ as the starting point;
   (b) Save the trajectory between $p_i$ and $p_{i+1}$;

# 3   Experiments

The experiments investigate the ability of STRAGEN to reproduce a certain gait from the positions generated for the robot. The robot used in the experiments has six limbs, each with three degrees of freedom, i.e. three joints. Of these three joints, two remained free and the most extreme joint remains with its angle set at 100 degrees, which comes to a total of 12 variables controlled by the system.

Three databases were used to perform the experiments and represented three different gaits: wave, medium and trot, for speeds of slow, moderate and fast respectively. These bases were generated from the model by Arena et al. [5]. This model was implemented in C++ programming language and validated with the results shown in [5] and with the help of the Gazebo simulator [9] which was made suitable for the simulation of dynamic and outdoor environments. These databases contain the postures of the robot during the execution of a particular gait for complete step, states being collected every 330 milliseconds. A posture is defined by the angular position of the 12 free joints of the robot.

## 3.1  Noise

This stage of the experiment tests the ability of STRAGEN to deal with noisy data. Out of the three original databases, nine new databases were created, so for each gait three databases were prepared, one for each noise level. The noise was generated with a Gaussian function with a mean of 0 and a standard deviation of 0.001, 0.01 and 0.1 applied to the original data (Table 1). The STRAGEN set-up was: the pruning parameter was set to 0.8; the motor babbling procedure was not used; three control points, each chosen for each third of the total of training samples; the initial learning rate was 0.1 and the final one 0.001; the maximum number of victories for the winner neuron was 40; the neighborhood and activity group were taken as the entire vector of characteristics; there was no subgroup of activity. The stopping criterion of the training was for the number of connections in the network not to increase after 300 iterations.

**Table 1.** Experimental Setup for the three Gaits

| Setup | Gait | Noise | Activity Threshold | Dynamic Time Warping |
|-------|------|-------|--------------------|----------------------|
| 1 | Wave | 0.001 | 0.900 | $6.0103 \times 10^{-6}$ |
| 2 | Wave | 0.010 | 0.890 | $5.5686 \times 10^{-4}$ |
| 3 | Wave | 0.100 | 0.460 | $1.6560 \times 10^{-1}$ |
| 4 | Medium | 0.001 | 0.540 | $7.0740 \times 10^{-6}$ |
| 5 | Medium | 0.010 | 0.550 | $6.6158 \times 10^{-4}$ |
| 6 | Medium | 0.100 | 0.465 | $1.9200 \times 10^{-1}$ |
| 7 | Fast | 0.001 | 0.700 | $4.3887 \times 10^{-6}$ |
| 8 | Fast | 0.010 | 0.660 | $3.2041 \times 10^{-3}$ |
| 9 | Fast | 0.100 | 0.480 | $1.8443 \times 10^{-1}$ |

Algorithm DTW (Dynamic Time Warping) [10] was used to make the comparison between the trajectories generated by STRAGEN from noisy data and the original noise-free trajectories. Each scenario was run 30 times, the results (Figure 1) were generated for a free joint. The noise of 0.1 is high enough to mix two samples that were previously represented by different neurons. Thus, the activation threshold needed to be reduced so that each neuron represented a larger region of space. Consequently fewer neurons come to represent a trajectory, implying there was a reduction in the quality of the resulting trajectory (Table 1).

In all situations, STRAGEN managed to recover the original trajectory. Particularly in the situations where the noise applied was higher (0.1), lines 3, 6 and 9 of Table 1, STRAGEN managed to recover the original trajectory satisfactorily. With a noise level of 0.01 and 0.001, the trajectories generated by STRAGEN were very similar to the originals (Table 1).

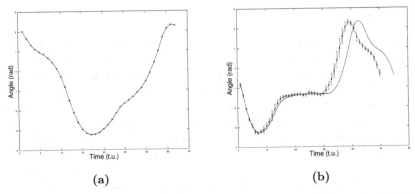

(a)                                      (b)

**Fig. 1.** Results for the highest levels of noise, gaussian noise with standard deviation (a) 0.01 in medium gait and (b) 0.1 in wave gait

## 3.2  Three Gaits one Data Base

At this stage of the experiment, the data for the three gaits were stored in one database at random, with no information on the sequences of the states in each trajectory. STRAGEN generated each of the three trajectories from the points stored. STRAGEN parameters are the same as in Section 3.1, except for the activation threshold, set to 0.65. We ran STRAGEN 30 times, and in all of them, it generated the three trajectories completely. Probably two factors contributed to the success of STRAGEN: the high dimensionality of the samples with discriminating information; and the capture of the distinct way the postures, expressed by the values of joint angles, vary for each gait. Therefore STRAGEN presented a crucial emergent property: a different synchronism between limbs for different gaits. Figure 2 illustrates the relationship of proximity between the neurons resulting at the end of training by STRAGEN.

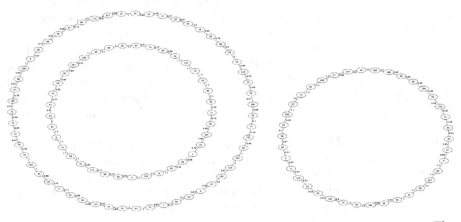

**Fig. 2.** Each node in the graph represents one STRAGEN neuron, thus a state. The figure shows the three gaits.

# 4   Conclusion

This article dealt with a model of Self-Organizing Map of variable topology that can generate state trajectories, STRAGEN, which was applied to the problem of controlling the locomotion of legged robots. The most notable contribution of STRAGEN is its ability to construct any kind of state trajectory and from this trajectory to control the robot gait. Each one of the trajectories is constructed autonomously by STRAGEN from the set of postures, which may be noisy or belongs to different gaits. During the experiments, to build any kind of trajectories only the activity threshold needs to be determined.

Two interesting issues to be investigated in the future are: the creation of a mechanism for transition between gaits, and the automatic adjustment of the activity threshold for a desired trajectory.

# References

1. Sproewitz, A., Moeckel, R., Maye, J., Ijspeert, A.J.: Learning to move in modular robots using central pattern generators and online optimization. International Journal of Robotics Research 27(3-4), 423–443 (2008)
2. Nakamura, Y., Mori, T., Sato, M.A., Ishii, S.: Reinforcement learning for a biped robot based on a cpg-actor-critic method. Neural Netw. 20(6), 723–735 (2007)
3. Ijspeert, A.J., Crespi, A., Ryczko, D., Cabelguen, J.M.: From swimming to walking with a salamander robot driven by a spinal cord model. Science 315(5817), 1416–1420 (2007)
4. Ayers, J., Witting, J.: Biomimetic approaches to the control of underwater walking machines. Philosophical Transactions of the Royal Society A: Mathematical, Physical and Engineering Sciences 365(1850), 273–295 (1850)
5. Arena, P., Fortuna, L., Frasca, M., Sicurella, G.: An adaptive, self-organizing dynamical system for hierarchical control of bio-inspired locomotion. IEEE Transactions on Systems, Man, and Cybernetics, Part B 34(4), 1823–1837 (2004)
6. Ijspeert, A.J.: Central pattern generators for locomotion control in animals and robots: a review. Neural Networks 21(4), 642–653 (2008)
7. Ijspeert, A.J., Hallam, J., Willshaw, D.: Evolving swimming controllers for a simulated lamprey with inspiration from neurobiology. Adaptive Behavior 7(2), 151–172 (1999)
8. Benante, R., Araujo, A.: Self-organizing maps to generate state trajectories of manipulators. In: IEEE International Conference on Systems, Man and Cybernetics, ISIC, vol. 1, pp. 1590–1595 (October 2007)
9. Koenig, N., Howard, A.: Design and use paradigms for gazebo, an open-source multi-robot simulator. In: IEEE/RSJ International Conference on Intelligent Robots and Systems, vol. 3, pp. 2149–2154 (2004)
10. Keogh, E.J., Pazzani, M.J.: Derivative dynamic time warping. In: First SIAM International Conference on Data Mining, SDM 2001 (2001)

# Visualising Clusters in Self-Organising Maps with Minimum Spanning Trees

Rudolf Mayer and Andreas Rauber

Institute of Software Technology & Interactive Systems
Vienna University of Technology, Austria
http://www.ifs.tuwien.ac.at/~mayer

**Abstract.** The Self-Organising Map (SOM) is a well-known neural-network model that has successfully been used as a data analysis tool in many different domains. The SOM provides a topology-preserving mapping from a high-dimensional input space to a lower-dimensional output space, a convenient interface to the data. However, the real power of this model can only be utilised with sophisticated visualisations that provide a powerful tool-set for exploring and understanding the characteristics of the underlying data. We thus present a novel visualisation technique that is able to illustrate the structure inherent in the data. The method builds on minimum spanning trees as a graph of similar data items, which is subsequently visualised on top of the SOM grid.

## 1 Introduction

The Self-Organising Map [2] (SOM) is a prominent tool for data analysis and mining tasks. It's main characteristic is a topology-preserving mapping (vector projection) from a high-dimensional input to a lower-dimensional output space. The output space is often a two-dimensional, rectangular lattice of nodes, which offers a convenient platform for plotting the topology of the high dimensional data for subsequent analysis tasks.

However, to fully exploit the potential of SOMs for data analysis and mining, it has to be combined with visualisations that additionally uncover the properties of the map and underlying data, e.g. cluster boundaries and densities. In this paper, we thus propose a novel technique that is able to visualise the similarity relationships. It is based on constructing a minimum spanning tree, which is then visualised on the SOM grid. This visualisation indicates, by connections across the map, which parts of the SOM are similar, and thus can uncover groups or clusters of related areas on the map. We compare this novel method with earlier visualisation techniques, and evaluate the benefits of the new method.

The remainder of this paper is organised as follows. Section 2 gives an overview on the SOM and its visualisations. Section 3 then introduces the concept of minimum spanning trees, and details how they can be applied to Self-Organising Maps. In Section 4, we present an experimental evaluation of the method on two benchmark datasets. Finally, Section 5 provides a conclusion.

K. Diamantaras, W. Duch, L.S. Iliadis (Eds.): ICANN 2010, Part II, LNCS 6353, pp. 426–431, 2010.

# 2   Self-Organising Map and Visualisations

The SOM performs both a vector quantisation, i.e. finding prototypical representatives in the data, similar to k-Means clustering, as well as a vector projection,
i.e. a reduction of dimensionality. The SOM projection is, as faithfully as possible, preserving the topology of the input data, i.e. items located close to each
other in input space will also be mapped close to each other on the map, while
items distant in the input space will be mapped to different regions of the SOM.

The SOM consists of a grid of nodes (or units), each being associated with a
model vector in input space. The grid (or lattice) is usually two-dimensional, due
to the convenience of visualising two dimensions and the analogy to conventional
maps. The nodes are commonly arranged in rectangular or hexagonal structures.
The model vector of node $i$ is denoted as $m_i = [m_{i1}, m_{i2}, ...m_{in}]^T \in \Re^n$, and is
of the same dimensionality as the input vectors $x_i = [x_{i1}, x_{i2}, ...x_{in}]^T \in \Re^n$.

After initialisation of the model vectors, the map is trained to optimally describe the domain of observations. This process consists of a number of iterations
of two steps. First, a vector $x$ of the input patterns is randomly selected. The
node with the model vector most similar to $x$ is computed, and referred to as
winner or best matching unit (BMU) $c$.

In the second step, the SOM is learning from the input sample to improve
the mapping, i.e. some model vectors $m_i$ of the SOM are adapted, by moving
them towards $x$. The degree of this adaptation is influenced by two factors. The
*learning rate* $\alpha$ determines how much a vector is adapted, and should be a time-
decreasing function. The *neighbourhood function* $h_{ci}$ is typically designed to be
symmetric around the BMU, with a radius $\sigma$; its task is to impose a spatial
structure on the amount of model vector adaptation.

As noted earlier, the SOM grid itself does not reveal much information about
the relationships inherent to the data, besides their location on the map. A set
of visualisation techniques uncovering more of the data and map structure has
thus been developed. They are generally superimposed on the SOM, focusing on
different aspects of the data.

Some methods rely solely on the **model-vectors**. Among them, *Component
Planes* are projections of single dimensions of the model vectors $\mathbf{m}_i$. With increasing dimensionality, however, it becomes more difficult to perceive important
information from the many illustrations. The *U-Matrix* [7] shows local cluster
boundaries by depicting pair-wise distances of neighbouring model vectors. The
Gradient Field [4] has some similarity with the U-Matrix, but applies smoothing over a broader neighbourhood. It uses a vector field style of representation,
where each arrow points to its closest cluster centre.

A second category of techniques take into account the **data distribution** on
the map. Labelling techniques plot the names and categories of data samples. Hit
histograms show how many data samples are mapped to a unit (c.f. the textual
markers in Figure 1, where units with no marker contain no data inputs, and
are so-called interpolation units). More sophisticated methods include Smoothed
Data Histograms [3], which show data densities by mapping each data sample to
a number of map units. The P-Matrix [6] depicts the number of samples that lie

within a sphere of a certain radius around the model vectors. The density-graph method [5] shows the density of the dataset on the map. It also indicates clusters that are close to each other in the input space, but further apart on the map, i.e. topology violations. The graph is computed in input space, and consists of a set of edges connecting data samples which are 'close' to each other. Closeness can be fined based on a $k$-nearest neighbours scheme, where edges are created to the $k$ closest peers of each data sample. A second approach connects samples with a pairwise distance below a threshold value $r$, i.e. the samples within the hyper-sphere of radius $r$. The parameters $k$ and $r$ thus determine the density of the resulting graph. To visualise the graph, all samples are projected onto the SOM grid, and connecting lines between two nodes are drawn if there is an edge between any of the vertices mapped on those two nodes.

# 3   Minimum Spanning Tree Visualisation

A *spanning tree* is a sub-graph of a connected, undirected graph. More precisely, it is a tree, i.e. a graph without cycles, that connects all the vertices together. A graph can have several different spanning trees. By assigning a weight to each edge, one can compute an overall weight of a spanning tree. A minimum spanning tree is then a spanning tree with the minimum weight of all spanning trees.

The weights assigned to the edges often denote how *unfavourable* a connection is. A Minimum Spanning Trees then represents a sub-graph which indicates a favoured set of edges on the graph. Applied to SOMs, a Minimum Spanning Tree can be used to connect similar nodes with each other, and can thus visualise related nodes on the map. A graph on the SOM can be defined by using either the input data samples or the SOM nodes as vertices. The weights of the edges are computed by a distance metric between the vectors of the vertices, i.e. the input vectors or the model vectors, respectively.

When constructing the MST with the SOM nodes, it can be visualised by connecting lines between the two nodes that represent the vertices in each edge of the MST. When using the input data samples, first the best-matching-unit of each of the vertices is computed, and then again these two nodes are connected by a line. An illustration of these two visualisation technique is given in Figure 1(a) and 1(b). It can be observed that in both versions, sub-groups emerge.

The tree, by definition, fully connects all vertices, which, at first glance, makes it more difficult to spot the clusters. In Figure 1, this is especially the case when using the SOM nodes as vertices. Thus, a slight modification of the visualisation indicates the weights of the edges via the line thickness. We define the thickness as inverse proportional to the distance of the two nodes, i.e. to the weight of the edge, normalised by the maximum distance in the tree. Therefore, edges in the tree between very similar vertices are indicated by thick lines, while thin lines indicate a large distance. This approach is illustrated in Figure 1(c) and 1(d). It can be observed that the clusters are now visually much more separated than before.

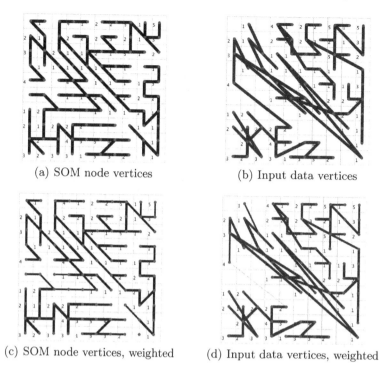

(a) SOM node vertices

(b) Input data vertices

(c) SOM node vertices, weighted

(d) Input data vertices, weighted

**Fig. 1.** MST visualisation, two sources of vertices (Iris dataset, 10x10 nodes)

# 4   Experimental Evaluation

We evaluate our visualisation method by applying it to two benchmark datasets. The first is the Iris dataset [1], a well-known reference dataset, describing three kinds of Iris flowers by four features: sepal length, sepal width, petal length, and petal width. The classes contain 50 samples each. One class is linearly separable from the remaining two, which in turn are not linearly separable from each other. This separation can be easily seen in the MST visualisation in Figure 1. Connections concentrate within the one separable class in the lower-left corner, and the two other classes in the rest of the map. Only one connection cuts across the boundary, as an implication of the full connectivity of the MST. Applying the line-thickness weighting clearly reveals the separation.

A comparison to the density graph is given in Figure 2. With a $k$ value of 1, both visualisation reveal similar information. The MST visualisation seems clearer when it comes to within cluster relations, e.g. in the upper-right area. With a $k$ of 1, the density graph doesn't indicate the relations between the many nodes that form small sub-graphs with one other node. With higher $k$, the display of local relations is traded for a better display of the cluster density.

In the display of the MST visualisation based on the model vectors of the SOM, the separation is not so apparent. While the MST considers all vertices, in a SOM, as mentioned earlier, there is often a number of nodes that do not

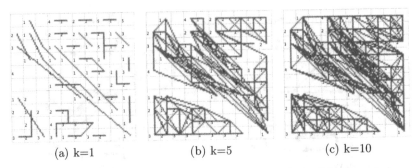

(a) k=1                  (b) k=5                  (c) k=10

**Fig. 2.** Density Neighbourhood Graph on Iris Dataset (10x10 nodes)

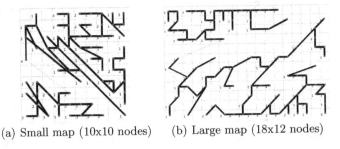

(a) Small map (10x10 nodes)    (b) Large map (18x12 nodes)

**Fig. 3.** MST visualisation on Iris dataset, SOM node vertices, weighted lines, no interpolation nodes

hold any data samples, but serve as interpolation units along cluster boundaries. The model vectors of these nodes are located in an area in the input space that is either very sparsely populated, or not populated at all. To alleviate this problem, the user can select a mode that skips these interpolation nodes. Illustrations of the previously mentioned map, and a larger map, are given in Figure 3. Applying this filtering technique, the cluster structure is now more clearly visualised.

The second dataset is artificially created[1], to demonstrate how a data analysis method deals with clusters of different densities and shapes when these different characteristics are present in the same dataset. It consists of ten sub-datasets that are placed in a 10-dimensional space; some of the subsets live in spaces of lower dimensions. Figure 4 shows the visualisations of this dataset: (a) depicts the SOM nodes based MST visualisation, with weighted line thickness. As in this map the number of interpolation nodes is very high, only the variant skipping interpolation nodes yields a clear illustration. The MST on the input data is given in (b), compared to the neighbourhood density graph in (c). The two variants of the MST visualisation show very similar structures, with just minor differences. Compared to the density graph, the MST visualisation better depicts the relation between the subsets in the centre and upper-right corner.

---

[1] The dataset can be obtained at http://www.ifs.tuwien.ac.at/dm/dataSets.html

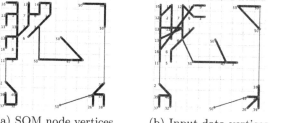 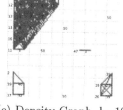

(a) SOM node vertices          (b) Input data vertices          (c) Density Graph, k=10

**Fig. 4.** Visualisations of the artificial dataset: MST (a), (b) and density graph (c)

## 5   Conclusions

We presented a visualisation technique for Self-Organising Maps based on Minimum Spanning Trees. The method is able to reveal groups of similar items, based on graphs built either of the input data, or the SOM nodes.

We evaluated the visualisation, and compared it to the density graph method, and found it to reveal similar information. The visualisation is not dependent on a specific user parameter, which is beneficial for novice users. The method operating on the SOM node vertices generally has lower computation time than the density graph method, as the number of nodes in a SOM is generally a magnitude smaller than the number of data samples. This variant can also be computed when the training data is not available. The visualisation can be superimposed on other techniques, such as the U-Matrix or Smoothed Data Histograms, which enables the display of various types of different information at once, without having to compare different figures.

## References

1. Fisher, R.A.: The use of multiple measurements in taxonomic problems. Annual Eugenics 7(Part II), 179–188 (1936)
2. Kohonen, T.: Self-Organizing Maps. Springer, Heidelberg (2001)
3. Pampalk, E., Rauber, A., Merkl, D.: Using Smoothed Data Histograms for Cluster Visualization in Self-Organizing Maps. In: Proceedings of the International Conference on Artifical Neural Networks, Madrid, Spain. Springer, Heidelberg (2002)
4. Pölzlbauer, G., Dittenbach, M., Rauber, A.: Advanced visualization of self-organizing maps with vector fields. Neural Networks 19(6-7), 911–922 (2006)
5. Pölzlbauer, G., Rauber, A., Dittenbach, M.: Graph projection techniques for self-organizing maps. In: Proceedings of the European Symposium on Artificial Neural Networks, Bruges, Belgium. d-side publications (2005)
6. Ultsch, A.: Maps for the visualization of high-dimensional data spaces. In: Proceedings of the Workshop on Self-organizing Maps (2003)
7. Ultsch, A., Siemon, H.P.: Kohonen's Self-Organizing Feature Maps for Exploratory Data Analysis. In: Proceedings of the International Neural Network Conference. Kluwer Academic Press, Dordrecht (1990)

# Elementary Logical Reasoning
# in the SOM Output Space*

Jorge Ramón Letosa** and Timo Honkela

Adaptive Informatics Research Centre
Aalto University of Science and Technology
P.O. Box 15400, FI-00076 Aalto

**Abstract.** In this paper, we consider how to represent world knowledge using the self-organizing map (SOM), how to use a simple recurrent network (SRN) to device sentence comprehension, and how to use the SOM output space to represent situations and facilitate grounded logical reasoning.

## 1 Introduction

The self-organizing map (SOM) is a well known neural network algorithm. The map is typically a 2-dimensional array, the nodes of which become specifically tuned to various input signal patterns or classes of patterns in an orderly fashion [1]. The SOM provides a means for modeling concept formation and symbol grounding [2,3]. It also can be used for implicit representation of conceptual hierarchies [1]. In this paper, we focus on the question how to conduct basic logical reasoning within the SOM framework. Moreover, we wish to connect the level of representing knowledge propositionally with its representation in the form of natural language sentences. The framework would also allow multimodal grounding of the knowledge (see e.g. [4]) but we do not address the issue here.

In a *related work*, Duch has provided an overall view and motivation on neurocognitive modeling of linguistic processing [5]. In relation to conceptual modeling, he states that each node in a neurally plausible semantic network is a neural circuit, with similarities and associations between concepts resulting from sharing some common elements or mutual activations that are responsible for semantic priming [5]. Consistent with this line of thought, Miikkulainen developed already some time ago a system for story comprehension using the SOM as a conceptual memory [6]. Later, the model has been extended to include recurrent processing of sentence structures [7]. In a recent work, Mayberry and Miikkulainen have introduced a new connectionist model called InSomNet [8]. Their results show that InSomNet learns to represent semantic dependencies accurately and generalizes to novel structures. The InSomNet system interprets sentences nonmonotonically, generating expectations and revising them, priming

---

* The work has been supported by the Academy of Finland.
** Visiting from the University of Zaragoza, Spain.

K. Diamantaras, W. Duch, L.S. Iliadis (Eds.): ICANN 2010, Part II, LNCS 6353, pp. 432–437, 2010.

future inputs based on semantics, and properly coactivating multiple interpretations of expressions [8].

Frank has presented a model in which basic logical operations can be represented as a certain kind of Venn diagram manipulations on the SOM surface [9]. Our current work is closely related to Frank's approach. We verify his experimental results, provide some extensions, and build further the underlying theoretical framework. Starting with a model basically focused in the use of self-organizing maps to carry out knowledge representation based on the comprehension of situations from a story created from the combination of basic propositions and the study about how to extract inferences from this representation [10], Frank adds a sentence comprehension model [11,9] based on a microlanguage that intends to learn how to relate a set of input sentences with the microworld situations represented onto a SOM map, and accomplish some kind of abstraction learning in the sentence comprehension.

As the *main objectives* in this paper, we consider how to represent propositionally defined situations using the SOM, how to represent the processing and structural representation of related sentences using recurrent neural networks, and how to evaluate the comprehensibility of the sentences in the framework of this methodology. We also consider how logical reasoning can be conducted using the SOM output space as grounding for the propositional elements. We present the underlying theory and methodology as well as an illuminative experiment.

# 2  Methods

The objective of this work is threefold: (1) to represent world knowledge using the self-organizing map (SOM), (2) to use a simple recurrent network (SRN) to device sentence comprehension, and (3) to use the output space to represent situations and facilitate grounded logical reasoning. We will apply set theory and fuzzy set theory [12], clause logic, neural networks (specifically simple recurrent neural networks [13] and the self-organizing map [1]).

The degree of fit between an input value and a particular prototype in the SOM is interpreted as an membership value in the fuzzy set theory. We also assume that the proportional size of the distribution on the map related to a specific input approximates the probability of this input. Furthermore, we assume that the distributions on the map can be interpreted as fuzzy Venn diagrams allowing for basic set-theoretic operations (see e.g. [14]). Venn diagrams show possible logical relations among a finite collection of sets.

Simple recurrent network is a variant multilayer perceptrons. In a simple recurrent network, a set of context units is added to the three-layer network. The connections from the hidden layer to context units allow the network to model time-dependent phenomena and perform tasks like sequence prediction. [13]

## 2.1  World Knowledge Representation

In order to implement world knowledge, we shall begin by constructing a defined microworld framework in which a set of situations takes place. After defining the

**Table 1.** Examples of the basic events in the microworld

| No. | Name | Meaning |
|-----|------|---------|
| 1 | 70s | In the 70s decade. |
| 2 | 80s | In the 80s decade. |
| 3 | lcSuccess | LC gets success. |
| .. | ... | ... |
| 15 | bdHome | BD is at the home country. |
| 16 | bdEurope | BD is in Europe. |
| 17 | accompanied | He is/they are accompanied. |

microworld and its constraints, we explain how the microworld knowledge can be represented by means of the help of the Self-Organizing Maps.

Following the model presented in [10], the knowledge of a microworld is learned implicitly by means of training a set of example situations that fulfill the microworld definition; each one of them is created from combining the events such as presented in Table 1. Thus, the SOM output of the model is expected to reflect the inherent regularities, constraints and the *a priori* probabilities of occurrences of the concrete events within the microworld. This serves as a kind of "experience" the system has after being trained with a set of microworld example situations.

After training, a situation in the microworld is represented by a high-dimensional vector of $n = 150$ components (a SOM map). This implementation in which a situation is contained in a vector of fixed size of $n$ elements allows a representation in which $n$ is independent of the size of the example set, although, at the same time, by reducing the dimensionality from $k$, size of the example set, 227 in this case, to $n = 150$, some of the information contained in the previous example situations set may be lost. A situation vector is in the form $s(p) = (s_1(p), s_2(p), ..., s_n(p))$, where every $s_i(p)$ has a value between 0 and 1 for every event $p$ ($p$ can, in fact, be any combination of events) that indicates the extent to which the component, or more precisely, the cell in the SOM, is a part of the representation of $p$ ([9]). As it can be observed in Fig. 1, the pattern representing *"lcHome"* overlaps with the pattern in which *"lcWrites"*, showing that if LC is writing a book, LC is at the home country.

In general, a situation can be represented on a map so that it is possible to obtain the probability of occurrence of such situation and any combination of

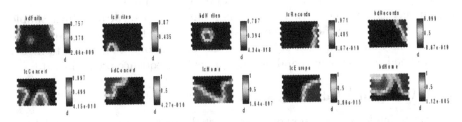

**Fig. 1.** A subset of the component planes of a situation map

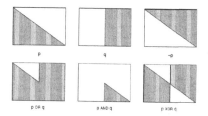

**Fig. 2.** Basic logical reasoning at the SOM output level

situations by means of fuzzy set theory. Taking the example shown in Fig. 2 where $p$ and $q$ are situations with a probability of 0.5 each one in the microworld and taking into account the equations $s_i(\neg p) = 1 - s_i(p)$ and $s_i(p \wedge q) = s_i(p)s_i(q)$ every logical combination of situations can be represented.

Since there is no one-to-one correspondence between propositions and dimensions in the taken representation of situations, we use *belief values* in order to figure out the results that are given as situation vectors. Let $X = (x_1, x_2, ..., x_n)$ be a situation vector, with $n$ as the number of situation-space dimensions. As a result of training the SOM, the probability (the probability estimate is approximated) that situation $X$ occurs in the microworld equals the fraction of the map it covers ([9]). The belief values $\tau$ for a situation $X$ and for a situation $p$ in $X$ are defined as:

$$\tau(X) = \frac{1}{n}\Sigma_i x_i. \quad \tau(p|X) = \frac{\Sigma_i s_i(p)x_i}{\Sigma_i x_i}. \tag{1}$$

## 2.2   Sentence Comprehension

Next, we convert sentences from a microlanguage to the representation of the corresponding microworld situation.

The *microlanguage* used in the experiments consists of 13 words: *LC, BD, and, is, gets_success, fails, performs_concert, writes_book, records_CD, at_home, in_Europe, single, accompanied*. With these words and following the rules of the grammar in Table 2, 396 different sentences can be obtained by associating each of them with a microworld situation.

Microlanguage sentences are transformed into situational vector representations by training a simple recurrent neural network [13]. The input layer of the network consists of 13 units, one for each word in the microlanguage. The hidden layer has 50 units and the output layer 150 units, one for each dimension of the situational space.

The words of a sentence are processed one-by-one, so only one of the input units is active at any moment. This way, the output of the network can be observed at any moment and it is possible to analyze how the representation of the situations gets defined as the sentence gets completed.

Belief values are useful in measuring the performance of the model after the network has been trained. The belief value of a situation $X(p)$, represented by

**Table 2.** Grammar of the microlanguage

| | |
|---|---|
| S | → NP VP |
| NP | → LC \| BD \| LC and BD \| BD and LC |
| VP | → Action [Place \| and is State \| and Result] |
| | → is Place [and Action \| and State \| and Result] |
| | → is State [and Action \| Place \| and Result] |
| | → Result [and Action \| Place \| and is State] |
| Action | → writes_book \| performs_concert \| records_CD |
| Place | → at_home \| in_Europe \| at_home and in_Europe \| in_Europe and at_home |
| State | → single \| accompanied |
| Result | → gets_success \| fails |

the output for a certain sentence, should be larger than the a priori belief value of the situation $p$ corresponding to that sentence:

$$compr(p) = \frac{\tau(p|X(p)) - \tau(p)}{\tau(p|p) - \tau(p)}. \tag{2}$$

When $\tau(p|X(p)) > \tau(p)$, the comprehension score is higher than 0 and the network reflects a comprehension of the sentence, having the ideal case when $\tau(p|X(p)) = \tau(p|p)$, and the score is 1. On the other hand, when the score is negative the network is misunderstanding the sentence and there is no comprehension when the result equals 0.

## 3   Experiments

In the following, we describe the experiments conducted in this work including both the formation of the self-organizing map of the situations and simple recurrent network model of the sentences describing the situations in a microworld.

The example situations set constitutes the input of the SOM and consists of 227 example situations that follow the microworld constraints so that every situation in this set is obtained by one or more propositions combined. Each of the input example situations is a vector $\mu = (\mu_1, \mu_2, ..., \mu_m)$, $m = 17$, which is the number of events in the microworld, so that a component $\mu_i$ is equal to 1 if it is the case of the example situation or 0 if it is not.

The SRN network is trained with a set of 368 sentences that are presented to the network randomly. The rest of the sentences are not trained and they are used as a test set. After training and calculating the comprehension scores for the sentences present in the training set, the percentage of comprehended sentences is 89.7% and the mean of the score is 0.3931. In the other hand, a set of 20 sentences not presented to the network during the training but referring to situations in the microworld that were already present in the training set are considered as well, obtaining a score mean of 0.3330 within the 18 of the 20 sentences that were comprehended. Finally, a set of 8 sentences not presented describing new situations resulted in a score mean of 0.3799 and 7 of this set of 8 sentences had a comprehension score above 0. Furthermore, the results show how the short sentences lead to higher comprehension scores than the long ones.

# 4 Conclusions

In this paper, we have described an approach which enables representation of situations in a microworld using the self-organizing map algorithm and processing of sentences that describe the situations using simple recurrent network. We have also considered how to conduct basic logical reasoning at the output level of the self-organizing map in a Venn diagram like manner. The approach seems to facilitate well a grounded approach for modeling story comprehension. The present study is based on a microworld in which the number of different situations and sentences is small. Future research is needed to test how well the methodology scales up to large real-world applications.

# References

1. Kohonen, T.: Self-Organizing Maps. Springer, Heidelberg (2001)
2. Gärdenfors, P.: Conceptual spaces: The Geometry of Thought. MIT Press, Cambridge (2000)
3. Honkela, T.: Self-Organizing Maps in Symbol Processing. In: Hybrid Neural Systems, pp. 348–362. Springer, Heidelberg (2000)
4. Harnad, S.: The symbol grounding problem. Phys. D 42(1-3), 335–346 (1990)
5. Duch, W.: Neurocognitive informatics manifesto. In: Proc. of IMS 2009, pp. 264–282 (2009)
6. Miikkulainen, R.: Subsymbolic Natural Language Processing: An Integrated Model of Scripts, Lexicon, and Memory. MIT Press, Cambridge (1993)
7. Mayberry, M.R., Miikkulainen, R.: SARDSRN: a neural network shift-reduce parser. In: Proc. of IJCAI 1999, pp. 820–825. Morgan Kaufmann, San Francisco (1999)
8. Mayberry, M.R., Miikkulainen, R.: Incremental nonmonotonic sentence interpretation through semantic self-organization. Technical Report AI08-12, Department of Computer Sciences, University of Texas at Austin
9. Frank, S.L.: Sentence comprehension as the construction of a situational representation: A connectionist model. In: Proceedings of AMKLC 2005, International Symposium on Adaptive Models of Knowledge, Language and Cognition, pp. 27–33. Helsinki University of Technology, Espoo (2005)
10. Frank, S.L., Koppen, M., Noordman, L.G.M., Vonk, W.: Modeling knowledge-based inferences in story comprehension. Cognitive Science 27(6), 875–910 (2003)
11. Frank, S.L.: Sentence comprehension without propositional structure. In: Modeling language, cognition and action, pp. 119–128. World Scientific, New Jersey (2005)
12. Zadeh, L.A.: Fuzzy sets. Information and Control 8, 338–353 (1965)
13. Elman, J.L.: Finding structure in time. Cognitive Science 14(2), 179–211 (1990)
14. Harris, J.: Fuzzy Logic Applications in Engineering Science. Springer, Dordrecht (2006)

# Adaptive Critic Design with ESN Critic for Bioprocess Optimization

Petia Koprinkova-Hristova[1] and Guenther Palm[2]

[1] Bulgarian Academy of Sciences, Institute of Control and System Research, Sofia, Bulgaria
pkoprinkova@icsr.bas.bg
[2] Institute of Neural Information Processing, University of Ulm, Ulm, Germany
guenther.palm@uni-ulm.de

**Abstract.** We propose an on-line action-dependent heuristic dynamic programming approach based on recurrent neural network architecture – Echo state network (ESN) – as critic network within the frame of adaptive critic design (ACD), to be used for adaptive control. Here it is applied to the optimization of a complex nonlinear process for production of a biodegradable polymer, briefly called PHB. The on-line procedure for simultaneous critic training and process optimization is tested in the absence and presence of measurement noise. In both cases the optimization procedure succeeded in increasing the productivity and in proper training of the adaptive critic network at the same time.

**Keywords:** Adaptive critic design, Action dependent heuristic dynamic programming, Echo state network, PHB production process.

## 1 Introduction

Reinforcement learning (RL) is introduced as a method of artificial neural network training "by experience", rather than "by examples". Created initially to mimic animal behavior in an attempt to explain Pavlovian conditioning, RL is also recognized as an approximation of Bellman's dynamic programming method [1] that is well known in the control community. During the last thirty years theoretical developments in this field (a very exhaustive retrospective can be found in [9]) have lead to methodologies known as neuro-dynamic programming [2] and adaptive critic designs (ACD) [13] also commonly known as Adaptive Dynamic Programming. The core of the methods is the approximation of Bellman's equation or value function (which is the discounted sum of future rewards) using neural networks (also called "heuristic adaptive critic"). Having such well-trained critic networks allows solving dynamic programming or RL tasks in a forward manner. Different training schemes for adaptive critic design depend on the presence or absence of a model of the environment [13]. In both cases the critic's training is done using temporal difference (TD) error [20] thereby mimicking the brain's ability to learn how to predict future outcomes on the basis of previous experience without awaiting the final results of future actions. The key component of ACD training and solving the task of behavioral optimization is the backpropagation method essentially based on the chain rule of derivative calculation [22].

K. Diamantaras, W. Duch, L.S. Iliadis (Eds.): ICANN 2010, Part II, LNCS 6353, pp. 438–447, 2010.

Usually the critic is trained off-line since it needs a collection of a variety of data from the beginning to the end of several process runs. Combination between off-line and on-line learning is also considered [15]. True on-line applications of ACD approaches, however, need very fast training algorithms [16]. In highly non-linear environments the necessity for additional feedback connections arises, which further complicates the on-line training. In such cases the application of backpropagation trough time (BPTT) [22] is an alternative. However, it is impossible to be used in an on-line mode. Instead of that the Extended Kalman Filter (EKF) method [4] is usually applied, which is more complicated and resource demanding. Hence it is crucial to work towards finding simply trainable recurrent network structures for ACD schemes.

The recently proposed ESN structure [4, 5, 10] incorporates a dynamic reservoir generated randomly and easily trainable output neurons. The less complex and much faster Recursive Least Square method (RLS) [4] can be applied for their on-line training. Moreover, the derivative calculation with respect to the ESN inputs (that is needed for gradient descent), requires much less computational effort, because of the ESN structure that naturally separates the reservoir from its input and output connections. In our previous investigations we applied this approach to a robot control task for obstacle avoidance [8]. Two approaches to ESN training were investigated: with and without initial intrinsic plasticity (IP) adjustment of the reservoir connectivity as it was proposed in [8]. The results definitely showed that initial IP adjustment improved the stability of further ESN on-line training and that ESNs are a good candidate for an on-line trainable critic network.

In the present work on-line training of ESN critic for solving the optimization task of a complex nonlinear process of biopolymer production is further investigated. There are examples of ACD applications to re-optimization of a biotechnological process [3] but the critic network was trained off-line using sufficiently rich data. In our present work the training and optimization procedures are applied on-line, ordering a cycle of critic training with an optimization cycle one after another. Two cases are investigated: one without noise in state variable measurement and one with 1% measurement noise. In both cases the critic is able to cope with the process behavior and to predict future outcomes sufficiently accurate so that its predictions can be used for further optimization. In both cases the increase of productivity is bigger and the number of training cycles is significantly smaller in comparison to results obtained in [6] where the critic was a backpropagation network without recurrent connections.

## 2 Problem Statement

### 2.1 ACD Approach

The ACD approach also called neural dynamic programming or heuristic dynamic programming [2, 13] is an approximation of the classical dynamic programming in which the Bellman equation is approximated by a neural network that is then used to predict the future utility function to be minimized by adjusting control actions. The scheme for on-line training of ACD without known process model (that is analog to the RL task) is given on Figure 1 below.

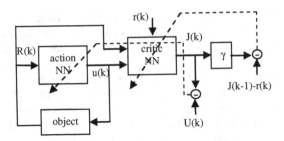

**Fig. 1.** ACD scheme (adopted from [18]). Dashed lines represent the training cycle.

The vector $R(k)$ represents the object state vector, $u(k)$ is the control variable, $r(k)$ is the binary reinforcement signal that indicates "success=0" or "failure=-1" of the present control strategy. The critic NN has to be trained to predict the utility function $U(k)$ by approximating Bellman's equation as follows:

$$J\big(R(k),u(k)\big)= \sum_{t=0}^{k}\gamma^{t}U\big(R(t),u(t)\big) \tag{1}$$

where $\gamma$ is discount factor taking values between $0$ and $1$.

In [18] both neural networks (action and critic) are trained by backpropagation using the following errors to be minimized:

$$e_{c}(k)= \gamma J(k)-\big(J(k-1)-r(k)\big) \tag{2}$$

for the critic network and

$$e_{a}(k)= J(k)-U(k) \tag{3}$$

for the action network.

## 2.2 Echo State Networks

ESNs are a kind of recurrent neural networks that arise from so called "reservoir computing approaches" [10]. The basic ESN structure is shown in Figure 2 below.

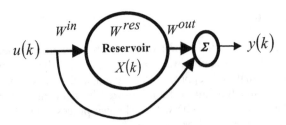

**Fig. 2.** Echo state network structure

The ESN output vector $y(k)$ for the current time instance $k$ is usually a linear function of its input and current state

$$y(k) = f^{out}\left( W^{out}[u(k), \quad X(k)] \right) \qquad (4)$$

Here, $u(k)$ is a vector of network inputs and $X(k)$ a vector composed of the reservoir neuron states; $f^{out}$ is a linear function (usually the identity), $W^{out}$ is a trainable $n_y \times (n_u + n_X)$ matrix (here $n_y$, $n_u$ and $n_X$ are the sizes of the corresponding vectors $y$, $u$ and $X$). The neurons in the reservoir have a simple sigmoid output function $f^{res}$ (usually $tanh$) that depends on both the ESN input $u(k)$ and the previous reservoir state $X(k-1)$:

$$X(k) = f^{res}\left( W^{in}u(k) + W^{res}X(k-1) \right) \qquad (5)$$

$W^{in}$ and $W^{res}$ are $n_u \times n_X$ and $n_X \times n_X$ matrices that are randomly generated and are not trainable. There are different approaches for reservoir parameter production [10]. A recent approach used in the present investigation is proposed in [17]. It is called intrinsic plasticity (IP) and suggests initial adjustment of these matrices, aiming at increasing the entropy of the reservoir neurons outputs.

ESN training can be done in an off-line or an on-line mode. For on-line training, the RLS algorithm [5] was proposed. It is claimed that it converges fast and it is less computationally expensive in comparison to BPTT-EKF methods [14].

Another useful property of ESNs is the simplified calculation of derivatives of its output with respect to its inputs (needed further for action network training) due to separation of the reservoir from the readout.

Indeed, the partial derivative of $y(k)$ with respect to the input vector $u(k)$ depends only on the input and output weights and on the current reservoir's state. In comparison to typical layered neural networks with feedback connections there is no need to account for the structure of the internal reservoir. Hence the ESN structure allows faster and easier calculation of "ordered" derivatives [22] on-line.

## 2.3  PHB Production Process

The object under consideration here (PHB production process) is a kind of mixed culture cultivation biotechnological process. Mixed culture systems are quite common in nature: the human body, waste water treatment, ecosystems are some well known examples. In such systems one microorganism assimilates substrate A and converts it to metabolite B which is converted by another microorganism to metabolite C. Since the change in culture conditions affects all microorganisms differently it is difficult to control them in an optimal way. That is why they are extremely difficult for dynamic analysis and control strategies in typical industrial applications. Subject of our optimization here is a mixed culture system where sugars (glucose) are converted to lactate by the microorganism *L. delbrueckii* and then the lactate is converted to PHB (poly-β-hydroxybutyrate) by the microorganism *R. euthropha*. The main product obtained – PHB – is a biodegradable polymer used as thermoplastic in food and drug industry. The main purpose of the process control strategy is to maximize the final product of the process (PHB) accounting for the needs and mutual relations of both microorganisms in the culture. By now several approaches to this problem are known. In [21] quite a complete mathematical model of the process has been developed and different control strategies were exploited separately or in combination. Several intelligent control approaches are also applied to this process: optimization of the glucose and ammonium time profiles is done using neural networks for process model and feed-back controller in [11]; based on the available expert information about the proper process control strategies three fuzzy rule-bases for the time profiles of the three main control variables (dissolved oxygen, glucose and nitrogen source concentrations) are synthesized in [7]; in [12] genetic algorithm optimization is applied for the same purpose; in [6] the ACD approach using layered critic architecture without feedback was applied to synthesis of glucose concentration optimal time profile, but it is reported to suffer from very slow convergence.

The PHB production process was modeled by a system with seven nonlinear ordinary differential equations details of which can be found in previous works [7, 21]. In present study the aim was to optimize set point time profiles of all three variables used as control inputs - dissolved oxygen $(DO^*)$, glucose $(S^*)$ and nitrogen source $(N^*)$ concentrations. The previously developed model is used as process simulator as it is difficult to make multiple real on-line experiments with such kind of processes.

## 3    Results and Discussion

In the present investigation the action dependent heuristic dynamic programming is applied. The main goal is to maximize the process outcome, i.e. the target product PHB (denoted by $Q$ here) by the end of the process. The utility function is:

$$U(k) = \sum_{t=0}^{k} Q(t)V(t) \tag{6}$$

The reinforcement signal indicates the failure $(r(k)=-1)$ when the working volume $V$ of the bioreactor is filled over its limit (3.5 liters). Otherwise $r(k)=0$.

Vector $R(k)$ includes all the main process state variables, i.e.:

$$R(k) = \left( X_1(k), S(k), P(k), X_2(k), N(k), Q(k) \right) \tag{7}$$

where $X_1$ and $X_2$ denote concentrations of two microorganisms and $P$ – the intermediate metabolite (lactate) concentration The control vector is created by the three optimized set points:

$$u(k) = \left( S^*(k), N^*(k), DO^*(k) \right) \tag{8}$$

We suppose that the all concentration controllers work properly and are able to follow their set points. The applied control scheme is described in more detail in [7, 21]. The on-line critic training and optimization algorithm in program-like code is shown below:

```
γ=0
initialize ESN and other variables
start training cycles
   for t=0 to t_f
      simulate the process state variables
      if it is critic training cycle
         if it is first critic training cycle
            do IP improvement of ESN critic network
         else
            train ESN critic network
         end
      else it is action training cycle
         use ESN critic to predict utility function
         do optimization of three set point profiles
      end
   end
   if the action training cycle is just finished
      increase γ
      switch to critic training cycle
   else
      switch to action training cycle
   end
end
```

For the ESN critic training and simulation a Matlab toolbox from [19] with our improvements for IP training as in [17] was used. The critic network has 9 inputs, 10 reservoir neurons and 1 output. The reservoir neurons have tanh output function. Instead of a complex action network here we have only time profiles of the set points of the sugar, nitrogen and dissolved oxygen concentrations that have to be adjusted during the training phase. The initial set point profiles were taken from [7]. The training procedure is the same described in section 2. After every action training iteration parameter $\gamma$ is increased by $0.001$ and its final value after 1000 iterations is $0.5$.

Figure 3 presents the initial and trained time profiles of all three variables set points as well as the initial and final product outcome for two training procedures (with and without noise). The achieved increase of the final product concentration is summarized in Table 1. The table also compares these results with those from previous work [6] where backpropagation network critic without feedback connections was used. In [6] it was noticed that the MLP critic is unable to learn precisely to predict the future outcomes on-line. In fact the optimization procedure works more like simple BPTT gradient optimization and hence is very slow. This is mainly because the RL approach developed in [18] is intended for cases where the punish/reward signal is received at the end of the process. However the more common dynamic programming approach must be able to solve true optimization tasks with utility functions that accumulate intermediate rewards too (as in the case considered here). The number of iterations needed in the case of ESN critic is considerably lower having in mind that in [6] for each time step and hence for each training data point the critic training procedure is repeated several times (according to the algorithm in [18]). In contrast, the ESN critic was just trained after the first iteration and without repeating of training

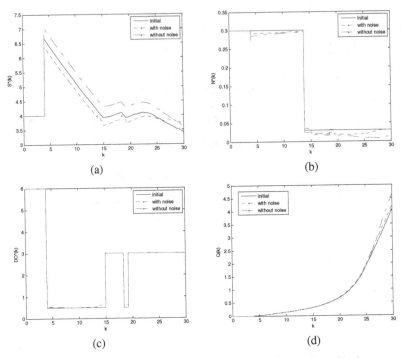

**Fig. 3.** Optimization results for: (a) sugar's concentration set point profiles; (b) nitrogen source concentration set point profiles; (c) dissolved oxygen concentration set point profiles; (d) product concentration.

data points. The product outcome is increased significantly in the case of optimization procedure using ESN critic and without measurement noise but even in the case of 1% measurement noise the optimization procedure with ESN critic network still outperforms the procedure in [6].

**Table 1.** Comparison of product outcome after optimization and needed iterations number

|                 | g/l  | % increased | iterations needed |
|-----------------|------|-------------|-------------------|
| initial outcome | 4.06 | --          |                   |
| in [6]          | 4.15 | 2.13        | over 3000         |
| without noise   | 4.64 | 14.28       | 1000              |
| with 1% noise   | 4.22 | 3.92        | 1000              |

Figures 4 and 5 present the critic training results after first iteration and at the end of iterations. The mean square errors in both cases are summarized in Table 2. As can be seen from the figures, at first iteration the ESN critic is trained almost perfectly even in the presence of measurement noise – result that is hard to be achieved on-line. Even after 1000 iterations and simultaneous optimization that changes control variables and hence the overall process state variables behavior, the ESN critic still copes with on-line training well enough to be used for optimization purposes.

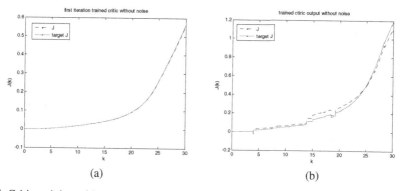

**Fig. 4.** Critic training without noise: (a) critic output after first iteration; (b) critic output at the end of learning

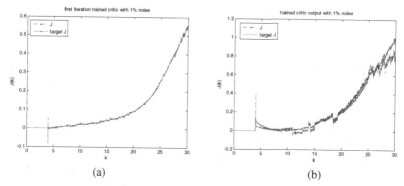

**Fig. 5.** Critic training with 1% noise: (a) critic output after first iteration; (b) critic output at the end of learning

**Table 2.** ESN critic's training mean square errors

|  | After first training iteration | At the end of training |
|---|---|---|
| without noise | $4.5512*10^{-5}$ | $9.3449*10^{-4}$ |
| with 1% noise | $3.1805*10^{-4}$ | $0.012$ |

## 4  Conclusions

In the present paper an ACD optimization approach with ESN critic is tested by simulations on optimization of a complex nonlinear system - a bioprocess for biopolymer production. It is shown that the proposed training procedure of ESN critic – a combination between initial IP training of the reservoir and RLS for the reservoir readout at the next iterations – is able to learn to predict future outcomes and to optimize the process simultaneously. The approach also demonstrated measurement data noise tolerance. The comparison with previous attempts to optimize the same process using ACD with backpropagation critic [6] definitely confirmed the superiority of the ESN critic in the ACD scheme.

The presented initial tests of the proposed new combination of ACD with ESN critic open a new direction of work that could allow true on-line critic training in ACD schemes thus revealing a promising area of investigations towards its real-time embedded application of adaptive control of complex nonlinear real-world systems.

**Acknowledgments.** This work was partially supported by the Bulgarian National Science Fund under the Project No DTK 02/27 "Increasing the efficiency of bio-fuel purpose ethanol production" and by DFG project No PA 268/24-1 "Biologically inspired reinforcement learning in artificial neural networks for the control of complex systems".

# References

1. Bellman, R.E.: Dynamic Programming. Princeton Univ. Press, Princeton (1957)
2. Bertsekas, D.P., Tsitsiklis, J.N.: Neuro-Dymanic Programming. Athena Scientific, Belmont (1996)
3. Iyer, M.S., Wunsch II, D.C.: Dynamic reoptimization of a fed-batch fermentor using adaptive critic designs. IEEE Trans. on Neural Networks 12(6), 1433–1444 (2001)
4. Jaeger, H.: Tutorial on training recurrent neural networks, covering BPPT, RTRL, EKF and the "echo state network" approach. GMD Report 159, German National Research Center for Information Technology (2002)
5. Jaeger, H.: Adaptive nonlinear system identification with echo state networks. In: Advances in Neural Information Processing Systems (NIPS 2002), vol. 15, pp. 593–600. MIT Press, Cambridge (2003)
6. Koprinkova-Hristova, P.: ACD Approach to Optimal Control of Mixed Culture Cultivation for PHB Production Process – Sugar's Time Profile Synthesis. In: Proc. of the IEEE Intelligent Systems IS 2008 Methodology, Models, Applications and Emerging Technologies, Varna, Bulgaria, September 6-8, vol. II, pp. 12-29–12-32 (2008)
7. Koprinkova-Hristova, P.: Knowledge-based approach to control of mixed culture cultivation for PHB production process. Biotechnology and Biotechnological Equipment 22(4), 964–967 (2008)
8. Koprinkova-Hristova, P., Oubbati, M., Palm, G.: Adaptive critic design with echo state network. In: 2010 IEEE Int. Conf. on Systems, Man and Cybernetics SMC 2010, Istanbul, Turkey, October 10-13 (2010) (accepted paper)
9. Lenardis, G.G.: A retrospective on adaptive dynamic programming for control. In: Proc. of Int. Joint Conf. on Neural Networks, Atlanta, GA, USA, June 14-19, pp. 1750–1757 (2009)
10. Lukosevicius, M., Jaeger, H.: Reservoir computing approaches to recurrent neural network training. Computer Science Review 3, 127–149 (2009)
11. Patnaik, P.R.: Neural network designs for poly-$\beta$-hydroxybutyrate production optimization under simulated industrial conditions. Biotechnology Letters 27, 409–415 (2005)
12. Patnaik, P.R.: Genetic algorithmic optimization of PHB production by a mixed culture in an optimally dispersed fed-batch bioreactor. Int. J. Boiautomation 13(3), 27–46 (2009)
13. Prokhorov, D.V.: Adaptive critic designs and their applications. Ph.D. dissertation. Department of Electrical Engineering, Texas Tech. Univ. (1997)
14. Prokhorov, D.: Echo state networks: appeal and challenges. In: Proc. of Int. Joint Conf. on Neural Networks (IJCNN), Montreal, Canada, pp. 1463–1466 (2005)

15. Prokhorov, D.: Toward effective combination of off-line and on-line training in ADP framework. In: Proc. of the 2007 IEEE Symposium on Approximate Dynamic Programming and Reinforcement Learning (ADPRL 2007), pp. 268–271 (2007)
16. Prokhorov, D.: Training recurrent neurocontrollers for real-time applications. IEEE Trans. on Neural Networks 18(4), 1003–1015 (2007)
17. Schrauwen, B., Wandermann, M., Verstraeten, D., Steil, J.J.: Improving reservoirs using intrinsic plasticity. Neurocomputing 71, 1159–1171 (2008)
18. Si, J., Wang, Y.-T.: On-line learning control by associationand reinforcement. IEEE Trans. on Neural Networks 12(2), 264–276 (2001)
19. Simple and very simple Matlab toolbox for Echo State Networks by H. Jaeger and group members, http://www.reservoir-computing.org/software
20. Sutton, R.S.: Learning to predict by methods of temporal differences. Machine Learning 3, 9–44 (1988)
21. Tohyama, M., Patarinska, T., Qiang, Z., Shimizu, K.: Modeling of the mixed culture and periodic control for PHB production. Biochemical Engineering Journal 10, 157–173 (2002)
22. Werbos, P.J.: Backpropagation through time: What it does and how to do it. Proceedings of the IEEE 78(10), 1550–1560 (1990)

# Correcting Errors in Optical Data Transmission Using Neural Networks

Stephen Hunt[1], Yi Sun[1], Alex Shafarenko[1], Rod Adams[1], and Neil Davey[1],
Brendan Slater[2], Ranjeet Bhamber[2], Sonia Boscolo[2], and Sergei K. Turitsyn[2]

[1] Biological and Neural Computation Research Group, School of Computer Science
University of Hertfordshire, Hatfield, Herts. AL10 9AB UK
http://homepages.feis.herts.ac.uk/~nngroup/
{s.p.hunt,y.2.sun,a.shafarenko,r.g.adams,n.davey}@herts.ac.uk
[2] Photonics Research Group, School of Engineering and Applied Science
Aston University, Birmingham B4 7ET, UK
http://www.ee.aston.ac.uk/research/prg/
{slaterbm,bhambers,s.a.boscolo,s.k.turitsyn}@aston.ac.uk

**Abstract.** Optical data communication systems are prone to a variety of processes that modify the transmitted signal, and contribute errors in the determination of 1s from 0s. This is a difficult, and commercially important, problem to solve. Errors must be detected and corrected at high speed, and the classifier must be very accurate; ideally it should also be tunable to the characteristics of individual communication links. We show that simple single layer neural networks may be used to address these problems, and examine how different input representations affect the accuracy of bit error correction. Our results lead us to conclude that a system based on these principles can perform at least as well as an existing non-trainable error correction system, whilst being tunable to suit the individual characteristics of different communication links.

**Keywords:** Error correction, classification, optical communication, adaptive signal processing.

## 1 Introduction

Fibre-optic data links are near ubiquitous in high-speed and long-distance data communications. Links of this type are subject to a combination of random processes and deterministic or quasi-deterministic effects, all of which can serve to degrade their performance [1]. Some of these arise as a result of the properties of the materials and equipment used, whilst others are a consequence of the design of the communication system and the regime under which it operates. Each installed fibre-optic link has a set of individual specific transmission impairments all its own: a characteristic signature of corruptions and distortions it applies to the transmitted signal, and an individual pattern of errors it introduces into the digital data stream.

A system that can repair some of these distortions by post-processing the received signal, or that can separate line-specific distortions from non-recoverable errors, is potentially of great value. It has already been shown that overall system performance

K. Diamantaras, W. Duch, L.S. Iliadis (Eds.): ICANN 2010, Part II, LNCS 6353, pp. 448–457, 2010.

can be improved by employing a variety of post-processing techniques, such as tuneable dispersion compensation and electronic equalization (see [2-5] and references given in those sources). Post-processing techniques can be applied to signals in the optical domain and in the electrical domain (after conversion of the signal into an electric current). The use of electronic signal processing for amelioration of transmission impairments is attractive, and has become popular due to recent advances in high-speed electronics. A system that can be adapted to the characteristics of different data links, as proposed here, is of even greater value, as it may be tuned to give the best results for an individual link, and re-tuned as its characteristics change, which inevitably happens over time.

In this ongoing project we have applied machine learning techniques to the problem of adaptive signal post-processing in optical data communication systems. To the best of our knowledge this is the first project in which such techniques have been applied to this particular problem, although neural networks have been applied to the analysis of performance in an optical channel [6].

In earlier work [7] we have demonstrated the feasibility of bit-error-rate improvement by adaptive post-processing of received electrical signals. Here we considerably extend our analysis. We use a much bigger data set, with data drawn from two different channels. We also use data in which the error rate, using energy thresholding, is much higher than before. This gives our classifier a more challenging task, with more errors to identify.

## 2  Background

Optical data communications rely on the modulation of a visible-light or infra-red carrier wave to transmit a digital data stream over a fibre-optic link. There are a number of different schemes for modulating a carrier wave, but in this work we assume the simplest form of Amplitude Shift Keying, in which a 1 is represented by the light source being on, and a 0 is represented by the light source being off [1] (unsurprisingly this is known as On Off Keying). At the receiving end the light is converted into an analogue electrical signal by a photodiode, typically after some filtering.

In order to correctly reproduce the digital signal that is sent along the link the received signal is compared with a decision threshold, allowing discrimination between logical 1s and 0s. There are several ways that this can be done: for example the output current may be examined at an optimized sample point within the time slot for transmitting a single bit, or the current may be integrated over some time interval and this value may be used for comparison purposes. The precise method employed depends on the design of the receiver.

Here we assume that the classification is performed using current integrated over the entire time taken to transmit a single bit. Note that the approach we propose and describe here is generic and can be adapted to any receiver design. To minimize the bit-error-rate, we propose a method that permits the receiver to be adjusted to cope with the specific transmission impairments for a given link. This is achieved by applying learning algorithms based on the analysis of sampled currents within bit time slots and adaptive correction of the decisions taking into account accumulated information gained from analysis of the signal waveforms.

## 3  Description of the Data

The data used in these experiments is derived from a simulation of a multiplexed optical communications link carrying data bits on five parallel channels. On Off Keying is used to encode the bits for transmission, and the data values are a series of floating point numbers, each representing the amplitude of the signal received at a specific point in time.

In this work we use data from two of the five channels, which we refer to as Channel 1 and Channel 2. Each channel has its own characteristics and here we do not mix the two data sets. Each data set consists of a sequence of samples representing 114,681 transmitted bits. It is worth noting that Channel 2 is not segmented in a manner that aligns well with the original bit boundaries, and hence may be harder to decode (see Figure 5).

Each bit in the original signal is represented by a waveform, captured as a sequence of 32 floating point numbers: the signal amplitude at each of 32 equally spaced sample points during a single bit time slot. The waveform representing a sequence of 5 consecutive bits is shown in Figure 1. As already explained, a bit may be classified according the cumulative amplitude of the light wave. For each of the simulated light pulses in our data we know the original bit that it represents. Therefore the data consists of 32-ary vectors each with a corresponding binary label.

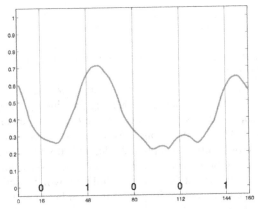

**Fig. 1.** An example of the intensity pattern for a stream of 5 bits - 0 1 0 0 1

Figure 2 gives an example of a bit that is misclassified. The middle bit of the sequence is a 0 but is identified from its cumulative amplitude (henceforth referred to as its *energy*) as a 1. This is due to the presence of two 1's on either side and to jitter. It would be difficult for any classifier to rectify this error.

However there are other cases that can be readily identified by the human eye, and so may be amenable to automatic identification. Figure 3 illustrates an example where a misclassification occurs, even though the bit pattern seems obvious to the human observer. The central bit is misclassified as a zero based on its energy.

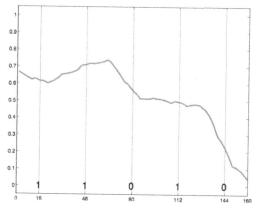

**Fig. 2.** An example of a difficult error to identify. The middle bit is meant to be a 0, but jitter has rendered it very hard to see.

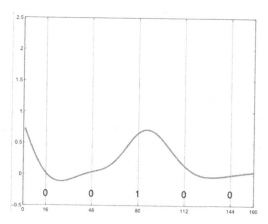

**Fig. 3.** The peak amplitude of the central bit is low, and it is classified as a zero from its energy. To the human eye it is 'obvious' that it should be classified as a 1

## 3.1 Representation of the Data

The raw data may be pre-processed in a number of different ways before presenting it to the classifier. A single bit may be represented as a 32-ary vector (referred to here as the *Waveform-1* representation), or as a single cumulative amplitude value (the sum of the 32 values, referred to as the *Energy-1* representation). In order to improve classification accuracy we may also want to use information that may be present in adjacent bits. We thus create windowed input representations, in which values representing 3 contiguous bits are concatenated together, with the target output being the label of the central bit. The simplest approach (referred to as *Waveform-3*) is to use a 96-ary vector made up of the raw values for three consecutive bits. An alternative (referred to here as *Energy-3*) is to construct a vector comprising 3 consecutive

Table 1. The different data representations employed

| Name | Arity | Description |
|------|-------|-------------|
| *Energy-1* | 1 | The energy of the target bit |
| *Energy-3* | 3 | The energy of the target bit and one bit either side |
| *Waveform-1* | 32 | The waveform of the target bit |
| *Waveform-3* | 96 | The waveform of the target bit and the waveforms of the bits on either side |
| *E-W-E* | 34 | The waveform of the target bit together with the energy of the bit on either side |

energy values. The third such representation we have used (referred to as *E-W-E*) employs a 34-ary vector, made up of the 32-ary vector of the bit being classified and the energy values of the bits either side of it in the data stream. Table 1 gives a summary of all the different data sets.

## 3.2 Setting the Threshold

In order to find an optimum energy threshold for each channel we conduct a simple search for the value that produces the lowest bit error rate across the whole data stream for that channel. Due to the aforementioned misalignment in Channel 2 its error rate is much higher than that of Channel 1, with around a quarter of the bits being misclassified from their energy. In order to facilitate an analysis of the data we use the optimal threshold to divide it into two disjoint subsets: those bits that are correctly classified by comparing their *Energy-1* value with the optimum threshold for the channel in question, and those that are mis-classified. We call these two subsets the *easy* and *hard* bits.

## 3.3 Visualization Using Principal Component Analysis (PCA)

As each data point is a 32-ary vector of floating-point numbers it must be projected onto a lower dimensional space for visualization purposes. We use PCA to produce a linear projection onto a 2 dimensional space that preserves as much of the variance in the data as possible. Figure 4 shows this projection for the Channel 2 data set.

In this projection there is a roughly linear separation between the patterns classified as 0 and as 1. This is an expected consequence of using a threshold. The separation is not an exact straight line because the thresholding takes place in a different data space to the data in the projection. The distribution of the hard cases is interesting. In the left hand side of the projection (which contains the easy zeroes) the *hard ones* occupy a distinct area – on the lower side and near the boundary, whereas the *hard zeroes* occupy the higher area on the other side of the boundary. A substantial proportion of the *hard* bits are spatially separable from the *easy* bits with which they are being confused, suggesting that a trainable classifier may be of use.

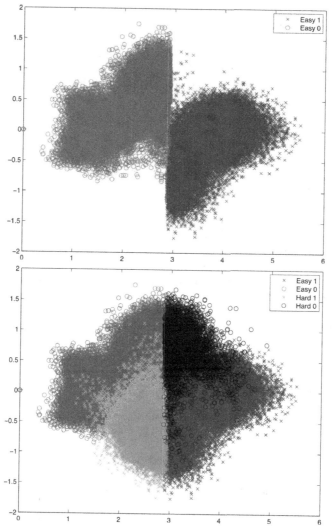

**Fig. 4.** Projection of the Channel 2 data into a 2-D space based on PCA. The upper plot shows just the *easy* bits and the lower plot shows the data for all bits.

# 4  Classifier Used

The classifiers employed in an optical data communications system need to be very fast under normal operating conditions. Simplicity is therefore a virtue. The main classifier we use in this work is a simple single layer neural network (SLN), comprising a single artificial neuron with a weighted input for each feature in the data vector. The SLN's *weight vector* can therefore be thought of as a vector in the input space, and the *decision boundary* for the classifier is a hyperplane in the input space that is normal to the weight vector. Training the *SLN* is an iterative process of modifying the position of the decision boundary by modifying the weight vector, in an attempt to find the best solution to the problem of classifying input vectors into 1s and 0s. This is a simple, convex optimization problem. For the purposes of this work we use an *SLN* implemented using the NetLab toolbox for MatLab [8]. However, in an optical telecommunications system the classifier will have to function with great speed, and therefore will need to be implemented in hardware (probably using analogue devices); simplicity is therefore a virtue.

# 5   Experiments

As the two channels have different characteristics they are treated separately. For each channel the bit stream is divided into a training set and a test set. As is normally the case it is sensible to validate the selection of the test set by choosing different training/test sets and then to report the mean accuracy across the different test sets. To this end we perform 10-fold cross-validation of the test set selection.

We segment the data into 10 test sets. In the first data set (Channel 1) each distinct segment has 10,831 easy cases and 637 hard ones. We therefore construct 10 different training set / test set pairs. Hence each training set includes 103,212 cases and each test set has 11,468 cases in total. In each case an *SLN* is trained on the training set and then tested on the corresponding test set.

For the *Energy-1* data set we do not perform cross validation, but simply set the threshold that gives the best result over the whole data set, which can be done deterministically (see Figure 1), this represents the baseline performance.

## 5.1   Results for Channel 1

The results reported here are therefore (with the exception of *Energy-1*) evaluations on averages over the 10 different test sets. The main results are given in Table 2.

Table 2. The results for Channel 1

| Datasets | Mean Accuracy ± Standard Deviation (%) | Error Rate (%) |
|----------|----------------------------------------|----------------|
| *Energy-1* | 94.45 | 5.05 |
| *Energy-3* | 97.37 ± 0.13 | 2.63 |
| *Waveform-1* | 98.30 ± 0.12 | 1.70 |
| *Waveform-3* | 98.97 ± 0.13 | 1.03 |
| *E-W-E* | 98.36 ± 0.11 | 1.64 |

These results are in accord with our earlier results on smaller data sets. We observe:

- The addition of the energy of the adjacent bit either side of the target bit (*Energy-3*) almost halves the baseline error rate.
- *Waveform-3* gives best performance, reducing the original error rate by nearly four fifths.
- The more information the classifier is given (the arity of the data) the better is the performance. This suggests that all the information used here is useful.

## 5.2   Results for Channel 2

The results for Channel 2 are interesting. The main results are given in Table 3.

**Table 3.** The results for Channel 2

| Datasets | Mean Accuracy ± Standard Deviation (%) | Error Rate (%) |
|---|---|---|
| *Energy-1* | 74.30 | 25.70 |
| *Energy-3* | 87.00 ± 0.24 | 13.00 |
| *Waveform-1* | 98.15 ± 0.08 | 1.85 |
| *Waveform-3* | 98.85 ± 0.12 | 1.15 |
| *E-W-E* | 98.24 ± 0.09 | 1.76 |

These results here are more dramatic. We observe:

- The addition of the energy of the bit either side of the target bit (*Energy-3*) again almost halves the error rate.
- *Waveform-3* again gives best performance, significantly reducing the original error rate. In fact the performance is returned to one that is similar to Channel 1, even though this is a much noisier channel.
- The more information the classifier is given the better is the performance.
- The neural network manages to overcome the alignment problem by using a *weighted* sum of the inputs rather than just a straightforward sum, as used by the thresholder.

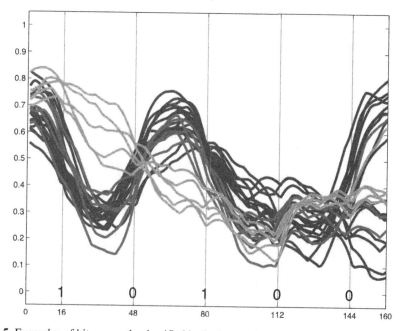

**Fig. 5.** Examples of bits correctly classified by both neural network and the thresholder (blue), by the Neural network but not the thresholder (red) and by neither (green)

To give a visualization of what is happening Figure 5 shows some instances of the 5 bit sequence 10100, where the middle bit is being classified. This is data from Channel 2 and the misalignment of the waveform is evident – it is shifted to the left by about half a bit width. In blue there are 50 instances of bits correctly classified by both the thresholder and the neural network, 5 instances, in red, where the thresholder is incorrect but the neural network is able to classify it correctly and in green 5 instances that neither classifier could correct. The neural network has learnt the shape of a wave representing a one and is able to use this to correct the red bits.

## 6 Discussion

Fast and accurate signal post-processing in optical data communications systems is a challenging problem with commercial relevance. The challenge from a computational standpoint to provide a classifier that is sufficiently accurate to reduce bit error rates and fast enough to operate in real time. As a consequence we have restricted our investigation to an SLN employing input representations that are simple to obtain from a 'raw' sampled data stream. On the large data sets analyzed here we have shown we can reduce the error rate by about 80% on a channel where the original error rate was about 5%. But on the channel where misalignment caused the baseline error rate to be 25% we could eliminate almost all of these errors and return the error rate to just over 1%.

A further benefit of the method proposed here is that the weight vector of an SLN is trainable, so an individual classifier can be tuned to fit the characteristics of a specific fibre-optic link, and a new weight vector can be found each time the characteristics of the link change sufficiently that the bit error rate rises above an acceptable level. This may be achieved by re-tuning an adjustable classifier in place, or simply by replacing an existing classifier with a new one that performs better.

## References

[1] Senior, J.H.: Optical Fiber Communications: Principles and Practice, 3rd edn. Pearson Education Limited, London (2009)
[2] Bulow, H.: Electronic equalization of transmission impairments. In: Optical Fiber Communication Conference and Exhibit, OFC 2002, pp. 24–25 (2002)
[3] Haunstein, H.F., Urbansky, R.: Application of Electronic Equalization and Error Correction in Lightwave Systems. In: 30th European Conference on Optical Communications (ECOC), Stockholm, Sweden (2004)
[4] Rosenkranz, W., Xia, C.: Electrical equalization for advanced optical communication systems. AEU - International Journal of Electronics and Communications 61, 153–157 (2007)
[5] Watts, P.M., Mikhailov, V., Savory, S., Bayvel, P., Glick, M., Lobel, M., Christensen, B., Kirkpatrick, P., Song, S., Killey, R.I.: Performance of single-mode fiber links using electronic feed-forward and decision feedback equalizers. Photonics Technology Letters, IEEE 17, 2206–2208 (2005)

[6] Wu, X., Jargon, J.A., Skoog, R.A., Paraschis, L., Willner, A.E.: Applications of Artificial Neural Networks in Optical Performance Monitoring. J. Lightwave Technol. 27, 3580–3589 (2009)

[7] Hunt, S.P., Sun, Y., Shafarenko, A., Adams, R.G., Davey, N., Slater, B., Bhamber, R., Boscolo, S., Turitsyn, S.K.: Adaptive Electrical Signal Post-processing with Varying Representations in Optical Communication Systems. In: Proceedings of the 11th International Conference on Engineering Applications of Neural Networks (EANN 2009), pp. 235–245 (2009)

[8] Nabney, I.T.: Netlab: Algorithms for Pattern Recognition. Springer, London (2002)

# Adaptive Classifiers with ICI-Based Adaptive Knowledge Base Management

Cesare Alippi, Giacomo Boracchi, and Manuel Roveri

Dipartimento di Elettronica e Informazione
Politecnico di Milano, Milano, Italy
{alippi,boracchi,roveri}@elet.polimi.it

**Abstract.** Classification systems meant to operate in non-stationary environments are requested to adapt when the process generating the observed data changes. A particularly effective form of adaptation in the abrupt perturbation case suggests to release the obsolete knowledge base of the classifier (or training set), and consider novel samples to configure the new classification model. In this direction, we propose an adaptive classifier based on a change detection test used both for detecting changes in the process and identifying the new training set (and, then, the new classifier). A key point of the proposed solution is that no assumptions are made about the distribution of the process generating the data. Experimental results show that the proposed adaptive classification system is particularly effective in situations where the process generating the data evolves through a sequence of abrupt changes.

**Keywords:** Adaptive Classifiers, Change Detection Tests.

## 1 Introduction

In the real world, data coming from industrial or environmental processes change their statistical behavior over time due to thermal drifts, aging effects, transient and permanent faults. This evolutionary nature is particularly evident in sensors subject to stress such as in X-ray detectors (due to the invasive nature of the radiation), electronic noses (due to thermal and humidity effects, as well as degradation of the active film) and monitoring system working in harsh environments (e.g., presence of water, dust, etc). Whenever a change occurs subsequent data violate that stationary hypothesis traditionally assumed in the design of the application solution, here assumed to contain a classifier. As a consequence, the classifier accuracy degrades, possibly impairing the quality of service of the application.

The need to deal with nonstationary conditions or *concept drift* [1][2] led to the development of classification systems able to adapt their knowledge base (i.e., training set) and in turn their parameters or model family to track the process evolution. In particular, [3] suggests the "instance selection" approach to trade-off accuracy and computational complexity. There, classifiers provide a classification value of a given input by relying on a subset of the knowledge base representing the current state of the process. In the same direction, FLORA and FLORA2 [4] suggest to remove a fixed 20% of the training samples (e.g., the oldest training pairs) from the knowledge

K. Diamantaras, W. Duch, L.S. Iliadis (Eds.): ICANN 2010, Part II, LNCS 6353, pp. 458–467, 2010.

base when a change is suspected (i.e., when the accuracy of the classifier decreases below a user-defined threshold). Differently, [5] suggests to adapt the knowledge base over the last samples which are assumed to contain supervised patterns.

A different and effective approach is proposed in [7] where the Just-in-Time (JIT) adaptive classifier integrates a change detection test to detect the change and an adaptive knowledge management phase removes obsolete training samples and inserts fresh ones. A soft version extends JIT classifiers to address the smooth drift case [8].

JIT classifiers consider the CI-CUSUM [6] test both to assess the stationary hypothesis and identify the training samples relevant to the classifier. Recently, a novel change detection test based on the Intersection of Confidence Intervals rule (ICI) has been proposed in [9]. The test appears to be very promising as it guarantees a higher detection ability with lower detection latency and a contained computational complexity compared to the CI-CUSUM test. Moreover, the ICI test revealed to be very reliable in critical situations where only a reduced data set is available to configure the test. Whichever test we consider to detect the change, a mechanism to automatically update the test and the training set after each change detection is required.

This work provides such a mechanism by presenting a change-detection refinement procedure that adaptively identifies, once a change has been detected, the data subset representing the new process state. The novelty of the proposed approach resides in the change-detection refinement procedure which identifies the training subsequence coherent with the current state of the process. The joint use of an adaptive classifier and the change detection test allows us for improving the accuracy in stationary conditions and promptly reacting to abrupt changes in non-stationary ones.

The structure of the paper is as follows. Section 2 introduces the change-detection refinement procedure. The ICI-based JIT adaptive classifier dealing with both stationary and nonstationary situations is presented in Section 3. Experimental results are finally given in Section 4.

## 2  Adaptation via Change Detection Test

Let $X : \mathbb{N} \to \mathbb{R}^d$, $d \in \mathbb{N}$ be a stochastic process generating data from two different classes of unknown *pdf*. Denote by $O_T = \{x(t),\ t = 1,...,T\}$ the sequence of data (observations) measured up to time $T$, and assume that the data are independent realizations of $X$. Assume also that the initial $T_0$ observations have been generated in a stationary condition, and that the classification system uses $O_{T_0}$ observations as training set. Since the focus is on abrupt changes, we assume that, after time $T_0$, the process $X$ either does not change or evolves through a sequence of stationary states (whose change times need to be detected with a suitable test).

### 2.1  Detecting Changes Using the ICI rule

The change detection tests presented in [9] require a preliminary feature extraction followed by a statistical technique, the Intersection of Confidence Intervals (ICI) rule [11], [12] to assess the process stationarity.

At first we compute the sample mean and the sample variance over non overlapping subsequences of $v$ observations. Thanks to the Central Limit Theorem and to an ad-hoc transformation of the sample variance suggested in [13] both features $z_j$ are Gaussian distributed

$$z_j(s) \sim \mathcal{N}\left(\mu_j(s), \sigma_j^{\,2}\right), \quad s = 1, \ldots, T/\nu, \quad j = 1, 2, \tag{1}$$

where $s$ indicates the subsequence index and $j$ is the feature index. The ICI rule, combined with a polynomial smoothing operator applied to $\{z_j(s)\}_s$, is then used to identify possible changes in $\mu_j$ (i.e., the expected values for the sample mean and the transformed sample variance) and, in turn, in the stationarity of $X$. Experiments show that the ICI change detection test outperforms state-of-the-art solutions both in terms of reliability and computational complexity [9]. A relevant characteristic of this test is that it relies only on the tuning parameter $\Gamma > 0$, which does not depend on the change.

## 2.2  Change-Detection Refinement Procedure

Figure 1 a) shows the average Detection Latency ($DL$), measured as the number of observations required to detect an occurred change, over $T^*$, the time instant where the change occurs. It comes out that the later the change occurs, the larger is the number of observations (generated in the novel status of $X$) needed to detect it with the ICI detection test. Of course, this is an undesirable behavior which needs to be addressed to make the test effective in the long run. Such delays cannot be analytically compensated during an on-line data analysis, as they depend on the pdf of $X$ before and after the change. Moreover, Figure 1 a) suggests that, once the change has been detected, the estimate of $T^*$ can be improved by executing the ICI change detection on shorter observation sequences. This is the motivating idea of the change-detection refinement procedure, which is briefly described in the following and detailed in Algorithm 1.

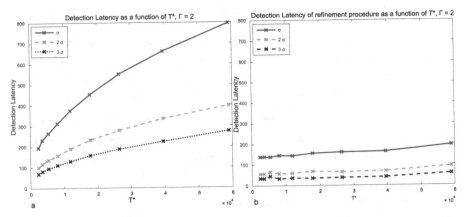

**Fig. 1.** Detection Latency ($DL$) as a function of process change time $T^*$: data are processed in subsequences of $\nu = 20$ observations, $\Gamma = 2$, and the stationary state is $X \sim \mathcal{N}(\mu, \sigma)$. Each curve represents changes in the process obtained by increasing $\mu$ of $\sigma, 2\sigma, 3\sigma$. Results have been averaged over 500 executions. **a)** The ICI change detection test (i.e., $DL$ considering $\hat{T}$); **b)** the output of refined procedure (i.e., $DL$ considering $T_{refined}$).

---

**Algorithm 1. Change-detection refinement procedure**

---

1.  Let $\hat{T}$ be the ICI change detection test output;

2.  Compute $T_1 = T_0 + (\hat{T} - T_0) / \lambda$ ;

3.  $i = 1$; continue = true;

4.  **while** (continue == true){

5.      Apply ICI change detection test to $[0, T_0] \cup [T_i, \hat{T}]$ ; let $\hat{T}_i$ be the result;

6.      Compute $T_{i+1} = T_i + (\hat{T} - T_i) / \lambda$ ;

7.      **If** ( $\min(\{\hat{T}_j\}_{j=1,\dots,i}) < T_{i+1}$ )

8.          continue = false; }

9.  Define $T_{refined} = \min(\{\hat{T}_j\}_{j=1,\dots,i})$ ; (Define $T_0 = \hat{T}$ ).

---

Whenever the ICI change detection test reveals a process change in $\hat{T}$, the refinement procedure analyzes the previous observations to identify a more accurate estimate of the change time $T^*$. Operatively, the analyzed interval $[T_0, \hat{T}]$ is split in two intervals $[T_0, T_1]$ and $[T_1, \hat{T}]$ whose lengths are determined by the parameter $\lambda > 1$ (line 2), and then the ICI change detection test is run on $[0, T_0] \cup [T_1, \hat{T}]$ (line 5) providing (a possible) detection $\hat{T}_1$. This is considered a more accurate estimate of $T^*$, as the test operates on a shorter sequence w.r.t. the former detection. The procedure is then iterated by further splitting $[T_1, \hat{T}]$ (line 6), until the earliest detection is reached by the leftmost interval bound (line 7). An illustrative example of the change-detection refinement procedure is shown in Figure 2.

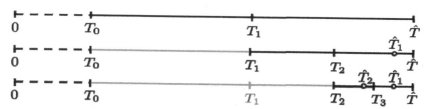

**Fig. 2.** Change-detection refinement procedure: an example with $\lambda = 2$. Initially (first line) a change is detected in $\hat{T}$, and the refinement starts by computing $T_1$. The test is thus executed on $[0, T_0] \cup [T_1, \hat{T}]$, resulting in a detection at $\hat{T}_1$ (second line). This procedure is iterated computing $T_2$ and running the ICI change detection test on $[0, T_0] \cup [T_2, \hat{T}]$. The procedure is terminated when $T_3 > \hat{T}_2 (= \min\{\hat{T}_j\})$. The output is $T_{refined} = \hat{T}_2$, and $[T_2, \hat{T}]$ is assumed to be generated by $X$ in the novel (stationary) state.

Note that this procedure provides the estimate $T_{refined}$ of $T^*$ which is expected to be less affected by the systematic delays shown in Figure 1 a). It comes out that the observation interval $[T_{refined}, T_0]$ can be considered as being generated by $X$ in the new stationary state. Figure 1 b) shows that the change-detection refinement procedure effectively reduces $DL$ when $T^*$ increases.

## 3  ICI-Based Adaptive Classifier

The joint use of the ICI change detection test [9] and the change-detection refinement procedure allows us for devising a novel classification system following the philosophy of the JIT soft adaptive classifier delineated in [7]. Similarly to the JIT soft classifier, classification is performed with a $k$-NN classifier, while stationarity of $X$ is monitored through the ICI change detection test.

---

**Algorithm 2. ICI-based adaptive classifier (x)**

1.  $I_0 = \{1, .., T_0\}$, $Z_0 = \{(x(t), y(t)), t \in I_0\}$;

2.  estimate $k$ by means of LOO on $Z_0$;

3.  configure the ICI change detection test using $O_{T_0}$;

4.  $t = T_0 + 1$;

5.  **while** (1) $\{$

6.     **if** (new knowledge on $x(t)$ is available) $\{$

7.        $I_t = I_{t-1} \cup \{t\}$;

8.        $Z_t = Z_{t-1} \cup \{(x(t), y(t))\}$;

9.        update $k$ using Equation (3) of [7]. $\}$

10.    **else** $\{$

11.       $I_t = I_{t-1}$;

12.       $Z_t = Z_{t-1}$; $\}$

13.    **if** (ICI test $(x(t))$ == " $X$ is NOT stationary") $\{$

14.       run the change-detection refinement procedure (Algorithm 1);

15.       configure the ICI change detection test using $[T_{refined}, T_0]$;

16.       set $I_t = \{t \in I_t, t > T_{refined}\}$;

17.       set $Z_t = \{(x(t), y(t)), t \in I_t\}$;

18.       estimate $k$ by means of LOO on $Z_t$; $\}$

19.    classify $x(t)$ using $k - NN(x(t), k, Z_t)$;

20.    $t = t + 1$; $\}$

---

The proposed ICI-based adaptive classifier is presented in Algorithm 2. More in detail, the sequence $Z_T = \{(x(t), y(t)), t \in I_T\}$ consists of all the supervised couples $(x(t), y(t))$ *available* and $I_T$ contains their observation time instants. Define $I_0 = \{1, \ldots, T_0\}$ so that $Z_0 = \{(x(t), t(t)), t \in I_0\}$ is used as the initial training set for both the $k$-NN and the ICI change detection test (line 1). In particular, the initial value of $k$ is estimated by means of the Leave-One-Out (LOO) technique (line 2), while the ICI change detection test is configured on the initial training set $O_{T_0}$ (line 3).

After the initial configuration phase, the algorithm works on-line by classifying upcoming samples and by introducing, whenever available, new supervised data $(x(t), y(t))$ into the knowledge base of the classifier. In this case (line 6), the algorithm stores the time instant $t$ when the sample has been received (line 7), it includes the pair $(x(t), y(t))$ in the knowledge base of the classifier (line 8) and updates the parameter $k$ according to Equation (3) of [7] (line 9). In stationary conditions, the classification accuracy can be always increased by introducing additional supervised samples during the operational life [10]. When $x(t)$ carries no additional information, $I_t$ and $Z_t$ are not updated (lines 11-12) and $x(t)$ is classified (line 19).

When the ICI change detection test does not identify changes in the data generating process, the current sample $x(t)$ is simply classified by the $k$-NN classifier (line 19) by using the current knowledge base $Z_t$, and the current value of $k$. On the contrary, when the test detects a variation in the subsequence containing $x(t)$ (line 13), the change-detection refinement procedure is executed (line 14) and produces $T_{refined}$. The change detection test is then reconfigured on the sequence $[T_{refined}, t]$ (line15), which is seen as generated by $X$ in the novel status. This information is then exploited to remove the training samples that have been acquired before $T_{refined}$ both from $I_t$ and from $Z_t$ (lines 16-17). This is the main difference w.r.t. the JIT adaptive classifiers presented in [7] and [8] where the window size was either a-priori fixed by the user (as in [7]) or adapted to keep only those training samples that have been acquired in a state of the process compatible with the current one. The new value of $k$ is then estimated by means of the LOO technique (line 18). Finally, $x(t)$ is classified by relying on the updated knowledge base (line 19).

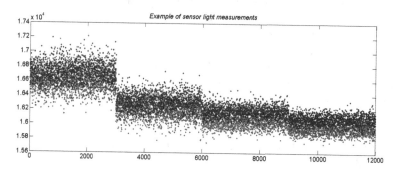

**Fig. 3.** An example of dataset for Application D2

## 4 Experiments

The performance of the proposed adaptive classification system has been compared with those of JIT [7] and JIT soft [8] when classifying both synthetically generated data (Application D1), and measurements coming from photodiodes (Application D2).

*Application D1* contains three classification datasets each of which presenting a change in stationarity: *abrupt, transient, stairs*. A dataset is composed by 200 sequences of 12000 real-valued observations drawn from two equiprobable Gaussian-distributed classes $(\omega_0, \omega_1)$ that, in the initial stationary state, are distributed as $p(x \mid \omega_0) = N(0,3)$, and $p(x \mid \omega_1) = N(4,3)$. In the *abrupt* dataset, a change occurring at observation 6001 increases the mean of both classes by 15. In the *transient* dataset, the mean of both classes increases by 3 at observation 4001 and then returns to the original values at observation 8001. The *stairs* dataset is characterized by a concatenation of changes at observations 3001, 6001 and 9001, each one increasing of 6 the classes' mean.

*Application D2* refers to a dataset composed of 28 sequences of measurements taken from couples of photodiode sensors. Each sequence is composed of 12000 16-bit measurements (6000 per sensor). We tested the algorithms by classifying the observations according to the sensor. An example of such a sequence is shown in Figure 3.

The effectiveness of the three classifiers is measured by the classification error at time $t$, which corresponds to the percentage of correct classification of $x(t)$ computed over the whole dataset. Figure 4 shows these percentages averaged over a window of the 200 previous values.

We impose a minimum training set of 80 observations for the ICI-based classifier. The JIT soft has been configured with a minimum training set size of 80 observations for the classifier and 400 for the test (as required in [8]), while the JIT requires 400 observations both for the classifier and the test (as stated in [7]).

The length of the initial training set is set to $T_0 = 500$ samples; after time $T_0$ we provide each classifier with 1 supervised observation out of 5 to update the knowledge base. We set $\Gamma = 2$ in the ICI change detection test and $\Gamma_{refinement} = 3$ in the change-detection refinement procedure to reduce the false positives when the test is repeated several times. In the change-detection refinement procedure we also set $\lambda = 2$.

Plots of Figure 4 show a comparison among the classification errors of the three considered classifiers. In stationary conditions (i.e. before the change), the classification error typically decreases thanks to the introduction of additional supervised samples. Thus, any detection (false positive) results in an unnecessary removal of up-to-date training samples, which may significantly reduce the classification accuracy. In particular, the JIT soft shows the highest classification error due to the fact that false positives significantly reduce the training set size (this effect is less evident in JIT since, after a change is detected, the training set is composed of at least 400 samples). On the contrary, the ICI-based classifier guarantees a lower classification error since, as stated in [9], the ICI change detection test is more robust to false positives than CI-CUSUM.

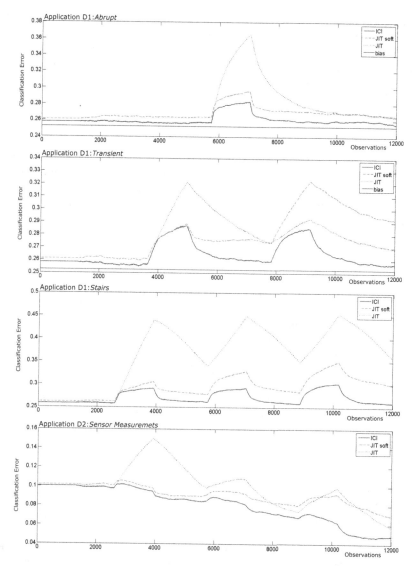

**Fig. 4.** Experimental results on applications D1 and D2. The classification error has been averaged over a window of 200 values

In nonstationary conditions (i.e., an abrupt change occurs in the data generating process), the ICI-based classifier shows the lowest classification error thanks both to the prompter detection provided by the ICI test [9] and the change-detection refinement procedure, which identifies a timely knowledge base subset of observations representative of the new status. We emphasize that the ICI-based classifier provides an adaptive training set evolving with the process and the occurring changes, whereas in JIT classifiers the CI-CUSUM test is configured with a fixed window containing the last 400 observations. This latter, after an abrupt change, might then contain samples not coherent with the current state of the process and, hence, produce a loss in classification accuracy, as presented in Figure 4 (Abrupt).

When the nonstationary behavior is characterized by a sequence of abrupt changes (the *transient* and *stairs* datasets in Figures 4 (Transient and Faults)), the improvement provided by the ICI-based classifier is even more evident: after the first change, the ICI-based classifier successfully adapts both the classifier and the test to the novel operating conditions and thus the test is ready to detect further changes. Conversely, after the first change, the JIT and the JIT soft cannot successfully adapt to the novel operating conditions and this affects the detection abilities on subsequent states. It is interesting to note that, in the *transient* dataset, the JIT classifier outperforms JIT soft and this is justified by the fact that the obsolete knowledge may still be present in the training set and the test configuration after the first detection.

Experiments run on photodiode sensor data Figure 4 (Sensor Measurements), shows classification errors in line with the *stairs* synthetically generated datasets.

## 5  Conclusions

The paper suggests an ICI adaptive classifier able to effectively react to abrupt changes in an unknown data generating process. The novel content is the definition of the change-detection refinement procedure that allows the integration of the ICI–based change detection test within the JIT framework. Such a procedure provides an effective way to identify, in nonstationary conditions, the training samples coherent with the current state of the process that can be used to configure the test and to update the knowledge base of the classifier.

Experimental results show that the proposed classification system provides higher classification accuracy than the traditional JIT and the JIT soft adaptive classifiers on both synthetically generated sequences, and light sensor measurements presenting abrupt perturbations.

## References

1. Helmbold, D.P., Long, P.M.: Tracking drifting concepts by minimizing disagreements. Machine Learning 14(1), 27–45 (1994)
2. Kuh, A., Petsche, T.: Learning Time Varying Concepts with Applications to Pattern Recognition Problems. In: Petsche, T. (ed.) Conference Record Twenty-Fourth Asilomar Conference on Signals, Systems and Computers, 1990, vol. 2, p. 971 (1990)
3. Tsymbal. A.: The problem of concept drift: definitions and related work. Technical Report: Trinity College, Dublin, Ireland, TCD-CS-2004-15 (2004)
4. Widmer, G., Kubat, M.: Learning in the presence of concept drift and hidden contexts. Machine Learning 23(1), 69–101 (1996)
5. Klinkenberg, R.: Learning drifting concepts: example selection vs. example weighting, Intelligent Data Analysis. Special Issue on Incremental Learning Systems Capable of Dealing with Concept Drift 8(3) (2004)
6. Alippi, C., Roveri, M.: Just-in-time adaptive classifiers—Part I: Detecting nonstationarity changes. IEEE Transactions on Neural Networks 19 (2008)

7. Alippi, C., Roveri, M.: Just-in-Time Adaptive Classifiers–Part II: Designing the classifier. IEEE Transactions on Neural Networks 19(11), 2053–2064 (2008)
8. Alippi, C., Boracchi, G., Roveri, M.: Just in time classifiers: Managing the slow drift case. In: Proc. of the IEEE 2009 International Joint Conference on Neural Networks 2009, June 14-19, pp. 114–120 (2009)
9. Alippi, C., Boracchi, G., Roveri, M.: Change Detection Tests Using the ICI rule. In: Proc. of the IEEE 2010 International Joint Conference on Neural Networks, June 18-23 (2010)
10. Fukunaga, K.: Introduction to Statistical Pattern Recognition. Academic, New York (1972)
11. Goldenshluger, A., Nemirovski, A.: On spatial adaptive estimation of nonparametric regression. Mathematical Methods of Statistics 6, 135–170 (1997)
12. Katkovnik, V.: A new method for varying adaptive bandwidth selection. IEEE Transactions. on Signal Processing 47(9), 2567–2571 (1999)
13. Mudholkar, G.S., Trivedi, M.C.: A Gaussian Approximation to the Distribution of the Sample Variance for Nonnormal Populations. Journal of the American Statistical Association 76(374), 479–485 (1981)

# Multi Class Semi-Supervised Classification with Graph Construction Based on Adaptive Metric Learning

Shogo Okada and Toyoaki Nishida

Dept. of Intelligence Science and Technology, Graduate School of Informatics, Kyoto University
Yoshida-Honmachi, Sakyo-ku, Kyoto 606-8501 Japan
{okada_s,nishida}@i.kyoto-u.ac.jp

**Abstract.** This paper proposes a graph based Semi-Supervised Learning (SSL) approach by constructing a graph using a metric learning technique. It is important for SSL with a graph to calculate a good distance metric, which is crucial for many high-dimensional data sets, such as image classification. In this paper, we construct the similarity affinity matrix (graph) with the metric optimized by using Adaptive Metric Learning (AML) which performs clustering and distance metric learning simultaneously. Experimental results on real-world datasets show that the proposed algorithm is significantly better than graph based SSL algorithms in terms of classification accuracy, and AML gives a good distance metric to calculate the similarity of the graph. In eight benchmark datasets, 1 to 11 percent is attributed to the improvement of classification accuracy of state of the art graph based approaches.

## 1 Introduction

Semi-supervised learning, typically transductive learning, deals with classification tasks through utilizing both labeled and unlabeled examples [1]. Semi-supervised learning (SSL) has proved effective in a lot of practical classification tasks, since it is often easy to obtain unlabeled data and labeled data are very scarce. Among current research on semi-supervised classification, Transductive Support Vector Machines (TSVMs) [2] aim to optimize the margins of unlabeled examples as well as labeled samples. TSVMs implemented the low density separation assumption (cluster assumption) by pushing away from samples. These methods assume that most of the data, both labeled and unlabeled, should be far away from the decision boundary of the target classes.

Numerous semi-supervised learning methods such as [3,4,5,6,7] use graph-based approaches. These approaches make the manifold assumption that most of data lie on a low-dimensional manifold in the input space. The advantage of a graph approach is that we can use any similarity criteria. This paper focuses on the improvement of the semi-supervised classification (SSC) performance of graph based approaches. The classification performance depends on the similarity measure of the graph. The weights of edges are defined locally in a pair-wise parametric form using functions that are essentially based on a distance metric such as radial basis functions (RBF).

In this paper, we propose an approach that constructs graphs based on a distance metric optimized by the metric learning approach. In our approach, a semi-supervised metric learning approach is used to optimize the distance between nodes (edges of the

K. Diamantaras, W. Duch, L.S. Iliadis (Eds.): ICANN 2010, Part II, LNCS 6353, pp. 468–478, 2010.

graph). We use the Adaptive Metric Learning (AML) approach [8] for this purpose. The key idea in AML is to integrate metric learning and clustering in a joint framework so that the separability of the data is maximized in the low-dimensional space. We also use Robust Multi-class Graph Transaction (RMGT) [7] as a graph based SSL method. In RMGT a nonparametric algorithm is used to learn the entire adjacency matrix of a symmetry-favored k-NN graph. The nonparametric algorithm makes the constructed graph highly robust to noisy samples and capable of approximating underlying clusters.

The contribution of this paper is to show that a SSC approach based on constructing of a graph by AML is effective for semi-supervised classification of real data. We report that the SSC approach by constructing a graph based on AML gives good semi-supervised classification performance. Experimental results on eight real-world datasets show that RGMT with AML is significantly better than RGMT algorithms and state-of-the-art graph based approaches in terms of classification accuracy.

## 2   Related Work

This research is mainly related to two groups of research. One is the graph based semi-supervised classification approach. The other is distance metric learning research in machine learning. We briefly review some state-of-the-art of research.

There is much research for graph based semi-supervised classification. These techniques can be found in the comprehensive survey [9]. Well known graph based approach using the traditional k-NN graph are the Local and Global Consistency method [5] and the Gaussian Field and Harmonic Function [1]. [7] proposed the nonparametric algorithm that made the constructed graph highly robust to noisy samples and was capable of approximating underlying submanifolds or clusters. Experimental results in [7] show RMGT is significantly better than the graph-based semi-supervised learning algorithms including in [1,5]. In [7], radial basis functions based on Euclidean distance are used. On the other hand, our approach gives higher classification accuracy by using the distance which is optimized by metric learning for the radial basis function.

The other major group of related works is distance metric learning research in machine learning, which can be classified into three major categories, supervised distance metric learning [10,11], unsupervised distance metric learning [12,13,14] and semi-supervised distance metric learning [8,15]. In this paper, we focus on a semi-supervised classification task by using a large amount of unlabeled data. Thus we use semi-supervised distance metric learning approaches or unsupervised distance metric learning approaches to implement our proposed method.

These metric learning algorithms project observed data onto a low-dimensional manifold. However, the projection may not correlate with a particular classification task. In [8], Ye et.al proposed an Adaptive Metric Learning algorithm (AML), which performs clustering and distance metric learning simultaneously. AML projects the data onto a low-dimensional manifold, where the separability of the data is maximized. Ye et.al proposed AML as a clustering and semi-supervised clustering approach. On the other side, we use AML to optimize the distance metric of the graph. We show that graph construction based on AML improves semi-supervised classification accuracy.

## 3   Proposed Approach

In this section, we explain the algorithm of proposed approach. The concept of the proposed approach is described in Figure 1.

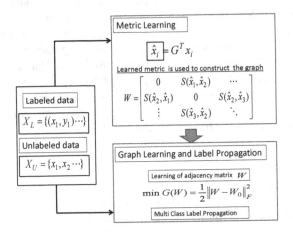

**Fig. 1.** Proposed semi-supervised classification framework

### 3.1   Adaptive Metric Learning for Initialization Graph

Let $X$ denote a data set with $n$ samples, $\{x_j\}_{j=1}^n \in \mathbb{R}^m$. By using linear transformation $G \in \mathbb{R}^{m \times l}$, each $x_i$ in the m-dimensional space is mapped to a vector $\hat{x}_i$ in the l-dimensional space: $G : x_i \in \mathbb{R}^m \rightarrow \hat{x}_i = G^T x_i \in \mathbb{R}^l$ $(l < m)$.

We use orthogonal transformations for $G : G^T G = I_l$ as in [8]. $I_l$ is an identity matrix of size $l$. The distance measure is defined as the Mahalanobis distance measure :

$$d_M(\hat{x}_i, \hat{x}_j) = \sqrt{(\hat{x}_i - \hat{x}_j)^T \hat{\Sigma}^{-1} (\hat{x}_i - \hat{x}_j)} \qquad (1)$$

where $\hat{\Sigma}$ is the covariance matrix as follows:

$$\hat{\Sigma} = \frac{1}{n} \sum_{i=1}^n G^T (x_i - \mu)(x_i - \mu)^T G + \lambda G^T I_m G \qquad (2)$$

where $\lambda > 0$ is a regularization parameter. By using this new distance measure (Equation (1)), K-means clustering is applied to assign $\{\hat{x}_i\}_{i=1}^n$ in $K$ disjoint clusters, $\{C_j\}_{j=1}^K$ which minimizes the Sum of Squared Error (SSE). The minimization problem of the SSE is transformed to the maximization problem of Sum of Squared Intra-cluster Error (SSIE). SSIE can be formulated as follows:

$$\text{SSIE}(\{C_j\}_{j=1}^K) = \frac{1}{n} \text{tr}(L^T X^T G(\hat{\Sigma})^{-1} G^T X L). \qquad (3)$$

where $tr()$ stands for the matrix trace operator. Let $L \in \mathbb{R}^{n \times K}$ be the cluster indicator matrix defined as follows:

$$F = \{f_{i,j}\}_{n \times K}, \text{where } f_{i,j} = 1, \text{iff } x_i \in C_j$$
$$L = F(F^T F)^{-\frac{1}{2}}. \tag{4}$$

The maximization problem is solved in the EM framework which updates G and L iteratively to find a local optimal solution. The adaptive metric learning problem can be formulated to maximize SSIE. For a given transformation matrix G, the maximization problem specified in Equation (3) reduces to the maximization of $tr(L^T \tilde{K} L)$. This is equivalent to a kernel K-means problem [16] with $\tilde{K}$ as the kernel. For a given $L$, we can compute the optimal $G$, by computing the $QR$ decomposition of the matrix $\Sigma^{-1} XLL^T X^T$. G consists of the first $l_p$ eigenvectors of the matrix $\Sigma^{-1} XLL^T X^T$. The algorithm of AML is presented in Table 1.

**Table 1.** Algorithm 1:Adaptive Metric Learning

---

**Input:** $X, K, l_p$
**Output:** $G, L$

**Step 1.** Use constrained K-means to obtain the initial weighted cluster indicator matrix $L$ by using labeled and unlabeled data.
**Step 2.** Compute the optimal $G$ by using QR decomposition. Obtain $G$ composed of first $l_p$ eigenvectors of the matrix $\Sigma^{-1} XLL^T X^T$.
**Step 3.** Update $L$ by running constrained Kernel K-means [16].
**Step 4.** Repeat (Step 2.) and (Step 3.) for the trace of Equation (3) is increasing. When the trace converges or decrease, iteration of the algorithm is stopped.

---

In K-means (Step 1.) and the kernel K-means (Step 3.), we perform constraint clustering [17] by using labeled data. Details of the algorithm and its theorem are described elsewhere in the literature [8].

### 3.2 Graph Based Semi-Supervised Classification

We use Robust Multi-class Transductive Learning [7] for semi-supervised classification. In this approach, we first construct a symmetry-favored k-NN graph. We use $G$ which is optimized by AML for calculation of the similarity between nodes of symmetry-favored k-NN graph. Secondly, a nonparametric algorithm is used to learn the entire adjacency matrix of a symmetry-favored k-NN graph. Thirdly, to address multi-class semi-supervised classification, label propagation is formulated on the learned graph.

**Graph Construction by AML.** Let us start by defining an asymmetric $n \times n$ matrix:

$$\mathbf{A}_{i,j} = \begin{cases} \exp(-\frac{d_M(\hat{x}_i, \hat{x}_j)^2}{\sigma^2}), & \text{if } j \in \mathcal{N}_i \\ 0, & \text{otherwise} \end{cases} \tag{5}$$

$\mathcal{N}_i$ saves the indexes of $k$ nearest neighbors of point $x_i$. Here, we use the orthogonal transformation matrix $G$ of $m \times l_p$ dimensions, where $l_p \geq K - 1$. We use $l_p$ eigenvectors for $G$ for the following reason. Although, $G$ is composed of the first $K - 1$ eigenvectors in the original AML algorithm [8], when the distance metric is not approximated in the first $K - 1$ eigenvectors, we need more eigenvectors to give an good distance metric for the classification of data. We find that optimal $l_p$ differs depending on the kind of input data. We do not use the fixed value $K - 1$ to calculate the similarity $A$, but propose an approach to estimate the parameter $l_p$ automatically.

The parameter $\sigma$ is empirically estimated by $\sigma = \sum_{i=1}^{n} d_M(x_i, x_{ik})$ where $x_{ik}$ is the k-th nearest neighbor of $x_i$. Based on matrix $\mathbf{A}$, we can define the weighted adjacency matrix $\mathbf{W} : \mathbf{W} = \mathbf{A} + \mathbf{A}^T$. Note that in this case the requirement $\mathbf{W}_{ii} = 0$ is satisfied automatically since there is no self-loop edge [18].

**Learning of adjacency matrix W.** Suppose a pair set:

$$\mathcal{T} = \{(i,j)|i = j) \text{ or } x_i \text{ and } x_j \text{ are differently labeled}\}$$

and define its matrix form.

$$\mathbf{T}_{i,j} = \begin{cases} 1, \text{if } (i,j) \in \mathcal{T} \\ 0, \text{otherwise} \end{cases} \tag{6}$$

In the RMGT algorithm, only the differently labeled relationships are employed. Learning doubly-stochastic $\mathbf{W}$ subject to differently labeled information is formulated as follows,

$$\min \ \mathcal{G}(\mathbf{W}) = \frac{1}{2} \| \mathbf{W} - \mathbf{W}^0 \|_F^2$$

$$\text{s.t.} \sum_{(ij) \in \mathcal{T}} \mathbf{W}_{ij} = 0, \mathbf{W}\mathbf{1} = \mathbf{1}, \mathbf{W} = \mathbf{W}^T, \mathbf{W} \geq 0, \tag{7}$$

where $\| \cdot \|_F$ stands for the Frobenius norm. Equation (7) falls into an instance of quadratic programming (QP). In order to solve the problem, we can obtain

$$\mathbf{W}^* = \mathbf{W}^m - (t^m + \frac{2\mathbf{1}^T\mathbf{T}\mu^m}{|\mathcal{T}|}) + \mu^m\mathbf{1}^T + \mathbf{1}\mu^{m^T}$$

$$\mathbf{W}^{m+1} = \lceil \mathbf{W}^* \rceil_{\geq 0}, \tag{8}$$

where the operator $\lceil \mathbf{W}^0 \rceil_{\geq 0}$ zeros out all negative entries of $\mathbf{W}^*$, and $|\mathcal{T}| = n + l^2 - \sum_{k=1}^{K} l_k^2$. In Equation (8), $t_m$ and $\mu_m$ are described in [7].

**Multi-Class Label Propagation.** Consider the first $l$ samples as labeled and the remaining $u = n - l$ ones as unlabeled. Graph Laplacian as $\mathbf{L} = \mathbf{D} - \mathbf{W}$, where $\mathbf{D} \in \mathbb{R}^{n \times n}$ is a diagonal degree matrix such that $\mathbf{D}_{ii} = \sum_{j=1}^{n} W_{ij}$. Given the multi-class labeled data $(x_i, \mathbf{Y}_i)_{i=1}^{l}$, we aim to learn a class assignment $\mathbf{F}_i \in \mathbb{R}^{1 \times K}$ for each unlabeled data point $x_i$ $(i = l + 1, \ldots, n)$. In matrix form, the global classification result is obtained by $\mathbf{F} = [\mathbf{F}_l^T, \mathbf{F}_u^T] \in \mathbb{R}^{n \times K}$ in which $\mathbf{F}_l = \mathbf{Y}_l$ is the known class assignment and $\mathbf{F}_u \in \mathbb{R}^{u \times K}$ is the target variable. Note that $\mathbf{F}_u$ is in a soft range of the hard label values 0 and 1.

A cost function under the multi class setting is as follows:

$$\mathcal{Q}(\mathbf{F}) = \sum_{k=1}^{K} \mathbf{F}_{.k}^T \mathbf{L} \mathbf{F}_{.k} = tr(\mathbf{F}^T \mathbf{L} \mathbf{F}) \tag{9}$$

Let $\mathbf{L} = \begin{bmatrix} \mathbf{L}_{ll} & \mathbf{L}_{lu} \\ \mathbf{L}_{ul} & \mathbf{L}_{uu} \end{bmatrix}$ and $\mathbf{1}_l$ and $\mathbf{1}_u$ be $l-$ and $u-$dimensional $1-$entry vectors. The minimization problem of $Q$ is as follows:

$$\min \mathcal{Q}(\mathbf{F}_u) = tr(\mathbf{F}_u^T \mathbf{L}_{uu} \mathbf{F}_u) + 2tr(\mathbf{F}_u^T \mathbf{L}_{ul} \mathbf{Y}_l)$$
$$s.t. \mathbf{F}_u \mathbf{1}_c = \mathbf{1}_u, \mathbf{F}_u^T \mathbf{1}_u = n\omega - \mathbf{Y}_l^T \mathbf{1}_l. \tag{10}$$

Finally, $\mathbf{F}_u$ such that minimize $\mathcal{Q}$ is obtained as follows:

$$\mathbf{F}_u = \mathbf{F}_u^0 + \frac{\mathbf{L}_{uu}^{-1}\mathbf{1}_u}{\mathbf{1}_u^T \mathbf{L}_{uu}^{-1} \mathbf{1}_u}(n\omega^T - \mathbf{1}_l^T \mathbf{Y}_l - \mathbf{1}_u^T \mathbf{F}_u^0), \tag{11}$$

where $\mathbf{F}_u^0 = -\mathbf{L}_{uu}^{-1}\mathbf{L}_{ul}\mathbf{Y}_l$ is just the multi-class version of the harmonic function proposed in [6], $\omega$ is the class posterior probability vector and all factors are equal to $1/K$. Details of the algorithm and its theorem are described in the literature [7].

**Estimating the Number of Dimensions $l_p$.** To estimate the number of dimensions $l_p$ of $\mathbf{G}$, an appropriate criterion is required to measure the quality of the resultant $l_p$. To find a specific number of $l_p$, we compute $SSIE$ (Equation (3)).

We search the specific number of $l_p^*$, such that the corresponding $SSIE$ is maximized. The search range of value $l_p$ is described in the next equation.

$$l_p = K - 1 + (m - K + 1)\frac{p}{p_{max}}, \quad \text{where } p = (0, \dots, p_{max}) \tag{12}$$

We set $p_{max}$ as 4 in the following experiment. We summarize the proposed SSC algorithm in Figure 2.

# 4   Experiments

In this section, several experiments were performed to test our algorithm in comparison with baseline approach: RMGT, AML (Constraint clustering version). We compared all algorithms on eight benchmark data sets, including Iris, Glass, Letter (a-d), Soybean Large (Soybean), Segment, and Wine from UCI Machine Learning Repository [19] and two image data sets: USPS handwritten data and Yale Face B (YaleFaceB). In addition, we compared proposed approaches with state-of-the-art graph-based semi-supervised learning approaches by referring to the experimental result in [7] on USPS handwritten data.

For YaleFaceB data, we reduced image size from 648*480 to 40*30. For Soybean Large data, instances with an unknown value are removed. For Letter data, the first 4 letters ga, b, c, dh were selected. The details of the data set are described in Fig.3

**Table 2.** Algorithm 2:SSC with Graph based on AML

| |
|---|
| Input: $X, K, Y_l$ |
| Output: $Y_u$ |
| |
| **Step 1.** Perform AML upon a set of all data points and obtain $\mathbf{G}$ of $m \times l_p$. |
| **Step 2.** Repeat Step 1. with changing dimension $l_p$ of $\mathbf{G}$ to find the special parameter $l_p^*$. |
| **Step 3.** Construct a k-NN symmetry Graph by using the optimized metric $d_M(\hat{x}_i, \hat{x}_j)$. |
| **Step 4.** Learn the adjacency matrix $\mathbf{W}$ by running the procedure in Section (3.2). |
| **Step 5.** Compute graph Laplacian $\mathbf{L}$ from $\mathbf{W}$. Use graph Laplacian $\mathbf{L}$ and the known class assignment $\mathbf{Y}_l$ to propagate label information to the unlabeled data with Equation (11). |

**Table 3.** Data sets used in our experiment

| Data set | Dimension | Instance | Class |
|---|---|---|---|
| Iris | 4 | 150 | 3 |
| Glass | 6 | 214 | 6 |
| Letter | 16 | 3096 | 4 |
| Segment | 19 | 2310 | 7 |
| Soybean | 35 | 562 | 15 |
| USPS | 256 | 2007 | 10 |
| Wine | 13 | 178 | 3 |
| Yale Face B | 1200 | 5850 | 10 |

## 4.1  Experimental Setting

We randomly chose labeled samples such that they contain at least one labeled sample for each class. We performed 30 trials with the changing labeled dataset, and calculated the error rates for the proposed approach, RMGT, and AML. For the baseline algorithm RMGT, we used RMGT with nonparametric adjacency matrix learning to compare approaches. We denote them as RMGT(W).

We carried out two versions of the proposed approach: without and with estimation of $l_p$ in Section 3.2. We denote this as Proposed (No Est.) and Proposed (Est.), respectively. Proposed (No Est.) performed RMGT with graph construction by using $G$ which is composed of $K - 1$ eigenvectors. To compare all method fairly, $k$ of k-NN graph was set as 20 in both RMGT(W) and our approach and $\lambda$ of the parameter of AML was set as 100 in both AML and our approach.

## 4.2  Experimental Results

By using the USPS dataset, experimental results of graph based algorithms are described in [7]. We referred to the experimental results in [7] and compare the proposed approach with the referred algorithms. We describe the experimental results of the other seven datasets in the next section.

**Experimental Results with USPS dataset.** SSC experiments are performed by setting of the number of labeled samples [20, 40, 60, 80, 100] in USPS dataset. We denote these

**Table 4.** Average classification error rates on USPS

| Error Rate (%) | 20 labels | 100 labels |
|---|---|---|
| LGC*[5] | 33.10±5.40 | 17.23±1.29 |
| SGT*[4] | 30.37±5.48 | 15.79±1.33 |
| QC*[1] | 34.24±5.18 | 18.77±1.22 |
| GFHF*[1] | 57.28±7.81 | 22.04±2.64 |
| GFHF+CMN*[6] | 32.31±5.41 | 17.07±1.89 |
| LapRLS*[3] | 37.22±5.28 | 17.68±1.86 |
| AML [8] | 28.90 ±3.57 | 28.60± 1.30 |
| RMGT(W) | 22.53± 4.49 | 12.18 ± 1.54 |
| (RMGT(W)*)[7] | (22.52±5.08) | (12.20±0.86) |
| Proposed (No Est.) | 27.57± 5.46 | 17.82 ± 1.32 |
| Proposed (Est.) | **21.29±4.56** | **10.94± 1.39** |

methods as RMGT(W)*, LGC*, SGT*, QC*, GFHF*, GFHF+CMN*, LapRLS*. These algorithms are Local and Global Consistency (LGC) [5], Quadratic Criterion (QC) [1], Gaussian Fields and Harmonic Functions (GFHF) plus the post-processing: Class Mass Normalization (CMN) [6], Laplacian Regularized Least Squares (LapRLS) [3], and Superposable Graph Transduction (SGT) [4].

Table 4 shows the results with 20 and 100 labeled samples. We denote the referred methods and it's results as (Method name)* in the table. The table shows that the result of RMGT(W) which we implement is equal to RMGT(W)* obtained in [7]. We observe that the proposed approach with estimation of $l_p$ is superior to the other methods, which demonstrates that the graph construction based on metric learning and the graph learning technique improves semi-supervised classification performance.

We calculated the error rates for the proposed approach, RMGT, and AML with the number of labeled samples increasing from 20 to 100. The results are displayed in Fig.2. Again, we observe that the proposed approach is significantly superior to the

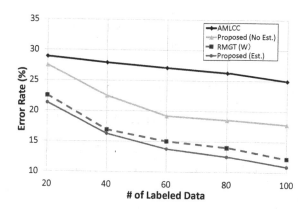

**Fig. 2.** Dependency of error classification ratio according to number of training example

other methods, which demonstrates that the graph construction based on AML improves graph-based semi-supervised classification performance.

**Experimental results of the other seven datasets.** SSC is performed by using the other seven datasets and it is performed in the two cases where labeled data is few (6 to 20) or many (50 or 100). The results are displayed in Table 5. We can observe from the table that in terms of accuracy, the proposed approach with estimating $l_p$ improves RMGT(W) on 4 data sets under the condition that labeled data is few and 5 data sets under the condition that labeled data is many. We can also observe that the proposed approach does not improve RMGT(W) on Soybean data sets and makes SSC accuracy of RMGT(W) worse on the Glass dataset.

From Table 5, RMGT(W) has a high classification accuracy on the Glass dataset and the accuracy is much better than that of AML. In this case, the graph based on AML makes the accuracy worse. From this result, construction the graph based on AML improves SSC accuracy under the condition that the classification accuracy of AML is high, or that of RMGT is low.

### 4.3 Discussion of $l_p$ Estimation

From Table 5, the proposed approach using an $l_p$ estimation is superior to the approach without estimating it in five datasets except Glass and Yale B. To discuss how the estimation of $l_p$ depend on classification accuracy, we calculate the classification accuracy by varying $p$ of Equation (12).

Figure 3 and Figure 4 show different values of the $SSIE$ or error rate by varying the number of $p$ on Wine and Yale Face B datasets. As we can see from Figure 3, the

**Table 5.** Average classification error rates with a few labeled data

| Error Rate (%) | Iris | | Glass | |
|---|---|---|---|---|
| | 6 labels | 50 labels | 12 labels | 50 labels |
| AML | 13.05±13.37 | 4.39±1.75 | 29.55±5.35 | 17.96±5.15 |
| RMGT(W) | 12.45±5.12 | 2.85±1.75 | **16.93±5.54** | **5.26±2.98** |
| Proposed (No Est.) | 8.50±10.50 | 7.08±7.88 | 18.67±6.94 | 7.52±3.67 |
| Proposed (Est.) | **6.29±4.20** | **2.48±0.99** | 18.52±5.29 | 7.96±2.82 |

| Error Rate (%) | Letter | | Segment | |
|---|---|---|---|---|
| | 8labels | 100 labels | 14 labels | 100 labels |
| AML | 45.23±14.90 | 34.16±0.22 | 55.37±8.17 | 50.18±13.59 |
| RMGT(W) | **28.52±2.97** | 10.26±2.51 | 29.45±5.10 | 18.69±8.35 |
| Proposed (No Est.) | 48.86±8.30 | 35.07±6.20 | 25.69±5.82 | 18.30±7.14 |
| Proposed (Est.) | **28.48±3.00** | **10.08±2.49** | **23.50±4.67** | **16.12±5.23** |

| Error Rate (%) | Soybean | | Wine | | Yale Face B | |
|---|---|---|---|---|---|---|
| | 30labels | 100labels | 6 labels | 50labels | 20 labels | 100labels |
| AML | 50.86±11.06 | 46.48±9.64 | 52.41±22.38 | 25.01±4.81 | 11.40±4.10 | **0.27±0.46** |
| RMGT(W) | **28.52±2.97** | **13.06±2.27** | 29.51±2.86 | 22.47±2.28 | 13.04±8.08 | **0.26±0.56** |
| Proposed (No Est.) | 34.97±4.0 | 17.40±2.62 | 34.51±5.25 | 24.52±4.98 | **1.82±4.17** | **0.25±0.34** |
| Proposed (Est.) | **28.48±3.00** | **13.02±2.28** | **21.91±5.57** | **10.93±3.51** | 3.05±4.52 | **0.25±0.34** |

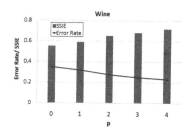
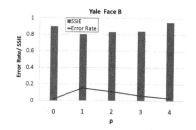
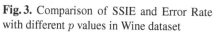

**Fig. 3.** Comparison of SSIE and Error Rate with different $p$ values in Wine dataset

**Fig. 4.** Comparison of SSIE and Error Rate with different $p$ values in Yale B data set dataset

maximum value of $SSIE$ and the minimum value of error rate are achieved when the value of $p$ is equal to five. The result shows that searching a specific number of $l_p^*$ which maximizes $SSIE$ gives the best classification accuracy in the Wine dataset. The results of Iris, Letter, Soybean,and Segment indicated a similar tendency with the result of Wine.

On the other hand, as we can see from the Figure 4, the maximum value of $SSIE$ and the minimum value of error rate are achieved when the values of $p$ are different. The result of USPS and Glass indicated a similar tendency with the result of Yale Face B. The $l_p$ estimating approach does not always give the best classification accuracy. In future work, we have to discuss the approach to estimate $l_p$.

### 4.4  Future Work

The experimental result shows that graph construction by using metric learning improves the classification performance. In this paper, though we use RMGT for a graph based SSC algorithm and the AML to optimize distance metric of data, we can connect any graph approach and metric learning approach.

Our final goal is to implement the SSC algorithm for high dimensional structure data such a time-series data, scene image data and power point slide data including image and text data. To realize this, we try to implement various combination algorithms on each graph based SSC approach and each metric learning approach, and test what kind of the combination algorithm is effective for the classification task.

## 5  Conclusion

This paper proposed the SSC algorithm based on graph construction by AML. We reported that the proposed graph based approach, implemented by constructing a graph based on AML gave good semi-supervised classification performance. Experimental results on real-world datasets showed that the proposed approach was significantly better than comparative algorithms in terms of classification accuracy.

# References

1. Chapelle, O., Scholkopf, B., Zien, A.: Semi-supervised learning. MIT Press, Cambridge (2006)
2. Joachims, T.: Transductive inference for text classifcation using support vector machines. In: Proc. ICML (1999)
3. Belkin, M., Niyogi, P., Sindhwani, V.: Manifold regularization: A geometric framework for learning from labeled and unlabeled examples. The Journal of Machine Learning Research 7, 2434 (2006)
4. Wang, J., Chang, S., Zhou, X., Wong, S.: Active microscopic cellular image annotation by superposable graph transduction with imbalanced labels. In: Proc. IEEE Conference on CVPR (2008)
5. Zhou, D., Bousquet, O., Lal, T., Weston, J., Schökopf, B.: Learning with local and global consistency. In: NIPS 2004, pp. 595–602. The MIT Press, Cambridge (2004)
6. Zhu, X., Ghahramani, Z., Lafferty, J.: Semi-supervised learning using Gaussian fields and harmonic functions. In: Proc. ICML, vol. 20, p. 912 (2003)
7. Liu, W., Chang, S.F.: Robust multi-class transductive learning with graphs. In: Proc. IEEE Conference on CVPR, pp. 381–388 (2009)
8. Ye, J., Zhao, Z., Liu, H.: Adaptive distance metric learning for clustering. In: Proc. IEEE Conference on CVPR (2007)
9. Zhu, X.: Semi-supervised learning literature survey. Technical report, Computer Science, University of Wisconsin-Madison (2006)
10. Globerson, A., Roweis, S.: Metric learning by collapsing classes. Advances in Neural Information Processing Systems 18, 451 (2006)
11. Goldberger, J., Roweis, S., Hinton, G., Salakhutdinov, R.: Neighbourhood components analysis. In: Advances in Neural Information Processing Systems, pp. 513–520 (2004)
12. Fukunaga, K.: Introduction to statistical pattern recognition. Academic Press, New York (1990)
13. Tenenbaum, J., Silva, V., Langford, J.: A global geometric framework for nonlinear dimensionality reduction. Science 290(5500), 2319 (2000)
14. Roweis, S.T., Saul, L.K.: Nonlinear dimensionality reduction by locally linear embedding. SCIENCE 290, 2323–2326 (2000)
15. Zha, Z.J., Mei, T., Wang, M., Wang, Z., Hua, X.S.: In: Proc. International Joint Conferences on Artificial Intelligence (IJCAI)
16. Dhillon, I., Guan, Y., Kulis, B.: Kernel k-means: spectral clustering and normalized cuts. In: Proceedings of ACM SIGKDD, p. 556. ACM, New York (2004)
17. Wagstaff, K., Cardie, C., Rogers, S., Schrodl, S.: Constrained k-means clustering with background knowledge. In: Proc. ICML, pp. 577–584 (2001)
18. Zhou, D., Bousquet, O., Lal, T., Weston, J., Schölkopf, B.: Semi-supervised learning by maximizing smoothness. J. of Mach. Learn. Research (2004)
19. Blake, C., Merz, C.: UCI repository of machine learning databases (1998)

# Genetically Tuned Controller of an Adaptive Cruise Control for Urban Traffic Based on Ultrasounds

Luciano Alonso[1], Juan Pérez-Oria[1], Mónica Fernández[1], Cristina Rodríguez[1], Jesús Arce[1], Manuel Ibarra[1], and Víctor Ordoñez[1]

[1] Electronic Technology, Systems Engineering and Automatics Department, University of Cantabria, Santander, Spain
{alonso,oria,monica,cristina,arce,ordonez}@teisa.unican.es

**Abstract.** Currently, Adaptive Cruise Controls on the market can only run at high speeds and distances. This makes them useless in urban traffic, where most traffic accidents occur. In the present work, a controller for an adaptive cruise control (ACC) system for urban traffic based on ultrasonic sensors is optimized using Genetic Algorithms. The use of ultrasonic sensors limits their operating range to distances and speeds typical of urban traffic. The proposed system uses the distance between vehicles as measured by the ultrasonic sensor to estimate the relative velocity and acceleration, thus requiring no interaction with the electronics of the car, except for the actuation on acceleration and braking systems. The system is capable of acting on the acceleration and braking systems throughout all its operating range, thereby constituting an additional emergency braking system. With this system both comfort and safety are improved.

**Keywords:** Genetic Algorithms, Artificial Intelligence, Adaptive Cruise Control, Automatic Control, Ultrasonic Transducers.

## 1 Introduction

In this paper, a linear controller for the speed and distance to the vehicle ahead is proposed, an Adaptive Cruise Control plus an Emergency Braking system, using ultrasonic sensors. The advantages of ultrasonic sensor are their low cost and their capability to detect pedestrians on the road.

The use of ultrasonic sensors limits the distance range to a few tens of meters due to the high attenuation of acoustic waves in air, and the low response time due to the speed of sound. In addition, atmospheric conditions like changes in temperature and humidity along with the wind and turbulence, may adversely affect its operation [1]. Despite this, the results of this and previous works of the authors indicate that this system would be used for this purpose in urban traffic [2].

The controlled system is highly non-linear, and a Genetic Algorithm is used for tuning of the controller to minimize the distance with the preceding vehicle avoiding collisions.

## 2 Mathematical Model of the Longitudinal Dynamics

To verify the operation of the control system, a mathematical model of the longitudinal dynamics of the vehicle has been used [3]. In the range of distances and relative

K. Diamantaras, W. Duch, L.S. Iliadis (Eds.): ICANN 2010, Part II, LNCS 6353, pp. 479–485, 2010.
© Springer-Verlag Berlin Heidelberg 2010

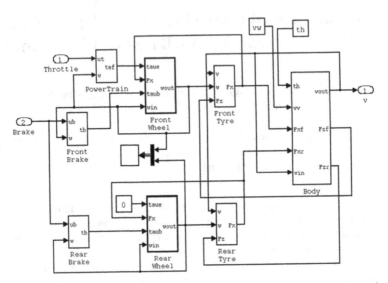

**Fig. 1.** Block diagram of the mathematical model of longitudinal vehicle dynamics

speeds typical of urban traffic, the lateral and vertical forces are negligible. The block diagram of the model is shown in Figure 1. The inputs to the system are the actions on the accelerator and brake with values between 0 and 100, wind speed and road gradient. The output is the speed of the vehicle. In this work wind speed and road gradient are assumed both zero. Likewise, a dry tarmac is considered, which influences the friction between tire and road [4]. Using this model the control system could be easily modified to take into account the road conditions. Several simulations of different acceleration and braking maneuvers have been carried out, and the results have been compared with experimental data provided by manufacturers of vehicles with similar features, allowing confirming their validity.

## 3 Speed vs. Braking Distance

Several parameters affect the braking distance: initial speed, driver's reaction time (between 0.75 and 1 second), state of the road, or visibility. An automatic system based on ultrasonic sensors as proposed would reduce this distance by eliminating the problem of visibility and the driver's reaction time, allowing moving at shorter distances while maintaining or even increasing security by preventing human error. The safe distance would be reduced to the vehicle's braking distance.

In order to obtain the relationship between vehicle speed and braking distance, several simulations can be performed at different initial velocities, and adjust the results by a curve. However, in this work a mathematical relationship is obtained from a physical point of view. Considering that during the braking action the only present forces are the frictions of tires on the road neglecting aerodynamic drag, from the kinematical equation of uniformly accelerated motion, it is obtained for the braking distance $d_s$:

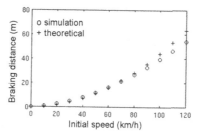

**Fig. 2.** Braking distance versus initial speed obtained by simulation and by the theoretical expression (1).

$$d_s = \frac{v_0^2}{2 \cdot \mu \cdot g} \tag{1}$$

$g$ being the acceleration due to gravity, $v_0$ the initial speed, and $\mu$ the coefficient of friction between tire and road considering that is close to one [4] on a dry tarmac. Figure 2 shows the difference between expression (1) and braking distances obtained by simulation for initial speeds between 0 and 120 km/h (maximum allowed in Spain). As shown, at low speeds the results are very similar, but for increasing speeds, the simulation provides smaller distances. This is because the expression (1) does not take into account factors such as aerodynamic drag, especially important at high speeds, as mentioned above.

## 4  Ultrasonic System

For measuring the separation distance between vehicles, an ultrasonic system based on a emitter-receiver transducer of 43 kHz has been used. The time elapsed since the emission until receiving the echo is measured (time of flight). This time is proportional to the distance between vehicles, related both quantities by the speed of sound, which depends on the temperature, relative humidity and wind speed [1, 2]. When the distance is greater than 12 m. or there is no vehicle in front, the ultrasonic system reports a fixed distance of this value, preventing in this form an uncontrolled acceleration (the braking distance at 50 km/h is about 11 m.). The process is repeated each 0.2 seconds, enough for obtaining and processing the ultrasonic signal, but could be reduced improving the performance of the system. The relative speed and relative acceleration are estimated from consecutive measurements of the distance.

## 5  Control System

This work proposes a control system which aims to minimize the difference between the separation distance and the braking distance at the current speed. The principal advantage of the proposed system over actual systems is that only the relative distance provided by the ultrasonic system is used for the control, reducing the interaction with the vehicle to the actions on the accelerator and on the brake. Because the absolute speed is not used by the controller, it is necessary an offline tuning using a mathematical model, or the data of braking distance at different speeds provided by manufacturers. Control law implemented by the system is as follows:

$$v = k_d \cdot d + k_s \cdot s + k_a \cdot a$$

$$ac = \begin{cases} v & v > 0 \\ 0 & v \leq 0 \end{cases} \qquad br = \begin{cases} 0 & v \geq 0 \\ -v & v < 0 \end{cases} \tag{2}$$

$v$ being the control action (bounded between -100 and 100), $d$ the relative distance, $s$ the relative speed and $a$ the relative acceleration. $k_d$, $k_s$ and $k_a$ are constants of proportionality, which must be determined with the aim to get the objective above mentioned. $ac$ and $br$ are the actions on the accelerator and the brake.

Figure 3 shows the block diagram used for simulation of the control system. It can be seen the controlled rear vehicle, the ultrasonic system which performs sampling of the relative distance, the controller and the vehicle in front. Also can be seen one block that provides the security distance and one block that calculates the cost function that we want to minimize, which in turn is given by the expression:

$$J = \frac{1}{T} \int_0^T \left( \frac{d - d_s}{10} \right)^2 dt \tag{3}$$

$T$ being the total time simulated. This cost function depends on the result of a simulation of a complex non-linear system, which makes necessary a special optimization method. A Genetic Algorithm is used in this work.

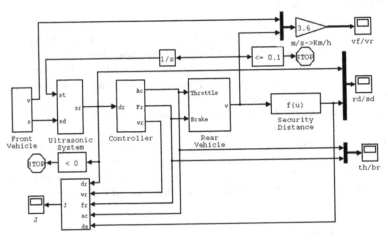

**Fig. 3.** Block diagram used for the simulation of control system

# 6   Genetic Optimization of the Controller

As it is well known, Genetic Algorithms (GA) came in the 70s [5], so called because they are inspired by the evolution of species and genetic and molecular basis. The function of a GA is to find the optimum (maximum or minimum) of an arbitrarily complex function of several variables, based on probability. In GA an initial random population of candidate solutions to an optimization problem, called individuals or chromosomes, evolves toward better solutions. Traditionally, solutions are represented as binary strings, but other encodings are also possible. At each iteration or generation, the fitness value of every individual in the population is evaluated. The fitness function is problem dependent, and measures the quality of the candidate solutions. Then several individuals are randomly selected from the current population, with a probability according to their fitness, and randomly recombined and mutated to form a new population. The new population is then used in the next iteration. Usually, the algorithm terminates when either a maximum number of generations has been produced, or a fitness level has been reached.

This paper seeks the control law that minimizes the cost function of expression (3) when the preceding vehicle performs random steps (ideal) of acceleration and deceleration. An individual is an array $[k_d, k_s, k_a]$ of real values called *genes*. An initial population of 20 individuals in the range [0, 20] x [0, 20] x [0, 20] is randomly created. The fitness of each individual $f(x_i)$ is its position in a list ordered from highest to lowest cost. The probability of each individual to be selected for crossover is proportional to its fitness according to the expression (4). An array of cumulative probabilities is created from the probabilities of each individual.

$$p(x_i) = \frac{f(x_i)}{\sum_{k=1}^{N} f(x_k)} \tag{4}$$

To select an individual for crossover, a random number is generated. The interval in the array of cumulative probability to which this number belongs indicates the selected individual. By this method, two parents are randomly selected from the population. Then a random number is generated and compared with the probability of crossover, which is selected to be 0.8. If this number is greater than the probability of crossover the selected individuals move on to the next generation without crossing. But if the number is less than the probability of crossover, selected individuals are crossed to generate two new individuals according to the following expressions:

$$x_i^{n+1} = \alpha \cdot x_i^n + (1-\alpha) \cdot x_j^n$$
$$x_j^{n+1} = \alpha \cdot x_j^n + (1-\alpha) \cdot x_i^n \tag{5}$$

where $\alpha$ is an array of three random numbers, each one affecting to a gene. The subscript indicates the individual and the superscript indicates the generation.

Then, for each offspring a new random number is generated and compared with the probability of mutation, which is selected to be 0.2. If this number is greater than the probability of mutation, the offspring is passed to the next generation without mutation. But if the number is less than the probability of mutation, the offspring is mutated by adding a random number to each gene, and then passed to the next population.

At each generation, the individual with better fitness passes directly to the next generation (elitism). To complete the population of the next generation, repeatedly apply the operators of selection, crossover and mutation. Then the new population replaces the previous one and the process begins again. The algorithm terminates after 50 generations.

The convergence of the algorithm can be seen in Figure 4, in which both the minimum cost and the average cost for each generation are shown. The values of $k_d$, $k_s$ and $k_a$ for the best individual obtained are 1.145, 10.823 and 0.454 respectively, and the minimum cost J is 0.061.

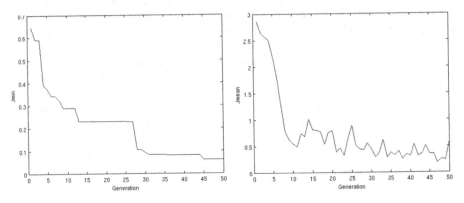

**Fig. 4.** Minimum (left) and mean (right) cost for each generation

# 7  Results

Figure 5 shows the simulation for the best individual found. In the graph above the relative distance between vehicles and the safety distance for actual speed can be seen. The relative distance is always lightly greater than the safety distance, and is adapted to the speed of vehicles.

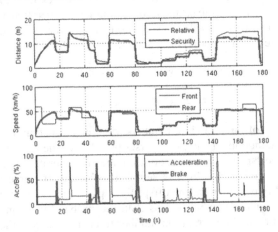

**Fig. 5.** Top: distance between vehicles and braking distance. Centre: speed of both vehicles. Bottom: actions on the accelerator and the brake.

In the central graph the speed of both vehicles are observed. Vehicle in front realizes ideal steps of acceleration and brake, and the rear vehicle adjusts its speed at the speed of the vehicle ahead. Finally, in the bottom graph actions on the accelerator and brake are represented.

To verify performance under more realistic conditions a new simulation has been carried out, in which the leading vehicle accelerates and brakes smoothly. Figure 6 presents the results of this simulation. As can be seen, the controlled vehicle is capable of adjusting its speed and the separation distance to the vehicle ahead. This indicates a good behaviour of the vehicle to circulate in urban traffic conditions, using the genetically tuned controller. The system presented would improve driving comfort and enhance the vehicle's active safety, preventing accidents or minimizing potential damage to other vehicles, and what is more important to pedestrians.

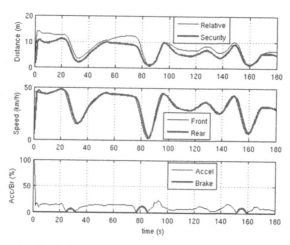

**Fig. 6.** Results of the simulation for the best individual and realistic acceleration and brake

**Acknowledgments.** This work has been carried out under CYCIT project DPI2007-64295, funded by the Spanish MICINN.

# References

1. Álvarez, F.: Ultrasonic emission encoding with complementary sequences for outdoor use. PhD Thesis, University of Alcalá, Spain (2006)
2. Alonso, L.: Contribution to the study of ultrasonic systems and its application to intelligent vehicle active safety. PhD Thesis, University of Cantabria, Spain (2009)
3. Short, M., Pont, M., Huang, Q.: Simulation of Vehicle Longitudinal Dynamics. Technical Report ESL 04-01, Embedded Systems Laboratory, University of Leicester (2004)
4. Pacejka, H.B.: Tyre and vehicle dynamics. Butterworth-Heinemann Ltd., Butterworths (2002)
5. Holland, J.H.: Adaptation in Natural and Artificial Systems. The MIT Press, Cambridge (1992)

# Adaptive Local Fusion with Neural Networks

Ahmed Chamseddine Ben Abdallah[1], Hichem Frigui[1], and Paul Gader[2]

[1] CECS Department, University of Louisville, Louisville, KY 40292, USA
[2] CISE Department, University of Florida, Gainesville, FL 32611, USA

**Abstract.** We propose a novel method for fusing different classifiers outputs. Our approach, called Context Extraction for Local Fusion with Neural Networks (CELF-NN), is a local approach that adapts Artificial Neural Network fusion method to different regions of the feature space. It is based on a novel objective function that combines context identification and multi-algorithm fusion criteria into a joint objective function. This objective function is defined and optimized to produce contexts as compact clusters via unsupervised clustering. Optimization of the objective function also provide an optimal local Neural Network for fusion within each context. Our initial experiments on semantic video indexing have indicated that the proposed fusion approach outperforms all individual classifiers and the global Neural Network fusion method.

**Keywords:** Neural Networks, Classifier fusion, Local fusion, Clustering, Classification.

## 1 Introduction

For complex detection and classification problems involving data with large intra-class variations and noisy inputs, perfect solutions are difficult to achieve, and no single source of information can provide a satisfactory solution. As a result, combination of multiple classifiers (or multiple experts) is playing an increasing role in solving these complex problems [1,2,3], and has proven to be a viable alternative to using a single classifier. Classifier combination is mostly a heuristic approach and is based on the idea that classifiers with different methodologies or different features can have complementary information. Thus, if these classifiers cooperate, group decisions should be able to take advantages of the strengths of the individual classifiers, overcome their weaknesses, and achieve a higher accuracy than any individual's.

Methods for combining multiple classifiers can be classified into two main categories: global methods and local methods. Global methods assign a degree of worthiness, that is averaged over the entire training data, to each classifier. Local methods, on the other hand, adapt the classifiers' worthiness to different data subspaces. Intuitively, the use of data-dependent weights, when learned properly, provides higher classification accuracy. This approach requires partitioning the input samples into regions during the training phase [3,4,5]. Then, the best classifier for each region is identified and is designated as the expert for this region [6].

K. Diamantaras, W. Duch, L.S. Iliadis (Eds.): ICANN 2010, Part II, LNCS 6353, pp. 486–491, 2010.
© Springer-Verlag Berlin Heidelberg 2010

In [7], we proposed a generic framework for context-dependent fusion, called Context Extraction for Local Fusion (CELF), that jointly optimizes the partitioning of the feature space and the fusion of the classifiers. CELF uses a simple linear aggregation to assign fusion weights to the individual classifiers. This may not be the optimal way to combine the algorithms within each context. In this paper, we generalize CELF to use non linear aggregation. In particular, we propose using local Neural Networks that are adapted to different contexts.

The rest of this paper is organized as follows. The proposed algorithm, called CELF-NN, is presented in Section 2. Section 3 presents the experimental results on a video data collection. Finally, we provide the conclusions in Section 4.

## 2    Local Fusion with Neural Networks

Given $N$ training observations with desired output $\mathcal{T} = \{t_j | j = 1, \ldots, N\}$ that were processed by $K$ algorithms. Each algorithm $k$ extracts its own feature set, $\mathcal{X}^k = \{\mathbf{x}_j^k | j = 1, \ldots, N\}$, and generates confidence values, $\mathcal{Y}^k = \{y_{kj} | j = 1, \ldots, N\}$. The $K$ feature sets are then concatenated to generate one global descriptor, $\mathcal{X} = \bigcup_{k=1}^{K} \mathcal{X}^k = \{\mathbf{x}_j = [\mathbf{x}_j^1, \ldots, \mathbf{x}_j^K] | j = 1, \ldots, N\}$.

Fig. 1 displays the architecture of the proposed approach called CELF-NN. This figure highlights the two main components of the training phase, namely,

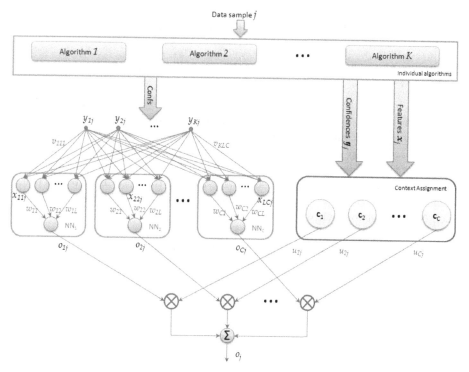

**Fig. 1.** Architecture of the proposed CELF-NN

context extraction and decision fusion. The context extraction step uses both the features extracted by various algorithms to partition the training input samples into $C$ different contexts, i.e, each training sample $j$ is assigned to each context $j$ with a fuzzy membership $u_{ij}$. The decision fusion step uses the confidence values assigned by the individual algorithms to adapt a two-layers Neural Network to each context. Each network has $K$ input (the $K$ classifiers' decision), $L$ hidden neurons in the hidden layer, and one output. In the following, $f$ is the activation function. $v_{kli}$ is the weight that connects the $k^{th}$ input to the $l^{th}$ neuron (of the hidden layer) of the $i^{th}$ Neural Network. $\omega_{il}$ is the weight that connects the $l^{th}$ neuron to the output of the $i^{th}$ Neural Network. $x_{lij}$ is the output of the $l^{th}$ neuron (of the hidden layer) in the $i^{th}$ Neural Network for the sample $j$. And $o_{ij}$ is the output of the $i^{th}$ Neural Network for the sample $j$. Finally, the final output $o_j$, for the sample $j$, is the weighted aggregation of the $C$ Neural Networks' output, i.e.,

$$o_j = \sum_{i=1}^{C} u_{ij} o_{ij} \,. \tag{1}$$

CELF-NN partitions the feature space and learns the weights of the different Neural Networks simultaneously by optimizing the following objective function.

$$J_{NN} = \sum_{j=1}^{N} \sum_{i=1}^{C} u_{ij}^m \|\mathbf{x}_j - \mathbf{c}_i\|^2 + \alpha \sum_{j=1}^{N} \sum_{i=1}^{C} u_{ij}^m (o_{ij} - t_j)^2, \tag{2}$$

subject to

$$\sum_{i=1}^{C} u_{ij} = 1 \,\forall j, \quad \text{and} \quad u_{ij} \in [0,1] \,\forall i,j. \tag{3}$$

The first term in (2) is the objective function of the Fuzzy C-Means (FCM) algorithm [8]. It seeks to partition the $N$ samples into $C$ clusters, and represent each cluster by a center $\mathbf{c}_i$. Each sample $\mathbf{x}_j$ will be assigned to each cluster $i$ with a membership degree $u_{ij}$. The second term in (2) attempts to learn the weights of the different Neural Networks. When both terms are combined and $\alpha$ is chosen properly, the algorithm seeks to partition the data into compact and homogeneous clusters (called also contexts) while learning optimal weights for each Neural Network within each cluster.

To minimize $J_{NN}$ with respect to the centers $\mathbf{c}_{ik}$, we fix $\mathbf{U} = [u_{ij}]$, $\mathbf{V} = [v_{kli}]$, and $\mathbf{W} = [\omega_{il}]$, and set the gradient to zero. We obtain

$$\mathbf{c}_{ik} = \frac{\sum\limits_{j=1}^{N} u_{ij}^m \mathbf{x}_{jk}}{\sum\limits_{j=1}^{N} u_{ij}^m} \,. \tag{4}$$

Minimizing $J_{NN}$ w.r.t the membership degree $u_{ij}$, we fix $\mathbf{C} = [\mathbf{c}_{ik}]$, $\mathbf{V} = [v_{kli}]$, and $\mathbf{W} = [\omega_{il}]$, and set the gradient to zero. We obtain

$$u_{ij} = \frac{1}{\sum_{l=1}^{C}(D_{ij}/D_{lj})^{1/(m-1)}}, \tag{5}$$

where

$$D_{ij} = \|\mathbf{x}_j - \mathbf{c}_i\|^2 + \alpha(o_j - t_j)^2 . \tag{6}$$

In (6), $D_{ij}$ can be viewed as the total cost when considering point $\mathbf{x}_j$ in cluster $i$. This cost depends on: (i) the distance between the considered point and the cluster's centroid $\mathbf{c}_i$; and (ii) the deviation of the combined algorithms' decision from the desired output.

To adjust the weights of the different layers of the Neural Networks, we fix $\mathbf{C} = [c_{ik}]$, and $\mathbf{U} = [u_{ij}]$, and optimize $J_{NN}$ with respect to $o_{ij}$ using gradient descent methods. Given a constant $\eta$, It can be shown that the weights need to be adjusted using:

$$\Delta\omega_{il} = \eta\delta_{o_{ij}}x_{lij} \quad \text{and} \quad \Delta v_{kli} = \eta\delta_{x_{lij}}y_{kj}, \tag{7}$$

where $\delta_{o_{ij}} = 2\alpha u_{ij}^m(t_j - o_{ij})f'_{o_{ij}}$, $\delta_{x_{lij}} = f'_{x_{lij}}\delta_{o_{ij}}\omega_{il}$, and $f'$ is the derivative of the activation function $f$. In this paper, we use the bipolar sigmoidal and $f'_o = (1 - o^2)/2$.

The resulting algorithm is summarized below.

---

CELF with NN fusion

**Inputs:** $\mathcal{X}$, $\mathcal{Y}$, $\mathcal{T}$, $C$, $m$, $\alpha$, $L$, and $\eta$.
**Outputs:** $\mathbf{U}$, $\mathbf{C}$, $\mathbf{W}$, and $\mathbf{V}$.

1: Initialize $\mathbf{U}$, $\mathbf{W}$, and $\mathbf{V}$.
2: **repeat**
3:    Update $\mathbf{C}$ using (4).
4:    Update $\mathbf{U}$ using (5).
5:    Update $\mathbf{W}$ and $\mathbf{V}$ using (7).
6: **until** parameters do not change significantly
7: **return** $\mathbf{C}$, $\mathbf{U}$, $\mathbf{W}$, and $\mathbf{V}$

---

# 3  Experimental Results

To illustrate the performance of the proposed adaptive fusion, we use it to label MPEG-1 movies from the TRECVID-2002 data collection [9].

This collection consists mainly of Internet Archive of advertising, educational, industrial, amateur films produced between 1930 and 1970 by corporations, non-profit organizations, and trade groups. This collection included a total of 73.3 hours of video data partitioned into a search test set (40.12 hours); a feature development set (training and validation; 23.26 hours); a feature test set (5.07 hours); and a shot boundary test set (4.85 hours). For our experiment, we used the feature development set for training and the feature test set for testing and evaluation. Each shot in this collection can belong to one (or more) of the 10 semantic concepts: 'Outdoors', 'Indoors', 'Face', 'People', 'Cityscape', 'Landscape', 'Text Overlay', 'Speech', 'Instrumental Sound', and 'Monologue'. For all data, we used the shot boundaries provided by NIST [9].

The goal of our experiment is to illustrate that the proposed context dependent fusion is a framework that can improve the performance by partitioning the feature space into disjoint regions and identifying local expert algorithms for each region. Thus, we did not attempt to optimize the feature extraction nor the classifier design components. We simply use a set of generic MPEG-7 descriptors (namely, the Color Structure Descriptor (CSD), the Scalable Color Descriptor (SCD), the Edge Histogram Descriptor (EHD), and the Homogeneous Texture Descriptor (HTD)) [10] and a simple $k-$NN classifier [11]. Other descriptors and classifiers can be easily integrated into our approach. In particular, the following set of low-level multi-modal descriptors are extracted and used to construct the low-level feature space for context extraction.

CELF-NN was used to partition the feature space into 20 clusters. Since we are using only visual features, we only use the first 6 semantic concepts as the last 4 concepts require textual and audio features.

For comparison purposes, we fuse the 4 classifiers ($k-$NN based on CSD, SCD, EHD, and HTD) using global Neural Network. The performance of the different classifiers and fusion algorithms is measured in terms of the 'Mean Averaged Precision (MAP)' [12]. and is reported in Table 1.

**Table 1.** MAP values for the individual classifier and the fusion algorithms averaged over the test data

|          | CSD  | SCD  | EHD  | HTD  | Neural Network | CELF-NN |
|----------|------|------|------|------|----------------|---------|
| Outdoors | 0.58 | 0.64 | 0.72 | 0.58 | 0.74           | 0.81    |
| Indoors  | 0.22 | 0.23 | 0.31 | 0.29 | 0.25           | 0.37    |
| Face     | 0.21 | 0.23 | 0.33 | 0.32 | 0.33           | 0.41    |
| People   | 0.28 | 0.35 | 0.40 | 0.37 | 0.38           | 0.46    |
| Cityscape| 0.40 | 0.48 | 0.49 | 0.39 | 0.52           | 0.54    |
| Landscape| 0.08 | 0.08 | 0.16 | 0.12 | 0.15           | 0.21    |

We note that, for all concepts, the proposed CELF-NN approach outperforms all individual classifiers and the global fusion. For some concepts, the global Neural Network fusion is not able to improve the result of the individual classifiers. The improved performance of CELF-NN is due to the context identification and the adaptation of the fusion to each context.

## 4    Conclusions

In this paper, we have proposed a new multi-algorithm fusion method, called CELF-NN, and applied it to the semantic video indexing problem. This approach is local and adapts the Neural Network fusion method to different regions of the feature space. The different regions, or contexts, correspond to groups of keyframes that share common low-level semantics descriptors. Our initial experiments have indicated that the proposed fusion approach outperforms the individual algorithms and the global fusion of these algorithms.

In the current implementation of CELF-NN, only 2-class problems are supported. Future work will include adaptation of CELF-NN to support fusion for the general multi-class case.

**Acknowledgments.** This work was supported in part by U.S. Army Research Office Grants Number W911NF-08-0255 and W911NF- 07-1-0347, and by NSF awards No. CBET-0730802 and CBET-0730484.

# References

1. Gader, P.D., Mohamed, M.A., Keller, J.M.: Fusion of handwritten word classifiers. Pattern Recogn. Lett. 17(6), 577–584 (1996)
2. Huang, Y.S., Suen, C.Y.: A method of combining multiple classifiers-a neural network approach. In: Proc. Int. Conf. on Pattern Recognition and Computer Vision, vol. 2, pp. 473–475 (1994)
3. Kuncheva, L.I.: Switching between selection and fusion in combining classifiers: An experiment. IEEE Trans. Systems, Man, and Cybernetics 32(2), 146–156 (2002)
4. Mandler, E., Schurmann, J.: Combining the classification results of independent classifiers based on the dempster-shafer theory of evidence. Pattern Recognition and Artificial Intelligence, 381–393 (1988)
5. Ho, T.K., Hull, J.J., Srihari, S.N.: Decision combination in multiple classifier systems. IEEE Trans. Pattern Analysis and Machine Intelligence 16, 66–75 (1994)
6. Verikas, A., Lipnickas, A., Malmqvist, K., Bacauskiene, M., Gelzinis, A.: Soft combination of neural classifiers: A comparative study. Pattern Recognit. Lett. 20, 429–444 (1999)
7. Frigui, H., Gader, P., Ben Abdallah, A.C.: A generic framework for context-dependent fusion with application to landmine detection. In: SPIE Defense and Security Symposium, Orlando (2008)
8. Bezdek, J.C.: Pattern Recognition with Fuzzy Objective Function Algorithms. Plenum Press, New York (1981)
9. Smeaton, A.F., Over, P.: The trec-2002 video track report (2002)
10. Manjunath, B.S., Salembier, P., Sikora, T.: Introduction to MPEG 7: Multimedia Content Description Languag. John Wiley, Chichester (2002)
11. Fix, E., Hodges, J.: Discriminatory analysis: Nonparametric discrimination: Small sample performance. Technical Report 11, USAF School of Aviation Medicine, Randolph Field, Texas (August 1952)
12. Trec-10 proceedings appendix on common evaluation measures. Technical report (2002), http://trec.nist.gov/pubs/trec10/appendices/measures.pdf (Retrieved March 30, 2007)

# A Controlling Strategy for an Active Vision System Based on Auditory and Visual Cues

Miranda Grahl[1], Frank Joublin[2], and Franz Kummert[1]

[1] Cor-Lab, Bielefeld University, D-33615 Bielefeld, Germany
mgrahl,franz@cor-lab.uni-bielefeld.de
http://www.cor-lab.uni-bielefeld.de
[2] Honda Research Institute Europe GmbH, D-63073 Offenbach, Germany
Frank.Joublin@honda-ri.de
http://www.honda-hri.de

**Abstract.** It is still an open question how preliminary visual reflexes can be structured by auditory and visual modalities in order to recognize objects. Therefore, we propose a new method for a controlling strategy for an active vision system that learns to focus on relevant multi modal aspects of the environment. The method is bootstrapped by a bottom up visual saliency process in order to extract important visual points. In this paper, we present our first results and focus on the unsupervised generation of training data for a multi-modal object recognition. The performance is compared to a human evaluated database.

**Keywords:** adaptive learning, active vision, object recognition.

## 1 Introduction

Active vision starts from retinal filtering and is understood as a process that actively interacts with the environment in order to control the gaze towards relevant aspects like objects. Most object recognition systems suffer from training with hand annotated data resulting in an inflexibility regarding spontaneous changes. So far, little work has been done in the computational modeling of an object recognition process, which automatically extracts a structure of auditory and visual cues in order to gain an object representation. Object recognition in an online learning scenario features a wide range of challenges. This means to build up a system that incrementally learns the structure of a demonstrated object. The ability to enhance the visual sensitivity on repeated exposures to multi-modal sources like movements of the mouth and speech requires the integration of bimodal signals. In addition, this requires a mechanism which selects stimulus driven relevant visual and auditory features in an initial learning phase in order to define unsupervised learned classifiers. Walter and Koch [1] propose a model that links a bottom up attention model to an object recognition system with an attentional modulation. This approach focuses on visual perceptual properties of the environment. In order to maintain object constancy for an object recognition, Newell [2] proposes that a constancy can be achieved by a

K. Diamantaras, W. Duch, L.S. Iliadis (Eds.): ICANN 2010, Part II, LNCS 6353, pp. 492–497, 2010.

multi sensory representation and refers to the interaction with haptic cues. Xiao [3] studies the effect of task irrelevant sound on the oculomotor system. The analysis with different pitch deviants shows that the smooth pursuit ability increases with an increasing of the pitch. Lehmann [4] investigates the influence of past audio-visual object representations on an unimodal object recognition task. The criteria of memory performance and accuracy are improved if an object has been perceived in both modalities. Molholm [5] also suggests that an audio-visual representation leads to a faster and more accurate object detection performance and hypothesizes that auditory input modulates the processing in regions of the lateral occipital cortex. This challenges to find features that link the auditory and visual part of an object. Furthermore, a system needs to discriminate relevant information from irrelevant information automatically. Roy et. al [6] addresses the problem of finding significant features for the learning of auditory and visual cues between objects and speech. This approach uses the mutual information as clustering criterion and selects images and speech segments according to their mutual information maximization. A few approaches have been suggested to estimate audio-visual correlations [7], [8]. In contrast to this methods, our approach researches the correlation of auditory and visual properties from an active vision perspective and therefore focuses on space variant regions. In section 2, we present a system architecture for the control of an active vision system. Section 3 focuses on the correlation of auditory and visual properties with respect to center activity. A conclusion about the performance of unsupervised generation of training data is given in section 4.

## 2    System Architecture

In the following, the architecture [9] (fig. 1) is described with respect to the shown components. At each time when the camera moves onto a new position and tracks the scene for a defined time, the field of vision is processed with visual filters. The central region of the observed scene is correlated with auditory cues. The visual filtering is initially determined by predefined filters (6) and results into a saliency map. In relation to the new position, the movement is defined by a saccade logic (7) that calculates the center position by using the saliency map. The extraction of the most important point defines the camera movement. The moment of the movement is determined by a timer logic (8) that defines a new saccade and the system reevaluates the scene center. During the track of the scene, the system separates the acquired sound in active and non active audio segments. In a first learning phase the audio signal is not classified and is not accessible for the saliency computation with a weighting by auditory classifiers. The properties of the active audio segments are correlated with visual properties of the camera center and serves as criterion for retaining auditory and visual segments. The correlation computation provides a basis to extract visual and auditory segments in order to cluster them (11, 12) and to prepare classes for learning of an auditory classifier and for additional visual saliency filters. The correlation computation (9) is carried out during the tracking and

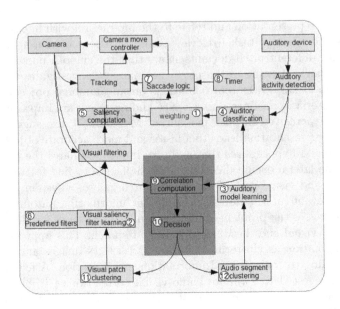

**Fig. 1.** An active vision system that attends on multi-modal relevant aspects. In the initial phase, the gaze selection of the architecture is reactive and the controlling strategy is defined by [10]. This model extracts visual salient points of the environment. An object classification based on auditory characteristics requires an associative learning of visual and auditory concepts (e.g. mouth/speech, hand/knocking). Therefore a learning of additional visual saliency filters (2) and auditory classifiers (3) are proposed. The association of learned concepts is defined by a weighting (1) of the relative importance of *visual saliency filters* that determines the saliency computation.

results in a statistic that provides indications about the mutuality of visual and auditory properties. The decision (10) of retaining single segments depends on the observed mutuality and extracted visual regions and auditory segments that have been correlated in particular. In this paper, we focus on part 9 and 10.

## 3    Selection of Relevant Visual and Auditory Segments

The proposed selection mechanism serves as a criterion for what to learn and suppresses the processing of noise with respect to missing coherence of auditory and visual information. Hershey et. al [7] define temporal synchronous observations of audio $a_t$ and visual signals $v(x, y)_t$ as *Mutual Information I* (1). Both events at timestamp $t$ are drawn independently from a joint Gaussian process with variances $\hat{C}_{A_t}$ and $\hat{C}_{V(x,y)_t}$ belonging to a joint covariance matrix $\hat{C}_{AV(x,y)_t}$.

$$I(x, y)_t = -\frac{1}{2} \log \left( \frac{|\hat{C}_{A_t}| \cdot |\hat{C}_{V(x,y)_t}|}{|\hat{C}_{AV(x,y)_t}|} \right). \tag{1}$$

This approach suffers from a constant time averaging and hence temporal changes of $I$ are not adapted. Therefore, we use the method proposed by Rolf

[8]. We investigate in the analysis of the audio energy $a_t$ and motion activity $v_t$ defined by the difference of intensity images with respect to center activity $w(x, y) = exp\left(\left(-x^2 - y^2\right)/\sigma^2\right)$. For $\hat{C}_{V(x,y)_t}$ we estimate a threshold $\hat{\gamma}_t$ (2) during the tracking:

$$\hat{\gamma}_t = \hat{\gamma}_{t-1} + \beta \cdot (\gamma_t - \hat{\gamma}_{t-1}) \text{ with } \gamma_t = \sum_{x,y} w \cdot \hat{C}_{V(x,y)_t} . \tag{2}$$

Those regions that don't exhibit significantly a large variance of $v_t$ are removed for a further correlation computation:

$$\hat{C}_{V(x,y)_t} = \begin{cases} 0, & \text{if } \hat{\gamma}_t > \hat{C}_{V(x,y)_t} \\ \hat{C}_{V(x,y)_t}, & else \end{cases} \tag{3}$$

Active acoustic segments are obtained by applying a fixed threshold. After each tracking step $k$ the observed mutuality is summarized with $I_k = \sum_{x,y} w \cdot I(x, y)_t$. In order to select relevant visual and auditory events $\hat{r}_{v,a}$ that have been correlated, $I_k$ is evaluated after each tracking sequence (4). Firstly, the thresholding step ensures that visual and auditory information are removed that obtain low correlation activity. The threshold $\theta_1$ is adapted by removed correlation measurements during the whole observation of the scene. The filtering includes a second threshold $\theta_2$ and is determined by a randomization step $Ir_k$ computed in parallel. For this $a$ is drawn from a normal distribution with $\sigma$ and $\mu$ estimated from origin active acoustic segments.

$$\hat{r}_{v,a} = \begin{cases} 1 & \text{if } I_k > max(\hat{\theta}_1, \theta_2) \\ 0 \text{ and } & \hat{\theta}_{1_k} = \hat{\theta}_{1_{k-1}} + \beta \cdot (\hat{\theta}_{1_k} - \hat{\theta}_{1_{k-1}}) \text{ else} \end{cases} \tag{4}$$

If the estimated $I_k$ yields a higher mean value as the estimated $\theta_1$ and the randomized correlation $\theta_2$, than the visual and auditory information are selected as relevant. Otherwise the correlation is caused by noise.

# 4  Results

The manual classification contains the separation between relevant and not relevant information of the sequences. The next saccade movement is determined by a saliency map that is computed by color, motion and orientation. An inhibition of return leads to a gaze selection to locations that have not been attended before. A new saccade is triggered each second. The *Mutual Information* $I$ is weighted with $\alpha = 0.05$ and $w$ is defined with $\sigma = 0.1/$cut-off $= 0.5$. The threshold for motion activity $\hat{C}_{V(x,y)_t}$ and $\hat{\theta}_1$ are adapted with $\beta = 0.5$. In order to analyze the performance of our approach, we use a dataset that is manually classified by humans into relevant and irrelevant patches. The dataset is recorded under laboratory conditions and shows a speaking person. The dataset comprises sequences of images with sound. Figure 2 shows a set of visual patches marked as relevant and irrelevant. As our thresholding criterion (4) contains a random parameter,

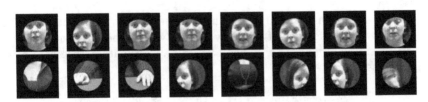

**Fig. 2.** Example dataset of relevant and irrelevant information (upper/bottom row). For the evaluation, the sequences are extracted in a predefined step with our algorithm. They contain always the last image and the sound information from start to the end of the tracked scene. The image view is restricted according $w$. The labeling criterion is defined by the appearance of redundant information of both modalities. This means if the sequence contains a mouth and is coherent with speech, the sequence is marked as relevant. Otherwise the sequence is marked as irrelevant. We conducted our analysis on 105 tracking sequences $k$. Sequences without any sound activity are removed from the dataset. By the manual annotation, we get 35 relevant combinations of auditory and visual information and 70 not relevant combinations.

**Table 1.** Evaluation results: The true positive error $tp$ and false negative error $fn$ describes those patch combinations that are selected as important and unimportant from relevant ones. The false positive error $fp$ and true negative error $tn$ describes those patch combinations that are selected as important and unimportant from irrelevant ones.

|  | tp | fn | tn | fp | relevant | irrelevant |
|---|---|---|---|---|---|---|
| relative | 0.46 | 0.54 | 0.83 | 0.17 | | |
| average total | 16 | 19 | 58.2 | 11.8 | 35 | 70 |
| $d_\mu$ | | 26 | 39.4 | 251.2 | 217.1 | |
| $d_\sigma$ | | 17.6 | 31.4 | 165.8 | 148.4 | |

we repeated our analysis for five times on the dataset. The results are averaged by the number of trails. Compared to the manually annotated data, our automatic approach finds 46 % (table 1) of the dataset that are selected as relevant ($tp$). Our method classifies 54 % combinations as not relevant. The $fn$ error shows a loss of training data. This does not implicate an influence of a further clustering step. The most difficult task for an object recognition system consists in the unsupervised description of not relevant information. The $tn$ error is 83 % and shows the effectiveness of our approach. Most irrelevant combinations are identified. Only 17 % are detected as relevant. Hence an unsupervised extraction of valid training data is ensured for a further clustering step. An additional analysis of the spatial distribution of center views of selected and rejected information shows a difference in the different conditions. This similarity is measured by the euclidean distance $d$ between the centers resulted from a sequence $k$. The results show that in case of the $tp$ the average distance is smaller than in the case of $fp$. This means the accepted visual information from false wise accepted correlation events are distributed to center reference and can not share common features. In contrast to this, the visual fields that are evaluated as $tp$ provides a basis for a common feature representation reasoned by the low $d_\mu$.

# 5 Conclusion

This paper introduces an active vision architecture that is bootstrapped by a visual bottom up process and a correlation computation. A threshold adaptation takes place during the tracking and removes not significant aligned audio-visual events. The results provide a significant discrimination of relevant auditory-visual information. The investigation in the analysis with respect to center reference provides a preliminary clustering and a basis for learning of visual saliency filters.

**Acknowledgments.** The work described was supported by the Honda Research Institute Europe.

# References

1. Walther, D., Koch, C.: Modeling attention to salient proto-objects. Neural Networks 19, 1395–1407 (2006)
2. Newell, F.N.: Cross-modal object recognition. In: Calvert, G., Spence, C., Stein, B.E. (eds.) The handbook of multisensory processes, pp. 123–139. MIT Press, Cambridge (2004)
3. Xiao, M., Wong, M., Umali, M., Pomplun, M.: Using eye-tracking to study audio-visual perceptual integration. Perception 36(9), 1391–1395 (2007)
4. Lehmann, S., Murray, M.M.: The role of multisensory memories in unisensory object discrimination. Cognitive Brain Research 24(2), 326–334 (2005)
5. Molholm, S., Ritter, W., Javitt, D.C., Foxe, J.J.: Multisensory visual-auditory object recognition in humans: a high-density electrical mapping study. Cerebral Cortex 14, 452–465 (2004)
6. Roy, D.: Learning Audio-Visual Associations using Mutual Information. In: Proceedings of International Workshop on Integrating Speech and Image Understanding, pp. 147–163 (1999)
7. Hershey, J., Movellan, J.: Audio-vision: Using audio-visual synchrony to locate sounds. In: Advances in Neural Information Processing Systems, pp. 813–819 (1999)
8. Rolf, M., Hanheide, M., Rohlfing, K.: Attention via synchrony: Making use of multimodal cues in social learning. IEEE Transactions on Autonomous Mental Development, 55–67 (2009)
9. Grahl, M., Joublin, F., Kummert, F.: A method for multi modal object recognition based on self-referential classification strategies. European Patent Application, No. 09177019.8, pending (2009)
10. Itti, L., Koch, C., Niebur, E.: A model of saliency-based visual attention for rapid scene analysis. IEEE Transactions on Pattern Analysis and Machine Intelligence 20(11), 1254–1259 (1998)

# A One-Layer Dual Neural Network with a Unipolar Hard-Limiting Activation Function for Shortest-Path Routing*

Qingshan Liu[1] and Jun Wang[2]

[1] School of Automation, Southeast University, Nanjing 210096, China
qsliu@seu.edu.cn
[2] Department of Mechanical and Automation Engineering
The Chinese University of Hong Kong, Shatin, New Territories, Hong Kong
jwang@mae.cuhk.edu.hk

**Abstract.** The shortest path problem is an archetypal combinatorial optimization problem arising in a variety of application settings. For real-time applications, parallel computational approaches such as neural computation are more desirable. This paper presents a new recurrent neural network with a simple structure for solving the shortest path problem (SPP). Compared with the existing neural networks for SPP, the proposed neural network has a lower model complexity; i.e., the number of neurons in the neural network is the same as the number of nodes in the problem. A simple lower bound on the gain parameter is derived to guarantee the finite-time global convergence of the proposed neural network. The performance and operating characteristics of the proposed neural network are demonstrated by means of simulation results.

**Keywords:** Recurrent neural networks, global convergence in finite time, shortest path problem.

## 1 Introduction

The shortest path problem is concerned with finding the shortest path from a specified origin to a specified destination in a given network while minimizing the total cost associated with the path. The shortest path problem is an archetypal combinatorial optimization problem with widespread applications in a variety of settings. The applications of the shortest path problem include vehicle routing in transportation systems [1], traffic routing in communication networks [2,4], and path planning in robotic systems [3]. Furthermore, the shortest path problem also has numerous variations such as the minimum weight problem, the quickest path problem, the most reliable path problem, and so on.

---

* The work described in the paper was supported by the Research Grants Council of the Hong Kong Special Administrative Region, China, under Grants CUHK417608E and CUHK417209E.

K. Diamantaras, W. Duch, L.S. Iliadis (Eds.): ICANN 2010, Part II, LNCS 6353, pp. 498–505, 2010.

Since Tank and Hopfield's seminal work [5], neurodynamic optimization has been a major area in neural network research. In the literature, recurrent neural networks for solving shortest path problems have been widely investigated [6,8,9,10]. In [8], Wang investigated the primal and dual neural networks for solving the shortest path problems. In [9], based on the primal-dual optimization approach, a discrete-time recurrent neural network with global convergence was constructed to solve the shortest path problems. These investigations have shown the sufficient potentials for the neural network approach to the shortest path problem.

This paper presents a recurrent neural network with lower implementation complexity to solve the shortest path problem. The proposed neural network can solve the routing network problem with global finite-time convergence. Furthermore, the proposed network is realizable in parallel digital circuits.

## 2  Problem Formulation and Model Description

We consider the shortest path from vertex 1 to vertex $n$ in a directed graph $G$ with $n$ vertices, $m$ edges, and a cost $c_{ij}$ associated with each edge $(i; j)$ in $G$. Based on the edge path representation, the primal shortest path problem can be formulated as a linear integer program as follows:

$$
\begin{aligned}
\text{minimize} \quad & \sum_{i=1}^{n} \sum_{j=1}^{n} c_{ij} x_{ij}, \\
\text{subject to} \quad & \sum_{k=1}^{n} x_{ik} - \sum_{l=1}^{n} x_{li} = \begin{cases} 1, & \text{if } i = 1 \\ 0, & \text{if } i = 2, 3, \ldots, n-1 \\ -1, & \text{if } i = n \end{cases} \\
& x_{ij} \in \{0, 1\}, \ i, j = 1, 2, \ldots, n,
\end{aligned}
\tag{1}
$$

where $x_{ij}$ denotes the decision variable associated with the edge from vertices $i$ to $j$, as defined below

$$
x_{ij} = \begin{cases} 1, & \text{if the edge from vertices } i \text{ to } j \text{ is in the path;} \\ 0, & \text{otherwise.} \end{cases}
$$

If an optimal solution exists and unique, we may solve the above integer program as the following linear program:

$$
\begin{aligned}
\text{minimize} \quad & \sum_{i=1}^{n} \sum_{j=1}^{n} c_{ij} x_{ij}, \\
\text{subject to} \quad & \sum_{k=1}^{n} x_{ik} - \sum_{l=1}^{n} x_{li} = \delta_{i1} - \delta_{in}, \\
& x_{ij} \geq 0, \ i, j = 1, 2, \ldots, n,
\end{aligned}
\tag{2}
$$

where $\delta_{ij}$ is the Kronecker delta function defined as $\delta_{ij} = 1 (i = j)$ and $\delta_{ij} = 0 (i \neq j)$.

By the duality of convex program [11], we see that the dual shortest path problem is as follows:

$$
\begin{aligned}
&\text{maxmize}\quad y_n - y_1,\\
&\text{subject to } y_j - y_i \le c_{ij},\ i,j = 1,2,\dots,n,
\end{aligned}
\tag{3}
$$

where $y_i$ denotes the dual decision variable associated with vertex $i$ and $y_i - y_1$ is the shortest distance from vertex 1 to vertex $i$ at optimality.

According to the Karush-Kuhn-Tucker (KKT) conditions [11], the proposed recurrent neural network for solving the dual shortest path problem can be described as follows:

$$
\epsilon\frac{dy_k}{dt} = -\delta_{k1} + \delta_{kn} - \sigma\sum_{i=1}^{n}\sum_{j=1}^{n}(\delta_{jk} - \delta_{ik})g(y_j - y_i - c_{ij}),\ k = 1,2,\dots,n,
\tag{4}
$$

where $\epsilon$ is a positive scaling constant, $\sigma$ is a nonnegative gain parameter, $\delta_{ij}$ is defined in (2), $g(v)$ is the unipolar hard-limiting activation function defined as

$$
g(v) = \begin{cases}
1, & \text{if } v > 0,\\
[0,1], & \text{if } v = 0,\\
0, & \text{if } v < 0.
\end{cases}
\tag{5}
$$

The proposed neural network (4) has one-layer structure only with $n$ neurons (same as the number of decision variables in the dual shortest path problem (3)). Compared with the primal neural networks [6,7,8] with $n^2$ neurons and the primal-dual neural networks [9] with $n^2+n$ neurons, the proposed neural network herein has lower model complexity with one order fewer neurons. The proposed neural network has the same model complexity as the dual neural networks [7,8]. Nevertheless, the parameter selections for the dual neural networks therein are not straightforward, whereas the proposed dual neural network herein is guaranteed for exact optimal solutions if the single gain parameter in the model is larger than a derived lower bound, as will be discussed in the ensuing section.

## 3   Global Convergence

In this section, the finite-time global convergence to optimality of the proposed recurrent neural network (4) is proved with a derived lower bound of the gain parameter $\sigma$. Throughout this paper, we always assume that the optimal solution set is not empty and solutions are finite.

Denote $y = (y_1, y_2, \dots, y_n)^T$, $b = (c_{11}, \dots, c_{1n}, c_{21}, \dots, c_{2n}, \dots, c_{n1}, \dots, c_{nn})^T$ and $c = (1, 0, \dots, 0, -1)^T \in \mathbb{R}^n$, then the neural network in (4) can be written as the following vector form

$$
\epsilon\frac{dy}{dt} = -c - \sigma A^T g(Ay - b),
\tag{6}
$$

where $g(v) : \mathbb{R}^{n^2} \to \mathbb{R}^{n^2}$ and its component is defined as that in (5), $A = M - E$ with

$$M = \begin{pmatrix} I \\ I \\ \vdots \\ I \end{pmatrix}, E = \begin{pmatrix} e & o & \cdots & o \\ o & e & \cdots & o \\ \vdots & \vdots & \ddots & \vdots \\ o & o & \cdots & e \end{pmatrix},$$

in which $e = (1, 1, \ldots, 1)^T \in \mathbb{R}^n$ and $I$ is the identity matrix.

Let $\psi(y) = c^T y + \sigma e^T \phi(Ay - b)$, where $\phi(v) = (\phi_1(v), \phi_2(v), \ldots, \phi_m(v))^T$ and $\phi_i(v) = \max\{0, v\}$. Then its generalized gradient is $\partial\psi(y) = c + \sigma A^T K[g(Ay - b)]$, where $K(\cdot)$ denotes the closure of the convex hull. That is, the neural network in (6) is a gradient system of energy function $\psi(y)$. Since $\psi(y)$ is convex, the minimum point of $\psi(y)$ corresponds to the equilibrium point of neural network (6). In addition, if the gain parameter $\sigma$ is large enough, the optimal solution of problem (3) can be obtained. Next, we give the finite-time global convergence of the proposed neural network.

**Theorem 1.** *If $\psi(y)$ has a finite minimum, then the state variables of (6) (or (4)) are globally convergent to an equilibrium point in finite time with any $\sigma \geq 0$.*

*Proof:* From the assumption, the equilibrium point set of neural network (6) is not empty. Let $\bar{y}$ be an equilibrium point of neural network (6), then there exists $\bar{\gamma} \in K[g(A\bar{y} - b)]$ such that

$$c + \sigma A^T \bar{\gamma} = 0.$$

Consider the following Lyapunov function:

$$V(y) = \epsilon \int_0^1 (y - \bar{y})^T [F(\bar{y} + t(y - \bar{y})) - F(\bar{y})]dt + \frac{\epsilon}{2}\|y - \bar{y}\|^2, \qquad (7)$$

where $F(y) = c + \sigma A^T g(Ay - b)$ and $\|\cdot\|$ denotes the Euclidian norm. We have

$$\partial V(y) = \epsilon \{K[F(y)] - K[F(\bar{y})] + y - \bar{y}\},$$

where $K[F(y)] = c + \sigma A^T K[g(Ay - b)]$.

Similar to the proof of Theorem 3 in [12], we have

$$\dot{V}(y(t)) \leq - \inf_{\eta \in K[F(y)]} \|\eta\|^2, \qquad (8)$$

and any state trajectory of neural network (6) is globally convergent to an equilibrium point.

Suppose that $y(t)$ is not an equilibrium, so that $c + \sigma A^T \gamma \neq 0$, where $\gamma \in K[g(Ay - b)]$. Since the set $K[g(Ay - b)]$ is nonempty and compact, the set $K[F(y)]$ is also nonempty, compact and $0 \notin K[F(y)]$. Thus, $\inf_{\eta \in K[F(y)]} \|\eta\|^2$ is a positive constant, denoted as $\beta$. Then, from (8), we have

$$\dot{V}(y(t)) \leq -\beta.$$

Integrating both sides of previous inequality from $t_0 = 0$ to $t$, it is easily to verify that $V(y(t)) = 0$ for $t \geq V(y(t_0))/\beta$. From (7), it follows that $V(y(t)) \geq \epsilon \|y - \bar{y}\|^2/2$, then we have $y = \bar{y}$ for $t \geq V(y(t_0))/\beta$. That is, $x(t)$ is globally convergent to an equilibrium point in finite time. □

From above analysis, the proposed neural network is guaranteed to reach an equilibrium point in finite time. To obtain the optimal solution of the dual shortest path problem in (3), the following theorem reveals the relationship between the optimal solution of problem (3) and the equilibrium point of neural network (4).

**Theorem 2.** *Any equilibrium point of neural network (4) is an optimal solution of the dual shortest path problem (3) and vice verse, if $\sigma > \sqrt{2}$.*

*Proof:* The proof is similar to that of Theorem 2 in [12] and omitted here.    □

Combining Theorems 1 and 2, the state variables of neural network (4) are globally convergent to an optimal solution of the dual shortest path problem (3) in finite time if $\sigma > \sqrt{2}$.

## 4    Simulation Results

Consider a shortest path problem with $n$ being 20. The origin and destination vertices are, respectively, vertices 1 and 20. The network topology is shown in Fig. 1, where the solid lines indicate the shortest path and the dash lines indicate the existing arcs.

**Fig. 1.** Network topology and the shortest path in the example

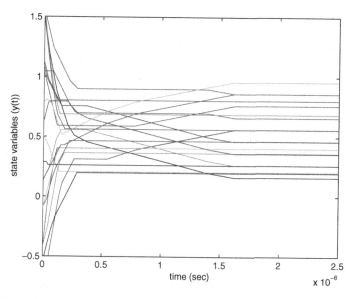

**Fig. 2.** Transient behaviors of the state variables of the neural network (4) in the Example

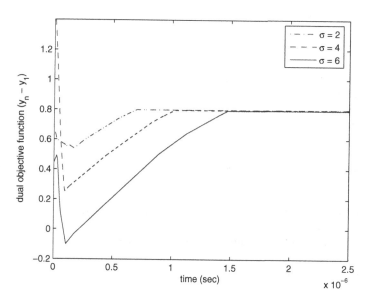

**Fig. 3.** Convergence of the dual objective function of the neural network (4) in the Example

This shortest path of this problem is $\{n_1, n_4, n_7, n_{10}, n_{12}, n_{17}, n_{20}\}$; i.e., $\{a_{14}, a_{47}, a_{7,10}, a_{10,12}, a_{12,17}, a_{17,20}\}$. Let $\epsilon = 10^{-6}$, Figs. 2 and 3 show the simulation results of the neural network constructed from the dual linear programming (3). Specifically Fig. 2 depicts the convergence of the state variables with $\sigma = 2$. Fig. 3 shows the convergence of the dual objective function $y_n - y_1$ (i.e., $\sum_{i=1}^{n} \sum_{j=1}^{n} c_{ij}x_{ij}$ in the primal shortest path problem) with three different values of $\sigma$. The optimal dual solution needs post-processing to decode the optimal primal solution in terms of edges. According to the Complementary Slackness Theorem: given the feasible solutions of $x_{ij}$ and $y_i$ to the primal and dual problems, respectively, the solutions are optimal if and only if 1) $x_{ij} = 0$ is implied by $y_j - y_i < c_{ij}$ and 2) $x_{ij} = 1$ is implied by $y_j - y_i = c_{ij}$ for $i, j = 1, 2, \ldots, n$. In this example, after post-processing, the optimal primal solution is obtained as high lighted by the dark lines in Fig. 1.

## 5    Conclusions

This paper presents a recurrent neural network with a unipolar hard-limiting activation function for solving the shortest path problem in its dual form. The dual neural network is guaranteed to be globally convergent to the optimal solutions in finite time if its single gain parameter is larger than a derived lower bound. A numerical example with simulation results is given to illustrate the effectiveness and performance of the proposed neural network.

## References

1. Bodin, L., Golden, B., Assad, A., Ball, M.: Routing and scheduling of vehicles and crews: The state of the art. Comput. Oper. Res. 10(2), 63–211 (1983)
2. Ephremides, A., Verdu, S.: Control and optimization methods in communication network problems. IEEE Transactions on Automatic Control 34(9), 930–942 (1989)
3. Jun, S., Shin, K.: Shortest path planning in distributed workspace using dominance relation. IEEE Trans. Robot. Automat. 7, 342–350 (1991)
4. Antonio, J.K., Huang, G.M., Tsai, W.K.: A fast distributed shortest path algorithm for a class of hierarchically clustered data networks. IEEE Trans. on Computers 41, 710–724 (1992)
5. Tank, D., Hopfield, J.: Simple neural optimization networks: An a/d converter, signal decision circuit, and a linear programming circuit. IEEE Transactions on Circuits and Systems 33(5), 533–541 (1986)
6. Wang, J.: A recurrent neural network for solving the shortest path problem. IEEE Transactions on Circuits and Systems-I 43(6), 482–486 (1996)
7. Wang, J.: Primal and dual assignment networks. IEEE Transactions on Neural Networks 8(3), 784–790 (1997)
8. Wang, J.: Primal and dual neural networks for shortest-path routing. IEEE Transactions on Systems, Man, and Cybernetics-A 28(6), 864–869 (1998)
9. Xia, Y., Wang, J.: A discrete-time recurrent neural network for shortest-path routing. IEEE Transactions on Automatic Control 45(11), 2129–2134 (2000)

10. Liu, Q., Wang, J.: A one-layer recurrent neural network with a discontinuous activation function for linear programming. Neural Computation 20(5), 1366–1383 (2008)
11. Bazaraa, M., Sherali, H., Shetty, C.: Nonlinear Programming: Theory and Algorithms, 3rd edn. John Wiley & Sons, Hoboken (2006)
12. Liu, Q., Wang, J.: A one-layer recurrent neural network for convex programming. In: Proc. IEEE International Joint Conference on Neural Networks, pp. 83–90 (2008)

# Optimizing Hierarchical Temporal Memory for Multivariable Time Series

David Rozado*, Francisco B. Rodriguez, and Pablo Varona

Grupo de Neurocomputación Biológica (GNB)
Dpto. de Ingeniería Informática, Escuela Politécnica Superior,
Universidad Autónoma de Madrid. Calle Francisco Tomás y Valiente,
11, 28049 - Madrid, Spain
{david.rozado,F.Rodriguez,pablo.varona}@uam.es
http://www.ii.uam.es/~gnb

**Abstract.** Hierarchical Temporal Memory (HTM) is an emerging computational paradigm consisting of a hierarchically connected network of nodes. The hierarchy models a key design principle of neocortical organization. Nodes throughout the hierarchy encode information by means of clustering spatial instances within their receptive fields according to temporal proximity. Literature shows HTMs' robust performance on traditional machine learning tasks such as image recognition. Problems involving multi-variable time series where instances unfold over time with no complete spatial representation at any point in time have proven trickier for HTMs. We have extended the traditional HTMs' principles by means of a top node that stores and aligns sequences of input patterns representing the spatio-temporal structure of instances to be learned. This extended HTM network improves performance with respect to traditional HTMs in machine learning tasks whose input instances unfold over time.

**Keywords:** Sequence Encoding, Motion Analysis, Multidimensional Signal Processing, Neural Network Architecture, Pattern Recognition.

## 1 Introduction

Hierarchical Temporal Memory (HTM) [1], [2] is a conexionist paradigm with a novel set of bio-inspired assumptions encapsulating theories about neocortical function into a set of algorithms [3]. HTM theory incorporates the hierarchical organization of the mammalian neocortex into its topological architecture [4], [5]. HTM also uses spatio-temporal codification as a way to encapsulate and learn the structure and invariance of problems' spaces [6]. Spatio-temporal coding and hierarchical organization are well documented principles of information processing in living neural systems [7], [8].

---

* This work was supported by grants from 'Consejería de Educación de la Comunidad de Madrid' (C.A.M), the 'European Social Fund (E.S.F.)' and the 'Ministerio de Ciencia e Innovacion': MICINN BFU2009-08473, TIN 2007-65989 and CAM S-SEM-0255-2006

K. Diamantaras, W. Duch, L.S. Iliadis (Eds.): ICANN 2010, Part II, LNCS 6353, pp. 506–518, 2010.

HTM hypothesizes that time is used by the neocortex as a supervisory signal for clustering together spatially different input patterns that tend to present themselves close together in time. The usage of temporal integration minimizes storage requirements and reduces the need for supervised training.

The theoretical aspects of the HTM paradigm were throughly described in [2], [9]. An up to date version of the theory with a probabilistic model of temporal aggregation and feedback information flowing from parent nodes to children nodes to disambiguate noisy inputs can be found in [1]. HTM algorithms can be used to solve problems on different domains: pattern recognition, control theory or behavior generation among others [10]. In this paper we center our attention to HTMs applied within the realm of temporal pattern recognition.

The main objective of an HTM network trained for pattern recognition is the development of invariance capabilities [11]. That is, given a set of categories, each one of them represented by a set of instances, the system should learn to properly separate the category-space using a small subset of training instances from each category set. After training, the system should be able to generalize and properly assign the correct categories to unseen instances from the category space.

HTM algorithms perform robustly in traditional machine learning tasks such as image recognition [11]. Problems where HTM excel are those with an inherent spatio-temporal structure and whose instances are represented completely at any given time instant. For problems where an instance is composed of a time series of spatial arrangements, HTMs performance is not as robust.

In this paper we develop a feature for HTMs to perform better on learning tasks whose instances unfold over time: we modify the HTM's top node by enabling it to store sequences of spatio-temporal input patterns arriving at the top node over time. This top node also performs similarity measurements among incoming sequences in order to map unseen instances to known categories. The rationale for using sequences to map stimuli to categories has been justified in [12], [7], [13].

We illustrate the performance of our modified HTM system in the problem of sign language recognition. Sign language is used by deaf people to communicate by means of using sequences of hand movements instead of speech. Sign Language constitutes a good fit for the type of problem that we wanted to tackle: category spaces whose instances are composed of an ordered sequence of spatial arrangements. Therefore, we chose a data set containing time series of hand movements representing signs from Australian Sign Language (ASL) as a proof of principle that our expanded HTM system can perform well on problems whose instances develop over time.

## 2   HTM Formalism

HTM's network topology consists of a set of layers arranged in a hierarchy, Fig. 1(a). Each layer is composed of one or several computational nodes operating in discrete time steps. Nodes are related through children-parent relationships. Each node throughout the hierarchy possesses an intrinsic receptive field formed

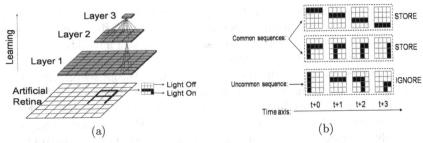

(a)                                          (b)

**Fig. 1. HTM Basis.** Panel *a* shows an HTM's topology containing 3 layers. Each layer is composed of one or several nodes. Bottom level nodes are fed with input from a sensor, in this case an "artificial retina". Figure adapted from [3]. Panel *b* shows instances of 2-Dimensional spatial coincidences from a small receptive field in an artificial retina. The spatial coincidences in the first two rows do not have a high pixel-to-pixel similarity but since they appear often in a sequence they are temporally adjacent, so an HTM node clusters them into the same temporal group. Non frequent sequences of spatial coincidences are not clustered together. Figure adapted from [2].

by its children nodes or, in the case of bottom level nodes, a portion of the sensors' input space. Nodes of HTM networks can receive many types of input vectors that specifically encapsulate the input space properties of the receptive field to which they are exposed. All nodes through-out the hierarchy, except the top node, carry out unsupervised learning.

Each node in an HTM network can be thought of as composed of two critical elements: a *spatial pooler* and a *temporal pooler*. These two identifiers serve as abstractions to refer to the form by which input vectors received during training are partitioned and stored into sets of temporally adjacent vectors. All nodes start off with their spatial and temporal poolers empty. Nodes undergo two modes of function during their lifetime: a training mode and an inference mode.

During the training mode, a node stores input vectors coming from children nodes that are different enough, according to a threshold, from the vectors already stored on its spatial pooler. These input vectors are also referred to in the HTM literature as *spatial coincidences* [11].

When the spatial pooler is full or a sufficiently large number of training iterations has been carried out, the node creates a time-adjacency matrix. Each row and each column of this matrix represents a spatial coincidence, and the intersection between a row and a column maintains a probability value indicating the likelihood of a spatial coincidence, represented by the row, transitioning into the spatial coincidence, represented by the column, in the next time step.

Training is completed when a time-adjacency matrix' modification coefficient falls bellow a certain threshold. The node initiates then a segmentation algorithm that uses the transition frequencies stored in the time adjacency matrix to cluster the vectors in the spatial pooler into groups according to how frequently they tend to follow each other in time. These temporally adjacent groups are stored in the temporal pooler of the node. The rationale for this is the fact that input patterns with a large spatial distance might be closely related or have a common cause if they tend to follow each other in time repeatedly, Fig. 1(b).

After the node spatial pooler has been partitioned into temporal groups, the node switches its state from training mode towards inference mode. During inference mode, the node continues to receive input vectors, but it does not perform any more learning of new vectors, it just calculates to which temporal group the incoming input vector most likely belongs. This is done by calculating the similarity between the incoming input vector and the vectors stored in the temporal groups. The node then emits an output vector containing as many elements as temporal groups are stored on its temporal pooler. Each element of the output vector could indicate a probability value of that temporal group being active. In a simplified version of the system, all elements of the output vector can be binary with all elements of the vector being 0s except for the element representing the temporal group to which the node believes the actual input vector belongs, which contains a 1. This vector is propagated toward the node's parent node. Fig. 2(a) shows the stages a node goes through during its life time.

In traditional HTM, the network's top node functions in a slightly different fashion to the rest of the nodes in the hierarchy. The top node does receive input vectors from children nodes, but it does not perform temporal aggregation of the data and it does not emit output vectors. During training, a signal is given to the top node as a cue about the particular category to which the system is being exposed to at a particular time instant. The top node just maps incoming input vectors to the signaled category in a supervised fashion.

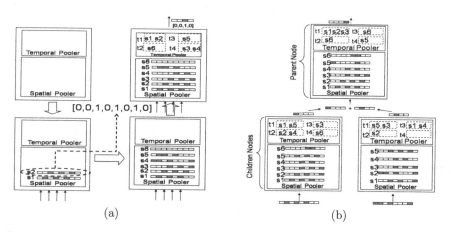

(a)                                         (b)

**Fig. 2. Node inner-workings.** Panel $a$ shows how a node starts out with its spatial and temporal poolers empty. Input vectors formed by 1s and 0s (s1,s2...,s6) received during training are stored in the spatial pooler. After training, the time adjacency matrix is used to determine the temporal groups of the node (t1,...,t4). During inference mode, the node maps input vectors to temporal groups and emits the corresponding output vector. In Panel $b$, a parent node aggregates output vectors from children nodes to form its own input vector. These aggregated patterns from several children nodes constitute the spatial coincidences of a parent node's input space.

Training starts off on the bottom level layer and propagates throughout the hierarchy one layer at a time, with parent nodes transitioning into training mode right when their children nodes initiate their inference mode. First, only nodes at the bottom layer of the hierarchy are active and in training mode, the rest of the nodes in the hierarchy are silent. Once the bottom layer has completed its training mode, its nodes are switched to inference mode, and the nodes starts to emit output vectors, which conform the input data for the nodes higher up in the hierarchy. Parent nodes aggregate incoming vectors from several children nodes, Fig. 2(b), and use this aggregated pattern as their input vector.

When all the nodes in all the layers of the hierarchy have undergone their training mode, training for the whole network has been completed and the network is ready to perform inference.

# 3    Proposed Extension for the HTM Formalism

We have developed a version of the HTM theory as proposed in [2]. Message passing from children nodes to parent nodes nodes is implemented using binary vectors, containing just 1s and 0s in each element without feedback from parent nodes. This binary vector indicates which temporal group is active at a time. This extended HTM formalism has been developed in order to adjust the system to the specific needs of multivariable time-series problems whose instances develop over time.

The fundamental modification of our local HTM system with respect to traditional HTM networks is the modification of the network's top node whose task in original HTM algorithms is simply to map incoming vectors from children nodes to categories. The newly defined top node stores instead complete sequences of spatio-temporal input vectors in its *sequential pooler* and maps those sequences to categories.

Besides storing sequences of input vectors during training, the top node also performs similarity measurements among incoming sequences during both training and inference. The similarity calculation is needed in order to map unknown incoming sequences to the sequences already stored in the top node. Similarity measurements are carried out by sequence alignment using dynamic programming [14] as explained below.

We have tested our approach in the problem of Sign language recognition. Sign language recognition is fundamentally different from previously tried out problems within the HTM community, [11]. Most problems undertaken by HTMs, [10], consist of instances whose spatial configuration are fully represented at any time instant. Sign language is composed of sequences of spatial arrangements over time that together constitute a sign. At any given time $t$, the complete representation of the sign is not available, just a particular spatial arrangement of the hands. It is the particular temporal sequence of hand arrangements what constitutes a sign. The fundamentally different nature of this kind of problem and the poor performance of traditional HTM networks to deal with it justified the undertaking of modifications within the HTM inner-workings. Figure 3(a)

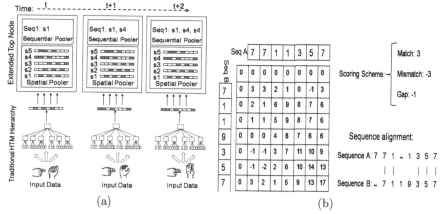

(a)                                                    (b)

**Fig. 3. Extended Top Node.** Panel *a* shows how the top node stores sequences of spatial coincidences during training in its sequential pooler. First the node stores on its spatial pooler the set of spatial coincidences to which it is exposed to during training. Then it learns common sequences of those spatial coincidences. Panel *b* shows how the extended top node uses sequence alignment using dynamic programming to measure similarity among two sequences. The external row and column represent 2 sequences formed by spatial coincidences units. The score at the bottom right of the matrix indicates the top global alignment between both sequences. A scoring scheme was used to score matches, gaps and mismatches in the alignments.

illustrates how the learning of a sign comes about over time in our modified top node by storing the sequence of spatial coincidences that follow each other in time during the "utterance" of the sign.

# 4    Example Application: Sign Language Recognition

We illustrate the extended HTM formalism on a data set consisting of several instances from sign language. The data set was obtained from [15] and it was captured using a pair of electronic data gloves[1] containing accelerometers and sensors to track 11 channels of information for each hand: x, y and z spatial coordinates of the hand, the roll, pitch and yaw rotation angles of the wrist and a bend coefficient for each finger. A particular configuration of all the channel variables at one instant in time is referred to in this paper as a frame.

When a user puts on this gloves and performs a particular sequence of hands movements representing a sign, the gloves provide dynamic data representing the spatio-temporal transitions of the tracked variables as they oscillate over time while the hands "utter" a particular sign. A total of 95 different sign-categories with 27 sign-samples per category were recorded from a single volunteer native signer using ASL [15].

---

[1] Data Gloves from 5DT Fifth Dimension Technologies (http://www.5dt.com).

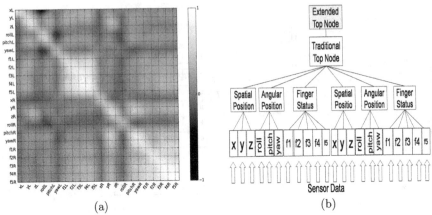

(a)                                      (b)

**Fig. 4. Optimal Network Topology.** Panel *a* shows a cross-correlation matrix of the 22 channels from the data set. This matrix was used to find the optimal topology of the network since highly correlated input channels should be grouped in the network's lower layers. All the fingers of each hand are highly correlated as wells as the x,y and z coordinates of each hand and the roll, pitch and yaw angles of the wrist. Panel *b* shows what was determined to be the optimal HTM network topology for the illustrated problem of sign recognition.

For each simulation, the data was automatically partitioned in a random fashion into two sets, 90% of the available data became the training set and the remaining 10% became the test set. The partitions were different for each simulation and were determined ad-hoc right before each simulation. This prevented over-fitting during the search for optimum HTM training parameters.

We created an HTM topology formed by 3 layers as shown in Fig. 4(b) that proved to be the one that optimized the performance of the network over several alternative network designs as explained below. The bottom layer nodes received their input data from the 11 channels of input data coming from each glove. Several topologies were tried out varying the number of layers, nodes, fan-in edges, fan-out edges, spatial-pooler specificity coefficients and clustering coefficients for the nodes.

The original data contained intrinsic noise, making it necessary to filter the data. For each channel an average value for each category was determined. Then, when any instance differed significantly from the category average, the difference was subtracted from the absolute values for that particular instance. This procedure visibly reduced noise deviations in the data set.

Since the original data contained continuous variables, the next filtering step was to discretize the continuous input values into discrete input values. That is, the continuous input space had to be converted into a discrete input space. For each channel, the range of possible values was segmented into a finite number of regions. Each region represented a particular discrete value of the input space. If the value of a continuous variable from an input channel fell into a particular region, the channel adopted the discrete value associated with that region.

$$H(X) = \sum_{n=1}^{N} (p_i \cdot \log(p_i))$$

$$p_i = \frac{|x_i|}{\|X\|}$$

$$\|X\| = \sum_{1}^{N} (x_i)$$

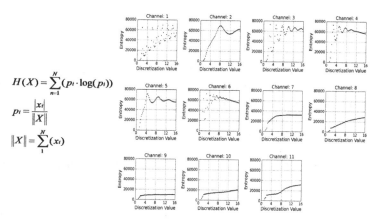

**Fig. 5. Entropy analysis of left hand** Determining the right partitioning values, $\nu$, to transform the continuous input variable into $\nu$ discrete states. The optimum $\nu$ according to simulation trials coincided with low entropies when comparing different $\nu$ values' impact on performance. The entropy of a sequence of values in a channel $X = x_1, x_2, x_3, ..., x_N$ is defined by the formula in the figure with $p_i$ being the probability of value $i$, $|x_i|$ being the number of times value $x_i$ occurs and $|X|$ being the length of the sequence.

An entropy analysis for each channel was performed in order to determine the proper segmentation value for each channel, Fig. 5. That is, in how many discrete segments the continuous variable should be divided in order to minimize entropy. The optimal parameters suggested by the entropy analysis and confirmed by manual supervision settled down on segmentations values between 2-6 regions for each channel.

The input data's absolute x, y and z coordinates of the hands is sometimes not enough to completely describe a sign. Other variables such as first and second derivatives of the x, y, and z coordinates further describe a particular sequence of hand movements. Therefore, we used derived data from the absolute values provided by the data set and performed simulations using the derived velocity and acceleration information corresponding to the x, y and z variables.

Since our Extended HTM formalism consisted of a top node that stored sequences of spatio-temporal patterns, we needed some means to perform comparisons among stored and incoming sequences in order to determine similarity. The need for a measurement of similarity was two-fold: It was needed during training in order to determine which sequences to store and which ones to disregard, in case of high similarity to an already stored sequence. A similarity measurement was also needed during inference to determine which sequence, from the set of stored sequences in the sequential pooler of a top node had the highest degree of similarity to an incoming input sequence. We measured sequence similarity by performing sequence alignment using dynamic programming. Dynamic programming has been successfully used by the bioinformatics research community to calculate the degree of similarity between genetic sequences [14]. Dynamic Programming sequence alignment consists of using a scoring matrix to align two sequences according to a scoring scheme by tracing down the optimal global alignment, Fig. 3(b).

Combinations of different HTM networks that exploit different data representations improves the performance of the algorithm. Therefore, a method was needed in order to carry out the combination of the results of several simulations. We settled down with a simple aggregated sum of results from different simulations as a way of pooling the results of several simulations into a combined result, Fig. 6(a). That is, each trained HTM network was tested by making it to perform inference over a set of unseen instances. For each inference over an unseen instance, a rank of sequences stored in the sequential pooler of the top node which were similar enough to the input instance was generated. Every sequence in the rank had a particular score and category associated with it. The score was the result of performing a global alignment between the input sequence and this specific sequence stored in the sequential pooler. Pooling the results of several simulations simply consisted of adding all the scores associated to a certain category in the similarity rank generated for each input instance, Fig. 6(b).

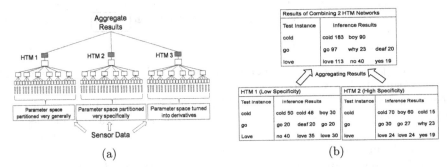

(a)                                         (b)

**Fig. 6. Aggregation of Results.** The results of HTM networks with different configuration parameters and fed with different data representations can be pooled to improve overall performance, Panel *a*. Panel *b* shows how the results tables of two different HTM network simulations can be combined into a single table by adding up the scores associated to each category in the similarity rank.

We measured the performance of the algorithms by testing what percentage of unseen signs' instances were assigned to their proper categories after training. Two types of measurements were used: Measurement A indicated the percentage of times the algorithm correctly first guessed an unseen utterance of a sign. Measurement B indicated the percentage of times the algorithm guessed the correct category of the unseen instances within its top three guesses.

Several simulations were carried out with different network parameters. The optimal topology used in the simulations was that of Fig. 4(b). The results of the simulations using a traditional HTM network were poor, just above 30% for Measure A, since they are not optimized to handle patterns unfolding over time. The addition of our own node with sequence storage and sequence alignment capabilities proved to be of critical importance with results jumping up to the

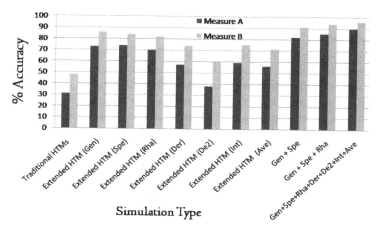

**Fig. 7. Comparison of Simulations Performance under different arrangements.** Measure A refers to the percentage of times the simulation correctly first guessed the appropriate category of an unseen instance. Measure B refers to the percentage of times the simulation correctly guessed the appropriate category of an unseen instance within its top 3 guesses. Aggregated results of several simulations are indicated with the + operator.

70-80% range for Measure A. Figure 7 provides a summary of results for different simulation types.

In Fig. 7, 'traditional HTMs' simulation type refers to HTMs as described in [2]. The rest of the simulations were carried out with the expanded top node as described previously in this paper. Several simulations with different data representations were carried out: Simulations optimized for specificity (Spe) or generalization (Gen), simulations using derived data from the original x, y and z coordinates: derivatives (Der), second derivatives (Der2), integrals (Int), averages (Ave) and simulations using data just from the right hand (Rha).

Simulations combining several single type simulations improve inference's performance. Combination of results from individual networks are referred to in Fig. 7 as addition of the specific tags associated with each simulation type.

# 5  Discussion

HTMs perform successful pattern recognition over data sets whose instances' spatial components are perceived completely at a particular time instant, for instance, image recognition [11]. That is, through one single flash-shot, the system perceives the whole spatial representation of an instance from a category.

Instances whose composition unfolds over time as a particular timed sequence of spatio-temporal configurations of input variables have not been shown in the literature to be as robustly recognised by existing HTMs networks [10]. Our data set consisted of precisely that: instances of sign language composed by an ordered sequence of frames.

Traditional HTM algorithms as described in the literature perform poorly on our selected dataset, Fig. 7. This comes about because of the specific nature of our tackled problem which is fundamentally different from image recognition. In our data set, each frame considered in isolation does not represent any particular sign just a flash-view spatial arrangement of the hands in space. Only the appropriate sequence of spatial arrangements over time uniquely constitutes a sign. The top node in traditional HTMs just tries to guess the proper category of an instance for every given frame during the performance of a sign. But a given time frame or arrangement of the 11 channels of information for each hand can be shared by several signs and hence the poor results.

To overcome the traditional HTMs shortcomings, our Extended HTM formalism creates a top node whose main task is to store sequences of spatio-temporal input vectors as incoming input instances unfold over time 3(a).

A cross correlation analysis was performed in order to find out correlations among input channels, Fig. 4(a). This information was used to design the optimal network topology, Fig. 4(b). HTMs work better if highly correlated channels are grouped locally in the lower levels of the hierarchy [2], leaving the upper layers to find out more complex, distant or not so obvious correlations. Accordingly our network topology grouped in its bottom layers those variables that were highly correlated according to Fig. 4(a).

A critical aspect for the performance of the algorithm is the degree of granularity used for the discretization of the continuous input space. The discretization process represents a trade-off between specificity and generalization capabilities of the network. Excessive granularization, that is, partitioning the continuous input space into too many regions, increases the specificity of the learning, but leads to over-fitting and less generalization abilities of the network. Obviously, the more instances available for training, the higher the degree of specificity that can be reached, but our data set was constrained to just 27 samples for each sign. On the other hand, a very unspecific partition of the input space, favors generalization capabilities but also decreases the specificity of the network, that is, the number of false positives increases. An entropy analysis was performed, Fig. 5, to find out the optimum degree of granularity needed to transform the continuous input space into a discrete space.

The types of errors committed for different simulations were different in terms of sensibility and specificity. Simulations optimized for generalization improved the sensibility with the cost of getting too many false positives. Simulations optimized for specificity were very accurate in terms of always getting true positives, yet they would miss several true positives due to their lack of generalization capabilities. Too much specificity also lead to an explosion in terms of storage and processing requirements.

The relatively good results of simulations using just information from the right hand (Rha) 7 are due to the fact that in Australian Sign Language most signs are perform just with the right hand while the left hand stays still.

Performing several simulations for different data representations of the data set and then using a pooling system to aggregate the results of different network simulations improves overall performance, Fig. 7. This is due to the fact that some granularizations, or data representations, are optimal just for the recognition of some signs with no obvious optimal data representation for all signs. Therefore, combinations of HTM networks that exploit different data representation overcomes this limitation.

Our approach improves performance of HTMs significantly for recognition of multivariable time series. There is however a trade-off since the sequence alignment methodology used by our modified top node is NP-hard underlining the high computational costs of this approach.

The results of applying our method on the ASL Date Set, Table 7 are slightly worse than those obtained by cite [16] which achieves accuracy percentages of up to 96%. However, the method described by [16] is intrinsically of a highly supervised nature, since the features to be matched by the algorithm were previously defined by the author. The nature of our algorithm is fundamentally different since it is highly unsupervised in its feature learning methodologies and therefore highly adaptable to a wide array of problems.

Other authors have recently used HTMs for Polish sign language recognition [17]. These authors have used a video based recognition approach while we used data captured with a data glove. Although in [17] they get slightly better results for Polish Sign Language than our algorithm for ASL, around 94%, they also fed the HTM algorithm with additional channels about movement type, and visemes [17] something which our data set lacked [17]. Also their training set contained more instances for each sign, 40, as opposed to our data set which only contained 27.

In summary, our reformulation of the top node in an HTM system by providing it with sequence storage and alignment capabilities improves performance when used upon classifying signs from a data set containing Australians sign language data recorded using electronic gloves. This approach can be easily generalized for machine learning applications where the patterns to be learned also unfold over time.

# References

1. George, D., Hawkins, J.: Towards a mathematical theory of cortical micro-circuits. PLoS Comput. Biol. 5(10), e1000532 (2009)
2. Hawkings, J.: Hierarchical temporal memory, concepts, theory, and terminology. Numenta, Tech. Rep. (2006)
3. George, D., Jarosy, B.: The HTM learning algorithms. Numenta, Tech. Rep. (2007)
4. Mountcastle, V.: The columnar organization of the neocortex. Brain 120(4), 701–722 (1997)
5. Douglas, R.J., Martin, K.A.: Neuronal circuits of the neocortex. Annual Review of Neuroscience 27(1), 419–451 (2004)
6. Dean, T.: Learning invariant features using inertial priors. Annals of Mathematics and Artificial Intelligence 47, 223–250 (2006)
7. Rabinovich, M.I., Varona, P., Selverston, A.I., Abarbanel, H.D.I.: Dynamical principles in neuroscience. Reviews of Modern Physics 78(4), 1213+ (2006)

8. Pöppel, E.: A hierarchical model of temporal perception. Trends in Cognitive Sciences 1(2), 56–61 (1997)
9. Hawkings, J.: On Intelligence. Cambridge University Press, Cambridge (1991)
10. Numenta: Problems that fit htm, Numenta, Tech. Rep. (2006)
11. George, D., Hawkins, J.: A hierarchical bayesian model of invariant pattern recognition in the visual cortex. In: Proceedings of 2005 IEEE International Joint Conference on Neural Networks, IJCNN 2005, July 4-August, vol. 3, pp. 1812–1817 (2005)
12. Abeles, M.: Corticonics: neural circuits of the cerebral cortex. Henry Holt and Company (2004)
13. Rodríguez, F.B., Huerta, R.: Analysis of perfect mappings of the stimuli through neural temporal sequences. Neural Netw. 17(7), 963–973 (2004)
14. Giegerich, R.: A systematic approach to dynamic programming in bioinformatics. Bioinformatics 16(8), 665–677 (2000)
15. Kadous, M.W.: Australian sign language signs data set, UCI Machine Learning Repository, Tech. Rep., http://archive.ics.uci.edu/ml/datasets/
16. Kadous, M.W.: Temporal classification: Extending the classification paradigm to multivariate time series. Ph.D. dissertation, The University of New South Wales (2002)
17. Tomasz Kapuscinski, M.W.: Computer Recognition Systems 3, vol. 57, pp. 355–362. Springer, Heidelberg (2009)

# Solving Independent Component Analysis Contrast Functions with Particle Swarm Optimization

Jorge Igual[1], Jehad Ababneh[2], Raul Llenares[1], Julio Miro-Borras[1], and Vicente Zarzoso[3]

[1] Universidad Politecnica de Valencia, Camino de Vera s/n,
46022 Valencia, Spain
[2] Jordan University of Science and Technology
22110 Irbid, Jordan
[3] Laboratoire d'Informatique, Signaux et Systèmes de Sophia Antipolis
06903 Sophia Antipolis Cedex, France
jigual@dcom.upv.es

**Abstract.** Independent Component Analysis (ICA) is a statistical computation method that transforms a random vector in another one whose components are independent. Because the marginal distributions are usually unknown, the final problem is reduced to an optimization of a contrast function, a function that measures the independence of the components. In this paper, the stochastic global Particle Swarm Optimization (PSO) algorithm is used to solve the optimization problem. The PSO is used to separate some selected benchmarks signals based on two different contrast functions. The results obtained using the PSO are compared with classical ICA algorithms. It is shown that the PSO is a more powerful and robust technique and capable of finding the original signals or sources when classical ICA algorithms give poor results or fail to converge.

**Keywords:** Independent Component Analysis, Particle Swarm Optimization.

## 1 Introduction

Independent Component Analysis (ICA) and its most popular application Blind Source Separation (BSS) is a very active research area. The theoretical problem has been clearly stated since a long time [1]. In this paper we will concentrate in the linear noiseless instantaneous model $\mathbf{x} = \mathbf{A}\mathbf{s}$ where $\mathbf{x}$ is the observed vector that is a linear transformation (matrix $\mathbf{A}$ ) of a random vector $\mathbf{s}$ whose components are statistically independent. In BSS terminology, $\mathbf{x}$ is the mixture vector, $\mathbf{A}$ is the mixing matrix and $\mathbf{s}$ is the source vector. Many ICA algorithms can be decomposed into two steps; in the first one, the second order statistics are exploited, imposing the decorrelation of the signals (whitening step). The second step consists in the estimation of an orthogonal matrix that imposes the independence, being necessary the use of higher order statistics. In matrix notation,

$$\mathbf{y} = \mathbf{B}\mathbf{x} = \mathbf{U}\mathbf{W}\mathbf{x} \tag{1}$$

K. Diamantaras, W. Duch, L.S. Iliadis (Eds.): ICANN 2010, Part II, LNCS 6353, pp. 519–524, 2010.
© Springer-Verlag Berlin Heidelberg 2010

where $\mathbf{W}$ is the whitening matrix and $\mathbf{U}$ is the orthogonal one. The whitened vector is expressed as $\mathbf{z} = \mathbf{WAs}$, with $E[\mathbf{zz}^T] = \mathbf{I}$, and the uncorrelated unit variance constraint $E[\mathbf{yy}^T] = \mathbf{I}$, being $\mathbf{y}$ the recovered or estimated sources.

The independence hypothesis must be approximated and, as a consequence, the estimation of the sources is transformed in an optimization problem defined by a contrast (cost) function that is minimum when the estimated sources are as independent as possible, i.e., the matrix $\mathbf{BA}$ equals the product of a permutation (order indeterminacy) and a diagonal matrix (scale indeterminacy). We present in this paper the Particle Swarm Optimization PSO approach to solve the ICA problem. The use of the PSO to solve the ICA problem is proposed to overcome the trapped-in-local-optimum problems of gradient descent traditional approaches. Although PSO and ICA are very active research areas, there are few works about the application of PSO in ICA; see, e.g., [5], [6], and they are focused in some particular part of the ICA solution, not in a general analysis of cost functions.

## 2 Contrast Functions in ICA

### 2.1 Mutual Information

The Mutual Information MI is defined as the Kullback-Leibler divergence or relative entropy between the joint density and the product of the marginal distributions; it is non negative and equals to zero only if the distributions are the same, i.e., MI is a contrast function for ICA:

$$MI(\mathbf{y}) = KL(\mathbf{y}; \prod_i p(y_i)) = \int p(\mathbf{y}) \log \frac{p(\mathbf{y})}{\prod_i p(y_i)} d\mathbf{y} \tag{2}$$

It is related to the differential entropy, $MI(\mathbf{y}) = \sum_i H(y_i) - H(\mathbf{y})$, where the differential entropy of a random variable $u$ is defined as $H(u) = -\int p(u) \log p(u) du$, that can be seen as a measure of the randomness of the variable $u$. Using $H(\mathbf{y}) = H(\mathbf{x}) + \log |\det \mathbf{B}|$, the contrast, up to an additive constant term, can be expressed as:

$$MI(\mathbf{y}) = \sum_i H(y_i) - \log |\det \mathbf{B}| \tag{3}$$

with the advantage that only one dimensional distributions are involved instead of multidimensional densities. In the case where the observations are first whitened, i.e., $\mathbf{y} = \mathbf{Uz}$, $E[\mathbf{zz}^T] = \mathbf{I}$, we only have to estimate the remaining orthogonal matrix, and the contrast is reduced to the sum of the marginal entropies of $\mathbf{y}$:

$$MI(\mathbf{y}) = \sum_i H(y_i) \quad , E[\mathbf{yy}^T] = \mathbf{I} \tag{4}$$

As a conclusion, ICA can be interpreted as a minimum entropy method under the whitening assumption. Hence, the MI contrast is equivalent to find the marginal distributions as far as possible from Gaussianity.

## 2.2 Higher Order Cumulants

The cross-cumulants are equal to zero for independent variables. In ICA, it means that $C_{ij}(s) = \sigma_i^2 \delta_{ij}$ , $C_{ijkl}(s) = k_i \delta_{ijkl}$ with $\delta_{ij} = 1$ for $i = j$ and $\delta_{ij} = 0$ otherwise, $\delta_{ijkl} = 1$ for $i = j = k = l$ and $\delta_{ijkl} = 0$ otherwise, $\sigma_i^2$ is the variance and $k_i$ is the kurtosis of the source component $s_i$ , i.e., $k_i = E[s_i^4] - 3E^2[s_i^2]$. Then, if there is no prior knowledge about the kurtosis, the contrast function $J_{cum}$ is:

$$J_{cum} = -\sum_i C_{iiii}^2(\mathbf{y}) \tag{5}$$

This is equivalent up to a constant to $\sum_{ijkl \neq iiii} C_{ijkl}^2(\mathbf{y})$ since $E[\mathbf{yy}^T] = \mathbf{I}$. JADE algorithm [4] approximates the independence by minimizing a smaller number of cross cumulants, $\phi_{JADE} = \sum_{ijkl \neq ijkk} C_{ijkl}^2(\mathbf{y})$.

# 3   Particle Swarm Optimization for ICA

PSO is a stochastic optimization technique that was first introduced in 1995 by Eberhart and Kennedy [5]. It is a global optimization algorithm that simulates the swarming behavior of birds, bees, fish, etc. The PSO has a comparable performance to other stochastic optimization technique like genetic algorithm (GA) and simulated annealing. A major advantage of the PSO is its ease of implementation in both the context of coding and parameter selection.

The PSO starts with an initial population of individuals (to be termed swarm of particles). Each individual (particle) in the swarm is randomly assigned an initial position and velocity within the solution space. The position of the particle is an N-dimensional vector that represents a possible set of the unknown parameters to be optimized. Each particle in the swarm starts from its initial position at its initial velocity in order to find the position with global minimum (or maximum). During the algorithm search, the velocity and position of each particle is updated based on the individual and the swarm experience according to:

$$v_{mn}^t = v_{mn}^{t-1} + U_{n1}^t(0, \varphi_1)(pbest_{mn}^t - x_{mn}^{t-1}) + U_{n2}^t(0, \varphi_2)(gbest_{mn}^t - x_{mn}^{t-1})$$
$$x_{mn}^t = x_{mn}^{t-1} + \Delta t \, v_{mn}^t \tag{6}$$

where $v_{mn}$ and $x_{mn}$ represents the velocity and position of the $m$-th particle in the nth dimension, respectively. The superscripts $t$ and $t$-$1$ denote the time index of the current and the previous iterations, $U_{n1}^t(0,\varphi_1)$ and $U_{n2}^t(0,\varphi_2)$ are two different, uniformly distributed random numbers in the intervals $[0, \varphi_1]$ and $[0, \varphi_2]$, respectively. These random numbers are generated at each iteration and for each particle. The first term in (6) indicates that particle's current velocity depends on its previous velocity while the other two terms represent the effect of the individual (particle's best position (pbest)) and the swarm experience (neighborhood best position (gbest)) on the behavior of the particle. $\Delta t$ represents a given time step (usually chosen to be one). The goodness of the new particle position (possible solution) is measured by evaluating a suitable contrast or fitness function.

In this article, Clerc's constriction method is used [6]. It consists on a strategy for the placement of constriction coefficient ($\chi$) by which the whole equation (6) is multiplied. This coefficient is used to control the convergence of the particle, prevent explosion and ensure convergence.

$$\chi = \frac{2}{\varphi - 2 + \sqrt{\varphi^2 - 4\varphi}} \tag{7}$$

where $\varphi = \varphi_1 + \varphi_2 > 4$. The parameter $\varphi$ is commonly set to 4.1 and $\varphi_1 = \varphi_2$ which result in an approximate value of 0.7298 for $\chi$.

## 4   Results and Discussion

In this section, the use of Clerc's constriction PSO method to solve the optimization problem in ICA is demonstrated and different simulation examples are presented. In our implementation of the PSO algorithm, a swarm size of 25 particles, 500 iterations, $\varphi_1 = \varphi_2 = 2.05$, $\chi = 0.7298$ and circular population topology were used. The results obtained are compared with classical ICA algorithm FastICA [7]. In order to test the performance of the algorithm with different but standard signals, we use the benchmarks proposed in the ICALAB package [8]. The ICA contrasts analyzed are the sum of the marginal entropy and the fourth order cumulant (kurtosis), corresponding to equations (4) and (5), respectively. It is worth mentioning that the elements of the PSO output vector are reshaped to form the demixing matrix B in equation (1), which is then normalized and made orthogonal before used in the contrast function in order to impose these constraints on the demixing matrix. The PSO output is an N-dimensional vector (position of the particle with best fitness) that represents a possible set of all the elements of the matrix **B** in equation (1). The reshaping is necessary to transfer the vector into a square matrix.

In the first example, 10 sparse (smooth bell-shape) sources that are approximately independent are randomly mixed. Some ICA algorithms have failed to separate such sources, so we want to test if PSO can overcome these difficulties. The corresponding recovered signals using the PSO and the two different contrast functions are shown in the Figures 1 and 2. The recovered signals are in a very good agreement with the

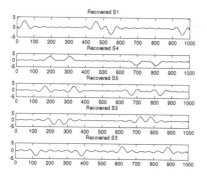

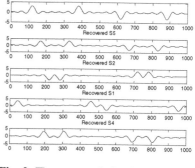

**Fig. 1.** The recovered signals of Example 1 using PSO and the entropy contrast function

**Fig. 2.** The recovered signals of Example 1 using PSO and the cumulant contrast function

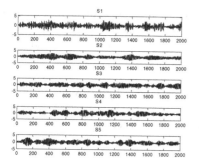

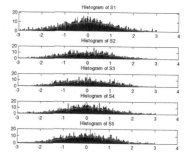

**Fig. 3.** The original signals of Example 2

**Fig. 4.** The Histogram of the signals in Example 2

original signals (we do not show them for the lack of space) with a different ordering and some of them with a change of sign. The recovered signals using FastICA algorithm are also in comparable agreement with the original signals.

Five fourth order colored sources with a distribution close to Gaussian belonging to the same ICALAB package were used in the second example. This is the most challenging case, since the signals are close to Gaussian distribution and ICA algorithms can estimate at most one Gaussian component. Figure 3 shows the original signals of Example 2.

The histograms of the sources are shown in Figure 4 to indicate proximity to Gaussianity. The recovered signals of Example 2 using the PSO with the kurtosis contrast function are shown in Figure 5.

Comparing the signals in Figure 3 and 5, it can be seen that the proposed methodology was successful in recovering some of the original signals with acceptable quality and the other signals with poor quality. On the other hand, the FastICA algorithm has completely failed to separate the mixed signals of this example. The algorithm in the ICALAB package only outputs one signal and does not give any output for the remaining signals. In addition, the algorithm outputs the statement "Too many failures to converge. Giving up". This example shows the robustness of PSO compared to

524     J. Igual et al.

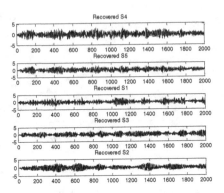

**Fig. 5.** The recovered signals of Example 2 using PSO and the kurtosis contrast function

classical optimization techniques. In order to assure this result, other ICA algorithms based on other optimization paradigms (gradient based and versions of it) was tested and confirmed this result, which is in agreement with the comments included in the ICALAB toolbox "This is a rather difficult benchmark".

**Acknowledgments.** This work has been partially funded by the Valencia Regional Government (Generalitat Valenciana) through project GV/2010/002 (Conselleria d'Educacio) and by the Universidad Politecnica de Valencia under grant no. PAID-06-09-003-382.

# References

[1] Cardoso, J.F.: Blind Signal Separation: statistical principles. Proceedings of the IEEE 86(10), 2009–2025 (1998)

[2] Krusienski, D.J., Jenkins, W.K.: Nonparametric density estimation based ICA via PSO. In: Proc. ICASSP 2005, vol. IV, pp. 357–360 (2005)

[3] Liu, C.C., Sun, T.Y., Li, K.Y., Hsieh, S.T., Tsai, S.J.: Blind Source Separation using cluster PSO technique. In: Proc. 25th IAESTED Artificial Intelligence and Applications, pp. 289–294 (2007)

[4] Cardoso, J.F., Souloumiac, A.: Blind beamforming for non Gaussian signals. Proc. Inst. Elec. Eng. 140(6), 395–401 (1993)

[5] Kennedy, J., Eberhart, R.C.: Particle swarm optimization. In: Proceedings of IEEE International Conference on Neural Networks, Piscataway, NJ, pp. 1942–1948 (1995)

[6] Clerc, M., Kennedy, J.: The particle swarm—Explosion, stability, and convergence in a multidimensional complex space. IEEE Trans. Evol. Comput. 6, 58–73 (2002)

[7] Hyvarinen, A., Oja, E.: A fast fixed point algorithm for independent component analysis. Neural Computation 9(7), 1483–1492 (1997)

[8] Cichocki, A., Amari, S., Siwek, K., Tanaka, T., Phan, A.H., Zdunek, R.: ICALAB – MATLAB Toolbox Ver. 3 for signal processing

# Binary Minimization: Increasing the Attraction Area of the Global Minimum in the Binary Optimization Problem

Yakov Karandashev[1,2] and Boris Kryzhanovsky[2]

[1] Moscow Institute of Physics and Technology (SU), Dolgoprudny 141700, Russia
[2] Center of Optical Neural Technologies SRISA RAS, Vavilova St., 44/2, Moscow 119333
Yakov.Karandashev@phystech.edu, kryzhanov@mail.ru

**Abstract.** The paper deals with the minimization of a quadratic functional in the configuration space of binary states. To increase the efficiency of the random-search algorithm, we offer changing the functional by raising the matrix it is based on to a power. We demonstrate that this brings about changes of the energy surface: deep minima displace slightly in the space and become still deeper and their attraction areas grow significantly. The experiment shows that use of the approach results in a considerable displacement of the spectrum of sought-for minima to the area of greater depths, while the probability to find the global minimum increases abruptly (by a factor of $10^3$ in the case of a two-dimensional Ising model).

**Keywords:** binary minimization, global minimum, random search, Ising model.

## 1 Introduction

The goal of the paper is to make a random-search procedure used in binary-minimization problems more effective.

The problem of binary minimization can be formulated as follows: there is $N \times N$ symmetrical matrix $T_{ij}$ with zero diagonal, the goal is to find $N$-dimensional configuration vector $S_m = (s_1^{(m)}, s_2^{(m)}, ..., s_N^{(m)})$ ($s_i^{(m)} = \pm 1$, $i = \overline{1, N}$,) that ensures a minimum for the energy functional $E_1(S)$ :

$$E_1(S) = -c_1 \sum_{i=1}^{N} \sum_{j=1}^{N} T_{ij} s_i s_j , \quad c_1^{-2} = N(N-1) \sum_{i=1}^{N} \sum_{j}^{N} T_{ij}^2 \tag{1}$$

where normalization coefficient $c_1$ is introduced to allow us to correctly compare the results for different matrices.

For minimization we use the Hopfield model [1] which is the basis of most today's algorithms of binary optimization. The model is a one-dimensional system of $N$ spins whose interactions are governed by the energy functional $E_1(S)$ . Only conventional (asynchronous) behavior of the Hopfield model is considered: we compute the local field $h_i = -\partial E_1(S)/\partial s_i$ that acts on an arbitrary spin (*i*-th spin):

K. Diamantaras, W. Duch, L.S. Iliadis (Eds.): ICANN 2010, Part II, LNCS 6353, pp. 525–530, 2010.
© Springer-Verlag Berlin Heidelberg 2010

$$h_i = c_1 \sum_{j \neq i}^{N} T_{ij} s_j .$$
(2)

If the spin is in an unstable state ($h_i s_i < 0$), then the spin changes its state in accordance with the decision rule $s_i = \text{sgn}\, h_i$. The procedure is applied successively to all neurons until the network comes to a stable energy-minimum state $S_m$.

This minimum $S_m$ is very likely to be a local one despite our wish to find the deepest (global) minimum of the functional. That is why we have to turn to random search which involves descents from different random initial configurations repeated until the minimum of a specific depth (probably a global minimum) is reached. Below we will denote this simple algorithm as SRS (Standard Random Search) and use it for comparison with the algorithm we offer.

The problem of binary minimization is NP-complete in the general case. For this reason heuristic methods are used to solve it [1-3]. Because of a large number of local minima, such methods do not work efficiently, though allow acceptable solutions. Despite of these difficulties, heuristic methods based on random search have found wide use in binary-optimization problems. Usually [4-9], one tries to make the random-search procedure more efficient by changing the algorithm of the descent down the surface described by functional $E_1(S)$. A good review of the methods is given in papers [4-6].

In contrast to that approach, we offer alteration of the surface itself rather than the dynamics of the descent by increasing the radius of the attraction area of the global minimum (and other minima that are almost as deep as the global one). Following the theory developed in [11], we consider the simplest kind of alteration which involves raising matrix $T$ to power $k$ ($k = 2, 3, \ldots$). The approach proved quite effective: the change of the surface increases the chance of finding the global minimum by $10^3$ times and makes the spectrum of the sought-for minima move far into a deeper-depth region.

## 2  Surface Transformation

*Basic relation.* Before coming to the question of surface transformation, let us define basic relations involving the depth of a global (local) minimum.

The first relation deals with the limitation on the depth of a minimum. Let $S_0 = (s_1^{(0)}, s_2^{(0)}, \ldots, s_N^{(0)})$ be a configuration corresponding to global minimum $E_0 = E_1(S_0)$. Following to [12] the matrix $T$ can be represented as

$$T = T_0 + T_1, \quad \text{where} \quad T_0 = r_0 \sigma_T S_0^+ S_0, \quad T_1 = T - T_0, \quad r_0 = -E_0,$$
(3)

and $\sigma_T$ is standard deviation of elements $T_{ij}$ (for the simplicity sake we assume that mean value of $T_{ij}$ is equal to zero). Then by using statistical physics methods [13] we can state that the following limitation on the depth of a minimum are true:

$$1 \geq r_0 \geq r_c \quad \text{and} \quad -1 \leq E_0 \leq E_c = -r_c \ , \quad \text{where} \quad r_c = \frac{1}{2\sqrt{\alpha_c N}} \qquad (3)$$

and $\alpha_c \approx 0.138$ is the threshold value of the load parameter [13].

The second necessary expression relates the depth and width of a minimum. As shown in [3], the width of minimum $E_0$ increases with its depth. Correspondingly, the chance to find this minimum grows exponentially as $P(E_0) \sim \exp\left(-NE_c^2 / E_0^2\right)$.

The result is that we have determined two formulas: a) the deeper the minimum $E_0$, the greater the weight $r_0$ of an addition to configuration $S_0$ in the initial matrix $T$ and the higher the probability of finding the minimum, b) point $S_0$ can be a minimum only if $r_0 \geq r_c$, that is, if the depth of the minimum $|E_0|$ is greater than the value $|E_c|$.

These formulae set the direction of our efforts to improve the efficiency of the random-search algorithm: energy surface should be altered so that the global minimum will become deeper and, therefore, the chance to find it will grow.

All of the above conclusions have to do with configuration $S_0$ corresponding to the global minimum. However, they are true for any extreme $S_m$ of functional $E_1(S)$.

*Surface transformation.* A surface defined by functional $E_1(S)$ can be transformed only by changing the corresponding matrix. Let us put matrix $M = T^k$ into expression (1). Here $T^k$ is a matrix resulted from raising matrix $T$ to power $k$ and zeroing its diagonal elements. Correspondingly, the surface determined by functional $E_1(S)$ turns into the surface described by functional $E_k(S)$:

$$E_k(S) = -c_k \sum_{i=1}^{N} \sum_{j=1}^{N} M_{ij} s_i s_j \ , \quad c_k = \frac{1}{\sigma_M N(N-1)} , \qquad (4)$$

where $\sigma_M$ is the standard deviation of the elements of matrix $M$. Transformation of the global minimum is taken as a basis for all considerations. It is clear that when we alter the surface, the minimum moves with its depth and attraction area changing. We will show below that when parameter $k$ is small ($2 \leq k \leq 5$) this transformation causes the minimum to change its depth noticeably and to move slightly.

Correspondingly we offer a two-stage algorithm of minimization. The first stage suggests a descent over surface $E_k(S)$ and finding configuration $S_m^{(k)}$ which brings functional $E_k(S)$ to a minimum. The second stage involves correction: we descend over surface $E_1(S)$ from point $S_m^{(k)}$ to the nearest minimum $S_m$ of functional $E_1(S)$. The method of descending surface $E_k(S)$ is exactly the same as that described above: we compute the local field $h_i^{(k)} = -\partial E_k(S)/\partial s_i$ at the $i$-th spin:

$$h_i^{(k)} = c_k \sum_{j \neq i}^{N} M_{ij} s_j \qquad (5)$$

and if $h_i^{(k)} s_i < 0$, then the spin's state changes as $s_i = \operatorname{sgn} h_i^{(k)}$.

**Algorithm DDK** ( *Double Descent* with parameter $K=2, 3, \ldots$ )
**begin**

    **Step 1.** Random Initialization ( random state $S$ generation )

    **Step 2.** Descent over landscape $E_k$ from $S$ to minimum $S_m^{(k)}$

    **Step 3.** Correction: descent over landscape $E_1$ from $S_m^{(k)}$ to minimum $S_m$

**end algorithm**

**Fig. 1.** DDK algorithm of random search using a two-stage descent

Using this two-stage descent, we realized the random-search method whose short description is given in Fig. 2. Below we will refer to it as DDK (Double Descent algorithm with parameter $K = 2, 3, \ldots$ ). To avoid misunderstanding, note that when $k = 1$, the transformed functional $E_k(S)$ is identical to the original one $E_1(S)$, and the DDK method does not differ from the common SRS ( $DD1 \equiv SRS$ ).

To ground the DDK algorithm, we turn to the case when $k = 3$. We will show that the surface transformation makes the global minimum significantly deeper, while its position changes only slightly.

*The deepening of the minima.* Let us consider energy $E_{30} = E_3(S_0)$ at point $S_0$. In view of relations $S_0 T_1 S_0^+ = 0$ and $\sigma_M = N\sigma_T^3$ we get from (4):

$$E_{30} = NE_0^3 - \frac{1}{N^3 \sigma_T^3} \sum_{i=1}^{N} \sum_{j \neq i}^{N} (2Nr_0 \sigma_T T_1^2 + T_1^3)_{ij} s_i^{(0)} s_j^{(0)} . \tag{6}$$

It follows from (6) that when $N \gg 1$, energy $E_{30}$ can be regarded as a normally distributed quantity with the mean $\overline{E}_{30}$ and relatively small standard deviation $\sigma_E$:

$$\overline{E}_{30} = NE_0^3 , \qquad \sigma_E \approx (1 - r_0^2)\sqrt{4r_0^2 N + 1} / N . \tag{7}$$

Since $\overline{E}_{30} / E_0 = r_0^2 N \geq r_c^2 N \approx 1.76$, the minimum should be expected to become deeper after surface transformation ( $E_{30} < E_0$ ). The probability of that event is given by the expression:

$$\Pr\{E_{30} < E_0\} = \frac{1}{2}(1 + erf \ \gamma_3) \quad \text{where} \quad \gamma_3 = \frac{E_0 - \overline{E}_{30}}{\sqrt{2}\sigma_E} . \tag{8}$$

From $r_0 \geq r_c$ it follows that $\gamma_3 \geq 0.25\sqrt{N}$, hence the probability of the minimum deepening $\Pr\{E_{30} < E_0\}$ approaches unit with growing $N$. In other words, the surface transformation is most likely to cause the minimum to deepen considerably, which, according to [3], leads to the probability of finding it growing with $N$ exponentially.

*The shift of the minimum.* The average distance of the shift can be represented as $d_k = N \Pr\{s_i^{(0)} h_i^{(k)} < 0\}$, where $\Pr\{s_i^{(0)} h_i^{(k)} < 0\}$ is the probability of spin $s_i^{(0)}$ and local field $h_i^{(k)}$ having different directions given configuration $S_0$. For our case of $k = 3$ we can get the following expression:

$$d_3 = \frac{N}{2}(1 - erf\,\eta_3), \quad \text{where} \quad \eta_3 \approx \frac{N\sqrt{N}E_0^3}{(1-r_0^2)\sqrt{2}}. \tag{9}$$

It is seen that the shift of the minimum is not large: given $|E_0| \geq |E_c|$, we get that $\eta_3 \geq 1.7$, which means that $d_3 \leq 0.008N$.

Relations $\overline{E}_{30} / E_0 \geq 1.76$ and $d_3 \leq 0.008N$ are in accordance with experiment.

## 3  Experimental Results and Discussion

The DDK algorithm efficiency was evaluated for $k = 2 \div 7$. The experimental results for the matrices of the two-dimensional Ising model are given in Table 1. The first column holds data for the SRS algorithm. The other columns hold data for the DDK algorithm. To evaluate the efficiency of the algorithm, we picked three characteristics: the first row contains deviation $\delta E = (\overline{E}_m - E_0) / E_0$; the second the probability of entering the energy interval $[E_0, 0.99E_0]$ in the close vicinity of the global minimum; the third the probability of hitting the global minimum.

**Table 1.** Comparison of the DDK algorithm efficiency with the results of using the SRS algorithm performed for a two-dimensional Ising model with $N = 100$

|  | SRS | DD2 | DD3 | DD4 | DD5 |
|---|---|---|---|---|---|
| Deviation $\delta E = (\overline{E}_m - E_0) / E_0$ | 16% | 11% | 6% | 10% | 5% |
| Probability of entering the energy interval $[E_0, 0.99E_0]$ | $2.8 \times 10^{-5}$ | $2.3 \times 10^{-3}$ | $1.1 \times 10^{-2}$ | $5.6 \times 10^{-3}$ | $2.5 \times 10^{-2}$ |
| Probability of hitting the global minimum $P_k(d=0)$ | $2.4 \times 10^{-6}$ | $3.8 \times 10^{-4}$ | $2.1 \times 10^{-3}$ | $1.2 \times 10^{-3}$ | $4.1 \times 10^{-3}$ |

It is seen that the results for $k = 5$ little differ from the results for $k = 3$. When $k > 5$, the results become worse. That is why a further increase of $k$ does not make much sense: as $k$ grows, the efficiency of the algorithm falls and computations begin consuming too much time. It seems that the efficiency provided by the DDK algorithm only grows with $k$. However, it does not make sense to raise the matrix to power endlessly and expect the probability of hitting deep minima to grow. Functional $E_2$ exhibits chimera minima which are deeper than the global minimum of the initial functional $E_1$. The higher the power of the matrix, the more chimera minima the corresponding functional holds and the deeper they are. It should be also noticed that raising the matrix to a power may result in the global minimum becoming invisible at all.

Comparison shows that the surface transformation increases the optimization algorithm efficiency significantly. In particular, the use of the DD3 method allows the following improvements: probability of hitting the global minimum increases by almost $10^3$ times and reaches quite a reasonable value of $\sim 0.2\%$; the difference between the average energy $\overline{E}_m$ and the energy of the global minimum decreases by three times; the probability that $E_m \in [E_0, 0.99E_0]$ grows by several hundred times.

Besides, the superiority of the DDK algorithm over the SRS one only grows with increasing dimensionality $N$.

**Acknowledgments.** The research was supported by the RFBR grant #09-07-00159.

# References

1. Hopfield, J.J.: Neural Networks and physical systems with emergent collective computational abilities. Proc. Nat. Acad. Sci. USA 79, 2554–2558 (1982)
2. Hopfield, J.J., Tank, D.W.: Neural computation of decisions in optimization problems. Biological Cybernetics 52, 141–152 (1985); Hopfield, J.J., Tank, D.W.: Computing with neural curcuits: A Model. Science 233, 625–633 (1986)
3. Kryzhanovskii, B.V., Magomedov, B.M., Mikaelyan, A.L.: A Relation Between the Depth of a Local Minimum and the Probability of Its Detection in the Generalized Hopfield Model. Doklady Mathematics 72(3), 986–990 (2005)
4. Hartmann, A.K., Rieger, H. (eds.): New optimization Algorithms in Physics. Wiley-VCH, Berlin (2004)
5. Duch, W., Korczak, J.: Optimization and global minimization methods suitable for neural networks. KMK UMK Technical Report 1/99; Neural Computing Surveys (1998)
6. Hartmann, A.K., Rieger, H.: Optimization Algorithms in Physics. Wiley-VCH, Berlin (2001)
7. Litinskii, L.B.: Eigenvalue problem approach to discrete minimization. In: Duch, W., Kacprzyk, J., Oja, E., Zadrożny, S. (eds.) ICANN 2005, Part II. LNCS, vol. 3697, pp. 405–410. Springer, Heidelberg (2005)
8. Smith, K.A.: Neural Networks for Combinatorial Optimization: A Review of More Than a Decade of Research. INFORMS Journal on Computing 11(1), 15–34 (1999)
9. Boettecher, S.: Extremal Optimization for Sherrington-Kirkpatrick Spin Glasses. Eur. Phys. Journal B 46, 501 (2005)
10. Kryzhanovsky, B.V., Kryzhanovsky, V.M.: The shape of a local minimum and the probability of its detection in random search. In: Filipe, J., Ferrier, J.-L., Andrade-Cetto, J. (eds.) Lecture Notes in Electrical Engineering, vol. 24, pp. 51–61 (2009)
11. Karandashev, Y.M., Kryzhanovsky, B.V.: Transformation of Energy Landscape in the Problem of Binary Minimization. Doklady Mathematics 80(3), 927–931 (2009)
12. Kryzhanovsky, B.V.: Expansion of a matrix in terms of external products of configuration vectors. Optical Memory & Neural Networks 17(1), 62–68 (2008)
13. Amit, D.J., Gutfreund, H., Sompolinsky, H.: Spin-glass models of neural networks. Phys. Rev. A 32, 1007–1018 (1985); Annals of Physics 173, 30–67 (1987)

# An Artificial Immune Network
# for Multi-objective Optimization

Aris Lanaridis and Andreas Stafylopatis

Intelligent Systems Laboratory,
School of Electrical and Computer Engineering,
National Technical University of Athens,
Zografou 15780, Athens, Greece

**Abstract.** This paper presents a method for approximating the Pareto front of a given function using Artificial Immune Networks. The proposed algorithm uses cloning and mutation to create local subsets of the Pareto front, and combines elements of these local fronts in a way that maximizes the diversity. The method is compared against SPEA and NSGA-II in a number of problems from the ZDT test suite, yielding satisfactory results.

**Keywords:** Artificial Immune Networks, Pareto Front, Multiobjective Optimization, Computational Intelligence.

## 1   Introduction

Finding the Pareto front of a given function is a complex task since both the Pareto optimality and the diversity of the proposed solutions must be simultaneously addressed. Analytical methods are often computationally infeasible, rendering Evolutionary Algorithms a dominant approach in the field. In this paper we suggest a method of approximating the Pareto front of a given function based on Artificial Immune Networks.

The proposed method evolves a population of candidate solutions using cloning and non-uniform mutation, and evaluates the population using both Pareto-dominance and distribution criteria. Our method is tested on the well-known ZDT Test Suite [5], and the solutions suggested are compared to the NSGA-II [2] and SPEA [3] algorithms.

The rest of the paper begins by giving an overview of the Artificial Immune Networks in Section 2. Sections 3 discusses the concepts of Pareto dominance and the diversity of the Pareto front. The algorithm is presented in Section 4 and the experimental results are listed in Section 5.

## 2   Artificial Immune Networks

The immune system consists of a complex of cells, molecules and organs, whose primary function is to limit the damage that invading pathogens cause to the host organism. To confront these invaders (antigens), the organism secrets receptor

K. Diamantaras, W. Duch, L.S. Iliadis (Eds.): ICANN 2010, Part II, LNCS 6353, pp. 531–536, 2010.
© Springer-Verlag Berlin Heidelberg 2010

molecules called antibodies which bind with the invading antigen. The shape of the antibodies can change to better match with the corresponding antigen through a process known as Clonal Selection. For each antibody a number of clones are created and mutated at a high rate. The clones that better match the antigen survive while the ones that do not die out. Gradually, this leads to antibodies of higher ability to match the invading antigen.

Another critical addition to the biological model of the immune system is Jerne's theory of the Immune Network. According to this, antibodies can recognize and eliminate other antibodies, even in the absence of antigens. To avoid recognizing its own antibodies as invaders, the immune system must ensure that antibodies not only match antigens, but do not match other antibodies already present in the organism. This means that the network must ensure the diversity of its antibody population, by removing antibodies that are too similar to already existing antibodies and replacing them by new ones.

Based on the biological principles described above, a multitude of corresponding computational models have been developed (we refer the reader to [7] for a thorough analysis). All of them address the problem by maintaining a evolving population of antibodies. Throughout the evolution, some antibodies are randomly created, some evolve according to the Clonal Selection process, and some die according to the Immune Network principles. The fact that the Immune Network addresses both the quality and the diversity of the population simultaneously makes it particularly suitable to multiobjective optimization problems.

## 3    Pareto Dominance and Diversity Evaluation

### 3.1    Pareto Dominance

In what follows, let us consider an optimization problem with $k$ objectives that are all, without loss of generality, to be minimized and equally important. Let $f : \mathbf{X} \to \mathbf{Y}$ be the function that is to be optimized. This function performs a mapping of a *decision vector* $x = \{x_1, x_2, \ldots, x_n\}$ in the *decision space* $\mathbf{X} \subseteq \mathbb{R}^n$ to an *objective vector* $y = \{y_1, y_2, \ldots, y_k\}$ in the *objective space* $\mathbf{Y} \subseteq \mathbb{R}^k$.

Each decision attribute $x_j$ takes values in the interval $X_j = [l_j, u_j]$, hence the decision space is the Cartesian product of those intervals, namely $\mathbf{X} = X_1 \times X_2 \times \ldots \times X_n$. Accordingly each attribute $y_j$ of the objective space lies in $Y_j = [L_j, U_j]$ and thus $y \in \mathbf{Y} = Y_1 \times Y_2 \times \ldots \times Y_k$.

Given two such objective vectors $y^1, y^2 \in \mathbf{Y}$, we say that $y^1$ Pareto-dominates $y^2$ if $y^1$ is smaller than $y^2$ in at least one attribute and not larger in any of the others, that is

$$y^1 \succ y^2 \Leftrightarrow \{(\exists j : y_j^1 < y_j^2) \wedge (\forall j : y_j^1 \leq y_j^2)\} \tag{1}$$

Accordingly, we can say that solution $x^1$ is better than $x^2$ if the corresponding mapping $y^1$ dominates $y^2$, that is $x^1 \succ x^2 \Leftrightarrow f(x^1) \succ f(x^2)$. Given this equivalence, for the remaining of the paper, each time a solution $y^i$ in the objective space is selected as optimal, it is implied that the corresponding vector $x^i$ in the decision space is also selected.

An objective vector $y^i$ (and the corresponding $x^i$) is considered optimal if it is not dominated by any other vector in the objective space. The goal of the algorithm is to find a set of such mutually non-dominated solutions, each representing a different trade-off between the multiple objectives. This set of vectors is called the Pareto front of the function, denoted $\mathbf{P}$, while the set of the corresponding decision vectors is called the Pareto set $\mathbf{S}$.

### 3.2 Diversity Evaluation

To evaluate the diversity of the proposed solutions, we use the S metric, a common diversity criterion proposed by Zitzler in [6]. Specifically, given a candidate Pareto front $\mathbf{y}$, we select a reference point $y^{ref}$ dominated by all points in $\mathbf{y}$. We then calculate the hypervolume dominated by all members in $\mathbf{y}$ bounded by $y^{ref}$. This volume is used as an indicator of the diversity of the suggested Pareto front.

Formally, for a given $y^i \in \mathbf{y}$, the region dominated by $y^i$ and bounded by $y^{ref}$ is the set

$$R(y^i, y^{ref}) = \{y | y^i < y < y^{ref}, y \in \mathbb{R}^k\} \qquad (2)$$

The region dominated by all points in $\mathbf{y}$ and bounded by $y^{ref}$ we be the union of all such sets for $1 \leq i \leq m$. That is

$$R(\mathbf{y}, y^{ref}) = \cup_{1 \leq i \leq m} R(y^i, y^{ref}) \qquad (3)$$

The value of the metric $S(\mathbf{y}, y^{ref})$ is equal to the Lebesgue integral of the set $R(\mathbf{y}, y^{ref})$. The details of Lebesgue integration are omitted here for brevity.

The selection of the reference point used to compute $S(\mathbf{y}, y^{ref})$ is arbitrary. Zitzler suggests that we use as such the vector consisting of the maximum values of all attributes in the objective space, that is $y^{ref} = \{U_1, U_2, \ldots, U_k\}$. This number has widely been employed in the literature and is also used here.

# 4  Algorithm

The artificial immune network proposed here attempts to approximate the Pareto front of a given function by maintaining a population of antibodies $B$. Each antibody $b^i \in B$ represents a point $x = \{x_1, x_2, \ldots, x_n\}$ in the decision space of the problem. This section explains how each antibody evolves by mutation, and how the antibodies are combined to form the complete Pareto front of the function.

### 4.1  The Pareto Cloud

Let $b$ be an antibody, representing a point in the decision space and $f(b)$ the corresponding mapping in the objective space. Then, the non-uniform mutation operator (described in [1]) acts on $b$ producing a variant $b'$. The point $b'$ may be situated anywhere in the decision space, but as time progresses and the mutation rate decreases, it becomes more likely that it will be closer to the original $b$. As a result, its corresponding mapping $f(b')$ will be closer to $f(b)$ as training progresses.

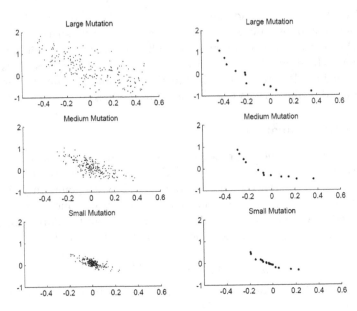

**Fig. 1.** The effect of non-uniform mutation

Given the above, if **C** is a set of mutated clones of the antibody $b$ and $f(\mathbf{C})$ the set of their corresponding mappings in the objective space, the points in $f(\mathbf{C})$ will form a 'cloud' surrounding the point $f(b)$. The exact shape of this cloud depends on the objective function, but in general it will become smaller (covering less volume around $f(b)$) as time progresses.

Among the points that make up this cloud, we select the ones that are not dominated by any other point in the cloud, thus composing the Pareto front **P** of the cloud. The corresponding points in the decision space are also stored as **S**, where $f(\mathbf{S}) = \mathbf{P}$. A number of points from this local Pareto front will be selected to form the whole Pareto front of the function. Figure 1 gives an illustrative example of clouds formed around a point situated at $[0, 0]$ and the corresponding local Pareto fronts produced for various mutation rates

## 4.2   Evolution of the Network

Given a number of antibodies having the form described above, a population **B** consisting of $N_B$ such antibodies is randomly initialized, with each antibody given a value in the decision space **X**. Then, for a given number of generations, the following procedure is repeated:

For each antibody $b^i \in \mathbf{B}$ a set of clones is created, and the clones undergo a non-uniform mutation process, producing a set of mutated clones $\mathbf{C}^i$. The number of clones $N_C$ will be constant and defined as a parameter of the training. Among the mutated clones $\mathbf{C}^i$, the ones whose mappings are situated on the Pareto front of the set $f(\mathbf{C}^i)$ are selected, forming a local Pareto front $\mathbf{P}^i$ of the antibody. After the process has been repeated for all the antibodies, we construct the union set $\mathbf{P}^* = \cup_{1 \leq i \leq N_B} \mathbf{P}^i$ of all the local Pareto fronts $\mathbf{P}^i$ of the antibodies. The Pareto front $\mathbf{P}$ produced by the algorithm will be a subset of $\mathbf{P}^*$, which will be extracted in two steps.

First, we must remove dominated points that may result from the union of the local Pareto fronts. Second, we must select only the best $N_B$ antibodies, to prevent a size explosion that would render the problem computationally infeasible after the first few generations. The selected points are the ones that maximize the diversity metric defined in Section 3. Given all of the above, the algorithm is formulated as follows.

**Step 1.** [Network initialization] In the beginning $N_B$ antibodies are created. Each is initialized to a random point in the decision space.

**Step 2.** [Candidate Pareto set] The candidate Pareto set is initialized to $\emptyset$. For each antibody a number of clones are created and mutated. The ones situated on the local Pareto front are added to the candidate Pareto set.

**Step 3.** [Remove dominated points] We remove the dominated points that may result from the union of local Pareto fronts.

**Step 4.** [Keep best points] If the number of points in the candidate Pareto set is larger than $N_B$, the $N_B$ points that maximize the diversity are selected.

**Step 5.** [Refresh antibodies] At this point, each of the antibodies is re-initialized to a point in the Pareto set. If the size of the Pareto set is smaller than $N_B$, new antibodies are randomly created to cover the desired number.

**Step 6.** [Loop] Repeat the procedure from step 2 until the desired of number of generations is completed.

# 5 Experiments

In this section our algorithm is tested on four problems from the well-known ZDT Test Suite, described in [5]. The results are compared against the NSGA-II [2] (a state-of-the-art algorithm) and SPEA [3] algorithms. To compare the performance of the algorithms, we use two metrics. The first measures the mean Euclidean distance of the proposed points to the true Pareto front, and the second the deviation of the proposed solutions. A description of these metrics is given in [2].

Our model was trained for 200 generations, using a population of $N_B = 40$ antibodies and $N_C = 200$ clones for each antibody. The dependency of non-uniform mutation on time was set to $d = 2$. The number of samples of the ideal Pareto front in the performance metric was set to $h = 500$, since both competing algorithms used this number in evaluating their performance.

Table 1 lists the results obtained by the 3 algorithms. Specifically, (a) illustrates the values obtained for the distance metric and (b) the values of the diversity metric. These values correspond to the average values of different runs of each algorithm (10 runs for our algorithm). The variance between different runs was negligible for all algorithms and is therefore omitted for brevity.

**Table 1.** Result Comparisons

(a) Distance Metric

| Problem | Immune | NSGA − II | SPEA |
|---------|--------|-----------|------|
| ZDT1 | **0.0009** | **0.0009** | 0.0018 |
| ZDT2 | 0.0010 | **0.0008** | 0.0013 |
| ZDT3 | **0.0024** | 0.0434 | 0.0475 |
| ZDT6 | **0.0041** | 0.2965 | 0.2211 |

(b) Diversity Metric

| Problem | Immune | NSGA − II | SPEA |
|---------|--------|-----------|------|
| ZDT1 | **0.2009** | 0.4632 | 0.7845 |
| ZDT2 | **0.2536** | 0.4351 | 0.7551 |
| ZDT3 | **0.4584** | 0.5756 | 0.6729 |
| ZDT6 | **0.1495** | 0.6680 | 0.8494 |

The results listed show the performance of the proposed algorithm to be very satisfactory. In the distance metric, our algorithm surpasses SPEA in all problems and NSGA-2 in two out of four problems. Our method also outperforms both NSGA-2 and SPEA in diversity for all problems.

The results listed do not necessarily mean that the proposed algorithm is better that NSGA-II or SPEA. All 3 algorithms converge very closely to the true Pareto front of the functions, so the differences in their performance may not be fully indicative of their quality in general. However, the fact that our algorithm compares favorably to a state-of the-art algorithm and a classic one shows that it is a promising method for Pareto front approximation.

# References

1. Michalewicz, Z.: Genetic Algorithms + Data Structures = Evolution Programs. Springer, New York (1992)
2. Deb, K., Pratap, A., Agarwal, S., Meyarivan, T.: A fast and elitist multi-objective genetic algorithm: NSGA-II. IEEE Trans. Evol. Comput. 6(2), 181–197 (2002)
3. Zitzler, E., Thiele, L.: Multiobjective evolutionary algorithms: A comparative case study and the strength pareto approach. IEEE Trans. Evol. Comput. 3(4), 257–271 (1999)
4. Zitzler, E., Laumanns, M., Thiele, L.: SPEA2: Improving the strength pareto evolutionary algorithm. Tech. Rep. 103, Gloriastrasse 35, CH-8092 Zurich, Switzerland (2001)
5. Zitzler, E., Deb, K., Thiele, L.: Comparison of multiobjective evolutionary algorithms: Empirical results. IEEE Trans. Evol. Comput. 8(2), 173–195 (2000)
6. Zitzler, E.: Evolutionary algorithms for multiobjective optimization: Methods and applications. Ph.D. dissertation, Swiss Federal Institute of Technology (1999)
7. Garrett, S.M.: How Do We Evaluate Artificial Immune Systems? MIT Press Evolutionary Computation 13(2), 145–178 (2005)

# Author Index